THE FIFTIES

Also by Douglas T. Miller

JACKSONIAN ARISTOCRACY: CLASS AND DEMOCRACY IN NEW YORK, 1830–1860

THE BIRTH OF MODERN AMERICA, 1820–1850

THEN WAS THE FUTURE: THE NORTH IN THE AGE OF JACKSON, 1815–1850

THE FIFTIES:

The Way We Really Were

DOUGLAS T. MILLER
and MARION NOWAK

DOUBLEDAY & COMPANY, INC., Garden City, New York
1977

Portions of *The Fifties* appeared in *The Journal of Popular Culture* in slightly different form.

Grateful acknowledgment is made for permission to include excerpts from the following copyrighted publications:

"School Days" by Chuck Berry copyright © 1957 by Arc Music Corporation. Reprinted by permission of The Goodman Group Music Publishers.

"Shake, Rattle and Roll" copyright © 1954 by Progressive Music Co., Inc. Copyright and all rights assigned to Unichappell Music, Inc. International Copyright Secured. All Rights Reserved. Used by permission.

"Wear My Ring Around Your Neck" copyright © 1958 by Elvis Presley Music and Rush Music Corp. Unichappell Music, Inc., Administrator. International copyright secured. All Rights Reserved. Used by permission of Chappell Music Company.

"I've Got A Woman" copyright © 1954 by Progressive Music Publishing Co., Inc. Copyright assigned to Unichappell Music, Inc. Belinda Music, Publishers. International copyright secured. All Rights Reserved. Used by permission of Chappell Music Company.

Library of Congress Cataloging in Publication Data

Miller, Douglas T
The fifties.

Bibliography
Includes index.
1. United States—Social life and customs—1945–1970. 2. United States—Social conditions—1945– I. Nowak, Marion, 1948– joint author. II. Title.
E169.02.M485 973.92
ISBN 0-385-11248-3
Library of Congress Catalog Card Number 75-36602

PRINTED IN THE UNITED STATES OF AMERICA
FIRST EDITION

To our sisters,
Lena Nowak and Nan Reale

ACKNOWLEDGMENTS

Over the years many people have aided us in working on *The Fifties*. Early drafts of the book were read in whole or in part by our friends Gilman Ostrander, Richard Moss, Peter Levine, Larry Finfer, Norman Pollack, William Hixson, David Bergmann, Carolyn and Donald Fermoyle, Harry Reed, Larry Rudner, Charles Gregory, and B. J. Wendell Moose. The book has benefited from their varied suggestions. We are thankful for the generosity of our friend John Humins in allowing us to tape his superb collection of fifties records. We are also indebted to Marion's father, Cass Nowak, for giving us numerous hard-to-find fifties journals, magazines, and books. In our research we were assisted by the courteous staffs of the libraries of Michigan State University, the State University of New York at New Paltz, Saint Francis Xavier College in Antigonish, Nova Scotia, Sandy Cove and Digby, Nova Scotia, and the New York Public Library. For financial aid to Douglas, we wish to thank Michigan State University and the American Philosophical Society. For permission to use material from our earlier published articles in the *Journal of Popular Culture,* we thank the Popular Culture Association. We are obliged to Betty Uphaus for her excellent typing of the original manuscript. We are indebted to Michael Darner for his friendship and jacket photo. To Virginia Barber and Larry Jordan, we are deeply grateful. Their encouragement, patience, and helpful editorial comments have been invaluable. Finally, though acknowledgment is made in the footnotes and bibliography to the innumerable authors we read in researching *The Fifties,* more specific thanks should be given to the following writers whose works we found to be of particular importance: Frederick Lewis Allen, Jacques Barzun, Daniel Bell, Saul Bellow, Arthur Bestor, John Brooks, Bruce Cook, Fred J. Cook, Lawrence Cremin, Carl Degler, W. E. B. DuBois, Ralph Ellison, Marynia Farnham, Leslie Fiedler, Betty Friedan, Erich Fromm, John Kenneth Galbraith, Allen Ginsberg, Eric Goldman, Paul Goodman, Gordon Gow, Robert Griffith, Thomas Griffith, Robert Heilbroner, Jules Henry, Will Herberg, Irving Howe, Jack Kerouac, Martin Luther King, Jr., Paul Landis, Max Lerner, Richard S. Lewis, Robert Jay Lifton, Robert Lindner, Lawrence Lipton, Ferdinand Lundberg, Richard Dyer MacCann, Norman Mailer, Kate Millett, C. Wright Mills, Norman Moss, Lewis Mumford, Vladimir Nabokov, Jeff Nuttall, Vance Packard, Linus Pauling, Norman Vincent Peale, David Riesman, Michael Paul Rogin, J. D. Salinger, Arthur Schlesinger, Jr., Charles Silberman, Ernest Sternglass, I. F. Stone, William Styron, Harvey Swados, Thomas Szasz, Harold Vatter, Peter Viereck, Ben Wattenberg, James Wechsler, Lynn White, Jr., William H. Whyte, Jr., Lawrence S. Wittner, and Howard Zinn.

DOUGLAS T. MILLER
MARION NOWAK

Murphy's Pond, Cape Breton Island, Nova Scotia
July 27, 1976

CONTENTS

For me there is something melancholy, something tragic, in all this, as though the world were living somehow in expectation of the earth's giving way under its feet, and were seeking not orderliness but forgetfulness. I see this not only in the careworn, wrinkled faces but also in a fear of any serious thinking, in an aversion from any analysis of the situation, in a convulsive craving to be busy, and for external distractions. The old are ready to play with toys, "if only to keep from thinking."

ALEXANDER HERZEN

Introduction

Hula hoops, bunny hops, 3-D movies. Davy Crockett coonskins, chlorophyll toothpaste, 22 collegians stuffed into a phone booth. Edsels and tail-finned Cadillacs. Greasy duck's-ass hairdos, leather jackets, souped-up hot rods, dragging, cruising, mooning. Like crazy, man, dig? Kefauver hearings, Howdy Doody, Kukla, Fran and Ollie. Bridey Murphy, Charles Van Doren, Francis Gary Powers. *The Catcher in the Rye, The Power of Positive Thinking; Howl, On the Road.* Patti Page, Pat Boone, Vic Damone; Little Richard, Chuck Berry, Elvis Presley; The Platters, The Clovers, The Drifters; Bill Haley and the Comets, Danny and the Juniors. Mantle, Mays, Marciano. Pink shirts, gray flannels, white bucks. I LIKE IKE.

THE FABULOUS FIFTIES!—or so 1970s nostalgia would lead one to believe. A 1972 issue of *Newsweek*, complete with Marilyn Monroe cover, explored this phenomenon under the heading "Yearning for the Fifties: The Good Old Days." "It was a simple decade," *Newsweek* writers recalled, "when hip was hep, good was boss." That same year *Life* magazine reminisced about "The Nifty Fifties"—"it's been barely a dozen years since the '50s ended and yet here we are again, awash in the trappings of that sunnier time."[1]

This wistful view of the fifties first became evident about 1971 and 1972. It quickly exploded into a national craze that still pervades the popular images of the mid-century era. Numerous examples of fifties nostalgia exist in the seventies. It was the theme of movies like *American Graffiti, The Last Picture Show, Let the Good Times Roll,* and *The Way We Were.* Television shows "Happy Days" and "Laverne and Shirley" recreated an idyllic fifties world of youth and innocence. The TV show "M*A*S*H" even managed to make people a little homesick for the Korean War. By February 1976, the fifties rock-and-roll parody *Grease* began its fifth season. It had become Broadway's longest running show by far, and this despite the fact that it never had name stars, hit songs, or a high budget.[2]

Popular music in this post-Beatles period also saw a major revival of fifties rock. By the mid-seventies Elvis Presley, Chuck Berry, Rick Nelson, Fats Domino, Little Richard, and Bill Haley again were drawing mass audiences. Record companies were reissuing fifties hits on special golden-oldies LPs, and many radio stations were devoting several hours daily to an oldies format. The fifties musical revival spawned contemporary groups such as Sha-Na-Na, Flash Cadillac and the Continental Kids, and Vince Vance and the Valiants. These groups not only sang the oldies, they also revived the greaser look. Vince Vance even got himself arrested while attempting to steal an Edsel hubcap. Nightclubs too have cashed in on nostalgia. Across the country, clubs have featured old music and special trivia nights with questions such as "Who played James Dean's girlfriend in *Rebel Without a Cause?*"[3]

Another sign of the fifties fad has been in clothing. Leather motorcycle jackets, picture sweaters, pedal pushers, pleated skirts, and strapless evening dresses have been hot items in the last few years. In 1973, Monique, the New York *Daily News* fashion reporter, announced: "the feeling of the fifties that will rule a large part of the fashion next fall is already apparent." A year earlier Cyrinda Foxe, a Marilyn Monroe look-alike modeling a dress from a fifties collection, claimed that "people just go crazy when I walk down the street! The fifties were so much sexier."[4]

What does all this nostalgia mean? Periods of intense longing for an earlier era indicate that people are discontented with the present. Excessive, sentimental nostalgia generally occurs during times of perceived crisis. Such has been the case in the seventies. The rise of the fifties enthusiasm coincided with widespread disillusionment and a growing conservatism. For many people the 1950s came to symbolize a golden age of innocence and simplicity, an era supposedly unruffled by riots, racial violence, Vietnam, Watergate, assassinations. People numbed by the traumas of the sixties and seventies, desiring to forget the horrors of presidential crime, soaring prices, Cambodian bombings, Kent State, My Lai, the Manson case, the Chicago Convention, the murders of two Kennedys, Martin Luther King, and Malcolm X, yearned for a quieter time. As a Cleveland oldies-but-goodies disc jockey put it, "my audience wants to forget its problems and return to—or at least recall—those happy high-school times—the prom, no wars, no riots, no protests, the convertibles and the drive-in." Another DJ even saw the fifties music revival as a way to bridge the generation gap. "I get the feeling that through this music some of the kids are finding a back-door way of getting together with their parents."[5] Nostalgia, then, is a pleasant distraction. One imagines the past, and so overlooks the present.

Additionally, since we live in a society that prizes youth over age, there is a natural tendency for nostalgia on the part of the aging generation. For those who grew up in the fifties, the happy images of that decade are a positive reassurance—a reclaiming of fading youth. Then too in the mid-seventies the general realization that energy, prosperity, and growth are not limitless undoubtedly makes Americans a more retrospective, nostalgic people. We may die tomorrow, but we wish to remember it as a good world while it lasted.

But whatever the reasons for the fifties revival, the image of that decade conveyed by current nostalgia is badly distorted. The artifacts of the fifties are still with us. The facts are less clear. Looking back on that period, people today see it as a time of fun and innocence, a soda-shop world with youth as its only participants. They recall Bo Diddley and Buddy Holly, but ignore Joe McCarthy and John Foster Dulles. Nostalgia is highly selective. No one is staging a House Un-American Activities Committee revival, or longing for the good old days of nuclear brinksmanship and the deadly H-bomb tests.

Certainly, there was some fun in the fifties—the Coasters' songs, Lenny Bruce's nightclub routines, Sid Caesar's TV antics. But in retrospect it was essentially a humorless decade, one in which comic Mort Sahl could raise national ire by cracking a single J. Edgar Hoover joke. Much of what strikes observers as quaint now—Nixon's Checkers speech, Norman Vincent Peale's homilies, or tailfinned Cadillacs—were grotesque realities at the time. It was more an era of fear than fun. The bomb, communists, spies, and Sputnik all scared Americans. And fear bred repression both of the blatant McCarthyite type and the more subtle, pervasive, and personal daily pressures to conform.

Astute social critics have found the fifties anything but the good old days. To the late Paul Goodman it was an "extraordinarily senseless and unnatural" time. American society, in his words, was "a Closed Room with a Rat Race as the center of fascination, powerfully energized by fear of being outcasts." To Michael Harrington the decade "was a moral disaster, an amusing waste of life." Norman Mailer bluntly described the fifties as "one of the worst decades in the history of man."[6]

A generation has passed since the second half of the twentieth century began. Yet, despite the nostalgic revival, in some ways that era now seems ancient history. The fifties can be compared to the 1920s. Both postwar periods were relatively prosperous and highly conservative. In both decades radicalism was singularly suspect and nearly driven out of existence by Red scares and witch hunts. Fatherly Republican Eisenhower was only a more popular version of the Harding/Coolidge-type politician.

Even the economic aftermaths of the two periods have similarities. The Great Depression can be blamed on the economic policies and practices of the twenties. No such devastating collapse followed the fifties of course. But the inflation-recession syndrome and ecological and energy crises of the seventies are rooted in the reckless, wasteful, exploitative, growth-oriented policies of the fifties and sixties.

There is, however, an important difference between the twenties and the fifties. The moods of the two decades were divergent. Ironically, though prohibition existed throughout the twenties, sobriety, in the broadest sense, was more a fifties phenomenon. The Eisenhower years were tired, dull, cautious, and anxious, in a word more "normal" than the "normalcy" of the Harding-Coolidge era. The fifties witnessed much less happy nonsense, much more conformity. International tensions and conflicts were far greater than had been the case during the relatively isolationist twenties. The daily reality of the cold war caused persons to fear international communism and, more importantly, internal communist subversion. Such fears put a premium on conformity. Bourgeois values reasserted themselves in a manner which would have pleased a twenties fundamentalist. Domesticity, religiosity, respectability, security through compliance with the system, that was the essence of the fifties.

Other major factors distinguished the mid-century years not only from the twenties but from all previous periods of American history —TV, suburbia, superhighways, and the triumphant auto. None of these things were new in the fifties; even television as an invention goes back to the 1930s. But up to the late 1940s TV, suburbia, and superhighways were just aspects of American life; after that they became dominant factors.

As late as 1946, there were only 7,000 television sets in use throughout the nation. By 1960 they numbered over 50 million. TV's conquest was swift. In 1952 *TV Guide* magazine was founded. The TV dinner was introduced in 1954, and by 1956 Americans for the first time were spending more hours watching their sets than working for pay.[7]

With similar speed, suburbia, cars, and highways became central features of the postwar American scene. Though the urge to escape urban congestion, crime, or other ills had given rise to suburban communities as early as the nineteenth century, such residences up through the close of World War II attracted only a small portion of the population, usually the rich. Then suddenly, beginning in the late 1940s, came a massive suburban building boom. Throughout the country, tract-built developments sprang up, the Levittowns and Park Forests. There was a massive middle- and lower-middle-class exodus from the cities. A bulldozed landscape appeared, consisting of tiny ranch houses on 50-foot tracts surrounded by shopping centers, schools, churches, and parking lots. The cities were left to deteriorate. Between 1950 and 1960 the number of U.S. homeowners increased by over nine million, reaching an incredible 32.8 million. And just as they had chosen the private-family house,

Americans also opted for the private-family automobile as never before. During the decade the number of registered cars increased by over 21 million. To facilitate the driving urge and link suburbs to cities, the federal and state governments undertook colossal road-building projects, including a 40,000-mile Interstate Highway System. Little attention was paid to the great social and aesthetic problems engendered by this reliance on the auto. The result was the breakdown of mass transportation, pollution, congestion, depletion of fossil fuels, ugliness, and frequent fatalities.[8]

These things were accepted as the price of progress. In fact most Americans seemed to believe that the good life had arrived. The poverty of the Depression years and the disruptions of World War II were in the past. Wife, kids, cars, a house—the American dream fulfilled, or so many thought.

"Meet the Typical American," announced a 1954 *Reader's Digest* article. "The average American male stands five feet nine inches tall, weighs 158 pounds, prefers brunettes, baseball, beefsteak and French fried potatoes, and thinks the ability to run a home smoothly and efficiently is the most important quality in a wife." The average American woman, the article continued, "is five feet four, weighs 132, can't stand an unshaven face." This typical female preferred marriage to a career. As the average weights of men and women might suggest, many Americans were on the heavy side. The prevalent styles encouraged this. Women in pleated skirts falling a few inches below the knees were expected to be shapely in a plump sort of way. Bikinis were largely limited to the girlie magazines. But big breasts, symbols of motherhood, were definitely in vogue. For men, excess flab was easily concealed beneath baggy pleated pants, suits and shirts that did not follow body lines, boxer shorts and bathing trunks, Bermudas with knee-length socks. So in this decade of suburban prosperity, many people carried paunches as if they were symbols of success.[9]

The goals of these "average" Americans were not radical. What George Meany said of organized labor in the mid-fifties would have applied to most groups: "We do not seek to recast American society. We do seek an ever-rising standard of living by which we mean not only more money but more leisure and a richer cultural life."[10]

Leisure and culture—Americans took to these as never before. About one sixth of all personal income was spent on leisure pursuits. In record force people painted-by-numbers, drank, gardened, watched TV, traveled, listened to music, hunted and fished, read *Reader's Digest* condensed books. Doing-it-oneself became a national fad. Everything from home permanents to boat building had millions of amateur practitioners. In 1954 it was reported that 70 per cent of all wallpaper bought was hung by novices, while some 11 million weekend carpenters drilled, sawed, and sanded some 180 square miles of plywood with their 25 million power tools. In California, the Pan Pacific Do-It-Yourself Show even exhibited separate pieces of fur that could be assembled into a do-it-yourself mink coat. For persons of a more sedentary nature, American industry produced quantities of amusing junk—cigarette lighters that played "Smoke Gets in Your Eyes," whiskey-flavored toothpaste, mink-trimmed clothespins, Venus toothpicks, Jayne Mansfield hot-water bottles.[11]

Americans could do just about anything. Or so at least they were told in hundreds of books purportedly revealing the secrets of how to make love, how to tap one's secret source of strength, how to mix a good martini, how to get thin or fat, how to be popular, powerful, famous, rich.

But it was *Culture* that American boosters boasted of most. "Once in a great while a society explodes in a flood of new ideas, new tastes, new standards," claimed Fenton Turck in a 1952 *Reader's Digest* article. "A fresh and exciting age emerges, alive with expanding opportunities. Today's Americans are living in one of these extraordinary periods." Turck talked of a great flowering of culture. As evidence of this he cited such things as increased attendance at concerts, opera, and theater. Art museums, opera companies, and symphony orchestras all multiplied in the fifties, as did the sale of quality paperbacks and classical records.[12]

Culture had status appeal and an increased portion of the population had both the leisure and money to dabble in it. Perhaps the apogee of the era's culture boom was reached in April 1960, when the Parke-Bernet Galleries held a huge art auction to benefit the Museum of Modern Art. The New York City auction room was linked via closed-circuit TV to similar rooms in Chicago, Dallas, and Los Angeles. The auction was a great success; an Utrillo went to a Dallas millionaire for $20,000, a Cézanne to a New York collector for $200,000. Bidding on a Hans Hartung had reached the $10,000 level before anyone noticed it was hung upside down. "We're ready for our renaissance," claimed poet Louis Untermeyer at mid-decade. "Westward the course of culture!"[13]

In addition to celebrating American culture and living standards, many people saw the United States in the middle of the twentieth century as having a peculiar and providential mission. "We are living in one of the great watershed periods of history," asserted Democratic presidential nominee Adlai Stevenson in the 1952 campaign. This era "may well fix the pattern of civilization for many generations to come. God has set for us an awesome mission: nothing less than the leadership of the free world." The editors of *Fortune* felt the same. "There come times in the history of every people," they wrote, "when destiny knocks on their door with an iron insistence." In American history, as they read it, destiny had so knocked three times: "Once when we faced the seemingly impossible odds of British power to gain our independence: once at Fort Sumter, when we faced the bloody task of preserving our union: and it is knocking today [1951]. . . . Our outlook is the same as it was at the time of the Revolution, and again at the time of the Civil War: the shape of things to come depends on us: our moral decision, our wisdom, our vision, and our will."[14]

That America would succeed in fulfilling its God-given mission few doubted. The future was bright. "Our spiritual road map," predicted philosopher Morris Ernst, "will carry the direction pointers: 1976–This Way–Energy, Leisure, Full Rich Life."[15]

Yet despite the varied and frequent versions of "America the Beautiful," doubts and anxieties were also present. The fifties was a time of tensions and insecurities. Early in the decade the usually optimistic Norman Vincent Peale spoke of an "epidemic of fear and worry" in the United States. "All doctors," he declared, "are having cases of illness which are brought on directly by fear, and aggravated by worry and a feeling of insecurity." For some Americans the greatest anxieties stemmed from the cold war. "Our nation," warned a late-fifties civil defense pamphlet, "is in a grim struggle for national survival and the preservation of freedom in the world." And of course there was the constant threat of nuclear destruction which left people, in the words of one mid-fifties observer, "in a state of suspension, waiting to see whether the Bomb is going to fall or not."[16]

For other people, the speed of social and economic change generated uncertainties and cast doubts on old certitudes. The new prosperity and changing lifestyles, while materially benefiting many, caused insecurities. Traditional ethnic neighborhoods were breaking down as newly prosperous people fled to suburbia. Yet this very mobility created rootlessness. Many people simply discovered that abundance was not enough. In any case Americans became quite self-critical and made best sellers of books telling them of their shortcomings.[17]

In this light, some of the most important social and cultural phenomena of the fifties are more understandable. The overwhelming emphasis on the family gave people a sense of place and personal identity. The massive return to religion provided individuals with a sense of security; it reassured them that the traditional moral verities were still valid. Sustained and successful attacks against progressive education were another manifestation of the search for traditional, absolute values. So too was the intellectual emphasis on consensus. Historians, sociologists, and other social scientists played down conflict and instead stressed the harmonious and enduring nature of American democratic values. Blacks and other nonwhites, who did not share equally in America's bounty, were assured by the white media that they never had it so good. Generally speaking, neither racial nor economic classes were recognized. Critics of this celebrated consensus, whether from right or left, tended to be treated as psychological deviants suffering from such cliché ills as status anxiety or authoritarian personality. Nonconformists and rebels were subject to harsh conformist pressures. No wonder then that bipartisan banality flourished. Both major political parties clung tenaciously to the same center, maintaining the status quo while mouthing provincial Protestant platitudes and preparing for Armageddon.

The Fifties tells the story of this complex decade. Having lived through the sixties and half of the seventies, we are far enough removed from the mid-century era to attempt a detached evaluation. For more than five years now, we have immersed ourselves in the study of the fifties, reading literally thousands of popular magazines, scholarly journals, highbrow and lowbrow literature, newspapers, comics, pamphlets, government documents, and numerous other published sources. We have taught graduate seminars on the social and cultural history of the fifties, discussed the decade with many people, stayed up nights watching TV reruns of fifties movies and shows, and collected literally hundreds of fifties songs.

We are professional historians trying to understand an important period of America's recent past. Yet, while *The Fifties* is a scholarly book, it is also a personal one. Both of us lived through that era. In many respects these were formative years for us, and on occasion we have drawn upon personal experiences to illustrate some of the decade's major social and cultural trends.

In the broadest sense, of course, all history is personal—an interpretation of people and events as perceived by the historian. History is as much art as it is a social science, though the canons of theoretical historical objectivity have long tended to obscure this fact. Knowledge of history is fascinating and essential to survival. Yet history will always be impressionistic. There certainly are patterns. They are like the impressionist's picture—the focus is raised slightly above the canvas. Look too close to compute the process and you lose it. To pretend that history is some sort of science that can be quantified and computerized is incredibly naive. History just does not happen that way, not neatly, efficiently, all ready for punch cards. It is lush and enigmatic, and eminently a subjective study. As historians, we interpret events and make moral judgments. We consciously falsify nothing, and hopefully the reader will find our interpretations to be educated, humane, and stimulating. They remain, however, our personal judgments.

An important aspect of writing history is the influence that the historian's values and prejudices has on his or her work. Put in a simple syllogism one could say: All historians are people; all people have biases; therefore, all historians have biases. Our particular biases undoubtedly will become apparent. But let us make our position clear at the outset. This book is not a nostalgic celebration of the "nifty fifties." We simply do not see the Eisenhower years as the "happy days" of innocence and youth. Like many individuals who have been radicalized during the sixties and seventies, we still dream of a better America, a real democracy freed from the taints of racism, sexism, and exploitation. And while Mailer's earlier quoted remark about the fifties being "one of the worst decades in the history of man" strikes us as extreme (and sexist), we would have preferred a decade that was less materialistic, militaristic, frightened, conformist, conservative, stuffy, trivial.

The chapters that follow are topical. Each chapter, as much as possible, is developed chronologically. Our subject is the social and cultural history of the ten years from 1950 to 1960. At the same time we are aware that to write about a particular decade is to risk oversimplification. While there were important characteristics and trends peculiar to that era, most of the period's social and cultural manifestations had roots in earlier American history and have continued beyond 1960. When Frederick Lewis Allen described the twenties in *Only Yesterday,* he was able to begin at the beginning of the decade and end with the end of it, because, according to his interpretation, it was a unique decade in the nation's history, commencing with the close of World War I and culminating with the 1929 crash. The same cannot be said of the fifties.[18]

If one were attempting a precise periodization, the fifties could well be divided into three parts: 1948–53, 1954–57, 1958–60. These three periods might then be labeled "The Age of Fear," "The Era of Conservative Consensus," and "The Time of National Reassessment."

The Age of Fear: The post-World War II era really begins around 1948. By then the nation had essentially adjusted to a peacetime economy; depression had not recurred and people were coming to believe in the possibility of perpetual prosperity. At the same time, the cold war had become a debilitating reality. A chronology of terror began unfolding. In 1948 a communist coup was successful in Czechoslovakia and the Soviets blockaded western access to Berlin. That same year in the United States, talk of treason and communist infiltration became commonplace, especially after a former New Deal State Department official, Alger Hiss, was accused by Whittaker Chambers of having passed secrets to the Russians. The following year, 1949, the Soviets exploded their first atomic bomb and Mao Tse-tung's communist forces were victorious in China. Early in 1950 President Harry S Truman announced plans to begin development of a hydrogen bomb (it was perfected by 1952); Senator Joseph McCarthy added the loudest voice to the already sizable outcry of anticommunist witch hunters. Nineteen fifty also saw the conviction of Alger Hiss for perjury, the arrest and trial of Ethel and Julius Rosenberg as atomic spies (they were executed in 1953), the outbreak of the Korean War, and Senator Estes Kefauver's televised criminal investigations that dramatically revealed the extent and power of organized crime.

Such events shocked and frightened people, and the last years of Truman's presidency proved a trying time—a period of suspicions, accusations, loyalty oaths, loathings, extreme chauvinistic Americanism. Republicans, attempting to regain power, were not averse to charging the Democrats with being "soft on communism," though in reality both parties were excessively anticommunist. Tensions raised by Korean fighting, supposed communist infiltration, spy trials, loyalty investigations, inflation, crime, and the bomb reached near hysteric proportions in the early fifties. Dissent was suppressed, conformity demanded. With the exception of a few legitimate espionage cases, none of which really endangered national security, *most victims of the anti-red mania were guilty of little more than holding unpopular opinions.* Not only the national government, but thousands of local communities as well felt obliged to search out and destroy suspected subversive views. Teachers, government workers, entertainers, and many others were dismissed. Textbooks were censored and libraries closed.

Yet such fear and repression, plus prosperity, also made Americans seem united under a national faith. Seeing the world in dualistic terms of good versus evil, people celebrated the United States as the bastion of freedom, democracy, and "people's capitalism." Intellectuals defended America and searched for enduring consensual values of the country's past and present. A noncritical conservative consensus emerged offering hope and reassurance during this age of fear. The widespread emphasis on religion and the family gave further solace. The combined anxiety and hope of this period is well illustrated in the title of a 1950 song—"Jesus Is God's Atomic Bomb."

The Era of Conservative Consensus: The conservative consensus and celebration of America continued into the mid-fifties, and fortunately for national nerves the fears and anxieties began to ebb. Several factors contributed to this: the death of Stalin and the end of the Korean War in 1953; the downfall of Senator McCarthy in 1954; the Geneva summit conference with the Soviets in 1955; the lack of new spy sensations after 1950; continued prosperity; and, above all, the election of Eisenhower to the presidency.

When Ike was first elected in 1952, one Pennsylvania housewife remarked: "It's like America has come home."[19] And so it seemed to millions. While politics traditionally means conflict, Ike appeared to people as above politics. He was the heroic general come to unite the nation in peace and prosperity as he had defended it earlier in war. Democratic presidents Roosevelt and Truman had for 20 years emphasized a politics of class strife and crisis. With Eisenhower came the appearance at least of a politics of unity and classlessness. His boyish grin and downhome homely face, his simple sincere platitudes about home, mother, and heaven, his circumlocutions when difficult issues came up, all these things endeared him to millions and made him a symbol, not of party, but of national consensus. Americans, tired of constant crises and the hysteria of the age of fear, found in Ike a symbol of hope and confidence.

And so, by the mid-fifties there came a brief happy moment—the quintessential fifties—prosperous, stable, bland, religious, moral, patriotic, conservative, domestic, buttoned-down. Huge tail-finned cars sold in record numbers, *The Power of Positive Thinking* and *The Man in the Gray Flannel Suit* sat atop the best-seller lists, and the "Spirit of Geneva" seemed to diffuse itself over the globe. Domestically no problem appeared more pressing than the specter of juvenile delinquency, though in reality young people overwhelmingly accepted the values of their elders and dedicated themselves to the bourgeois goals of security, sociability, domesticity. They went steady, married young, had lots of children, lived the conforming life of "togetherness."

Crises still existed. Poverty, racism, sexism, and militarism all threatened America. But Eisenhower and most citizens tried to ignore such ills. The sting seemed gone from the times, and a cheerful nation overwhelmingly re-elected Eisenhower in 1956. Just before that election, David Riesman and Stewart Alsop visited a new suburb south of Chicago to poll voters. They found people vague about politics but liking Ike. "Most of the people we spoke to were young housewives, often interrupted in their midday television program. . . ." They were educated but complacent. "As one looked over that flat Illinois prairie at all the signs of prosperity," generalized Riesman, "it was not hard to see why these people were so bland politically and responded to the same qualities in Ike. . . . These people were not self-made men who remembered their struggles against hardship but, rather, a society-made generation who could not believe society would let them down. . . ."[20] These were the model fifties figures—suburbanized, bureaucratized, smug, secure.

The Time of National Reassessment: Eisenhower's second term quickly revealed how precarious the mid-fifties plateau of repose actually was. Even before that new term began, America's foreign relations suffered major setbacks. Just prior to the 1956 elections, fighting broke out in Egypt and Hungary. In late October, Anglo-French-Israeli forces invaded the Suez region of Egypt in an attempt to regain the canal which Egyptian leader Gamal Abdel Nasser earlier had nationalized. Third World anticolonial resentment and threatened Soviet intervention convinced the Eisenhower administration that the invasion must be ended. America pressured Britain, France, and Israel to withdraw. They did so. However, these nations' humiliation embittered them toward the United States. Western unity seemed seriously weakened. During these same tense days of late October and early November 1956, the Soviet Union, taking advantage of the dissent among the Western powers, harshly crushed an anticommunist uprising in Hungary that had broken out only a week before the Suez war. For a few weeks the world hovered on the brink of nuclear war. And while both crises were over at about the same time as Eisenhower's November re-election, they greatly intensified international tensions. Suez and Hungary clearly revealed the 1955 Geneva summit to be only a temporary thaw in the cold war.

Less than a year later, the domestic tranquillity of the mid-fifties was also disrupted. In September 1957, American racism was shockingly unveiled when the school-integration issue reached crisis proportions in Little Rock. Eisenhower, who was not sympathetic to the civil rights movement, reluctantly was forced to send troops into that city to insure compliance with the Supreme Court's 1954 desegregation decision. But the ugly scenes in front of Central High School laid bare for Americans and the world this nation's deep-seated racial tensions.

Then a month later in October 1957, the Soviets launched Sputnik I, the world's first earth-orbiting satellite. Americans were profoundly shocked. National self-confidence seemed shattered in the light of this demonstrated Soviet superiority in space science. Calls for an expanded arms race accelerated. American affluence, once the nation's pride, now was blamed for enfeebling the populace. Progressive education, which had been on the defensive throughout the decade, was quickly demolished as people demanded intellectual discipline with more emphasis on science, mathematics, and language.

Sputnik clearly struck the major blow against mid-fifties tranquillity. But other developments in the last three years of Eisenhower's presidency added to American doubts and increased the national penchant for soul-searching. At about the same time as the Soviet space successes, the American economy began to slump. By the spring of 1958, a major recession existed; unemployment had climbed to 7.7 per cent of the total labor force, the highest rate since 1941. That same year congressional committees disclosed conflict-of-interest violations by presidential appointees and charges of influence-peddling by Vice-President Nixon's former campaign manager. Even Ike's closest, most trusted and influential adviser, Sherman Adams, was dismissed for taking bribes. Adams, it was revealed, had accepted expensive gifts from Bernard Goldfine, a wealthy businessman with cases pending before the government. On tour in Latin America that year, Nixon was spat upon, jeered, and stoned. A year later, Charles Van Doren, a handsome young instructor from Columbia University, scion of an eminent literary family, revealed to investigators that the brilliance he had displayed in winning vast sums on a TV quiz show was fake. The show had been rigged. At about the same time famed disc jockey Alan Freed, the self-appointed father of rock and roll, became involved in a payola scandal. Among other revelations were exposés of widespread cheating in schools and of a group of New York cops working for a burglary ring.

By May 1960, when the Soviets announced that Francis Gary Powers had been shot down in a U-2 spy plane over Russian territory, the American propensity for critical self-evaluation had become obsessive. A presidential Commission on National Goals, which Eisenhower had established after Sputnik, produced a ponderous report, *Goals for Americans*. The Rockefeller Brothers Fund issued their own version, *Prospect for America. Life, Look,* the New York *Times* and other mass-circulation publications featured articles and whole issues discussing national purpose and the future role of America. Leading social and political writers began turning out books with titles like *America the Vincible* and *What Ivan Knows and Johnny Doesn't.*

Much of the national debate focused on dissatisfaction with the quality of American life. Conformity and materialism, critics argued, had dulled Americans into a complacent averageness. "Our goal has become a life of amiable sloth," complained *Time* editor Thomas Griffith in 1959. "We are in danger of becoming a vibrating and mediocre people." "Looking at some of the institutions we nourish and defend," Robert Heilbroner noted, early in 1960, "it would not be difficult to maintain that our society is an immense stamping press for the careless production of underdeveloped and malformed human beings, and that, whatever it may claim to be, it is not a society fundamentally concerned with moral issues, with serious purposes, or with human dignity."[21] Such laments swelled into a national chorus of self-reproach as Americans once more showed themselves to be an anxious, self-conscious people.

Yet there remained an underlying note of hope in this intramural abuse. Most doubters viewed their disparagements as enterprises of self-correction. "America the Beautiful" would soar once more if only we could speed up economic growth, put a man on the moon, develop a more flexible military establishment, rekindle a spirit of national self-sacrifice, and so on and so on. John F. Kennedy's 1960 campaign epitomized the schizophrenic national mood of doubt and hope. In this, many others concurred. Walter Lippmann stated in July 1960, "We're at the end of something that is petering out and aging and about finished." He was not unhappy about this; rather he sensed that a new and better day was coming. Arthur Schlesinger, Jr., already active with the Kennedy people, also lamented the late fifties but foretold "a new epoch" of "vitality," "identity," and "new values . . . straining for expression and for release."[22]

The fifties, then, is not a neat single unit. The decade began with terror and affluence uniting a people under a national faith. The mid-fifties, desperately tired of crises, continued that faith in a more casual and relaxed manner. Yet by 1960, that mask of faith was drawn aside to reveal a changing face: regretful, doubting, yet also looking in hope to a rebirth.

In the chapters that follow, we have attempted to understand the most significant social and cultural developments of these important, intriguing years.

NOTES

1. *Newsweek,* October 16, 1972, cover and pp. 78–82; *Life,* June 16, 1972, cover and pp. 38–46.

2. Shaun Considine, "*Grease* Slides Into Its Fifth Year," New York *Times,* February 15, 1976, Section 2, p. 5.

3. Richard R. Lingeman, "There Was Another Fifties," New York *Times Magazine,* June 17, 1973, pp. 26–38; *Newsweek,* October 16, 1972, pp. 78–82; *Life,* June 16, 1972, pp. 38–46. Natalie Wood played Dean's girlfriend in *Rebel.*

4. New York *Times,* March 11, 1973, p. 6; Monique is quoted in Lingeman, "There Was Another Fifties," p. 27; Cyrinda Foxe is pictured and quoted in *Life,* June 16, 1972, pp. 44–45.

5. The Cleveland disc jockey was Dick Liberatore. He is quoted in Lingeman, "There Was Another Fifties," p. 27. The second DJ was Dick Biondi of Chicago who is quoted in *Life,* June 16, 1972, p. 39. See also James Joslyn and John Pendleton, "The Adventures of Ozzie and Harriet," *Journal of Popular Culture,* VII (Summer 1973), 23.

6. Paul Goodman, *Utopian Essays and Practical Proposals* (New York, 1962), pp. 204–5, 234; Michael Harrington is quoted in *Newsweek,* October 16, 1972, p. 78; Norman Mailer is quoted on the title page of John Montgomery, *The Fifties* (London, 1965).

7. Russel B. Nye, *The Unembarrassed Muse* (New York, 1970), p. 406; Ben J. Wattenberg, *This U.S.A.* (Garden City, 1965), p. 248; Martin Mayer, "Television's Lords of Creation," *Harper's,* November 1956, p. 25.

8. Editors of *Time-Life, This Fabulous Century,* vol. VI, *1950–1960* (New York, 1970), pp. 156–73; Daniel Snowman, *America Since 1920* (New York, 1968), pp. 126–27; Jeff Greenfield, *No Peace, No Place* (Garden City, 1973), pp. 25–27; William O'Neill, ed., *American Society Since 1945* (Chicago, 1969), pp. 16–18.

9. "Meet the Typical American–Male and Female," *Reader's Digest,* February 1954, pp. 34, 36; *Life,* March 20, 1950, p. 120; *Fortune,* October 1953, pp. 135, 137.

10. *Reader's Digest,* June 1955, p. 38.

11. Reuel Denney, *The Astonished Muse* (Chicago, 1957), pp. 22–23; Eric Larrabee and Rolf Meyerson, eds., *Mass Leisure* (Glencoe, Ill., 1958), pp. 270–73; Frederick Lewis Allen, *The Big Change* (New York, 1952), p. 273; *The Unicorn Book of 1954* (New York, 1954), pp. 277, 280–81; Reed Whittemore, "The Cuteness of Well-Being: the Gift Shoppe," *Esquire,* October 1958, p. 68; Russell Lynes, *A Surfeit of Honey* (New York, 1957), p. 129; *Time,* October 6, 1952, p. 115.

12. Fenton B. Turck, "The Great American Explosion," *Reader's Digest,* November 1952, pp. 83–85; see also Albert Karson and Perry E. Gianakos, eds., *American Civilization Since World War II* (Belmont, Cal., 1968), p. 229; John Brooks, *The Great Leap* (New York, 1966), pp. 178–79; Louis Kronenberger, *Company Manners* (Indianapolis, 1954), pp. 225–26; Peter F. Drucker, "The Myth of American Uniformity," *Harper's,* May 1952, p. 74.

13. Brooks, *Great Leap,* p. 185; Untermeyer is quoted in *Time,* April 23, 1956.

14. Adlai E. Stevenson, *Major Campaign Speeches, 1952* (New York, 1953), pp. 248, 262; Editors of *Fortune, U.S.A.: The Permanent Revolution* (New York, 1951), pp. xvi–xvii.

15. Morris L. Ernst, *Utopia 1976* (New York, 1955), pp. 147–76.

16. Norman Vincent Peale, *The Power of Positive Thinking* (New York, 1952), p. 124; *A Guide to Fallout Protection for New York Schools* (New York, n.d., ca. 1959), p. 3; Robert Langbaum, "This Literary Generation," *American Scholar,* 25, Winter 1955–56, 94.

17. Examples of widely read fifties books critical of aspects of American society would include: David Riesman et al, *The Lonely Crowd* (Garden City, 1955 ed.); William H. Whyte, Jr., *The Organization Man* (Garden City, 1956); Vance Packard, *The Status Seekers* (New York, 1959); William J. Lederer and Eugene Burdick, *The Ugly American* (New York, 1958).

18. Frederick Lewis Allen, *Only Yesterday* (New York, 1957 ed.). Eric Goldman in writing about the period from the close of World War II to the mid-fifties describes this as a unique and "crucial" decade. His interpretation, however, is questionable, and his periodization strikes us as artificial. Goldman, *The Crucial Decade and After* (New York, 1960).

19. Editors of *Time-Life, The Fabulous Century,* p. 34. After Ike was installed in office one minister, Reverend James Miller of Los Angeles, offered up a prayer which began: "Now that virtue has been restored to high places." Goldman, *Crucial Decade,* p. 239. Norman Mailer described the whole Eisenhower phenomenon this way: "Came the Korean War, the shadow of the H-Bomb, and we were ready for the General. Uncle Harry gave way to Father, and security, regularity, order and the life of no imagination were the command of the day." Quoted in Lawrence Goldman, "The Political Vision of Norman Mailer," *Studies on the Left,* IV (Summer 1964), 131.

20. Riesman is quoted in Elting E. Morison, ed., *The American Style* (New York, 1958), pp. 359–60.

21. Thomas Griffith, *The Waist-High Culture* (New York, 1959), pp. 166–67; Robert L. Heilbroner, *The Future As History* (New York, 1960), p. 199.

22. Walter Lippmann, "Interviewed by Howard K. Smith," *New Republic,* July 25, 1960, pp. 19–24; Arthur Schlesinger, Jr., *The Politics of Hope* (Boston, 1962), pp. 81–93.

One does not have to search far to find evidence that American social and cultural life was changing in the late fifties. Books like *Peyton Place* and the first American edition of *Lady Chatterley's Lover* were published; sick jokes and black humor became popular; the Beats attracted national attention. On a more serious level poverty, racism, and sexism were rediscovered. Among college students, by fifties end panty raids and "grassers" were beginning to give way to demonstrations against ROTC, war, the bomb, and racial inequality. In 1959, for example, some 30,000 blacks and whites participated in a "Youth pilgrimage" to Washington to pressure for faster school desegregation. As reporter James Wechsler remarked at the time, this was "one of the largest signs of life exhibited by the younger generation in recent years." James Wechsler, *Reflections of an Angry Middle-Aged Editor* (New York, 1960), p. 116.

1

Sinister Sweets and More Insidious McCarthyisms

One evening in 1950 a Houston couple entered a Chinese restaurant. The woman, a radio writer, wanted the proprietor's help in producing a program on recent Chinese history. Overhearing their conversation, a nearby man rushed out, phoned the police, and informed them that people were "talking Communism." The couple was immediately arrested and jailed for 14 hours before the police concluded they had no case. At about the same time a policeman in Wheeling, West Virginia, discovered some penny-candy machines dispensing goodies with tiny geography lessons. One lesson, under the hammer-and-sickle Soviet flag, read: "U.S.S.R. Population 211,000,000. Capitol Moscow. Largest country in the world." "This is a terrible thing to expose our children to," pronounced city manager Robert Plummer when informed. He quickly had the sinister sweets removed to protect the innocent from knowledge of the Soviet Union.[1]

Retrospectively, one can laugh at such events, dismissing them as isolated instances of American nuttiness. But such behavior was far from rare or even odd in the fifties. Monogram Pictures canceled a film on Longfellow with the explanation that Hiawatha had tried to stop wars between Indian tribes, and people might see this as propaganda for the communist "peace offensive." A foundation offered $100,000 support for research into the creation of a device for detecting traitors. The U. S. Immigration services, in an attempt to prove an alien was a communist, had a witness testify that the alien preferred soccer to football. What "an insult to this country," added the witness. In Pasadena a three-year-old girl was hired as a model for an art class at a tax-supported college. Her mother was told the child could not be paid unless she signed a loyalty oath. Since the child could not write, she was never paid. The anticommunist compulsion had seized the national mind.[2]

These are fairly harmless examples. But the damage done by anticommunism went far deeper than stealing a kid's few bucks or prosecuting penny-candy machines. Much anticommunism was neither so funny nor so ephemeral. The trivial actions of the witch hunters obscure the infinitely more important functions of real and manipulated anticommunism in destroying the left, discrediting any radical alternatives to the status quo, ensuring a rigid foreign policy and a tense period of cold war, and aiding the eight-year reign of conservative Republicanism. It is essential to know something of the depth and persuasiveness of the anticommunist impulse in order to understand the United States from the late 1940s to the present. We are still the unfortunate heirs of an irrational anticommunist legacy.

The threat of communist ideology loomed so large in the American imagination that the reflex action of opposing it struck no one as ideology but only as one of the "givens," the essences of life. Truly, anticommunism was an invisible ideology, an unperceived taint.[3] And like an unperceived taint, in the years from the late forties through the mid-fifties, it became an hysterical pandemic. Most Americans accepted its effects quite willingly, believing their nation to be locked in a death struggle with evil communists bent upon world domination and willing to use any means to achieve that end, including internal subversion. In a 1954 national survey, over half of those interviewed agreed that all known communists should be jailed. Civil liberties were considered far less important than ending the Red menace; 58 per cent of the populace questioned in this survey favored finding all communists "even if some innocent people should be hurt." Seventy-eight per cent thought it a good idea to report to the FBI neighbors or acquaintances whom they suspected of being communists. Anyone appearing at all strange or different was liable to be accused of being a communist. This did produce many amusing anecdotes. But, again, the humor found in our distance from the event is hardly the major point. The threat appeared in the way Americans showed a willingness to rub out their own freedoms in pursuit of a force that threatened to rub out their freedoms.[4]

Excessive, emotional anticommunism has too often been explained away as a defensive postwar reaction to the Soviet challenge, or as a response to the anticommunist demagoguery of Joseph McCarthy. Such an interpretation overlooks the deep-rooted anti-radicalism in this nation's history; twentieth-century anticommunism is just one more manifestation of this. From the 1790s when the United States first established a workable constitutional government to today, radicalism has been in disrepute.

Several related factors account for this. First, this has generally been a stable society dominated by people of wealth and standing; thus, the sanctity of private property and free enterprise always have been prevailing American values. Such views have been propagated by the propertied interests and by institutions influenced or controlled by these interests such as the schools, the churches, the professions, the press, and the politicians. Ever since the late 1820s when organized labor began to question the emergent capitalist system, challenges to that system have been harshly, sometimes violently, rejected. For generations, elites have effectively equated Americanism with free enterprise, and in the popular mind, socialism and communism have been emotionally dismissed as "un-American" and unworthy of legitimate consideration as alternatives to capitalism.

Anticommunism also feeds on the historic notion of American uniqueness and greatness. "We the American people," intoned a mid-nineteenth-century editorialist, "are the most independent, intelligent, moral and happy people on the face of the earth." Such views, and they abound throughout this nation's history, insist on the clear superiority of the American people and the American way of life. God or History selected this chosen people to perfect an ideal society in the New World, an Eden uncontaminated by Old World corruption. Americans have historically identified their greatness with such concepts as democracy, individualism, godliness, and free enterprise. Communism was the apparent antithesis of all this—a despotic, collectivist, godless, alien ideology.[5]

A final contributing cause to America's long-standing anti-radicalism is the belief, widely held during various periods of history, that threatening conspiracies are at work trying to destroy this virtuous republic. From the seventeenth-century actual witch hunts to their twentieth-century figurative counterparts, Americans often have explained afflictions in conspiratorial terms. Virtually all nations and peoples have resorted to blaming supposed conspiratorial groups for the ills and evils tormenting them. But Americans seem particularly prone to this type of scapegoating. Believing their nation's history to be the progressive unfolding of a divine plan in which individual effort was rewarded by material success, spiritual salvation, or both, Americans have never taken well to adversity. Consequently, during times of crises, often generated by wars or rapid change, Americans have been quick to account their miseries the result of a diabolical, alien group. If ills could be interpreted as the result of a vast, well-organized yet cleverly disguised conspiracy, then guilt and anxiety over one's failures are relieved and it is unnecessary to actually deal with the real problems. In American history various groups on occasion have served such scapegoat roles: witches, Masons, Catholics, abolitionists, anarchists, Jews. But from 1917 on, America's conspiratorial phobia has centered on communists.[6]

Capitalist countries throughout the world took alarm at the successful communist revolution in Russia. Though the infant Soviet state could not conceivably have posed any military or economic threat, the United States joined England, France, Germany, Italy, and Japan in sending troops into Russia in an attempt to crush the nascent Bolshevism. This failed. Then the American government, under the prodding of President Woodrow Wilson's Attorney General A. Mitchell Palmer and the young anti-radical sleuth J. Edgar Hoover, began to search for Reds at home. They conducted a series of largely illegal raids against suspected communists. Through 1919 and 1920 the irrational Red Scare raged; virtually every ill confronting America was blamed on Bolsheviks.[7]

The frenzied post-World War I Red Scare soon passed blandly

into the normalcy of the Harding-Coolidge years. But unreasonable anticommunism was never far from the surface of American life. Such hysteria emerged again in 1938 with the founding of the House Un-American Activities Committee (HUAC). In the first few days of the committee's existence, witnesses charged some 640 organizations, 483 newspapers, and 280 labor unions with being communistic. Witnesses even questioned the loyalty of the Boy Scouts, the Camp Fire Girls, and child movie star Shirley Temple. Headed by conservative Democrat Martin Dies, this committee pioneered techniques and charges that would later be associated with Joseph McCarthy. These included guilt by association whereby a person's loyalty would be judged on the basis of his or her friendships, relations, or organizational connections; using the communist issue to attack liberals; harping on communists in government; pretending reliable evidence when none existed; and drawing on the supposed expert testimony of ex-communists eager to prove their redemption.[8]

The wartime alliance of convenience between the United States and the Soviet Union temporarily subdued anticommunism. But soon after World War II, as relations between the two superpowers rapidly deteriorated, fears of an internal communist threat re-emerged with renewed vehemence. More than ever right-wing propaganda equated all liberalism with the Red menace. In the 1946 congressional elections, Republicans, making frequent use of that equation, gained a majority for the first time in 18 years. Newly elected on the basis of anticommunist smear campaigns were, among other Republicans, Richard Nixon, Karl Mundt, and Joseph McCarthy.

The immediate postwar years were frustrating times. Domestically, people suffered from inflation, unemployment, strikes, racial tensions, fear of renewed depression, and the general dislocations caused by the rapid attempt to adjust from war to peace. International affairs were also extremely worrisome as it quickly became clear that the great sacrifices of the war years had not brought instant tranquillity.

In March 1947, President Harry S Truman, genuinely concerned about supposed Soviet aggressions and seeking to head off Republican attacks on the patriotism of Democrats, committed the United States to a policy aimed at defeating communism abroad and at home. On March 12, 1947, he announced what became known as the Truman Doctrine: "It must be the policy of the United States to support free peoples who are resisting attempted subjugation by armed minorities." This policy pledged the nation to the cold war—a reliance on maintaining military superiority in a world pictured as irreconcilably divided into camps of good and evil. Less than two weeks later, on March 22, the President launched his domestic war against communism. Truman issued Executive Order 9835 initiating a loyalty review program with the stated purpose of effecting "maximum protection" to "the United States against infiltration of disloyal persons into the ranks of its employees."

Though Truman would later complain of the "great wave of hysteria" sweeping the nation, his commitment to victory over communism, to completely safeguarding the United States from external and internal threats, was in large measure responsible for creating that very hysteria. Between the launching of his security program in March 1947 and December 1952, some 6.6 million persons were investigated. Not a single case of espionage was uncovered, though about 500 persons were dismissed in dubious cases of "questionable loyalty." All of this was conducted with secret evidence, secret and often paid informers, and neither judge nor jury. Despite the failure to find subversion, the broad scope of the official Red hunt gave popular credence to the notion that the government was riddled with spies. A conservative and fearful reaction coursed the country. Americans became convinced of the need for absolute security and the preservation of the established order.[9]

Not to be outdone by the federal government, states, cities, and counties set up their own loyalty programs. So too did many corporations, educational institutions, and labor unions. Publicly pledging allegiance to God, country, and constitution, while abjuring communist affiliations, became a basic feature of American life. Under the guise of loyalty checks, conservatives ferreted out not communists but liberals, New Dealers, radical labor leaders, civil rights activists, pacifists, atheists.

From the time of Truman's 1947 executive order through the early fifties, a series of external events contributed to the growing internal anticommunist mania. In 1948 a communist coup succeeded in Czechoslovakia and the Soviets blocked allied ground entry into Berlin. Nineteen forty-nine was more shocking as China, which Americans had always regarded as practically their own, became communist. To make matters worse, the Soviets exploded their first nuclear weapon, breaking the American monopoly. Then in June 1950 fighting broke out in distant Korea. For the next three years U.S. troops fought North Korean and Chinese communists to a frustrating stalemate in a war Americans were told was necessary to stop Soviet-sponsored aggression and avoid a Munichlike appeasement.

While troubles abroad deeply disturbed Americans, domestic witch hunting in the late forties and early fifties had equally disquieting effects. On July 20, 1948, a federal grand jury indicted 11 leaders of the Communist party of the United States. They were charged with conspiracy to advocate the overthrow of the U. S. Government by force. The defendants were not proved to be agents of the Soviet Union; nor were they even charged with engaging in espionage. In a much publicized ten-month trial that began in January 1949, the prosecutors established that the communist leaders advocated the principles of Marxism-Leninism, which in the atmosphere of the time was enough to convict them.

On January 21, 1950, Alger Hiss was convicted of perjury following two of the most sensational and highly publicized trials in American history. The Hiss case first came to national attention in August 1948 when at an HUAC hearing Whittaker Chambers, a confessed ex-communist, accused Hiss of having been a party member while employed in the State Department during the 1930s. Initially Chambers' charges were vague. But with prodding from Nixon and other committee members, he soon told a story of stolen documents passed from Hiss to himself to the Soviets. Though Hiss could not be tried for espionage due to the statute of limitations, a New York grand jury indicted him for perjury. A first trial ended in a hung jury. A second much publicized and still controversial trial resulted in Hiss' conviction.[10]

The Hiss case convinced millions that Republican charges of 20 years of Democratic treason must be true. Here in Hiss, the handsome, urbane, Harvard-educated, eastern aristocrat, Republican politicians and right-wing superpatriots had the perfect symbol of New Deal, Fair Deal treachery. The Hiss case, declared Richard Nixon, was only "a small part of the whole shocking story of Communist espionage in the United States."[11]

On February 3, 1950, only two weeks after Hiss' conviction, the British Government announced the arrest of Dr. Klaus Fuchs, a high-level atomic scientist who had worked at Los Alamos during the war. Fuchs confessed to having spied for the Soviet Union. Investigators linked him to Americans Harry Gold, Morton Sobel, and Julius and Ethel Rosenberg. All of these Americans were arrested, tried, and convicted of conspiracy to commit espionage. Gold and Sobel received long jail terms. The Rosenbergs were executed.[12]

These events of 1949–50 shocked and stunned Americans. How could Russia have the Bomb? How could China have fallen to the communists? How many Alger Hisses must there still be in government?

The mass media encouraged such questioning. Even before the heyday of McCarthy, articles appeared in major magazines with titles such as "How Communists Get That Way," "How the Russians Spied on Their Allies," "Trained to Raise Hell in America: International Lenin School in Moscow," "Communists Penetrate Wall Street," "Why I Broke with the Communists," "Reds Are After Your Child," "How Communists Take Over." Anticommunist, anti-Soviet books glutted bookstores—Victor Kravchenko, *I Choose Freedom*, Hamilton Fish, *The Red Plotters*, Richard Hirsch, *The Soviet Spies*, Louis Budenz, *This Is My Story*, Richard Crossman, ed., *The God That Failed*, to name but a few. *I Led Three Lives*, Herbert Philbrick's story about his role as communist turned FBI informer, was serialized in some 500 newspapers. Hollywood turned out such thrillers as *I Married a Communist, The Red Menace, The Iron Curtain, The Conspirator, Guilty of Treason*, and *I Was a Communist for the FBI*.[13]

The popular image of a communist conveyed by such massive propaganda was that of a nearly superhuman daemon, a devious and highly skilled fiend, the master of techniques of hypnotic intellectual seduction who would be more than a match for ordinary mortals operating under the lawful ways of democracy. Consequently, Americans became quite tolerant of extralegal vigilante violence committed against supposed Reds. Henry Wallace's Progressive party presidential campaign in 1948, falsely labeled a communist movement by both major parties and the press, was constantly harassed. Speakers were heckled, egged, and stoned; meetings were broken up. On one occasion a Wallace supporter, Robert New, was murdered at a public rally. The killer received a three-year sentence for manslaughter. Similarly, in the summer of 1949, a concert by the black singer Paul Robeson held in Peekskill, New York, to benefit a civil rights organization that had been placed without a hearing on the attorney general's subversive list, was brutally disrupted. Hundreds of casualties resulted.[14]

No wonder, then, Americans bought some three million copies of Mickey Spillane's 1951 thriller *One Lonely Night.* In this novel the author's gutsy American hero Mike Hammer brags "I killed more people tonight than I have fingers on my hands. I shot them in cold blood and enjoyed every minute of it. I pumped slugs in the nastiest bunch of bastards you ever saw. . . . They were Commies. . . . They were red sons-of-bitches who should have died long ago. . . . They never thought there were people like me in this country. They figured us all to be soft as horse manure and just as stupid."[15]

While the brutal Mike Hammer was fictional, muscular ex-marine Joseph R. McCarthy, the junior senator from Wisconsin, was all too real. On February 9, 1950, less than a week after the Fuchs story broke and while Americans were still inflamed over Hiss, China, and the Soviet bomb, McCarthy, holding an old laundry list while addressing the Wheeling Women's Republican Club, announced, "I have here in my hand a list of 205 that were known to the Secretary of State as being members of the Communist party and who, nevertheless, are still working and shaping policy in the State Department." With these words began McCarthy's national anticommunist career. In the following five years he would take the already existing mania to new heights of irrational hysteria.[16]

But it needs to be emphasized again that McCarthy did not create the national paranoia over communism. He merely capitalized on it. His rhetoric and tactics, though extreme, were well within the already established framework of cold war politics. In fact, many Democrats inadvertently furthered McCarthy's cause through their own exaggerated depiction of the communist threat. For example, Truman's last attorney general, J. Howard McGrath, in an address some two months after McCarthy's Wheeling diatribe, claimed: "There are today many Communists in America. They are everywhere—in factories, offices, butcher shops, on street corners, in private business—and each carries in himself the germs of death for society." These communists, he warned, "are busy at work—undermining your Government, plotting to destroy the liberties of every citizen, and feverishly trying, in whatever way they can, to aid the Soviet Union." Such speeches, of course, coincided with McCarthy's claims that the Truman administration was "soft on communism."[17]

From Wheeling on February 9, McCarthy went on to repeat his charges in Salt Lake City the following night and in Reno on February 11, though now claiming 57 as the number of known communists in government. He also sent President Truman an insulting telegram demanding of the man who had already initiated the largest loyalty check in American history that he do something about the communists in the State Department. McCarthy's repetitive charges soon attracted national attention. On February 20, 1950, he brought his show to the floor of the Senate where for nearly six hours he spewed forth accusations. Now he professed to have 81 documented cases of communists in the State Department.

These were grave charges. The Senate responded by establishing a special investigative committee headed by conservative Maryland Democrat Millard Tydings. For several months this committee carefully sifted through evidence, took testimony, ran down leads. Without exception McCarthy's cases proved false. They were based on rumor, gossip, lies. Most had been drawn from old and already discredited files. When the Tydings committee report was made public on July 17, 1950, McCarthy was bluntly exposed for the falsifier he was. "At a time when American blood is again being shed to preserve our dream of freedom," began the report, "we are constrained fearlessly and frankly to call the charges, and the methods employed to give them ostensible validity, what they truly are: a fraud and a hoax. . . . They represent perhaps the most nefarious campaign of half-truths and untruths in the history of this republic. For the first time in our history, we have seen the totalitarian technique of the 'big lie' employed on a sustained basis."[18]

In a saner time such a report might have squelched the upstart senator. But in the absurdity of the early fifties, it had the reverse effect. Republicans generally, and many other persons, treated the Tydings committee disclosures scornfully, as a whitewash of communist infiltration. McCarthy went on, more reckless than ever, gaining power, causing chaos and fear. When Senator Tydings came up for re-election in November 1950, a McCarthy-backed unknown, John Butler, defeated him.[19] Two years later when Eisenhower's popularity gave the Republicans control of Congress as well as the White House, McCarthy was rewarded with the chairmanship of his own investigative committee.

We have tried to give some indication of the cultural beliefs and fears that could cause a lying bully like McCarthy to gain such power. With all the apparent proofs of subversion—the Hiss case, the Rosenbergs, Truman's witch hunting—people were ready to believe him. Maybe McCarthy had not turned up a spy—yet—but he was on to something. People believed that communists and communist sympathizers had to be driven out of government even if this necessitated a McCarthyite disregard of civil liberties.[20] To a frightened populace there was something reassuring about the blustering McCarthy with his names, numbers, and endless charges. He appeared to millions as the great American avenger—heroic "Tail Gunner Joe" out to beat traitors and spies into submission, to smite the communist anti-Christ. So what if a few wrong toes were stepped on? The cause was just.

McCarthy built up a large popular following. He also collected a most influential one. Various groups and individuals saw in McCarthyism a movement useful to their own purposes. To the superpatriots of the American Legion and the Veterans of Foreign Wars, McCarthy stood for their ideal of real 100 per cent Americanism. To weighty Catholics such as Francis Cardinal Spellman or layman Joseph P. Kennedy, Catholic McCarthy was defending both America and the church against atheistic subversion. Protestant fundamentalists such as J. B. Matthews and Daniel A. Poling also saw McCarthy as a religious savior. To Poling, president of the World's Christian Endeavor Union and chairman of the All American Council to Combat Communism, McCarthy was the modern Messiah leading Americans out of the wilderness of subversion. The China lobby, the powerful propaganda operation financed by Chiang Kai-shek's Nationalists and wealthy right-wing Americans, saw in McCarthy's attacks on the State Department a means of reversing what they considered a disastrous Far Eastern policy. Well-heeled businessmen and Texas oil millionaires such as Hugh Roy Cullen, Clint W. Murchison, and H. L. Hunt financially supported McCarthy as the scourge of the liberals. Such men cheered when the Wisconsin senator assailed as communists the "whole group of twisted-thinking New Dealers [who] have led America near to ruin at home and abroad." To the fascist fringe of the American right, the followers of people like Gerald L. K. Smith, Joseph P. Kamp, and Upton Close, McCarthy was a brother with the power to carry out the purges they had long advocated.[21]

The Hearst, McCormick, and Scripps-Howard newspapers favorably publicized McCarthy's charges and crusades. The New York *Daily News* and the Dallas *Morning News* also supported him. So too did prominent magazines such as the *Saturday Evening Post, U.S. News & World Report,* and the *American Mercury.* Syndicated columnists Westbrook Pegler, George Sokolsky, Fulton Lewis, Jr., and David Lawrence were all pro-McCarthy. But even papers not ostensibly in McCarthy's camp fostered the notion that the senator was discovering real espionage. In the atmosphere of terror of the time, his fabricated charges were front-page, banner-headline stuff. Denials or complete proof of the falsehood of McCarthy's allegations might eventually appear on page 17, squeezed between two girdle ads. But in the meantime McCarthy would have captured page one with yet another big lie. New York *Times* columnist Peter Kihss finally felt obliged to warn that "the reading public should understand that it is difficult if not impossible to ignore charges by Senator McCarthy just because they are usually proved exaggerated or false."[22]

Published stories the least bit unfavorable to McCarthy evoked the senator's wrath. When the generally pro-McCarthy *Time* magazine ran a slightly censorious article in 1952, McCarthy wrote *Time:* "I am sure you will agree that the policy of *Time* magazine to throw pebbles at communism generally but to then parallel the *Daily Worker*'s smear attack upon individuals who start to dig out dangerous secret Communists, is rendering almost unlimited service to the Communist cause and undermining America." McCarthy harshly attacked reporters regularly critical of him such as Drew Pearson and James Wechsler. In Pearson's case, McCarthy, in addition to his usual verbal abuse (he called Pearson a "Moscow-directed character assassin"), actually kneed the columnist in the groin and punched him about the head when the two accidentally encountered one another in the cloakroom of Washington's Sulgrave Club on December 12, 1950. Though Pearson brought suit against McCarthy, nothing came of it. In fact, McCarthy was able to pressure Adams Hats to stop sponsoring Pearson's popular radio program. Pearson continued to oppose McCarthy. But few other reporters were courageous enough to stand up against the senator's intimidating tactics. The press, therefore, until McCarthy's downfall became evident, was overwhelmingly pro-McCarthy.[23]

In Congress, politicians should have seen more clearly than the public McCarthy's evil nature. Congressmen, after all, witnessed his terrorizing ways daily. Why then was he given such power? For one thing he had staunch allies in the conservative wing of the Republican party. Republican senators like Robert Taft of Ohio, Homer Capehart and William Jenner of Indiana, Everett Dirksen of Illinois, Charles Potter of Michigan, Karl Mundt of South Dakota, and California's Richard Nixon were in basic agreement with McCarthy. Like him they believed that in both foreign and domestic matters the Democrats had been "soft on communism" and that subversives continued to fill key government positions. Nixon is a good example. He had risen to prominence in the late forties by exploiting the communist menace, his fame stemming from the fact that he was the most persistent prosecutor of Alger Hiss on the House Un-American Activities Committee. His campaigns invariably smeared opponents as pinkos or dupes. Even after attaining the respectability of the vice-presidency, Nixon remained, in Adlai Stevenson's words, "McCarthy with a white collar." As Stanley Plastrik noted, "Nixonism is McCarthyism with its nails pared and cleaned, its 5 o'clock shadow shaved off. It is McCarthyism systematized, made palatable for the respectable and decent." For Nixon and his ilk, then, McCarthyism was attractive and useful. It was both a way back to power and a way to discredit New Deal liberalism and left-wing intellectuals.[24]

Even moderate Republicans, though not always in agreement with McCarthy's tactics, felt that he could be used for practical political purposes. After all, through 1952 at least, all his charges of communists in government were direct assaults on the Democrats. The vote-getting power of McCarthyism, exhibited as early as 1950, was an important consideration. Consequently, in 1952, McCarthy's coattails were nearly as used as Ike's. In the age-old tradition of American politics, Republicans did not mind stirring up hate and fear if it brought them votes and power.

After Eisenhower's election in 1952, however, McCarthy kept flailing away at his favorite target, even though his wild punches now were hitting Republicans. But the popular Ike believed that the executive branch of government had no right to interfere with legislators. He also hated to dirty his hands in politics. To pleas that he silence McCarthy, Ike replied: "I just will not—I *refuse*—to get into the gutter with that guy." With no backing from the President, other administrators felt helpless. For a time, Secretary of

State John Foster Dulles almost looked like McCarthy's errand boy. In general the administration seemed demoralized by his savage onslaught.[25]

Democrats should have united to a man against the Wisconsin senator. Time and again he slandered them and their party. In a Charleston, West Virginia, speech he stated: "The hard fact is that those who wear the label—Democrat—wear it with the stain of an historic betrayal." Yet as late as February 1954, the Senate passed an appropriation bill for the continued funding of McCarthy's investigating committee by a vote of 85 to 1. Only Arkansas Democrat William Fulbright dissented. Guilt and fear had undermined the Democrats. Many actually believed some of the reckless charges of having been too lax on the communist issue, and certainly the Hiss case had a demoralizing effect. Others learned too well the lesson of Tyding's defeat. Opposition to McCarthy could result in political suicide. It is not that individual Democrats (and some Republicans, too) failed to attack McCarthy; many did. What was lacking was a sustained, co-ordinated attack of sufficient magnitude to succeed.[26]

More typical of Democratic tactics was the continuation of Truman's 1947 strategy, trying to assert their party's anticommunist credentials. Stevenson, campaigning in 1952, spoke of how effectively the Democrats had exposed the communists "before the junior Senator from Wisconsin suddenly appeared on the scene and began his wild and reckless campaign." Unquestionably this was an attempt by Democratic politicians to co-opt the issue, snatch it from GOP hands, and make it—and especially the power involved—their own. In retrospect it is clear that this tactic only confirmed in the public mind McCarthy's contention that there was a menace. Liberal Democrats, very fearful of being considered fellow-travelers, often went to extremes on the communist issue. Hubert Humphrey actually introduced a bill to outlaw the Communist party altogether. Paul Douglas, the liberal Illinois senator, supported Humphrey, claiming that Republicans kept the Communist party in existence "to smear Democrats like myself. We liberals must destroy the Communists if this dirty game is to stop." Such a liberalism, of course, was simply self-defeating.[27]

The anticommunist political atmosphere of the time was evidenced by the wide range of witch-hunting activity and legislation not directly attributable to the Wisconsin senator. In 1951 Congress overwhelmingly passed the McCarran Internal Security Act. This required communist and so-called communist-front organizations to register with the government and to clearly label all their mail and literature as communist. This act, by establishing a five-member Subversive Activities Control Board with the authority to investigate the thoughts and beliefs of citizens, sanctified internal repression. Its most totalitarian provision was first proposed by Humphrey, Douglas, and other liberals. The board set up concentration camps and authorized the government to lock up communists and other suspected subversives any time a national emergency was proclaimed.

In addition to McCarthy's own Government Operations Committee, which he illegally used for probing supposed subversive activities, two other congressional committees—HUAC and the Senate Internal Security Committee—were also active in the Red-hunting business. The FBI and the CIA naturally were involved too. Then in April 1953, President Eisenhower bestirred himself to issue Executive Order 10450, establishing a loyalty program even more sweeping and strict than Truman's 1947 measure. By Ike's order, all new government employees and workers in firms with government contracts regardless of position were to be investigated. Any derogatory information, no matter what its source (always kept secret), was grounds for dismissal. Furthermore, all those cleared by field investigations during Truman's administration had to undergo another full investigation, during which they were suspended without pay.

McCarthy then was far from alone in pushing the anticommunist issue to extremes. He was a recognizable product of an irrational system. He ranted and raved in a rough manner, but so did many others in and out of government. For instance a best-selling 1952 book, *U.S.A. Confidential* by newsmen Jack Lait and Lee Mortimer, was filled with puerile, racist, Red-baiting drivel of the most lascivious sort: "Female card-holders [Communist party] are required to show their loyalty to the cause through indiscriminate intercourse wherever it will do the most good. . . . Sex is offered as an inducement to comrades for attending meetings. Most soirees of the faithful end up with vodka toasts in dim candlelight. Negro men get the first choice of white women. An indoctrinated girl may whimsically turn down a white man, but never a Negro: That is racial intolerance. Many Negroes join up only for that purpose and pass the word along to their friends. The Red bed-battalion is also committed to romancing unioneers in sensitive industries." But, they added, "judging from the looks and odor of the revolutionists, we prefer to remain capitalists."[28]

For years McCarthy spewed forth similar slander. But his was more effectively vicious, because he named names and hurt numerous innocent people. Since he made his most outlandish charges within the confines of the Senate, he was immune from libel suits or other prosecution.

After nearly five years of irresponsible actions—forcing from the State Department the only knowledgeable Far Eastern experts, weakening the Voice of America, purging from United States overseas libraries books by Theodore Dreiser, Archibald MacLeish, Arthur Miller, Arthur Schlesinger, Jr., and hundreds of other "dangerous" authors, disrupting the army base at Fort Monmouth, New Jersey, defaming thousands—McCarthy fell from grace. The downfall began with a 35-day Senate investigation into alleged attempts to gain preferential treatment from the army for his young assistant, Private G. David Schine. The televised hearings gave millions of Americans the opportunity to see for themselves the bludgeoning manner of the unprincipled communist hunter as he attacked the army's dignified top brass. His popularity lessened. Even before the hearings closed, the Senate got up the nerve to start an inquiry of its own into McCarthy's conduct as a senator. Finally on December 2, 1954, his colleagues by a vote of 67 to 22 condemned him. Though he retained all his senatorial privileges, McCarthy's power did not survive censure. Always a heavy drinker, he imbibed more after this. His health deteriorated, and on May 2, 1957, he died.

Liberal intellectuals, then and now, refer to McCarthyism and McCarthy as temporary insanities. They believe that basically the American people are too rational and decent to long tolerate extremism of either right or left. They cite McCarthy's demise as a return to the usual pluralistic democratic consensus.[29]

Such an interpretation seems wrong on two counts. First, McCarthy's fall from power resulted more from external events than from an upsurge of human decency. Such factors as Eisenhower's election in 1952, the end of the Korean War and the death of Stalin in 1953, and the absence of new spy sensations after the Rosenberg case all helped to reduce tensions and thereby lessen

McCarthy's appeal. By 1954 the nation had sustained some eight years of intense witch hunting. It could not confront and sustain the high pitch of fear indefinitely. Millions of Americans wanted a time to rest, to forget the bomb and internal subversion. The fatherly general was in the White House; prosperity appeared to abound; the terror and urgency of the recent past seemed gone. With or without McCarthy, a degree of calm over the issue of communist subversion undoubtedly would have returned to American life by the mid-fifties.

Second, and more important, McCarthyism did not completely end with McCarthy; it merely slumbered. Even after the Army-McCarthy hearings, a Gallup poll revealed that only 51 per cent of the public opposed him while 36 per cent supported him. These figures, though showing a decline in popularity for McCarthy, still represented a devoted following of millions. As late as 1958, a Richard Rovere article in *Esquire* critically assessing McCarthy's career caused an outrage. "The furies descended," Rovere later recalled. "I have half a file drawer of suggestions that I walk into the Atlantic Ocean until my hat floats, that I ask God's forgiveness for my acts of desecration, that I buck for the next Stalin Prize, and so forth. . . . The letters were ugly, threatening, in many cases vile. . . . Three hundred subscriptions, or a lot, to *Esquire* were canceled."[30]

Long after McCarthy's condemnation, funds for HUAC and the Senate Internal Security Committee came regularly without much debate. When HUAC was first made a standing committee in 1945 (as distinct from its original status as a special committee), 186 members had opposed this action; by 1958, when a vote again was taken, the opposition had declined to one. The Communist party by the late fifties had dwindled to a few thousand members, a high proportion of whom were probably FBI agents. But FBI head Hoover and the congressional anticommunists put forth the bizarre theory that the Communist party became more menacing as its numbers dropped. A small party of truly dedicated Bolsheviki, Hoover held, was a worse danger than a massive but unenthusiastic one. So the witch hunts, though less frequent, continued. As Republican Senator Barry Goldwater said in 1959: "I am not willing to accept the idea that there are no Communists left in this country; I think that if we lift enough rocks, we will find some." The atrocities also continued. For example, in 1956, John W. Powell, who had edited the *China Monthly Review* from 1945 to 1953, was sentenced to 260 years in prison and fined $130,000. His offense was publishing and circulating a magazine opposed to American involvement in the Korean War and to support of Chiang Kai-shek.[31]

In effect the nation's politicians had censured McCarthy's clumsy and ineffective tactics, not his values. His fall in no way curbed the underlying anti-radicalism and anticommunism. As liberal Senator Wayne Morse stated at the time of McCarthy's condemnation: "In the Senate there is no division of opinion among liberals, conservatives, and those in between when it comes to our united insistence that as a Senate we fight the growth of the Communist conspiracy."[32]

Virulent anticommunism was central to American culture on all levels. Academic psychiatrist Robert Lindner, writing in 1956, described communism as "a haven for neurosis and a refuge for neurotics." On a more basic level, Marvel comic hero Captain America warned: "Beware, commies, spies, traitors, and foreign agents! Captain America, with all loyal, free men behind him, is looking for you, ready to fight until the last one of you is exposed for the yellow scum you are."[33]

The McCarthy phenomenon coincided with the country's post-World War II emotional breakdown. This hysteria peaked in the early fifties. As soon as a degree of composure was restored, McCarthy lost his power to dominate the national scene. Anticommunism continued, but became less intimidating. People felt a greater sense of security. They could relax with Ike and material possessions. By the late fifties McCarthy-type anticommunism came to be identified with the extreme right—with groups such as the John Birch Society (founded in 1958). Not that this right was insignificant, as was demonstrated in 1964 when Goldwater won the Republican nomination for President, or when former McCarthyite, Red-baiter Richard Nixon won the presidency in 1968 and 1972.[34]

In recent years the anticommunist impulse has been toned down, though it still profoundly affects American attitudes and policies. But the fact that hysterical belief in the Red menace reached its historic heights at mid-century makes it most important to the decade of the fifties. Its impact on that era can be seen in a variety of ways: the conformity, the search for security, the sizable return to religion, the celebration of the family and middle-class virtues, the absence of an effective left, the docility of labor unions, the "silent generation" of college students, the widespread political apathy, the cold war, the arms race, the reliance on nuclear supremacy.

Writing at the meridian of McCarthy's influence, Lewis Mumford warned that "in the name of freedom we are rapidly creating a police state; and in the name of democracy we have succumbed, not to creeping socialism but to galloping Fascism."[35] Mumford's statement was prophetic. The adverse effects of anticommunism from the late forties to the present have been great. Critical dissent has been constrained. National debate on basic issues has been hindered. Civil liberties have been widely violated, and a premium put on unquestioning Americanism. Absolute internal security and containment have remained fundamental U.S. objectives, while being "soft on communism" continues to be a serious, and frequently used, political charge. America is a nation poised on the knife edge of violence and hate. Millions of persons in the late forties and fifties became convinced that all our troubles stemmed from a communist conspiracy. Though their proportionate numbers have undoubtedly diminished, millions still believe this. These legions look for the simple, blunt action of a Captain America, Mike Hammer, Joe McCarthy to crush the demon once and for all. It is impossible to understand United States history since World War II without comprehending the pervasive nature of the anticommunist phobia.

NOTES

1. Elmer Davis, *But We Were Born Free* (Indianapolis, 1954), pp. 14–15, 35; Eric F. Goldman, *The Crucial Decade and After* (New York, 1960), p. 213.

2. Goldman, *Crucial Decade*, pp. 213, 258–59; Earl Latham, *The Communist Controversy in Washington* (Cambridge, Mass., 1966), p. 2; Robert M. Hutchins, *Some Observations on American Education* (Cambridge, Eng., 1956), pp. 65, n. 1, 70; Fred J. Cook, *The Nightmare Decade* (New York, 1971), p. 20.

3. This anti-ideology ideology was carried to extremes by American intellectuals. See Chapter Eight, pp. 223–25.

4. Samuel A. Stouffer, *Communism, Conformity, and Civil Liberties* (Garden City, 1955), pp. 40–46. The Stouffer study, sponsored by the Fund for the Republic and conducted both by the Gallup Poll and the National Opinion Research Center, asked interviewers who claimed to know a communist just how they could tell. Some typical replies were: "He was always talking about world peace" (Oregon woman). "Would not attend church and talked against God" (Pennsylvania woman). "I saw a map of Russia on a wall in his home" (locomotive engineer, Michigan). "I suspected it from his conversation and manner.

He was well educated and had a high disregard for the mentality of others" (Georgia lawyer). "Her activities in distributing literature about the United Nations" (Indiana woman). "He brought a lot of foreign-looking people into his home" (Kansas woman). Stouffer, pp. 176–78.

5. Michael Parenti, *The Anti-Communist Impulse* (New York, 1969), pp. 55–73.

6. Robert Goldston, *The American Nightmare: Senator Joseph R. McCarthy and the Politics of Hate* (Indianapolis, 1973), pp. 1–6, 30; Roberta Strauss Feurlicht, *Joe McCarthy and McCarthyism* (New York, 1972), pp. 30–40; David Brion Davis, ed., *The Fear of Conspiracy* (Ithaca, 1971), pp. 1–9; Richard O. Curry and Thomas M. Brown, eds., *Conspiracy: The Fear of Subversion in American History* (New York, 1972).

7. Robert K. Murray, *Red Scare* (Minneapolis, 1955); Roberta Strauss Feurlicht, *America's Reign of Terror: World War I, The Red Scare, and the Palmer Raids* (New York, 1971).

8. August R. Ogden, *The Dies Committee* (Washington, D.C., 1945), Walter Goodman, *The Committee* (New York, 1968), pp. 3–117; Eric Bentley, ed., *Thirty Years of Treason* (New York, 1971), pp. 3–51.

9. The anticommunist issue of the Truman years is well treated in Richard M. Freeland, *The Truman Doctrine and the Origins of McCarthyism* (New York, 1972); Alan D. Harper, *The Politics of Loyalty* (New York, 1969); and Athan Theoharis, *Seeds of Repression* (Chicago, 1971); Robert Griffith, "American Politics and the Origins of 'McCarthyism,'" in Griffith and Theoharis, eds., *The Specter* (New York, 1974), pp. 2–17.

10. Despite extensive study, the question of Hiss' innocence or guilt remains unsolved. Hiss himself to this day denies any guilt, and many serious critics of the case question the authenticity of the evidence used to convict him. The case is treated in Alistair Cooke, *A Generation on Trial* (New York, 1950); Earl Jowitt, *The Strange Case of Alger Hiss* (Garden City, 1953); Meyer Zeligs, *Friendship and Fratricide* (New York, 1967). Accounts by leading participants: Alger Hiss, *In the Court of Public Opinion* (New York, 1957); Whittaker Chambers, *Witness* (New York, 1953); and Richard M. Nixon, *Six Crises* (Garden City, 1967).

11. Nixon is quoted in Robert Griffith, *The Politics of Fear: Joseph R. McCarthy and the Senate* (Lexington, 1970), p. 48. For a similar use of the Hiss case see J. B. Matthews, "Communism and the Colleges," *American Mercury*, May 1953, p. 114.

12. Like the Hiss case, the Rosenbergs' conviction and execution has not settled quietly into history's pages. For a sampling of recent studies see Walter and Miriam Schneir, *Invitation to an Inquest* (Garden City, 1965); Allen Weinstein, "Agit-Prop and the Rosenbergs," *Commentary*, July 1970, pp. 18–75; Louis Nizer, *The Implosion Conspiracy* (Garden City, 1973); Robert and Michael Meeropol, *We Are Your Sons* (Boston, 1975).

13. A more complete list of articles, books, films, and other forms of anticommunist propaganda is in Albert E. Kahn, *High Treason: The Plot Against the People* (New York, 1950), pp. 329–32.

14. Freeland, *Truman Doctrine*, pp. 298–306; Westchester Committee for

a Fair Inquiry into the Peekskill Violence, *Eyewitness: Peekskill U.S.A.* (New York, 1949); Kahn, *High Treason*, pp. 285–90, 342–47. O. John Rogge, *Our Vanishing Civil Liberties* (New York, 1949).

15. Mickey Spillane, *One Lonely Night* (New York, 1951), p. 171. See also Christopher LaFarge, "Mickey Spillane and His Bloody Hammer," in Bernard Rosenberg and David Manning White, eds., *Mass Culture* (Glencoe, Ill., 1957), pp. 177–82.

16. Cook, *Nightmare*, pp. 147–56. After the Wheeling speech, much controversy developed over whether McCarthy had claimed to have the names of 205 or 57 communists. Though both figures were false and irrelevant, Cook's evidence in support of the larger number seems conclusive.

17. McGrath is quoted in Theoharis, *Seeds of Repression*, pp. 136–38.

18. Griffith, *Politics of Fear*, pp. 152–87; Richard H. Rovere, *Senator Joe McCarthy* (New York, 1959), pp. 145–59.

19. McCarthy and his staff played a very large role in the Maryland election. One of their tactics was the distribution of 500,000 copies of a four-page leaflet accusing Tydings of undermining the American effort in Korea and featuring a doctored photo showing Tydings in close consultation with communist leader Earl Browder.

20. The widespread fear of communist subversion that helped give McCarthy a large popular following was reflected in a 1954 national survey. A few examples will suffice: An Illinois farmer claimed communists "are scattered all over our big factories and are working underground in all of them." "They have positions in the government," a Pennsylvania florist said of communists, "especially in science. They steal our secrets and give them to Russia." A Massachusetts woman believed "Communists get children into cellars, educating them in warfare, and training them to go into secret places." An Indiana housewife envisioned communists "creeping in places and . . . poisoning the minds of young people in education with things that are contrary to the Bible." Stouffer, *Communism*, pp. 158–64.

21. The McCarthy quote is in Goldman, *Crucial Decade*, p. 144; Cook, *Nightmare*, pp. 275–97, treats McCarthy's supporters. See also *Time*, April 12, 1954, p. 51; I. F. Stone, *The Haunted Fifties* (New York, 1963), pp. 23–25, 30; Donald F. Crosby, "The Politics of Religion," and Peter H. Irons, "American Business and the Origins of McCarthyism," in Griffith and Theoharis, eds., *Specter*, pp. 18–38, 72–89.

22. Kihss is quoted in Michael Paul Rogin, *The Intellectuals and McCarthy* (Cambridge, Mass., 1967), p. 255. See also Theoharis, *Seeds of Repression*, p. 15; Douglass Cater, "The Captive Press," *Reporter*, June 6, 1950, pp. 17–20; Davis, *Born Free*, pp. 147–77.

23. The McCarthy attacks on *Time* and Pearson are treated in Cook, *Nightmare*, pp. 326–29, 572–73; *Time*, July 7, 1952, p. 48; James A. Wechsler, *Reflections of an Angry Middle-Aged Editor* (New York, 1960), pp. 175–93.

24. Stevenson is quoted in Cook, *Nightmare*, p. 459; the Plastrik article is in *Dissent*, II (Winter 1955), 91; Rogin, *Intellectuals and McCarthy*, pp. 216–23.

25. Ike is quoted in Emmet John Hughes, *The Ordeal of Power* (New York, 1964), p. 81.

26. McCarthy is quoted in Cook, *Nightmare*, pp. 462–63.

27. Adlai E. Stevenson, *Major Campaign Speeches of Adlai E. Stevenson, 1952* (New York, 1953), pp. 213–19; Douglas is quoted in Cook, *Nightmare*, pp. 18–19. See also Griffith, *Politics of Fear*, pp. 111, 120–21.

28. Jack Lait and Lee Mortimer, *U.S.A. Confidential* (New York, 1952), p. 52.

29. Typical of such a view is this quote from Arthur Schlesinger, Jr., in John Blum et al, *The National Experience* (New York, 1963), p. 774: "By the end of the decade the atmosphere of the McCarthy era seemed dim, remote and improbable. Though traces survived in occasional committees, laws, oaths, and interdictions, as well as in wrecked lives, the robust tradition of American civil freedom had begun at long last to reassert itself." Another good example is this quote from Arthur S. Link, *American Epoch* (New York, 1963), p. 746: "McCarthy's decline was perhaps as much symptom as cause. Except for a determined minority on the far right, Americans were beginning to realize by 1955 that there were more important problems—or more interesting diversions—than the search for Communists in government. Common sense was reasserting itself."

30. Cook, *Nightmare*, pp. 534–37; Rovere, *Senator Joe McCarthy*, pp. 236–37.

31. Lawrence S. Wittner, *Cold War America* (New York, 1974), p. 182; Wechsler, *Reflections*, pp. 44, 161–62 discusses the theory of the Communist party and contains the Goldwater quote; *Nation*, December 1, 1959, p. 487.

32. Morse is quoted in Howard Zinn, *Postwar America, 1945–1971* (Indianapolis, 1973), p. 157.

33. Robert Lindner, *Must You Conform?* (New York, 1956), pp. 87–93, 116–17; Captain America is quoted in Leslie A. Fiedler, *An End to Innocence* (Boston, 1955), p. 46.

34. Though Nixon spoke proudly of his "silent majority" and his publicity people boasted that this was the "new" Nixon, one has only to recall former Vice President Spiro Agnew lashing out at what he termed the "effete corps of impudent snobs who characterize themselves as intellectuals" to understand the continuity between the "old" and "new" Nixon and his following. Agnew is quoted in Cook, *Nightmare*, p. 575.

For a sampling of best-selling, right-wing diatribes—all variants of the communist conspiracy thesis—see J. Edgar Hoover, *Masters of Deceit* (New York, 1958); Col. Victor J. Fox [pseud.], *The Pentagon Case* (New York, 1958); Billy James Hargis, *Communist America: Must It Be?* (Tulsa, 1960); John A. Stormer, *None Dare Call It Treason* (Florissant, Mo., 1964); Medford Evans, *The Assassination of Joe McCarthy* (Belmont, Mass., 1970).

35. Lewis Mumford, *In the Name of Sanity* (New York, 1954), pp. 7, 155; see also Eric Bentley, "Joseph McCarthy, Superstar," *Village Voice*, June 7, 1973, pp. 33–34.

2

Learning to Love the Bomb

"My son and his family, who live in California not too far from the atomic-bomb testing grounds in Nevada, are becoming used to seeing a flash and some minutes later feeling the house rock," a woman told the *Reader's Digest* in 1952. "One night recently he woke from a sound sleep and asked, 'What's that?' 'Oh, go back to sleep,' said his wife. 'It's only an atomic bomb.' My son settled back. 'All right. I was afraid one of the kids had fallen out of bed.'"[1]

By 1950, the nuclear bomb was an integral part of American culture. It was much more than the underpinning to an international cold war. From the first it was a power so huge and raw it obliterated any and all moral trappings. Systems of good and evil, sensitivity to cruelty or the ridiculous, all became distorted to the wielder of atomic arms. Moral, ideological, even pragmatic concerns weakened. The American mind was reshaped in many ways. For with the bomb the cold war was not a conflict over ideology nor over maintaining any global power balance. It was about upsetting that balance. It was about using sheer power to get more sheer power.

One vital sign of the way this nuclear power reshaped American culture appeared in the basic concept of war. With such deadly possibilities, no one wanted war any more. We needed peace. So the United States embarked on a program of "waging peace." This consisted of building up as much destructive capability as possible. Many other national problems, whether moral or economic, were neglected as the country concentrated on military confrontation. The cold war itself went through flux and change. In the fifties, it reached terrifying points on the edge of war, then cooled. The Sputnik controversy transformed the conflict into a competition over aerospace and science education. Early in the sixties, President Kennedy would heat up the cold war all over again. In later years, when the cold war's tensions were funneled into Vietnam, or eased by the end of that war and détente, the nuclear threat seemed to subside. That, though, was only a perceived relaxation. If anything, the military and atomic escalations begun in the fifties accelerated madly. They still careen forward today.[2]

Those ever-increasing races for the superior edge over the Soviets were at first viewed rather hazily. Nuclear bombs might be terrifying instruments. John Hersey introduced America to the horror in his 1946 *Hiroshima*. Yet that horror had its hypnotic appeal. When only the United States had the bomb, it seemed to promise world domination. After the Soviets got their bomb, Americans looked to nuclear arms to maintain the dominating edge. As the crude tool of that maintenance, our bomb again appeared good.[3]

The cold war, moreover, had a salutary effect on the economy. Anyone could see how affluent the country had become since the advent of World War II. The continuing postwar military habit helped even more. In the fifties, the country grew richer as business and government became increasingly intertwined. Mort Sahl, at decade's end, commented, "one of these days, General Motors is going to get sore and cut the government off without a penny."[4]

Given nuclear weaponry, one would expect that conventional arms industries might become obsolete. Actually, the opposite became true. The military-industrial complex was already strong at mid-decade. By 1957, the aircraft industry alone was the nation's biggest single employer. Through the subcontracting system it sank roots in virtually every congressional district. This represented only one of many military-related industries. Americans in general came to have a vested interest in the cold war.[5] The cold war thus became a factor with a triple potential: for patriotism, for profit, and for destruction.

Regrettably, arming the cold war was too often pursued to excess, both emotionally and economically. A retrospective study of fifties media uncovers innumerable stories about the latest brilliant defense measure. Many of these seem ridiculous today. Most have vanished from use—if they ever did enjoy a practical use. One finds a surprising number of expensive dead ends. The nuclear bazooka, the F3H jet, the atomic artillery shell, or the pills and nostrums devised to cure radiation poisoning are only a few examples. Whatever became of the Vertijet, shown on a 1957 *Life* cover in takeoff straight up in the air?[6]

In the latter fifties, military and congressional spokesmen publicized various "missile" and "bomber" gaps. America, they claimed, was lagging behind Russian attack capabilities. These arguments were always couched in mock-rational, heavily emotional terms: fear of conquest and of being second were the major feelings summoned. These arguments were used to justify even more arms spending. By 1960, all the gaps but one proved to be false. These fake gaps had been manufactured to stimulate various arms businesses and to increase the military. The only genuine "gap" of the fifties was that created by the Sputnik satellite.[7] By that time (late 1957) Americans were accustomed to responding against phantom lags and gaps. They knew their cues. Not only did Sputnik imply superior Soviet science; not only did it trigger the silly issue of international prestige: Sputnik might even forecast attack from outer space. Such overt and covert fears explain the truly hysterical reaction in the United States to a superior (if somewhat pointless) Soviet achievement. At last, here was a visible Soviet triumph to confirm years of anxiety.

The process of pumping money through the military complex has been vital to the nation's economy since the beginning of World War II. By the mid-fifties, the country's major growth industry was sophisticated technological weaponry. America's superior nuclear muscle had to be preserved at all costs. This was one of the early distortions the bomb made in the national character. Americans had long felt they had a manifest destiny for global superiority. But owning the atomic bomb exaggerated that faith. People became willing to accept anything in order to remain the strongest. Both international aggression and a changed economic system did not seem high prices to pay. Such excesses did not even seem disproportionate to the popular mind.

Nor were these cultural consequences regarded as evil or threatening for much of the decade. General James Gavin, one of the shapers of national military policy since the late forties, expressed a fairly typical official opinion. He felt the transformation was a good thing: "If we believe as we profess to believe in the superiority of our competitive system, and thus believe that American industry reflects this competition at its best, then our military services should be intimately associated with American industry."[8] Gavin's comment is a simple demonstration of logic: if A and B, then C. Yet it manages to at once describe and mask an economic reality. The competitive economy, that is, was being eclipsed by cold war spending. It never entirely turned away from its World War II retooling. Government support increasingly went to military industries. In order for the economy to remain afloat, America had to make ever more war (hot or cold). To decelerate was to invite recession or, worse, depression. This represented a major and damaging turnabout in the American economic system.

That Gavin could describe such a crucial change so blandly is another symptom of the bomb culture. It points to the way official sources tried to manage vital information. The intent of such news management was controlling public opinion. One of its most significant concerns was the potential harm caused by radioactivity. The atomic age naturally began in ignorance. Little was known about the radiation A-bombs generated. One of the few sure facts was that a large dose was harmful. Other effects, such as long-term or small-dosage ones, were not clearly known or understood. It became too easy, therefore, for U.S. officials to take the next step. That is, the lack of evidence about subtle radiation led officials to conclude it posed no danger at all.[9] Both domestic and foreign nuclear behavior since then has been motivated by this too hasty decision.

The official nuclear attitude was more complicated than this, of course. But essentially, its whole thrust was to convince people both to trust the bomb and to be in terror of it, a most interesting contradiction. The conflict seemed to boil down to people needing to fear Soviet bombs, while trusting American ones. For example, the *Reader's Digest* said in 1955, "it all adds up to this: whereas fallout from big bombs in wartime might become highly dangerous, there is no significant evidence that fallout from U.S. atomic tests now being carried out will be hazardous either to people now or to future generations."[10]

Out of such reassurance rose the whole drive to make our bomb both everyday and palatable. Nuclear bombs were depicted as casual, even friendly. Nuclear euphemisms sprang up: the "sunshine unit" as a measure of Strontium-90 levels, small nuclear bombs affectionately dubbed "kitten bombs." The phenomenon of human bodies being tossed around by blast effects was referred to as "translation" or "displacement." The H-bomb was originally publicized as the "humanitarian bomb," though this was so obviously ludicrous that its permanent nickname, the "clean" bomb, seemed semantically pure in contrast. *Look* magazine tried to make the bomb seem familiar and cozy by comparing its size to that of the average living room. That magazine also showed the bomb as considerate and thrifty, "one of the cheapest forms of destruction known to man."[11]

These examples are not merely the clever word games of big business and government. Such bland semantics reveal a very real process: the violence being wrought upon language as upon the minds of its audience. People were not only being asked to repress their fears, they were expected to be happy with the bomb. Given the jolliness of words like "kitten bomb" or the living-room metaphor, it is no exaggeration to say they were expected to enjoy the bomb. The New York *Times* travel section even ran one feature called "Watching the Bombs Go Off."[12]

This official attitude struck a popular chord. Many people responded with terrific optimism. One reason for this reaction was individual fear. Persons needed to disarm their anxiety by making the bomb understandable. Often the effort was simply associated with small businesses. A Salt Lake City fast-food stand advertised a "tasty uranium burger, 45¢," and a uranium sundae made of ice cream, sherbet, whipped cream, pineapple, and jelly beans. A teenage girl on the Jackie Gleason TV show, "The Honeymooners," called her boyfriend "Atomic Passion." The opening of Pigeon Forge golf course in Tennessee was publicized with atomic golf balls. Oak Ridge scientists injected a few with Cobalt-60 pellets, and a blindfolded caddy located them with a Geiger counter. In 1959, the Las Vegas Chamber of Commerce heralded the advent of "cleaner bomb testing" with the crowning of Miss Atomic Blast. Her coronation bikini bra featured an 88-karat diamond called Spellbound, and on the panties another diamond called Spirit of Hope.[13]

Mere public relations wordcraft, however, could not have single-handedly made people accept the bomb. "One of the most important concepts of twentieth-century invention," Frederick Lewis Allen felt, was "the idea that man could produce materials to order . . . superior to what nature could produce." The effort to make the bomb commonplace, indeed glamorous and loved, was all made easier by Science. Science, many people felt in the fifties, could really do anything, so much so that we did not need dull, dirty old nature any more. "Amazingly real plastic plants" eliminated the need for the real article, *Science Digest* excitedly wrote, "and are completely washable." Chemistry also helped produce real plants. As mechanized agriculture led to more farm-factories, the use of chemicals increased. A *Fortune* article, "The Dawn of Farming's Chemical Age," praised the pesticides DDT, chlordane, aldrion, 2,4-3 and 2,4,5-T (all since linked to both gross and subtle environmental damage). "Organic Farming—Bunk" sneered the *Reader's Digest,* attacking non-chemical agriculture as total quackery.[14]

Science would surely continue to make nature more superfluous than ever. Philosopher Morris Ernst predicted in his 1955 book, *Utopia 1976,* that by that year we would enjoy plastic autos and tires lasting for decades, solar energy, and quick-grow chemical beef. Ernst also predicted weather control by 1976. This would say "halt to the Torrid Zone in its northward march . . . arable land will become available in the now Frozen North." And "man will be master. Weather will be his servant." RCA's David Sarnoff predicted small atomic generators for every home, to provide a lifetime of power. "Before 1980, ships, aircraft, locomotives and even automobiles will be atomically fueled," Sarnoff said.[15] If it could be imagined, it could be achieved.

Nuclear science, instead of being used to blow everybody up, would evolve into the greatest miracle of all. It would make a new peaceful world. "Atom Roots Out Corn," said *Business Week. National Geographic* added "Bombarded Foods Stay Germ-Free As Others Rot," with lush pictures comparing gamma-ray bombarded hot dogs, potatoes, bread, and oranges to their rotting natural twins. The rise of nuclear medicine seemed to confirm atomic optimism. For instance, patients with suspected thyroid gland disorders were given "atomic cocktails" with radioactive iodine that would show up on an X-ray. Such beneficial services as electricity would surely be provided by the Atoms for Peace program so well-publicized after 1953. Project Plowshare, announced late in the decade by Atomic Energy Commission head Willard F. Libby, would put nuclear explosives to peaceful uses. Its list of possibilities included earth moving to gouge out harbors and canals, strip mining, and electrical energy.[16]

But the link between bomb testing and material luxury was being established in the American mind long before Project Plowshare. In 1952, a *Holiday* reporter watched a bomb test. He described it at length for the magazine. He wrote about the desert, the crowd of reporters, the beauty of the blast. Then, inexplicably, he concluded: "Despite secrecy, the good living which is *Holiday*'s theme is closer than the eternal desert where the experiments take place. Perhaps not tomorrow, but maybe the day after, the ships will sail, the craft will fly, and there will be a fission-powered society of less work, more leisure."[17] This person's mental leap from bomb test to nuclear leisure might leave us gasping. But such dazzling expectations were not unusual. Looking back, one can say that to trust the bomb was to mentally jump over certain problems. One especially sees this happening in fifties information about atomic attack. At times, it seemed the populace could overcome nuclear harm by a simple act of will. This attitude was especially revealed in official documents for civilians about nuclear war. These may appear retrospectively naive. They certainly express some startling ideas.

You Can Survive, published in 1950, is one of the earliest of such pamphlets. This booklet is still found in some public libraries. It is civil defense at its most simplistic. Survival, it notes, is virtually ensured if you "KNOW THE BOMB'S TRUE DANGERS. KNOW THE STEPS YOU CAN TAKE TO ESCAPE THEM!" Avert contamination, it urged, by "simply taking refuge inside a house or even by getting inside a car and rolling up the window." Of course, "should you happen to be one of the unlucky people right under the bomb, there is practically no hope of living through it." Proceeding as though its entire audience would surely live through impact, *You Can Survive* went on to minimize radiation sickness. The pamphlet used a fascinating approach to this. It combined scientific information with a genial tone. After exposure to fallout, "you most likely would get sick at your stomach, and begin to vomit. However, you might be sick at your stomach for other reasons, too, so vomiting won't always mean you have radiation sickness. . . . About two weeks later most of your hair might fall out. By the time you lost your hair you would be good and sick. But in spite of it all, you would stand better than an even chance of making a complete recovery, including having your hair grow back in again."[18]

Survive's was a hale and hearty message, simultaneously warning and soothing the reader. This, true, was one of the earliest civil defense booklets. Consequently much of its information soon would become obsolete. But one factor it represented never became obsolete: the official's perceived need to disguise facts. Much of the above quote from *Survive* is a semantic dodge. Instead of passing on solid statistics, or genuine information on self-conduct in time of atomic attack, the government wrote one's hair "might fall out," that one has "better than an even chance" of recovering from severe radiation sickness. The bomb was not all that dangerous. Another section of *You Can Survive* attempted to prove "your chances of living through an atomic bomb attack are much better than you may have thought. At Nagasaki, almost 70 per cent of the people a mile from the bomb lived to tell their experience." Their lives were improved by the bomb too. For "today thousands of survivors of these two atomic attacks live in new houses built right where their old ones stood."[19]

"I cannot tell you when or where the attack will come or that it will come at all," Harry Truman told the nation early in the decade, in starting a nationwide atomic civil defense program. "I can only remind you that we must be ready when it does come." The semantic thrust of his words alone shows how average people were being softened up to accept nuclear terrorism. Consider just the impact of his final "when it does come"—not "if." As a civil defense pamphlet would later announce, "much of the threat of war can be erased by a prepared civilian population. A population that has *planned* to survive will survive."[20]

Basic to this program of civil defense, to the act of will involved (bombs can't hurt me, I've planned to survive), was "pre-attack planning." A manual called *Atomic Attack* suggested everyone should buy a Geiger counter and learn how to use it. All glass, the booklet insisted, should be replaced with plexiglass or lucite immediately. Children should be taught to fall "instantly" to the floor, face down, elbows out, eyes shut. The author advised parents to have their children practice atomic falling each night at bedtime. The mass media participated in the whole civil defense effort too. In 1951, the Los Angeles *Mirror* conducted Operation Wakeup, in which planes dropped 2 million leaflets on the city, proclaiming that if an atomic bomb had been included in the shower, the populace would be very unfortunately dead.[21]

The private fallout shelter also began to creep into the popular imagination. In California, a whole variety of shelters were available by 1950. They ranged from the economical $13.50 foxhole model to the luxurious $3,500 version with phone and Geiger counter. Mrs. Alf Heiberg generously built a huge shelter big enough to accommodate from 100 to 150 of her neighbors. A Los Angeles woman named Colhoun contracted for a shelter at her home, and the groundbreaking was turned into a Hollywood-style celebration. Actress Adele Mara, before cheering starlets, gift-laden advertisers, proud neighbors, and reporters, smiled for the cameras and dug up a little of Mrs. Colhoun's earth. "It will make a wonderful place for the children to play in," beamed Mrs. Colhoun. "And it will be a good storehouse too. I do a lot of canning and bottling in the summer."[22]

This whole shelter impulse only increased in magnitude during the fifties. After a brief mid-decade flirtation with such alternatives as mass evacuation, it became the major civil defense concern. A national policy on shelters was articulated by the end of the decade. It held that "in the event of nuclear attack, fallout shelters offer the single best non-military defense measure for the protection of the greatest numbers of our people. Furthermore, a nation with adequate fallout protection is a nation which would be more difficult to successfully attack." *Life* touted the communal possibilities of municipal shelters, where neighboring families would be safe for many post-attack months. Such shelters, presumably, would be jointly financed by federal and local governments. Added Dr. Edward Teller, "it is necessary to provide every person in the U.S. with a shelter."[23]

To popularize this notion, a number of late-decade publicity stunts were staged. Honeymooners Mr. and Mrs. Melvin Minnison participated in a typical stunt in Miami. The newlyweds spent two weeks in a 22-ton steel and concrete 8-by-14-foot shelter 12 feet underground. They found it hot, in the high eighties. But they had a phone to call up their friends, and a radio. After their simulated survival, the contractor gave them a genuine two-week trip to Mexico. The Minnisons also got their picture in *Life*.[24]

Hiding in holes, not necessarily actual solid shelters, came to be expected of large portions of the population. In New York City at special sirens everyone was required to head for the nearest public shelter. Usually this was a subway. Tunnels and basements were many locales' public shelters. The shelter program, like some atavistic burrowing urge, actually increased in frenzy into the early sixties as Kennedy accelerated the cold war. The Kennedy administration touted more personal home shelters, revived the artificial arms gap scares, and even researched such panaceas for a post-attack America, such as the fallout suit. In 1961, Dr. Willard F. Libby told the nation in a widely syndicated feature that in the event of nuclear attack, 90 to 95 per cent of the population would be saved by shelters.[25]

That salvation would even extend to the quality of national life. With pre-attack planning and family shelters, atomic conflict would only temporarily disrupt America. "DENIES NUCLEAR WAR WOULD WIPE OUT CIVILIZATION," headlined the St. Louis *Post-Dispatch* in 1959.[26] With shelters, civil defense urged us to believe, the effects of war would be only transitory.

The shelter appeal has persisted for certain affluent groups. Standard Oil of New Jersey installed a giant complex of executive shelters inside a carved-out mountain in upstate New York. Their shelter includes separate facilities for lower-echelon clerks. A vast system of natural caves in the High Falls, New York area also houses a fallout shelter complex. Space in the shelters within has been sold to affluent businessmen. The shelters are costly, well-appointed, and constantly guarded. These are far from the only examples of the continuing shelter impulse. Many private homes maintain their shelters, regularly changing the food and water supplies. California also possesses remote shelter complexes for the rich.[27] One reason these persist is the seventies fear of possible nuclear terrorism by small nations or political extremists. But the fifties fascination with shelters is primarily responsible.

What this enthusiastic and unfeeling official message did to the American mind is all too clear. There are dozens of stories about the distorted mentality produced solely by the shelter program. The question "Would you let a neighbor into your shelter?" was actually, vehemently controversial. The citizens of Beaumont, California, resolved to arm themselves to repel the potential refugees fleeing atom-bombed Los Angeles. One man announced he was setting up a machine gun in front of his home shelter. A Jesuit priest proclaimed self-defense a traditional Christian tenet. A person had a right to use violence to keep the neighbors out of the family shelter, he said.[28] Christianity, certainly, has never been immune to grotesque cultural purpose. But if just the idea of sharing a fallout shelter so brutalized concepts of religion, imagine the full mutilating impact on thought and feeling of the entire optimistic bomb culture. Violence gradually was becoming an expectation.

Children, too, were taught the atomic optimism of civil defense. Early in the decade, a teacher of third- and fourth-graders wrote, "we spent some time . . . on the peacetime potentialities of atomic energy. We compiled large individual booklets and had an extensive bulletin board display. . . . When our civil defense leader came to call and explain how to care for ourselves in the event of a nuclear disaster, I found that none of the children was upset or fearful." Many school districts incorporated courses to "enable the pupil to meet disaster and survive" into academic programs. Air-raid drills were regular events. The drills were explained as a defense measure.[29] Yet their real thrust was to accustom kids to nuclear weaponry as a commonplace. One child of the fifties recounted his school's particular form of air-raid drill: they would lie on the floor and stick their heads under the lockers. He later recalled that he believed this would make him invulnerable to atomic attack.

His was a fairly unusual confidence, perhaps instilled by intervening years. More typically, children of the fifties remember their fear. Many continue to expect holocaust. Urban children learned whether their home area was a prime military target. They practiced every variation of bomb drill. They ducked under the tables and desks, tucked into protective huddles, filed with a partner into hallway or basement, and in some areas were practice-evacuated. They also participated in "suggested student activities" related to nuclear war. One teacher's guide suggested these activities: "draw on a map of your city the zones of damage due to the explosion of high-yield nuclear weapons." "Plot a fallout pattern for 20 KT and

20 MT weapons." "Make a list of common diseases that would be valuable as warfare agents."[30]

Zones of damage? Fallout pattern? Germ warfare? Here was where the first chinks appeared in the official armor. The optimism and assurance of such children's lessons could never hide that most basic fact: what was being discussed was death and destruction. Being "upset or fearful" was a natural, sensible reaction. Educators, however, regarded the fear as infantile behavior, to be replaced by a more mature acceptance. No alternative was taught. For lack of any choice, kids listened to these monolithic lessons. This, in addition to the banal violence saturating TV, inured the young to the aggressive, cruel, and absurd. Not surprisingly in this time of waging peace, many kids grew up expecting holocaust. They were often more aware than their elders of the delicate possibilities of total destruction.

Children are helpless against the whims and contradictions of their culture. For kids, to whom the whole bomb-culture message was a thing to be inhaled like air, defense security could not help but get garbled up with terror. Adults, more accomplished at psychological defense, had an easier time of it. They could dodge the great fears and moral questions with more deftness than their offspring. So that, for much of the decade, nuclear weapons protests were stifled. Critical analyses of the nature of American defense measures were few and far between. Most were suppressed or distorted by the media. This was partly an emotional defense measure. Americans wanted to avoid the full weight of atomic implications. The military aspects were no exception.[31] With nuclear war seemingly inevitable, all that military spending had to be capable of saving our lives. It *had* to.

Unfortunately, saving lives was not the aim. American defense measures in the cold war came to depend on a three-pronged effort. First was a defensive missile ring around the cities plus early-warning systems. Added to this was a massive retaliatory power—best exemplified by the Strategic Air Command, with planes always in the air, armed, ready to destroy an attacker's cities. The third prong was civil defense. It all sounded quite thorough. But the tiny flaws in the facade would, under the slightest scrutiny, yawn into chasms of error and betrayal. An air officer, commenting in 1954 on the mission of SAC, noted it was "not our policy to protect this country, for that . . . would interfere with our retaliatory capabilities."

One critic dubbed such a response "spasm war": war solely as vicious retaliation against hostage populations.[32]

While the SAC might be bombing the enemy, at least we would be saved by those early-warning systems and the missile interceptors ringing the cities. But, as General Earl Partridge told *U.S. News & World Report*, the missile bases themselves were prime targets. Said Partridge, "I wouldn't feel too secure in any city under attack." Of enemy bombers, he noted, "some will get through." These missile bases were often located with little or no consideration of fallout patterns and prevailing winds. At Spokane, for instance, only two of nine Atlas sites were on the safe downwind (east) side. All nine sites at Topeka were within 100 miles upwind of the million-plus Kansas City area population.[33]

Well, anyhow, there were always shelters. Or were there? By the end of the fifties, Congress and the federal government had refused to subsidize the financing of shelters. The emphasis, finally, fell on the individual homeowner. Excluded were renters, the poor, apartment dwellers, and other similar groups. These people would have to make do with public shelters, located in places like basements, subways, passages, and stairwells.

But this was not the gravest news. A number of critics writing late in the decade conceded the shelters then proposed would protect people from radiation. But that was inadequate. Even government officials expected the most dangerous thing about the bombs to be not fallout but what they called "mechanical effects." As Bertrand Russell explained, "in a firestorm, the misinformed refugees in deep shelters would either be incinerated or die from lack of oxygen." Some shelters did not even hold up to more conventional tests of heat. The California shelter belonging to AEC head Dr. Willard F. Libby caved in during a brush fire.[34]

Rarely did the civil defense debate seriously consider the type of world the nuclear survivors would emerge to find. That earlier headline from the *Post-Dispatch* about civilization triumphant was fairly typical. The whole insistence that civilization-as-we-know-it would easily survive was dumb, cruel, and deceptive. Only occasionally did government personnel admit to the adverse possibilities. Val Peterson briefly served as Eisenhower's Civil Defense administrator. After leaving the post he said "if nuclear war occurs, it is going to be stark, elemental, brutal, filthy, and miserable." Services, food supplies, and communications would be utterly disrupted. Peterson voiced "contempt for anybody who attempts to minimize the sheer destructiveness and desolation that will befall humankind if these weapons are dropped." But Peterson's words were not widely reported. Nor were those of John N. Wolfe, an AEC scientist. Wolfe testified before Congress on the predictable ecological effects of thermonuclear war. He foresaw fires over enormous areas of forest and grassland, radiation poisoning of soil rendering it inarable, vast soil erosion, the creation of huge dust bowls. Insects would swarm. There would be human starvation and pestilence. Such predictions, rationally arrived at and emotionally terrifying, were shared among many scientists but minimized in the media. One might also cite an early sixties Rand study that experienced the same obscure fate. The study had predicted that a 3,000-megaton attack on U.S. cities would lead inescapably to the death of 80 per cent of the population.[35]

But most often such logical horror gave way before more cheerful voices. Civil defense, finally, amounted to just what Peterson held in contempt. It was an attempt to minimize the brutality of atomic war. It tried to show war as not terribly dangerous and as easily survivable—providing everybody bought the right stuff and obeyed the right orders. It denied any alternative but the warlike course. Only at decade's end, and then only painfully and slowly, were other questions widely asked.

As C. Wright Mills wrote late in the fifties, "the immediate cause of World War III is the preparation of it." Bomb testing was the most notorious preparation. Between 1951 and 1958, the United States exploded 122 nuclear bombs of various sorts. Also in the decade, the U.S.S.R. set off 50 known explosions, and Great Britain 21. The tests created radioactive fallout that had never existed previously. But, just as in other areas of the bomb culture, the public had difficulty determining the issues. Here, perhaps, their curiosity was the greatest. Just how dangerous was fallout? A military man wrote reassuringly in a 1952 *Collier's* that fallout caused "only 15 percent" of the estimated 140,000 Hiroshima deaths.[36] Yet Hiroshima had suffered only one blast. The war already taking place in the American imagination would not be so modest, nor would it use bombs as small as the Hiroshima and Nagasaki ones. Thus the way was open for far more dire predictions about their effect.

One expression of this was the long procession of doomsday fiction, dealing in various ways with the world after nuclear holocaust. Nevil Shute's *On the Beach* is one of the most memorable of these. The book is set in Australia. A quick atomic war has recently taken place between the distant superpowers. Only those on the Australian continent have survived at all, and they are doomed by the vast amounts of radioactivity. Shute allowed his characters a measure of dignity through euthanasia pills. Not so Walter Miller in *A Canticle for Leibowitz.* Miller's book, a science fiction classic, presents a future Earth that has been atom-bombed back into medievalism. It is a world of ignorance, superstition, violence, and rare oases of priestly order. Casually, too, Miller includes a sizable brute population of freaks and mutants, grotesquely disfigured descendants of humanity.[37]

The possibility of deformity grew ever more prominent in the mass consciousness. Many photo magazines carried pictorial essays on horrifying laboratory experiments. One such feature, in the *National Geographic,* showed lab mice with huge malignant tumors, induced experimentally. *Life* showed photos of disfigured survivors of Hiroshima and Nagasaki.[38] But these things, while real, did not quite answer the most fearful public questions. As *Canticle for Leibowitz* hinted, could fallout create human monsters? Did fallout cause congenital or genetic damage? These were perhaps the most terrifying fears of all to a society oriented toward children and bodily perfection.

Even official commentators tended to confuse lay people on these matters. The confusion occurred for several reasons. First, there was a beginning scientific lack of knowledge about radiation, although this became less and less so over the years. Scientists themselves, being human, were subject to the same numbings and fascinations as the rest of us. They too were and are capable of repressing sensitivity and fear, of being hypnotized by the vast potential of nuclear energy. This would explain why existing knowledge of radioactive dangers tended to be minimized, if not forgotten.[39] Such relatively unconscious processes became even more dangerous when linked to the official attempt to control public opinion.

A 1955 article in *Reader's Digest* gives much of the AEC version on fallout. "The scare stories about this country's atomic tests are simply not justified," the article states, though it never clearly establishes why this is so. Currently, that magazine wrote, no danger existed of radioactive build-up from U.S. tests. Even if such a build-up occurred, and the fallout did unaccountably cause human mutations, "some experts believe that mutations usually work out in the end to improve the species." But even such a vaguely ominous possibility was denied. "The total fallout from all tests would have to be multiplied by a million to produce visible deleterious effects except in areas close to the explosion itself."[40]

The AEC, in effect, was telling the public "if we can't see any problem now, no problem exists." There were many expressions of this ideal. Strontium-90 was the new element produced by nuclear blasts. This radioactive substance, the commission said, had only one potential hazard to humans. The element tends to replace calcium in the body, chiefly in the bones and teeth. AEC drew a scenario in which beef cattle eat grass that retains fallout sifted from the skies; in turn, people could in odd circumstances be harmed by "the ingestion of bone splinters which might be mingled with muscle tissue during butchering and cutting of the meat." Only cattle took in the element, it seemed. Their bones provided the only foreseeable danger from Strontium-90. News features on other aspects of nuclear explosives supported similar conclusions. One of these was the idea that fallout shelters would save civilization. In 1958, Dr. Edward Teller and Dr. Albert Latter published an article in *Life* called "Why Nuclear Bomb Tests Must Go On." They insisted "American tests are leading to the development of a clean bomb." The word "clean" was operational. It implied that such tests were reducing the radioactivity bombs produced. That is, by continuing to test nuclear bombs we were diminishing the radioactive threat rather than increasing it. The article was accompanied by a photo of five grinning Air Force officers, standing under a detonating nuclear air burst. The photo was captioned "none was hurt by blast or fallout."[41] The next logical step was clear: not only was the bomb harmless to the average citizen, it scarcely hurt those directly experiencing it.

Eventually, to receive even a massive radiation dose came to seem benign. At Hiroshima, commented Nobel Peace Prize winner Dr. H. J. Muller, "there were survivors who got as much [radioactivity] as they could stand and then reproduced and we saw that their offspring looked about normal. It doesn't mean that they were, but they were enough normal to get by—and the human race as a whole, if it got by, would eventually recover." Other scientists were far more abrupt in interpreting data to lay persons. In the *Life* article mentioned in the previous paragraph, Drs. Teller and Latter referred to a group of Pacific natives in the Marshall Islands who had been exposed accidentally to test fallout. Four of the women were pregnant. "One baby," they wrote, "was born dead, but the other three were quite normal. There is no evidence that the stillbirth was due to radiation effects. . . . Statistically, one in four is not an unusual ratio."[42]

Undoubtedly such remarks, even with their retrospective shock, originally bore a complex impact. Some people regarded these as forthright assessments, if a little brashly put. Others were appalled at the harshness these men revealed. A less delicate balance between these effects appeared in the reaction to Herman Kahn. In the late fifties and early sixties Kahn, a Rand scientist, published several books on the topic of thermonuclear war. He also advised national policymakers on this subject. Kahn became rather notorious for his blandness in calculating the anonymous death of millions. For many, he came to personify the myth of the amoral, unfeeling, almost mad scientist.

Kahn was, of course, not at all alone in his impersonal musings. Many persons made similar public assessments. Thomas E. Murray, an AEC member, delivered a speech in 1958 after he had left the commission. Americans, he announced, were too afraid of war. A total war was nothing to worry about, Murray said, because "neither ourselves nor the Soviet Union could possibly survive." He conceded that limited war was the true danger because "the Soviet Union could inflict this kind of piecemeal defeat on us." One could also look to General James Gavin's definition of the difference between a liberal and a conservative defense policy. The conservative, he wrote, favored atomic weapons of the "largest yield possible" to smash the enemy in a single blow. Liberals—and he considered himself one—preferred the idea of small tactical nuclear weapons, literally tens of thousands of them, to be scattered by all the armed services. Anything else, Gavin felt, was inefficient and impractical.[43] Gavin's liberal/conservative contrast also gives a very good idea of the utter lack of alternatives in the fifties vision. You hit them with some big bombs, or else you hit them with more little bombs. Period.

Not surprisingly, then, some Americans began to feel their leaders were unconcerned about them. People began to question the goodness of the bomb. It was rather jarring to look at the leaders Americans had in this newly skeptical light. Too often, these leaders were not elected officials at all. They could not be affected by public opinion. They were experts universally consulted by all elected officials of whatever party, or they were appointees. Sometimes these powerful men were business people, or worked intimately in a government post with business firms. Sometimes they were military career men who never needed to acknowledge the electorate. Popular opposition, such as there was, could not stop them. To the traditional three branches of the government was added a fourth, uncontrollable one.

The psychic consequences were great. Americans in general felt powerless, helpless, nervous. Many other factors had contributed to these emotions: the Red scare, the spread of corporate bureaucracy into daily life, mass conformity. But the nuclear threat motivating the cold war was the medium helping these factors succeed. Americans were manipulated by and through the bomb. They backed away from the threats of war and McCarthyism, and rushed instead into dreams of domesticity, religion, material conformity. Their leaders encouraged this turning away from both political power and autonomy. These leaders may have been guilty of confusing the country, of distorting facts and stealing choices from their public. But, in the end, their acts were not difficult to achieve. The American people were very easy to lie to.

Exceptions did occur. Fortunately, fear encouraged not just apathy but, in some few, an awareness of the official deception—and so, rebellion. This society had been rendered falsely moral in its blindness to the bomb. The only truly moral people became those opposing its brutality. The bomb culture was just beginning to produce the schism of later years. On one side stood an obedient mass of nervous consumers; on the other, a small alternative countering force, conceived in adversity.

One important class of nuclear protesters was scientists. These were highly educated men, literally a small enclosed elite, who often worked in the government's nuclear programs. J. Robert Oppenheimer was the first such protester to become famous. One of the developers of the H-bomb, he lost his security clearance simply for questioning the morality of such destructive research. Essentially he was accused of not being "enthusiastic" enough. Ralph Lapp, while also not a pacifist nor a proponent of nuclear disarmament, intelligently criticized official abuses of atomic energy. One of his most notable efforts was his 1956 *Voyage of the Lucky Dragon.*[44] This work is a sympathetic report about the accidental irradiation of some Japanese fishermen in an early American H-bomb test. Lapp also scored the blundering and arrogance of U.S. spokesmen during the incident.

Linus Pauling is one of the most outstanding of the scientists who came to speak for pacifism. Pauling tirelessly argued the necessity of nuclear disarmament. He was the most prominent scientist decrying the danger of bomb testing. Pauling tried to present clear and cogent analyses of nuclear issues. The decade's most complete scientific refutation of test safety and AEC deception is his 1956 book *No More War!* Quoting the Strontium-90 bone-splinter comment, Pauling reminded the reader this element does not simply seek the bones of cattle. It also replaces calcium in the human bones (where blood cells are made) and in the teeth. It can induce such cancers as leukemia. Continuing bomb testing both increased the amount of Strontium-90 in the world and posed a palpable danger to the very young and old.

Pauling deplored AEC statements about a supposed threshold level of radioactivity exposure. The threshold issue was and remains a major controversy. Through most of the fifties, scientists felt that humans could safely receive small doses of some dangerous products, such as radiation. Pauling emphasized there was no proof of such a threshold of safety in radiation exposure. He was particularly worried about the potential of genetic damage. "*Any radiation,*" he stressed, "*is genetically undesirable.*"[45]

Questioning the threshold concept led Pauling to other immediate problems. If radiation jeopardized people at even tiny trace levels, bomb testing must not be as harmless as claimed. Pauling attacked Teller and Latter's myth that fallout could be multiplied by a million before deleterious effects were noticed. He calculated in 1956 that birth defects all over the world had already vastly increased due to test fallout. "We may say that each year of bomb testing at the present rate is carried out with the sacrifice of 15,000 children, who would be born healthy and who would lead normal lives if the bomb tests had not been carried out that year," he charged. "Perhaps the testing of one large superbomb required the sacrifice of only 1,500 children. Perhaps it requires the sacrifice of 15,000 children or more. . . . The only debatable point is whether the victims of bomb-testing should be counted in the thousands, hundreds of thousands, or millions."[46]

The work of Linus Pauling pointed the way for further nuclear protest. A few exposés of government suppression began to appear in print. In 1959, *Nation* magazine reported the AEC was refusing to make public a report showing that Strontium-90 levels in the bones of American babies up to age four had doubled in the one-year period ending December 1957. This report was the third part of "Project Sunshine." The study, on skeletal absorption of the cancer- and leukemia-causing element, had been launched in 1953. Its first two sections were never made available to the general public. They were only printed in a technical magazine with a highly limited circulation. Some exposés of AEC suppression only made the papers too late to have any effect. Such was the case in 1956, when AEC chairman Lewis Strauss suppressed a report that opposed the building of the Fermi reactor. Fermi was slated for the highly populated Detroit area, on a major watershed. Strauss kept the report secret until the construction permit had been approved and building commenced.[47] It was only in the late fifties that AEC's interest in nuclear proliferation became obvious to lay people. Any bureaucracy would react in much the same way: protecting its vested interests when the public interest was contradictory. Too often, consequently, AEC suppressed unfavorable reports, silenced critical scientists and technicians, and in the end fostered dangerous policies in order to protect itself. In the latter fifties, some few reporters did examine this issue. Regrettably, the American press in general refused to be inspired by their example.

The knowledge provided by scientists like Pauling helped the work of two larger bodies of dissenters. Both groups worked to ban bomb tests and for a system of nuclear disarmament. Members of the old left made up the first group. Because of the communist witch hunts of the era, these people were generally distrusted no matter what they did. The French-originated Stockholm Peace Petition (a brief apolitical call for nuclear disarmament) was nationally circulated by the left in 1951. The Los Angeles *Times* advised: "if anyone comes to your door . . . with a petition sponsored by an association called Partisans for Peace—don't sign it! If you really want peace, that is. This petition is straight from Moscow. . . . What should you do [to the bearer of the petition]? Don't punch him in the nose, or slam the door in his face. Reds are used to that. The thing to do is ask him for his credentials of identification; get his name and address if you can, take a good look at him, and then telephone the FBI." W. E. B. DuBois, who was one of the organizers of this circulation (and not yet a member of the Communist party), found himself and four coworkers indicted by the federal government for failure to register as agents of a "foreign principle." After a lengthy court fight, they were all acquitted because of absolute lack of evidence. Clearly much of the legal battle was merely expensive harassment. But, emphatically, the "foreign principle" involved was never perceived outside of the courts as another government. Rather it was the "foreign" notion of peace.[48]

Yet another group of nuclear protesters in fifties America were more religious in orientation. These were often affluent, educated Quakers. They always affirmed their love of country in wording their dissent. Attempting to dramatize the abuses of power and humanity of the bomb culture, these people found media indifference and distortion, kangaroo court justice, and often physical violence. Jim Peck was beaten by two legionnaires in daytime Manhattan. Kenneth Calkins was struck by a truck in a Wyoming ICBM sit-in.[49]

The courts offered the legal version of such violence. Earle Reynolds led a crew sailing his *Phoenix* into the Bikini test zone. He was protesting both bomb testing and the legality of American control of the zone. Reynolds' trial was distorted and irregular from the start. The judge displayed thorough and constant prejudice against Reynolds. The experience of Wilmer Young, an elderly Quaker, is fairly typical of the distortion newspapers applied to peace agitation. Young participated in a series of civil disobedience protests at missile base sites. After his arrest Young realized very few papers were mentioning that protest. Those that did only offered condescending jokes about Young's age. They implied Young (and his beliefs) were just laughably senile.[50]

A. J. Muste, also participating with Young in this series of protests, was easily the most important peace leader in the decade. He had been prominent in pacifist movements throughout the twentieth century. Muste's actions and essays form the link between the traditional pacifists and the new uprush of young rebels late in the decade. In 1952 he published a pamphlet called *Of Holy Disobedience.* "A general appeal to American youth," it urged the young to resist conscription, regimentation, and war, to adopt Thoreau's and Gandhi's principles of pacifist "Holy Disobedience." In the morally insensible bomb culture, he stressed, "*disobedience becomes imperative.*" There are striking parallels between his words and those of later New Leftists. One also finds echoes of Muste in the sayings of such influential people as Lenny Bruce. As Bruce once said, "The Ten Commandments don't say, 'Thou shalt not kill sometimes.' "[51]

Fifties America may have been afraid of nuclear war, may have quietly hungered for an end to violence. But its approach to the protesters' calls for peace, feeling, morality was too fragmented and alienated. In a way, it was a capsule of the alienation and confusion of modern times. In this nation scared of war, engaged in the highly charged concept of waging peace, seeking desperate security, pacifists were considered utter fools. The best illustration of this comes from Jim Peck's 1958 autobiography, *We Who Would Not Kill.* During World War II Peck had been imprisoned as a conscientious objector along with a young man named Lowell Naeve. Naeve's cell was alongside that of convicted killer Louis Lepke. At one point the c.o. tried to explain to Lepke what pacifism meant. But the mobster had trouble understanding him. Then Lepke suddenly exclaimed, "You mean they put you in here for not killing?" and "he laughed and laughed."[52]

By 1957, the year before Peck's book was published, AEC members were admitting within the commission that somewhere between 2,500 and 13,000 cases of genetic defects had already been produced in the newborn by fallout. Teller and Latter, however, blithely estimated the life of the entire human race had been shortened, on the average, "only" by two days due to fallout. Other scientists produced higher estimates. On March 30, 1958, Dr. Libby and Dr. Pauling debated fallout problems on Edward R. Murrow's TV program "See It Now." Pauling spoke first, sharply criticizing the government for a nuclear policy that doomed literally millions throughout the world well into the future. Surprisingly, Libby agreed with Pauling's predictions. But, he said, testing had to continue. The "public interest," or the AEC's concept of it, was paramount, Libby said. If necessary, a patriotic excuse could be found. As another scientist commented elsewhere, "I think we have to face the fact that there is damage [to people from fallout] and then say it is worth it, because if you don't have the tests, you are running a risk of far worse damage by the loss of freedom and democracy."[53]

"The young complacents of America, the tired old fighters, the smug liberals, the shrill ladies of jingoist culture—they are all quite free," wrote C. Wright Mills in 1958. "Nobody locks them up. Nobody has to. They are locking themselves up." This deadening of human sensibility was one of the major results of the bomb culture in America. Feeling became not so much wrong as irrelevant. In a very important sense, the quintessential man of the fifties became the bomber pilot. He was a highly trained technician, a sophisticate who could kill anonymous hundreds without hating them or, indeed, feeling anything at all except pleasure for a mission accomplished. Reporters interviewing the men who flew the Hiroshima and Nagasaki missions were pleased to find them "normal, friendly, and well-adjusted." The man who had gone on the Hiroshima mission and later developed such severe mental problems he was institutionalized was explained away: he had suffered from emotional maladjustment long before Hiroshima. He was abnormal in his anguish.[54]

Clearly, though, the simplistic pilot model did not allow for human variations. Human personality is subtle and complicated; no less so the personality of a whole modern culture. In this emotional, anxious age, a wide range of reactions to the bomb threat emerged. For some, the danger of imminent annihilation became so large it nearly vanished. Such people lived with virtually no fear of the bomb at all: it was too much to worry about. Other persons experienced intense and almost constant anxiety. They were sure nuclear war was immediately imminent. Official science threw the blame for this fear back on the individual worrier. The best that doctors and psychiatrists did was to prescribe tranquilizers or civil defense work, treating the symptoms rather than the disease. For the average person, the constant potential of faceless national suicide imbued every waking moment with fear. Many Americans, however, were to some degree able to swallow their feelings and obey the official voices. That was the new normalcy. Americans avoided seeing the nuclear issue straight on.

Their fears did emerge more indirectly. The fiction of holocaust and deformity was one expression of such fears. The novels and comics that predicted genetic monsters represent a degree of rebellion against officialdom. By fantasizing a future filled with freaks and horrors, Americans rejected the nuclear safety message. Unfortunately, their shrewd assessment of the big lie was rarely followed by more intense action.

Instead of intensifying, people's nuclear feelings were spread thin in an almost superstitious manner. An alternative to the printed fiction of holocaust was the science fiction film. The genre enjoyed a great transformation as well as a vast popularity in the fifties. Sci-fi movies differed from their earlier counterparts in one vital respect. Nearly every plot hung on the strange rise of a terrible and novel threat. Often, some horrible creature would appear without warning to ravage the countryside. Such movies confirmed the viewer's repressed suspicions about reality. That is, these films insisted there was something to worry about in the insidious bugaboos of the times (fallout or communists). Often the lurking-monster theme was forwarded with no obvious statement of radioactive or Red subversion. *The Blob* is an example. But fallout did serve as a direct topic, too. *Godzilla* was a huge mutant created by Strontium-90. *The Incredible Shrinking Man* was exposed to an atomic mist and so doomed to eternally dwindle away.[55]

A few movies went on to depict the aftermath of atomic war. In *Panic in the Year Zero* one family tried to survive a nuclear holocaust in the California wilds. *Panic* ended optimistically. World peace was mysteriously restored and a new calendar inaugurated to symbolize the world's rebirth—"the year zero." Some other films played tricks with audience beliefs by making the sole survivors interracial: often one white woman, one white man, one black man. The most famous of these movies was *The World, the Flesh and the Devil.*[56] All these films had one thing in common: distractingly, more of their energy was sunk into race innuendoes than into the problems of surviving.

Relatively junky movies alone were not the only signs of the new normalcy. Also integral to this attitude was the way people tried to hedge their bets against death. The diversions of the fifties—the extreme sex myths, endless material consumerism, TV—all drew Americans away from having to consider the consequences of their nuclear behavior. In order to avoid thinking with sensitivity about nuclear war, both sensitivity and peace had to be redefined. Feeling became irrelevant. Peace became a foreign notion. But, like any forbidden notion, it murmured to people too sweetly, at once an evil fantasy and an unspoken longing.

That intense longing turned out to be useful in the development of another part of the bomb culture: the nuclear power plant. The nuclear bomb had bribed Americans with the illusion of total security against war. The nuclear reactor bribed Americans too: this time offering inexhaustible energy. And the idea of harnessing all that sophisticated violence for peaceful uses seemed to fulfill people's wildest dreams. Such luxurious promise had long been a part of the bomb culture anyway. "With the device of the reactor," said the *Walt Disney Story of Our Friend the Atom*, "we hold the Atomic Genie under safe control. He comes forth at the beckoning of modern science—a smiling, magic servant to all mankind. He promises to grant us three wishes. The decision is ours. What should we wish for? What do we need most?" This miraculous promise was not reserved for children alone. As a supporter of nuclear power plants stated in 1957, "atomic energy can be applied to peaceful purposes without serious hazard to the public or its employees."[57] The bomb culture began to grow more subtle. As the decade drew to a close, nuclear bombs would appear more and more evil. But the bomb culture itself was changing in response; it was repressing its nasty bombs and assuming a benign air. It was transforming into the atomic-age culture.

To make such a transition, it was important that nuclear power plants be carefully differentiated from nuclear bombs in the public mind. This was how it came to be admitted that bombs destroyed. In contrast, nuclear reactors were publicized with the positive imagery of safety and affluence. Utility companies first began to build the privately owned atomic installations in 1956. At that time the plants came to be depicted as harmless, kind, and beneficent. Their operations were presented as offering endless cheap power (cheaper than fossil-fuel-generated electricity) and also freedom from the unpleasant pollution of such fossil-fuel operations. Not only did nuclear power plants promise limitless inexpensive energy. "It is abundantly clear," the AEC stated in mid-decade, "that radiation is by far the best understood environmental hazard." This hazard was in utter control around nuclear facilities. The area around the plants was so safe, indeed, that proponents of the plants adopted an aggressive tack: they dubbed persons unhappy with its proximity "nervous neighbors."[58]

That supporters of nuclear energy felt they had to strike out with such an aggressive label is important. It creates a suspicion that there might be something hiding beneath the publicity about safety, economy, and affluence. This is a facade that one hesitates to strip away, simply because the promise of nuclear power is so enticing. One longs for a simple solution to the world's energy crises. Yet, sadly, the possible danger is too great. This area must not remain unexamined. And "danger" is the correct word in context; for too long the safety question surrounding nuclear power plants was minimized or shoved aside.

One way this was achieved was through public relations. In manipulating facts, nuclear interests could also manipulate people. One minor example concerned the artists' conceptions of planned atomic facilities, which often showed the future plant to be free of smokestacks. In fossil-fuel plants, these stacks notoriously dispersed unpleasant pollutants into the air. To depict nuclear power plants as lacking such stacks was a very subtle deletion. Yet when the plant was completed, it would have stacks. These would then be explained as "for ventilation purposes only." The ventilation argument was not exposed until the early sixties. The stacks, it was revealed, release waste gases that are mildly radioactive.[59]

This was a relatively small hint about nuclear problems. A larger one began in 1958 at Bodega Head, California. Pacific Gas and Electric announced it would build a nuclear power plant on a site there. The San Andreas Fault was only a thousand feet away. PGE denied the volatile possibilities of combining an earthquake zone with an atomic installation. It is appalling to note that only many years of determined court battles by environmentalists succeeded in stopping the proposed plant.[60]

The careless selection of a plant's site provided many people's first introduction to the perils of such a peaceable industry. If firms were willing to place reactors in relatively risky locations, what other chances were they taking? Some few people began to worry about the larger impact of reactor problems. Specifically, some people worried about the results of a severe accident in a reactor.

In 1957, the AEC ordered a report about the consequences of accidents in a reactor. When the study, called the Brookhaven Report, emerged, its findings were frightening. An accident in a nuclear reactor could never lead to a nuclear explosion. But the Brookhaven Report found that a "credible" accident, in which a reactor's core melted down and then the core container was breached, would spew toxic, highly radioactive material into the surrounding countryside. In this accident, the report predicted immediate death of 3,400 people, severe injury of 43,000 more, and $7 billion in damage. By 1964, the typical reactor had increased fivefold in size. The report was revised taking this into account. Its new conclusions predicted 45,000 killed; injuries and damages increased proportionately. This later report was suppressed by the AEC, only becoming available in the mid-seventies because the Union of Concerned Scientists obtained it under the Freedom of Information Act.[61]

It is true that the chance of such an accident is statistically small. But the consequences would be disastrous. The safety issue, however, was repressed for a long time. One major reason this occurred was because people in general—whether lay folk, nuclear protesters, or nuclear engineers—were disarmed by the Atomic Genie's promise. Nuclear protesters were chiefly worrying about atomic weaponry. Like any other Americans they wanted to believe in a peaceful atomic age. In those years, furthermore, no patterns existed for broad-scale dissent in America. Protest was both stifled and unfamiliar. The ban-the-bomb people had to rediscover the techniques as well as a morality and vocabulary of dissent.[62] Protest, of course, is still stifled in America. But the sixties and seventies gave the culture models of successful protest and long-term ideals to further those goals. Nuclear dissent would surge in the mid-seventies. It is important, though, to remember its early and difficult origins. Its problems were far greater in an age when environmentalists and leftists alike were regarded as nuts.

Crucially, many of the arguments of the mid-seventies nuclear dissenters reflected back on nuclear policies coined in the fifties. In February 1976, several nuclear engineers very dramatically resigned their posts in protest of official nuclear acts. These were three General Electric engineers and an engineer of the Nuclear Regulatory Commission (NRC, which in 1975 took over the AEC's regulatory functions). At the time, the three former GE workers charged virtually every nuclear power plant in operation had serious safety defects. Often these defects existed in the safeguard systems within the plants, those systems intended to prevent accidents. Bob Pollard, the former NRC engineer, pointed specifically to the Indian Point No. 2 and No. 3 plants on the Hudson River, New York. Indian Point No. 2 was already in operation; No. 3 was under construction. Pollard had quit when his intramural protests about the inefficient safety systems at both plants went unheeded. All these engineers charged that NRC (and before that AEC) habitually licensed nuclear power plants with poor safety designs, hoping the problem would be corrected some day. A malfunction in the safety system of a nuclear reactor is especially dangerous because accidents happen so very quickly, literally within seconds. The accidents that have already taken place—such as the 1976 Brown's Ferry, Alabama, accident, the Chalk River, Ontario, one in the early sixties, and the core meltdown of the Fermi reactor near Detroit later in the decade—occurred due to a combination of error and unexpected failure of the safety features. Yet apathy persists. When an NBC-TV reporter filmed a program on the Indian Point plants in February 1976, he interviewed one of Indian Point No. 2's engineers. The man refused to express worry about accident problems in the plant. "It can't happen here," he said.[63]

But even if the accident and safeguard issues were resolved, other questions remain. The mere presence of a nuclear power plant may be dangerous. Part of the threat comes to the surrounding ecosystem. For many years a corollary to the existence of atomic installations was an apathy about their effects on the countryside. In the fifties, no one had firm proof of ecological pollution from atomic power plants. Nor did anyone want such proof. It was a full eight years between the establishment of the Oak Ridge atomic installation and the request that TVA make an ecological survey of its impact. The facility at Hanford in Washington State was built in the mid-forties. Studies of its impact were not made until the late sixties. Hanford released its waste water into the Columbia River. Scientific studies revealed radiation concentrated throughout the entire Columbia ecosystem. Duck-egg yolks were found to have 40,000 times the radiation borne in the river water. Adult swallows had 75,000 times the radiation. Caddis fly larvae bore 350,000 times the radiation of the water. It cannot be assumed this radiation was harmless.[64]

Wildlife considerations were far from the only pollution problem. In the early seventies, Dr. Ernest Sternglass studied infant mortality statistics in the Hanford area. Comparing the rates for 1943, before the facility had opened, with 1945 when it was producing the plutonium for test bombs, Sternglass discovered some disturbing facts. Benton County, where Hanford is located, showed an infant mortality jump of 160 per cent. Rates in Umatilla, the adjoining county to the south, went up 60 per cent. Franklin County directly to the east showed a jump of some 50 per cent and Walla Walla, southwest of Franklin, showed an increase of 10 per cent. At this time, infant mortality on the whole in the state of Washington was on the decline. Sternglass also reported similar patterns of rises and declines in infant mortality corresponding to rises and falls in radioactive releases from atomic plants *of all types* across the country. He has even linked infant mortality to emissions from the little TRIGA reactors owned by many colleges. Sternglass also suspects a corresponding shortening of old people's lives due to such releases.[65]

Sternglass' work has terrifying implications. Not surprisingly, controversy continues in the nuclear community about this issue. Essentially, though, Sternglass was pursuing the implications of ideas first publicly forwarded by Linus Pauling. Both scientists have in effect accused the nuclear interests of killing babies. This is a highly charged emotional concept. Many people prefer to denigrate the entire issue simply because of this volatile feeling. Yet the reader is reminded that Pauling's conclusions about bomb test toxicity were quietly conceded by the AEC in the fifties (though only just before the international atmospheric test ban). The trace radiation from bomb tests, that is, did kill babies. That this was so, of course, does not prove Sternglass' accuracy. He is not considered to have proved his conclusions, but rather to have found an intensely disturbing *correlation.* Some nuclear activists agree with Jonathan Bingham, a New York representative; Bingham said, this "appears to be the only explanation currently available" for those infant mortality rises. Others, such as *Environment* editor Sheldon Novick, say Sternglass is, simply, "wrong."[66]

The Sternglass controversy is just a small part of a larger nuclear safety issue. Nor, frightening as it is, is it the most serious one. Many of the nuclear power policies pursued since the mid-fifties are giant scandals. But the disposal of radioactive wastes was (and remains) a scandal evolving into a tragedy.

Much of the environmental activism budding in the late fifties began with the question of how atomic facilities disposed of their waste. In 1958, the *Saturday Evening Post* carried an article called "Gangway for the Atomic Garbage Man!" The piece told of the only east coast firm licensed to transport and dump radioactive wastes. These highly toxic byproducts were trucked by the firm to various dumping sites. The "hottest" were sunk into the ocean. "Gangway" rather casually revealed that vast amounts of hot wastes were being dumped into Boston Harbor.[67]

Incredibly, this was the first New Englanders had heard of an unclassified operation going on since 1946. In 1959, Grace Des Champs wrote in the *Nation* that the dumping site was located 12 miles from Boston and 30 miles northwest of Cape Cod. The site was also in a fishing area. "Unknown tons" of hot wastes had been dumped into water with a depth of 250 feet. Up to that time, AEC claimed all such dumping always went into at least 6,000 feet of water. Des Champs, one of the leaders of an ad hoc citizens' group opposing the waste operations, also noted the steel-and-cement containers used had a brief life expectancy. Some technicians predicted they would last only ten years.[68]

That citizens' group, the Lower Cape Committee, succeeded in getting AEC to move the dumping operations much farther out to sea. Additionally it managed to prevent another dumping license being granted for a nearby site, and, in 1960, blocked the building of a "nuclear park" near Falmouth, Massachusetts. The Lower Cape Committee also got AEC to examine the impact of the sea dumping. The containers had apparently held. No radiation was found in the area. At that time, James Muldoon, a Boston lawyer who was a member of the Lower Cape Committee, charged, "the fatal and inexcusable defect in the public health philosophy of the nuclear scientists is that they are primarily concerned with how much radiation a man can stand, and not how perfectly he can be protected against all radiation."[69]

The radioisotopes in the Cape dumping apparently had a relatively short toxic life—probably 300 years. Most of the reactor material being transported or dumped, however, posed a greater danger. Plutonium is one of the raw materials transported to nuclear reactors as fuel. It is the most carcinogenic material known. A speck of plutonium the size of a grain of pollen will cause lung cancer. If less than three per cent of a typical 50-pound shipment of plutonium escaped, it would be capable of causing 100,000 lung cancers. It would remain toxic for many thousands of years. Plutonium was and is shipped to processing plants and then reactors via truck and train. The element was also shipped by air until federal law forbade this in summer 1975. Plutonium and all fuels and wastes from reactors are transported large distances across the country. Many shipments were and are trucked through highly populated areas, such as midtown Manhattan.[70]

The waste products of reactors are a mix of many radioisotopes.

But they pose no less a threat. Their radioactivity will persist for tens of thousands of years. Controversy persists well into the seventies over the adequacy of shipping containers against accidental rupture. But even the development of a technology of container safety would fail to answer the most serious question of all. What is to be finally done with radioactive waste? The most toxic byproducts of reactors will remain dangerous for about two hundred thousand years. They must be meticulously isolated from the environment for all that time. What social institution can promise to last that long? Even if the human race did have a permanent religious or military class to guard these elements, what means could they use to achieve this? No permanent facilities exist for the storage of such enormously dangerous wastes. Only temporary facilities have been created since the fifties. These include the water dumping sites, cause of much environmental controversy, and the tanks near reactors, which by the latter seventies will be nearly filled.[71] In the truly long view, these sparse measures are risky and ridiculous. Americans have created an atomic legacy that, in terms of human history, is practically permanent.

The late fifties and early sixties did witness a number of localized environmental triumphs in addition to the Bodega Head and Cape Cod controversies. For instance, certain New England towns were able to ban transport of hot wastes through their borders. Dumping of radioactive wastes in the sea off Houston was banned. Some journalists produced exposés of atomic power abuses. In a few areas in the sixties, local citizens groups blocked proposed nuclear facilities.[72] But no wider concerted effort against nuclear power problems arose in the fifties or early sixties. It would be deferred for well over a decade, and the plants would proliferate.

"It appears a certainty," said one nuclear scientist in the early seventies, "we will have a serious nuclear accident before the year 2000." Nuclear power is a technology of jeopardy. It permits no mistake. Human error is rendered disproportionately dangerous. Just as nuclear bombs implied the evolution of war beyond human abilities to recuperate, nuclear power plants represent the evolution of technology beyond human abilities of complete control. Yet the reactor program begun in the fifties projects 1,200 atomic plants for the year 2000. Other possible energy sources, such as solar power, are cruelly underfunded. Only the monolithic answer of nuclear energy is pursued. As A. J. Muste warned in 1959, "modern technology is not equipped with a safety valve."[73]

Why, then, do people still desire nuclear power? Only part of the answer rests with the profitability of nuclear energy. Utilities wishing to have nuclear facilities could obtain them with heavy subsidies from the federal government. That is, the taxpayers paid for private utilities to switch to nuclear energy. There is a consequent arrogance among the nuclear interests. Gene Bryerton noted this in quoting from *INFO,* a nuclear trade magazine: "They [lay people] believe in the declared marvels of the latest deodorant, and of all the other declared wonders propounded over and over on the radio and television and in the magazines and daily press, from the time they get up until bedtime. They have come to prefer authority because it takes so much less mental wear and tear than to choose or to decide." That statement itself represents a fascinating elliptical process: nuclear ethics first helping to destroy Americans' autonomy, then scorning them for it. Another side of this attitude is the behavior of the AEC and, now, the NRC. It cannot be expected that bureaucracies with a vested interest in nuclear energy could admit it to be unworkable or dangerous. Much the same is true of the companies involved in nuclear power. Atomic energy, right now, is a good business. One is ironically reminded of a 1951 cartoon in the *Bulletin of the Atomic Scientists.* Two newscasters are depicted wearing gas masks and broadcasting from a flaming ruin. The caption reads: "And so it is evident that the end of our civilization is at hand. Goodnight—and here is Lyle Van for the Pure Oil Company."[74]

But business factors are not the only ones forwarding the nuclear fascination. Deep emotional strains contribute too. These have been elaborately overlooked for years. Since the late forties Americans have been barraged with praise generally for scientific and technological endeavors, and specifically for the "Atomic Genie." People came to think of nuclear power as the highest and best evolution of science. They also anticipated the fruits of the atomic age with relish. The bomb's cultural lessons, moreover, helped condition Americans to risky and violent authoritarian behavior. We at once recognized and minimized our danger: "It can't happen here." Beginning in the fifties, we embraced a way of life that rendered us all nuclear victims. Americans began their entanglement with the atomic age by learning to stop worrying and love the bomb.

NOTES

1. "Life in These United States," *Reader's Digest,* October 1952, p. 52. The same story in different trappings appears in other sources—for instance, in the February 5, 1951, *Time,* p. 11, only this variation involved absorbed gamblers in a Las Vegas casino. The *Digest,* February 1957, p. 34, printed a cartoon about a perfume sales counter, captioned "The first whiff is good, but it's the fallout that gets 'em." *Saturday Evening Post,* January 11, 1958, p. 48, ran a cartoon depicting an atomic high chair for babies ("no fall-out").

2. Worthwhile secondary sources were Bert Cochran, *The War System* (New York, 1965), and, to a lesser extent, Howard Zinn's *Postwar America* (Indianapolis, 1973), and Lawrence S. Wittner's *Cold War America* (New York, 1974).

The term "official" is used to refer to government spokespeople, politicians, military men, and scientists following or forwarding the "party line"—since for all practical purposes there was little differentiation between the two major political parties regarding the arms, space, and energy races. This definition loses its apparently amorphous nature when the lack of widespread public dissent in the fifties comes clear. Much more so than today, there *was* an official reality that was rarely contradicted.

3. John Hersey, *Hiroshima* (New York, 1946), originally published in *The New Yorker* magazine. Also see "Preview of the War We Do Not Want," *Collier's,* October 27, 1951, special issue on the main "events of World War III." Also of interest are Dean Acheson's remarks in the July 13, 1950, New York *Times.* He announced the United States did not intend to refrain from using atomic weapons simply because it would be called a war criminal.

4. Sahl quoted in Editors of *Time-Life* Books, *1950–1960* (New York, 1970), p. 229; see also James Clayton, ed., *Economic Impact of the Cold War* (New York, 1970). I. F. Stone noted in 1957 that 60 per cent of the national budget would go to the military.

5. Al Toffler, "The Airpower Lobby," in Henry V. Christman, ed., *A View of the Nation* (New York, 1960), pp. 177–78; Clayton, ed., *Economic Impact,* p. 4. Eisenhower coined the term "military-industrial complex" as a warning in his 1960 farewell address, though the first major exposé of this new force in American life was C. Wright Mills' seminal study *The Power Elite* (New York, 1956).

6. "The New Vertijet's Straight-Up Flight," *Life,* May 20, 1957, pp. 136–40; Lt. Gen. James Gavin, *War and Peace in the Space Age* (New York, 1958), pp. ix, 256. Cochran, in *War System,* tells about one Rear Admiral Harrison, who insisted the Navy continue its contracts with McDonnell Aircraft and Westinghouse for the F3H jet fighter. The F3H had crashed in 17 tests. A total of $320 million was spent on this jet. The Navy eventually admitted this was a total waste. Upon his 1955 retirement, the admiral went on to become vice president of McDonnell. This is scarcely an isolated incident.

As the *Nation* noted April 11, 1959, by that year America had stockpiled 75,000 nuclear weapons, quite a considerable glut.

7. See also the discussion of Sputnik in our chapter "Showdown at the Little Red Schoolhouse." Much of Gavin's *War and Peace* worries about the threat of Soviet space capabilities in attacking and spying. See also Harvey Swados, "The Brain Market," *Nation,* March 8, 1958, pp. 209–10, on Sputnik hysteria.

8. Gavin, *War and Peace,* p. 256.

9. The most thorough discussion of press control appears in A. J. Liebling, *The Press* (New York, 1959). This is an anthology of Liebling's fifties columns from *The New Yorker.* As he pointed out, reporters are no less gullible than anyone else. They are merely more dangerous in their gullibility, particularly when coupled with conservative publishers. Ralph Gleason noted some recent results of such management of news in the November 7, 1974, *Rolling Stone.* He wrote on public figures who believe "that the image is more real than reality, and thus everything they do is aimed at structuring the image rather than dealing with the truth." Our point is that the media offered little encouragement to anyone in challenging such thinking. News reporting in the fifties was distinguished mainly by its concurrence with official news management. When information is limited and controlled in this fashion, people cannot make judgments based on complete facts—that is, they cannot make true judgments.

10. "The Facts About A-Bomb 'Fall-Out,' " *Reader's Digest,* June 1955, pp. 22–24.

11. Gene Bryerton, *Nuclear Dilemma* (New York, 1970), p. 6; Doris Lessing, *The Four-Gated City* (London, 1969), p. 330; "First Picture of Atom Bomb," *Look,* May 3, 1951; "Atomic Weapons Will Save Money," *Look,* October 10, 1950, p. 34; Ralph Lapp, "Nuclear War," in John M. Fowler, ed., *Fallout* (New York, 1960), p. 161—an excellent anthology on many aspects of nuclear power. Lapp, *Voyage of the Lucky Dragon* (New York, 1958), p. 197. *Nation,* March 21, 1959, p. 241. The "cheapest form of destruction" argument was also a great way to combat fears about military overspending.

12. Jim Peck, *We Who Would Not Kill* (New York, 1958), p. 208—he also recalls the full-color postcards sold in the Southwest showing nuclear blasts. Also see "Uranium Makes a Wilder West," *Life,* July 19, 1954, pp. 12–13—largely about the rush to uranium prospecting.

13. *Life,* July 19, 1954, p. 14; *Time,* August 15, 1955, p. 40; Sheldon Novick, *The Careless Atom* (Boston, 1969), p. 54.

14. Frederick Lewis Allen, *The Big Change* (New York, 1952), p. 120; *Science Digest,* May 1951, p. 95; Jacques Barzun, *God's Country and Mine* (Boston, 1954), p. 135; "The Dawn of Farming's Chemical Age," *Reader's Digest,* February 1954, p. 113 (condensed from *Fortune*); Carl Degler, *Affluence and Anxiety* (Glenview, Ill., 1968), p. 178; R. I. Throckmorton, "Organic Farming—Bunk," *Reader's Digest,* October 1952, pp. 45–48.

15. Morris L. Ernst, *Utopia 1976* (New York, 1955), pp. 39, 77, 72–75; David Sarnoff in Editors of *Fortune, The Fabulous Future* (New York, 1956), pp. 17, 18.

16. "Atom Roots Out Corn," *Business Week,* September 20, 1952, p. 162; "Bombarded Foods Stay Germ-Free As Others Rot," *National Geographic,* September 1958, p. 311; Heinz Haber, *The Walt Disney Story of Our Friend the Atom* (New York, 1956), p. 124; U. S. Atomic Energy Commission press release, March 9, 1959, on Project Plowshare.

17. "Our Atomic Tomorrow," *Holiday,* August 1952, p. 5.

18. U. S. National Security Resources Board, *You Can Survive* (Washington, D.C., 1950), pp. 3–6, 8, 12; also see "Radiation—Minor Bomb Hazard?", *Science Digest,* March 1951, p. 77, in which an AEC member "thinks it best to regard the casualties of any atomic explosion as the result of mechanical destruction."

19. National Security Resources Board, *Survive,* pp. 8, 12. Another interesting article is Capt. Richard P. Taffe, "I'm Not Afraid of the A-BOMB," *Collier's,* January 26, 1952, pp. 14, 41, in which Taffe calculates that "only 15 percent" of the Hiroshima deaths—according to his figures, only 21,000 people—occurred due to radiation. This was intended to prove the A-bombs were no more scarey than conventional ones, just bigger.

20. Athan Theoharis, *Seeds of Repression* (Chicago, 1971), p. 64; Office of Civil Defense Mobilization, *Disaster Readiness in Undergraduate Education* (Nashville, 1960), p. 69.

21. John L. Balderston, Jr., and Gordon Hewe, *Atomic Attack: A Manual for Survival* (Los Angeles, 1950); "Operation Wake Up," *American Mercury,* January 1953, p. 38. See also "How One Hospital Prepares for Atomic Disaster," *Look,* February 13, 1951, pp. 36–41; and Fletcher Knebel, "We're Wide Open for Disaster," *Look,* February 27, 1951, p. 29.

22. "Place to Hide," *Time,* December 13, 1950, p. 21; *Time,* September 25, 1950, p. 112; *Time,* February 5, 1951 on Mrs. Colhoun.

23. One look at any urban rush hour would be enough to convince anyone of the idiocy of a mass evacuation program. But it was the highway automobile interests' way of cashing in on the cold war while seeking patriotic publicity. See, for instance, the Caterpillar ad "Big Reason for Better Roads," *Saturday Evening Post,* January 25, 1958, p. 81. National policy on shelters is found in OCDM, *Individual and Family Survival Requirements* (Washington, D.C., November 1959), p. 147, wherein Teller's public relations nickname, "Father of the H-bomb," appears.

24. "Their Sheltered Honeymoon," *Life,* August 10, 1959; see also *Nation,* August 29, 1959, p. 82, on a similar experiment at Princeton University involving a larger family; also Fred J. Cook, *The Warfare State* (New York, 1962), p. 321; OCDM, *The Family Fallout Shelter* (Washington, D.C., 1959), pp. 2, 4–6, 13, 14, 18. The latter with its plans for five basic shelters became the standard booklet. It has been reissued several times since 1959.

One of the most crucial points in the shelter reassurances was the way the country seemed to feel it could buy its way out of any dilemma. Jules Feiffer recognized this in his 1959 cartoon story "Boom!" Feiffer's tale is set in a world where there are so many bomb tests the sky fills with big black floating specks. People are terrified and anxious. Then the government announces the development of a big black floating speckproof filter, on sale everywhere. The world is able to buy the filters and relaxes into a golden age of materialism, art, and arms. "Boom!" appears in Feiffer's *Passionella* (New York, 1959).

25. Wittner, *Cold War*, p. 214; Cook, *Warfare*, p. 321.

26. *Post-Dispatch* is quoted by John Fowler in his final essay in *Fallout*, p. 182, from a UPI dispatch.

27. Wittner, *Cold War*, p. 214; Sonny Klienfield, "Gimme Shelter," *New Times*, January 23, 1976, pp. 50–54. Klienfield wrote of all the abandoned shelters from the fifties and early sixties, now used for parties, wine cellars, or, mostly, nothing. He also wrote of one chemist who recently built a $24,000 four-bedroom shelter adjoining his house in New York State.

28. Cochran, *System*, pp. 35–36; Wittner, *Cold War*, p. 214.

29. OCDM, *Disaster Readiness*, pp. 86–89.

30. Ibid., pp. 76–78, 129. Also see Civil Defense Education Project, *Education for National Survival*, a 1956 pamphlet for teachers.

31. See A. Alvarez, *The Savage God* (London, 1971). This book is an examination of suicide. Alvarez comments that for society today "every perspective closes with the possibility of international suicide by nuclear war," and this awareness shapes much of our social behavior.

32. I. F. Stone, *The Haunted Fifties* (New York, 1963), pp. 80, 122; also see Norman Moss, *Men Who Play God* (New York, 1958), chapter five, "Men with a Mission"; and James Michener's aggressive *While Others Sleep* condensed in the October 1957, *Reader's Digest*, pp. 70–243—justification for SAC.

33. "Two-Hour Warning Against Sneak Attack," *U.S. News & World Report*, September 6, 1957, pp. 77, 83, interviewing Partridge; *Nation*, January 30, 1960, p. 89, quoting Dr. James E. MacDonald, University of Arizona, on the potential of nuclear attack on cities; Cochran, *System*, p. 35.

34. Bertrand Russell's introduction to Fred Cook, *The Warfare State*, p. viii; also see Cook's remarks on p. 320; Wittner, *Cold War*, p. 214.

35. Cochran, *System*, p. 35; Wolfe is quoted in Fowler, *Fallout*, pp. 178–80. It is estimated in Fowler that "the incidence of leukemia after a [widespread] nuclear attack would be staggering." The populations of Hiroshima and Nagasaki, which each suffered only one bomb, over the years have shown increases of several kinds of cancer. Different varieties appeared gradually as time elapsed. Robert Jay Lifton's stunning and thorough book, *Death in Life* is an examination of the Hiroshima survivors. Lifton writes primarily about emotional effects of the bombings, but also refers to physical effects (pp. 104–5, for instance). The Japanese had been making surrender overtures for months when the Hiroshima bomb and then the totally unnecessary Nagasaki bomb were dropped. These overtures, however, had failed to offer the total surrender Truman wanted. As the Air Force's Strategic Bombing Survey concluded, Japan would have surrendered within five months without nuclear bombing but with blockades, conventional bombing, and very small American losses. In other words atomic-bombing the cities was unnecessary even from a military standpoint. See Wittner, *Cold War*, pp. 12–14, on the opposition of Eisenhower and others; *Bulletin of the Atomic Scientists*, November 1949, p. 324; Takashi Nagai, *We of Nagasaki; the Story of Survivors in an Atomic Wasteland* (New York, 1958), written for an American audience.

36. C. Wright Mills, *The Causes of World War III* (New York, 1960), p. 59; Fowler, "Bombs and Their Products," in *Fallout;* Taffe, "I'm Not Afraid," *Collier's,* p. 41.

37. Nevil Shute, *On the Beach* (New York, 1957); Walter Miller, *A Canticle for Leibowitz* (New York, 1959).

38. *National Geographic,* September 1958, about radiation and lab animals; "What Will Radioactivity Do to Our Children?", *U.S. News & World Report,* May 13, 1955, p. 72; "When Atom Bomb Struck—Uncensored," *Life,* September 29, 1952, pp. 19–21, photos by Japanese of Hiroshima and Nagasaki devastation "for any people who live in the not illogical fear of being caught themselves in an atomic blast."

39. Lifton discusses the "psychic numbing" of scientists' minds in *Death in Life.* H. J. Muller, Nobel Prize winner, had discovered in the late forties gross genetic defects produced in fruit flies by radiation. Some defects, he found, did not appear in first-generation offspring of exposed flies, but did in later generations. Muller, by the latter fifties, was a supporter of continued bomb testing. See "What Will Radioactivity Do?", *U.S. News,* and Richard S. Lewis, *The Nuclear Power Rebellion* (New York, 1972), probably the best of the books about abuses of nuclear power. Also see Novick, *Careless,* pp. 131–33, on pollution hazards from uranium mines. Up to 1959, people drinking water from the Animas River received three times the maximum permissible exposure to Radium-226 and Strontium-90 because tailings from the mines washed into the stream. Both water and crops in the San Miguel River area were found to contain high concentrations of Radium-226. By 1960, Novick points out, over 1,000 active uranium mines operated in the United States alone. Neither AEC, state, nor federal agencies accepted jurisdiction over them. Some mines were found to have atmospheric concentrations of radon (and its daughters) 59 times the permissible level. Under such conditions in thirties Germany, many miners died of lung cancer and other respiratory diseases attributed to the radon gas. Nothing was done about these conditions in the United States until 1967, when the first enforceable standards were formulated. Many other blunders with radioactive materials can be cited. These appear in Novick and in Lewis, *The Nuclear Power Rebellion.*

40. " 'Fall-Out,' " p. 23.

41. Linus Pauling, *No More War!* (New York, 1958), pp. 119–32; Edward Teller and Albert Latter, "Why Nuclear Bomb Tests Must Go On," *Life,* February 10, 1958, pp. 67–70; Novick, *Careless,* p. 98.

42. "What Will Radioactivity Do to Our Children?", *U.S. News,* May 13, 1955, p. 72; Teller and Latter, "Why Tests," pp. 119–32.

43. Norman Moss devotes a chapter to Herman Kahn in *Men Who Play God,* especially see p. 243. Kahn's most famous book is *On Thermonuclear War* (New York, 1960). See also *Reader's Digest,* June 1955, pp. 129–30; Kurt Vonnegut, *Wampeters, Foma and Granfalloons* (New York, 1974), p. 98; Gavin, *War and Peace,* pp. 250–52. Gavin, in 1956, estimated an atomic assault on Russia would produce "on the order of several hundred million" deaths, extending into Japan and the Philippines, and "well back up into Western Europe," p. 176.

44. On Oppenheimer see Stone, *Haunted,* p. 80, and A. J. Muste, "Mephistopheles and the Scientists," in Nat Hentoff, ed., *The Essays of A. J. Muste* (Indianapolis, 1967), pp. 370–79; Lapp, *Voyage of the Lucky Dragon,* in addition to his essay in Fowler, *Fallout,* his other books and contributions to such publications as *Bulletin of the Atomic Scientists.* In the latter seventies, Lapp has emerged as a proponent of nuclear power plants to solve the energy crisis. Also see Ben Shahn and Richard Hudson, *Kuboyama and the Saga of the Lucky Dragon* (New York, 1965), primarily a series of Shahn's pictures based on the irradiation of the fishermen and Kuboyama's death.

45. Pauling, *No More War!,* pp. 119–32.

46. Ibid., pp. 370–79, 68, 70–73. Pauling includes a table "Estimated Effect of Bomb Tests on Future Generations," p. 71. Also see "Latest About Aftereffects of A-Bomb," *U.S. News,* May 13, 1955, pp. 65–66.

47. Walter Schneir, "Strontium-90 in U.S. Children," *Nation,* April 25, 1959, p. 355; Bryerton, *Dilemma,* pp. 45–46.

48. W. E. B. DuBois, *I Take My Stand for Peace* (New York, 1951), pp. 7, 14–16; DuBois, *In Battle for Peace* (New York, 1952), pp. 25–37, 88. The New York *Herald-Tribune* editorialized in 1951 that "the DuBois outfit was set up to promote tricky appeal of Soviet origin. . . . This thing came straight out of the Cominform." An integral part of the cold war's witch hunting was the labeling of leftist and pacifist work as part of Russia's campaign of "adroit world-wide propaganda"—see, for instance, Michener, *While Others Sleep.*

49. Peck, *We Who Would Not Kill,* pp. 180–81, 183–84, 190–93; Bradford Lyttle, "On Nonviolent Obstruction," in Paul Goodman, ed., *Seeds of Liberation* (New York, 1964), p. 126—this is an anthology of selections from *Liberation* magazine.

50. Wilmer Young, *Visible Witness,* a Pendle Hill pamphlet reprinted in Staughton Lynd, ed., *Nonviolence in America* (New York, 1966); Earle Reynolds, *The Forbidden Voyage* (New York, 1961), on the 1958 sailing of the *Phoenix* into the Bikini test zone; Albert Bigelow, "Why I Am Sailing into the Pacific Bomb Test Area," in Goodman, *Seeds,* pp. 145–49; also see *Nation,* April 19, 1958, p. 334, on Bigelow's intention to sail the 30-foot ketch *Golden Rule* into the Eniwetok test grounds. Bigelow and his crew were arrested at Hawaii despite repeated attempts to sail. They intended to question both bomb tests and the legality of the American presence in the Pacific.

51. A. J. Muste, *Of Holy Disobedience,* a Pendle Hill pamphlet reprinted in Hentoff, *Muste.* Bruce quoted in Arthur Steuer, "How to Talk Dirty and Influence People," *Esquire,* November 1959, p. 155.

Many other modes of protest were being rediscovered in the late fifties, prompted by the nuclear arms situation. Juanita Nelson, "A Matter of Principle," in Goodman, *Seeds,* writes about tax resistance. Kay Boyle, "The Triumph of Principles," in *Seeds,* noted rising protest activity among students and artists, particularly mass demonstrations of civil disobedience. See also Rev. Maurice McCracken, "Pilgrimage of a Conscience," in Lynd, *Nonviolence.* The publication of *Dissent* magazine had been one of the first signs of intellectual discontent with conformist America. The publication of *Liberation* (which continues to appear) tied together old left, religious left, and many young New Leftists.

52. Peck, *We Who Would Not Kill*, pp. 18–19.

53. Cook, *Warfare*, pp. 320–21; "What Will Radioactivity Do?", p. 73.

54. Mills, *Causes*, pp. 148–49; one such bomber interview appears in Frank W. Chinnock, *Nagasaki: The Forgotten Bomb* (New York, 1970), a book that confuses listing dreadful nuclear casualties with sensitivity; see also Lifton, *Death in Life*, p. 411; Moss, *Men Who Play God*, chapter five, "Men with a Mission," and remarks by Alvarez in *Savage God*. Jeff Nuttal's entire *Bomb Culture* (New York, 1968) deals primarily with the problem of the artist in a world of malevolent technology. We found ourselves influenced by his comments to the point of using his term "bomb culture" throughout this chapter. See also George S. Stevenson, "Antidote for Atomic Jitters," New York *Times Magazine*, May 13, 1951, p. 13–article by a psychiatrist who understands nuclear jitters as symptoms of personal guilt, a neurotic problem "on the individual level."

55. Brian Murphy, "They Came from Beneath the Fifties," *Journal of Popular Film*, 1 (Winter 1972), 31–38, also discusses monster movies and the paranoiac fifties style, particularly in terms of anticommunism; "Huge Props to Shrink a Man," *Life*, May 13, 1957, p. 149, on *Incredible Shrinking Man*. *Godzilla* was the first in a long series of Japanese monster films of tremendous popularity in the United States. These films continue to be made and have introduced a huge cast of creatures representing many degrees of good and evil. In some more recent films, for instance, Godzilla is the heroic monster defending Japan against other monsters; in *Destroy All Monsters*, a group of the monsters band together to repel invaders from outer space. Generally each film includes the figure of an heroic Japanese, often a child, who innocently creates a sympathetic alliance with the monster and tames it. When Americans appear, they are frequently in bumbling and insensitive authoritarian roles. The Japanese person is always far more instrumental in easing the danger. In effect, this is a symbolic conquest of the American atomic threat. For a more extended discussion of science fiction films in the fifties see Chapter 12, pp. 334–37.

56. Chris Steinbrunner and Burt Goldblatt, *Cinema of the Fantastic* (New York, 1972), pp. 221–34. Another race-anxious holocaust film was *Five*.

57. Haber, *Our Friend*, p. 113; C. Rogers McCullough, ed., *Safety Aspects of Nuclear Reactors* (Princeton, 1957), p. ix.

58. William E. Leuchtenberg, *The Great Age of Change* (New York, 1964), p. 23; U. S. Atomic Energy Commission, *18 Questions and Answers About Radiation* (Oak Ridge, 1960), p. 21.

59. Novick, *Careless*, p. 100; Bryerton, *Dilemma*, p. 42.

60. Bryerton, *Dilemma*, p. 7; Novick, *Careless*, pp. 36–38. Plans for Bodega Head were abandoned in 1964.

61. Barry Commoner, "A Reporter At Large; Energy–II," *New Yorker*, February 9, 1976, p. 42; also McCullough, *Safety Aspects*, pp. 25–28, 140–42. The Brookhaven reports are referred to in most of the literature about nuclear power after 1957; authors Novick, Bryerton, and Lewis all discuss them in

various contexts. Plant hazards, however, were dismissed earlier, see George L. Weil, "Hazards of Nuclear Power Plants," *Science*, March 4, 1955, p. 315. The Commoner article is an excellent brief summary of nuclear reactor operations and problems, as well as discussing solar energy. Commoner points out nuclear power may well become economically unfeasible within a decade, as fuel and safety system costs rise. His article is probably the best introduction to the issues for the reader with little time. Of the books we have read on the subject of nuclear power plants, Lewis' *Nuclear Power Rebellion* is the most comprehensive.

62. Commoner, "Reporter," pp. 42–43; Bryerton, in *Dilemma*, pp. xiii, 7, refers to nuclear dissent during the sixties. His book began as journalistic coverage of a proposed nuclear plant in New York State.

63. Pollard and the Indian Point plants were featured in a segment of *Sixty Minutes*, CBS-TV, February 15, 1976; Bryerton, *Dilemma*, pp. 21–25; Novick, *Careless*, pp. 1–10; the New York *Times*, February 22, 1976, wrote about Pollard and the GE engineers in *Week in Review* section. The New York *Times*, February 29, 1976, carried several articles in different sections on nuclear power abuses. These ranged from coverage of the Brown's Ferry, Alabama, accident to the irradiation of convicts' testicles for experimental purposes.

64. Novick, *Careless*, p. 100; Bryerton, *Dilemma*, pp. 42–47. The plants produce a large "inventory" of radioactive fission products, emitted as gas. These include Strontium-90, Iodine-131 that seeks muscle tissue, and Tritium, which substitutes for hydrogen at any point in the body.

65. Ernest Sternglass, *Low-Level Radiation* (New York, 1972); see also Sternglass, "The Death of All Children," *Esquire*, September 1969, special insert in protest of ABMs; Cook, *Warfare*, p. 320; Joel Griffith, "Fallout and Infant Mortality," *Village Voice*, November 23, 1973, p. 19. The most controversial portion of Sternglass' work deals with emissions from nuclear power plants. But he is also concerned with test fallout and fallout from nuclear weaponry in wartime, as in the *Esquire* insert.

66. As Pauling said, even if only a few infant deaths and defects occurred because of nuclear bombs, "the moral problem would remain the same." See also Griffith, "Fallout and Infant Mortality," p. 19.

67. John Kobler, "Gangway for the Atomic Garbage Man!", *Saturday Evening Post*, January 25, 1958, pp. 36, 73.

68. Grace Des Champs, "'Hot' Dumping Off Boston," *Nation*, September 19, 1959, pp. 143–46; Novick, *Careless*, pp. 36–37.

69. E. J. Kahn, Jr., "Our Far-Flung Correspondents," *New Yorker*, October 1960, pp. 104–24, writes about Des Champs and the entire Cape Cod dumping controversy; also "Sea Disposal of Atomic Wastes," *Bulletin of the Atomic Scientists*, April, 1960, p. 141, a letter from several members of the Lower Cape Committee protesting the dumping. It is signed by Albert Szent-Gyorgy, Frederick G. Keyes, and Allan M. Butler. The letter concluded: "We believe it is essential that the control of sea disposal of atomic wastes be taken from the AEC and placed in the hands of the Public Health Service."

70. Larry Kraftowitz, "Stop Trucking Radioactive Material Through Our Streets," *Village Voice*, February 9, 1976, pp. 46–47; Commoner, "Reporter," pp. 43, 47.

71. Commoner, "Reporter," pp. 41, 43–47; Kraftowitz, "Stop Trucking," p. 46.

72. Gerald McCourt, "Test Case on Atomic Waste," *Nation*, August 1, 1959, pp. 43–44, about New Britain, Connecticut, the third New England town to ban shipment of radioactive goods inside its borders. At this time Houston was attempting to institute a similar ban. Additionally, Houston eventually succeeded in convincing AEC against dumping hot wastes in the sea nearby. The Mexican government had proved particularly hostile to the idea. We have found no indication of the feelings of the Canadian government about the matter. The Boston dumping, after citizen protests, was moved off the Nova Scotia shore.

73. Bartle Bull, "Ecofreaks," *Village Voice*, June 21, 1973, p. 7; Bryerton, *Dilemma*, pp. 124–25; Anna Mayo, "Atoms of the Night," *Voice*, July 12, 1973, pp. 19–20 and "Will Powdered Seaweed be the Next Cult Food?" *Voice*, July 12, 1973, p. 24; Muste, "Getting Rid of War," in Hentoff, *Muste*, p. 390. See also "AEC Files Show Effort to Conceal Safety Perils," New York *Times*, November 10, 1974, front page, and Lewis, *Rebellion*, pp. 56–61. Another source of peripheral interest is Rachel Carson's *Silent Spring*, which does not deal with nuclear power but laid the cultural groundwork for such work.

74. *Bulletin of the Atomic Scientists*, October, 1951, p. 303. By the mid-seventies, with the cold war's apparent dwindling, any imminent thermonuclear conflict between the major powers seemed unlikely. But the fifties policy that had placed such weaponry in many foreign countries under American auspices was becoming cause for worry. Some observers wondered when more volatile nations would seize such weapons for their own use. A number of nations, for instance India, possessed nuclear weapons by the mid-seventies. The possibility of nuclear terrorism seemed to grow greater. Some predicted it would come from extremist groups who would build their own bombs. Others foresaw tiny yet angry nations triggering the nuclear war. That, actually, was the origin of the end-all war in Shute's *On the Beach.* See Walter Pincus, "Congress and Tactical Nukes," *New Republic*, October 12, 1974, p. 19.

Experts now believe that at least 70 per cent of all cancers are caused by man-made environmental problems, from radiation through asbestos to polyvinyl chloride plastic. See "The Public Be Damned," *Rolling Stone*, November 21, 1974, p. 38, and Joe Klien, "The Plastic Coffin of Charlie Arthur," *Rolling Stone*, January 15, 1976, pp. 42–47.

3

Ain't Nobody Here but Us Protestants, Catholics, and Jews

Americans admired Jacques Maritain, the French neo-Thomist theologian, and he in turn liked them. When he delivered a series of lectures at the University of Chicago in 1956, he proclaimed "that if a new Christian civilization, a new Christendom is ever to come about in human history, it is on American soil that it will find its starting point."[1]

Many Americans shared Maritain's vision. Henry Luce, head of the *Time-Life* empire, was one. Writing in a book optimistically entitled *The Fabulous Future: America in 1980*, Luce envisioned a religious renaissance bringing peace and plenty. Unlike Orwell's 1984 nightmare, the Lucean America of 1980 combined "free enterprise" with "humanitarianism" and "science" in an evolutionary "collaboration with God." "Collaboration with God," he wrote, "in the *whole* of evolution—this is a vision so new that it may even be regarded as dangerous in its sweep. For it is nothing less than at last to Christianize Atlas, to unchain Prometheus on his own recognizance, to create a greater Renaissance which shall not become pagan, and to suffuse Lord Russell's dark, icy cosmology with the light and warmth of Christian love and sacrifice and hope."[2]

That optimistic predictions about America's future stressed religion was not surprising. Religious interest was at an all-time high during the fifties. As a *Time* magazine reporter claimed in 1954, "today in the U.S. the Christian faith is back in the center of things."[3] Increased religious concern became evident during World War II, though declining somewhat immediately after the war. Then in the late forties and early fifties a great change began. Church attendance soared. Membership lists swelled with new converts. In 1940 less than half the population belonged to institutionalized churches, but by the late fifties over 63 per cent were officially enrolled. Actually an even larger portion of the population identified themselves as church members. Seventy-three per cent answered "yes" to a national survey asking "Do you happen at the present time to be an active member of a church or a religious group?" In questionnaires inquiring "What is your religion?", about 96 per cent of those responding identified themselves as Protestants, Catholics, or Jews.[4]

Signs of the religious boom were everywhere. Huge billboards dotted the countryside urging people to "bring the whole family to church." These were sponsored by a national layman's committee, "Religion in American Life." This organization by the mid-fifties received some six million dollars' worth of free advertising annually. Early in 1955 the American Legion launched a well-publicized, well-organized, and well-financed campaign to bring the nation "Back to God." Helping to open the crusade, President Eisenhower solemnly proclaimed: "Recognition of the Supreme Being is the first, the most basic, expression of Americanism. Without God, there could be no American form of government, nor an American way of life."[5]

The prestige of religious leaders was great. The leading popularizers—Rev. Billy Graham, Rev. Norman Vincent Peale, and Bishop Fulton J. Sheen—each had his own television and radio programs. *Time* magazine frequently featured theologians and revivalists in their cover stories, and other popular magazines relied heavily on clerical contributions. Elmo Roper made a series of national surveys in the forties and fifties. From a list of leadership groups that included government, Congress, business, labor, and religion, Roper asked people "Which one of these groups do you feel is doing the most good for the country at the present time?" When he first made this survey in 1942, religious leaders were third behind government and business; only 17.5 per cent named that group as "doing the most good." By 1947, however, religious leaders were first; 32.6 per cent saw them as doing most good as opposed to 18.8 per cent choosing business leaders, 15.4 per cent government leaders, 10.6 per cent labor, and 6.7 per cent Congress. By 1957, 46 per cent of those surveyed picked religious leaders as "doing the most good." As the Roper report concluded: "No other group—whether government, congressional, business, or labor—came anywhere near matching the prestige and pulling power of the men who are the ministers of God."[6]

Skyrocketing Bible sales were another good index of the religious revival. Between 1949 and 1953 the yearly distribution of Bibles rose 140 per cent, reaching the incredible figure of nearly ten million Bibles a year by 1953. Stories from the Bible became common features in the comic sections of Sunday newspapers. A *Reader's Digest* writer, Fulton Oursler, rewrote the Bible in *Digest* style; it was syndicated in numerous newspapers with great success. When the Revised Standard Version of the Bible was published in 1952, it headed the best-seller list, selling two million copies the first year.[7]

Religious books other than the Bible also sold incredibly well. In 1953, booksellers reported one out of every ten books vended was religious. *Publisher's Weekly*, January 23, 1954, related that "the theme of religion dominates the non-fiction best sellers in 1953." That same year the two most popular works of fiction had religious themes. Second only to the Bible in book sales from 1952 to 1955 was Norman Vincent Peale's *The Power of Positive Thinking*. On the New York *Times* non-fiction best-seller list for over three years, mostly at the top, this book had sold over 2,000,000 copies by 1955. Besides the regular edition, a special child's version was published as well as a "new Deluxe Pocket Edition" advertised as being "bound handsomely in genuine Stardite . . . stamped in gold with flexible binding . . . wrapped attractively in cellophane . . . printed on fine white Bible paper." Other best-selling religious works included Catherine Marshall's account of her minister-husband, *A Man Called Peter* (1951); by 1955 this had sold some 1,300,000 copies as well as serving as the inspiration for a popular movie. Bishop Fulton Sheen's *Life Is Worth Living* (1953), being transcripts from his TV show and "dedicated to our Heavenly Mother who stands behind me at every telecast," sold a quarter of a million copies in two years. Bookstores even featured such offerings as *The Power of Prayer on Plants* and *Pray Your Weight Away.* And the fiction in popular magazines such as the *Saturday Evening Post* invariably gushed with religiosity.[8]

Contributions to religious causes reached a record $3.4 billion by 1957, and a major religious building boom occurred, particularly in the burgeoning suburbs. The value of new religious buildings jumped from $409 million in 1950, to $868 million in 1957. Ministers spoke proudly of their new "plants." Even drive-in churches appeared, modeled on the success of drive-in movies. One Presbyterian drive-in in Venice, Florida, offered to carry the communion grape juice to those cars whose passengers were unable to walk to the communion table. This drive-in, according to its pastor, "with its loudspeakers set among the trees, provides an extra spiritual dimension, brought on by the sun, the pines and the birds."[9]

As might be expected, popular entertainment was affected by the religious vogue. Jukeboxes blared "Our Lady of Fatima," "I Believe," "The Man Upstairs," "It Is No Secret What God Can Do." Radio stations began pausing not only for station breaks but for moments of meditation. The Southwest Conference colleges started opening football games with a prayer. Movies such as *The Robe,* based on Lloyd Douglas' best-selling novel, and Hollywood's first Cinemascope production, Cecil B. DeMille's 1956 extravaganza, *The Ten Commandments,* made Christianity vivid and dramatic for millions. The movie version of *A Man Called Peter* was billed as a film in which "Religion can be fun." The hero, the Reverend Peter Marshall, was pictured in ads looking like a gray-flanneled young executive. *"He was a first-name kind of guy,"* read the ads. *"He was everybody's kind of guy. . . . He was God's kind of guy."*[10]

Previous periods of religious enthusiasm in American history have generally affected only certain segments of the population—usually lower- and middle-class Protestants. In the fifties, however, all faiths and all classes were influenced: Protestants, Catholics, and Jews, rich and poor, old and young, intellectuals and illiterates, suburbanites and city dwellers, farmers and small-town people, blacks and whites.

On college campuses, amid the fraternities and football, the beer parties and panty raids, religion too was in evidence. Throughout the country, colleges and universities added new departments of religion or substantially enlarged existing ones. Writing on this phenomenon in *Newsweek*, a reporter claimed that "no fad was the renewed interest in religion." To illustrate this he cited the cases of Donn Moomaw, an all-American football player at UCLA who was working with Billy Graham, and of Fred McPhee, Princeton's football captain and a religion major. "Religious courses on most campuses," he concluded, "were well subscribed, and religious-emphasis weeks were a big hit with students." At Wheaton College a revival was held for 39 straight hours. During that time it was observed "teachers closed classrooms and joined the steady stream to the altar." On a more prestigious level, Harvard Divinity School was raised from a moribund state in the early fifties to become the nation's most respected seminary with a 700 per cent larger endowment and such eminent theologians as Reinhold Niebuhr and Paul Tillich on the staff.[11]

Religious interest was great among intellectuals. However, it differed markedly from the popular religious enthusiasms of the day. Instead of the gospel of success and happiness with a little help from "the Man Upstairs," intellectuals were concerned with neo-orthodox theology and existentialism. Kierkegaard was rediscovered and popularized. Theologians Niebuhr, Tillich, Maritain, Martin Buber, and Karl Barth had a prominence with the intellectual elite that no religious thinkers had possessed since the days of Jonathan Edwards. Religious writers, ideas, and themes became commonplace in high-level intellectual journals such as *Partisan Review*, *American Scholar*, and *Commentary*, as well as in the liberal news magazines, *The Nation*, *The New Republic*, and *The Reporter*.[12]

The theology admired by intellectuals was conservative. As *Time* magazine noted in the caption beneath a picture of Niebuhr, "Sin is back in fashion"—not the committing of it, but the recognition of it. "The forces of evil," intoned Union Theological Seminary's head, Henry Pitney Van Dusen, "are always gaining ground, and must be stopped again and again." According to the neo-orthodox theologians, the great errors of modern man were placing too much faith in human goodness and the inevitable progress of history. As Niebuhr wrote: "One cannot understand the spiritual climate of our time if one does not see how catastrophically modern man's experience of contemporary history has refuted all the secular securities which had been established irrefutably in the past two centuries. . . . Modern experience has refuted the conceptions of human nature held by the nineteenth century even more catastrophically than the conceptions of history. Evil seems so inextricably mixed with good."[13] This brooding theology with its rejection of liberal idealism fitted well with the conservative consensus of fifties intellectuals.

But such a heady and pessimistic theology was not for the mass of Americans. A much more popular manifestation of the religious surge was what one writer has called the "Piety along the Potomac." Despite the First Amendment, politics and religion have always mixed in America; never more so than in the fifties. There were many illustrations of this. In January 1953 when President Eisenhower was inaugurated, the parade of floats representing the 48 states was headed by an amorphous "float to God"—a church-like (but non-denominational) building, bearing enlarged photographs of scenes of worship, surrounded by mottoes in Gothic script: "In God We Trust" and "Freedom of Worship." A writer for the *Episcopal Church News* described the float as looking "like nothing whatsoever in Heaven above, or in the earth beneath, except possibly an oversized model of a deformed molar left over from the dental exhibit."[14]

In 1952, a few months before God's float, the Supreme Court reached a decision, reversing one of 1948, allowing for released time from public schools for religious instruction. Justice William O. Douglas wrote in the decision: "We are a religious people whose institutions presuppose a Supreme Being." Congress, in June 1954, enacted legislation adding "under God" to the pledge of allegiance. That same year they also passed a bill authorizing the construction of a "Prayer Room for Congressmen" near the Rotunda. The new room, complete with a stained-glass George Washington kneeling in prayer, opened in March 1955. "In God We Trust" was adopted as the national motto in 1956, with neither debate nor a single dissenting vote in the House or Senate. That same year the sum of $250,000 was awarded to the Postal Department for special "Pray For Peace" cancellation dies. Pompous piety became so thick in Washington that one doubting newsman, speaking of Secretary of Defense Charles Wilson, said: "I like Charlie. He's the only man in the Administration who doesn't talk about God."[15]

The central symbol of the nation's political piety was the President himself. Though not an official church member until after his election, Eisenhower more than made up for this with his frequent religious pronouncements. Ike's faith was a simple one; it was just faith. "Our government makes no sense," he declared during the 1952 campaign, "unless it is founded in a deeply felt religious faith, and I don't care what it is." On another occasion he told the people, though "I am the most intensely religious man I know, that does not mean I adhere to any sect." In still another speech the President assured Americans that this nation was "the mightiest power which God has seen fit to put upon His footstool." In 1954, Ike told the nation to spend July Fourth as a day of penance and prayer. He himself went fishing in the morning, played 18 holes of golf in the afternoon, and bridge at night.[16]

But millions of Americans loved the simple, reassuring piety the President epitomized. Billboards in California proclaimed: "Faith in God and Country; that's Eisenhower—how about you?" The President's Washington pastor wrote of his famous parishioner: "It may not be too much to say that through his personal conduct and expression he has become the focal point of a moral resurgence and spiritual awakening of national proportions." A *Reader's Digest* writer agreed that was what Eisenhower was about. He has "one consuming ambition: He is determined to use his influence and his office to help make this period a spiritual turning point in America, and thereby to recover the strength, the values and the conduct which a vital faith produces in a people."[17]

There were two main reasons for the religiosity of fifties politics. First, it was simply good politics. Democrats as well as Republicans tried to appear godly. With a snide reference to Ike's favorite leisure activity, Adlai Stevenson, the Democratic standard-bearer, told voters in the 1952 campaign: "Some of us worship in churches, some in synagogues, some on golf courses. . . . Yet, we are all children of the same Judaic-Christian civilization, with very much the same religious background." But Republicans, with Eisenhower at their head, seemed more successful in identifying their cause with God's. The Republican National Committee solemnly declared Republican Eisenhower to be "not only the political leader, but the spiritual leader of our times." Other Republican bigwigs tried to cash in on the identification of piety with the President. Vice-President Nixon, for example, kept the hand-written prayer that Ike had delivered at his first inaugural framed and hanging in a prominent place on his office wall. Secretary of State John Foster Dulles publicly claimed that "there is no way to solve the great perplexing international problems except by bringing to bear on them the force of Christianity."[18]

The second and more significant reason for the close identification of religion with politics was the cold war. Communists were our mortal enemies and they were atheists. Religion, therefore, came to seem essential in the fight against communism, and it is not surprising that the religiosity of the era became entwined with superpatriotism. This was amply evident in the "Back to God" crusade of the American Legion. Speaking on behalf of that body, Nixon asserted that "among the great privileges we enjoy [which the communists had to forego] is the privilege of hearing President Eisenhower pray at the beginning of his inauguration." "Since Communists are anti-God," FBI boss J. Edgar Hoover warned, "encourage your child to be active in the church"; or as Senator Joseph McCarthy proclaimed: "the fate of the world rests with the clash between the atheism of Moscow and the Christian spirit throughout other parts of the world."[19]

From such a position it was only a short step to making a religion of democracy itself. Some people took that step. Professor J. Paul Williams of Mount Holyoke College argued in *What Americans Believe and How They Worship:* "I can see no escape from the conclusion that, in the present world situation, America runs a grave danger from lack of attention to the spiritual core which is the heart of her national existence. If we are to avoid this danger, democracy must become an object of religious dedication. Americans must come to look on the democratic ideal . . . as the Will of God." Williams recommended not only that democracy be taught as religion in churches and synagogues, but that government agencies be set up because a "systematic and universal indoctrination is essential." He also wanted schools to "open indoctrination of the faith that the democratic ideal accords with ultimate reality—that democracy is the very Law of Life." Others agreed with Williams. A conference on "The Scientific Spirit and Democratic Faith" issued a report claiming that "a working democracy would be modern religion at work. . . . If we really set to work to integrate the values which we recognize as democratic values in life, we will have done a religious job."[20]

Such a blending of secular frustrations with spiritual aspirations helps explain not only political religiosity but also the general surge in religious interest throughout the nation. Patriotism and religion seemed synonymous. Atheists or agnostics were not tolerated. A survey in 1954 indicated that a majority of Americans (60 per cent) would not permit a book by an atheist to remain in a public library. That same survey found 84 per cent of the people believing that atheists should be excluded from teaching in colleges or universities. The popular attitude toward avowed communists was only slightly more repressive. Sixty-six per cent of those surveyed would remove their books from libraries, and 89 per cent would keep them out of higher education. A Gallup poll in 1958 revealed that four out of five of the American electorate would refuse to vote for an atheist for President under *any* circumstances.[21]

Such intolerance of unbelievers was unusual in the United States. In other eras of American history, even periods of religious revival, atheism was not uncommon and certainly not considered treasonable. In the twenties for instance, the heyday of Aimee Semple McPherson and Billy Sunday, people like Clarence Darrow and H. L. Mencken achieved fame and fortune ridiculing the foibles of the fundamentalists. In the fifties, however, with the exceptions of Paul Krassner who published the satiric, militantly atheistic *Realist* for a few thousand readers and an occasional comic such as Lenny Bruce who told Jesus jokes, public ridicule of religion was rare. In a 1956 article in *Harper's*, an agnostic, Elinor Goulding Smith, talked about the lack of freedom she felt in the fifties. She had not experienced this in the thirties or forties. "Freedom of religion" in the America of the mid-fifties she defined as: "You can have any you like, but you gotta pick one." "I speak in what I fear is a lonely voice," she concluded, "for a return to a real respect for one another's beliefs—or disbeliefs."[22]

Fear, then, was probably the major cause of the phenomenal return to religion. People turned to religion in record numbers to find hope in an anxious world. Believing that "atheistic Communism" threatened America both without and within, Americans saw the world in terms of good and evil, godly and godless. The insecurity brought on by hydrogen bombs and atomic spies made the churches seem the mainstay of traditional values. Despite the diverse denominations and the major differences between Protestantism, Catholicism, and Judaism, there seemed to be a basic unity to religion in America. Religious organizations played down doctrinal differences and stressed common moral values and religion in general.

Unlike the intellectuals, the majority of Americans did not want religion to remind them of their frailties or to criticize the status quo. Religion was seldom seen as a vehicle for social reform in the fifties. Very few churches practiced the social gospel and, in general, reformist movements such as Christian Action were weakened or disbanded. Churchmen were urged to avoid social activism. "Is our church competent to determine all relationships in social and economic life?" asked the president of the Foundation of the Presbyterian church, J. Howard Pew. His answer was a resounding no. Religion upheld the secular order. "If there is a safe prediction about religion in this society," wrote C. Wright Mills, "it would seem to be that if tomorrow official spokesmen were to proclaim XYZ-ism, next week 90 per cent of religious declaration would be XYZ-ist. . . . Religious spokesmen would reveal that the new doctrine did not violate those of the church. As a social and as a personal force, religion has become a dependent variable. It does not originate: it reacts."[23]

What most Americans did want from religion was a sense of well-being, the assurance that as members of a church or synagogue they shared an esteemed place in society. The message of the churches was to be a pleasant one. The following excerpt from a bulletin put out by the Protestant Council of New York City as a guide to their radio and television speakers was typical of American religion generally:

> Subject matter should project love, joy, courage, hope, faith, trust in God, good will. Generally avoid condemnation, criticism, controversy. In a very real sense we are "selling" religion, the good news of the Gospel. Therefore admonitions and training of Christians on cross-bearing, forsaking all else, sacrifices, and service usually cause the average listener to turn the dial. Consoling the bereaved and calling sinners to repentance, by direct indictment of the listeners, is out of place. . . . As apostles, can we not extend an invitation, in effect: "Come and enjoy our privileges, meet good friends, see what God can do for you!"[24]

In no way was this message better illustrated than in the pervasive popularity of the cult of reassurance as preached by Norman

Vincent Peale and his imitators. Peale's message was not new. It drew from two traditional strains of American thought: the rags-to-riches, self-help philosophy of the Horatio Alger school and the psychological, self-help philosophy of positive thinking popularized in the 1920s and 1930s by such people as Émile Coué and Dale Carnegie. But the message seemed more relevant to America of the 1950s. With the threat of annihilation a daily reality, people were ready to listen to someone who told them that everything would turn out all right. Peale brought that message to millions.

He did not begin the post-World War II cult of reassurance. It started with the publication of Rabbi Joshua Liebman's *Peace of Mind* in 1946. This book had been originally delivered as a series of lectures aimed at helping people rid themselves of inner tensions. Simon and Schuster, the publishers of *Peace of Mind,* were astounded when the book reached the best-seller list and remained there for over three years. By the early fifties Liebman's book, which combined religious faith with a simplified Freudian psychology, had sold over a million copies. Publishing houses, sensing a good thing, rushed out similar tracts. Claude Bristol's *The Magic of Believing* (1948) quickly went through seventeen printings. Such best sellers followed as Peale's *A Guide to Confident Living* (1948), Georgia Harkness, *Prayer and the Common Life* (1948), James Keller, *You Can Change the World!* (1948), Elton Trueblood, *Alternative to Futility* (1948), Bishop Sheen's *Peace of Soul* (1949), Harry Overstreet's *The Mature Mind* (1949), Peter Marshall, *Mr. Jones, Meet the Master* (1949), and Peale and Smiley Blanton, *The Art of Real Happiness* (1950).[25]

By the time Peale published *The Power of Positive Thinking* in 1952, the cult of reassurance was in full flower with Peale as its high priest. His success had come slowly at first. He began writing guides to a happy life through Christian living and applied psychiatry during the depression years. But his early tracts, *You Can Win* (1938) and *Faith Is the Answer* (1940), the latter done in collaboration with his Freudian psychoanalyst colleague, Smiley Blanton, reached disappointingly small audiences. By the late forties, however, Peale's ascent to sensational prominence had begun. *A Guide to Confident Living* quickly sold over half a million copies. Speaking engagements multiplied, and Peale, deliberately seeking the largest popular audience, spoke everywhere—commencements, business banquets, Rotaries, testimonial dinners, American Legions.

He became a virtual industry getting his message across through sermons, books, greeting and Christmas cards, long-playing records, magazine articles, newspaper columns, radio and TV appearances. Peale founded his own magazine, *Guideposts*, which by the late fifties had a circulation of 800,000. His regular sermons at his Marble Collegiate Church on Fifth Avenue drew capacity crowds, filling the main part of the church plus two packed chapels where he was taped in on closed-circuit TV. Under the auspices of the National Council of Churches, Peale appeared on national television and was heard on national radio Mondays through Fridays and twice on Sunday. His weekly syndicated newspaper column was carried in about 100 dailies. He also had a regular weekly question-and-answer page in *Look*. In 1954 he was named to a list of "Twelve Best U.S. Salesmen."[26]

Peale was not really a theologian or philosopher. His books and sermons were of the "how to" variety, in the American tradition of "How to Lose Weight Without Dieting" or "How to Speak French Without Studying." One of Peale's books or sermons was much like another. Paragraphs or whole chapters could be shuffled with no great loss or confusion. Sample sermon titles were "The Key to Self-Confidence," "How to Feel Alive and Well," "Ways to Improve Your Situation," "Wonderful Results of Faith Attitude," "Live with Joyous Vitality." In these Peale talked about particular personal problems that could easily be overcome through "faith-attitudes," "confidence-concepts," "energy-producing thoughts," "Two fifteen-minute formulas," a "Three-point program," "Seven simple steps," "Eight practical formulas," "Ten simple, workable rules," and on and on. To illustrate how well the handy "Ten rules" would work, Peale gave numerous examples of specific people who had successfully applied them. The examples tended to be of wealthy business executives, outstanding athletes, or high-ranking military officers.[27]

The underlying assumption of Peale's teaching was that nearly all basic problems were personal, the result of inner conflicts and especially "negative thinking." We "manufacture our own unhappiness," he told readers. "By our thoughts and attitudes we distill out of the ingredients of life either happiness or unhappiness for ourselves." "Unhappiness" could be avoided by following one of his simple formulas. As he wrote in the introduction to *The Power of Positive Thinking*, "you do not need to be defeated by anything, . . . you can have peace of mind, improved health, and a never-ceasing flow of energy. . . . By using the techniques outlined here you can modify or change the circumstances in which you now live, assuming control over them rather than continuing to be directed by them. . . . You will become a more popular, esteemed, and well-liked individual." For example, Peale related the story of a woman who "happened to be of the Jewish faith." She had a drunken, unemployed husband and a mother-in-law who "whined and complained" continually. But by getting up every morning and repeating "I believe" three times, all this changed. In just ten days her husband got a job and stopped drinking; her mother-in-law stopped complaining.[28]

Much of Peale's appeal was blatantly materialistic. "ARE *YOU* MISSING THE LIFE OF SUCCESS?" asked an ad for *The Power of Positive Thinking*. "Norman Vincent Peale's great best seller . . . is GUARANTEED to bring it to you! Make people like you. . . . Increase your earnings." Peale's writings were filled with stories of rags to riches achieved through following one of his simple formulas. In one case a businessman with a floundering operation followed Peale's advice and took "God in as a partner." His business immediately boomed and now, according to Reverend Peale, he tells other businessmen "that if they will take God as a partner in their business they will get more good ideas than they can ever use, and they can turn those ideas into assets." In another instance Peale told of a door-to-door vacuum-cleaner saleswoman who was doing poorly until she began saying to herself before calling at each house: "If God be for *me*, who can be against *me*?" Her luck changed. "Now she declared, 'God helps me sell vacuum cleaners.'" And Peale concluded, "Who can dispute it?"[29]

For factory laborers there were no such things as bad jobs or exploitive economic conditions. Discontent came from individual maladjustments. "Determine to like your work. Then it will become a pleasure, not drudgery." All a worker needed to do, according to Peale, was to find the right rhythm. "A machine is an assembling of parts according to the law of God. When you love a machine and get to know it, you will be aware that it has a rhythm. It is one with the rhythm of the body, of the nerves, of the soul. It is in God's rhythm. . . . There is a rhythm of the stove, a rhythm of the typewriter, a rhythm of the office, . . . a rhythm of your job. So to avoid tiredness and to have energy, feel your way into the essential rhythm of Almighty God and His works." Undoubtedly such a conservative economic philosophy explains why United States Steel put up $150,000 to subscribe to Peale's *Guideposts* for some 125,000 employees.[30]

For problems that were obviously not the result of internal maladjustments, Peale had the ostrich solution—ignore them. Thus, although asserting that "no one has more contempt for Communism" than himself, he recommended that no one should talk about communism or anything else that was "negative." When the "hear no evil, see no evil" technique failed, Peale resorted to bland reassurances and faith. On one of his TV shows a child who was frightened by the destructive power of the new hydrogen bombs was brought before Peale. He put his hand on her head and said: "Don't be afraid; God will take care of you; no H-bomb will fall on New York."[31]

Peale was a staunch individualist who emphasized that personal problems were unrelated to the larger social context. He also believed in laissez-faire economics.[32] Yet in his preaching he stressed a modified version of the suburban social ethic. On several occasions he told readers of the virtue of meshing "into the group." Hard work, so basic to the traditional Protestant ethic, was not stressed. "There is no virtue," he wrote, "in overtrying." Many of his examples illustrated this. In one he told of a "go-getter-type businessman" who worked continually and claimed that "everything depends on me." But a good physician showed him the error of his ways and he slowed down. "He learned to delegate authority. . . . He stopped fuming and fretting. He got peaceful. And . . . he does better work. He is developing a more competent organization." Certainly in reading or listening to Peale one did not get the idea that laboring had much to do with achieving one's goals. "Success," "happiness," "health," "wealth," "prestige," "popularity," "emotional security," and "self-assurance" all could be had if one simply memorized and repeated one of Peale's 40 "health-producing, life-changing, power-creating Thought Conditioners," or some of his assorted "spirit lifters."[33]

Such an optimistic, shallow, non-sectarian religion undoubtedly eased many personal tensions in the age of Korea, McCarthy, and Sputnik. It was a pragmatic religion—it worked, at least according to Peale's numerous testimonials. It was also purportedly "scientific," clothed in the jargon of simple psychiatry and psychology. Peale himself assured: "Religious faith is not something piously stuffy but is a scientific procedure for successful living."[34] Not only did the cult of reassurance blend science with religion, but it also promised quick solutions to basic problems, and solutions that did not in any way require altering the status quo. Furthermore, the promised plenty did not have to await some far-off millennium. It could be had here and now.

To an anxious middle-class populace, such simple assurances came at the right time. Peale reached immense audiences as he rode high on the wave of religious revival. His success bred many imitators. Reassurance preachers told frustrated, confused people that with faith, God's help, and a positive attitude they could achieve anything. As in the popular song of the time, people were urged to "accentuate the positive." "Religion produces more serenity than all the phenobarbital and reserpine and other drugs we shall ever discover," claimed the Reverend George Crane. "It is a fact that active church people live longer and suffer less ulcer, less high blood pressure—than do folks who never attend a religious meeting." "Jesus," assured the Reverend Irving Howard, "recommended faith as a technique for getting results; Jesus recommended faith as a way to heal the body and to remove any of the practical problems that loom up as mountains in a man's path." By saying the two words, "I believe" every morning, testified another reassurance preacher, one gets "a running start for my day, and for every day."[35] This faith, often with a little assist from martinis and Miltowns, helped sooth anxious young executives, suburban housewives, resentful small businessmen, and myriad others. Norman Vincent Peale and the cult of reassurance had become central to American popular culture.

Another figure central to American religion and culture was the revivalist Billy Graham. Like Peale, Graham moved millions in the 1950s. Coming from a background of stern, southern God-fearing evangelism, Graham was converted by an itinerant revivalist in the summer of 1936, the year he graduated from high school. This conversion happened just in time, as he later recalled, for although he "never touched a girl in the wrong way," he did remember being "pretty wild." Graham spent the next seven years attending three different fundamentalist colleges. In 1943 he graduated from Wheaton outside Chicago. After a brief period as a Baptist minister in a small Illinois town, Graham became a full-time evangelist under the auspices of the Youth for Christ organization in 1945. For the next three years, he traveled the country urging youthful delinquents to make "decisions for Christ."[36]

His first national fame came in the fall of 1949 when he opened what was to be a three-week "Christ for Greater Los Angeles Crusade." The crusade began packing people in. Hearst's newspapers puffed Graham; a well-known radio personality and a gangster henchman of mobster Mickey Cohen were among those converted. The revival was extended to eight weeks. By the time it closed, Graham had preached to some 350,000 persons. Until Los Angeles, Billy Graham had been just another evangelist—younger and handsomer than many, but not markedly different from others on the revival circuit. After Los Angeles this changed. Billy Graham became the central voice of the revival.[37]

He also became a big-time business, incorporated in 1950 as The Billy Graham Evangelistic Association, which by the mid-fifties had an annual budget of over $2 million, a large office building staffed by 125 secretaries plus numerous other associates and functionaries. Like Peale, Graham used all available media. Besides his preaching he authored two best sellers, *Peace with God* (1953) and *The Secret of Happiness* (1955). He had a TV series and a Sunday afternoon radio program, "The Hour of Decision," broadcast over three networks by some 850 stations in the United States and abroad and heard by an estimated 20 million people. His daily newspaper advice column, "My Answer," was carried in 200 papers with a daily readership of about 28 million. His organization also produced and distributed films showing Graham at work.[38]

But it was the crusades themselves that remained the key to Graham's success. When he was first making it as an evangelist, Graham used lots of gaudy ads, as in the L.A. crusade when he billed himself as "America's Sensational Young Evangelist" appearing in a "Mammoth Tent Crusade" with "Glorious Music, Dazzling Array of Gospel Talent. 22 Tremendous Nights." But after his fame, this changed. Discreet posters pictured the revivalist with the words "Hear Billy Graham." As his public relations man, Jerry Beavan, explained: "When you see an advertisement for a Cadillac, it just says Cadillac and shows you a picture. Billy is like a Cadillac. We don't have to explain."[39]

As befitted the Cadillac of preachers, Graham's crusades became the most carefully planned and heavily financed in the history of revivalism. No crusade would be held in a city until the Association had secured the support of the leading Protestant churches and the business and civic leaders in the area. Two months before a scheduled campaign, the first of Graham's workers would arrive to mobilize the local preachers and laymen into an efficient Christian army. Anywhere from 1,000 to 3,000 would be assigned to the choir. About 1,000 were carefully trained as counselors, and another 1,500 were selected as ushers. Posters and street banners were hung; ample TV, radio, and newspaper publicity was arranged; special "Dayglo" bumpers with extra strong adhesive were distributed. A few days before the opening Graham himself would arrive.[40]

The goal of the Graham crusade was individual conversion. At this he was very effective. His well-paced harangues, relying heavily on the Bible, produced results. Often thousands would rise to come forward and make "decisions for Christ." At that point the well-oiled organization went to work. As a potential convert rose from the audience, he or she would immediately be joined by a Graham worker of the same sex and similar age who would lead the way to the "Inquiry Tent." These converts were given packets of literature and "inspirational talks." Then a counselor would work with each individually. Before leaving the tent the convert was asked to fill out a card giving name, address, occupation, age, church membership or preference. Converts also were asked to check one of the four categories of decision: "1) Acceptance of Christ as Savior and Lord; 2) Reaffirmation of Faith; 3) Assurance of Salvation; 4) Dedication of Life." The cards became the basis for the follow-up campaign by both the Graham organization and local ministers.[41]

Graham's faith was not identical to Peale's. It was more literal and biblical, less bland and "scientific." It stressed sin, not psychology. Conversion was the key. Christian conversion, he once claimed on a TV show, could solve the problem of the hydrogen bomb.[42] Certainly the majority of those who crowded into his crusades in New York, Detroit, New Orleans, Chicago, and other cities did not tend to be the same people who found solace in *Positive Thinking*. Peale reached the metropolitan middle classes. Graham appealed more to the lower classes, especially those rooted in rural and small-town fundamentalist doctrines. He reaffirmed their literal Bible faith.

Yet, while the reassurance preachers and the revivalists reached somewhat different audiences, the resulting religious faiths had much in common. Both taught a simplistic, optimistic, non-denominational, non-liturgical, man-centered faith, promising salvation and worldly success. Both were closely tied to American culture and identified the nation's struggle against "atheistic Communism" as God's battle. Both beliefs were conservative, emphasizing the individual and eschewing social activism or any altering of existing institutions. Both owed their phenomenal success to the anxieties of the age.

As world tensions began to ease in the mid-fifties, following the end of the Korean War, the death of Stalin, the demise of Senator McCarthy, and the Geneva summit conference, there appeared indications that the popular religious revival was ebbing. By the late fifties, publishers were no longer wary of putting out books by atheist writers such as Bertrand Russell and Julian Huxley. Aldous Huxley, Julian's brother, suggested at that time in the *Saturday Evening Post* that the true revival of religion would not come about through evangelistic mass meetings or "the television appearances of photogenic clergymen." It would come, he predicted, through the use of drugs which allowed "large numbers of men and women to achieve a radical self-transcendence."[43] Titillating and blatantly sexual novels like *Peyton Place* (1956) crowded religious tracts off the best-seller lists. Similarly, songs such as "Baby Let Me Bang Your Box" and "Honey Love" were coming to seem more relevant to many young people than "The Man Upstairs." Even books critical of the churches such as Harry Golden's *Only in America* (1958) became best sellers. At the same time younger writers were rebelling with the Beats or delving into black humor. Sick, irreverent jokes became commonplace.

Perhaps the clearest sign that all was not well within the churches despite the return to religion was the increasing criticism of that religion made by theologians themselves. Ministers began wondering whether the sticky, sweet piety that permeated the nation wasn't just fluff. Was it really religion when Ike had his float to God or when Hollywood sex goddess Jane Russell cooed that God was a "Livin' Doll"? Many theologians thought not. They saw few signs of deep religious conviction, many of religiosity. People were seeking religion, but was it for the right reasons? Or was it, as Catholic archbishop Patrick A. O'Boyle believed, that people turned "to religion as they would a benign sedative to soothe their minds and settle their nerves." Churchmen questioned the cult of God as "a friendly neighbor who dwells in the apartment just above." Such a God, a writer for *Christian Century* concluded, "is a foolish idol fabricated from out of the proud imaginations of the human spirit, a childish projection of granddaddy." Other clergymen lamented the fact that religion seemed to be a "culture religion," waving the American flag while remaining socially inert.[44]

One of the most telling critiques of fifties religiosity by a theologian was the influential 1955 study, *Protestant-Catholic-Jew* by Will Herberg, a professor of Judaic studies at Drew University. Herberg, like many serious religious thinkers, saw a false quality to the revival. He called it "religiousness without religion, a religiousness with almost any kind of content or none, a way of sociability or 'belonging'; rather than a way of reorienting life to God. It is thus frequently a religiousness without serious commitment, without real inner conviction, without genuine existential decision." But he saw the revival as more than just a grasping at straws in a time of crisis. Religion was, he believed, the major means by which Americans identified themselves. Earlier in American history, persons had identified themselves ethnically; they were English, Irish, Italians, Poles, Germans, and so on. But by the fifties, Herberg believed, this was no longer so. The cutting off of immigration in the 1920s had led to the breaking down of ethnic culture, customs, language, and identity. Society had become homogenized, suburbanized. People became simply Americans. "But," Herberg asked, "what kind of Americans? They could not be simply shapeless integers. . . . They wished to belong to a group. But what group could they belong to?" The answer he found was the religious group. "Religious association now became the primary context of self-identification and social location." Thus instead of a series of ethnic communities, Herberg saw America in terms of Protestant, Catholic, and Jew. "It becomes virtually mandatory for the American to place himself in one or another of these groups. . . . For being a Protestant, a Catholic, or a Jew is understood as the specific way, and increasingly perhaps the only way, of being an American and locating oneself in American society."[45]

A revival of religion as a way of "belonging" or as a means of achieving "peace of mind" was hardly a revival to challenge society, let alone alter it. Little wonder then that even at its height the fifties revival remained superficial and often downright silly. America remained a secular, materialistic society.

By 1962, even Norman Vincent Peale realized that "the great postwar return to religion" was ebbing. In an article in *Reader's Digest,* he asked: "Can Protestantism Be Saved?" He was not so sure any more. Though such a conversation is fictitious, one can almost hear Peale saying to Graham: "Billy, we blew it."[46]

NOTES

1. Jacques Maritain, *Reflections on America* (New York, 1958), p. 188.
2. Editors of *Fortune, The Fabulous Future: America in 1980* (New York, 1956), pp. 194–98.
3. *Time,* April 19, 1954, p. 62.
4. Will Herberg, *Protestant-Catholic-Jew* (Garden City, 1960), pp. 47–50; Martin E. Marty, *The New Shape of American Religion* (New York, 1959), pp. 6–15; Paul Blanshard, *God and Man in Washington* (Boston, 1960), pp. 14–15.
5. *Life,* April 11, 1955, p. 138; New York *Herald Tribune,* February 22, 1955.
6. William Lee Miller, *Piety Along the Potomac* (Boston, 1964), pp. 126–27; Herberg, *Protestant,* p. 51.
7. C. Wright Mills, "A Pagan Sermon to the Christian Clergy," *The Nation,* March 8, 1958, p. 201; *Time,* April 21, 1952, p. 54, October 6, 1952, p. 50; *Life,* April 11, 1955, p. 138; Herberg, *Protestant,* p. 2; Miller, *Piety,* p. 127.
8. Miller, *Piety,* p. 127; Herberg, *Protestant,* pp. 68–69; William Lee Miller, "Some Negative Thinking About Norman Vincent Peale," *The Reporter,* January 13, 1955, p. 19; Louis Schneider and Sanford M. Dornbusch, *Popular Religion* (Chicago, 1958), p. 162; Eric F. Goldman, *The Crucial Decade and After* (New York, 1960), p. 305; Robert S. Brustein, "The New Faith of the *Saturday Evening Post,*" *Commentary,* 16 (October 1953), 367–69.
9. Blanshard, *God and Man,* p. 14; Herberg, *Protestant,* p. 50; *Life,* April 18, 1955, pp. 175–78.
10. *Life,* April 11, 1955, pp. 48, 140; A. Roy Eckardt, "The New Look in American Piety," *The Christian Century,* 71 (November 17, 1954), 1395; Gordon Gow, *Hollywood in the Fifties* (New York, 1971), pp. 17, 31; William H. Whyte, Jr., *The Organization Man* (Garden City, 1956), p. 282.
11. Herberg, *Protestant,* pp. 53–54; Reinhold Niebuhr, "Is There a Revival of Religion?", New York *Times Magazine,* November 19, 1950; *Newsweek,* November 12, 1953, p. 55; *Nation,* September 26, 1959, p. 169; *Look,* January 2, 1951, pp. 40–41; William Warren Bartley, III, "Religion at Harvard," *The New Republic,* April 21, 1958, pp. 10–17.
12. Marty, *New Shape,* p. 43; Herberg, *Protestant,* pp. 53–54; Miller, *Piety,* p. 125. A good example of the intellectual concern with religion was the sym-

posium on "Religion and the Intellectuals" which ran in four successive issues, February through May 1950, in *Partisan Review*.

13. *Time*, April 19, 1954, pp. 63, 66; Miller, *Piety*, pp. 146–47; Reinhold Niebuhr, "Varieties of Religious Revival," *New Republic*, June 6, 1955, pp. 13–16; Brand Blanshard, "Theology of Power," *Nation*, March 22, 1958, pp. 253–55; Marty, *New Shape*, pp. 43, 134.

14. Miller, *Piety*, pp. 43–44; Blanshard, *God and Man*, p. 21.

15. Blanshard, *God and Man*, pp. 14, 21–28, 100; Miller, *Piety*, p. 44; Marty, *New Shape*, p. 15; D. W. Brogan, "Unnoticed Changes in America," *Harper's Magazine*, February 1957, p. 33.

16. John Brooks, *The Great Leap* (New York, 1966), p. 351; Marty, *New Shape*, p. 38; Blanshard, *God and Man*, pp. 12–13, 32–33; Miller, *Piety*, pp. 45–46.

17. Miller, *Piety*, p. 19; Reverend Edward L. R. Elson, *America's Spiritual Recovery* (New York, 1954), p. 48; Stanley High, "What the President Wants," *Reader's Digest*, April 1953, pp. 2–4.

18. Adlai E. Stevenson, *Major Campaign Speeches of Adlai E. Stevenson, 1952* (New York, 1953), p. 282; *Time*, April 12, 1954, p. 85; Herberg, *Protestant*, p. 265; Miller, *Piety*, pp. 41–42, 166–72.

19. Miller, *Piety*, pp. 44–45; Fred J. Cook, *The Nightmare Decade* (New York, 1971), p. 149; Blanshard, *God and Man*, p. 106; Eckardt, "New Look in American Piety," p. 1396.

20. J. Paul Williams, *What Americans Believe and How They Worship* (New York, 1952), pp. 368–75; Marty, *New Shape*, pp. 82–83; Arthur Mann, "Charles Fleischer's Religion of Democracy," *Commentary*, 17 (June 1954), 557–65.

21. Samuel A. Stouffer, *Communism, Conformity, and Civil Liberties* (Garden City, 1955), pp. 32, 40–43; Blanshard, *God and Man*, p. 20.

22. Herberg, *Protestant*, p. 47; Elinor Goulding Smith, "Won't Somebody Tolerate Me?", *Harper's Magazine*, August 1956, pp. 36–38.

23. Marty, *New Shape*, p. 19; Mills, "Pagan Sermon," p. 200.

24. Whyte, *Organization Man*, p. 418; Mills, "Pagan Sermon," p. 200; Alan Valentine, *The Age of Conformity* (Chicago, 1954), p. 108.

25. Two excellent studies treating the history of positive thinking and its best sellers are Donald Meyer, *The Positive Thinkers* (New York, 1966), and Schneider, *Popular Religion*. See also Ralph Carey, "Best Selling Religion" (unpublished doctoral dissertation, Michigan State University, 1971); Paul Hutchinson, "Have We a New Religion?", *Life*, April 11, 1955, pp. 144, 147; Harry C. Meserve, "The New Piety," *Atlantic*, June 1955, pp. 34–36.

26. Lois Mattox Miller and James Monahan, "Pastor of Troubled Souls," *Reader's Digest*, June 1954, pp. 105–9; Meyer, *Positive Thinkers*, pp. 240–44; Hutchinson, "Have We a New Religion?", pp. 148–55; Miller, "Some Negative Thinking," p. 19; Arthur Gordon, *Norman Vincent Peale: Minister to Millions* (New York, 1958) is a laudatory biography.

27. The best example of Peale's "how to" technique is his all-time best seller *The Power of Positive Thinking* (New York, 1952); excellent critical evaluations are Miller, "Some Negative Thinking," pp. 19–24; Hutchinson,

"Have We a New Religion?", pp. 138–58; Meyer, *Positive Thinkers*, pp. 243–75; Warren Weaver, "Peace of Mind," *Saturday Review*, December 11, 1954, pp. 11, 50.

28. Peale, *Power*, pp. ix–x, 63, 128.

29. Miller, "Some Negative Thinking," p. 21; Peale, *Power*, pp. 102–3, 138–39.

30. Peale, *Power*, pp. 36, 197; Duncan Norton-Taylor, "Businessmen on Their Knees," *Fortune*, October 1953, pp. 253–54.

31. Peale, *Power*, p. 24; Miller, "Some Negative Thinking," p. 23.

32. Peale's own political convictions could be classified as pre-New Deal conservative. He opposed income and inheritance taxes, minimum wages, social security, and unemployment compensation. During World War II he personally endorsed a book charging President Roosevelt with being a dictator. In 1948 he supported General Douglas MacArthur for the presidency, and in the 1960 campaign he associated himself with a national organization opposing Kennedy's election on religious grounds, though he later withdrew his support for this because of public pressure. In most of Peale's writings, however, his politics are more implicit than explicit. See Meyer, *Positive Thinkers*, pp. 262, 267; Miller, "Some Negative Thinking," p. 24.

33. Peale, *Power*, pp. 80–81, 203, 226.

34. Ibid., p. 53.

35. Dr. George W. Crane, "Vitamin R(eligion) Doesn't Cost a Penny," Boston *Daily Globe*, July 18, 1956, p. 22; Herberg, *Protestant*, p. 266; Daniel A. Poling, "A Running Start for Every Day," *Parade: The Sunday Picture Magazine*, September 19, 1954.

36. Details of Graham's life up to 1955 can be found in the laudatory biography by Stanley High, *Billy Graham* (New York, 1956). This book was condensed for *Reader's Digest*, May 1957, pp. 70–75, 213–29.

37. *Time*, October 25, 1954, pp. 54–55; High, "Billy Graham," *Reader's Digest*, May 1957, pp. 219–23.

38. High, "Billy Graham," pp. 222–23; Carey, "Best Selling Religion," pp. 315–21.

39. *Time*, October 25, 1954, pp. 56–58.

40. Ibid.

41. Ibid.; High, "Billy Graham," pp. 227–28; William McLoughlin, Jr., *Modern Revivalism* (New York, 1959), pp. 472–95.

42. Niebuhr, "Varieties of Religious Revival," p. 14.

43. Aldous Huxley, "Drugs that Shape Men's Minds," in Richard Truelsen and John Kobler, eds., *Adventures of the Mind from the Saturday Evening Post* (New York, 1959), pp. 101–2.

44. *Time*, April 12, 1954, pp. 83, 85; Herberg, *Protestant*, pp. 266–67; Eckardt, "New Look in American Piety," p. 1396; Marty, *New Shape*, pp. 11–13; Valentine, *Age of Conformity*, p. 107.

45. Herberg, *Protestant*, pp. 27–41, 260.

46. Peale, "Can Protestantism Be Saved?", *Reader's Digest* (September 1962), pp. 49–54.

4

People's Capitalism and Other Edsels

The American economic system, according to most fifties observers, was a pretty wonderful thing. But what to call it? Surely "capitalism" was an inadequate label, conveying, as it did, a world of sweatshop laborers ruled by ruthless robber barons. Many people wondered if a more accurate descriptive phrase could not be found. William Nichols, the editor of *This Week,* the magazine supplement stuffed into many Sunday newspapers, decided to see. On March 4, 1951, he authored an article (later reprinted in *Reader's Digest*) entitled "Wanted: A New Name for Capitalism." "How shall we describe this system," Nichols asked, "imperfect, but always improving, and always capable of further improvement—where men move forward together, working together, building together, producing always more and more, and sharing together the rewards of their increased production?" He proposed a few possible choices: "the new capitalism," "democratic capitalism," "economic democracy," "productivism." But, not entirely satisfied with any of those, he asked readers to submit their own suggestions and included a handy coupon for that purpose. A surprising 15,000 coupons came back. "Never in my whole editorial experience," Nichols later recalled, "have I touched so live a nerve."[1]

At about the same time that Nichols was attempting to rename capitalism, three very popular books appeared offering explanations of the new economic system. The editors of *Fortune* wrote of *U.S.A.: The Permanent Revolution;* Peter Drucker told of *The New Society,* Frederick Lewis Allen of *The Big Change.* Each study related a similar story: In the United States we have never had it so good. Our industrial society, in Drucker's words, was "*beyond Capitalism and Socialism. It is a new society transcending both.*" Not since the precrash days of Hoover and Calvin Coolidge was such lavish praise bestowed on the business community. "It is not the capitalists who are using the people," claimed the Luce men at *Fortune,* "but the people who are using the capitalists. Capital has become, not the master of this society, but its servant." "U.S. capitalism," they continued, "is *popular* capitalism, not only in the sense that it has popular support, but in the deeper sense that the people as a whole participate in it and use it."[2]

Like most books of the early fifties, there was a sense of cold war urgency to these studies. The United States, the bastion of freedom and capitalism, was being derided, not just by our communist enemies but even by many of our European friends whom we were generously helping back on their feet. These people did not understand—capitalism was fine here. Maybe not perfect, but damn good, and, even more important, it was self-correcting. "Karl Marx," asserted the *Fortune* editors, "based his philosophy on the fatalistic assumption that what he described as the inherent defects of capitalism are above the will of men to affect them. It has remained for the history of U.S. Capitalism, beginning as early as the 1870s, to show that the moral convictions of men can change the course of capitalist development."[3]

Allen's book, the most popular of the three, while not quite so naive as the *Fortune* study (at least he implied that the New Deal had something to do with making capitalists responsible), told a similar success story. *The Big Change* is subtitled "America Transforms Itself 1900–1950." Allen chose as his theme "the changes which have taken place in the character and quality of American life by reason of what might be called the democratization of ou economic system, or the adjustment of capitalism to democrati ends." From the days of the Carnegies, Rockefellers, and Morgan when "America seemed in danger of becoming a land in which th millionaires had more and more and the rest less and less," Alle unfolded a tale of unrevolutionary but steady change leading to th nearly classless utopia of mid-century. By his own figures over quarter of all American families had to subsist on less than $2,000 year and nearly half on less than $3,000. Nevertheless, he went o to paint a picture of one big happy middle class. "We had brough about a virtually automatic redistribution of income from the well to-do to the less well-to-do."

Even more impressive "than the narrowing of the gap in *incom* between rich and poor has been the narrowing of the gap betwee them in their ways of living." To prove this he gave two memorabl examples. First he noted that in 1949 some 543 million pairs o nylon stockings were sold—enough to provide every woman ove 14 with nine or ten pairs. This led him to exclaim: "How is tha for an example of the dynamic logic of mass production producin luxury for all?" His second example of the "convergence be tween the ways of living of rich and poor" involved workme standing about a New York City street excavation. Allen notice that one of the men held an iron rod "presumably used for pryin off manhole covers. . . . I looked twice to see what he was doin with that rod. He was practicing a graceful golf stroke."[4]

None of these three studies denied that big business dominate American life. But that was fine because big business was benevo lent. "When I was growing up," Allen approvingly quoted Ralp Coghlan of the St. Louis *Post-Dispatch,* "the word 'soulless' corpo ration was a very common term. . . . Well, in my lifetime I hav seen a remarkable change in this. I don't know whether it could b said that corporations have obtained souls, but at least they hav obtained intelligence." "Modern management exhibits," the *Fortune* editors lyricized, "a sense of responsibility toward its employees, not only to prevent or anticipate the demands of labor unions . . . but for the simple, obvious, and honest reason that a satisfied loyal group of employees is at least as much of an asset as a modern plant or a vital piece of machinery." These editors actually believed that "the problem, indeed, may be to prevent management from becoming overgenerous."[5]

Under such a benevolent system these prophets foresaw the dawning of an era of harmony between labor and management. Strikes, claimed Allen, were no longer regarded "as class warfare but as a sort of game played between two teams, one of which has numbers on its side while the other has authority and money." The *Fortune* editors concurred: "Never have left-wing ideologies had so little influence on the American labor movement as they have today." The difference between European workers and American, they all asserted, was that here laborers had a personal stake in the general economy. "In this country," Drucker proclaimed, "*one out of every eight workers—other than farm hands—has a direct investment in industrial securities.*" Even the American Federation of Labor house organ *Labor's Monthly Survey*, noted the *Fortune* writers, "ran an admirable treatise on investment and small estate management." They were all pleased that, as Allen stated, "very few Americans seriously propose any *really wholesale* change in our evolving system."[6]

Numerous other observers of the mid-century American scene agreed—capitalism had united with democracy in what had to be at least the second greatest story ever told. "Easy Street," puffed *Time* correspondent Thomas Griffith, "now stretches from coast to coast." Adlai Stevenson, during his 1952 campaign, joined the chorus: "The United States at mid-century stands on the threshold of abundance for all." To Republican Henry Luce that threshold was already crossed: "In mid-twentieth-century America, bread is a drug on the market. Our problem is not to get bread, but to get rid of bread." Even visiting French neo-Thomist Jacques Maritain chimed in about our "economic humanism":

> The vital, pragmatic, completely unsystematic pressure exercised by the American people and the American soul on the structures of our modern industrial civilization is transforming from within the inner dynamism and historical trends of the industrial regime. It is causing this regime to pass beyond capitalism. The people have thus vanquished the inner logic of the industrial regime considered in its first historical phase, and have, almost without knowing it, inaugurated a really new phase in modern civilization.[7]

Businessmen themselves, however, seemed somewhat reluctant to bask in the praise or to share the optimism. The era of the Great

Depression with its dual horrors of economic collapse and government intervention was still too vivid a memory. Though prosperity was in evidence, many business leaders had come to accept the inevitability of another crash. If by some miracle a crash could be averted, what was to prevent the entire system from being sapped by "creeping socialism?" Although "that man in Washington" was dead, his Missouri running mate remained in the White House as the fifties opened. Business laments were frequent. The American economic system, claimed the president of United States Steel at an April 21, 1950, luncheon meeting in Baltimore, was "in deadlier peril than it has been in my lifetime." Even after Eisenhower and the Republicans presumably ended the "twenty years of treason," business leaders were not entirely happy. As late as 1955 the newly elected president of the National Association of Manufacturers announced "creeping socialism is now walking," and concluded "we're already well on our way to the achievement of the Communist State as blueprinted by Marx."[8]

But such rhetoric was less common by the mid-fifties, and one suspects that it continued only as a kind of ritual. Most businessmen by that time had come to believe they really were the good guys. Not only did numerous social observers tell them this, but the Eisenhower administration as well. Ike's first cabinet reflected the probusiness views, consisting of, as TRB* of *The New Republic* quipped, "eight millionaires and a plumber." The plumber, Secretary of Labor Martin Durkin (he had been president of the plumber's union), resigned a few months later. Other cabinet members quickly let business know where the administration stood. Even before taking office as Secretary of Defense, Charles Wilson, then president of General Motors, told the Senate Armed Services Committee that "what was good for our country was good for General Motors and vice versa." In 1953, Secretary of Commerce Sinclair Weeks assured the annual gathering of the National Association of Manufacturers that "a climate favorable to business has most definitely been substituted for the socialism of recent years." Even our foreign policy, Eisenhower promised, would "be based on the need for America to obtain profitable foreign markets and raw materials to sustain her economy." Industrial leaders breathed a sigh of relief. "The United States has had a close call," U.S. Steel presi-

* TRB is an unidentified Washington columnist who reports regularly in *The New Republic.*

1. The 1959 Blossomtime Queen of Benton Harbor, Michigan, with her court.

2. Automobile production soared in the fifties as the private car became America's principle means of transportation. Here cars roll off the end of a Ford assembly line.

3. A student protest at Colby College, Waterville, Maine, in 1954. Defiant frosh, '58, rose up in arms and burned their name-signs.

DEDICATION

THE SPIRIT OF W. H. S.

We, the Staff, dedicate the 1957 CARDINAL to the spirit of Worthington High School.

Here is a spirit found in classrooms, school organizations, social events, athletic contests, and wherever Cardinals congregate; a spirit reflected as Worthington students leave the campus to take their place with the new and challenging situations of life.

4. The dedication page of the 1957 high school yearbook, Worthington, Ohio.

5. The pill habit antedated the huge mid-decade success of the first tranquilizers. Here, in 1950, an Anahist executive stands beside one day's production: nine million antihistamines.

"One nice thing about television, you don't have to pick out where to look."

7. Senator Joseph McCarthy browses through his brief-case in April 1950.

8. Julius and Ethel Rosenbe being driven to the death house by police van on Apr 5, 1951. The original wire service caption read "Deatl Rewards Their Spying."

dent Clifford Hood noted soon after Ike was safely ensconced in Washington. "It was taken on a long detour toward Socialism. . . . We have turned and now face toward private capitalism."[9]

In such a climate businessmen could not help but feel good. They too began telling the world of the glories of American capitalism. Public relations people became a permanent part of large corporations and helped spread the word about industrial altruism. In the 20 years from 1944 to 1964 the number of public relation firms jumped from 100 to 1,500. Corporate-made movies and corporate-employed speakers told schoolchildren and Rotary clubbers about America's great manufacturing enterprises. Boy and Girl Scouts, little leaguers, and other wholesome youth groups became the beneficiaries of local corporate charity, and in many communities new symphony orchestras, art museums, and civic centers publicly proclaimed the spirit of philanthropic business. In case the message was not clear, some companies spelled it out more bluntly. "General Electric," read the bold headlines of a two-page *Harper's* ad (January 1956), "has a billion-dollar belief in U.S. progress."

The annual company reports to stockholders became glossier, artier, more dazzling. No longer were they filled with just dry statistics. Companies began including big colored pictures, cartoons, comic strips, phonograph records, even sample merchandise. One corporation, Charles Pfizer and Company, had their annual report reprinted in the New York *Times,* the Chicago *Tribune,* and the Los Angeles *Times* "for [in their words] the many thousands of newspaper readers who may not have had an opportunity to see just how a typical American corporation reports to its owners." The report filled an entire section of the Sunday *Times.* In the early fifties, Standard Oil of New Jersey and General Electric pioneered in encouraging large attendance at annual stockholders' meetings. Other companies followed suit and soon these annual gatherings, complete with fried-chicken boxed lunches, looked more like family reunions or pep rallies than serious business affairs.[10]

The apotheosis of the probusiness mentality emerged as one of the great myths of the fifties—"People's Capitalism." The expression came into vogue in 1956, though the ideas behind it were implicit in the early fifties capitalist eulogies of Allen, Drucker, and the *Fortune* editors. In another two-page General Electric ad picturing a happy gathering of stockholders (*Harper's,* August 1956), the headline read: "PEOPLE'S CAPITALISM—What makes it work for you?" It announced: "Our American brand of capitalism is distinctive and unusually successful because it is 'people's capitalism': all the people share in its responsibilities and benefits." The ad went on to list the eight characteristics of people's capitalism: 1) opportunity for each individual to develop to his highest potential; 2) high volume at prices within reach of all; 3) high wages, high productivity, high purchasing power; 4) constant innovation combined with the scrapping of the obsolete; 5) consumer credit and installment sales; 6) leisure through a short "highly productive" work week; 7) a "broad share ownership of American business"; 8) competition as the spark of our economy.

The term "people's capitalism" was coined by the Advertising Council. Early in 1956 the Council prepared an exhibit under that title to be shown internationally under the auspices of the United States Information Agency. The exhibit was first set up in February 1956 at Union Station in Washington, D.C., where Eisenhower and other dignitaries viewed it. Later the program toured Latin America, Europe, Africa, and Asia. It contrasted America of 1776 with 1956 by showing a crude log cabin alongside "a modern steel prefabricated five-room house, including all the modern labor-saving appliances." Display cards in the exhibit made the point that 60 per cent of American families owned their own homes and 75 per cent of American farmers owned their own land. Cards further asserted that 70 million Americans had savings accounts; 115 million had life insurance policies; 10 million owned shares in American companies. In other words the USIA announced: "in the United States almost everybody is a 'capitalist.'"[11]

The major emphasis of the people's capitalism propagandists was on the wide distribution of stock ownership. "The economy of the United States," claimed M. Nadler in a 1956 pamphlet, "is rapidly assuming the character of what may be termed 'People's Capitalism,' under which the production facilities of the nation—notably manufacturing—have come to be increasingly owned by people in the middle and lower income brackets." Big businesses like United States Steel, certified the president of that company, Roger Blough, in a January 1957 speech, "are owned by millions of people in all walks of life." Marx's ideal is realized in America, affirmed the author of an Esso corporation pamphlet, *The Story of Creative Capital.* "Yes, the people own the tools of production. . . . How odd to find that it is here, in the capitalism he reviled, that the promise of the tools has been fulfilled." Edward Maher, writing for *Reader's Digest,* agreed. "This is a new kind of capitalism for the world to contemplate—capitalism for the many, not for the few. Communism or socialism will have a hard time matching it."[12]

Most of these assertions, of course, were advertising and public relations fantasies. Actually the percentage of the population owning stock was lower in 1956 than in 1930. Only 3.5 per cent of employed persons were stock owners (about the same percentage as in the twenties and thirties). Among industrial workers fewer than 1.5 per cent held securities and few of them owned as much as $1,000 worth. According to Victor Perlo, an economist who investigated the people's capitalism claims, any one of several rich families—Rockefellers, du Ponts, Mellons—owned much more stock than "all the wage earners in the U.S." In fact "the market value of Rockefeller holdings in a single corporation, Standard Oil of New Jersey, was twice the market value of all the holdings of all American wage earners." There was no evidence of any significant widening of the concentrated ownership and control of the corporate structure. As the Senate Committee on Banking and Currency reported in 1955, "less than one per cent of all American families owned over four-fifths of all publicly held stocks owned by individuals." With power so imbalanced, even those small investors who did exist had no influence whatever in corporate affairs. Perlo correctly concluded in regard to people's capitalism that "the widespread diffusion of this theory signifies only the effectiveness of organized propaganda."[13]

Perlo's refutation of people's capitalism claims, published in a scholarly journal in 1958, in no way dampened the ardor of the public love affair with big business. It's ironic, a *Life* reporter mused, that "of all the great industrial nations, the one that clings most tenaciously to private capitalism has come closest to the socialist goal of providing abundance for all in a classless society." To Peter Drucker it did not even make sense to talk of this country as a middle-class society since "a middle class has to have a class on either side to be in the middle."[14] The admen agreed. "Gimbel's takes note of a new trend in American living," headlined a big ad for that department store in the New York *Times*, January 10, 1954: "The 'Booming Middle Class' is taking over—and no longer are we living up to the Joneses (Chauncy Montague Jones et familia)—we're living down to the Joneses (Charlie Jones and the wife and kids). It's bye-bye, upstairs chambermaid—ta, ta liveried chauffeur—good riddance to the lorgnette, limousine, and solid-gold lavatory. The new Good Life is casual, de-frilled, comfortable, fun—and isn't it marvelous. Gimbel's is all for the bright, young, can't-be-fooled Charlie Joneses."

Even liberal intellectuals not easily taken in by the ads or the people's capitalism propaganda developed positive theories regarding the American economy. Former New Dealers Adolf Berle and David Lilienthal, noted critics of big business in the thirties, became staunch defenders of the corporate giants in the fifties. Berle wrote positively of what he termed *The 20th Century Capitalist Revolution,* claiming among other things that "the corporations have a conscience." "Bigness," argued Lilienthal, once the controversial head of TVA, was wonderful. "In U.S.A. 1952, Bigness in industry is itself one of the most effective ways—sometimes the only effective way—to maintain competition." In fact, he concluded, "bigness can be an expression of the heroic size of man himself as he comes to a new-found greatness."[15]

Historians, who had attacked the robber barons so mercilessly in the thirties, now elevated those same nabobs to the role of industrial statesmen. Allan Nevin's biography of John D. Rockefeller made even that crotchety and crooked magnate into an American savior.[16]

But the most influential of the liberal intellectuals when it came to explaining the marvels of capitalism was John Kenneth Galbraith. Here was a realist. He did not celebrate people's capitalism. Nor did he accept the idea that competition kept business in line—the most basic assumption of economists and corporate executives alike. In 1952 Galbraith published *American Capitalism,* putting forth his theory of "countervailing power."

American Capitalism tried to show why the economic system worked so well even though it fit no traditional theories. Galbraith admitted that most major industries were dominated by a few giant companies—oligopoly. But like Lilienthal and Berle he welcomed bigness; it was more efficient, more productive, and provided more funds for research. Unlike most others, however, Galbraith was willing to admit that an oligopolistic economy was not a competitive one. The price differential between Camels, Luckies, and Chesterfields, or between Chevrolets, Fords, and Plymouths, was minimal and was far more the result of collusion than of free competition. How then was the power of big business kept in check? Galbraith's answer was simple. If put in Newtonian terms it might read: "original power begets an equal and opposite countervailing power." In Galbraith's own words: "Private economic power is held in check by the countervailing power of those who are subject to it. The first begets the second." That is, power was inevitably checked by a corresponding power, and these powers working at cross purposes made the system function for the common good. Best of all this was a "self-generating" phenomenon. Thus "in the ultimate sense it was the power of the steel industry, not the organizing abilities of John L. Lewis and Philip Murray, that brought the United Steel Workers into being."

Galbraith's examples of actual working countervailing powers were few, but he repeated them often. There was, of course, organized labor to protect workers in major industries. There also existed the buying power of large retailers—A&P, Sears Roebuck, and so on—acting as a check on high prices for the consumer. Finally, there was the power of the farmer who with the aid of government price supports was able to counter the power of the giant food producers.

Galbraith's theory of the role of government was interesting. Like the two Roosevelts, he saw the state as a referee stepping in to protect those unable to protect themselves with minimum wage and maximum hour laws, social security, farm price supports. And like the classical economists and Marxian communists, he ultimately saw the state as at least shrinking if not entirely withering away. This would take place once sufficient countervailing powers were operative. As Galbraith wrote: "Given the existence of private market power in the economy, the growth of countervailing power strengthens the capacity of the economy for autonomous self-regulation and thereby lessens the amount of over-all government control or planning that is required or sought." This was a reassuring theory. Liberals and conservatives alike loved it. Like the Constitution itself, or Madison's famed Federalist ten, the countervailing power thesis conjured up an image of self-interested factions checking and balancing one another and in so doing producing an ideal economy where all benefit.[17]

Galbraith's assessment of the economic system, recognizing as it did both the dominance of the giant corporations and the absence of competition, was more realistic than those of Allen, Drucker, Berle, or other business apologists. Yet it was basically flawed. He either ignored or minimized many things. For instance, Galbraith overlooked the fact that there could be collusion between supposedly countervailing powers; the fact that big business maintained a disproportionate amount of power; the fact that under this supposedly benign system millions lived in utter poverty; the fact that inflation wiped out savings and lowered the living standards of millions; the fact that millions of able-bodied persons remained unemployed; the fact that the whole system was subject to periodic declines in the business cycle; the fact that waste and environmental exploitation were basic to the prosperity; and, most basic, the fact that the prosperity of the era rested primarily on cold war military spending.[18]

When one examines the actual workings of the American economic system in the 1950s, a quite different picture emerges from that painted by either Galbraith or the people's capitalism celebrants. To be sure, talk of prosperity was not altogether a fiction. The massive military spending of World War II ended the depression as no New Deal measures had come close to doing. Economists and business leaders feared a slump after 1945. But the spending of vast amounts by consumers, who had saved over $150 billion during the war, combined with the increasingly heavy outlays for defense led instead to continued economic growth. Per capita disposable consumption measured in 1960 dollars increased from $1,274 in the depression year 1940 to $1,824 by 1960. During those same years the Gross National Product (GNP) grew from about $100 billion annually to over $500 billion. By 1955, the United States, with but six per cent of the world's population, was producing nearly 50 per cent of the world's goods. Personal consumption reached record heights. In 1952 the Department of Commerce listed such consumption at $218 billion, including such items as $255 million spent on chewing gum, $235 million on greeting cards, $130 million on laxatives and cathartics, $38 million on stomach sweeteners, and $23 million on mouthwash.[19]

Big business was dominant and grew more so in the fifties. Between 1940 and 1960 the percentage of the total labor force classified as self-employed dropped from 26 to 11 per cent. Most people worked for giant corporations. In major industries a few huge firms controlled most business. In the manufacture of automobiles, agricultural machinery, tires, cigarettes, aluminum, liquor, meat products, copper, tin cans, and office machinery, three companies prevailed. In steel, chemicals, and dairy products, about six did. These corporate giants were well entrenched. Out of 1,001 largest manufacturing firms in 1951, all but nine were in existence at the end of the decade. Smaller companies merged with larger ones at the rate of about 800 a year. By the late fifties the top five per cent of American corporations received 87.7 per cent of all corporate net income. The big companies desiring stability tended to cooperatively manage such things as prices and markets. A *New Republic* reporter, for example, discovered that on three different occasions TVA received exactly identical bids on equipment from competitive firms. On one such bid for electrical cable, seven different companies listed the same price: $198,438.24.[20]

The major facet of the fifties economy disregarded by most of its defenders was the utter dependence on defense spending. War had ended the depression. War preparation, the Korean conflict, and more war preparation sustained prosperity in the postwar era. Government budgets for arms yearly ran to 15 or 20 per cent of the entire Gross National Product. Between 1947 and 1957, defense expenditures, exclusive of veterans' payments, totaled over $325 billion.[21]

It was not that economists totally overlooked this single most important economic expenditure. Rather they made two questionable assumptions: first, that if a more peaceful period came, much of the defense spending could be channeled into highways, housing, health, and welfare; second, that such expenditures were essential for national security and therefore not a proper area for economic debate. On this latter point, Galbraith stated quite typically that the United States "is being forced to spend for military purposes" and "obviously cannot [or should not] reduce these expenditures for reasons of fiscal policy."[22] Such thinking ignored the tremendously powerful military-industrial complex's vested interest in an arms economy. It also overlooked the fact that while the generally conservative Congress almost never balked at bills labeled defense, that body was not about to pump billions into welfare and public services. Thus it remained that the basic bulwark of the nation's much-vaunted prosperity was destructive weaponry. Hydrogen bombs, B-52 bombers, a nuclear navy, guided missiles—America the beautiful rested firmly on the potential Armageddon: death supporting life.

Another basic problem with the American economy was that it

depended on an ever-accelerating volume of consumer spending, much of it for luxuries. Three questionable tactics were employed to assure high levels of product consumption: massive advertising, credit buying, and planned obsolescence.

With price competition virtually eliminated, competitive activities took the form of salesmanship and advertising. Advertisers tried to convince the public that their product was of higher quality, finer style, better for you: "Be Happy Go Lucky"—"LSMFT—Lucky Strike Means Fine Tobacco," "Call for Phillip Morris," "I'd Walk a Mile for a Camel"—"Test Camels in your T-zone." Of all American businesses, tobacco companies devoted the highest percentage of their $4 billion earnings to advertising. In 1953–54, medical reports linked smoking to lung cancer and heart disease. Throughout the remainder of the fifties, companies bragged endlessly about how low in tar and how mild their brands were ("Pall Malls are longer, filters your smoke further and makes it mild.") Cancer which had been rare in the early twentieth century claimed 255,000 lives in 1957; lung cancer ranked first among types of cancer killers.

Advertising was big business and grew during the fifties at a faster rate than did the GNP. In 1955 some $8 billion was spent stimulating consumers to buy. By the end of the decade this rose to nearly $12 billion. Admen toyed with all kinds of motivational research. Subliminal ads, flashed so briefly on the screen they could only be perceived subconsciously, were also first explored at this time. The package often became more important than the product packaged.

One side effect of massive advertising expenditures was that it led to business control of the content on radio, TV, and to a slightly lesser extent in newspapers and magazines. These media became primarily vehicles for advertiser messages. But ads worked. As Robert Sarnoff, president of the National Broadcasting Company, claimed in 1956: "The reason we have such a high standard of living is because advertising has created an American frame of mind that makes people want more things, better things and newer things."[23]

To make certain that people could purchase the products that advertising convinced them they needed, credit was vastly extended in the fifties. Poverty, Henry Luce assured Americans in 1956, was merely the "habit of thinking poorly." There was no need to think poorly in the fifties. Even without the money you could have the goods. It was of course necessary to convince people that the old American habit of thrift was no longer a sacred virtue. Motivational researcher Dr. Ernest Dichter, in a bulletin to businessmen, described the problem of changing people's values from thrift to spending: "We are now confronted with the problem of permitting the average American to feel moral . . . even when he is spending, even when he is not saving, even when he is taking two vacations a year and buying a second or third car. One of the basic problems of prosperity, then, is to demonstrate that the hedonistic approach to his life is a moral, not an immoral one." In preaching an ethic of consumption and impulse-release, Madison Avenue unwittingly played a role similar to that of Henry Miller and the Beats—proclaiming the virtues of the uninhibited life. J. Walter Thompson, the nation's largest ad agency, even found a way to put old Ben Franklin to use in the battle against thrift by quoting Ben as having said: "Is not the hope of being one day able to purchase and enjoy luxuries a great spur to labor and industry?" This thought of Franklin's, the agency asserted, "appears to be a mature afterthought, qualifying his earlier more familiar writings on the importance of thrift."[24]

The admen were mostly successful in the battle against thrift. Installment purchases caused consumer indebtedness to soar during the fifties from $73 billion to $196 billion. Charge cards multiplied. By 1960, Sears Roebuck alone had over ten million credit accounts, one for every five American families. Revolving credit whereby one could remain indefinitely in debt up to a certain amount—say $500—became very popular. The special credit card was born in the fifties, beginning with the Diners Club founded in 1950. Though initiated to provide credit to a select few at a handful of New York's finest restaurants, the Diners Club proved so popular that its uses and membership were quickly extended. By 1958 it was billing over $90 million annually to some 750,000 members. The all-purpose American Express card was launched in the mid-fifties. Hotel chains, oil companies, car rental services, the phone company, and thousands of other businesses issued their own credit cards. Such cards stimulated buying. *U.S. News & World Report* noted that "the credit-card agencies believe a person is likely to spend more money if he buys with a credit card. One of the companies that issues the cards says that, on the average, people who charge purchases spend about 35 per cent more than those who pay cash."[25] The apparent bountifulness provided by credit obscured its essential function: creating affluence where none existed.

The third factor necessary to sustain consumer spending was planned obsolescence. "Just past the midmark of the 20th century," noted a 1956 *Business Week*, and "it looks as though all of our business forces are bent on getting every one to Borrow. Spend. Buy. Waste. Want." In Aldous Huxley's *Brave New World* sleeping children were indoctrinated with the message: "I do love having new clothes. But old clothes are beastly. . . . Ending is better than mending." The fifties fashion industry agreed. Addressing 400 fashion experts at a Fashion Group luncheon in 1950, B. Earl Puckett of Allied Stores insisted that "basic utility cannot be the foundation of a prosperous apparel industry. We must accelerate obsolescence." General Motors was credited by the *Business Week* article quoted above with having "adopted the annual model change, helping to establish the auto industry's renowned principle of 'planned obsolescence.'" Henry Ford, after all, had been a production man aiming to produce the same simple black car year after year. But Ford Motors had long since overthrown his ideas and joined the waste race of numerous poorly put together yearly models.[26]

Obtrusive advertising, massive personal indebtedness, mountains of junked cars, millions in military spending—a nice basis on which to build a lasting prosperity. Or was it? By the late fifties some former believers began to have their doubts. John Kenneth Galbraith was one. In 1958 he published *The Affluent Society*. The title suggested yet another paean to American prosperity such as his earlier *American Capitalism* had been. Indeed many superficial readers accepted it as such, and the term "affluent society" took its place beside "people's capitalism" in the lexicon of national self-congratulation. But a close reading of *Affluent Society* conveys a very different picture. At one point in the book, Galbraith described a typical family out for a drive in their "mauve and cerise, air-conditioned, power-steered, and power-braked automobile." They pass "through cities that are badly paved, made hideous by litter, blighted buildings, billboards, and posts for wires that should long since have been put underground." Finally reaching the country they find a roadside landscape "rendered largely invisible by commercial art." Undissuaded, they stop to picnic "on exquisitely packaged food from a portable icebox by a polluted stream and go on to spend the night at a park which is a menace to public health and morals. Just before dozing off on an air mattress, beneath a nylon tent, amid the stench of decaying refuse, they may reflect vaguely on the curious unevenness of their blessings. Is this, indeed, the American genius?"

Well, was it? Galbraith's answers were hard to swallow for those who had already swallowed the whole people's capitalism dream. His thesis was that, despite the plethora of privately produced consumer goods, the public sector of the economy was impoverished, causing the country to wallow in "an atmosphere of private opulence and public squalor." Schools suffered from crowding, inadequate facilities, and poorly paid teachers. Hospitals, mental institutions, clinics, and prisons were inadequate, understaffed, and overfilled. The air was becoming unbearable. Rivers already were open sewers. Natural resources were rapidly being exhausted. All this resulted from the concentration on producing goods for profit. With profit as the dominant value, desperately needed public services which brought no profit naturally lagged. Thus, we could produce endless numbers of cars, ever bigger, gaudier, more powerful. But we neglected the public services required by increased consumption of automobiles: safe highways, parking facilities, traffic controls, traffic police, hospitals, and numerous related needs. Galbraith summed this up well with another example: "The more goods people procure, the more packages they discard and the more trash that must be carried away. If the appropriate sanitation services are not provided, the counterpart of increasing opulence will be deepening filth. The greater the wealth the thicker will be the dirt. This indubitably describes a tendency of our time."

The solution Galbraith recommended for solving this problem of socioeconomic imbalance between the private and public sectors was for the government greatly to increase expenditures for public needs even if this meant higher taxes. The result, he predicted, would be a restoration of balance and an end to the related problems of unemployment and poverty. Actually there was little new in these proposals. Galbraith was really calling for a revived New Deal, only this time as a cure to the ills of affluence, not depression. But the book did much to stir the complacency of late-fifties economic thinking. Galbraith became an advisor to John F. Kennedy and helped plan some of the liberal reforms of the early sixties.[27]

Another factor rippling the calm surface of the economic consensus in the late fifties was the rediscovery of poverty. Early in the decade observers outdid one another in proclaiming all Americans to be prosperous, upwardly mobile middle class. *Esquire* even ran a chart, only half in jest, on "How to Tell a Rich Girl" from the rich-looking secretary. (The real rich girl wears plain pumps, goes to Europe with her real daddy, and wears white underwear.) When poverty was noticed at all it was generally assumed to be a temporary aberration; a few more years of an upswinging GNP and it would be eliminated. Thus David Riesman and Nathan Glazer in a 1955 essay related how "15 years of prosperity" had caused the "mass of underprivileged people" to "virtually disappear," though they did add as an afterthought (tucked in a footnote at the end): "To be sure, there are enclaves where the underprivileged can still be found as in the Southern Alleghenies or the rural Deep South."[28]

But by the late fifties, radical observers such as Michael Harrington and Harvey Swados began pointing out an entire culture of poverty amid America's plenty. In 1957 (a prosperous year), a study by Robert Lampmann of the University of Wisconsin revealed 32.2 million persons, nearly a quarter of the population, had incomes below government-proclaimed poverty levels. Millions more, while not starving, had minimal comforts. In the fifties only six in ten dwelling units had the basic plumbing facilities of private flush toilet, private bath, and hot running water; 50 per cent of the houses lacked central heating. In 1959, a quarter of the population had *no* liquid assets; over half the population had no savings accounts.[29]

Like "people's capitalism," "we're all middle class" was mythic. Not only did poverty persist, but the gap between rich and poor, if anything, increased in the decade. The top 0.5 per cent of individuals had 25 per cent of all personal wealth by 1955; this was up from 19.3 per cent in 1949. The top group owned 80 per cent of the corporate stock held by individuals and well over 90 per cent of corporate bonds. Harvard studies during the fifties found that upward mobility in the Soviet Union was as great as that in the United States. Even a *Fortune* investigation indicated that economic opportunities for workingmen were declining. Added to this was an average annual unemployment rate of nearly five per cent throughout the fifties, reaching as high as 6.8 per cent or 4.7 million people in 1958.[30]

Few persons read writers like Harrington and Swados. But Galbraith's best-selling *Affluent Society* also included a chapter on "The New Position of Poverty" which aimed to shatter the myth that "with increasing output poverty must disappear." And myth it was. As Galbraith stated, "the most certain thing about modern poverty is that it is not efficiently remedied by a general and tolerably well-distributed advance in income."[31] Unfortunately, however, it was not until the 1962 publication of Harrington's very influential *The Other America* that any sizable segment of the populace became at all concerned about poverty. For most people, poverty remained invisible.

The most commonly heard economic criticism in the late fifties did not concern poverty, unemployment, waste, environmental pollution, or dependence on armaments. It was that the GNP was not growing at a fast enough rate. Growth became the great panacea. Special, costly commissions of experts would huddle and issue wordy tomes calling for faster growth. The four per cent growth rate of the GNP must be raised to five per cent, claimed the 1958 report of the prestigious group funded by the Rockefellers. Perhaps there was a sense in the fifties that history was finally closing in on America; growth might stave off this process. Certainly there was a belief that the United States was in a growth race with the Soviet Union and that the fate of the free world depended on its outcome. Some government officials spoke of the need to step up the rate of growth to six or seven per cent. To continue our present laggard growth, asserted CIA head Allen Dulles at decade's end, was "virtually to commit economic suicide."[32]

And so, despite a growing national doubt, the decade ended economically as it began—spewing forth an ever-increasing volume of bombs, bazookas, bubble gum, cars and tanks, deodorants, crying dolls, hula hoops, pillows, and pollution. They called it people's capitalism. In reality it was a precarious prosperity maintained by cold war spending, highway and automobile building, sprawling suburbias, overeating, overbuying, forced premature obsolescence—always plagued by waste, unemployment, poverty, inequality, misuse of the environment, lack of public services, and the threat of annihilation.

NOTES

1. Nichols is quoted in Frederick Lewis Allen, *The Big Change* (New York, 1952), pp. 284–85, and in Jacques Maritain, *Reflections on America* (New York, 1958), pp. 112–13.

2. Peter Drucker, *The New Society* (New York, 1962 ed.; original ed. 1950), p. 351; Editors of *Fortune, U.S.A.: The Permanent Revolution* (New York, 1951), pp. 7–8, 67–68.

3. Editors of *Fortune, U.S.A.*, p. 69.

4. Allen, *Big Change*, pp. ix, 285–86, 209–33.

5. Ibid., p. 252; Editors of *Fortune, U.S.A.*, pp. 81–83.

6. Allen, *Big Change*, pp. 257, 290; Editors of *Fortune, U.S.A.*, pp. 95–96, 103; Drucker, *New Society*, p. 349.

7. Thomas Griffith, *The Waist-High Culture* (New York, 1959), p. 166; Adlai E. Stevenson, *Major Campaign Speeches, 1952* (New York, 1953), p. 117; Henry R. Luce, "A Speculation About A.D. 1980," in Editors of *Fortune, The Fabulous Future* (New York, 1956), p. 185; Maritain, *Reflections*, p. 23.

8. John Kenneth Galbraith, *American Capitalism* (Boston, 1956 ed.), pp. 2–5; Dan Wakefield, "Siobhan McKenna at the N.A.M.," in Henry M. Christman, ed., *A View of the Nation* (New York, 1960), pp. 216–22.

9. TRB and Wilson are quoted in Eric F. Goldman, *The Crucial Decade and After* (New York, 1960), p. 239; Weeks is quoted in Galbraith, *American Capitalism*, p. 4; Eisenhower is quoted in Thomas G. Patterson, ed., *Cold War Critics* (Chicago, 1971), p. 229. Secretary of Defense Wilson was later quoted in regard to unemployment: "I've always liked bird dogs better than kennel-fed dogs myself–you know one who'll get out and hunt for food rather than sit on his fanny and yell," Goldman, *Crucial*, p. 280; Hood is quoted in John Kenneth Galbraith, *Economics and the Art of Controversy* (New York, 1959 ed.), p. 36.

10. John Brooks, "From Dance Cards to the Ivy-League Look," *New Yorker*, May 18, 1957, pp. 76–103.

11. New York *Times*, February 14, 1956, p. 20, September 3, 1956, p. 14.

12. M. Nadler, *People's Capitalism* (New York, 1956), p. 5; Victor Perlo, " 'People's Capitalism' and Stock Ownership," *American Economic Review*, XLVII (June 1958), 333; Edward Maher, "The Spread of Grass-Roots Capitalism," *Reader's Digest*, June 1955, pp. 165–66.

13. Perlo, " 'People's Capitalism,' " pp. 335–47; Robert L. Heilbroner, *The Future as History* (New York, 1960), p. 125. Though "People's capitalism" was an adman's creation, scholars accepted it. See, for example, Max Lerner, *America as a Civilization* (New York, 1957), p. 267.

14. *Life*, May 16, 1955, p. 55; Peter Drucker, "The Myth of American Uniformity," *Harper's Magazine*, May 1952, pp. 70–77.

15. Adolf A. Berle, *The 20th Century Capitalist Revolution* (New York, 1954), pp. 113–14; David E. Lilienthal, "Our Anti-Trust Laws Are Crippling America," *Collier's*, pp. 15, 17, 23; see also Lilienthal, *Big Business: A New Era* (New York, 1953).

16. Allan Nevins, *John D. Rockefeller* (New York, 1959 ed.).

17. Galbraith, *American Capitalism.* The discussion is drawn from the entire book. See especially chapters 9–14. See also Bernard Rosenberg, "The Economics of Self-Congratulation," *Dissent,* I (Winter 1954), 92–102.

18. Galbraith mentioned poverty, inflation, and military spending but only in passing: *American Capitalism,* pp. 2, 183–84, 190–201.

19. Harold G. Vatter, *The U.S. Economy in the 1950's* (New York, 1963), pp. 3–8; George E. Mowry, *The Urban Nation* (New York, 1965), p. 203; Morris L. Ernst, *Utopia 1976* (New York, 1955), pp. 115–16; Arthur S. Link and William B. Catton, *American Epoch* (New York, 1963 ed.), pp. 592–95.

20. Ben J. Wattenberg, *This U.S.A.* (Garden City, 1965), pp. 146–47; Vance Packard, *The Status Seekers* (New York, 1959), p. 27; John Brooks, *The Great Leap* (New York, 1966), p. 344; Carl N. Degler, *Affluence and Anxiety* (Glenview, Ill., 1968), pp. 170–71; Ben B. Seligman, "Merger and Monopoly in the U. S.," *Dissent,* II (Spring 1955), 144; Vatter, *U.S. Economy,* p. 40; *New Republic,* May 25, 1959, p. 2.

21. Lerner, *America as a Civilization,* p. 267; Heilbroner, *Future as History,* pp. 133–34; John Kenneth Galbraith, *The Liberal Hour* (Boston, 1960), p. 19; Elting E. Morison, ed., *The American Style* (New York, 1958), p. 368.

22. Galbraith, *American Capitalism,* pp. 183–84; Lerner, *America as a Civilization,* pp. 341–46.

23. Brooks, *Great Leap,* pp. 86–94; *Fortune,* December 1953, pp. 130–31; *The Nation,* August 15, 1959, p. 6; Degler, *Affluence,* p. 174; David Cort, "Madison Avenue Jungle: Admen and Madmen," in Christman, ed., *View of the Nation,* pp. 222–30; *Dissent,* 3 (Spring 1956), 155; Vance Packard, *The Hidden Persuaders* (New York, 1957).

24. Luce, "Speculation About A.D. 1980," p. 186; Dichter and the Thompson agency are quoted in William H. Whyte, Jr., *The Organization Man* (Garden City, 1956), pp. 19–20.

25. Mowry, *Urban Nation,* p. 204; Whyte, *Organization Man,* p. 361; Brooks, *Great Leap,* p. 139; *U.S. News & World Report* is quoted in Richard Schickel, "The Credit Card Millionaires," in Christman, ed., *View of the Nation,* pp. 237–43.

26. *Business Week* is quoted in Kenneth Burke, "Recipe for Prosperity: 'Borrow. Buy. Waste. Want.'" in Christman, ed., *View of the Nation,* pp. 210–16; Puckett is quoted in *Time,* July 3, 1950, p. 72. See also *Coronet,* June 1953, pp. 23, 27; Griffith, *Waist-High,* pp. 164, 169–70.

27. The discussion of Galbraith is drawn from *The Affluent Society* (New York, 1958). The specific quotations are from pp. 199, 203, 201.

28. The *Esquire* chart is discussed in Schickel, "Credit Card Millionaires," p. 242; the Riesman and Glazer essay is in Daniel Bell, ed., *The Radical Right* (Garden City, 1963 ed.), pp. 90, 111.

29. Michael Harrington, "Slums, Old and New," *Commentary,* August 1960, pp. 118–24; Harvey Swados, *A Radical's America* (Boston, 1962), a collection of essays mostly from the fifties; the Lampmann study is noted in Brooks, *Great Leap,* pp. 135–37; Vatter, *U.S. Economy,* pp. 226–28; Gordon C. Lee, *An Introduction to Education in Modern America* (New York, 1957 ed.), pp. 31–32.

30. Vatter, *U.S. Economy*, pp. 36–39; Harvard and *Fortune* studies are both cited by Packard, *Status Seekers*, pp. 288, 291; Link, *American Epoch*, p. 600; Degler, *Affluence*, p. 169.

31. Galbraith, *Affluent*, pp. 250–58.

32. *Prospect for America: The Rockefeller Panel Reports* (Garden City, 1961), pp. 251–333; Dulles is quoted in Heilbroner, *Future as History*, p. 147.

5

The Paving of America

On February 5, 1956, the following ad appeared in the employment section of the New York *Times:*

> SALESMGR
>
> Intangible exp, must be able to move effectively at top mgmt level and effectively understand "Big Business" problems. Should be able to handle 12 martinis. . . .

Though the 12-martini requirement was an extreme, even for the fifties, the ad does illustrate a reality of the corporate economy. By mid-century big business was producing much more than goods and garbage. It was also shaping the lifestyles and values of millions of Americans.

An advanced technological society organized into giant corporations demands an increasingly high degree of social organization. It needs people who function smoothly in large groups; people who are willing to be commanded and who fit into the social machine without friction; people who want to consume more and more, and whose tastes are standardized and can be easily influenced and anticipated. By the 1950s American capitalism in conjunction with other social institutions—family, school, church, state—had produced such socialized individuals in abundance.[1]

Two of the most important, popular, and influential social criticisms of the fifties—David Riesman's *The Lonely Crowd* and William Whyte's *The Organization Man*—dealt with the emergence of this docile conformist character ideally suited for corporate America. To Riesman and his associates the dominant American type had changed from "inner directed" to "other directed." Inner-directed people were traditional self-reliant individualists who internalized adult authority. They judged themselves and others by such internalized self-disciplined standards. Other-directed people, in contrast, were those whose characters were formed chiefly by the examples of their peers. While inner-directed individuals felt guilty when violating their inner ideals, other-directed persons had no inner ideals to violate. Their morality came from the compulsion to be in harmony with the crowd. They felt guilty when deviating from group consensus. Such people, in this status-anxious time, emerged as uncritical conformists, unceasing consumers, and ideal members of the faceless corporate mass.[2]

Similarly, *Fortune* editor Whyte, in his careful examination of the "junior executive" type, uncovered impressive evidence that the traditional Protestant ethic of thrift, hard work, individualism, and competitive struggle—though still eulogized by Kiwanis and commencement speakers—had given way to a new social ethic. This value system was defined as "a belief in the group as the source of creativity; a belief in 'belongingness' as the ultimate need of the individual; and a belief in the application of science to achieve the belongingness."[3]

The assumption of the social ethic was that group-think and group-work were the norm. The individual asserting his or her will counter to the group was misinformed at best, but more likely maladjusted. The aim of group-work was consensus—a basic fifties ideal. The conference table, the workshop, the seminar, the project team all looked for unanimity. New or radical ideas were discouraged since such thoughts might upset group consensus. A handbook on "Conference Sense" put out in the early fifties by the Bureau of Naval Personnel well illustrates the intolerance of discordant thinking. Under a section on how to handle the person at odds with the group ("the Aggressor"), the conference leader was told to "place Donald Duck at your left [the blind spot]. Fail to hear his objections, or if you do, misunderstand them. If possible, recognize a legitimate objection and side with him. Object is to get him to feel that he belongs! If he still persists in running wild, let group do what they are probably by now quite hot to do, i.e., cut the lug down. They generally do it by asking Little Brother Terrible to clarify his position, then to clarify his clarification, etc., until our lad is so hot and bothered that he has worked himself into the role of conference comedian. Then soothe his bruised ego and restore him to human society by asking him questions that he can answer out of special experience."[4]

To assure that such errant individualists were avoided in the corporate structure, companies increasingly administered personality tests to prospective managerial employees or to those up for promotion. By 1952, one third of all U.S. corporations used such examinations and the number grew yearly. These tests aimed at scientifically determining how adjusted the individual was to the group. Those not properly integrated to other-directed values received the poorest score. Such tests served to reward the conservative conformist and to enshrine the status quo.

Even in hiring scientists, corporations looked for the nicely adjusted, yes-saying team man. An article by Lowell Steele in *Personnel* (May 1953) noted this trend: "While industry does not ignore the brilliant but erratic genius, in general it prefers its men to have 'normal' personalities. As one research executive explained, 'These fellows will be having contact with other people in the organization and it helps if they make a good impression. They participate in the task of selling research.'" Or as a company booklet from Socony-Vacuum Oil warned: "There is little room for virtuoso performances. Business is so complex . . . that no one can master all of it; to do his job, therefore, he must be able to work with other people."[5]

Besides the stress on cooperative belongingness, other aspects of the social ethic that Whyte observed included the decline of thrift in favor of time-buying consumption, the belief that one's fate was in the hands of the system but that the system was benevolent, and the striving not for the top in some rough-and-tumble nineteenth-century manner, but for a comfortable secure niche within the system. This last point was well illustrated in the mid-fifties Hollywood film *It's a Woman's World.* The movie was about an auto executive looking for a $125,000 per year general manager. Fred MacMurray, playing one of three people being considered, was the central character. Unlike the organization-man type who basked securely in the system allowing it to set his level in the organization, MacMurray portrayed a man who had fought his way tooth and claw through the ranks. Though he was now near the top, his success was portrayed as tragic. "I used to be at the bottom," he recalled, "and I was happy then." His rise had given him an ulcer and a nearly wrecked marriage, saved only by his not getting the big job. The theme was clear: you should not seek success; if you deserve it, it will seek you.[6]

Tom Rath, the hero of Sloan Wilson's 1955 best seller, *The Man in the Gray Flannel Suit,* expressed the same sentiment. When offered a top job by his boss, Rath replied: "I don't think I'm the kind of guy who should try to be a big executive. I'll say it frankly: I don't think I have the willingness to make the sacrifices. I don't want to give up the time. I'm trying to be honest about this. I want the money. Nobody likes money better than I do. But I'm just not the kind of guy who can work evenings and weekends and all the rest of it forever." The understanding boss accepted this, telling Rath "there are plenty of good positions where it's not necessary for a man to put in an unusual amount of work." Other popular literature reflected similar values. The advice Dr. Modesto gave to the sensitive and therefore miserable salesman in Alan Harrington's mid-fifties novel, *The Revelations of Dr. Modesto,* was the message of the age: "Look around and see who is the happy man. He is the one Just Like Everybody Else."[7]

For most middle-class youth coming to maturity in the 1950s, the values of the social ethic were already accepted. Homes, churches, and schools taught them that adjustment to the group was essential. The attitude of their peers meant everything. A study by Margaret Foster of third-grade readers used in the United States from 1900 to 1953 indicated that in the first two decades of the century the theme of "winning friends" occupied only four per cent of these books. By 1953, however, 35 per cent of the content reflected this theme. "Johnny wasn't doing so well at school," one mother confided to Whyte. "The teacher explained to me that he was doing fine in his lessons but that his social adjustment was not as good as it might be. He would pick just one or two friends to play with, and sometimes he was happy to remain by himself."[8]

Such indoctrination produced a generation of smooth, dull, cautious, savorless young men. These youths looked forward to a long, pleasant, rewarding relationship with a big company. They avoided the scary extremes of politics, morals, religion, emotion—feeling that to express such things was to risk future success. The company would provide security—a good salary, modest advancement, fringe benefits, responsibility but not too much—while they enjoyed the "good life" with wife and kiddies in suburbia. It was a modulated age; everyone seemed smothered in a blanket of inertia, apathy, and conformity. Even baseball players, noted Gay Talese in a 1958 New York *Times Magazine* article, had become respectable. "A new breed of players, couth and kempt, has brought a surprising look of respectability to baseball." Gone were the tobacco-chewing carousers, replaced by "tweedy" ball players who thought of "security," read *The Wall Street Journal*, and who wouldn't "think of tripping their mothers, even if Mom were rounding third on her way home with the winning run."[9]

The composite image of the organization man, then, was the gray-flanneled, bland, friendly junior executive who eschewed the ulcerous route to the executive suite in favor of a comfortable company niche and the good life in suburbia.

The ideal helpmate for this organization man was, of course, the organization woman. Like her spouse, the organization woman had arrived at her position through caution and playing games. Her games, though, centered more heavily on sex. Before marrying she had to carefully allow hints at her sexual promise, balancing on the fine line between puritanism and giveaway to win the big payoff—the wedding. In a culture that approved of such manipulative submissiveness, she was ready for the corporate message that would extend games throughout her lifestyle. A top executive was quoted in a 1951 *Fortune* article: "We control a man's environment in business and we lose it entirely when he crosses the threshold of his home. Management, therefore, has a challenge and an obligation to deliberately plan and create a favorable, constructive attitude on the part of the wife that will liberate her husband's total energies for the job." This businessman went on to note that happily the "younger generation of wives is the most cooperative the corporation has ever enlisted. Somehow they seem to give us so much less trouble than the older ones."[10]

To assure wifely compliance, corporations often ran special classes for management wives to instill in them a sense of belonging. In some firms executives were not hired, or promoted, unless their wives were judged as suitable company ornaments. Women's magazines featured such stories as "I Was a Company Wife" or "Management Bride" which presented the idea that the wife should be an adaptable and gregarious part of the whole system. Women's guides advised that the wife should help "sell her husband to his associates." The corporate wife was expected to adjust graciously to whatever demands the company put on her husband. She was to curb open intellectualism or the desire to be alone, avoid unseemly behavior, and, of course, forego any career or serious interest besides home, husband, and company. She was expected, however, to take an active role in women's community groups. The editors of *Fortune* portrayed "the successful businessman's wife" in 1951: "She has a favorite charity (the Children's Home perhaps or the Visiting Nurses Association); she belongs to the Arts and Literature Committee of the Women's Club, the Daughters of the American Revolution, and the Garden Club; she is a patroness of the Fine Arts Academy and the Little Theatre, and a charter member of the Wednesday Shakespeare Society." Like their husbands, younger women hoped hubby would have a happy but undemanding job. As Russell Lynes quoted a college girl: "I want my husband to be ambitious but not dangerously so. . . . I don't want him to have such a high executive position that it would ruin his health or personal relationships with his friends or family."[11]

The natural habitat of these well-adjusted organization couples was suburbia. Here they could mingle with like-minded young marrieds of similar background, income, and status. Like the corporation, fifties developments offered instant togetherness. "You *Belong* in PARK FOREST!" urged a 1952 ad for that huge suburban complex outside of Chicago. "The moment you come to town you know: You're welcome. You're part of a big group."[12]

Suburbia was not invented in the fifties. The yearning to escape the city because of its crowding, crime, poor health, and other real or imagined ills is nearly as old as the city itself. The desires to own a private house with land around it and to live among people of similar age and class were also long-standing aspirations. In the nineteenth century the industrial revolution in conjunction with romanticism caused a suburban upsurge throughout the Western world. In America architects from Andrew Jackson Downing to Henry Richardson and Frank Lloyd Wright designed some of their most beautiful houses for clients wanting rural retreats away from the squalor, noise, and pollution of the growing cities, yet close enough to be able to participate in urban commerce and culture. But up until about the 1920s suburban life was limited largely to the wealthy. Railroads, electric trolleys, and above all the motorcar accelerated suburban growth in the twenties, but the Depression and World War II checked this trend. As late as 1949 suburban living was a minor phenomenon confined to the fringes of cities in the Northeast, the Great Lakes region, and the West Coast. Such suburbs were generally quite attractive with substantial older houses designed to individual tastes, ample acreage for privacy and play, and usually open farm country separating the suburb from the city.

The fifties changed all this. On July 3, 1950, William J. Levitt was pictured on the cover of *Time*. The portrait showed him standing in front of a neat row of identical boxlike houses set up like Monopoly pieces on land newly bulldozed to a uniform flatness. The cover caption read: "HOUSE BUILDER LEVITT: For Sale: a new way of life." Levitt, who called his firm of Levitt and Sons "the General Motors of the housing industry," brought mass-production techniques to housebuilding. First on Long Island and then outside of Philadelphia, he turned farmlands into giant Levittowns. His houses were unvarying in floorplan, though there were four slight variations in exteriors and seven color choices, mostly pastels. Lots were of uniform size with a tree planted every 28 feet (two and a half trees per home). "The best house in the U.S.," bragged Levitt of his picture-windowed box complete with refrigerator, stove, Bendix washer in each kitchen, and an Admiral TV built into every living room. Deeds to Levitt's houses specified that no fences were to be built, lawns were to be mowed at least once a week in season, and laundry could be hung only on rotary racks, not on clotheslines, and never on weekends. So undeviating were these communities that when one man mounted a gargoyle on his house, it became such a famous sight that residents drove out of their way to show it to visitors. Such was the new suburban utopia.[13]

Demand for Levitt's houses ran far above supply. Other builders were quick to adopt his methods. Typical developers would buy up open land as cheaply as possible, clear it of any material impediments such as trees, brush, flowers, hills, swamps, even streams, install utilities, build roads, subdivide into tiny lots, construct a few model houses to show prospective buyers and then with prefabricated units construct the houses, sell, and come away with high profits. Many builders were irresponsible and built shoddily. Cesspools, typically used for sewage disposal, created health hazards and, not uncommonly, polluted water supplies. Bulldozed areas often eroded or became seas of mud. Even where construction and utilities were adequate, most of these new towns were left by their builders with no provisions for schools, churches, shopping, police, government, or other basic communal needs. Usually these developments were totally residential, and so were forced to levy high property taxes to supply even the most minimal public services.

Yet such communities grew at record rates. In 1950, 1.4 million new housing units were built, mostly in the suburbs. This rate kept up throughout the decade. These years saw an average of 3,000 acres of greenland *per day* bulldozed into suburban submission. Between 1950 and 1960 about 1.5 million persons moved to the suburbs from New York City alone. On a smaller scale this was happening around the country. During the decade, the consumer price index on all goods rose about ten per cent; suburban land values increased anywhere from 100 to 3,760 per cent. The 1960 census revealed that while central cities had grown about 25 per cent in population since 1950, the suburbs had increased over 50 per cent. Some suburban areas such as those around Detroit grew by nearly 130 per cent. It is also revealing that of the nation's largest cities only Los Angeles, which increased by about 50 per cent, experienced substantial growth. Since L.A. was and is really little more than a series of closely clustered suburbs, this was not surprising. Several central cities, including Detroit, St. Louis, San Francisco, and Washington, actually lost population, something unprecedented in the history of American cities.[14]

The whole process of suburbanizing the middle class was aided greatly by government policy. Through the Federal Housing Administration and the Veterans Administration, the government allowed millions of persons to purchase single-family homes with low down payments and long-amortization loans. In most cases the actual funds came from private sources—banks, building and loan associations, insurance companies—but the federal government guaranteed the mortgages. Approval for such loans had to come from both federal and private agencies; their loan policies made it virtually impossible to obtain funds for buying and restoring an older dwelling, especially within the central city. The result was that nearly all available funds went into suburban developments.

Life in most suburbias in the fifties mirrored the corporate ideal of human individualism submerged in mass-produced uniformity. With small lots, picture windows, thin walls, no fences, and few trees, privacy was minimal. It was not encouraged. People were expected to be outgoing, to "join the gang." As in the corporation, differences, even small ones, were disapproved. William Whyte, after investigating Park Forest in 1953, claimed that "an otherwise minor variation becomes blatant deviance; a man who paints his garage fire-engine red in a block where the rest of the garages are white has literally and psychologically made himself a marked man." Group pressures were so effective that suburbanites seemed to observers nearly as uniform as their houses. Urban Democrats became suburban Republicans; country Baptists became suburban Presbyterians. What made the sameness even bleaker was the similarity of age, income, and class outlook. Only the basic nuclear family was acceptable; most of the new suburbs were inhabited by young married couples between the ages of 25 and 35, usually with one child and a second on the way. Incomes averaged between $6,000 and $7,000. Suburbanites were tolerant of religious differences so long as one was a Protestant, Catholic, or Jew (though discrimination against the latter was not altogether absent). Church attendance was high, but religious affiliation seldom dictated group relations. Though many of these people were *new* middle class, they were *very* middle class. They were white. Tolerance did not extend to blacks in most of these bedroom havens. At no time in American history, with the abnormal exceptions of army or dormitory life, had such uniform one-class communities existed. Singles, childless couples, homosexual couples, extended families, old people, the rich, the poor, non-whites—all were avoided in those sterile, aseptic environments.[15]

One of the main reasons for the frantic "belongingness" in suburbia was the rootlessness most people felt. These were transient communities. Not only was everyone a newcomer, but few expected to remain in one place long since corporate policy prescribed frequent transfers of personnel, especially among younger management. In the Long Island Levittown, for instance, about 3,000 of the 17,600 dwellings changed hands annually. By 1958 some 33 million Americans moved each year. The average American pulled up stakes about every five years; for the suburbanite it was more like every three years, and annual moves were not unusual. To offset feelings of rootlessness people joined civic groups, planted gardens, did-it-themselves with elaborate equipment, held neighborhood backyard barbecues and regular get-togethers for such things as bridge, canasta, or even watching TV.[16]

Yet despite the almost forced brotherhood and the homogeneity of class, social snobbery and status striving were rampant. In many suburbs social pressure prevented blatant conspicuous consumption. Cadillacs were rare. But since these were transient communities where family background was unknown, social status was established by visible factors such as furnishings, consumption standards, jobs, club memberships, church affiliations, and so on. Little things like an especially fancy TV, power mower, or air conditioning became very important. An obviously costly touch such as gold-plated bathroom fixtures, or an extra bathroom, could score status points. In one suburban community after a new tax on toilets was levied (50¢ for the first, 25¢ for each additional), the residents, eager for the prestige that attached to owning many johns, phoned in to call attention to their tax liability. Some even claimed nonexistent toilets. Antiques were also popular since they gave their owners both a sense of status and brought a feeling of rootedness in the American heritage into the rootless split-level ranch house. Early Americana—spinning wheels, muskets, hitching posts, cobblers' tables, eagle crests—was very much in demand. While homes on a given block were invariably built alike and social pressure (or legal covenants) prevented major structural innovations, many large developments had houses in several price ranges.

It was not uncommon for a status-seeking couple to signify their improved finances by moving to a higher-priced house within the same suburb. Builders, aware of their customers' values, advertised homes to appeal to social snobbery. Using some French was a favorite technique. Thus a 1958 ad for a house in Manetto Hills, Long

Island, read: "C'est Magnifique! Une maison Ranch très originale avec 8 rooms, 2 1/2 baths . . . 2-Cadillac garage . . . $21,000. . . . No cash for veterans." Or homebuilders talked of "the living forum" or "reception galleria" instead of living room; bedrooms became "sleeping chambers," and a large lot a "huge 1/3 acre estate site." Development names like "Colonial Heritage Estates" or "Whitehills Estates" were also popular, even if heritage, hills, and estates were all lacking. Status hung on many fine threads.[17]

Except on weekends and evenings, suburban life was run by women. Adult males, other than TV repairmen, milkmen, mailmen, and the like were a rare sight during weekdays. It was left to the mothers to make suburban families function. But the predominant goal of these semi-matriarchies was the happiness and future success of the children.

Indeed the ostensible reason mentioned by most suburbanites for choosing such an environment was "for the sake of the kids"—a place for little Jane and Johnny to play, with green grass and clean air, safely away from gangs and street crimes, and with better schools. Most suburbias resembled nothing so much as giant nurseries.

How successful were these child sanctuaries? By most standards they would have to be judged failures, even for the children. While some big-city problems were avoided, new and often worse ills emerged in the wake of builders' bulldozers. There was a sterile sameness and unreality to suburban living. In escaping urban evils, suburbs created the illusion of a classless world segregated from reality. The uniformity of the economic strata and the absence of daily contact with the actualities of work drastically limited the educational role of the environment, putting the burden almost entirely on schools and family which themselves precluded the necessarily multifarious lesson. Even small towns where people actually farmed, fished, and tended stores, and certainly big cities, offered children an education in sheer humanity that was totally lacking in suburbia. The adult models visible to the suburban child were woman as mother-chauffeur, man as schizophrenic always rushing between roles of gray-flanneled urban job holder and casual suburban father.[18] In such an environment, where reality was often that which filtered through the TV screen, alienation was common. It is not surprising that middle-class suburban kids of the fifties formed the counterculture of the sixties.

Adults too suffered in such an environment. Craving acceptance, conforming to the group, judging others and oneself by peer reactions, status symbols, and market values left little room for individual self-awareness and growth. Wives, bored by baby talk and children's chatter, and husbands, frazzled by the rat race of job and commuting, joined in frenetic evenings and weekends of forced gaiety, ritual rounds of social pleasure. Group activity kept many from thinking about fading dreams. Yet individualism, if weakened, was still a basic part of the culture. Undoubtedly many people suffered from the conflict between the desire for personal autonomy and the pressures for collective conformity.

Numerous signs of tensions were evident. On August 7, 1959, New York *Times* reporter Austin Wehrwein summarized the findings of a medical and psychiatric study of one suburban community: "Life in growing suburbia, specifically in Englewood, New Jersey, is giving people ulcers, heart attacks and other 'tension-related psychosomatic disorders.'" Doctors "found that everything from crab grass to high taxes played a role in emotional difficulties." Drinking was very heavy in suburbia. But perhaps the clearest index of tensions there was the incredible rise in consumption of the new tranquilizer drugs such as Miltown and Thorazine. Apart from their use in mental hospitals, tranquilizers were almost exclusively a middle-class affair. Sales went from literally nothing in 1954 to $4.75 million in 1959 (1.2 million pounds of pills). The use of sleeping pills and, for those who could afford it, psychiatric help also skyrocketed. Thus, in all too typical American fashion, problems were not solved; people simply found artificial ways to bear them.[19]

If suburbia had damaged only suburbanites it would have been bad enough, but it did not stop there. The fifties flight to the suburbs spoiled the countryside and menaced the city as well. Open greenland between city and suburb, which had helped to make the original suburbs attractive, disappeared in developments, highways, shopping centers, and parking lots. Within the central city itself the suburban exodus left urban areas without an adequate tax base. Cities became the refuge for the numerous poor and some few rich, and since both poverty and prejudice excluded blacks from suburbia they concentrated in disproportionate numbers in segregated big-city slums. By 1960 half of the population of Washington, D.C. was black, as was about 40 per cent of Newark. In other major cities blacks made up anywhere from a quarter to a third of the population.

Government policy augmented urban problems. Beginning in the early fifties, federal tax policy allowed builders to depreciate construction costs over a seven- or eight-year period, encouraging shoddy buildings and a rapid turnover in ownership. Federally financed urban renewal (about $1 billion worth in the fifties) almost totally failed in its slum-clearing purpose. Old tenement dwellings were destroyed in favor of towering concrete apartments, office buildings, shopping centers, or colleges. Such projects made little improvement in the slums. Often livable, vital neighborhoods were destroyed.[20]

But the greatest single factor in subverting the virtues of both city and countryside was the object on which suburbia depended most, the automobile. Cars had made suburban escape possible, but at a very heavy price. As the nation became increasingly dependent on the private auto, public transportation was allowed to decline and in many cases was dismantled altogether. General Motors triumphed over common sense and the result was smog, creeping bumper-to-bumper traffic, decaying cities, divided by freeways, despoiled landscapes, time payments, and often early death.

In 1950 a record of more than 8 million cars and trucks were manufactured, and throughout the remainder of the decade, auto sales seldom fell below 7 million annually. By 1958 over 67.4 million cars and trucks were in use, more than one for every household. (Nearly 12 million families, mostly in suburbia, had two or more cars.) Vehicle miles traveled jumped from about 458 billion in 1950 to nearly 800 billion by the early sixties. In 1960 the census reported that 65 per cent of the working population drove to work; a mere ten per cent walked.[21]

Not only did Detroit produce more cars, but bigger, gaudier, faster, more lethal, and less practical ones. From the smooth curved lines and solid colors of the late forties, auto manufacturers' imaginations went berserk. Cars, already too big for basic space needs and ease of parking, became bigger and lower slung so that the slightest bump could smash the oil pan, muffler, or gas tank. Motors were advertised in terms of raw power—"Rocket 88," then "98." Soaring tail fins and enormous taillights became standard features. To counterbalance the sheer size and incredible horsepower of these gas-guzzling giants, manufacturers painted them in bathroom shades: not just one color but two, then three—colors with names like "Horizon Blue," "Robin's Egg Blue," "Crest Blue," "Dream Blue," "Passion Pink," "Sunset Pink," "Campus Cream," "Shell Gray," "Thistle Gray," "French Gray," "Lilac Mist." Matching seat covers and numerous interior gadgets were added. And for the final touch, manufacturers put on lots of chrome to panel the car off into its different pastel sections. Sex and power, the ads implied: the modern American dream.

And cars brought status too. "Obviously this is a car to attract attention," crooned the big type under the picture of a purple tail-finned Oldsmobile. "Its precedent-breaking beauty fully deserves all the applause owners are giving it. Men and women who have just recently moved up to a '58 Oldsmobile from another make are the loudest in their praise . . . proudest of their new possessions." Not to be outdone, a *Life* ad for the pretentious three-tone Packard (parked in front of an ostentatious house) read: "In the *new* Packard *you see the road but never feel it!* The *new* Packard has the world's most powerful V-8 engine. . . . Impressively styled . . . elegantly upholstered . . . distinctly color harmonized. . . . The *new* Packard is designed to *reflect your pride in the finest!*" Or there was the Edsel, "the smart car for the young executive or professional family on the way up."

But at the top of the heap sat the big one, Cadillac, with the world's longest tail fins. "At a conservative estimate," bragged a General Motors ad, "fifty per cent of all the motorists in America would rather own a Cadillac than any other automobile." Ads suggested that mere ownership of a Cadillac provided instant entry into High Society. (No wonder so many gangsters and morticians owned them.) To firm up its image as the highest-status car, Cadillac brought out the El Dorado Brougham. The least expensive Brougham cost $14,000 complete with vanity case, perfume bottle, lipsticks, dashboard tissue dispenser, and four gold-finished drinking cups: American baroque.[22]

Safety and practicality were not what the auto industry catered to. Style was. "The automobile business," testified American Motors president George Romney before a 1958 Senate committee, "has some of the elements of the millinery industry in it, in that you can make style become the hallmark of modernity." They did. Safe cars appeal only to "squares," William Mitchell, GM's styling director, told a *Fortune* reporter in 1956, "and," he added, "there ain't any squares no more." Most Americans accepted the industry's "dynamic obsolescence," turning in cars for the newest creation even before they prematurely fell apart. Companies spent millions on research, trying to anticipate or set style trends. The Chevrolet Division of General Motors, for example, hired seven psychologists in 1957 to investigate the effect of Chevy's "sounds and smells." The result of this program? Chevrolet's general manager proudly announced: "We've got the finest door-slam this year we've ever had —a big car sound." Almost nothing was spent on safety. We just build what the people want, shrugged the manufacturers. And so they did if it made a profit. (In King Farouk's case, Detroit turned out a customized special, complete with a horn that imitated the squeals and howls of dogs being mangled under the wheels.)[23]

Highway deaths mounted—over 40,000 a year by the late fifties. Millions more were injured, some maimed for life. When cars became involved in accidents the automatic assumption was that the driver was at fault. The fact that seat belts were unadvertised extra-cost options was ignored; so too were the faulty brakes on many models, particularly the 1953 Buick, or the inadequate tires as cars got heavier and heavier, or the fancy interior design that caused most accident damage, or the fact that the 1959 Corvair easily flipped over. Ralph Nader began his investigations of auto safety as a Harvard law student in 1957. Cornell University had launched a collision research program as early as 1951; their published research issued in 1954 proved conclusively that seat belts saved lives. Nobody listened. Even taking a look at the problem was suspect as Congressman Kenneth Roberts of Alabama found when he chaired a House subcommittee on traffic safety in 1956. In Congress he met either apathy or outright opposition. Needless to say, with no prodding from the powers in Congress, Roberts received minimal cooperation from the auto companies. Nothing was accomplished.[24]

The automobile industry had the world's most powerful lobby. Not only were they the biggest fish in a corporate sea of big fish, but they also spawned hundreds of other profit-making businesses. The steel, rubber, petroleum, and construction industries all grew rich and dependent on cars. Add to this motels, garages, automobile dealers, drive-ins, car-hops, and tourism generally, and one begins to see the power of the auto lobby. In 1958 receipts for some 56,000 motels and cabins reached $850 million. That same year

85,000 automobile dealers employed over 700,000 persons; 206,755 service stations gave 465,500 persons jobs and did over $14 billion worth of business; highway construction and maintenance costs that year alone came to $5.3 billion.[25]

The power of the auto lobby was borne out by the passage of the National Defense Highway Act in 1956, authorizing the building of a nationwide interstate highway system, designating over 40,000 miles of new high-speed, limited access roadways to be constructed at the cost of $41 billion.

This was a crucial decision. Up to the mid-fifties, alternative means of transportation existed. Rail and bus lines were extensive and, of course, far more efficient than private cars. It was estimated in 1956 that a single bus used effectively could eliminate the need for as many as 1,000 cars. As late as 1953, railroads were carrying about 1.5 million persons daily. But the rush to suburbia combined with massive automobile advertising and the search for status made most Americans opt for cars. And when new highways were neatly packaged by the Eisenhower administration as a defense measure everyone seemed satisfied. So a choice was made. Instead of modernizing the various forms of mass transportation necessary to have an efficient system, the nation chose to have all the eggs bouncing around in Chevies and Fords. As Lewis Mumford noted, people picked "General Motors, even if General Chaos" resulted. In 1956, before the new highway bill, U.S. roads already totaled over 4 million miles, some 40,000 square miles of pavement. After 1956 came the superhighways and soon more and more cars were crawling into the decaying cities, searching angrily for parking spaces. Other forms of transportation, with the exception of airplanes, were allowed to lapse. Trolley lines almost entirely disappeared; commuter trains and bus lines were sharply curtailed.[26]

By the late fifties some people began to sober up from the big auto binge. In 1958 it became evident that a growing portion of the population was developing an aversion to the giant Detroit dreamboats. Edsel failed. Other big cars would not sell. American Motors arose from a moribund state on the strength of the skyrocketing sales of the compact Rambler. Suddenly the big three auto manufacturers rushed to put out a smaller car. As one auto executive stated contemptuously, "if the public wants to lower its standard of living by driving a cheap, crowded car, we'll make it."[27] The dangerous Corvair was General Motors' first compact.

But the real cause of Detroit's change of heart was the growing popularity of the Volkswagen beetle. Beginning with a single dealer in 1950 who sold 330 cars, VW sales by 1957 were nearing the 200,000 mark. Here was an honest car. Though not built to withstand collisions with monster cars, the VW was well-built, small, cheap to buy and maintain, low on fuel consumption, responsive to the driver, and fun to drive. Was the VW the answer to America's transportation problems? Some people thought so. Edgar Snow claimed in 1955 that "if our present automobile owners overnight switched to Volkswagens it would have the effect of increasing available metropolitan parking space by about one-third, widening most streets and highways by ten-twenty feet, increasing national road capacities by about one-third, reducing passenger-car gas consumption by half, and enormously reducing traffic congestion—without any loss in average passenger load per car, legal cruising speeds and safety."[28]

This was wishful thinking. By the time American auto manufacturers modified the high horsepower emphasis in the early sixties the damage was done. Like new highway construction, smaller cars temporarily reduced the level of crisis; they in no way solved the problem. When the fifties ended, all parts of the nation had vast suburban belts. Highways with their space-consuming cloverleafs spanned the country, spawning more housing developments, shopping malls, motels, filling stations, Howard Johnsons—all with great sameness. Banks, offices, and factories were increasingly moved to suburbia. But instead of bringing anything of urban culture to the suburbs, this process only further undermined the central cities.

The future along the freeway America had chosen in the fifties had its prototype: Los Angeles. There, a once-efficient system of public transportation had been almost totally supplanted by the car. The central city had disappeared as L.A. spread out into an undifferentiated auto-addicted blob of single-family houses, offices, factories, fast-food restaurants, motels, gas stations, and shopping centers. Sections of the city were walled off by multilaned expressways, viaducts, and ramps on which traffic crawled at a snail's pace, producing a thick, deadly carbon monoxide smog. On one occasion in 1955 a record 74 vehicles were involved in a single gigantic smash-up. *Two thirds* of central L.A. was taken up by cement: streets, freeways, parking lots, and garages. Culture? One could drive out to Disneyland. It opened in the mid-fifties.[29]

NOTES

1. Erich Fromm, "The Present Human Condition," *American Scholar*, 25 (Winter 1955–56), 29–35; Erich Fromm, *The Sane Society* (New York, 1955), pp. 78–208; Robert L. Heilbroner, *The Future as History* (New York, 1960), p. 74.

2. David Riesman, Nathan Glazer, and Reuel Denney, *The Lonely Crowd: A Study of the Changing American Character* (abridged ed., Garden City, 1955); Dennis H. Wrong, "Riesman and the Age of Sociology," *Commentary*, 21 (April 1956), 331–38.

3. William H. Whyte, Jr., *The Organization Man* (Garden City, 1956), pp. 3–7.

4. Ibid., pp. 42–60, 189–201.

5. Ibid., pp. 231–35.

6. "It's a Woman's World" is discussed in Gabriel Gladstone, "Hollywood, Killer of the Dream," *Dissent*, II (Spring 1955), 166–70.

7. Sloan Wilson, *The Man in the Gray Flannel Suit* (New York, 1956 ed.), pp. 261–62; Dr. Modesto is quoted in *The Nation*, December 3, 1955, p. 484; Helen G. Kangieser, "A Note on Changing American Values as Seen in Contemporary Popular Literature" (unpublished paper, Center for International Studies, MIT, ca. 1956), claimed that fifties literature offered the individual two courses of action. "Feeling powerless to act alone, he may delegate his power to one to whom he feels psychologically close; or he may withdraw from the older power structure . . . in favor of the . . . value system of the group man." Similarly, Jerome Collins, "Changing Values in Best Sellers of the 1930–1935 and 1950–1955 Periods" (unpublished doctoral dissertation, Harvard University, 1957), found that fifties best sellers dealt more with "the individual within the organization;" more with the conflict of autonomy versus group benefits; more with religion as providing emotional security; and more with the horrors of men competing with women.

8. Margaret P. Foster, "A Study of the Content of Selected Third Grade Basic Readers Used in the United States from 1900 to 1953" (unpublished M.A. thesis, Wesleyan University, 1956); Whyte, *Organization Man*, pp. 425–29.

9. Gay Talese, "Gray-Flannel-Suit Men at Bat," New York *Times Magazine*, March 30, 1958, pp. 15, 17.

10. William H. Whyte, Jr., "The Wives of Management," *Fortune*, October 1951, pp. 86–87.

11. Whyte, *Organization Man*, pp. 287–88; John A. Schindler, M.D., *Woman's Guide to Better Living* (Garden City, 1958), p. 405; Vance Packard, *The Status Seekers* (New York, 1959), p. 122; Frederick Lewis Allen, *The Big Change* (New York, 1952), p. 254; Editors of *Fortune, U.S.A.: The Permanent Revolution* (New York, 1951), pp. 134–35; Russell Lynes, *A Surfeit of Honey* (New York, 1957), p. 108.

12. Quoted in Whyte, *Organization Man*, p. 314.

13. *Time*, July 3, 1950, pp. 69–71; Penn Kimball, "'Dream Town'–Large Economy Size," New York *Times Magazine*, December 14, 1952; William H. Whyte, Jr., "The Outgoing Life," *Fortune*, July 1953, p. 86.

14. Ben J. Wattenberg, *This U.S.A.* (Garden City, 1965), pp. 76, 244–45; Martin E. Marty, *The New Shape of American Religion* (New York, 1959), p. 98; *Fortune*, November 1953, pp. 128, 130; John Brooks, *The Great Leap* (New York, 1966), pp. 108–9; Harold G. Vatter, *The U.S. Economy in the 1950's* (New York, 1963), pp. 22–24; Carl N. Degler, *Affluence and Anxiety* (Glenview, Ill., 1968), pp. 186, 191.

15. William H. Whyte, Jr., "The Future, C/O Park Forest," *Fortune*, June 1953, pp. 126–27, 188–90; Whyte, "Outgoing Life," pp. 84–87; Whyte, *Organization Man*, pp. 310–97; Harry Gersh, "The New Suburbanites of the 50's," *Commentary*, March 1954, pp. 209–21; Gibson Winter, "The Church in Suburban Captivity," *Christian Century*, 72 (September 28, 1955), 1112–14; Stanley Rowland, Jr., "Suburbia Buys Religion," *Nation*, July 28, 1956, pp. 78–79; Marty, *New Shape*, p. 100. The fact that suburban communities were overwhelmingly middle class helps explain why so many 1950s social observers believed there only was one class; they saw America through suburban spectacles.

16. Whyte, "Future," p. 127; Whyte, *Organization Man*, pp. 298, 352; Packard, *Status Seekers*, pp. 6, 26.

17. Packard, *Status Seekers*, pp. 26, 62–69; example of the toilet tax is from *National Review*, August 30, 1958, p. 148.

18. I did not grow up in suburbia but rather in what A. C. Spectorsky termed "exurbia"—a rural ring at the farthest reaches of commuter trains or cars. I had the advantages of a colonial home that really was built in 1760 and a "large estate lot" that actually covered a dozen acres of hills, meadows, forest, swamps, and a river. But my father commuted; this I shared with suburban kids. Except in the longer days of summer, he usually left and returned in the dark, rushing dull-suited to who knew where. I had a vague perception that there must be something better than this. I can still remember one morning yelling after my disappearing train-bound father: "So long, sucker." He never forgot that and brought it up many times in later years. I guess he sensed it was true.—DTM.

19. Wehrwein's *Times* report is quoted in James A. Wechsler, *Reflections of an Angry Middle-Aged Editor* (New York, 1960), p. 26; Brooks, *Great Leap*, p. 141; *Time*, June 11, 1956, p. 47; Norman Vincent Peale, *The Power of Positive Thinking* (New York, 1952), pp. 187–88. A. C. Spectorsky, *The Exurbanites* (New York, 1955), pp. 154–63, 250–51, pictured the same tensions in the generally wealthier inhabitants of exurbia.

20. Brooks, *Great Leap*, pp. 111–17; Degler, *Affluence*, pp. 188–93; Jane Jacobs, *The Death and Life of Great American Cities* (New York, 1961); Editors of *Fortune, The Exploding Metropolis* (Garden City, 1957). The plight of the cities and the negative effects of urban renewal are treated further in Chapter 7, pp. 195–200.

21. Wattenberg, *This U.S.A.*, pp. 3, 256; Brooks, *Great Leap*, p. 121; Arthur S. Link and William B. Catton, *American Epoch* (New York, rev. ed., 1963), p. 607.

22. Fifties magazines are filled with car ads in all their pastel splendor; the ones referred to are from *The Saturday Evening Post*, May 3, 1958, p. 45; *Life*, April 18, 1955, p. 116, and May 16, 1955, p. 116; *Harper's*, July 1957, p. 73.

The best satire on fifties cars and the highway scene is Vladimir Nabokov, *Lolita* (New York, 1963 ed.), see especially pp. 207–8; see also John Keats, *The Insolent Chariots* (Philadelphia, 1958).

23. Romney is quoted in Ralph Nader, *Unsafe at Any Speed* (New York, 1965), p. 229; Mitchell is quoted in Jeffrey O'Connell and Arthur Myers, *Safety Last* (New York, 1966), p. 5; Chevy's sounds and smells and Farouk's car are covered in Keats, *Insolent*, pp. 58–75.

24. Ralph Nader, "The *Safe* Car You Can't Buy," *The Nation*, April 11, 1959, pp. 311–12; Nader, *Unsafe*, pp. 7, 10, 11, 42, 44–46, 79, 82, 113, 119, 236–38, 295–98, 313, 335–36; Margaret O. Hyde, *Driving Today and Tomorrow* (New York, 1954), pp. 14–15, 65, 78, 85; *Harper's*, August 1958, p. 80.

25. Brooks, *Great Leap*, p. 99; Link, *American Epoch*, pp. 607, 608, n. 11.

26. David Cort, "Our Strangling Highways," *The Nation*, April 28, 1956, pp. 357–59; Lewis Mumford, *The City in History* (New York, 1961), pp. 506–9.

27. Keats, *Insolent*, p. 230.

28. Edgar Snow, "Herr Tin Lizzie," *The Nation*, December 3, 1955, pp. 474–76; Harry Hammond, "Volkswagen Image," in Marshall Fishwick and Ray B. Browne, eds., *Icons of Popular Culture* (Bowling Green, Ohio, 1970), pp. 64–67; Keats, *Insolent*, pp. 222–25.

29. Mumford, *City in History*, pp. 479, 510; Cort, "Our Strangling Highways," p. 358.

6

The Happy Home Corporation and Baby Factory

Everybody got married in the fifties, or at least it was a supreme sign of personal health and well-being to be engaged in the social act of marriage and family-raising. "Whether you are a man or a woman," advised a widely read book called *The Woman's Guide to Better Living,* "the family is the unit to which you most genuinely belong. . . . The family is the center of your living. If it isn't, you've gone far astray." Men and women were marrying younger than ever. In 1950, census takers discovered, men's average marriage age was 22.0 and women's 20.3, a significant drop from 1940 figures of 24.3 and 21.5 respectively. More people were marrying. In 1955, family-living author Paul Landis estimated, 92 per cent of all Americans were or had been married, the highest record in national history. "Marriage is the *natural state* in adults," emphasized Landis.[1] In the 1950s, popular culture was saturated at all levels with this belief in the supreme wonderfulness of being married. It seemed so sane, healthy, *natural* for people to do that it became an absolute, unbending tenet of life.

In our culture, our view of marriage, domesticity, family life, home life has always been indelibly colored by our attitudes toward the sexes. Many trends of modern American history, though, led up to the particular reaction toward human relations that dominated fifties culture. For one thing, life in the twentieth century underwent a tremendous amount of technological change very quickly. These changes were accompanied by sweeping social transformations. Familiar verities vanished. As the world grew more fluid and less stable, anxiety and uncertainty spread.

Much of that anxiety was transformed into resentment of the social changes going on, both in and out of the context of human rights. In the first two decades of this century, major modifications were made in a flagrantly paternalistic culture. The First World War accelerated that change. More women moved into the professions, worked outside the home, participated in the cultural life of their communities and received advanced educational degrees. In 1920, the woman's suffrage amendment was ratified, signaling an important emotional turning point in both women's activism and the relations between the sexes.[2]

Clearly, the passage of the Nineteenth Amendment marked the end of the great feminist wave begun almost a century before. But the effects of its ebb were not immediately apparent. Women in the twenties did have a degree of choice about their lives. Alternatives to domesticity were few and difficult, but they did exist. Feminism encouraged women to forsake the domestic model and seek professional careers—legal, academic, medical. This choice was largely confined to young and affluent women. The housewife model itself changed in those years. The twenties saw the decline of the extended family. As the nuclear family rose, so did the consumer housewife. She, without servants, bought and prepared everything for the family. Another alternative, the twenties flapper, was not really a life model. But she did represent a new sensual attitude for women. The flapper and her man saw premarital sex as benefit, not damage. Even if this was limited to the women who could take advantage of better birth control, and even if the flapper turned into the consumer-housewife after marriage, that sensual attitude was an important change.[3] The very different rebellions of career woman and flapper never won over a majority of women. Many women resented, even feared, these figures. Still, they were popularly disseminated, often positive models.

The economic anxiety of the thirties, however, inevitably affected sex roles. The flighty flapper was now a useless ghost. Times demanded toughness. Necessity might force Mom to be the family's sole breadwinner, or a woman might have to postpone marriage for work. Yet her step into the work force was not at all on equal terms. Most females suffered from commerce's built-in discriminations—long hours, bad conditions, poor pay, no advance. The thirties was already a time of troubling failure, economic misery, and physical displacement. All these factors created a sexual uncertainty: the American man had difficulty proving himself as breadwinner, and in many instances the American woman was having to earn the living. So that to all the emotional upheavals of the thirties was added the conviction that a woman's working was a lousy thing, and a mere expedient. It was no more than a break in her real life as homebody.[4]

During World War II, record numbers of women moved into responsible positions. They replaced men at every level doing war work and business jobs. But meeting this challenge did not widely reinforce women's confidence. It only strengthened the belief in female work as temporary expedient. Already in the early forties, the models for female independence were disappearing. Thirties Hollywood produced films like *Mr. Smith Goes to Washington,* in which the wise and tough character played by Jean Arthur falls for Mr. Smith (James Stewart) because he is an equal, not a superior superman. By 1943, Ingrid Bergman was murmuring to Humphrey Bogart in *Casablanca:* "You'll have to do the thinking for both of us." Finally the whole erosion of paternalism came to be linked in the minds of women and men with the painful years of Depression and war—and eventually with all the shocks and traumas of the century.[5]

Two other major concepts also furthered this attitude. These two factors had been accumulating cultural force through the twentieth century. The first of these was Freudianism. Much of Freud's work posits the inferiority of the entire female sex. He regarded women as weaker physically and mentally, made less by their lack of a penis. He admitted, however, that the unhappy woman might want superiority. But he could only understand this in male-oriented terms. That is, the discontented female wanted to have a penis and be a man. Such resentment and longing he termed penis envy. Freud's theories also codify a vivid sexual symbolism, which represents a major contradiction within his work. Freud had tried to insist all cultures are different and mutable. But simultaneously his sexual rules and symbols were regarded as rigid and universal truths. All these sexual attitudes on Freud's part were nothing more than the sexual notions of his late-Victorian culture. Because he was able to rescue these notions as the rest of that culture passed away, and include them in a revolutionary and significant technique, sexual ideas that might otherwise have faded only appeared more vital, and even scientifically correct. In that sense, Freudian theory represents a conservative rear-guard action in sexual thought.[6]

As the trust for Freudian theory and technique percolated through modern American society, its nineteenth-century sexual attitude grew in impact. Gradually it would link up with the swelling reaction against the century's anxieties. Already by the mid-forties women's strength was being blamed for the century's shocks. Philip Wylie, in *Generation of Vipers* (1942), used very simplistic Freudian terms to blame the American female for a huge grab bag of social facts. These ranged from the cowardice of green soldiers, through the failure of modern religion and even to the Depression. Woman—more specifically, "Mom"—was responsible for *all* the ills and degeneracies of modern America, Wylie wrote. She was rapacious, dumb, greedy, rough, and used femininity as a bludgeon. Most of all she really wanted to be a man, or at least to emasculate all the men. She was taking over the country.[7]

Wylie's book was frequently reprinted after World War II and attained great popularity. But such Freudian works as his and the less brashly written *Modern Woman: The Lost Sex,* published in 1947 by Marynia Farnham and Ferdinand Lundberg, could never have attained their full impact without another widely disseminated concept of the century: functionalism. Originally, functionalism was developed as a device for social scientists. For instance, in the early years of anthropology, scholars could (and did) judge the behavior of unfamiliar peoples by their own Western cultural standards. Because of such erroneous comparisons, certain things that were very important in the original cultural context were wholly misinterpreted, even condemned. Functionalism tried to introduce objectivity. It got the social scientist to ask a simple question of a behavior or an artifact: "How does it function within this society?" One then simply described that function without imposing personal judgments. A large degree of subjectivity could then be eliminated.

By the 1950s, however, functionalism had been bent to serve other ends. As a basic social science method, it retained (and still possesses) great value. But during the forties and fifties, functionalism was bent toward non-objective cultural purposes. It was no longer used simply to describe.

One example of this misuse appeared in public education. Many school systems had misinterpreted the goals of progressive education to mean a student should be prepared for a future slot in life. Educators would look at a child's social position, and then project the child's future from that. A kid's education became functional training for that preplanned future. This demonstrates one way the functional technique was bent to nonobjective purposes.

Functionalism was similarly damaging when it came in contact with the sexual counterrevolution of the latter forties. Again the theory was employed as a predictive device. It was used to dictate how the sexes should function, according to precise ideals.

Not surprisingly, this revision of functionalism reflected Freudian sexual ideas. It helped further the assumption that all human behavior proceeds out of one's sex. Freudianism had always possessed a conservative face. Freud was more concerned with helping people adjust to the status quo than questioning society. Functionalism came to work in a very similar manner. Like Freudianism, it came to act not as teacher but as tyrant.[8]

The mass of people encountered this moralizing in the multitude of family counseling and family living documents so popular in the fifties. From such diverse sources as the public schools, newspaper advice columns, therapy sessions, popular magazines, and TV, they learned the very different characters men and women were supposed to possess. People were only happy if they were functioning properly, if they obeyed their sexual roles.

These ideas were all reinforced by the factors of time and history. By 1950, women under age thirty would have lived their lives with no feminist coevals. Feminists were aging ladies who had last been happy when they got the vote. Any large-scale tradition of female freedom of choice was being obliterated from memory. Most women only had the trials of their lifetime to remember.

Those difficulties had given many Americans a fantasy. They

longed for a stable, trouble-free domestic world. With war's end, the economy was at last both affluent and peaceful enough to support the dream. People could settle down and start families. When the GIs returned and found themselves competing with women, antifeminist sentiment surged. Not just women who worked only during the war but women who had held their jobs for years beforehand were frequently fired in favor of returning soldiers. Many of these same soldiers wanted to marry. So most women had no choice but to wed. Most welcomed the change.[9]

Still, the domesticity of the fifties might not have gone to such extremes if not for the way the war ended. The atom bombings of Hiroshima and Nagasaki, so resonant of Hitlerian evil, promised a long shock-filled future. These shocks did materialize, too: the immediate anti-Soviet cold war, frantic arms racing and, by 1947, Truman's introduction of the witch hunts that would soon be called McCarthyism. The American economy was being reshaped by the addiction to militarism and by the burgeoning corporations. The thoughts and opinions of mere individuals were being rendered irrelevant. To stand out was to be punished. As if decades of anxiety had not been enough, the postwar years only promised more and more fearful hate.

It was too much to deal with, and at last Americans had the time and money to escape their fears. People turned away from thinking about harsh realities. They turned instead to a nostalgic vision: the happy family huddling together against the visceral terror of modern times. A mock-Victorian vision of life became the great fifties American dream—Mom the homemaker, Dad the breadwinner, smiling determinedly in their traditional roles.

Instead of studying the errors and controversies of their world, Americans preferred to look at the rules to be followed in relations between the sexes. And these were standardized rules. The whole domesticating impulse of the fifties took its cues from nineteenth-century paternalism. Freud had conveniently packaged it; functionalism approved it. The impulse was based on a sexual world view in which men and women had characteristics so very different they were almost members of separate species. Every female was said to be ruled by the "female principle." Its ideals were embodied most of all in one word: nurture. That is, a woman's basic need was to be a wife, mother, and homemaker. Her only means of completion and fulfillment was in childbearing and in serving other people. As TV personality Allen Ludden noted in one of his teen-age advice books, "she knows that as a woman she will be doing a great deal more for others than will be done for herself." Mentally, woman was made to serve. She was emotional, irrational, gentle, obedient, cheerful, and dependent. Man, conversely, was rational, individualistic, unemotional, solid, and aggressive. He needed to struggle in the marketplace for both money and conquest. Every person fitted into an ordained part in marriage. There, Paul Landis wrote, "woman finds outlets for her emotions and protection from the harder forces of the world" and men plug into that outlet "to stimulate their ambition" in the world.[10]

The book that coalesced all these ideas into a solid body of thought appeared in 1947. *Modern Woman: The Lost Sex* won less fame in itself than had *Generation of Vipers,* to which it was similar in spirit. But this brilliant pastiche of Freudianism, functionalism, and distorted history achieved an astonishing amount of intellectual influence. Throughout the fifties, and even well up to the present time, one found phrases, sentences, even entire chapters from this source paraphrased in innumerable places. Such an extensive impact is rare for any artifact of popular culture. One can compare *Modern Woman: The Lost Sex* to other rallying points of popular culture: to McCarthy, around whom the Red scares coalesced, to Sputnik, which provided the central issue for educational reaction in the late fifties, to the film *Rebel Without a Cause* and the singer Elvis Presley, vital catalysts of a special teen-age identity. *Modern Woman* not only recognized the important cultural ideas of the twentieth century, its authors, Farnham and Lundberg, saw the tremendous misery and discontent of modern times. It is the way they focused this discontent that helped shape the fifties. True, people already felt women's strength and independence were responsible for a lot of unhappiness. And similarly, they already believed in the Freudian dichotomy of sexual personality. But *Modern Woman* directly blamed females. Philip Wylie had done this in *Generation of Vipers.* But his could be dismissed as an overemotional, popular work. *Modern Woman* was dense and cerebral. Its statements appeared more intellectual and scientific. If there was unhappiness and uncertainty in modern life, wrote Farnham and Lundberg, it had a sexual reason: modern woman had denied her femininity and her womanly role. Only by accepting her place as wife, mother, homemaker and by erasing her "masculine-aggressive" outside interests could woman be content. Man, similarly, must exercise his active and competitive role. The human halves linked together in that basic human wholeness, the natural marital state.[11]

There was something a bit wrong with people who avoided this *natural state*. First, they were unquestionably miserable. The *Reader's Digest*, in July 1956, published a story entitled, "You Don't Know How Lucky You Are to Be Married." The article, by Paul Gallico, described the "harrowing situation of single life" and "the snare of this so-called freedom." "There were irritations in my marriage I thought were intolerable until I found that life without them was even more so." This misery idea was extended further by Paul Landis, who said of those who never married: "Except for the sick, the badly crippled, the deformed, the emotionally warped and the mentally defective, almost everyone has an opportunity to marry."[12]

In *Modern Woman*, Farnham and Lundberg also considered the single person to be warped and defective. They had very specific ideas about unmarried adults and what should be done with them. For instance, "bachelors of more than thirty, unless deficient, should be encouraged to undergo psychotherapy." Far more dangerous than the single man, however, was the unmarried woman. Farnham and Lundberg suggested at one point in their book (italics theirs): *"all spinsters be barred by law from having anything to do with the teaching of children on the ground of theoretical (usually real) emotional incompetence*. . . . A great many children have been damaged psychologically by the spinster teacher who cannot be an adequate model of a complete woman." That incomplete woman was herself the damaging factor. Children, the authors felt, modeled themselves after their teachers; to hire a spinster teacher would only perpetuate future generations of incomplete spinster women. Such women were by definition unhappy and destructive. The authors' belief echoed through fifties culture. A Montana state senator declared in 1955, "children would be better off with high-school graduates teaching them than with [women] who go to a four-year teachers' college determined to remain teachers and old maids the rest of their lives."[13] When woman refused to follow her sexual function by pursuing unfeminine interests, she became that malignant quality, *The Lost Sex*. This was a skillful attack: it recognized the only way fifties-style domesticity could continue was with female cooperation. Woman's role was the base of the domestic and sexual pyramid. If she refused her acquiescence, the whole structure collapsed. She had to be compelled to submit.

But acquiesce she did, for quite a while. Women earnestly tried to live up to their proper role in the world. Farnham and Lundberg wrote in *Modern Woman* that only full-time mothers were right and healthy: "All mature childless women are . . . emotionally disturbed (as cause, or effect, or both) in some fashion, whatever the reason for childlessness." That threat was repeated frequently. If a woman lacked kids, she was sick, damaged, perverted. She really longed to be a man. (The reputation of feminism mirrored this notion: Farnham and Lundberg were among the very many who labeled feminism "masculinism.") The most efficient proof of one's femininity was to bear a child. In the fifties alone, the national population grew 18.5 per cent. "Of all the accomplishments of the American woman," *Life* prated in a special Christmas issue in 1956, "the one she brings off with the most spectacular success is having babies." A Harvard senior quite seriously related his marriage plans: "I'd like to have six kids. I don't know why I say that—it just seems like a minimum production goal."[14] Although most women did not seek to be baby factories to that great extent, they were told everywhere that only in child rearing and homemaking was their femininity confirmed.

This lesson was very powerfully reinforced by the publication of Dr. Benjamin Spock's *Common Sense Book of Baby and Child Care*. This book was first issued in 1946, and surprised its publisher by becoming a runaway best seller. It was reissued and revised many times, and still remains the best-selling baby book. The most unique thing about Spock's work was not his permissive attitude. Except for a brief time during the twenties and thirties, Americans have always been permissive toward their children, and Spock also insisted this be tempered with discipline. What was novel about Spock's stance was his virtual insistence that mothers should devote themselves full-time to child rearing. Any outside diversions, whether a job or a hobby, would only damage that malleable delicate being, the child, and make it a less perfect person. It was the responsibility of the mother if anything went wrong with the child, Spock insisted. This was not the unique philosophy of a baby doctor. It was merely a reiteration of many unspoken American ideas.

But his rendering them explicit had a most profound effect on the lives of millions of mothers.[15]

As women urgently tried to obey such injunctions, one crucial thing about woman's place was overlooked: What the American female did in the fifties was an historical novelty. Never before had so little been asked of so many. Child rearing alone had never before been a full-time job in any culture. In other societies, women performed many difficult chores. They simply could not devote all day to child care and housekeeping. By the fifties, the more difficult demands of woman's place had vanished. The average house was smaller in size, and less people lived in it. In all, there were fewer jobs demanding woman's energies—certainly not enough to absorb her full time. But even as the drudgery of woman's place decreased, its glorification increased. Women's many household tasks were puffed into things far more ennobling than they ever could be. The "complete" woman was not merely wife and mother, many publications said. Why, she was many professions all rolled up into one—doctor, nurse, chef, chauffeur, mistress, laundress, decorator, maid. This emphasis on the way wives embodied many professions seemed at times rather pathetic. It was almost as though, in being a little bit of everything, she was disguising her nothingness. Yet that had to be more and more disguised. As one pamphlet promised its teenage girl readers, things like homemaking and birthing "are very rich and rewarding experiences. You yourself feel more completely a woman as, indeed, you are."[16]

The complete woman joined her man in what was touted as a marriage of unprecedented democracy. A sure sign of the true "twentieth century democratizing of the American home," Paul Landis felt, was the increased sharing of housework by both spouses. This, he noted, was "strikingly shown" in a 1953 study of 18 tasks as performed in 543 households. Of the 18 tasks, however, only three (locking up at night, fixing broken things, and yardwork) even remotely approached 50 per cent male participation. Most of the tasks showed not even ten per cent male participation in such repetitive essentials as laundry, ironing, and cleaning.[17] The interpretation of this study shows a fair amount of emotional conflict existed over housework. Commentators knew women must perform housework or be unfeminine and incomplete; yet they wished to prove that America was a democracy even unto its marriages and homemaking. Landis' interpretation, in this light, offers a perfect balance. Credence is given both sides of the argument: yes, she is doing the housework, but no, she is not really a slave to the home.

The compassionate rhetoric of democracy sounded fine applied to other aspects of marriage. Pat Boone celebrated this pseudodemocracy in his 1958 best seller, *'Twixt Twelve and Twenty*. Dubbing his family "The Happy Home Corporation," Boone called his wife Shirley its executive vice-president. "I had always felt that one person had to have the final say—and that one had to be the husband," he wrote. "I do believe marriage is a fifty-fifty deal, but every corporation has to have a president who, when the chips are down, can say 'it's going to be this way.'" Similarly, Dr. John Schindler celebrated the "free," equal American wife, now an "active" partner in her marriage. Her active, equal part? "Her job is at once to understand *him*, to help him understand himself, to help him rise to *his* capacities."[18]

Such views were a subtle admission that women were perceived and treated unequally. Yet even this admission was denied rather than pursued. The distorted vision of equal sharing also came to effect beliefs about sexual intercourse. Here, more than anywhere, sex roles had to be maintained. Males were the aggressive partners, females the passive. Lovemaking had to be heterosexual. It had to be between people married to each other, and she a "good girl," a virgin until the wedding night. An unsatisfying sexual relationship, most emphatically, was the fault of the woman. "The smart woman will keep herself desirable. It is her duty to herself to be feminine and desirable at all times in the eyes of the opposite sex," wrote Lelord Kordel in *Coronet*.[19] Such an attitude represented a new sexual synthesis. In Victorian times, woman was either sexless saintly wife or sensual dirty whore. Fifties America maintained the premarital dichotomy of good girl versus bad girl. Yet it invested the wife with both ideals. Sexual repression was remodeled. A wife could enjoy sex as long as she obediently catered to her man. Doris Day's sexy propriety was the perfect mirror of this belief.

The 1953 publication of the Kinsey report, *Sexual Behavior in the Human Female*, documented that sexual fulfillment was as essential for woman's health as for a man's, and that role-playing in bed was not at all biologically necessary. Significantly, the report never received the attention it deserved and failed to stimulate much intellectual interchange. No one wanted to hear Kinsey's findings.[20]

What people did hear was the Freudian message. This insisted a man could only enjoy sexual success if his woman was passive or, better yet, awed. A *Reader's Digest* article in 1957 said that "What Every Husband Needs" was, simply, good sex uncomplicated by the worry of satisfying his woman. This, of course, was not the exclusive fifties view of sexual pleasure. Books like *Peyton Place*, movies like *Seven-Year Itch* dared to show women relishing guilt-free sexual encounters. But "dared" is the pivotal word: in the transitory fifties, the Victorian hostility to female sexuality still held true. Woman's sexual satisfaction was seen as either a daring controversy or a frivolity. The fifties version was slightly improved. At least it allowed coincidental enjoyment. "What Every Husband Needs" went on at great (and euphemistic) length about how women need not worry about never being sexually satisfied. It is remarkable in never once using the word "orgasm." "I talked to a woman a few years ago who had found a solution to this problem in a down-to-earth and very unselfish way. 'I never have that feeling . . . that wild emotion that many other women have. But my husband, he expects it. I love him. So I try to make him feel happy. . . .' Maybe her husband was missing something. But I had an idea it made no difference." And, in conclusion, Hannah Lees, the author, advised her sexually frustrated female readers to forget their little trouble and make "love a substitute for desire."[21]

The desire that women did feel was rated in quality too. *Modern Woman: The Lost Sex* led the way here. The book departed from popular attitudes in assuming women should enjoy making love. But first, the authors insisted, "we are saying that for the sexual act to be fully satisfactory to a woman she must, in the depths of her mind, desire deeply and utterly to be a mother. . . . If she does not so desire . . . it will be sensually unsatisfactory in many ways and will often fail to result in orgasm." Farnham and Lundberg, however, were forced to admit that some "masculine-aggressive" women who determinedly remained childless did have orgasms. But they followed the lead of Dr. Helene Deutsch in dubbing such women's pleasure "the malicious orgasm." Furthermore, again in a Freudian tradition, the two wrote that the only proper and normal female orgasm was vaginal. Clitoral orgasm, they said, indicated "lack of inner involvement, bespeaking a very definite lack of acceptance of femininity." (That these different orgasms actually exist has since been clinically disputed.) The clitoris, they claimed, was "completely external to the real genital apparatus of the fe-

9. Vice-President Nixon meets Sheba the lion in 1953. He later entered the lion's cage.

10. Originally printed under the headline "Los Angeles 'Crusade Against Communism': Sock then Ask," this picture shows Basil Gordon beaten in July 1950 for refusing to tell fellow auto workers whether he was a communist. Police made no arrests.

11. The Reverend Mr. Owen prepares to make "SIN" disappear in 1958. Magic tricks were a regular part of his sermons.

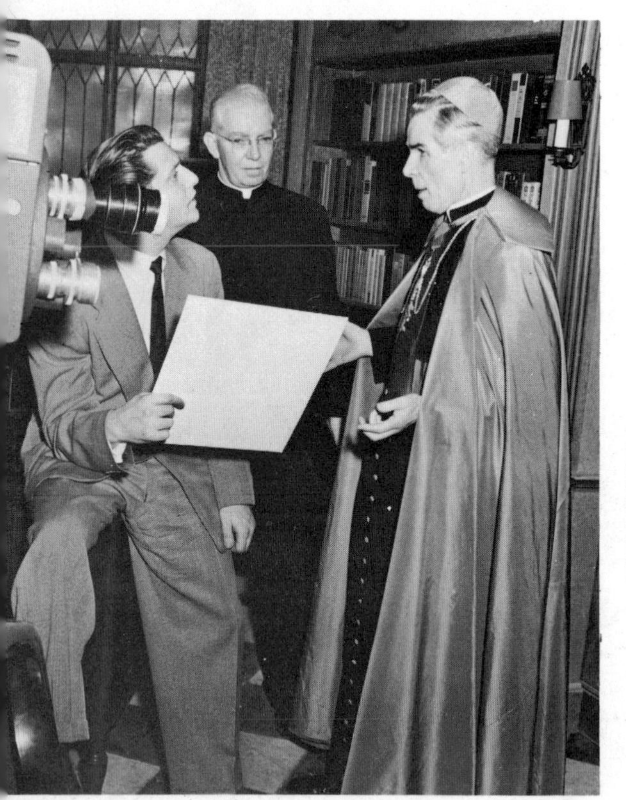

12. Bishop Fulton Sheen discusses details of his 1952 TV series "Life is Worth Living" with director Frank Bunetta and Msgr. Charles M. McBride.

13. The new Chryslers typified the 1957 American car models with their bigger-than-ever tail fins.

14. The proof of poverty was usually ignored by affluent Americans. This migratory worker camp in California, 1951, was just one type of slum where the poor were forgotten.

15. The giant homogeneous suburbs drastically changed the American landscape. Levittown, Pennsylvania, shown here in 1952, was one of the prototypes.

16. Novelist James Jones, shown here, claimed, "Every man should have enough knife to protect himself from every other man."

male."[22] That is, since the clitoris is not "real," neither are the feelings it produces. A fifties women's lesson: ignore the evidence of your sensuality. Play a sex game.

Sexuality was expressed in popular culture largely in a repressive manner. The most sexual female became the adolescent girl. Married women, in contrast, became less rather than more sexual. The focus on the unmarried girl was itself a repressive bind: she was the height of sexuality, yet it was forbidden to enjoy her, except in fantasy. The sex act itself was referred to only coyly or salaciously if at all. Such repressions in themselves contributed to a war between the sexes. Sexual satisfaction, especially for the unmarried, became a double bind. One wanted sex but feared punishment. Exploitation was a certainty. Bodies became battlegrounds, shooting ranges, scorecards. Behaviors besides satisfaction itself grew in importance. Conquest, titillation, deception, and manipulation were regarded as pleasurable in themselves.

At the same time a standardized image of sensuality grew in importance. That image stressed the secondary sexual characteristics of both sexes. Mannerism seemed ever more significant: walk, gestures, voice, dress, size of tits and hips. External appearance was a woman's proof of her sensuality. Men were expected to conform to a physical role, but women had to comply in that respect far more. When this became true, women inevitably turned to elaborate artifice. In the fifties, females followed innumerable awkward regimens. These ranged typically from cosmetic fashions and diet fads to children's trainer bras and ironclad or padded girdles. Allure could derive from any number of unnatural acts. For instance, the Indianapolis *News* advised:

> Warm Smile is An Attribute of Charm
> For this, train the upper lip by this method:
> 1. Stretch the upper lip down over the teeth. Say 'Moo-o-o-o.'
> 2. Hold the lips between the teeth and smile.
> 3. Purse the lips, pull them downward and grin.
> 4. Let the lower jaw fall and try to touch your nose with your upper lip.

> Months of daily practice are neccessary to eliminate strain from the new way of smiling, but it, too, can become as natural as all beguiling smiles must be.[23]

Just as a woman was expected to twist her body to an exaggerated ideal of femininity, she had also to warp her intelligence to that ideal. Education came to support that distortion, especially beginning in the years a girl reached puberty. Sexist educational practices were certainly nothing new in America. Only gradually did women receive equal education. By the mid-1900s, educators in America had come to feel students should be prepared for their future jobs in life. Since women were most properly wives and mothers, they had to learn feminine things. A distinct undercurrent of belief whispered that going beyond the high school level was a waste of time for girls anyway. The New York department store Gimbel's, for instance, advertised some campus clothing in 1952 with the riddle "What's college?" replying "That's where girls who are above cooking and sewing go to meet a man so they can spend their lives cooking and sewing."[24]

Lynn White, Jr., president of Mills College, led the public debate against educating women as one would educate men in his 1950 book *Educating Our Daughters*. White found "astonishing . . . the prevalent belief that higher education is something like spinach, which can profitably be absorbed without reference to the gender of the absorbent." Higher learning, he stressed repeatedly, was harmful to women. At best it was irrelevant because it did not help them in their inevitable futures as wives and mothers. College education was terribly "frustrating" to females, since few of them would ever get to use it anyway. Often, White mourned, it actually made them resent doing all the household tasks.[25]

White then outlined a college curriculum he considered appropriate to the women who insisted on attending college. His female students would first take "a firm nuclear course in the Family." Then they would go on to lots of housekeeping-type courses from cooking through child development to interior decoration. "Why not study the theory and preparation of Basque paella?" he mused at one point. He additionally emphasized that women should stay away from any field that employed men, so as not to threaten a male's livelihood. Just studying homemaking was fine. Wrote

White: "it is rumored that the divorce rate of home economics majors is greatly below that of college women as a whole."[26]

White's argument was quite representative of the way sexual prejudices filtered into education in the fifties. The argument as a whole always posited woman only according to her sexual role, her future as a wife and mother. Since a woman by definition could only be a wife and mother, she had to be trained to that end alone. Any other education would sabotage her. In one of his textbooks for a family-living course at the college level, Paul Landis stressed that college irreparably damaged many women's lives because they "placed too high a value" on getting a degree and so "missed the boat" of marriage. Landis reasoned a woman's greatest value lay not in herself but in her auxiliary status to her man. "It is known that each year's delay reduced the probability of a woman's marrying. . . . It is also known that college women in general have greater difficulty in marrying than the average run of population. Men are not interested in college degrees, but in the warmth and humanness of the girl they marry. . . . Men still want wives who will bolster their egos rather than detract from them."[27] That is, to educate women was to create cold, hostile shrews. It was thus a healthy and a virtuous thing for women to stay away from higher learning.

But this was America, the land where equal education was promised (even required) for all. To get around this mawkish democratic sentiment, special educational programs for women were encouraged. The process began at secondary level. Some of it was more a result of social life than education. Fifties adolescents imitated their elders with the mock marriage of going steady, and innumerable teen etiquette books urged girls to pretend they had little intelligence in order to flatter their boyfriends. But the school system did much to further sex-role pursuits. Sexually segregated elective classes had their effect. Girls took cooking, date appeal, marriage and family, or personal etiquette. Boys studied carpentry, auto mechanics, metalwork. Girls also might be counseled to study nurturant things after high school—home economics, primary education, even the "marriage" major at Mills College (where Lynn White was president). Or they might be discouraged from attending college at all. As *The Seventeen Book of Young Living* advised, girls "might do better to get a good business training so they can help fatten the family income while their husbands attend college."[28]

Conceptually, then, women were regarded as belonging in higher education in limited numbers and restricted programs. Women made up a far smaller percentage of college students than even in the twenties, and got fewer advanced degrees than in the twenties or thirties. At the crucial point of their last year in public school, teen-age girls were influenced in many cultural ways away from attending college. It was an influence irrelevant to girls who did not care about higher learning. But for those who cared about education and profession, it was destructive. Learning, for women in the fifties, often had little to do with education. The entire concept is summed up in a passage from a pamphlet intended to counsel high school girls. The booklet "deals with your concern with becoming feminine and suggests how—in the 1950s in the United States—you can learn what is essential to being a woman." Its title, simply, is *How to Be a Woman.*[29]

And this is the very point where the concept of femininity runs into trouble. What, after all, is this "natural" femininity if education destroys it? If women are, as Margaret Mead wrote, naturally "committed in every cell of their bodies for the mother role," then how can one learn How to Be a Woman? If this is such an inborn thing, why must it also be an acquired thing?

The artifice of how to be feminine persisted not just in determining women's education, but in jobholding. In the fifties, more women than ever joined the work force. By 1956, 22 million women held jobs, a full third of all the jobs in the nation, and half these female workers were married.[30] This was another contradiction. The popular image of women was as non-wage-earning homebodies, and yet women worked in huge numbers. But we have to look deeper: it was the way women worked, the jobs they chose or were given that tells.

"It is not that work is essentially masculine or feminine," Farnham and Lundberg had written in *The Lost Sex,* "but that the pursuit of a career (which is work plus prestige goal) is essentially masculine." Thus, a woman aspiring to a job involving large material reward, success, and promotion was undesirable and unwomanly. If a woman must work, it was felt, a non-prestige job was preferable, particularly if she was not competing in any way with men but rather working for men. "She gracefully concedes the top job rungs to men,"[31] wrote a *Look* reporter of the working woman.

The effect of such thinking on the female work force is quite statistically clear. Very few working women, less than six per cent, held any kind of executive position in the fifties. Some women performed jobs that could be pursued at home, such as writing or telephoning. A third of all working women had clerical jobs. Census takers in 1960 were surprised to learn the biggest job subcategory increase in the decade was "hucksters and peddlers." Likewise a large (and also female) increase showed in the similar classification "demonstrators."[32] That is, many women sold products like Avon or Tupperware.

Not only were the types of jobs filled concentrated at the bottom of the work hierarchy. Women's pay was grossly lower than that of men, whether at the clerical or professional levels. The census report on median incomes speaks most clearly. In 1959, median income for a white male with only a high-school diploma was $4,429, far higher than that of the white female college graduate, $3,758. Race only deepened the trap: the black male college graduate averaged $4,840, the black female college graduate only $3,708. Jacques Barzun clarified the American relationship between economic reward and social worth. While he was aware that few women in the early fifties earned as much as $6,000 a year, he claimed that a woman "was less valuable, less in demand than a man." Even more bluntly, Ian Fleming's popular character James Bond asserted that "women were for recreation. On a job, they got in the way and fogged things up with sex and hurt feelings and all the emotional baggage they carried around. One had to look out for them and take care of them."[33]

And this very attitude, that "on a job, they got in the way," affected women's work too. In researching this chapter we ran across dozens of little tales concerning female aggressiveness and incompetency, in every place from avant-garde literature to *Reader's Digest* condensations. An excellent example is a cheap science-fiction film called *From Hell It Came*, probably inspired by the far more masterful success of *Creature from the Black Lagoon*. This film tells the story of a vicious possessed tree stump that walks about terrorizing the Polynesian islanders. There are two women prominent in the movie: a scientist with both M.D. and Ph.D. (specializing in radiation studies and dermatology) and a trader who took over that post when her husband died some years before. The scientist is played by a pretty blond actress no more than 18 years old. The trader, who from all her dialogue is well into middle-age, looks about 30. The scientist finds herself pursued throughout the film both by the tree stump (which has worked up an inexplicable grudge against her) and a fellow researcher, a hefty male who embraces her and murmurs such scientific observations as "stop being a doctor first and a woman second. . . . Don't you want a husband and children like other women?" The trader, meanwhile, is portrayed as vacuous, always talking and always husband-hunting in a most grotesque manner. Although she has lived among the natives for many years, she has no knowledge of their culture and a lot of superficial scorn for their ways. At film's end, when the male researcher heroically kills the enraged stump (which is about to fling the teen-age scientist into the swamp), the two embrace and their colleagues note that it is time for "a stateside honeymoon." A foolish film, to be sure, but at the same time a great parable for attitudes about the competent woman in the fifties. Like the trader, the fifties woman was seen as totally trivial and a not-quite-whole entity. Like both the women, she was unable to cope with harsh realities. The two movie women, for instance, persisted in wearing full skirts and high heels on those long jungle treks. When the scientist was assaulted by the stump, she only flailed the air with her hands, even though a means of killing the thing was more available to her than anyone. Women, the film seemed to say, just could not handle anything. They were safer married.

Fantasy was not warning enough. The attack was multiple. Women with jobs were accused of wreaking all sorts of havoc. A working woman, Farnham and Lundberg insisted, "could only grudgingly give attention to her children." Not only was she a negligent mother but, as *From Hell It Came* suggested, a husband-hunter and an incompetent. The woman who took her job seriously, whether single or married, was "sexlessly modern," as Paul Landis wrote. Many commentators labeled her as sick, suffering from penis envy. In a 1954 *Esquire,* Merle Miller attacked "that increasing and strident minority of women who are doing their damndest to wreck marriage and home life in America, those who insist on having both a husband and a career. They are a menace and they have to be stopped. Let me be perfectly clear at the outset. I believe that if at five o'clock tomorrow all the married women in this country who have jobs were forced to resign, the republic would not only survive but would be considerably better off."[34]

The working mother also posed a serious danger to her family. Her offspring might become juvenile delinquents, atheists, communists, or worse. Sexual fears were used to bring women into line. An outstanding instance of this appeared in the 1956 *Life* "American Woman" issue, in an article written by Robert Coughlan. The feature raged against the "disease" of working women particularly when combined with "too democratic" households. One of Coughlan's central anecdotes concerned a family in which the wife worked; the unemployed husband helped with the housework. "Soon he began to take over the motherly role himself, and to overwhelm his children and preside over all the details of their lives. He was especially devoted to his small son. Then, to his horror, he found the boy wanting to dress in his mother's clothes. . . ." The father sought professional help for his son. The father was told to stop acting like a woman. "When he managed to limit himself to the fatherly role, she responded by becoming an excellent mother and the family settled into a healthy relationship."[35]

Even if the children did not turn into homosexuals overnight, women with jobs "are thrown into competition with their husbands," Landis wrote. "It is particularly difficult for the American male to maintain his self-respect while being outdistanced by his wife." Landis' comment indicates a number of factors about the myth of work. Never did he, or any other source, reveal any interest in a woman's self-respect. This humbling idea was far from the only critical one. Landis emphasized only the aggressive, emotionally repressive and competitive nature of a career: work as purely nasty. This was a very typical tack in fifties culture. It denied the many emotional pleasures men got out of their careers, the social satisfactions, excitement, and sense of purpose. When the work myth could pretend these feelings did not exist for men, it could also tell women not to expect such satisfactions. They would only be hardened and made cold by their work. Similarly, the entire dichotomy of home versus job did not have to be examined when such a myth was believed.[36] People would continue to accept the division: total emotional indulgence at home or total rational competition at work. Both ways were artificial; both ways denied the fullness of human character.

The function of the work myth was very similar to that of the special education idea. That is, women were intimidated. They believed work was a destructive pursuit, or that they should not pursue a satisfying interest. They believed they were less and deserved less. Most college women, thus, failed to use their education. Those record numbers of women who entered the work force were grossly underpaid and underpromoted. When the working woman could be perceived as a bored and frivolous butterfly, she did not deserve advances or rewards. When she was unfeminine—competitive, competent, tough—she similarly was mentally suspect, and again merited no reward. With such justifications, working women were not only given bottom-rung jobs and refused promotion. They were also denied job benefits. When women internalized the myth, they mistrusted one another and so avoided working unity. Lower-class women were the most economically disadvantaged. The female college graduate was doubly robbed, economically and educationally.

Many such women at every social level became frustrated and confused. The master stroke of the feminine mystique was to be able to explain away such restless women's discontent. We have already noted the skeleton of the argument: if a woman was discontented, it was for no reason other than her denial of her own femininity. Yet for her to embrace her femininity, woman had to deny her rationality and many emotional satisfactions. Women had a limited freedom to their emotions in the fifties, and at the same time became imprisoned by emotion. They were expected to trivialize their other mental strengths.

The belittling of women's capacities came from many cultural sources. One such source was romance magazines. These aimed mainly at lower-class and working-class females. Publications like *True Confessions* and *Modern Romance* fostered a murky confusion about the workings of the female body. The joking description of such magazines' fiction plots is all too true: "He kissed me and then a cloud came over everything and then I was pregnant." Such blurry depictions could only foster a woeful ignorance. This in turn was aggravated by the general mood of sexual repression. Women were expected not to know, and not to know both body and mind. The *Reader's Digest* suggested a fogging of women's mental capacities in talking about "the hardest decision for a woman to make." This turned out to be "when to reach middle age." *Good Housekeeping* helped shrink women's minds with such probing questions as "What is your family really like? What are its goals? Its needs? Its interests? If you know—with certainty—you will have a successful living room."[37]

The reverse side of encouraging such trivial thinking was discouraging major rational decisions. In late 1952, for instance, *Time* carried a brief anecdote about one Walter Mims of Tulsa, Oklahoma. Mims had struck a woman driver because "she signaled she was going to turn right and then she turned right." Similar woman-driver stories appeared in a multitude of forms in the fifties. These were so very common and so seemingly trivial that people still tend to dismiss their meaning. With the hindsight of a more sophisticated humor and of intervening years of feminist publicity, we find ourselves only bored by repetition of the tale of the woman driver. But in the fifties the woman-driver story was one of the most common means of attacking female capabilities. The brunt of the Mims anecdote is the point of the entire attitude toward woman as thinker: if a woman performs a responsible act correctly, it must be a mistake. It only remained for Freudian psychiatrist Leopold Stein to write in his 1959 book *Loathsome Women* that the good woman, "remaining at home . . . becomes best acquainted with the properties of familiar objects, and tends to concentrate her thinking on specific things in limited quantity." An abstract of that statement clarifies the whole pressure of culture on women: "her thinking . . . [is] limited."[38]

The feminine mystique was accompanied by a revived male mystique. Ideas about the role of the male became simplified and exaggerated just as they were regarding women. The extreme form the male mystique obtained in the fifties attempted to prove that men were the precise opposite of women. A man needed to struggle and compete. He had the freedom of his intellect, and conversely was the prisoner of intellect—although the idea of imprisonment with its implications of weakness would never appear in fifties popular culture.

What did appear is clearly exemplified by the writing of Mickey Spillane. One of America's best-selling novelists, Spillane turned sexual anxieties of the era into a formula that both profoundly influenced our culture and made him lots of money. His detective hero, Mike Hammer, occupies every Spillane novel as sexual and crime-solving superman. Hammer is always involved in immediate power struggles against evil. He always triumphs in his conquests, whether over women or crooks. He is unhandsome, craggy, hard-boiled. (Good looks, it seems, are rather effeminate.) All women become sexually excited in his presence. Hammer always masks his feelings with cool male strength. In *The Big Kill,* he remarks, "I gave him a taste of his own sap on the back of his hand and felt the bones go into splinters." The emotions this fifties hero does express are two: lust and hate. They are conveniently summed up in the expression "kill-lust." That is really the quintessential Spillane phrase, fully communicating the violent hit-and-run luxury of his sexual encounters and the sensual pleasures of his many murders. In Hammer, the active male principle of the Victorian period reaches its *reductio ad absurdum:* male shrunk to snarling rutting object.[39] But to say his popularity derived from such simplicity is not enough. That Spillane's books were and are so popular is a sign of the tenuous hold on reality of the myths of sexism. If people genuinely embodied such polarities of personality, Spillane would be without purpose. Hammer was popular because he enacted a daydream. He catered to the politically disarmed and sexually insecure, the ambiguous American who needed a powerful dose of artifice and reassurance.

This insecurity, emphatically, was closer to the genuine position of the American man than was the tough-guy image. One of the most common remarks about the American woman in fifties magazine articles was that she often seemed confused and paralyzed by modern society. This might be so. But man was no less paralyzed. In a time of A-bombs, witch hunting, and bitter corporate on-the-job competition, the workingman had to maintain a careful front. He could not afford any real-life indulgence of the Hammer fantasy. His relation to the company was one of subservience. There he had to display loyalty and dependence. He had to subdue his personality to another's and surrender his mental abilities to a stronger power. The American man, that is, had to act like a good old-fashioned wife. This was true for the corporate man as well as the man working on the line. Sexual role-playing, in such a society, was a distraction. Eyes fixed firmly on sex roles were averted from the real dangers and controversies of the world. Men, like women, chose to hem themselves into a narrow social space. If they could not have a genuinely stable world, they at least wanted the illusion of stability. When confusion seemed to intrude, the fault lay with emasculating women. To question that concept itself was a danger. It meant also questioning the whole cultural rat race.

"If people do not know *who* they are," wrote Arthur Schlesinger, Jr., "it is hardly surprising that they are no longer sure what sex they are." A fascination with what was felt to be sexual ambiguity also marked the decade. To be a homosexual, transsexual, or bisexual meant not fitting into that *natural state* of sexual polarities. Straight men and women who failed to conform to those opposites were subject to vicious pressures in the fifties. But for people who were not even sexually straight, the pressures were far more intense. Since they did not fit into conventional sex-role perceptions, they were regarded as sick and, of course, as terribly unhappy. *Time,* for instance, described the main character in a novel: "Tamara is a lesbian, too neurotically selfish for anything but a perverted counterfeit of love."[40]

As people who fell outside sexual conventions, homosexuals were perceived as fitting targets for sexual speculation and titillation. The widespread fascination with Christine Jorgensen's sex-change operation is just one instance of this. The most frequent reaction by the mainstream to gays was one of mixed fear and fury. Since Americans were unfamiliar with their sexual feelings, any anxiety about gays tended to be externalized. It was blamed on the gay. Homosexual men were perceived as aggressive threats. When this happened, several things were being communicated. First, this attitude indicated the pervasiveness of the superstition that sex partners always took active (conquering) or passive (submissive) roles. A second message proceeded out of this first one. When a straight man turned down a sexual request from a gay, he often felt angry and offended. Even hinting at such sexual intercourse was perceived as insult and conquest. The person who received the sexual advances of an aggressive male was weakened and desecrated. When this idea is placed in conjunction with the heterosexual proprieties of the time, we arrive at a disturbing discovery: one of the proofs of woman's inferiority was her sexually submissive role. To be the passive partner, the seduced person, was itself a low, weak thing. This is perhaps the most essential statement about woman's sexual role in the fifties. This crucial and contemptuous outlook is not always so clear in sources about heterosexual intercourse.

Often, the contempt for homosexuals manifested itself in varying degrees of violence. In the fifties, as before and still, rolling queers

—sexually luring, then beating and robbing gay men—was commonplace. The law quietly sanctioned this by labeling homosexuality a crime. Only recently, and then only in a very few locales, has it not been highly dangerous for a gay man to come out of the closet. Lesbians might not have to contend with physical attacks, but could expect more sublimated violence. They risked social ostracism if discovered, as did gay men. At the same time, because homosexuals were regarded as sick, they were subject to all sorts of cures. These expressed a subtle violence by seeking to extinguish gay sexuality. That is the case in the novel *Time* referred to. Tamara, at book's end, was married off. This proved to be not a tragedy but a benefit, reforming and purifying her. In general, the lesbian was perceived as weaker than the gay male. Therefore it was conceivable that she could be converted. She did not have to be killed. This fantasy appeared in Ian Fleming's *Goldfinger*. At the end of that novel, James Bond converted Pussy Galore from lesbianism with a good lay.[41]

Under such violent pressure from many sides toward a homogenized, pasteurized sex behavior, the undomesticated person, whether straight or gay, had to wear a mask of propriety. One aspect of the mask was the way self-aware homosexuals kept their sexuality hidden, closeted. Another sign of the American sexual disease was that teen-agers tormented themselves with fear of being gay. Homosexuality was a problem and a question. That this was so is indication enough of the artifice of sex roles. Instead of regarding human sexuality as a thing as flexible as human personality, everyone had to measure up to certain rigid rules. People had to pretend.

Another part of the pretense was the way undomesticated, professional women wore the mask of domesticity. The most ludicrous examples of this occurred when well-paid, hard-working, and accomplished Hollywood actresses posed fluttering about some fake studio kitchen, making cute little sandwiches and mock-dreaming of chintz curtains, picket fences, and diapers. In 1951, *Look* printed a publicity article entitled "The Many-Handed Woman." The feature was accompanied by a big composite picture, captioned "Movie star Barbara Britton beautifully portrays the American woman—in Swirl dress with . . . Modglin broom, O-Cedar mop, Stanley brush, Singer vacuum, scrub brush."[42]

The developing underground culture, too, only perpetuated sexual roles. Rock and roll music, for instance, kept singing the same old words, whether from Elvis ("I'll know you're mine by the ring around your neck") or Ray Charles ("She knows a woman's place is right there in her home"). Meanwhile that music was supporting young male rebellion against the dehumanizing status quo in such songs as "Charlie Brown," "Yakety Yak," and "Alley Oop." Movies about rebellion were also for men only. In Brando's fifties films, for instance, women were the guardians of domestic virtue and order. Mary Murphy in *The Wild One* and Eva Marie Saint in *On the Waterfront* are two instances of this. James Dean's films presented women in an equally Victorian fashion. In *Giant,* Dean worshiped Elizabeth Taylor on an emotional pedestal. In *Rebel Without a Cause,* he and Natalie Wood ran away from home—but only to set up a mock family with Sal Mineo as their "son."[43]

Anti-mainstream literature, too, preserved conventional attitudes about women. Paul Goodman's otherwise incisive classic *Growing Up Absurd* amazingly dismisses women entirely from any discussion of his central idea about "how to be useful and make something of oneself." He rather naively felt women already had a useful, maternal role. Therefore, "a girl does not *have* to, she is not expected to 'make something' of herself."[44]

The Beat writers similarly offered little hope to women. Ironically, their rebellion often was far more sexually reactionary than the domestic extremes of the fifties. Considering the culture's obsession with woman as domestic, it is not surprising many Beat writers came to identify women with all the sapping influences of commercialism, suburbia, and corporation. Beats tended to cast women in older sexual stereotypes. Lawrence Lipton, in his description of Beat life, *The Holy Barbarians,* depicted women wholly as clichés. He devoted an entire chapter to the sort of woman who hung around with Beats (who were men). The chapter was entitled "Loveways of the Beat Generation." Lipton noted such types as the kind of girl who liked to make love with black drug addicts, the rich girl flirting with poverty and rebellion, the earth mother, and the woman who needed a long succession of men and found casual Beat sex expedient. Jack Kerouac, the most famous of the Beat novelists, expressed an even more simplistic attitude. He saw woman either as the inferior temptress (such as Mardou Fox in *The Subterraneans*) or else as the saintly mother. His own mother appears in many of his works. Her ideal traits became his measuring stick so that he could write of another man's woman: "Now you see, man, there's *real* woman for you. Never a harsh word, never a complaint. . . . Her old man can come in any hour of the night with anybody and have talks in the kitchen, and drink the beer and leave any old time. This is a man, and that's his castle."[45]

Norman Mailer, who in the fifties acted as a go-between defending the Beat writers to the square world, amalgamated the sexual roles of one and the rebellions of the other most skillfully. He handled sex-as-incrimination in a manner more clear, Freudian, and artistic than any of his contemporaries. Mailer portrayed women as universally bitchy, greedy, vain, shallow, masochistic, and dependent. In *Barbary Shore* (1951), Lannie, one of the three female characters, moans, "You can't understand the peace of being with a man who looks at you as if you do not exist, so that slowly you're beaten beneath him and everything whirls and you're not there at all." In another brilliantly drawn passage, the sarcastically named Guinevere says: "'Oh honey . . . I'm so confused. Will you tell me what to do? Will you always tell me what to do?' His voice was balm, and I could see her drawing strength. 'I will tell you what to do. Over and over I will tell you what to do.'" In his famous essay "The White Negro" Mailer divorced "masculine" and "feminine" from their biological meanings. He applied them entirely in the abstract to certain men. In doing so he rendered the entire nature of fifties sex beliefs clear. To be female was to be inferior, defective, damaged: "If you flip, if you lose control, reveal the buried weaker more feminine part of your nature . . . your ear is less alive, your bad and energy-wasting habits are further confirmed, you are farther away from being with it. . . ." Finally, in *The Deer Park*, Mailer offered an image of the lovely, stupid, and vulgar Elena, with a "hole at the center of her soul."[46] Male discontent had boiled down to a strengthened sexual war. That woman had a damning flaw, a great "hole" in her psyche simply because of her corresponding anatomy, was the essence of the decade's sexual extremism.

Some women achieved a great deal in the fifties despite overwhelming difficulty. A few of these women managed to use the feminine mystique to their own advantage. But in doing so, they rarely could rise above its constrictions. In using the mystique, they came only to pander to it and became lessened because of it. One thinks of Lucille Ball, a comedienne of beauty and talent, obliterating her looks and belittling herself on "I Love Lucy." (Ball did gain tremendous economic power through this series, but she still is perceived as a foolish clown.) Marilyn Monroe is an even more obvious example. She so convincingly played the sex bomb that it destroyed all public regard for her considerable acting talent. The extreme experience of being a woman in fifties America intensely shaped the work of several important poets, such as Adrienne Rich, Sylvia Plath, Anne Sexton, and Diane DiPrima. But they, along with the few successful female painters and novelists, found themselves stigmatized. For instance, Helen Frankenthaler and Georgia O'Keeffe may have been major American talents—but they were described and treated like that Sunday dabbler, the woman painter.

Women in business did enjoy some successes, women in academia some triumphs. Two of the most significant of these were the 1959 publication of Eleanor Flexner's *Century of Struggle,* a history of American feminism, and the continuing work of Margaret Mead. But these few surfacing triumphs were far outweighed by the mass of suppression. The pressure was so great that one can only be awed at the strength and persistence of the successful woman in any field. For every Flexner and Frankenthaler, there were thousands who stifled their interests. The women who suffered the most economically were non-white lower class. But the women who were attacked the most by the culture were learned, middle and upper class. These women had been educated in a nation that valued economic power and personal autonomy, that had inculcated such values into these women—but then contradicted these lessons by barring them from satisfying goals. This frustration of earlier hopes was the reason for the tremendous discontent among women of apparent luxury. It also explains the initial elitist orientation of feminism in the sixties.

Such discontent soared through the fifties. Many women found the wife-and-mother role not at all as fulfilling as the mystique had promised. They found themselves trivialized by spending all their time with children; they found themselves expanding housework into a major operation; they found the demands of their role not enjoyable but boring and humiliating. This was not at all the case for every woman. We are not trying to universally condemn homemaking, nor to insult the housewife. What we are trying to say is that when homemaking becomes the only acceptable future for woman, when its trivial tasks are inflated into spiritually sanctified ends, a falsehood and an evil is being perpetrated. Psychological harm and economic exploitation will follow.

The moral problem was only aggravated by the terms of fifties sexism. The contempt with which female roles were reinforced was itself internalized by discontented women. Around mid-decade, many magazines began running articles about the astounding number of problems affluent American women were suffering. These ran the gamut from increased neuroses, through abortions attended by grief and guilt, to emotionally induced illnesses, divorce, and alcoholism. The overwhelming majority of such pieces were written by men. One typical article, written by a male doctor for *Coronet*, noted all sorts of "vague and disturbing" signs of psychosomatic illness. These appeared in women of the upper middle class, women with soft and undemanding lives. Most of these sufferers, he noted, had an extremely feminine appearance. For years they had cleaved strictly to the demands of the feminine mystique. They kept house, raised the kids, catered to the husbands. But instead of being fulfilled and content they were confused and hostile. "A mask of placidity," the doctor wrote, "hides an inwardly tense and emotionally unstable individual seething with hidden aggressiveness and resentment." He went on to make a judgment very typical of the genre. He concluded these women were unhappy because they were rejecting their femininity. Decades before, Freud had finally cried in exasperation, "What does woman want? Dear God, what does she want?" And this doctor echoed Freud's plaint when he wondered, "What, if anything, can be done to cure such women of their intense strivings for masculinity?"[47]

What indeed? This bland question was the dead end of all the sexual role games of the fifties. It represented the central issue of the sexual double bind: a woman is a free and equal human, but still she is only a lesser animal, fueled by her hormones and heart.

Such a root paradox, by fostering intense discontent and by being almost blatantly contradictory, would soon bring into being the new feminist wave of the sixties and seventies. But in the fifties its contradictory nature was ignored by most women and men. Americans had originally marched into domesticity to escape their fears and insecurities. But why did so many of them cling to such a damaging faith?

That men preferred the system is easier to see. Men themselves paid a price for the masculine myth. They had to deny much of their own character in conforming to the manly stereotype. Many men gave themselves so completely to the wearing role of breadwinner that they even paid with their lives, dying within a few years of retirement from the work force. But for the most part, men stuck with the sexual mystique because they benefited from it according to the cultural values of mid-century America. Men received the economic power so highly prized in America. They were deferred to not only on the large economic scale, but on every level. If woman had to be wife, man could be human. That was the thing that made it easy for men to continue: they were motivated constantly by the power that accrued to them—not merely economic power but far broader social sway.

The answer to the same question is more complicated for the American woman. First, fifties domesticity was a novelty not so much in its statement of sexual myth but rather in its extreme exaggeration. Initially it seemed only a sensible extension of past beliefs. But the passage of time and the march back into the home eradicated any memory of alternatives. By the time enough women felt unhappy because of the feminine mystique, no attractive options seemed to remain. There were, of course, certain advantages to the mystique. This was particularly the case for the wife of affluence. If she had no overweening ambitions, hers was a rather pleasant life. Minding the house and kids was a far simpler and less aggravating existence than sweating for a living in the company. The upper- or middle-class educated woman who was pleased with her domestic life was perhaps the best-off human being in the world. She had economic security, approval for her behavior from an entire culture, and personal contentment. But the major failure of the feminine mystique was in assuming her character to be all women's goal. The multitude of humans who were born female found themselves judged by her mythical limits.

In retrospect, it is both amazing and tragic that the very transparency of all this was not more obvious. Women and men were repeatedly urged to play their roles, like actors on a sexual stage. Both sexes suffered under the fifties version of sexuality, though women more so than men. The difference between a man's life and a woman's was the difference between having one's hands full and having one's hands tied. She was nothing but girlish Mommy and her man had to be only Big Daddy. The danger of this, of straight marriage as a norm, cannot be overemphasized. Its threat lies in the vanishing of choice. If woman's humanity is belittled, if heterosexuality is inevitable and alternatives are sick, if making life alone or as a single parent or in an extended family is ridiculed or, worse, never mentioned, these ways of life become incredibly difficult. Realistically, they no longer become possible: as far as the public imagination is concerned, they cease to exist. Marriage no longer becomes a voluntary experience of joy and fulfillment. Rather it is a no-exit cage. Humanity's condition is reduced to robot obedience.

By 1960, some few women had begun to speak against these extremes. Author Emily Kimbrough, in *Life*, asked a very simple question of employers. "Consider . . . the persistence of the qualifying phrase used by men about women, 'remarkable for a woman.' Why should it be remarkable that a woman can be successful in business? It seems to me far more remarkable that she is so seldom in the top position." Betty Friedan began working on her book *The Feminine Mystique* in the late fifties. And much of her writing was prefigured by the brilliant journalism of Eve Merriam, writing at this time for *The Nation*. Merriam, in an article entitled "Are Housewives Necessary?" saw the vast pressure on women to be happy home corporations and baby factories as profitable to the national economy: "There has to be a maw to cram all these products into, and Mrs. Total Housewife can provide it. . . . Thus, the woman who walks out of full-time housekeeping is forsaking generations to come."[48]

Yet a more successful criticism of sex role extremism would not be sparked until Betty Friedan published *Feminine Mystique* in 1963. Most women and most men would continue to explain their discontents in terms of the mystique itself. If one was frustrated or unhappy, it was because one could not prove oneself sexually. In spite of the many emotional and economic indications that the rules did not fit human character, people's desperate pursuit of sexual myths only continued throughout the decade. In 1960, the average marrying age remained identical to that of 1950—22.0 for men and 20.3 for women. The birth rate remained high, even as the divorce rate increased. People tried, very hard, to live up to the dream. Hardly anyone had questioned the basic sexual dichotomy—except, perhaps, to quibble about its class orientation as the Beats did. In January 1951, *True Story* published a novelette that sums up the monolithic message. Its words are strikingly similar to the writing of many thinkers even two decades later. And they possess an odd echo in Norman Mailer's fiction of the same year. Concludes the novelette: "'Yes, Burke,' I said, and it seemed to me I'd been saying it for years. And I want no more than to keep on saying it, all my life. THE END."[49]

NOTES

1. Dr. John A. Schindler, *A Woman's Guide to Better Living* (Garden City, 1958), p. 415; Ben J. Wattenberg, *This U.S.A.* (Garden City, 1965), p. 37—an analysis of the 1960 census; Paul H. Landis, *Making the Most of Your Marriage* (New York, 1955), p. 11. Landis was selected because he typifies the family-living authors of the fifties.

2. Estelle B. Freedman, "The New Woman: Changing Views of Women in the 1920s," *Journal of American History,* LXI (September 1974), 372–93; William H. Chafe, *The American Woman* (New York, 1974), pp. 25–27.

3. Freedman, "New Woman," pp. 377–78, 380, 389; June Sochen, *Movers and Shakers* (New York, 1973), pp. 27–28, 101–3.

4. Sochen, *Movers,* pp. 161–63, 172–73; Chafe, *Woman,* p. 51.

5. Betty Friedan, *The Feminine Mystique* (New York, 1963), pp. 100–1, 182–83; Sochen, *Movers,* p. 265.

6. Friedan, *Mystique,* pp. 103–25; Kate Millett, *Sexual Politics* (New York, 1973), pp. 239–56.

7. Philip Wylie, *Generation of Vipers* (New York, 1942).

8. Functionalism is discussed by Millett in *Politics* to a great extent (pp. 293–312) and also is crucial to Friedan's argument in *Mystique* (pp. 126–49). Friedan, however, mistakenly blames the functionalist technique and Margaret Mead for directly warping concepts of woman. This is inaccurate: First it was the abuse of the technique rather than the technique itself that was harmful; second, Mead herself was misinterpreted widely for the same reactionary purpose. Margaret Mead was never a supporter of paternalistic attitudes, and by the mid-fifties was strongly opposing sexism in the pages of *Life.* However, the way Mead was so very widely misinterpreted in the fifties was in itself a way of disarming her prestige as a brilliant and famous independent woman.

9. Friedan, *Mystique,* p. 185.

10. Allen Ludden, *Plain Talk for Women Under 21!* (New York, 1957), p. 1; Landis, *Your Marriage and Family Living* (St. Louis, 1954), p. 360—a high school textbook; *Making,* p. 28, a college textbook. Ludden also wrote a companion book entitled *Plain Talk for Men Under 21!*

11. Marynia Farnham and Ferdinand Lundberg, *Modern Woman: The Lost Sex* (New York, 1947). Friedan analyzes this work in her chapter on Freud, pp. 119–20.

12. Paul Gallico, "You Don't Know How Lucky You Are to Be Married," *Reader's Digest,* July 1956, pp. 134–36; Landis, *Making,* p. 11.

13. Farnham and Lundberg, *Modern Woman,* pp. 370–71; "Report Card," *Time,* March 14, 1955, p. 56.

14. Farnham and Lundberg, *Modern Woman,* pp. 364–65; "The First Baby," *Life,* December 24, 1956; David Riesman, "The Found Generation," *American Scholar,* 24 (Autumn 1956), 434.

15. Dr. Benjamin Spock, *The Common Sense Book of Baby and Child Care* (New York, 1946). Spock's book had a tremendous impact. Many millions of women literally raised their children by his book. Hundreds of writers about child care paraphrased and borrowed his ideas. His impact was not as broad as that of Farnham and Lundberg's, however, since they wrote explicitly not only about child rearing but about every aspect of contact between the sexes.

16. Philip Slater, *The Pursuit of Loneliness* (Boston, 1970), pp. 66–71; Friedan, *Mystique,* pp. 184–86; Farnham and Lundberg, *Modern Woman,* p. 171; Lawrence K. Frank and Mary Frank, *How to Be a Woman* (New York, 1954), pp. 65–66. In the copy of this booklet we consulted, a title page graffito captured the spirit of the whole booklet very shrewdly. Underneath "How to Be a Woman," someone scrawled "wear tight sweaters."

17. Landis, *Making,* pp. 74–75.

18. Pat Boone, *'Twixt Twelve and Twenty* (New York, 1958), pp. 83–84; Schindler, *Guide,* p. 405. See also Enid Haupt, *The Seventeen Book of Young Living* (New York, 1957), p. 201, where the teen-age girl audience is assured that while marriage is "a partnership," "there can be only one head of a happy home—and that is, by law, by taste, by census, and by women's intuition, the husband." Haupt, too, is an example of a very typical fifties phenomenon—the successful career woman who advises women away from public life and nondomestic interests. Mid-seventies versions of this phenomenon include singer Tammy Wynette ("Stand By Your Man") and Marabelle Morgan (author of *Total Woman*), both talented and competent women who preach female submissiveness while standing at the hubs of successful and vast businesses.

19. Lelord Kordel, "Husbands, Wives, and Other Women," *Coronet,* July 1953, pp. 131–36. This sort of logic, in only a slightly different light, can convolute itself to justify rape: "I couldn't help it, she provoked me with her constant desirability."

20. Sochen, *Movers,* pp. 203–7. One part of Kinsey's report did enter popular culture—the section about the failure of large percentages of educated women ever to have experienced orgasm.

21. Hannah Lees, "What Every Husband Needs," *Reader's Digest,* October 1957, p. 139. A corollary to this attitude was that the husband who had outside affairs usually did so because his wife was inadequate and had failed to cater to his sexual needs. Similarly, the wife was also faulted for male impotence—or else the man's mother was blamed. Another article by Lees, in the May 1957 *Digest,* is titled "How to Be Happy Though Incompatible."

22. Farnham and Lundberg, *Modern Woman,* pp. 266–67.

23. Indianapolis *News* quoted in *The New Yorker,* January 21, 1956. One could also cite a fascinating array of calisthenics having nothing to do with physical health—for instance, exercises to make the voice husky and sexy. When a woman is regarded as accessory to a man, the parts of her body too are re-

duced to the status of simple objects, as in the nylon stocking ad from the fifties advising "your legs are your most important accessory." *Life,* July 21, 1958, printed a letter from a Connecticut corset manufacturer who had "brought out the girdle with the padded stern to help American girls achieve the Brigitte Bardot 'corkscrew walk' you mentioned. . . . Since your story has been published dozens of men and women have urged me to rename my 'Young Derriere' the 'Brigitte Bardot Girdle.' Since I need her permission to do so, does she wear a girdle?" *Life* just replied: "No."

24. Gimbel's ad quoted in Sidonie Gruenberg and Hilde S. Krech, *The Many Lives of Modern Woman* (Garden City, 1952), p. 10.

25. Lynn White, Jr., *Educating Our Daughters* (New York, 1950), pp. 18, 57.

26. Friedan, *Mystique,* pp. 142, 148–50; White, *Educating,* pp. 77–78. White also suggested the middle-aged woman whose children had moved away should by no means seek an actual professional job, nor a compelling hobby. He insisted on deliberately frustrating interests: "A woman who wants some really novel experiences may start a campaign to rid her city or county of . . . the billboard." Of course, "the billboards will remain and multiply . . . but at least she will have had a rigorous adult education course in local politics. Then she can relax and devote herself to the alumnae activities of the institution from which she graduated." *Making,* pp. 115–17.

27. Landis, *Making,* pp. 59–60, 60–61, 75–76.

28. Haupt, *Seventeen Book,* p. 55.

29. Frank and Frank, *How to Be a Woman,* p. 3 and title page. See also Robert Hutchins, *Some Observations on American Education* (Cambridge, Eng., 1956), in opposition to the special education concept, and also the interview with Flo Kennedy in *Ms.,* February 1973, about her attempt to get into Columbia Law school in the mid-fifties. Also of interest is the October 16, 1950 *Life,* which contains several features about women's higher learning. They include a full-color picture story about Gulf Park By-the-Sea, a southern finishing college. The women at this school were never permitted to wear slacks, and so are shown participating in various activities like oil painting and sculpture, wearing pastel dresses and high heels. The popularity of such schools, *Life* noted, was rising. Another article in the issue included photos of Mills College's marriage majors.

30. "Women Hold Third of Jobs," *Life,* December 24, 1956, pp. 30–35. Noted the magazine, "patient and dexterous, she does well on repetitive, detailed factory work; compassionate, she becomes teacher and nurse." The accompanying photos show sewing machine operators, nurses, secretaries, food processors, chorus girls, and even executives.

31. Farnham and Lundberg, *Modern Woman,* p. 235; "A New Look at the American Woman," *Look,* October 16, 1956, pp. 35–42—the cover of this issue blurbed "The American Woman: She's Winning the Battle of the Sexes."

32. Wattenberg, *This U.S.A.,* pp. 168–69.

33. Jacques Barzun, *God's Country and Mine* (Boston, 1954), p. 317; Ian Fleming, *Casino Royale* (New York, 1953), p. 35.

34. Merle Miller is quoted in *Esquire,* July 1973, p. 126; Landis, *Making,* p. 53; Farnham and Lundberg, *Modern Woman,* pp. 228–29.

35. Robert Coughlan, "Changing Roles in Modern Marriage," *Life,* December 24, 1956, pp. 109–11. The reader interested in a summary of the various ideas about women in the decade should consult this issue. It includes every shade of opinion, from Coughlan's highly emotional Freudian attacks all the way to Margaret Mead's comments against paternalism. The bulk of the issue is weighted more toward the former. Cornelia Otis Skinner, for instance, opposes the working woman as silly. She cites "lady bullfighters" and bassoonists to illustrate her point.

36. Landis, *Making,* pp. 55, 60–61, 78; also Slater, *Pursuit,* pp. 72–74. Landis elsewhere advised married women they could indeed have a career "with only short interruptions." His idea of a short interruption? If the woman has a small family, "say two or three children—if they are born close together—take up only about 20 years of the mother's life."

37. "All About Eve," *Reader's Digest,* October 1957, p. 197; living room anecdote quoted in "Anticlimax Department," *New Yorker,* August 25, 1951, p. 65. See also any of the Rosamond Du Jardin romance books, for instance *The Real Thing* (New York, 1956).

38. *Time,* December 29, 1952, p. 72; Leopold Stein, *Loathsome Women* (New York, 1959), p. 77. For those interested in the subject of psychiatry as enforcer of the status quo and of male dominance, this book is most revealing. Stein's loathsome women are three patients whom he says are unable to fit into their feminine roles. One of them, a successful businesswoman, complains that since she has been going to him, she feels much more unhappy and miserable. That, he writes, is her own fault. Elsewhere, Stein compares his treatment of these patients to rape.

39. Mickey Spillane, *One Lonely Night* (New York, 1951); Malcolm Cowley, "Sex Murder Incorporated," *New Republic,* February 11, 1952, pp. 17–18; Charles J. Rolo, "Metaphysics of Murder for the Millions," in Bernard Rosenberg and David M. White, eds., *Mass Culture* (Glencoe, Ill., 1957), pp. 167–69. We are also indebted to an unpublished paper on Spillane's women by Kay Weibel.

40. Arthur Schlesinger, Jr., *The Politics of Hope* (New York, 1963), pp. 237–46—this section decries Americans' general loss of identity and therefore their sexual confusion. But its major focus is on "what has happened to the American male." *Time,* October 13, 1952, p. 118.

41. Mickey Spillane, in *Vengeance Is Mine* (New York, 1950), grapples with the homosexuality question. He is investigating a call-girl and blackmail ring when he meets the beautiful Juno Reeves, "queen of all the lesser gods and goddesses." While he is incredibly attracted to her, something about her repels him too. At book's end she turns out to be the blackmailer and murderer and Hammer, killing her, discovers she is a man in drag. He manages at once to penetrate her with his sexual bullets and eradicate her sexual threat. This is one of Spillane's most important books in terms of his sexual fantasies.

42. "The Many-Handed Woman," *Look,* April 24, 1951, p. 63.

43. Elvis Presley, "Wear My Ring Around Your Neck," recorded on RCA;

Ray Charles, "I've Got a Woman," Progressive, BMI. Joe Turner's song by Charles Calhoun, "Shake, Rattle, and Roll," is also of interest, as are the many wedding songs of the fifties and early sixties—"A Casual Look" and "To the Aisle" are good examples.

44. Paul Goodman, *Growing Up Absurd* (New York, 1960), pp. 13, 185–87, 52.

45. Lawrence Lipton, *The Holy Barbarians* (New York, 1959); Jack Kerouac, *On the Road* (New York, 1957), see p. 168. A Doris Day and Frank Sinatra movie called *Young at Heart* (1954) is a simple summary of all the things the Beats meant by the dangerous woman. Sinatra falls in love with bland, blond Day simply because she always nags him to press his pants, be on time, comb his hair, wear a necktie, and otherwise measure up to the middle class.

46. Norman Mailer, *Barbary Shore* (New York, 1951), pp. 157, 206 (see also pp. 129, 157); Mailer, "The White Negro," in *Advertisements for Myself* (New York, 1959), p. 351; Mailer, *The Deer Park* (New York, 1967)—this is the play version of the novel published in the fifties.

47. Dr. William G. Niederland, "Masculine Women Are Cheating Love!", *Coronet,* May 1953, pp. 41–44. See also Schindler, *Woman's Guide,* especially p. 401, the section entitled "Why Are So Many Women Failures?" Schindler estimates between 50 and 75 per cent of American medical practice dealt with emotionally induced illnesses, and three times as many women as men suffered from these.

48. Emily Kimbrough, "She Needs Some Years of Grace," *Life,* December 24, 1956, p. 28; Eve Merriam, "Are Housewives Necessary?", *Nation,* November 30, 1959, pp. 98–99. Merriam pointed out that the new domesticity was proving very profitable for many industries. This, of course, was no historical novelty. In *Century of Struggle,* Eleanor Flexner documented the way various interest groups (liquor, railroad, oil, and general manufacturing groups, particularly Swift meat packers, Gulf Refining, and American Express) actively interfered with the women's suffrage struggle, postponing its success by as much as 50 years.

49. "Girl in Trouble," *True Story,* January 1951, p. 87. Wattenberg notes (p. 41) that working women bore babies at a 50 per cent higher rate in 1960 than in 1950. Merriam published a book called *After Nora Slammed the Door* (Cleveland, 1964). This book has been unfairly eclipsed by Friedan's; Merriam's is both broader and more poetic.

7

Three-Fifths of a Person

"What ever happened to all those wonderful old Negro cooks?" a writer inquired in a 1952 *Holiday* magazine article on southern food. "Have all the Mammy Lou's and Uncle Ned's migrated north to play character parts for TV?"[1]

There has always been a great deal of tension between rhetoric and reality in the American experiment. This has been particularly true in racial matters: we proclaim true democracy but exclude non-whites from its sweep. By 1950, the tension this produced would bring American race matters to an uneasy, complex point.

The very space between people's words about ethnic equality and its facts underlined every aspect of this conflict. The most prominent ethnic concern in the decade was about "the Negro Problem," posed by the existence of a large black minority. For blacks, much of the twentieth century had been a moving toward the confrontation of bigotry. World War II itself had ostensibly been fought against a monstrous racist threat. But young black soldiers found themselves segregated during the war, treated as inferior. Ludicrously, they often had fewer privileges than the German POWs they might be escorting. To the anger this provoked in blacks was added an optimistic dimension. Some serious proposals against prejudice were being posed on the home front. In 1941, for instance, when A. Philip Randolph organized a huge march on Washington against job discrimination, Franklin D. Roosevelt headed it off by signing a Fair Employment order. In 1944, the NAACP won a long court fight to have the white-only voting primary rendered illegal. Black pride was strengthened, too, by the worldwide collapse of white colonialism, with independent nonwhite nations rising in its stead. These various steps prompted many American blacks to admit their bitter situation. To them, life was becoming daily more tender and difficult. One minor occurrence, in 1945, indicates this growing sensitivity. Walter Winchell asked a young black woman in Harlem how Hitler should be punished for his crimes against humanity. She replied, "Paint him black and send him over here."[2]

Black veterans returning from the First World War had also been eager to move against racism. But they were crushed by violence from the white power structure. The many anti-black race riots of 1919 and the rise of the Ku Klux Klan in the early twenties were two arms of the reaction. In the latter forties, though, genuine changes did seem to be eroding racism. By 1950, blacks were earning more than four times their 1940 wages. More legal breakthroughs had been secured, such as Truman's army desegregation order of 1948 and the Supreme Court decisions through 1950 that desegregated graduate schools in the South. Such trends appeared to persist in the fifties. The great migration of blacks out of the rural South accelerated. By 1960, for the first time in history, more blacks would be living in urban areas than rural. Moreover, in both 1957 and 1960, civil rights acts were passed by Congress, each concerned with improving black voting rights. Blacks, it seemed, had it better than ever. Such tangible changes led black reporter George Schuyler to optimistically note in a 1951 *Reader's Digest:* "the progressive improvement of race relations and the economic rise of the Negro in the United States is a flattering example of democracy in action."[3]

But what sort of gains had really been made? Did they continue to be made? It was true that by 1950 black wages had greatly increased. But this economic advance was not at all as great as the gains of whites. In 1950, white male workers earned a median wage of $2,982 compared to non-white males' $1,828, 61 per cent of the white median. By 1960, the situation was slightly worse. A median white male income of $5,137 could be compared to non-white earnings of $3,075, 60 per cent of the former. In the period between 1952 and 1963 the average income of black families nationally in relation to white ones *fell*, from 57 per cent to 43 per cent.[4] Similar patterns were true in every age, sex, and education group.

The major legal improvements of the forties, too, were more symbolic and rhetorical than tangible. That 1944 Supreme Court order against all-white primaries, for instance, was simply ignored in many parts of the South. Very few blacks got as far as graduate studies, making that series of desegregation orders relatively meaningless. Thurgood Marshall, visiting Korea as an NAACP lawyer, found the army desegregation order to have no effect on old lines of privilege. Perhaps the most gross display of the order's inadequacy appeared in courts-martial. Vastly disproportionate numbers of black GIs were convicted of all sorts of crimes, particularly the more serious ones like sleeping on duty. They also received much more severe sentencing. Marshall found that white soldiers charged with the same crimes that brought blacks severe penalties tended to be acquitted. In some cases acquittal went to whites who had not even defended themselves and had confessed.[5]

Through the fifties, mock attempts at equality continued to substitute for the actual thing. The civil rights acts of 1957 and 1960 were weak and difficult to enforce. In the book about the 1960 census, *This U.S.A.*, Ben Wattenberg noted the foreshortened earning power of blacks. His comment on this can be extended to the entire position of blacks and browns in America: "regardless of level of education, on an income standard the Negro today can still be counted as that 'three-fifths of a person' that the *unamended* Constitution declared him to be."[6]

All this puts the comments of a black reporter like Schuyler in a wholly different perspective. On one level his words seem to be a classic example of Uncle Tomming. He spent a lot of time in the *Reader's Digest* article making partial betterment, grudging gains and "nearlys" and "almosts" seem both thoroughly satisfying to non-whites and a whole struggle already won to whites. He was pleased about black health statistics that in any other context would be shocking: "today their life expectancy is 60 years, only eight years less than that of American whites." Schuyler went on to draw an international comparison: "The most 'exploited' Negroes in Mississippi are better off than the citizens of Russia."[7]

That Schuyler felt the need to employ this remark, though, is a clue to another level beneath his pleasantries. The "better off than the Russians" argument was heard in many quarters in those years. Its usual function was to smother dissent: how dare you complain since you are so much better off than. . . . During those years, blacks as well as whites were touched by the forced, frightened consensus seizing the land. But more factors than the pervasive threats of cold war, bomb, and McCarthy affected them. For blacks, flux and pressure were even greater than for whites. A population whose major occupation had been agriculture, and which was concentrated in the rural South, was being driven off the land by factory farming. Discarded by modernized agrobusiness, blacks headed by the millions for the urban industrial centers. Such a great migration had to have its message of hope, of promised and won opportunity. All these factors of conformity and longing melted together. This was why, in spite of the black militancy apparent in 1945, activism was delayed so many years. Americans in general withdrew from action. Weary of oppression, in flux, pushed into worried silence, blacks came to exaggerate a few tangible changes into rainbows of achievement. One cannot fight forever; nor when withdrawing or preoccupied can one identify rest with defeat. Changes must be happening; blacks had to believe this.[8]

Whites, too, wanted to think so of race relations. But this time the optimism existed for different reasons. In the late forties, Soviet diplomats began to use America's racism as a diplomatic device, to embarrass. This, after all, was a world where whites were a mere minority. The American consensus vision, moreover, demanded complete praise for American ideals and seemed to describe a country of freedom and hope. Racism was unflattering to these facades. It had to be officially decried. As one of Truman's attorney generals said, it "furnishes grist for the Communist propaganda mills, and it raises doubts even among friendly nations as to the intensity of our devotion to the democratic faith." In addition to being impractical on an international scale, discrimination also put a needless economic burden on local communities. To condemn part of the populace was a pragmatic error, as Frederick Lewis Allen warned.[9] All these practical, face- and money-saving considerations had prompted the forties legal breakthroughs. Genuine moral indignation, or the desire to right stupendous wrongs, had little to do with it. But at least these justifications proffered a dim recognition that racism did exist, and that it was somehow not very nice.

But racial awareness froze at that point for many years. To an extent, this happened because of the way Americans handled many problems in the fifties. A problem is recognized; it is acknowledged to be un-American and wrong; then it is pronounced to be vanishing—because people now care. Now you see it. Now you don't. The conflict is won with words alone. Liberal intellectuals helped further this habit. Max Lerner's statement is typical: "The Negro is entering into the full stream of our effort, helped by the great assimilative energies of an impersonal economy, a legal system which is ceaselessly being used on his side, and the conscience of decent men."[10] With the finest, kindest intentions, Lerner was acknowledging certain essential inequities in American life—and in terms strikingly like those of reporter Schuyler's. But curiously, given the context of each man's place in American culture, the two comments function in completely different ways. Lerner's remarks, in particular, both reveal and dismiss prejudice. Schuyler's article offered much more than a pandering everything-is-great vision of race relations. The reporter was providing a protective wall for blacks. His words were part of the withdrawal from activism, risk, and white incursion. Lerner, conversely, was trying to express concerned guilt. He was not challenging any of the basic ideas that forwarded the practice of racism. His view, essentially, was based on the dream of a middle-class world where crime was rare and could be handled in the courts with just ease; where all were swept up by the gains of industrial change; where all were equally rewarded for good work; and most of all where people were rational, kind, logical, sensitive, and decent. Lerner chose to neglect the realities of his world. He overlooked the way post-1945 economic gains had excluded fully a third of the people. He neglected the role of civil rights leaders in prodding "the conscience of decent men." Lerner also forgot that discrimination in the form of voter disfranchisement, job and wage inequities, segregated educational facilities, cultural notions of supremacy and a conveniently limited white conscience were the stuff of everyday living for blacks.[11] Like Schuyler, Lerner presented racism as a vanishing trifle. But because of his social and cultural position as a white, northern, influential intellectual, the impact of his words was quite different. He meant well. But in the last analysis his assurances were dangerous. They encouraged the idea the "Negro problem" was vanishing—by making Negroes invisible. At least mentally there were no more Negroes. Static smugness could be reinforced. Dynamic concern was discouraged.

Many prominent people, from politician to intellectual, made similar and nearly interchangeable statements in those years. The stifling of the old left, too, prevented any different voices from being widely heard. Any popular realization of widespread bigotry was blocked. Instead, only the perceived rise of black status outside the Deep South was highly publicized. Often, this was proved with a list of "firsts" or "breakthroughs." The unusual and brilliant successes of a very few blacks were held up as typical: Dr. Ralph Bunche, Althea Gibson, and Jackie Robinson were the most frequently mentioned. Such successes were held to be filtering down to less visible levels. *U.S. News & World Report* cited the "nearly 200" black professors teaching at white colleges, black congressmen in three states, black councilmen in 15 cities. The racial walls, as seen by the mass media, were tumbling down. Frederick Lewis Allen selected another biblical metaphor in titling his chapter on civil rights in *The Big Change* "Ol' Ark a-Moverin'."[12]

The condescension underlying such a semantic choice was inherent in much of the media approach to black rights. Opinions expressed in mainstream journalism are critical here. A few reporters attempted to write about racism with genuine feeling. But many more, and many publishers, were unable to get around the old racial notions. *U.S. News* approvingly quoted a white personnel officer who explained, "a few years ago it was almost impossible to place a Negro girl as secretary. Now it's getting harder to find really good secretaries, so employers are beginning to ask us for anyone who can do the job regardless of color." Vance Packard, in one of his books, felt black spending power was an index of their equality: "Advertisers are also enthusiastic champions of the Negro's right to consume the good things of American life. Negroes—as they have acquired skills and buying power—have become a $15,000,000 market."[13] There are certain unworded assumptions in these comments, dealing with preservation of privilege, with power and order. But perhaps the essential attitude was that blacks were not expected to realize how their new liberty was merely someone else's profit. They were, however, expected to be grateful.

With the vision of hindsight, we smile or tremble at such open talk. We are disturbed by the tone of these remarks, evoking an arrogant welfare department or the doling out of charity. We imagine anyone could see clearly the trickery involved. We think the way the power system refused to be budged by egalitarianism is betrayed, and that it stands revealed before its mass white audience. But in those times, it was not so obvious to the white mainstream that such statements were a ruse. The mainstream chose to be fascinated with other things. (Weren't most whites then delighted with the "right to consume"?) With games the daily stuff of life, self-examination was stifled. Only logical and passionate analysis, going beyond the feelings stirred by ideas like the "right to consume," would point to the actual beneficiaries of fifties-style black freedom: the same old whites.

For much of the decade, racism was seen by non-Southerners as existing only in the South. The secondary factors producing the distortion were, first, media coverage of the great events of modern racism, and second, the publicity surrounding active change. The 1954 Brown decision gave the rest of the country license to be appalled at the southern lifestyle. This was an unfair distraction from northern bigotry. But the South was scarcely blameless. Life for blacks in the South—particularly in rural areas in the Deep South—was a literal hell. Refined southern gentility rested on a system of brutality, cruelty, economic disadvantage, humiliation, sexual subjugation, and, of course, the utter theft of legal rights. But the simple mechanistic approach to problem solving that gripped the country in the fifties extended here too. The South, it was felt, could be cured of its racism with one simple device: the 1954 Supreme Court decision, *Brown* v. *Board of Education of Topeka.* It was actually expected that this order forbidding the racial segregation of southern schools would cause racist practices to melt away overnight.[14] When many in the South refused to have change imposed on them from outside, and instead became crueler and harsher than before, Northerners had even more excuse to be shocked and titillated.

And titillated they were. There was an intense fascination/repulsion in statements like Ross Barnett's: "The Negro is different because God made him different to punish him. His forehead slants back. His nose is different. His legs are different, and his color is sure different. . . . We will not drink from the cup of genocide." There were stories about the day-by-day inhumanity inherent in Jim Crow: the shooting of black prisoners when higher courts upset their rape convictions, the mob murders of Mack Parker and Emmett Till, lynching, disfranchisement, rape fantasies, miscegenation forced daily on black women. Sometimes it seemed that mobs would appear at the drop of a hat (or the transfer of one black student or the pronouncement of one demagogic speech).[15]

Events at Little Rock in 1957–58 served to underscore the nonsouthern attitude. Much of Arkansas, before this time, had been quietly integrating its schools. On September 2, 1957, with the Little Rock schools about to integrate, Governor Orval Faubus made a radio speech. Declaring that razor-toting blacks were planning mass attacks on whites, he closed the schools and called out the state militia. Faubus' demagoguery had the intended effect: segregationists were heartened to rally around the separatist cause. Mobs of whites rioted, preventing nine black students from entering Central High. Only when Eisenhower reluctantly sent in federal troops, late in the month, were the schools forcibly integrated. Because he procrastinated, the situation could only worsen. The world was treated to photos of dignified black youth walking calmly before jeering, hideous whites, and also to the image of one branch of government putting down a mob incited by another. Later, when Minnijean Brown, one of the nine students, was expelled permanently for defending herself from a bullying white girl, school officials felt the need to quell the anger of local whites. "She was fighting back—and that is impossible," one official announced. "The Negroes cannot afford to fight back."[16] The Kafkaesque double bind of the southern way of life was appalling. It provided many Americans their introduction to the idea of smug and insensitive authority and the caprice of law. Most of all, such violent events allowed a whole region to condemn itself.

So the South's image became a monolithic one. It neglected the way any geographical region varies, and the way people themselves vary. It particularly ignored the existence of the moderate Southerner, who believed in civil rights but often had been cowed or bullied into silence. Only rarely was a southern moderate treated approvingly in the northern media. Probably the favorite was

Harry Golden, the ex-New Yorker who published the *Carolina Israelite*. Golden created a wonderfully funny "VERTICAL NEGRO PLAN" to solve school segregation. Noting "VERTICAL SEGREGATION" had been virtually eliminated in the South—with blacks and whites alike walking through, standing, and purchasing in the same places—Golden explained that "it is only when the Negro 'sets' that the fur begins to fly." His was a simple solution: "provide *only* desks in all the public schools of our state—*no seats.*" Since no one would be sitting down, no one would get angry; moreover, it would save millions of dollars in furniture bills.[17]

Golden's humor was received with gratitude in the long, tense controversy. But more usually the southern moderate was regarded with scorn in the North. Just as southern extralegal violence introduced people to the arrogance of power, so would the questionable efficacy of moderation in the South eventually indict this as a means of change. Such groups as the white southern churchwomen might be sympathetic; they might help a few people out, but their basic inability to visualize, much less modify, essential corruption spoke against them. Too, many moderates were condemned for their moral cowardice. Golden himself lamented the silence of the southern moderate before the cruel indecency of leaders and hotheads. One of the great lessons of such events as Little Rock was the way moderation turned to silent passivity before bullies.[18] Such a spineless collapse during a true test of values certainly merited attack. But the message of the South as a total sink of iniquity in the fifties does deserve modification.

It was quite easy for Northerners to emit this message. The South's flaws, its viciousness, and fear were obvious. But it is especially crucial to place those evils in a larger context. In the fifties, a mood of moral apathy before demagogues prevailed. These were the years of security checks, of conformity trampling over personality, of individuality allowed only within a narrow norm. Most people did not stand up and protest this nationwide rape of autonomy. Nor did they protest when the few dissenters were punished, fired, harassed. People, whether moderate or conservative, justified these encroachments, or ignored them, and pandered to mass pressures. It is neither a flattering nor a pleasant thing to remember. Indeed just such mass cowardice has been true more often than not throughout American history. Why, particularly at this time of almost universal cowardice, should the South have been the only place labeled so sinful?

Essentially the blame fell disproportionately on the South because the North chose to ignore its own racism. Virtually a whole region was practicing what is called the externalizing of undesirable traits. Usually this idea is used in terms of social classes. An economically dominant group justifies its superiority by attributing its undesirable traits (emotionalism, sensuality) to an inferior group (blacks, women). If such traits appear in a member of the superior group, it is a sign of individual inferiority, not an indication of a universal human feeling.

Similarly, the North refused to see its own prejudices by insisting all bigotry lodged in the South. If such behavior cropped up outside the South, it was an aberration. The North, moreover, still fed off the moral self-congratulations accrued in the Civil War. Northerners continued to regard themselves as the great liberators of the slaves. The massive migration of blacks out of the rural South fed these dreams. Whites imagined they gave refuge to all those millions of hapless blacks fleeing the southern hell. Often it was as though such fancied refuge was quite enough, and alone proved the freedom of the North: we have given you liberty. Now shut up. This very self-satisfaction rose from the contrast between two behaviors: apparent southern blatancy versus apparent northern liberty. That is, what mattered was not the practice of discrimination, so much as one's public conduct. More, the conduct being judged was *white* behavior; what happened to blacks and how blacks were harmed by all this was secondary.

Jacques Barzun covertly admitted this early in the decade. Deploring the rising "militancy" of black people, he wrote of New York City "where handsome and expensively dressed Negroes—usually women—will arrogantly elbow white people out of their way and shout down expostulations." This, he added, "is almost the only instance of bad public behavior one notices traveling in America." When Barzun wrote this, the bad public behavior of segregated southern restaurants and washrooms, motels and schools was commonplace, as were lynchings and northern race incidents. Still, he felt, it would be difficult for white people to really emancipate blacks. So many blacks, Barzun felt, "are ignorant, irresponsible, unhygienic." The editor of the Des Moines *Register* accurately described the motivation behind such comments. He called it the northern "moral blind spot."[19] Certainly the symbolism of physical crippling is brought to mind: deafness, blindness, a voluntary dulling of the senses are compelling explanations for such persistent racial doublethink.

The blind spot was sustained not by day-to-day terrorism but more powerfully by a cultural belief in white supremacy running deep and insidious through America's culture and institutions. The white-is-right ethic was and remains subtly all-pervasive. Consider the standards of beauty: gentlemen preferring blondes (even phony blondes); flesh-colored Band-aids; lily-white children's dolls. Commercials pervaded the American consciousness. In them, success and attractiveness all were a white skin. Semantics also expressed this: think of "blackmail," "blackball," or "the blackest episode." Word concepts of blackness or darkness meant evil, corruption, or, as in the idea "blackballing," being inferior and outcast. Devil and outlaw both traditionally appear in black.

Television, a forties novelty, quickly saturated fifties households. It restated all the old racial clichés in its new way. At this time, a very few Hollywood films had begun to move beyond those clichés. TV networks countered that trend by airing the prefifties movies with their full complements of servile blacks, jungle savages, and brutal Indians. New series programs were scarcely more innocent. On prime-time TV, one could find all the servants (Rochester on Jack Benny's show), noble savages (Tonto on *The Lone Ranger*), lazy Mexican peasants (on *Zorro*) and wise old Orientals (*Charlie Chan*) of myth.[20] The only way TV attempted to circumvent these stereotypes was, eventually, to depict non-white people as little as possible.

In the late forties, some few Hollywood films began offering sympathetic portraits of black people acting like average members of society. Sometimes blacks were even shown troubled by problems that were real, as opposed to phony white-oriented problems like "passing." On the whole, however, Hollywood still created an absurd picture of race problems. There was, for instance, the long series of tragic mulatto women doomed by their racial taint. Usually these women were portrayed by white actresses such as Ava Gardner or Natalie Wood. A 1959 movie, *Band of Angels*, perhaps best summarizes the failure of Hollywood to adequately challenge racial beliefs. Black novelist John O. Killens remembers: "In one particular scene, Clark Gable, who was Sidney Poitier's good massa, was coming from New Orleans via the Mississippi River back to his plantation. When the boat neared the shore, all of his happy faithful slaves were gathered there singing a song of welcome to old massa. White people in the theater were weeping, some slyly, some unashamedly, at the touching scene, when suddenly my friend and I erupted with laughter, because we thought that surely, in the time of Montgomery and Little Rock, this must have been put in for comic relief."[21]

The major thing about Killens' reaction to this fantasy film was the way he could view it with wry, sardonic rejection. Such a reaction was only becoming openly, verbally possible toward the end of the fifties. Even then it was not widespread. More often, the total pressure of a white-is-right culture on non-whites was internalized to create terrible conflict and anguish. When well-being, beauty, and success are measured by white standards, non-whites are inevitably trapped. They feel love toward white people because they long to be like them; that is, to be beautiful and lucky. But they hate whites too. This happens not only because they can never become white, non-whites experience all the cruelty of their oppression daily. Humiliation is systematically applied.

The love/hate born in such a system was largely directed against the self. At mid-decade, Richard Wright would call this double bind the "abiding schism." Self-esteem was crippled.[22] In front of whites, blacks might twist themselves into caricatures to avoid being singled out: acting stupid, sloppy, servile, using bad grammar. Blacks also learned to suspect their own bodies—and so tried to conk kinky hair, or played the Dozens ("your mother is blacker than mine" as insult).

Such behaviors were signs of a very severe self-denial. One's own physical traits were undesirable. Therefore they were ridiculed. The self-obliteration this implied had a destructive effect. As one critic noted, "a person who has been attacked, violated, abused—especially over a long period of time—has, in fact, been doubly abused. First, by the act itself. Second, by the changes in his personality . . . wrought by his submissive position." These changes include the way non-whites' shortcomings and weaknesses were encouraged. One's personal failure, moreover, could be wholly blamed on white bigotry—which Bayard Rustin deplored as a "lamentable dodge." Yet the dodge came to be furthered by white liberal guilt, applauding even mediocre black achievements.[23] In all these fashions, the unworded racism ingrained in American culture first crippled the self-esteem of non-whites, then rewarded that crippling. One became used to the thousand little humiliations and accommodations of getting along in a white man's world. More, in getting used to it one became hostile to any idea of changing that world.

That any such conflict existed in non-whites was barely recognized in the culture. Often, when such frictions were seen, they were only recognized peripherally. They were regarded as mental disease. Such labeling, in the fifties, was a powerful way of indicating that something—a behavior, or an idea—was unacceptable to a contracting social order. Communists, for example, were labeled mentally ill, as were Beats, unmarried adults, teen-age non-virgin girls, and working mothers. Professing any unpopular notion proved one was mentally suspect. In these years, many whites felt that all blacks wanted integration. The idea that some blacks preferred segregation, or even the deplorable status quo, did not follow. It must be crazy.

A most revealing example of this whole labeling process began in a Harlem department store in September 1958. An autograph party was in progress for the author of a new book, *Stride Toward Freedom.* "Suddenly she shouted something about all 'the trouble' he had caused for the Negro people in fighting segregation," *Newsweek* later reported. Then Mrs. Isola Ware Curry, a 42-year-old black woman, stabbed Martin Luther King in the upper left chest. *Time* too sought to play up the craziness of the event. "Onlookers grabbed the deranged woman and held her for police as she babbled incoherently and shouted: 'I'm glad I done it.'" Both magazines noted the irony of such a near-successful attack in the midst of the North's largest black community. King was hospitalized. Mrs. Curry was indicted on a charge of attempted murder. But she never went to trial. Taken to Bellevue for observation, she was declared incompetent to be tried, and committed to New York's Matteawan State Hospital for an indefinite term. As an AP dispatch finally reported, "she never gave a coherent reason for the attack."[24]

One finds many disturbing undercurrents beneath these minimal news stories. Primarily, there is the question raised by that last AP comment on Mrs. Curry's motivation: to whom must her attack be coherent? In both magazine accounts of the attack, Mrs. Curry was quoted as having shouted something. Once she cried that King was causing blacks trouble with his activism. Again she announced she was glad she'd tried to kill him. That is, she had a motivation (however strange and ugly) for her act, and she expressed responsibility for that act.

Look again at the way these publications presented the Curry case. Her entire previous life was mentioned solely in terms of her moving from her native South back and forth to Harlem, as though she was an unstable Bedouin or vagrant. She was termed "deranged." She "babbled incoherently." These were serious judgments—written, moreover, before she had been committed. Having performed an almost incomprehensible act, she was tried for it in the media. As it turned out, that was her only trial.

Curry's case also illustrates the way a social order with little room for variation uses psychiatry to enforce consensus. That idea may be rephrased: security in fifties America depended on narrow, familiar cultural borders, carefully and fearfully guarded. To deeply examine the unfamiliar was also to threaten the familiar. One does not simply delve into Curry's ideas: the investigator at the same time unavoidably digs into her or his own psyche, and the culture's. Clearly the questions Mrs. Curry's case might summon were too intense, too dangerous. As Dr. Thomas Szasz has noted in his discussion of the issue, "I do not know what the psychiatric findings were in this case. But no matter what they were, they could not, *in themselves,* justify her commitment to a state hospital. . . . The point is that she broke the law, and something had to be done about her. Under the circumstances putting her away quietly was the socially preferred course of action."[25] She had to be labeled insane, to maintain the official version of sanity.

C. Wright Mills' concept of the unconscious conspiracy is also relevant here. Mills noted that a group of people with similar fears and goals need not articulate any conspiracy in order to act in concert. They simply had to perceive the same goals. In this instance there could well be a shared disinterest and fear of examining Curry's act in public. To have her judged insane concealed many problems. The function of this labeling was to deny her act any rationality or motivation. It denied any awareness in her of the very real tensions of the fifties racial scene (which she was verbalizing). It denied the intense inner harm wrought upon blacks by racism, the existence of a distinct black experience and of class hostilities within black life. It even denied she had done anything wrong.

After all, she never was tried. But most of all, in eradicating her legal right to trial, her commitment handily removed any need to expose all these things in court. Curry's commitment was a warning: just as we believe in only one kind of bigot (southern-style) we believe in only one black voice (middle-class, integrationist, educated). The possibility of anything else is suppressed.

All this harm was a matter of choice. Whites *chose* to remain blind to their own bigotry against non-whites. The suppression was individual, internalized as well as institutionalized. Racism was put outside. It existed, if at all, in some phantom elsewhere like the South or the mind of a deranged black.

Another way of regarding the phantom and the damage it caused to the national landscape is to examine American residential patterns in the fifties. Housing changed in a most important way in those years. Much of this change appeared to be due to rising affluence. But other more damaging processes were hidden in this affluence. Two million blacks moved out of the rural South in the fifties alone. Only 150,000 of these remained in the South. The rest concentrated primarily in the 12 big metropolitan areas of America. Driven off the land, they looked for freedom and opportunity. But they found, instead, the same old story: poor housing in closely defined areas, government apathy, and high rents. Slumlords welcomed the new black occupants: the profit potential was tremendous. Very often, such landlords pursued the short-term course. They raised the rent while cutting out services and repairs. City officials, too, simply did not care about a group lacking political clout. Without direct political representation, blacks found municipal services in their neighborhoods increasingly corrupt. The schools were poor, the cops crooked, the trash not picked up. Mix these together: rotting physical plants, little check against crime, few opportunities to rise, a subtle cultural system of racism, plus some half-hopeful, half-desperate immigrants. The frustrating pressure to fail, to suffer and rage is nearly total.[26]

Violence was a quick result. Usually this was directed against the most visible parts of the trap—the neighborhood, the self. Perhaps the most depressing proof of this came in the huge riots of the sixties. Then, blacks wrecked not white neighborhoods but their own; and most of the people killed (whether by black snipers or white National Guardsmen) were black.

Blacks could rarely escape all this urban corrosion for the suburban dream. The fifties suburbs had first been peopled by newly affluent Americans eager to spend their money and demonstrate status. But as whites fled the cities, blacks became the major force saving the cities from total abandonment. Yet because of the visible urban rot, they came to be identified as the destroyers of cities. Such identification only provoked more whites to run away. The new developments they fled to, those built after World War II, were intended to be segregated, and primarily whites only. A very few were blacks only. The federal government had a powerful hand in this. The FHA, for instance, refused to guarantee loans for racially mixed housing projects. An FHA refusal is one of the most effective means known of destroying a potential development. By 1960, suburbs had drawn millions of whites out of the cities at the time millions of blacks were being drawn into those cities. At decade's end, America was literally more racially segregated in residential terms than it had ever been before.[27]

Imagine some of the consequences of this. Blacks were generally restricted to certain tight, eroding areas. These areas then became stigmatized by the presence of their black residents. All the modern, sparkling suburbs simultaneously created a new housing ideal. In contrast, the cities looked dirty, dilapidated, rotting away in chunks. The consumer influence made itself felt too: urban oldness itself became bad. When oldness was also blackness—since the suburbs were a contrasting white—the city situation appeared even worse.

The cities' erosion, however, was not considered hopeless. A technological solution to human suffering was acknowledged. The urban renewal program, truly, is one of the plans most indicative of fifties mainstream values. The basic tenet of urban renewal was that racial ghettoes, slums, and most of all, poverty could be eliminated simply by tearing down the old area where these things flourished, and rebuilding anew. Not only would the neighborhoods be newer and therefore better. The former residents would be renewed too.[28]

Ideally, urban renewal programs intended to recreate new housing in place of the old. Generally this would be effected in the form of high-rise apartments for the poor. But often such plans proved ineffective in relocating the residents of a bulldozed area. Urban renewal destroyed far more housing than it ever rebuilt. Some localities' programs did include the building of "projects"—subsidized low-income housing. But as Michael Harrington would later observe, too often the projects quickly evolved into welfare dumping grounds. The way people were selected to live in these dwellings encouraged them to remain poor; a slight gain in income over the permissible level meant eviction. And the projects, with their towering heights and large populations, made community areas such as laundry rooms or playgrounds remote, unfriendly, and dangerous places. Anomie, impersonalization, aimless hostility, and violence—the concentrated habituation of poverty—resulted. Very often, however, urban renewal did not even pretend to this much aid for the displaced. In many cases the poor became urban refugees. They were replaced by parks, or trees, middle- or upper-income housing, by a university or a shopping center.[29]

It is true that not all those affected by such actions were blacks. Whites, especially elderly white women and ethnic minorities, suffered greatly too. But non-whites form a disproportionate percentage of the poor. Also urban renewal tended to focus more on the colored neighborhoods. When the University of Chicago was expanding in the mid-fifties, it demonstrated a not atypical selection. A "genteel poor" black neighborhood was condemned over an even poorer and more run-down white one. Too often, that is, "slum clearance" covertly meant "Negro clearance."[30] As a bumper sticker proclaimed at mid-decade, FIGHT BLIGHT. Already "blight" to many whites had become synonymous with "blacks."

In a society that praised upward mobility, affluent blacks inevitably sought more comfortable neighborhoods. Such families could never be sure what their reception might be in affluent all-white areas. Hostility of some sort was inevitable. Violence, too, remained a capricious possibility. Perhaps there might be no incidents. Or perhaps a family might be treated like that of William and Daisy Myers. The Myers family moved with their three children into Levittown, Pennsylvania, in 1957. They became the target of mobs who threw stones and burned crosses on their lawn. An obscene phone campaign was aimed at the Myers. The house directly behind theirs became a clubhouse for the segregationist forces, who played "Old Man River" at all hours on loudspeakers. The Myers family was lucky. After William Myers appealed to the state attorney general, that official indicted eight Levittowners for conspiring against the black family. Effectively, the harassment ended. One year later, they were accepted.[31]

To win even the most simple and expected rights was often nearly impossible for blacks. In the summer of 1951, Harvey E. Clark, a Fisk graduate and black veteran, tried to move his family's furniture into an already leased apartment in Cicero, Illinois. Police stopped the moving van, Clark later testified, and the chief of police struck Clark, telling him to leave town "or you'll get a bullet through you." An NAACP suit enjoined town officials from attacking Clark. On July 10 he tried to move in again. The following day a mob of 4,000 whites attacked the apartment house and spent the next four days tearing up trees, throwing torches, bricks, and flares at the building from outside, and, from the inside, throwing out furniture, tearing down walls, and ripping out plumbing. Police joked with them. The mayor and police chief were "out of town." The state militia finally drove off the mob at bayonet point, and a grand jury was organized to investigate. It eventually issued several indictments. Indicted were an NAACP attorney, the apartment owner, her lawyer, and her rental agent. They were charged with conspiracy to injure property by causing "depreciation in the market selling price." However, some months later a federal grand jury indicted seven Cicero policemen and officials. They were charged with violating or conspiring to violate the Clarks' civil rights. Four of the seven were convicted. Meanwhile the Chicago NAACP attempted to raise enough funds so the Clarks could replace their destroyed belongings.[32]

Such white riots were not early-decade flukes. A black family moving into a white neighborhood was not regarded as following the same status ideas whites so relished. Rather, their move often was treated as a destructive, malicious act. What *U.S. News* wrote about such moves is illustrative. That magazine's lead to the story of the Myers' move read: "A normally peaceful Northern community has been thrown into turmoil by the arrival of a Negro family in its all-white precincts. Stones have been thrown, police assaulted, demonstrators arrested and fined."[33] The most outstanding thing about these sentences is the way it dodges labeling who was the aggressor, who threw those stones and hit those cops. The juxtaposition of malicious violence with the word "Negro" hinted the damage was being done wholly by blacks. The Myers family, that is, was implied to be running roughshod over Levittown, smashing and burning.

Another *U.S. News* article, in 1958, was entitled "Latest Problems for Cities in North: Blockbusting." Blockbusting, here, meant the way one house on an all-white block would secretly be sold to blacks. Often, this triggered "white flight." The semantic implications of explosive aggression in the *U.S. News* story are grave. "In city after city," began the article, "white families are likely to wake up some morning to see a Negro family moving in next door. When it happens, chances are a 'blockbuster' has been at work—and before long the whole neighborhood may be Negro."[34] It was almost as though such an affluent family, trying to rise in society, was instead bringing with it the slum (that is, "Negro") contagion; drug addicts, no garbage pickup, street hookers, and collapsed property values could not be far behind.

And that—the value of property—was the core issue. Fear and hate of blacks usually goes hand in hand with a perceived economic threat. In many parts of America, poor whites have had to compete with poor blacks for unskilled jobs. Racism justified (at many levels) the keeping of blacks out of even such work. The problem in housing is somewhat different. Middle-class families have few major investments. Generally, their biggest one is the home. The "changing" of a neighborhood was perceived to endanger that investment. As long as this perception held on, so would the tension of integrating neighborhoods. In the fifties, rather often such values did suddenly plummet when a black family moved in—simply because the rest of the neighbors rushed to sell.

The continuing of racial tensions, however, did have its beneficiaries. The white families incumbent in a neighborhood wanted to maintain property values. A new black resident, motivated by upward mobility, also had a vested interest in the area's economic well-being. Falling property values hurt these blacks as much or more. Some people, though, did have a vested interest in challenging property values: realtors, bankers, suburban developers. What could give these groups more business, and faster, than to bust a city block and stampede all the owners? The creation of a ghetto, the downgrading of a more genteel neighborhood, the existence of a racial underclass are all profitable not only for urban slumlords. The pressure on the rest of the city by a racial ghetto guarantees business for every level of the housing interests.[35]

The detrimental effects of such a residential policy are clear. The white flight that began in the fifties left the cities with a poorer, shakier tax base. Human decline of the cities accelerated in diverse ways. The building of freeway systems dissected urban areas, so suburbanites could get in and out of town faster. Too, this emphasis on the suburban commuter's car hurt interurban transportation. More and more of the city was turned over to cars and pavement, and mass transit for those within towns was played down. Business and services began to flee the cities, following the white migration. In the fifties some critics predicted urban economic collapse, and an increasing anomie and hostility within the cities. At the time, they were usually dismissed as extremists. But their predictions seem to be coming true in cities like Detroit and New York.

All these negative effects are certainly not wholly attributable to racism. But racial grounds provided much of the emotional basis for the destructive urban policies. They served as a diversion from profiteering and ruin.

What happened in housing emerges as a fifties paradigm for changes in other areas. Education, in particular, can be examined as part of this pattern. The Brown decision pointed to southern segregation as destructive. But, in spite of great publicity, by 1960 not one black child attended school with white children in five southern states. In others, officials boasted openly of the barely token integration they had achieved. In the North, schools were also intensely segregated—but this time as a consequence of housing segregation, since most kids went to neighborhood schools. Only after 1960 did Northerners begin to realize how both the artificially created ghetto and the gerrymandering of school districts had produced such de facto segregation. This discriminatory pattern extended to school funding. Northern schools were almost as prejudicial in funding black schools as their southern counterparts.[36]

The effect of education in a northern black slum school was highly similar to the very situation the Brown decision decried. The segregated environment itself declared the black student inferior. "At an underprivileged school in Harlem," Paul Goodman wrote, "they used to test the intelligence of all the children at two-year intervals. They found that every two years each advancing class came out ten points lower in native intelligence. That is, the combined efforts of home influence and school education, a powerful combination, succeeded in making the children significantly stupider year by year; if they had a few more years of compulsory education, all would end up as gibbering idiots."[37]

The spectrum of prejudicial practices should be contrasted to fifties racial rhetoric. Recall Lerner's words about ever-improving race relations. The greatest source of tension in the decade was not so much oppression itself as the glowing rhetoric which promised the racial underclasses ever more equality, ever more freedom and uplift. These fantasies first fostered hope. But hope was stymied by realities, and this defeat brought bitterness, frustration, and suppressed rage. That frustration would eventually catalyze the civil rights and black power movements.

But first these terrible tensions manifested themselves in a long-term building of racial unrest. There were nine race riots in Chicago alone between 1945 and 1954. Hundreds of lesser racial incidents also occurred. Similar patterns of hostilities erupted in nearly every urban area.[38] Ironically, the mass media often did not report such incidents. The emotional process behind this not-reporting is interesting: the logic seemed to be that we were not racially prejudiced, therefore racial incidents did not occur, or were so insignificant as to be meaningless. For most of the fifties, such conflicts were denied by most of white society. Only in the latter fifties did this begin to change. And then only a very few people looked at tensions in the urban North.

Blacks, certainly, were not the only non-whites victimized by changing racism in the fifties. Much of American foreign policy in those years was directed against non-white peoples. One might cite the fury of many Americans when China was "lost" to Mao Tse-tung—as though the Chinese were the helpless wards, or even the property of the United States. The later forties and fifties, too, were the years of America's first commitment to containment in Southeast Asia. In Indochina, we took on a modern version of Kipling's "white man's burden," with all its implications of colonialism, paternalism, interference, and scorn. A profound disdain for Asians was visible in much of the writing on our Eastern involvement. American moral ambiguities were frequently resolved by blaming the oriental character. The Korean War, for instance, too often appeared to be some massive battle against the Yellow Peril. E. J. Kahn's non-fiction work *The Peculiar War* approvingly echoed the racism of the American GI in the field. He found the country a wasteland, and attributed its poverty and ugliness to Korean sloppiness rather than to the ongoing war. Never did he come close to examining why the country seemed dirty, degraded, unattractive. At one point, a sergeant told him, "Some gooks bugged out across the field. . . . We killed all of them." "That's what we're here for," added a PFC, "to kill the bastards."[39] The enemy here was never clearly defined as a soldier, nor even specifically as a communist. He was here (as he would be later in Vietnam) that impersonal entity, the gook, eradicated for that racial reason alone. Such notions would determine our Asian involvement for years to come.

One found a very similar attitude on the home front. In 1958, Hartmann Luggage ran an ad in *The New Yorker*. The copy touted the "superb taste and good judgment" of a Hartmann owner. The ad's photo showed an old oriental coolie, complete with strained facial expression and crooked posture, bent under a yoke bearing two big pieces of Hartmann luggage.[40] The only other possible link between the photo and the ad might be the summoning of a sophistication fantasy: a Hartmann owner is accustomed to casually traveling the world, the picture hints. That is the sole human significance of the coolie image. Ramifications of oppression and racism dwindle away, to be incorporated into one's worldliness.

The economic implications of racism emerge very clearly in studying the treatment of Mexican-Americans in the fifties. One of the very few people writing about discrimination against this group in those years was John Rechy. In a late-fifties issue of the *Nation*, Rechy recalled his childhood as a Mexican-American in Texas. He wrote of restaurant signs announcing "WE DO NOT SERVE MEXICANS, NIGGERS OR DOGS." He also wrote of the tourism ads, dreamy scornful pieces about Mexicans living in the "land of mañana." These quotes expressed a bigotry vital to business practice. In 1953 alone, I. F. Stone reported, about 483,000 Mexicans, many of whom had entered the United States as migrant workers, were deported "in a reign of terror and lawlessness." Among their numbers were American-born citizens of Mexican descent. They were expelled along with the native Mexicans. Stone found about the same number of Mexicans being simultaneously imported, to fill the agricultural need for cheap labor. The object was to maintain a constant population of low-paid and humble workers, too cowed to object to their ill treatment. This treatment—low pay, no health care, stoop labor, no schooling, bad food, and every sort of humiliation imaginable—was and remains the foundation for much of the American agrobusiness empires.[41] It continues, too, with the full cooperation of immigration and agriculture officials.

The American Indian was in the fifties more openly victimized than any of these non-white groups. While Latinos or Micronesians were virtually ignored by the media, Indians were discussed with relative frequency. Much of what happened to them in the decade, thus, is a matter of public record. Here, even more than for blacks, the economic exploitation that depended on racial bigotry was public knowledge. Actually, it was not usually regarded as exploitation but rather as a benefit to the red man. In these years the mass media accelerated its old-fashioned display of the Indian as senseless barbarian. Television was the major source. But the printed media also tended to reflect the same ideas.

A story in Eric Goldman's history of postwar America, *The Crucial Decade*, is a good introduction to Indian status. Goldman related the posthumous events surrounding the death of Sergeant John Rice, a Winnebago killed in Korean combat. Rice's body was refused burial in the Sioux City Memorial Park because he was not Caucasian. Truman invited Rice's widow to bury him in Arlington. He dispatched an Air Force plane for the body. "Harry Truman had rarely done anything more popular," Goldman exclaimed, and newspapers across the country praised such equality.[42] In retrospect this small story contains some buried shocks. Not only are the tokenism and the play for publicity irritating, but one is eerily reminded of the old cant about good Indians being dead ones. This example of democracy for a dead man was noisily hailed. Yet at the same time, under Harry Truman's administration and later Eisenhower's, the federal government joined with white moneyed interests to take natural resources from live Indians.

Former Bureau of Indian Affairs commissioner John Collier dubbed the federal policy toward native Americans an "Indian takeaway." It was hidden in a plan touted to benefit Indians. Actually two major programs were forwarded: termination and relocation. In the thirties, each tribe had organized into corporations. A new relationship between the federal government and the tribal corporations was then articulated. This was one of federal wardship and service. Wardship, with its implications to the white mainstream of charity, welfare, and control, would be ended by termination, which also dissolved a tribe's corporation. Relocation intended to take willing natives off the reservations, where poverty, illness, and alcoholism reigned, and relocate them in cities. There, they would ostensibly have more and better chances for affluence. Together the two programs sounded potentially good. Indians would now be citizens, not wards, with greater autonomy and opportunity than ever. They would have a chance to become assimilated.[43]

But to even lightly examine the realities behind these projects casts them in a different light. One first becomes suspicious after realizing that termination could not render Indians into citizens. They were already citizens. Relocation was verbalized as a method of giving Indians greater wealth and opportunity in the big cities. By mid-decade, experimental prototypes of the program obviously did not work. Indians who had been relocated in urban areas simply suffered in a different way. They found no great opportunities. But that did not seem to matter. "There is no doubt of the success of the Chicago experiment," observed a 1955 article in *Coronet*. "True, the present generation of relocated Indians, handicapped by lack of education and unfamiliarity with urban culture, fill the lesser jobs, live in the lesser neighborhoods. . . . Their children, of course, will make the great gains and flow most easily into their rightful place in the mainstream of American life."[44] That is, yes, there is no doubt the program has failed. But there is also no doubt it has succeeded. Relocated Indians are really better off because their children will get to be more like white people. Prompt and unquestioned failure and destruction were interpreted as unquestioned success. One wonders, then, where genuine success rested.

Such success went to the men who profited from the removal of Indians from their lands. It was in the forties and early fifties that various white economic interest groups began to realize Indian reservations were not all barren deserts. Many reservations were rich in natural resources: lumber, oil, grazing land, uranium, water. The termination process, wherein tribal holdings were equally divided among each individual, worked against the Indian owner. Without the tribal corporation and federal services, most individual Indians were too poor to hold on to those lands. They had to sell. Such interest groups as cattlemen, miners, agrobusiness farmers, or timber companies bought them out cheaply. Two of the first tribes slated for termination in the fifties were the Klamaths in Oregon and Wisconsin's Menominees. Each owned some of the country's richest lumber stands.[45]

One essential of each termination bill was that the tribe had to agree to be terminated. But tribes that refused were heavily pressured by the government. This was not merely a verbal pressuring. Arizona's Pimas, for instance, had their water supplies arbitrarily taken away in 1954 when they refused to terminate. The tribe was denied permission to dig irrigation wells. The Department of the Interior refused to recognize their Indian lawyer. They were helpless. Noted a reporter, "when Pima farmers get restive, threats are made to freeze their tribal funds or cut off the meager water they get from Coolidge Dam—which was built for them" but instead supplied big white-owned farms. Elsewhere, Paiute Indians never received the federal aid they were entitled to. The 172 full-blood Paiutes owned 45,000 acres of land newly found to be rich in oil and minerals. They had refused to be terminated.[46]

Such interest groups maintained powerful Washington lobbies, and the Indian affairs men acting for the Truman and Eisenhower administrations favored these lobbies. Some officials also had an unflattering race relations record. Dillon S. Myer, appointed Indian commissioner in 1950, previously had been the director of the internment camps where over 100,000 Japanese-Americans were imprisoned during World War II. (Although all the sabotage and espionage rings uncovered on the home front were run by Italian- or German-Americans, there were never any propositions to intern them in camps. No such plots by Japanese-Americans were ever discovered.) Other men high in the BIA hierarchy went there straight from lobbying against native tribal interests in the West. Ex-commissioner John Collier was the only Indian ever in that post. He charged that federal Indian policy was working only for the profit of a few. He said the BIA's "ruling purpose, harshly intensified by the present [Eisenhower] administration, has been to atomize and suffocate the group life of the tribes—that group life which is their vitality, motivation, and hope."[47]

Most racial minorities, though, were not so much suffocated as bypassed by the mainstream consciousness. The economic and emotional costs were only aggravated over the decade. Given any particular racial group, one saw a large poor lower class, its much smaller middle class pursuing white goals, a small body of liberal white humanitarians sympathizing with its plight and, most of all, a great mass of apathetic whites. The long and ponderous reversal of this state began with the sparking of civil rights activism at mid-decade. That first battle, the Montgomery bus boycott, could only catalyze broader efforts. Inevitably the ingrained prejudice of a whole culture had to be faced, and faced in both legal and cultural terms that touched all racial groups.

17. As this 1958 photo indicates, children learned early about sex roles and conspicuous consumption.

18. Elvis Presley, rock and roll idol of the fifties.

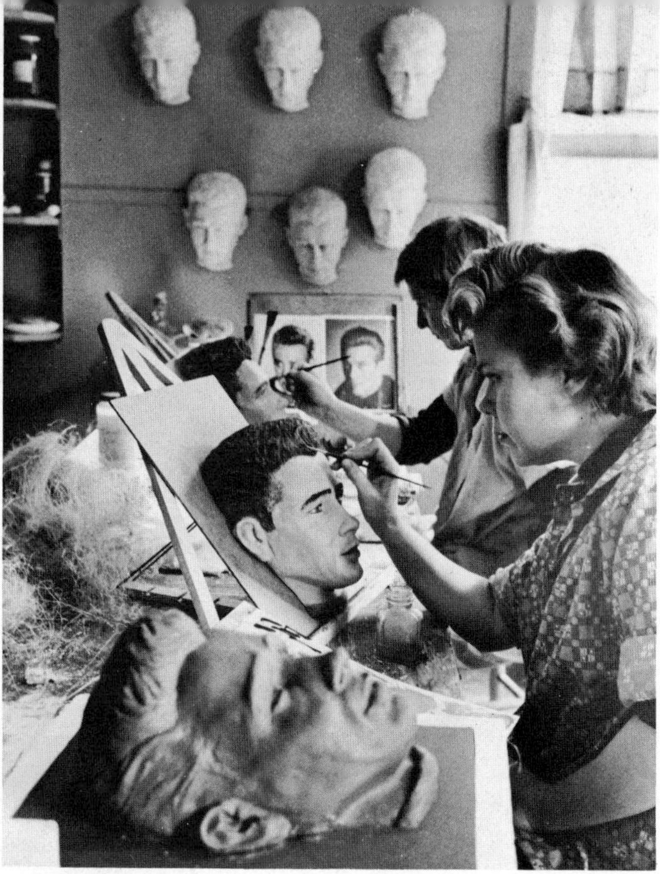

19. These women paint plaster ar Miracleflesh effigies of James De in 1956. Dean died in a 1955 au crash; his legend only grew.

20. Bogus quiz champ, Charles Van Doren.

21. A hostile crowd jeers at Elizabeth Eckford as she attempts to enter formerly all-white Central High School, Little Rock, September 1957.

22. The Reverend Martin Luther King, Jr., is mugged following his 1956 arrest during the Montgomery bus boycott.

23. Just after the launching of the first successful U.S. space satellite on January 31, 1958, a woman wears a missile hat.

24. This man digs a backyard bomb shelter in 1951.

One of the major events of the struggle took place long before the bus boycott. This was the 1952 publication of a major novel which even in its title spoke to cultural blindness. "I am an invisible man," wrote Ralph Ellison. "I am invisible, understand, simply because people refuse to see me." Much of *Invisible Man* is a guided tour through black lifestyles in America. It explored every path open to blacks: life in rural poverty, at the black southern college, northern city ways, even life in the "Brotherhood" (that is, the Communist party). In all these lives, Ellison relentlessly showed, black humanity was essentially betrayed. To whites, blacks were only a moving and breathing extension of their fantasies. The narrator of *Invisible Man* is ultimately deceived by the Brotherhood. Pursued by a religious destroyer, trapped in the race riot he had tried to end, he flees into the New York sewers. Discovering a secret room, he hides. His hermit life evokes the position of blacks early in the fifties: disillusioned, wanting big changes, hiding to rest. But this postponement was scarcely a defeat. Warned the writer: "It is incorrect to assume that, because I'm invisible and live in a hole, I am dead. I am neither dead nor in a state of suspended animation. Call me Jack-the-Bear, for I am in a state of hibernation." And, he softly added, "a hibernation is a covert preparation for a more overt action."[48]

As Ellison predicted, the overt moves soon began. Direct action, more than ever, became a way of dramatizing the need for both legal and attitudinal changes. This did not play down the vitality of legal changes. Rather, activism helped accelerate legal change. Even more it challenged racist consciousness. The first major event in this vein was sparked by a black woman in Montgomery, Alabama. Mrs. Rosa Parks, a seamstress, refused to yield her bus seat to a white who demanded it one Friday night in December 1955. At that time, Montgomery buses were segregated. Blacks had to sit in a few back seats. They could sit in other seats but had to vacate these upon white demand. The bus driver summoned a policeman who arrested Mrs. Parks.

All this was quite customary, including the arrest. Mrs. Parks, however, was well-respected in the large black community. Some local black ministers got together and decided to try to rally a boycott of the bus system around the fact of her arrest. It probably would have failed. But the town newspaper reprinted a boycott handout. The editors intended this as a joke. In this way notice was disseminated to blacks who would never have heard of it. The boycott worked. For over a year blacks united in the "Cradle of the Confederacy." They walked. They rode in car pools. The city harassed the car pools. Old laws were dug up to arrest boycott leaders. Unknown persons dynamited the leaders' homes. But eventually the boycott succeeded. The lesson of economic clout had been turned against its wielders; more important, one inspiring struggle for dignity had been won.[49]

This confrontation thrust Martin Luther King, Jr., into national fame and a life of activism. Crucially, the boycott centered on the issue of dignity. Many of the boycotters' specific complaints were against the humiliations of the bus system. For instance, blacks were required to board the bus in front, pay their fare, then get off and reboard at the back door. Often the driver simply drove off before they could get on again. Abuse and insults were customary from drivers to black passengers; this in addition to the insult of riding in the back and surrendering other seats. Boycott demands included the hiring of black drivers on black routes and a guarantee of courtesy. That such mild ideas were considered radical indicates the depths of the Jim Crow system. King, like the boycott itself, emerged in the national press as a humble, gentle, peace- and dignity-loving man. His professing total non-violence, even in the face of violence, made him a leader tailor-made to soothe white fears of black retaliation.[50] Too, he appealed to the mainstream belief in an ordered world. But King was unable, for those very reasons, to appeal to lower-class blacks who were divided from the black bourgeoisie.

Pacifism, with its big appeal to America's extrasensitivity to black aggression, was far from the only changing vision. A 1959 article in *Liberation* magazine, "Can Negroes Afford to Be Pacifists?" by Robert F. Williams, explained an alternative view. "In Montgomery," Williams wrote, "the issue was a matter of struggle for human dignity. Non-violence is made to order for that type of conflict." But non-violence, he insisted, was unrealistic in light of the daily brutalities facing blacks in the Deep South. In many places, "Negroes are faced with the necessity of combating savage violence. The struggle is for mere existence. The Negro is in a position of begging for life. . . . An open declaration of non-violence . . . is an invitation that white racist brutes will certainly honor."[51]

Williams then lived in Union County, North Carolina. The massive Ku Klux Klan organization there operated so openly it advertised clubhouse meetings in the local press and on the radio. Periodically, black sections were raided by the Klan. Police cars always headed the caravan. Appeals to high officials (even the President) to investigate police involvement had proved futile, Williams said. He explained that, after the appeals all failed, he had spoken of the situation on radio. In the speech, he simply announced that the era of passive acceptance of these raids was over. From then on Union County blacks would "meet violence with violence." Only then, when it was made clear that "turn-the-other-cheekism" was done with, did the raids cease. The mutual fear of violence, he concluded, had created peaceful co-existence.[52]

Williams, however, was asked to resign from the NAACP for making this statement. One is reminded of the expulsion of Minnijean Brown from Central High in Little Rock. Even self-defense, for a black, was impossible. It was seen as brutal aggression. These incidents begin to teach one of the most curious facts of American history: violence on the part of outgroups—radicals, non-whites—has always been wildly deplored. But most violence in this highly violent nation has been perpetrated to preserve the status quo, to destroy dissidence, to keep people in line.

All this is even more apparent in looking at reactions to the Black Muslims. A religious sect founded in the thirties, this strict group expanded greatly during the fifties. One reason was the rise within the organization of Malcolm X. His charisma and missionary methods—"fishing" for converts on street corners, disseminating the word through the newspaper *Muhammad Speaks*—drew thousands into the group. But another stimulus to Muslim membership was adverse media publicity. On July 10, 1959, Mike Wallace and Louis Lomax produced a TV commentary on the Black Muslims. Its title reflected its severe view: "The Hate That Hate Produced." Before that program, American membership was under 30,000. Within weeks it doubled. By 1961 there were 100,000 Black Muslims.[53]

The Muslim's appeal unquestionably lay in its insistence on black esteem. This was maintained by firm rules and tight discipline. Forbidden were gambling, smoking, drinking liquor, buying on credit, overeating, and being overweight. Sexual morality was extremely strict. No woman could be alone with any man except her husband. Women studied in special homemaking classes. Modest dress was also required. Members were urged to "buy black," to save money, to seek converts. Young men drilled in the paramilitary Fruit of Islam. They also trained in self-defense.

Most impressed by this imposed morality were lower-class blacks, from the very ghetto areas where self-discipline and ordered morality were eroded. The behavioral result was to transform castoffs of a white society into an alternate society of strong blacks. Malcolm X, for instance, was an ex-convict, converted in prison. Too, the Muslims attained a highly successful record of getting addicts off drugs and keeping them off without using substitute drugs.[54] An otherwise parodic pseudo-Islam does not discount the importance of the Black Muslims as one growing symbol of black strength at decade's end.

There were many other changes in black awareness in the fifties. The NAACP ceased to be the only organized group claiming to speak for non-whites. Its slow legal work lost its appeal to lower-class blacks—if it ever had any appeal to them. The group was strongly criticized for its white-middle-class orientation. By 1960, for instance, it had never elected one non-white president. By that year, too, the NAACP showed a big decline in membership.

The potential for individual betterment was also reassessed. The efforts of single blacks to rise on their own were proving pointless. Autherine Lucy's long unsuccessful mid-decade attempt to enter the University of Alabama vividly displayed the problem. Both students and faculty had indicated approval for her efforts. But because these people and any strong black group failed to unite behind her, bigoted students and locals repeatedly kept her out of school. Most effectively, this dramatized the futility of striving alone for any goals. Only a solid front could effect change and maintain it. This realization stimulated activity by CORE (the Congress on Racial Equality, formed in the forties). It also prompted the formation of SCLC (the Southern Christian Leadership Conference) late in the fifties, and in 1960 of SNCC (the Student Nonviolent Coordinating Committee).[55] The ferment within these groups would lead first to the widely publicized sit-ins for integration (implying assimilation), then to a questioning of the desirability of assimilation itself as a goal. Other things besides eating at a few lunch counters came to seem more important—like the vote and someone to vote for, like pride and economic power. All the varieties of black activism, furthermore, prompted other ethnic unions in years to come.

Whites, however, were hampered in understanding these bursts of activism. Many had been encouraged by the euphoric rhetoric of the early and mid-fifties to believe racism really was vanishing. What, then, were all these complaints about? By 1960, this uncomfortable and incomprehending reaction was the major response of the white middle class. Non-Southerners found ever more reasons to externalize their own bigotries as civil rights activism increased in the South. News photos of white punks and dignified blacks underscored that process. Some non-southern whites tried hard to be tolerant. Dick Gregory built a nightclub routine on such a stiff and nervous response: "Wouldn't it be a hell of a thing if this was burnt cork and you people were being tolerant for nothing?"[56] By the end of the fifties, only the faint beginnings of changing white ideas existed. The racial problem was still regarded by the mainstream as a "Negro problem" rather than a white one.

But some few whites did try to learn more. John Howard Griffin was one. His story is fascinating: blinded in the early forties, he was active nevertheless in helping Jewish children escape from the Nazis. He returned, completely blind, to the United States and settled in Texas with his family. In 1957 he regained his sight. He was horrified, when he could see, to realize the kinship between American and Nazi racism. Griffin took a medical treatment to darken his skin. He traveled through the Deep South for six weeks as a black. Then he wrote *Black Like Me*. Griffin feelingly illuminated the monstrous cruelty of the whole racial scene, the sexual exploitation, emotional destruction, arbitrary white violence. He also told of the ways blacks welcomed and helped each other. It is easy to laugh at this book, and dismiss it. Griffin's very honesty about his white life can be amusing. Having a big gourmet meal in a segregated restaurant, he wonders: "was there a place in New Orleans where a Negro could buy *huîtres variées?*"[57] It was the shock value of his act—the witness, transformed back and forth—that gave the book its vast importance. And this shock value would not have existed if it were not for one terrible truth. Even sympathetic liberals were bigoted enough to never have listened to black anguish. A white man had to say it. His six-week stint as a black was the only thing that could really convince many people.

"Today, in all too many northern communities," Martin Luther King wrote in 1958, "a sort of quasi-liberalism prevails so bent on seeking all sides that it fails to become dedicated to any side." Well into the sixties, when he was far more radicalized by this very quasi-liberalism, King would say "I have almost reached the regrettable conclusion that the Negroes' greatest stumbling block in the stride toward freedom is not the White Citizens' Council or the Ku Klux Klan, but the white moderate who is more devoted to 'order' than to justice . . . who constantly says 'I agree with you on the goal you seek, but I can't agree with your methods of direct action.'" Malcolm X, of course, had been saying this all along. The moderate wound up covertly supporting the racist, and this triggered black rage just as much or more. Some historians still have not learned this message. They write as though the rise of black consciousness (or any ethnic consciousness) came about because of "outside agitation" or because of white favors. It is much more factual to regard the changes as provoked by hundreds of years of oppression, topped off with the frustration of egalitarian talk and the fifties imperative to "go slow." No one, as Langston Hughes' character Simple would say, has ever been happy with partial equality.[58] Blacks, in 1960 as in 1950 or 1790, were still relatively "three-fifths of a person."

By the end of the decade, the United States was a far more racially segregated, racially tense country than in 1950. As it moved into the sixties, the nation would begin to pay with turmoil for those years of corrosive neglect. For so long, white Americans had turned away from the sore of bigotry. They turned to superficial mock answers. Change, true, seldom happens quickly in this world. But in the fifties, white Americans confused the ponderousness of history with a moral imperative for inertia. Worse, they chose to intensify an orderly evil. It was yet another contribution of the times to the dividing of people from each other.

By 1960, some few Americans, white youths among them, were beginning to question racial attitudes. But blacks especially were starting to define themselves, their own culture and experience. They formed a movement that would inspire many others. For blacks, the decade ended on a series of contrapuntal notes: the rage of frustration, the optimism of self-definition and successful activism, the determination to not just survive this time but prevail. It was a turning point of vision.

NOTES

1. Silas Spitzer, "Land of Plenty," *Holiday*, July 1952, p. 63.

2. Anne Braden, "The Southern Freedom Movement," *Monthly Review*, July–August 1956, pp. 11–13; Charles Silberman, *Crisis in Black and White* (New York, 1964), p. 60; Editors of *Year* Encyclopedia, *Pictorial History of the Black American* (New York, 1968), p. 57. During World War II, Red Cross blood was even segregated by donor.

3. Braden, "Movement," pp. 12–15; Ben Wattenberg, *This U.S.A.* (Garden City, 1965), pp. 250–73; George S. Schuyler, "The Phantom American Negro," *Reader's Digest*, July 1951, pp. 62–63; Lawrence S. Wittner, *Cold War America* (New York, 1974), p. 192; see also Eric Goldman, *The Crucial Decade* (New York, 1960), pp. 183–86; C. Vann Woodward, *The Strange Career of Jim Crow* (New York, 1955), pp. 120–22, 130–31.

4. Wattenberg, *U.S.A.*, pp. 271, 276–83; Lerone Bennett, *Confrontation: Black and White* (Baltimore, 1965), p. 173; John Brooks, *The Great Leap* (New York, 1966), p. 296; William Peters, *The Southern Temper* (Garden City, 1959), p. 227—the ratio of black to white wages was much lower in the South. Other indexes of inequality support the entire picture: one black doctor per 3,500 blacks compared to a national ratio of 1:750 (in Mississippi the ratio for blacks was 1:18,000). Blacks, with ten per cent of population, had access to one per cent of the hospital beds—Editors of *Fortune, U.S.A.* (New York, 1951), p. 169.

5. Thurgood Marshall, "Summary Justice—the Negro G.I. in Korea," *Crisis*, May 1951, pp. 297–304.

6. Wattenberg, *U.S.A.*, p. 283; Wittner, *Cold War*, p. 192.

7. Schuyler, "Phantom Negro," pp. 62–63.

8. Silberman, *Crisis*, pp. 7, 30; Wattenberg, *U.S.A.*, p. 273; Louis Lomax, *The Negro Revolt* (New York, 1962), pp. 69–70. As Lomax also points out, blacks too were part of the postwar baby boom. In the fifties, the black population increased 25 per cent compared to 18 per cent for whites. (See our chapter "Happy Home Corporation and Baby Factory" on the implications of domesticity as diversion). Silberman emphasizes that the number of farms in the nation dropped by a full third in the fifties alone (p. 30). Black farmers were the hardest hit: between 1954 and 1959 alone their numbers dropped 41 per cent. Sharecropping, once the predominant method of black farming, has virtually vanished, swallowed by the giant factory farms. During the decade, 4.5 million whites and 2 million blacks left rural areas for these reasons. Generally this has been discussed in a vacuum as if all these millions of people were uprooting themselves for the fun of it. Poor southern whites didn't get treated any better in the cities, either. See Albert N. Votaw, "The Hillbillies Invade Chicago," *Harper's*, February 1958, pp. 64–67. See also Lerone Bennett, *Confrontation*, p. 170: the period 1950–54, he feels, was one of "optative evasion" in which blacks, also caught up in the consensus, tried to wish their problems away.

9. Braden, "Movement," p. 14; Frederick Lewis Allen, *The Big Change* (New York, 1952), pp. 177, 266. Eric Goldman in *The Crucial Decade*, pp. 183–86, praises the practicality of army integration in too-lavish terms.

10. Max Lerner, in "Our Country and Our Culture: A Symposium," *Partisan Review*, XIX (Sept.–Oct. 1952); conservative intellectual Peter Viereck, for example, also tended to portray racism as a minor and occasional unfairness, a most transitory aberration. Jacques Barzun did not even admit to the basic tension between racism and consensus. He felt all Americans were "foreigners" with no "preconceived antagonism" toward any ethnic group. See William Hixson, "The Negro Revolution and the Intellectual" in Dwight Hoover, ed., *Understanding Negro History* (Chicago, 1968).

11. Michael Harrington, *The Other America* (Baltimore, 1964), pp. 9–10, 15–17.

12. See, for instance, the lists in "How Negroes Are Gaining in the U.S.," *U.S. News & World Report*, June 28, 1957, pp. 165–66; or "Negroes: Big Advances in Jobs, Wealth, Status," *U.S. News*, November 28, 1958, pp. 90–92; Lindsy Van Gelder, "Coffee, Tea or Fly Me," *Ms.*, January 1973, p. 87; James P. Mitchell, "The Negro Moves Up," *Reader's Digest*, December 1957, pp. 46–47—Mitchell was Secretary of Labor. His article denied the existence of any job discrimination whatsoever. For variety he picked less famous "firsts"—student body presidents, for instance. Ralph Bunche received 13 honorary degrees in the spring of 1951 alone. *Time*, July 17, 1950, pp. 74, 77, reported the protest of Alice Marble in *American Lawn Tennis* against Forest Hills' refusal to let Gibson play there. The USLTA maintained a color line well into the fifties. Such considerations of praise/prejudice are vital: someone like Gibson or Bunche is rendered a token person—a person only on a token basis.

13. "Negroes Gaining" and "Big Advances," *U.S. News;* Vance Packard, *The Status Seekers* (New York, 1959), p. 310. On p. 334, Packard seems to emphasize that discrimination is prompted by blacks and is somehow their fault; he quotes S. I. Hayakawa: "the secret of acting naturally [is] to forget as far as possible that one is Negro."

14. See, for instance, the tone in "Mississippi Justice," *Life*, April 3, 1950, p. 30, expressing surprises that a white was actually imprisoned for murdering three blacks. The article's emotions moved between righteous indignation and a rather distant horror, as though watching caged snakes eat mice. See also footnote 13; Bayard Rustin "Fear in the Delta," in *Down the Line* (Chicago, 1971), pp. 62–73; *Nation*, April 28, 1956.

15. Barnett is quoted in Robert Sherrill, *Gothic Politics in the Deep South* (New York, 1968), p. 174—this book, first published late in the fifties, was reissued in the mid-sixties under the title *The Accidental President*, to take advantage of the section on Lyndon Johnson; Peters, *Temper*, pp. 69, 83, 213, 219; Murray Kempton, *America Comes of Middle Age* (Boston, 1963), pp. 135–37; *Reader's Digest*, April 1956, pp. 57–62—including a box score demonstrating lynchings were in decline; I. F. Stone, *The Haunted Fifties* (New York, 1963), p. 61; see also *Time*, December 22, 1952, p. 18, on the death of Mr. and Mrs. Harry Moore. He was the NAACP coordinator for the state of Florida; their home was bombed. Southern violence was the focus of all these pieces. In the terrifying Mack Parker case, which came to symbolize southern justice for many Northerners, the FBI painstakingly assembled a dossier identifying those who

had kidnaped and lynched Parker. The Pearl River County, Mississippi, grand jury refused to even look at it.

16. Harry S. Ashmore, "The Untold Story Behind Little Rock," *Harper's*, June 1958, pp. 10–16—how Little Rock became an emotional symbol for all involved; David Wieck, "The Invention of Responsibility," anthologized from *Liberation* magazine in Paul Goodman, ed., *Seeds of Liberation* (New York, 1964), pp. 310–14; Sherrill, on p. 100 of *Gothic*, quoted Roy Harris announcing Little Rock was "the best" thing that could have happened to inspire the segregation forces. Eisenhower's slow, near-bungling approach to the situation has also been considered highly responsible for the dragged-out hostilities there.

17. Harry Golden, "Vertical Negro Plan," in John Hope Franklin and Isidore Starr, eds., *The Negro in Twentieth Century America* (New York, 1967), pp. 123–25.

18. Golden, "Leaderless Decency: The South Stalls Its Future," anthologized in Henry Christman, ed., *A View of the Nation* (New York, 1960), pp. 130–35. By 1974 the South would be more educationally integrated than any other part of the country, as the New York *Times* reported on its front page, May 12, 1974. In 1975, as hostility to integrating Boston schools continued unabated, a group of black and white South Carolina students would march on Boston in favor of integration. See also Wieck, "Intervention," and Richard A. Long, "Those Magnolia Myths," *Nation*, July 7, 1956, p. 17; Silberman, *Crisis*, p. 9.

19. Long, "Myths," p. 17; Jacques Barzun, *God's Country and Mine* (Boston, 1954), p. 98; the *Register* comment is in *Time*, June 4, 1956, p. 82; Larry Gara, in *The Liberty Line* (Lexington, 1961), discusses another aspect of this northern self-satisfaction: the mythology of the Underground Railroad, which has been vastly overblown to make it look as though far more Northerners participated than documentation could ever indicate. A chapter from Gara is anthologized in Hoover, ed., *Understanding Negro History*, which also includes a useful article by Leon F. Litwack, "The Abolitionist Dilemma," about racial prejudice in the antebellum North; also Irving Howe, "Reverberations in the North," *Dissent*, 3 (Spring 1956), 121–23.

20. These attitudes are examined further in our Chapter "TV's the Thing," pp. 361–62.

21. Gordon Gow, *Hollywood in the Fifties* (New York, 1971), pp. 95–101, and especially Edward Mapp, *Blacks in American Films* (Metuchen, N.J., 1972) quoting Killens. Mapp also lists Lawrence Reddick's description of black stereotypes in the movies—such as the happy slave, the sexual superman, the devoted servant, the superstitious churchgoer; examines the all-black musical as a one-dimensional view of the race (*Carmen Jones*, 1954, *St. Louis Blues*, 1958, *Porgy and Bess*, 1959). Also see our Chapter "Hollywood in Transition," pp. 330–33.

Many newspapers did not quite know how to handle the change from ignoring to accepting blacks. See especially *Time*, July 24, 1950, p. 62, which wonders just how a paper should report the subject of an interracial marriage, using as an example the 1950 marriage of a white heiress to a black social worker. Popular fiction, too, sometimes rather unpleasantly reflected and so disseminated bigotry. Ian Fleming filled out various James Bond plots with really dreadful racism. In *Live and Let Die* (1954), we are told the race riots of 1935 and 1943 were caused by voodoo excitement, and that the black underworld and all black workers are run by a black gangster who, conveniently, is also a Russian agent. See particularly Fleming's Chapter Five, "Nigger Heaven."

22. Richard Wright, *White Man, Listen!* (Garden City, 1957), pp. 79, 27–29.

23. Rustin, *Down the Line*, pp. 88–89; Silberman, *Crisis*, pp. 49–50; this subject has been extensively studied in recent years. It largely proceeds out of the writings of Frantz Fanon on the psychology of the oppressed. See also Thomas Szasz, *Law, Liberty and Psychiatry* (New York, 1964), p. 195, and Bruno Bettelheim, *The Informed Heart* (New York, 1960), which discusses the same processes in the context of the concentration camp.

We have assumed throughout this chapter that the reader is familiar with the basic notions of racism: that non-whites are childlike, emotional, physically powerful, and primitive inferiors. The particulars of course vary from race to race: thus, the drunken Indian, the hot-headed Puerto Rican, the sensual black. Another aspect of the self-reinforcing stereotype is the way it creates a circumscribed area within which there is freedom. For example, Indians are free to become alcoholic, encouraged by the stereotype. This is one of the very few outs in a trapped life. But in following it, the damaging stereotype is fulfilled. Similarly, in periods like the fifties, blacks were free to win success as, say, musicians. But such success also reinforced notions of natural rhythm.

24. "Incident in Harlem," *Newsweek*, September 29, 1958, p. 24; "Accident in Harlem," *Time*, September 29, 1958, p. 14; Szasz, *Law*, p. 193.

25. Szasz discusses Curry's case at length in *Law*, in a chapter entitled "Ethics and Psychiatry," pp. 193–98. We strongly recommend this book to anyone concerned about the issues involved, such as involuntary commitment, the rights of mental patients, even the criteria for commitment. Semantics are also fascinating in the context of mental "illness." American institutions like Matteawan are referred to as prison hospitals, with all the ramifications of healing and humanitarianism. Western writers disapprovingly refer to the same sort of place in the Soviet Union with honest bluntness: when it is in Russia, it is a penal asylum, a prison.

26. Silberman, *Crisis*, p. 7; Harrington, *Other*, pp. 137–54; Arthur S. Link, *American Epoch*, pp. 589–92.

27. Packard, *Status*, p. 88; see also *Time*, July 3, 1950, p. 68, on the plans of Joe Louis and builder Paul Trousdale to put up a 4,000-house development for blacks—an event so rare it even got mentioned in the news magazines; Lerner, *America as a Civilization* (New York, 1957), p. 517; *Time*, April 16, 1956, p. 24; Wattenberg, *U.S.A.*, p. 81.

28. Lomax, *Revolt*, pp. 69–70. We are also indebted to the remarks of LaVerne Blickley in her unpublished paper on urban renewal.

29. Silberman, *Crisis*, pp. 309, 311, 336; *U.S. News*, July 19, 1957, p. 88; Harrington, "Slums Old and New," *Commentary* (August 1960), pp. 120, 118–24. Sometimes slum clearance merely left an abandoned empty lot, the ultimate step in this war on poverty. Also see Lomax, *Revolt*, pp. 56–57.

30. Silberman, *Crisis,* pp. 311, 336.

31. "When a Negro Family Moved into a White Community," *U.S. News,* August 30, 1957, pp. 29–32; David B. Bittan, "Ordeal in Levittown," *Look,* August 19, 1958, pp. 84–85; also see *Time,* April 16, 1956, p. 24, on the John Rouse family in Detroit.

32. Wittner, *Cold War,* pp. 139–40; "Convictions in Cicero," *Newsweek,* June 16, 1952, pp. 34–35. See also Fletcher Martin, "We Don't Want Your Kind!", *Atlantic,* October 1958, p. 55. Innumerable incidents of racial/residential hostility occurred in the fifties. Anne Braden, the author of the article cited in footnote 2, and her husband Carl were similarly indicted in Louisville, Kentucky. They had helped friends who were black purchase a home in a white area. The prosecutor investigated the cross burnings, gunfire, and bombing of the house—by raiding the homes of the Bradens and their friends, seizing "communistic" literature, then indicting the Bradens and others for advocating sedition. Charles Abrams discusses this and many other cases all over the country in *Forbidden Neighbors* (New York, 1955).

33. "When a Negro Family," *U.S. News,* pp. 29–32.

34. "Latest Problems for Cities in North: Blockbusting," *U.S. News,* December 5, 1958, pp. 84–88; see also Leona D. Newkirk, "What's Up Town," *American Mercury,* July 1953, pp. 20–21, about the growing Puerto Rican population in New York, and how landlords were being deceived into believing these people were Caucasian even though they all have black relatives.

35. In the late sixties this was grotesquely accelerated by a combination of new laws concerning housing loans and welfare recipients and resultant FHA corruption. This subject has not been widely covered in the mass media. Read Brian D. Boyer, *Cities Destroyed for Cash* (Chicago, 1973).

36. Thomas I. Emerson, "Negro Registration Laws," *Nation,* March 19, 1960, p. 240; Silberman, *Crisis,* pp. 263–83.

37. Paul Goodman, *Growing Up Absurd* (New York, 1960), p. 79; Silberman, *Crisis,* pp. 263–83.

38. Wittner, *Cold War,* pp. 136–40.

39. E. J. Kahn, *The Peculiar War* (New York, 1952), pp. 9, 27. The most significant book to proceed out of this conflict is I. F. Stone's seminal, suppressed work *The Hidden History of the Korean War* (New York: 1952). It raises many important and unflattering questions about American involvement in Korea, indeed about the very beginnings of that conflict. One of the sidelights Stone briefly discussed (pp. 342–43) was the racism of American troops. When North Korean fighter pilots proved to be highly skillful at attacking UN forces, many refused to believe orientals could be flying those planes, and rumors began to circulate that the pilots were actually Poles, Germans, even renegade Americans —anything but Asians. But the most significant thing about this book is the similarity between American behavior in Korea and throughout Indochina in later years. The official lies, the reporters distrusting yet gobbling up those lies, the half-willing, half-reluctant administration, the use of napalm and saturation bombing against tiny hamlets with no military value, the indiscriminate destruction of both North and South are terrifying constants.

This book was reissued in 1969 by Monthly Review Press. Its original printing was not reviewed in the media, disappeared from libraries, and is most difficult to find. The new edition opens with a brief anecdote mentioning that when Stone was interviewing Che Guevara, he learned the U.S. embassy in Mexico had been destroying as many copies of *Hidden History's* Spanish edition as possible. Also of interest is Richard Falk, Gabriel Kolko, and Robert Jay Lifton, eds., *Crimes of War* (New York, 1970).

40. *The New Yorker,* June 7, 1958, p. 49.

41. John Rechy, "Jim Crow Wears a Sombrero," *Nation,* October 10, 1959, p. 211; Stone, *Haunted,* p. 34; Wattenberg, *U.S.A.,* p. 52. In Jack Kerouac's novels, such as *On the Road* and *The Dharma Bums,* there is a mystical romantic vision of Mexicans (and blacks too) that amounts to this: they're charmingly lazy, dirty, and superstitious and we like them that way.

42. Goldman, *Decade,* p. 183; see also James Warner Bellah, "Thirty-Nine Days to Glory," *Holiday,* September 1959, pp. 125–228—the "glory" of the title goes to Custer, whose last days are traced in this piece. Bellah idolized the man, praising the way he let his men rob Indian graves for "trinkets" a week before the Little Big Horn battle. Again, he is thrilled about Custer's brilliant tactics at the Little Big Horn, in sneaking up and then charging headlong to destroy what appeared to be a village of women and children. Bellah neglected, however, to point out that this was a Custer massacre technique already familiar to the Sioux, who this time used their village as a lure. The military strategy wins them the term "blood-hungry" in the article. Bellah summarily portrayed the entire event as a disgusting massacre that was the high point in all of Indian culture.

43. Blake Clark, "Must We Buy America from the Indians All Over Again?", *Reader's Digest,* March 1958, refers to the termination funds (which he feels Indians don't really deserve) as "big wampum"; John Collier, "Indian Takeaway," *Nation,* October 2, 1954, pp. 290–91; H. E. Fey, "Our National Indian Policy," *Christian Century,* June 1, 1955, p. 643; "Hapless, and Hopeless," *Newsweek,* April 2, 1956, p. 82.

44. Dorothy Van de Mark, "Raid on the Reservations," *Harper's,* February 1955, pp. 48–53; M. Golden and L. Carter, "New Deal for America's Indians," *Coronet,* October 1955, pp. 74–76.

45. Van de Mark, "Raid," p. 50. Termination, too, proceeded against one tribe at a time, thus scattering opposition. See also "Consultation or Consent?" *Christian Century,* January 27, 1956, pp. 183–84.

46. Van de Mark, "Raid," p. 50.

47. Collier, "Takeaway," p. 291. Also of interest is the way the situation cropped up in the *Time-Life* publications. Generally whatever issue was involved would be lightly passed over, with focus instead on colorful native costumes, or amusing but unfortunate native habits. See, for instance, two articles on the same page of the August 10, 1950, *Time,* p. 23: "Sky Father's Little Helper" and "The Case of the $12 Sheep." The former concerns water and rain; the latter four young Indian men (referred to as "bucks") who got drunk and stole one sheep, then wound up receiving a really huge prison sentence for it. While the article's last few sentences seem to express indignation, its earlier nattering about bucks and booze and reservations only creates a total effect of cynicism.

48. Ralph Ellison, *Invisible Man* (New York, 1952), pp. 3, 5, 11, 14, 25, 149–65.

49. See Martin Luther King, Jr., *Stride Toward Freedom* (New York, 1958). Rosa Parks' act quickly became one of the touchstones of black history. Innumerable books and articles open by repeating the story of her role.

50. Silberman, *Crisis,* p. 121.

51. Robert F. Williams, "Can Negroes Afford to be Pacifists?" in Goodman, *Seeds,* pp. 271–73.

52. Williams, "Can Negroes Afford," pp. 271–73. Following a race incident in Monroe, August 1961, Williams was charged with kidnaping a white couple. Williams fled the country to Cuba. During his stay there, he ran a radio program broadcast to the United States. Williams also lived in China and Tanzania. In 1969, he returned to Michigan. December 1975, the state of North Carolina finally succeeded in extraditing him to stand trial for the kidnaping charge. Mid-January 1976 all charges against Williams were dropped. "It's supposed to be a victory," Williams said at the time. "People expect me to say, 'Ah, yes—Black people can get justice.' " He went on to say he is considering a lawsuit against five North Carolina officials for violations of his civil rights during the sixties. As of mid-February 1976, charges against the other four defendants in the kidnaping case had not been dropped. William Kunstler, one of Williams' attorneys, planned to pursue this.

53. C. Eric Lincoln, *The Black Muslims in America* (Boston, 1961), pp. 107, 4, 17, 18, 22–26.

54. Lincoln, *Muslims,* pp. 146, 229, 81–82, 250.

55. W. Haywood Burns, *Voices of Negro Protest in America* (New York, 1963), pp. 44, 31–33, 42; E. Franklin Frazier, "The Negro," *Nation,* July 7, 1956, pp. 7–8; Lincoln, *Muslims,* p. 245. See also Mort Sahl quoted in *Esquire,* January 1959, p. 62.

56. *Life,* March 3, 1958, p. 92, showed one sign of aggravated racial hostility in the Deep South. The magazine quoted a Louisiana sawmill operator saying he didn't believe there would be an international nuclear war but "a war right here with the Negroes." Dick Gregory, *Nigger* (New York, 1963), facing p. 100.

57. John Howard Griffin, *Black Like Me* (New York, 1969 ed.), p. 11; Paul A. Freund, ed., *Experimentation with Human Subjects* (New York, 1970), pp. 172–73.

58. King, *Stride,* p. 200; see Silberman, *Crisis,* p. 355; Janet Harris and Julius W. Hobson, *Black Pride* (New York, 1969), pp. 112–21; Langston Hughes anthologized in Franklin and Starr, eds., *The Negro in Twentieth Century America,* pp. 149–51, from the New York *Post.*

8

Intellectuals: The Conservative Contraction

"An intellectual," Columbia professor Jacques Barzun defined in 1954, "is a man who carries a briefcase." That was a clear indication, for "if a man carries a briefcase, the odds are high that he is a scholar." In the 1950s such a definition was not quite so ludicrous as it sounds today. Like nearly everyone else, most intellectuals were staid, respectable, and conformist. "The good old days when it was enough to be against the government have gone," claimed ex-radical Granville Hicks in 1956, "and it is fortunate that the liberals, recognizing that fact, have grown responsible and moderate." Hicks went on to explain this change. First, there was the cold war which naturally called forth an intellectual rallying around the American flag. But second, and more important, Hicks found that "major evils have been eliminated or reduced in the past twenty years. We not only produce more goods than ever before; we distribute them more equitably, so that we have probably come closer than any other society in history to the abolition of poverty. . . . The underprivileged groups—women, aliens, Negroes—draw nearer and nearer to equal rights. In short many of the goals the radicals and reformers of the twenties set themselves have been or are being achieved."[1]

As in the 1930s, fifties intellectuals went searching for America. But unlike the thirties thinkers, who identified the common people as the real Americans and who seethed with radical indignation at the injustices those people suffered, fifties writers found a happy, homogeneous, prosperous middle-class populace and were pleased. It was as if intellectuals suddenly discovered that George F. Babbitt had virtues earlier intellectuals never recognized. They came to defend bourgeois values: stability, material possessions, propriety, social adjustment, family.

One of the first expressions of the changing intellectual temper in the post-World War II era was a 1947 essay, "America the Beautiful," that Mary McCarthy published in *Commentary*. Asserting that she and her fellow intellectuals liked and admired America, she wrote: "we preferred it to that imaginary America . . . of Caldwell and Steinbeck, dumb paradise of violence and detective story." This country was unmaterialistic. "Possessions, when they are desired, are not wanted for their own sakes but as tokens of an ideal state of freedom, fraternity, and franchise." And, she concluded (at the very time American foreign policy was helping to push the cold war into being): "passivity and not aggressiveness is the dominant trait of the American character."[2]

The attempt to understand and explain America's enduring virtues became an obsession in the fifties. "What, as a nation, are we all about?" asked the editors of *Fortune* in 1951. A good question, people thought, and numerous studies sponsored by government, universities, and business attempted answers. Academics joined with corporate executives in sessions of communal soul-searching. In 1950 a Harvard group looked into "The American Business Creed." The Corning Glass Company in 1951 brought together a variety of businessmen, government officials, and scholars for a conference on "Living in Industrial Civilization." In 1953 the government-financed Operations Research Office at Johns Hopkins investigated "Some Aspects of National Character." Several dozen prestigious scholars discussed "the American style" at a conference sponsored by MIT's Center for International Studies in 1957. And so it went throughout the decade. Individuals, too, produced sweeping reappraisals of American life such as Daniel Boorstin's *Genius of American Politics* (1953), David Potter's *People of Plenty* (1954), Louis Hartz's *The Liberal Tradition in America* (1955), Max Lerner's *America as a Civilization* (1957). Similarly whole issues of intellectual magazines—*The American Scholar, Commentary,* and *Partisan Review*—were devoted to asking, in the words of *The American Scholar* editors, "where we are, how we got here, and where we are going?"[3]

In the most famous of the journal symposia, *Partisan Review,* long the citadel of Trotskyite politics and literary despair, devoted three successive issues in 1952 to "Our Country and Our Culture." Its list of contributors reads like a who's who of fifties intellectuals. Articles appeared authored by (among others) Newtin Arvin, Leslie Fiedler, Norman Mailer, Reinhold Niebuhr, David Riesman, Lionel Trilling, Jacques Barzun, C. Wright Mills, Richard Chase, Sidney Hook, Irving Howe, Arthur Schlesinger, Jr., and Max Lerner. With but three exceptions among 24, these writers found the United States to be a mighty fine place. In introducing the symposium the editors clearly noted the dominant trend: "Until little more than a decade ago, America was commonly thought to be hostile to art and culture. Since then, however, the tide has begun to turn, and many writers and intellectuals now feel closer to their country and its culture." The editors went on to explain the nation's new positive image. "Politically there is a recognition that the kind of democracy which exists in America has an intrinsic and positive value: it is not merely a capitalist myth but a reality which must be defended against Russian totalitarianism. . . . Most writers no longer accept alienation as the artist's fate in America; on the contrary, they want very much to be a part of American life. More and more writers have ceased to think of themselves as rebels and exiles. They now believe that their values . . . must be realized in America and in relation to the actuality of American life."[4]

The great majority of scholarly reassessments of the national scene corroborated the *Partisan Review* celebration of American virtues. "Why should *we* make a five-year plan for ourselves when God seems to have had a thousand-year plan ready-made for us?" asked Daniel Boorstin. America, eulogized Max Lerner, is "the only fabulous country." To Peter Viereck the United States "is the highest fulfillment of the honorable ideals of socialism (though achieved—significantly—not by a socialist means but by a democratic capitalism)." "Our society," concurred Jacques Barzun, "fulfills more and more purposes, recognizes the desires of more and more different kinds of human beings. It gives me music, others cyclotrons, and still others camping sites or football games." Such national self-congratulations ran through fifties writings as a secular cult of reassurance, a kind of wishful cheer—we're great, we're great, we're great. . . .[5]

In embracing America, intellectuals also accepted the conservative mood of the Eisenhower years—an antirevolutionary foreign policy aimed at maintaining the international status quo by force of arms and nuclear threat, a domestic policy content with slight alterations of 20-year-old New Deal programs and a prosperity built on military spending.

This conservatism of the great majority of intellectuals was well illustrated by the immense enthusiasm they accorded Adlai Stevenson, the Democratic presidential nominee in 1952 and 1956. Since the time of the 1952 campaign, a vast mythology has surrounded Stevenson. Many intellectuals, even today, remember him as one of the great liberal champions of the twentieth century, a light in the dark days of McCarthyism. This is nonsense. Stevenson was an urbane, witty, charming patrician. But with the single exception of his mild 1956 protest against continued bomb testing, his stated positions varied very little from those of Eisenhower. He did not campaign as the champion of the poor or the working class. Nor did he take a strong stand in favor of civil rights. He did accept, however, the illiberal policies of containment abroad and anticommunist loyalty checks at home. Stevenson openly boasted of his party's conservatism. During the course of the 1952 campaign, he remarked that "the strange alchemy of time has somehow converted the Democrats into the truly conservative party of this country." It is not surprising, therefore, that Peter Viereck, intellectual leader of the "new" conservatives, greatly admired the "liberal" Democrat. "Adlai Stevenson," he claimed in 1953, "is rehabilitating the good name and self-confidence of American intellectuals at the very moment when they most needed rehabilitation against their own small but pestiferous Lumpen fringe." To Viereck, Stevenson was "the independent-souled intellectual now re-emerging at last. . . . 'Challenged' (in Toynbee fashion) by the Soviet crisis, America's free culture 'responds' superbly by producing . . . the maturer new intellectual."[6]

Like Stevenson, nearly all intellectuals considered themselves to be liberals. Yet their liberalism again, like Stevenson's, looked surprisingly like conservatism. Actually most Americans claimed to be liberal. "Out of some 140,000,000 people in the United States," wrote Robert Bendiner, "at least 139,500,000 are liberals to hear them tell it, 'liberal' having become a rough synonym for virtuous, decent, humane, and kind to animals." To be identified with the left in the fifties connoted alignment with communism, while the right signified blind reaction. So most persons clung to the liberal center. "Conventional political categories such as 'right' and 'left' are almost useless," stated the thinkers at *Fortune,* "both are scrambled together as an omelet."[7]

Most intellectuals were Democrats. However, this party, as one of its tacticians, John Kenneth Galbraith, noted, "has staked out little new ground in the last ten years; the idea-breeding, which created such a ferment in the thirties, came to an end with the war, and no one has seriously accused the Democratic party of having a new or dangerous thought for fifteen years." At the time this pleased Galbraith, for "in a country where well-being is general, the astute politician will be the one who stalwartly promises to defend the *status quo.*" Other noted academics agreed. David Riesman and Nathan Glazer, writing in the mid-fifties, professed that "there is room for change only within a narrow margin, if we interpret change in terms traditional among intellectuals." The only domestic problem of any importance, they believed, was the racial issue. But since they did not think that "the demand for tolerance of Negroes" could generate much political enthusiasm, they concluded that "for liberal intellectuals in the postwar era, the home front could not be the arena for major policies."[8]

Believing that the major problems of American life were already solved, intellectuals saw no need for an ideology. They were emphatic about this. "Totalitarianism is ideology, unity engineered from the top," said Barzun. "Democracy of the American brand is anti-ideology." Philip Rahv of the *Partisan Review* saw this as a healthy sign. American intellectuals had matured: "they have grown unreceptive to extreme ideas, less exacting and 'pure' in ideological commitment, more open to persuasions of actuality." The only intellectuals left with "Utopian illusions," according to Rahv, were "the few remaining fellow-travelers," and they were deluded. "American democracy looks like the real thing to the intellectuals. It is not a mere theory." Historian Boorstin wrote an entire book premised on the belief that this country had *always* been non-ideological.[9]

The most vehement exponent of "the end of ideology" was sociologist Daniel Bell. He argued that "the tendency to convert issues into ideologies, to invest them with moral color and high emotional charge, invites conflicts which can only damage a society." Such a position assumed that there were no *real* issues, and certainly no moral ones. Society was to be consensual; the status quo sanctified. The minor changes that were acceptable were those resulting from the pragmatic bargaining of politicians representing various interest groups. Wrote Bell: "one ultimately comes to admire the practical politics of a Theodore Roosevelt and his scorn for the intransigents."[10]

Intellectuals like Bell, Boorstin, and Barzun believed in pluralism, or as Barzun put it, "cohesion achieved by haggling." This was not conflict. It was practical politics conducted by adversaries who accepted the system and knew the rules. Having witnessed the rise of facism and communism, American intellectuals believed the extreme right and left were similar. Both were mass movements based on ideology. In the United States things were different. The experimental approach of the New Deal years had solved the nation's basic ills. Economic exploitation, they believed, was nearly nonexistent. Consequently, the Marxist scheme of conflict between two major classes did not apply. Instead of class struggle, they saw a jockeying among competing yet not incompatible power groups or interest blocs (business, labor, farmers, military, and so forth). Looked at in economic terms these were vertical groupings, not horizontal. They fit Galbraith's theory of countervailing power. The friction between groups was not social conflict between the haves and have-nots, but social competition among peer groups. Such competition was further removed from the dangers of emotional mass movements by the fact that each group was represented by an elite leadership. These various elites knew that logrolling and mutual back-scratching were the way the game was played. They weren't overly concerned with moral absolutes.[11]

Such a theory left no room for major innovations. Nor did it allow for the possibility that there might be groups—blacks, migrant workers, women, the aged, and so on—that were either outside the power structure altogether or not equal partners in it. The theory of pluralism, in fact, had much in common with classical liberalism. Both hypotheses recognized the force of self-interest, but assumed that various interests balanced each other, creating harmony without a single source of power. This would have been possible only if the actual power of various interests was relatively equal. This was not, of course, the case. But for fifties intellectuals, pluralist theory justified their lack of commitment to moral issues such as civil rights or nuclear disarmament. It sanctified also their disenchantment with "the masses" and mass movements.

The elitism and conservatism of the pluralist position can be illustrated by examining intellectual reactions to both McCarthyism and popular culture.

Some intellectuals were so reactionary they actually supported Senator McCarthy's hysterical witch hunting. Former radicals James Burnham, Whittaker Chambers, Max Eastman, John Flynn, and William Schlamm seemed to find in extreme anticommunism a means of purging their sense of guilt for former flirtations with Marxism. Younger right-wing intellectuals William Buckley and L. Brent Bozell saw in McCarthyism an effective bludgeon to attack liberals. Still others honestly believed the internal communist menace was real and that McCarthy was doing a good job of exposing it. Historian Leland Baldwin, for instance, called McCarthy a "likable chap" who did "an excellent thing for the country." Even Leslie Fiedler, though not pro-McCarthy, believed that "to assess McCarthyism justly means to admit that good and evil are divided, though not evenly, between ourselves [intellectuals] and our enemies [McCarthyites]; that there is not an entirely innocent 'we' opposed to an absolutely guilty 'they'."[12]

The overwhelming majority of intellectuals, however, strongly opposed McCarthy. But they did not always do so for the right reasons. Believing in pluralism—the politics of accommodation—they saw in McCarthyism a radical threat to social stability. They were only secondarily concerned with the damage McCarthy had done to innocent individuals and with the stultifying fear that McCarthyism spread. Instead they opposed McCarthyism primarily because they saw it as an ideological mass movement that by stirring up populist support threatened existing political elites and institutions. "The real problem," claimed former radical Will Herberg, "of which 'McCarthyism,' however understood, is but one aspect, lies in the portentous growth of *government by rabble-rousing*." To Fiedler, McCarthyism was "an extension of the American impulse toward 'direct democracy' with its distrust of authority, institutions, and expert knowledge."[13]

McCarthy, intellectuals were convinced, did not represent traditional conservatism. He was a radical whose roots went back to the Populist movement of the late-nineteenth century. According to sociologist Talcott Parsons, "the elements of continuity between Western agrarian populism and McCarthyism are not by any means purely fortuitous. At the levels of both leadership and popular following, the division of American political opinion over this issue *cuts clean across the traditional lines of distinction* between 'conservatives' and 'progressives.'" That was bad. Traditional lines were the stabilizing force of pluralist politics. The most revealing part of this argument was calling McCarthy a populist as a term of contempt. Up until the 1950s liberal intellectuals invariably looked upon populism and the Populist movement as a basic and positive part of the American liberal tradition. Populism, according to John Hicks, its major pre-fifties historian, represented a democratic reaction against plutocratic greed. Although defeated nationally in 1896, the Populist movement was credited with laying the groundwork for positive reforms during the Progressive era. In the 1950s, however, intellectuals became suspicious of any popular movement. The positive view of the Populists collapsed. To Richard Hofstadter, whose influential *Age of Reform* was published in 1955, populism was not issue-oriented. It was bred by anxiety over rapid change. It was to him a negative movement—emotional, self-righteous, moralistic, intolerant, individualistic, nostalgic, given to "conspiratorial theories." To fifties thinkers, then, populism, which had aimed at democratizing economics and politics, and McCarthyism, which aimed at destroying dissent, were nearly synonymous. Both represented a challenge to elitist leadership and gentlemanly compromise. The major impact of the McCarthy hysteria on the intellectuals, therefore, was to create a fear of radicalism and to discredit the entire radical tradition. And this, of course, was what McCarthy had wanted anyway.[14]

The intellectuals' fear of the masses and desire for an elite were also reflected in their reaction to popular culture. Fear that the industrialization and democratization of Western civilization would lead to a cultural leveling and the demise of true culture goes back at least as far as Edmund Burke. From Burke through later critics such as Tocqueville, Kierkegaard, Matthew Arnold, Ortega y Gasset, and T. S. Eliot mass society was attacked while the need for an aristocratic high culture and a cultural elite was upheld. This anti-populist view held sway among intellectuals of both the liberal-left and conservative-right in the 1950s. Even former or current Marxists, people such as Dwight MacDonald, T. W. Adorno, Erich Fromm, and Irving Howe, were appalled at the taste of the masses. "America," wrote Howe, "has entered the stage of kitsch, the mass culture of the middlebrows; literature and art have become estimable commodities." Believing in democracy, these scholars had assumed that when the masses were lifted above poverty the barriers between high and mass culture would vanish, naturally in favor of the former. So they could only be appalled that with the new prosperity the common man sat before the TV fascinated by Milton Berle and Gorgeous George. This disillusioned leftist intellectuals and tended to blunt their economic criticism of capitalist society, transforming it instead into a cultural censure of mass society. To Dwight MacDonald, society's most pressing problem was no longer poverty but the emergence of "a tepid, flaccid Middlebrow Culture that threatens to engulf everything in its spreading ooze."[15]

For those intellectuals already steeped in conservatism, the discovery of mass culture was less a disillusionment than an "I told you so." Mass man would always produce kitsch simply because human nature was corrupt and unimprovable. Society would eternally need a respected cultural elite. Peter Viereck, Walter Lippmann, Bernard Iddings Bell, Alan Valentine, and many others frequently lamented the vulgarity of popular culture—the banality of television, the violence and childishness of comics, the luridness of paperbacks, the shallowness of the press. Too much equality, they believed, threatened to sink America into a morass of materialistic junk with a culture at the level of *Reader's Digest* and the Book-of-the-Month Club. "Ours is a nation of new-rich people," wrote Bernard Iddings Bell, "well washed, all dressed up, rather pathetically unsure just what it is washed and dressed up for; a nation convinced that a multitude of material goods, standardized, furiously and expensively advertised by appeals to greed and vanity, will in themselves make life worth the living." More than ever, affirmed the intellectual elite, people like themselves were needed to set critical standards of opinion and taste. Such thinkers knew what they were expected to like: what was good music and literature. There was great concern with form, appearance, taste, with the result that high culture became increasingly arid and effete—a chasing after T. S. Eliot's footnotes or the Christian references in Ezra Pound's *Cantos*.[16]

Seeing middlebrow culture as kitsch and schmaltz, highbrows became excessively heady. They did not view art in terms of transcendence, experimentation, beauty, playfulness. Needless to say, they missed almost entirely the creative vigor of rock, jazz, *Mad* and E.C. comics, certain Hollywood movies, even some Madison Avenue advertising. They wanted depth, complexity, and above all symbolism. Literature and art were serious stuff, though not political unless of course conservative. The so-called new critics dominated, carefully separating literature from social problems and nearly crushing the creative impulse through critical analysis. The result was, as Paul Goodman wrote, that "the literary atmosphere for the reception of any deep-springing art, advance-guard or otherwise, was miserable." Or as Norman Mailer noted with despair: "everywhere the American writer is being dunned to become healthy, to grow up, to accept the American reality, to integrate himself, to eschew disease, to re-evaluate institutions."[17]

With only occasional exceptions, like Goodman and Mailer, most intellectuals, whether from the political right or left, hoped to stave off the barbarism of mass culture through the creation of an hierarchical elite. "Until the day dawns," wrote Bernard Iddings Bell, "when a democratic elite will be welcomed and listened to in this country, the American who would escape from slavery to crowd culture must expect to have a difficult time of it." Not only was a cultural elite desired, but a political one as well. Seymour Martin Lipset praised elitism as a protection "from the excesses of populism." Talcott Parsons was more specific. He called for a twofold elite: first, "politicians whose specialties consist in the management of public opinion"; and second, "administrators in both civil and military services." Although he believed intellectuals would be the most natural elite, as a realistic man he recommended that businessmen form a large part of the ruling class since "political leadership without prominent business participation is doomed to ineffectiveness and to the perpetuation of dangerous internal conflict." The general tenor of this intellectual conservatism is clearly reflected in a 1954 statement by Will Herberg: "What is needed today is a good, sound, responsible *conservatism.* . . . We need a new conservatism dedicated to the conservation of the American constitutional tradition of freedom and order and unalterably opposed to government by rabble-rousing from whatever direction it may come."[18]

Such conservative elitist attitudes naturally affected the literary, artistic, and scholarly productions of intellectuals. The dominant cultural values of the fifties were reflected in such things as new criticism; poetry by the Eliot, Pound, Stevens school; novels such as Herman Wouk's *Caine Mutiny,* J. D. Salinger's *Catcher in the Rye,* James Gould Cozzen's *By Love Possessed;* UN building and Lever House type architecture; atonal music and cool jazz; abstract expressionist art. Though diverse, such cultural artifacts had much in common. Where they were concerned with values these were deep, enduring conservative ones. Social protest was largely absent. Where such art was emotional, as in the case of abstract expressionism or cool jazz, it was not an emotionalism directed toward any particular social problem. More common in these works was a detached, self-conscious intellectualism. It was a heavy, humorless, serious culture.

The scholarly analyses of American society produced during the decade sought consensus and assiduously avoided any suggestion of conflict. Sociologists, from the beginnings of that discipline in the late-nineteenth century through the early 1940s, had always seen social conflict as a basic form of human interaction and the major cause of social change. In the post-World War II period, all this changed. Sociologists had come to see conflict as abnormal and dysfunctional. Even the study of conflict was eschewed in favor of searching for what holds societies together. The status quo was accepted as the norm and sociology became the tool to teach groups to adjust to the existing structure. Thus sociologists taught industrialists that social skills were all that was necessary for good employer-employee relations. One could not understand America "in terms of economic-interest group conflict," wrote Daniel Bell. W. W. Rostow agreed: "When one examines the classic sources of conflict within the national community—labor and capital, the farm and the city, regional interests, racial and minority groups—one finds each conflict has been softened . . . by the increased physical and social homogeneity of the society."[19]

Historians carried the conservative opposition to conflict to its logical extreme by imposing it on the nation's entire past. The course of American development, according to fifties chroniclers, ran almost as smoothly as a slickly polished slide. From Puritans to organization men, log cabins to suburban ranch houses, nothing much happened. Louis Hartz told how, lacking both a feudal aristocracy and a peasant-proletariat lower class, we developed stolidly within the safe confines of the Lockean liberal tradition. Daniel Boorstin agreed, though he expressed it in a more semantically cute way when he wrote of America's "seemlessness" and "giveiness." It was as if all American history had been chewed, swallowed, digested, and then spewed forth as giant tasteless Wonder bread—no caviar, no gruel, just Wonder bread. When conflicts were admitted, historians explained them away as psychotic aberrations, the results of status anxiety.[20]

The Puritans were made over to be just like you and me; they had sex and drank beer. The American Revolution? It was not really a revolution since it preserved the already well-established American way with an amazing lack of social disruption. That old story of a conflict between radical Jeffersonians and conservative Hamiltonians was said to be exaggerated. Both groups shared much in common; both were conservative. Hamilton, claimed fifties historians, was really a great American. Similarly they labeled the Jacksonian revolution a myth. The Whigs were actually more liberal, but both parties aimed at advancing capitalism. Besides, Webster and Clay were fine statesmen and Calhoun, while proslavery, was a genius when it came to defending minority rights. The Civil War, of course, presented something of a problem for consensus historians. Here was an undeniable conflict. But at least it could be blamed on the abolitionists, who needless to say suffered from status anxiety. The war they had so perversely triggered was held up as an example of the terrible consequences of taking a moral stand outside the pluralist consensus. And so it went. Robber barons became industrial statesmen; feminists, Populists and Progressives, anxious neurotics. Historical friction might imply present-day friction, and since *that* did not exist, our history had to be interpreted as uniform processed smoothness, like those fifties marvels Miracle Whip and Dairy Queen.[21]

Intellectuals celebrated a conservative consensus for a variety of reasons. The cold war coming close on the heels of World War II put a premium on agreement. Intellectuals as much as anyone perceived a need to support basic American values in the face of the supposed communist challenge. But intellectuals also lapsed into conservatism for reasons that went back to the period before the Second World War. Many prominent fifties thinkers had first achieved notoriety in the 1930s either in liberal or radical politics. For the former, the successes of the New Deal seemed complete, the need for further social change minimal. They were tired, self-satisfied, complacent. Stevenson was a natural leader for such persons. Furthermore, many of the thirties masses who had supported the New Deal coalition had themselves moved into suburbanized middle-class conservatism, thus shrinking the base of support for new liberal innovation.

For thirties radicals, or liberals who had flirted with radicalism, the picture was more complex. Communism, nearly all Americans in the fifties believed, threatened the nation. Yet many intellectuals had toyed with Marxism in the thirties. Were they not therefore guilty and partly responsible for the perilous position in which the United States stood at mid-century? A number of former radicals and even liberals thought so. They spoke in theological terms of guilt, penitence, and absolution. In repenting their former radicalism, people such as John Dos Passos, Max Eastman, James Burnham, and Whittaker Chambers simply did a total turnabout, becoming reactionary anticommunist crusaders. Still others, though continuing to call themselves liberals, also proclaimed their guilt. Diana Trilling, for example, in discussing the attacks against Robert Oppenheimer wrote of "the punishment we perhaps owe to ourselves for having once been so careless with our nation's security." Mary McCarthy recorded an incident where an anticommunist intellectual, mistakenly identified with the Communist party, had waited nine months for a passport. Instead of being outraged at this injustice the man welcomed it: "I am glad to suffer if our society can be safe." Intellectuals took seriously the false theory that the 1930s had been a "Red Decade." Writing in 1955, Talcott Parsons claimed "there has indeed been a considerable amount of Communist infiltration in the United States, particularly in the 1930's. . . . Most important was the fact that considerable numbers of the intellectuals became fellow-travelers." Such thinking naturally made intellectuals feel defensive and act conservatively.[22]

Leslie Fiedler's 1955 book, *End to Innocence,* excellently illustrates the stultifying sense of guilt from which liberals suffered. The "innocence" of Fiedler's title was the naive, sentimental faith in human betterment that liberals had believed in during New Deal days. Such an innocence, Fiedler maintained, had caused great harm by aiding world communism, covertly or overtly. "It was this belief," he claimed, "that was the implicit dogma of American liberalism during the past decades, piling up a terrible burden of self-righteousness and self-deceit to be paid for on the day when it would become impossible any longer to believe that the man of good will is identical with the righteous man, and that the liberal *per se* the hero."

Fiedler wrote in the first person plural, describing himself as a representative "liberal, intellectual, writer, American, Jew." Thus "we" are all guilty: "Who that calls himself a liberal is exempt from guilt?" Fiedler specifically defined the guilty "we" as those who supported "trade unionism, social security, and the rights of Negroes, Jews, and other minorities, including socialists and even Communists." The guilty "we," he further explained, were "those who believe or believed Sacco was innocent, who considered the recognition of the Soviet Union not merely wise strategically but a 'progressive' step, and who identified themselves with the Loyalist side during the Spanish Civil War." How such innocent activities and beliefs made liberals responsible for the Soviet threat, Fiedler did not say. But he did make the liberal need for repentance emphatically clear. "We have . . . done great evil" and must confess our past sins. "The confession in itself is nothing, but without the confession . . . we will not be able to move forward from a liberalism of innocence to a liberalism of responsibility." Such a repentant responsible liberalism obviously did not cause much of a ripple on the stagnating status quo of the Eisenhower years.[23]

Guilt was not the only silencer. Intellectuals were also quieted by grave doubts about human nature. Traditionally the mainspring of liberal activism has been a belief in human improvability. The Lockean-Jeffersonian credo maintained that people, though not perfect, were basically good, rational, and above all educable. But this faith seemed dubious to fifties liberals. The trap was that, in questioning human improvability, liberals lost much of their liberalism. The doctrine of original sin came into vogue. To talk positively of human nature in the fifties was to risk contemptuous dismissal as utopian. Liberal intellectuals therefore added a strong draught of conservative pessimism to their reformist brew.

Perhaps the most basic liberal text of the era was Arthur Schlesinger, Jr.'s, *The Vital Center* (1949). Historian Schlesinger saw modern liberalism as the only option—on one side of it stood a naive utopian radicalism, on the other an overly pessimistic conservatism. Both alternatives to "the vital center" could lead to totalitarianism. But the promised vitality of Schlesinger's liberalism was seriously tempered by his belief in "man's fallen nature." "The Soviet experience, on top of the rise of fascism," he wrote, "reminded my generation rather forcibly that man was, indeed, imperfect, and that the corruptions of power could unleash great evil in the world. We discovered a new dimension of experience—the dimension of anxiety, guilt and corruption." Neo-orthodox theology and Freudian psychology also taught liberals skepticism. "In the years after the Second War," Schlesinger concluded, "Americans began to rediscover the great tradition of liberalism— . . . the tradition of reasonable responsibility about politics and a moderate pessimism about man."[24]

Belief in original sin and guilt, or variants thereof, was part of a broader pattern of fear and anxiety clouding the mid-century American scene and causing a contraction of the liberal vision. "Western man in the middle of the twentieth century," noted Schlesinger, "is tense, uncertain, adrift. We look upon our epoch as a time of troubles, an age of anxiety. The grounds of our civilization, of our certitude, are breaking up under our feet." "Our civilization," professed psychiatrist Robert Lindner, "appears to have entered its terminal phase." Poet-playwright Archibald MacLeish wrote in 1955: "We have entered the Age of Despondency, with the Age of Desperation just around the corner. . . . In an Age of Despondency you look behind, like Job on his dungheap. . . . We Americans have begun, for the first time in our history, to look behind." "There is," added Max Lerner, "a crisis in the condition of society which is as grave as the crisis of survival wrought by the H-bomb. One finds a widespread belief . . . that there is a 'New Society' in which almost everything is degenerate and that America is its forerunner and carrier." To Louis Kronenberger it was an "unquiet age, an age not even of scars but of outright wounds."[25]

Such laments, like seventeenth-century jeremiads, were numerous and fashionable. Intellectuals and mortals alike feared the bomb and the very real danger of total annihilation; they feared technology; they feared loneliness and alienation; they feared fear. In the

1952 campaign Stevenson asserted that "the tragedy of our day is the climate of fear in which we live, and fear breeds repression." He had no solutions: "We will be still some time in a dark valley. I cannot promise easy delivery from the perils of this anguished age."[26]

For intellectuals there was a strong sense that events were out of kilter and that they personally and collectively had somehow lost control over history. Familiar with a past in which Americans through technology and force of will had seemed capable of shaping the future, intellectuals had difficulty coping with the cold war years. Events came at a frightening pace—the Soviet bomb, the fall of China, the Korean War, H-bombs, Third World revolutionary movements, Suez, Little Rock, Sputnik. Human control, certainly American control, appeared to be slipping. This sense of an uncontrollable future (as well as uncontrollable present) made intellectuals more fatalistic, more conservative. They turned their orientation from the future to the past and present. Louis Kronenberger noted this: "Today the worst kind of perplexity is added to anxiety: the future, which a while back we were all plotting, however desperately, like a game of chess, has now become something we can only gamble on, like a game of roulette." Lewis Mumford made a similar observation: "Our own leaders are living in a one-dimensional world of the immediate present." In such an insecure world most Americans, including intellectuals, clung to nostalgic traditional values, finding comfort in family, religion, and economic prosperity.[27]

Ironically many of the same scholars who lamented loudest about the anxieties of the age at other times were the booming singers of America the beautiful. They combined Kafkalike lyrics about an arbitrary, amoral universe with choruses of we've-never-had-it-so-good. With long faces they wrote of America's bountifulness, beauty, and promise. One can only conclude from this that either most intellectuals were schizophrenic or, more likely, that the pretty portraits they painted of America's happy classless consensus were a kind of ritual reassurance. As Delmore Schwartz put it, they were exhibiting "a flight from the flux, chaos and uncertainty of the present, a forced and false affirmation of stability in the face of immense and continually mounting instability."[28]

The anticommunist hysteria greatly augmented the fear that intellectuals felt. McCarthyism was not a primary cause of intellectual conservatism, but it certainly added to that don't-rock-the-boat mood. Even before McCarthy entered the fray in 1950, much anticommunist propaganda was directed against intellectuals. *Life*, on April 14, 1949, ran a two-page spread of 50 individual portraits under the headline: "Dupes and Fellow Travelers Dress Up Communist Fronts." Though admitting that few if any of the 50 were actual party members, *Life* asserted that "innocent or not, they accomplish quite as much for the Kremlin in their glamorous way as the card holder does in his drab toil." Pictured were such people as Albert Einstein, Mark Van Doren, Dorothy Parker, Norman Mailer, Arthur Miller, Langston Hughes, Leonard Bernstein, Aaron Copland, Clifford Odets, Louis Untermeyer, Lillian Hellman, Charlie Chaplin, and Ralph Barton Perry.

Intellectuals suffered most from the witch-hunting tactics of blacklisting, loyalty oaths, and special investigating committees. Universities, public schools, the press, the movie industry, radio and television, even the churches were periodically purged of suspected Reds by the superpatriots. Contemptuous terms—egghead, bleeding-heart liberal, fadistic liberal, dupe, pinko, fellow traveler—were frequently thrown at intellectuals. Under such pressures, thinkers, most of whom were already quite conservative, found it convenient to further temper their liberalism and conform their policies to the public mood of fear and hatred. "Since Communism questions our values," wrote journalist Thomas Griffith, "no one else must: fearing that someone may lose faith in our system, we redouble the publicity in its favor and discourage any questioning of it."[29]

Aiming to show the right that they too were good, loyal pro-Americans, intellectuals became excessively anticommunist themselves. James Rorty and Moshe Dexter, for instance, in their book *McCarthy and the Communists* (1954), though critical of McCarthy, tried to prove that they had better anticommunist credentials than the Wisconsin senator. They attacked McCarthy on the grounds that his methods aided communism. Adlai Stevenson campaigned as the true anticommunist who would help defeat the Red "anti-Christ" who "stalks our world." James Thurber wrote proudly of the "enormous contribution to patriotic propaganda on behalf of the security of the nation" that "writers and entertainers have made." "American writers," in Peter Viereck's words, "buzz into the market place in loud droves, proclaiming: 'Look, everybody; we've stopped being Irresponsibles.'" Scholars at all critical of American society often felt the need to preface any faultfinding with an apology. Alan Valentine's 1954 attack on conformity was typical. He began this study with the statement: "I believe there are things which should be said about America and that it is not unpatriotic to say them."[30]

Though timid criticisms of American life continued to be offered, many intellectuals found it expedient to forego any censure. A negative reaction to American culture, insisted Newtin Arvin, "is simply sterile, even psychopathic, and ought to give way, as it has done here in the last decade, to the positive relation. Anything else suggests too strongly the continuance into adult life of the negative Oedipal relations of adolescence." Intellectuals failing to fall into line with the conservative consensus often were attacked by their fellows as irresponsible. "The lowest form of intellectual life," charged Sidney Hook at the time McCarthy was close to dominating the country, "is led by left-bank American expatriates who curry favor with Sartrian neutralists by giving them the lowdown on the cultural 'reign of terror' [sic!] in America." Hook warned intellectuals not to forget "for a moment the total threat which communism poses to the life of the free mind." Intellectuals must give "dedicated support" if "free culture" was to survive.[31]

Under such pressures most intellectuals began to shun all causes since even the noblest of these—civil rights, peace—might also be backed by communists. They played it safe, refusing to join organizations, sign petitions, make commitments. No utopian ideals for them, just a standpat conformism. "The real adventure of existence," influential intellectual Norman Podhoretz asserted in a *New Leader* symposium on "The Younger Generation," "was to be found not in radical politics or in Bohemia but in the 'moral life' of the individual, within the framework of his efforts to do his duty and assume his responsibility in a world of adults." He went on to state that "to the younger generation, American society seemed on the whole a reasonably decent environment for the intellectual." Young people, he claimed, were discovering "that 'conformity' did not necessarily mean dullness and unthinking conventionality, that, indeed, there was great beauty, profound significance in a man's struggle to achieve freedom *through* submission to conditions. . . . The trick, then, was to stop carping at life like a petulant adolescent . . . and to get down to the business of adult living as quickly as possible." Looking around him, the pleased Podhoretz praised young people for marrying early and making firm commitments to careers. They were leading the "good life" as "poised," "sober," "judicious," "prudent" adults.[32] Freedom had come to mean the very things threatened by communism: regimentation, conformity, silencing dissent.

For those intellectuals who irresponsibly found fault with an economy based on warfare and waste, an arms stockpile sufficient for world destruction, a society rampant with racism, sexism, poverty, and exploitation, life was not easy. "We live in a climate so reactionary," Norman Mailer wrote in 1954, "that the normal guides to understanding contemporary American politics are reversed. . . . Radical political life has become difficult, and to hold the position of a libertarian socialist is equivalent to accepting almost total intellectual alienation from America." Mailer was right. There had occurred, in Philip Rahv's words, "the *embourgeoisement* of the American intelligentsia." This accounted, according to Rahv, "for the fact that the idea of socialism . . . has virtually ceased to figure in current intellectual discussion." Lionel Trilling went so far as to claim that "in the United States at this time liberalism is not only the dominant but even the sole intellectual tradition."[33]

When the existence of left-wing critics was recognized by the liberal intelligentsia, it was with contempt. To John Kenneth Galbraith, leftist protest was the "by-product of frustration." He characterized the typical protestor as "unreasonable, self-righteous, and violent," as opposed to his model liberal who was "persuasive, well-mannered, and ingratiating, and, in the end, disposed to a reasonable compromise." Granville Hicks called radicalism "a way of escape." In reviewing C. Wright Mills' *White Collar*, he lectured Mills to "drop the radical pose and get down to work." "Marx-baiting," Irving Howe noted, "has become a favorite sport in the academic journals." Even the non-radical *Nation* was too leftist for most intellectuals.[34]

In such an environment the organized left all but disappeared. The certainties of thirties Marxism were gone and most radicals of that era had long since renounced their radicalism. The Communist party in the fifties was a mere skeleton, serving more the needs of J. Edgar Hoover and the anticommunist right than those of the radical left. Almost no intellectuals retained communist affiliations. Even socialism as an organized force was moribund. In 1956 a few radicals sadly noted that "the decline of independent radicalism and the gradual falling into silence of prophetic and rebellious voices is an ominous feature of the mid-twentieth century. . . . Those who should furnish vision and direction are silent or echoing old ideas in which they scarcely believe themselves."[35]

In 1954 Irving Howe and others founded *Dissent*, a journal whose purpose was "to dissent from the bleak atmosphere of conformism that pervades the political and intellectual life of the United States; to dissent from the support of the *status quo* now so noticeable on the part of many former radicals and socialists; to dissent from the terrible assumption that a new war is necessary or inevitable." The *Dissent* people called themselves democratic socialists and radicals; some of them were. But most of the articles published were by liberals who only appeared radical in contrast to the conservatism of the self-proclaimed "liberals." Two years after the first *Dissent*, Dave Dellinger, A. J. Muste, Bayard Rustin, and others launched *Liberation*, a publication that prefigured much of the direct-action, non-violent protest of the sixties New Left. *Liberation* radicals were anti-Marxist pacifists, believers in civil disobedience as advocated and practiced by Thoreau and Gandhi. They favored utopian thinking, humanized technology, decentralized power, and participatory democracy. Neither *Dissent* nor *Liberation*, however, had much impact in the fifties.[36]

The best one can say about the intellectual left during that decade is that despite repression and alienation a few independent and sometimes brilliant thinkers continued to function—people such as C. Wright Mills, Erich Fromm, Herbert Marcuse, Barrington Moore, Wilheim Reich, Paul Goodman, Norman Mailer, Irving Howe, and Harvey Swados. And that out of the civil rights and pacifist activities of the later fifties the groundwork was laid for the radical revival of the 1960s. But on the whole, the left was in limbo.

As might be expected, the intellectual right fared much better. In the 1950s, for the first time since the days of William Graham Sumner, America produced a respected scholarly conservatism. The self-styled new conservatism could be dated from 1949 with the publication of Peter Viereck's *Conservatism Revisited.* In 1953 Russell Kirk's *The Conservative Mind* and Viereck's *Shame and Glory of the Intellectuals* appeared; Clinton Rossiter published *Conservatism in America* in 1956. Other new conservatives included Bernard Iddings Bell, the aged Walter Lippmann, John Blum, John Hallowell and the southern writers Allen Tate, Robert Penn Warren, and John Crowe Ransom. Longshoreman-philosopher Eric Hoffer, whose best-selling *True Believer* was published in 1951, helped popularize new conservative doctrine.

With the exception of a few reactionary intellectuals such as William Buckley,[37] the scholarly right was scarcely distinguishable from the liberals' "vital center." Both groups feared mass society and any form of populist democracy. "All mass movements," wrote Hoffer, in the era's most blatant and popular anti-populist treatise, "generate in their adherents a readiness to die . . . , all of them, irrespective of the doctrine they preach . . . , breed fanaticism, fervent hope, hatred and intolerances." To check the direct democracy of the "true believers," conservatives, like their liberal counterparts, advocated respect for traditional institutions and values, pluralist politics, and the need for cultural and political elites. Even more than liberals, conservatives stressed man's imperfect nature and the need for higher God-given or natural laws. It goes without saying that both groups were anticommunist and anti-radical.[38]

Peter Viereck's conservatism illustrates the closeness of the new conservative position to that of the liberals. Viereck wrote that "the conservative, politically descended from Burke, distrusts human nature and believes . . . in Original Sin, which must be restrained by the ethical traffic lights of traditionalism." He called himself a "value-conserving classical humanist." From the American past he admired historic conservatives—Hamilton, Gouverneur Morris, John Randolph, Rufus Choate, Calhoun. Yet he did not reject the Jeffersonian tradition and even accepted "the best of the revolution-preventing social reforms of the New Deal." Liberalism, he admitted, was deeply rooted in American life. "It is a question not of uprooting the great liberal part of America's complex and pluralistic heritage but of enriching it and deepening its shallow insights—now that it has grown stereotyped and complacent—with the insights of conservative dissent."[39]

Mid-century liberalism and conservatism, Tweedledum and Tweedledee. Not surprisingly, liberal sage Schlesinger praised books by Viereck and Rossiter and even called Hoffer's anti-intellectual *True Believer* a "brilliant and original inquiry into the nature of mass movements." Conservative Kirk in his turn praised Schlesinger as really a conservative at heart. "In our own day," wrote liberal historian Hofstadter in 1955, "there are some signs that liberals are beginning to find it both natural and expedient to explore the merits and employ the rhetoric of conservatism. They find themselves far more conscious of those things they would like to preserve than they are of those things they would change. . . . What appeals to me in the New Conservatism," he added, "is simply the old liberalism, chastened by adversity, tempered by time, and by a growing sense of reality." Locke was sobered by Hobbes, Rousseau replaced by Burke, as liberals and conservatives joined in congratulating one another on their maturity and realism, the timid applauding the timid for one another's timidity.[40]

By attacking radicals and praising conservatives, liberal intellectuals won a respected place in Eisenhower's America. No roach-infested garrets for these thinkers; they were scrubbed, suited, suburbanized as they went forth, briefcases bulging, to man the expanding universities or to take secure places in business, government, and publishing. A new age was dawning, thought Lionel Trilling. "Intellect has associated itself with power as perhaps never before in history." The editors of *Saturday Review* cheered the unity of business and intellect: "No sensible businessman would be prepared to do without the critical and analytical activity of the academic men; no sensible academician would be prepared to sacrifice the agreeable economic corollaries—scholarships, foundations, and subsidies—of a sound prosperity." To David Riesman and Nathan Glazer, the natural allies of the liberal intellectual were Wall Streeters and the military elite. After all, they asked, what intellectual issue "could be more crucial today than the outcome of the struggle between the Strategic Air Command and the Army Ground Forces?" The mass media, happy to discover that intellectuals were no longer bearded bomb-throwers, was ecstatic. Riesman bedecked *Time's* cover, and numerous articles praised the work of America's cultural and scholarly elite. "If the popular discovery of the intellectual in America continues at its present breakneck speed," joked Dan Wakefield in 1956, "we will soon see Arthur Schlesinger, Jr., replacing Phil Silvers on the back of *Life* with the invitation to try a Camel, and Mary McCarthy in a neck-and-neck race with Eudora Welty for the crown of 'Miss Rheingold.' "[41]

The dominant intellectual climate of the 1950s, then, was profoundly conservative. Proclaiming an end to ideology, intellectuals held dogmatically to an ideological pluralism, capitalism, anticommunism, and elitism. They were backward-looking Arcadians whose vision was bounded by the New Deal in the past and by that-which-was in the present. In championing an anti-utopian, hard-headed realism—a wheeler-dealer pragmatism and factionalism with little concern for ideas or morals—they helped lay the groundwork for the amoral policies of the sixties and seventies: Bay of Pigs, Vietnam, Watergate. The dreams of these thinkers were small, their social sympathies slight. They saw no other options than the accepted orthodoxy. As the no longer so self-satisfied Riesman wrote in 1958: "We have become a conservative country, despite our world-wide reputation for seeking novelty, in that we are unable to envisage alternative pictures for ourselves."[42]

In another 1958 essay Riesman questioned "whether liberalism in its traditional American form can survive if there is no radicalism against which to be moderate." He complained that the intellectuals with their vaunted realism were not producing "profound ideals" to motivate a new society. By the late fifties other formerly complacent intellectuals, aroused from lethargy by Sputniks, a slumping economy, and perhaps just boredom, made similar charges. *Time* foreign editor Thomas Griffith, looking back in 1959, saw the fifties as a period of disunity. "We have been like an orchestra playing all at once but with no particular melody and with brasses dominating. We need not so much to abandon our fiddles and cornets, as to be orchestrated again." "What a nine years it has been!" reminisced writer-critic Harvey Breit in 1960. "What an unholy, inactive lot we were during that time. Bitter, cynical, indifferent, supine, momentous events proceeded without us, the world advanced in spite of us, life ebbed and flowed in vast movements while we loafed on beaches and in television rooms. How sad for most of us, who rode out our nation's unconnection, remaining unconnected, solitary, alien, complacent."[43]

The anxious late-fifties mood of critical national and self-reappraisal brought about a great search for new goals. American development, alleged the massive Rockefeller Fund study, has "outrun our goals." Their findings aimed "to clarify the national purposes." What the nation needed, proclaimed TRB of *The New Republic* in September 1959, was "a sense of national purpose." Unfortunately most thinkers saw the need for goals only within the rigid context of fifties thinking: a domestic policy aimed at accelerating economic growth and a foreign policy based on containing and ultimately triumphing over communism. John F. Kennedy exemplified this with his call for national self-sacrifice, a faster growth rate for the GNP, and putting a man on the moon.[44]

But for a few intellectuals at least, the late fifties and early sixties brought a new sense that the true role of the thinker was to be utopian, to ask big questions, to stand apart from the status quo. New choices began to seem possible. As Paul Goodman told his fellow Americans in 1962, "if you do not do better, it is not because there are no alternatives, but because you do not choose to."[45]

NOTES

1. Jacques Barzun, *God's Country and Mine* (Boston, 1954), p. 201; Granville Hicks, "Liberalism in the Fifties," *American Scholar,* 25 (Summer 1956), 283–96.

2. Mary McCarthy, "America the Beautiful," is reprinted in her book *On the Contrary* (New York, 1961), pp. 6–19.

3. Editors of *Fortune, U.S.A.: The Permanent Revolution* (New York, 1951), p. viii; *American Scholar,* 25 (Winter 1955–56), 9; representative group studies of American character, life, and values include: Francis X. Sutton et al, *The American Business Creed* (Cambridge, Mass., 1956); Elting E. Morison, ed., *The American Style* (New York, 1958); Rockefeller Brothers Fund, *Prospect for America* (Garden City, 1961). Eric Larrabee, *The Self-Conscious Society* (Garden City, 1960) examines the fifties craze for self-examination and self-praise.

4. "Our Country and Our Culture: A Symposium," *Partisan Review,* XIX (May–June 1952), 282–84.

5. Daniel Boorstin, *The Genius of American Politics* (Chicago, 1953), p. 179; Max Lerner, "Our Country and Our Culture," *Partisan Review,* XIX (Sept.–Oct. 1952), 581–85; Peter Viereck, *Shame and Glory of the Intellectuals: Babbitt Jr. vs. the Rediscovery of Values* (Boston, 1953), p. 142; Barzun, *God's Country,* p. 88.

6. Adlai E. Stevenson, *Major Campaign Speeches, 1952* (New York, 1953), pp. 204–5; Viereck, *Shame and Glory,* p. 279. See also: Irving Howe, "Stevenson and the Intellectuals," *Dissent,* I (Winter 1954), 12–21; Richard Hofstadter, *The Age of Reform* (New York, 1955), pp. 13–14.

7. Bendiner is quoted in Viereck, *Shame and Glory,* p. 18; Editors of *Fortune, U.S.A.,* p. 113.

8. John Kenneth Galbraith, *Economics and the Art of Controversy* (New York, 1959 ed.), p. 111; John Kenneth Galbraith, *American Capitalism* (Boston, 1956 ed.), pp. 10–11; Riesman's and Glazer's essay is in Daniel Bell, ed., *The Radical Right* (Garden City, 1963 ed.), pp. 101–2. See also C. Wright Mills, "The Conservative Mood," *Dissent,* I (Winter 1954), 29–30; James A. Wechsler, *Reflections of an Angry Middle-Aged Editor* (New York, 1960), pp. 40–51.

9. Barzun, *God's Country,* p. 90; Philip Rahv, "Our Country and Our Culture," *Partisan Review,* XIX (May–June 1952), 304; Boorstin, *Genius.*

10. Bell, ed., *Radical Right,* pp. 56–57; Daniel Bell, *The End of Ideology* (New York, 1961).

11. Barzun, *God's Country,* p. 90; the essays in Bell, ed., *Radical Right* nearly all reflect pluralist theory; Galbraith's popular pluralist economic theory of countervailing power was put forth in his *American Capitalism.* See also Michael Paul Rogin, *The Intellectuals and McCarthy* (Cambridge, Mass., 1967), pp. 9–15.

12. Fred J. Cook, *The Nightmare Decade* (New York, 1971), p. 276; Leland DeWitt Baldwin, *The Meaning of America* (Pittsburgh, 1955), pp. 278–80; Leslie A. Fiedler, *An End to Innocence* (Boston, 1955), p. 51.

13. Will Herberg, "Government by Rabble-Rousing," *New Leader,* January 18, 1954, pp. 13–16; Fiedler, *End to Innocence,* p. 57.

14. Talcott Parsons' essay is in Bell, ed., *Radical Right,* pp. 175–99. *The Radical Right* is a representative collection of essays by influential social scientists of the 1950s, including Bell, Hofstadter, Riesman, Glazer, Viereck, Parsons, Seymour Martin Lipset, Alan Westin, and Herbert Hyman. In general the various authors treat McCarthyism as a radical threat to social order. Hofstadter, *Age of Reform,* pp. 3–130; the best treatment of this whole subject is Rogin, *Intellectuals and McCarthy.* See also Athan Theoharis, *Seeds of Repression* (Chicago, 1971), p. 225.

15. Irving Howe, "Our Country and Our Culture," *Partisan Review,* XIV (Sept.–Oct. 1952), 578; Dwight MacDonald, "A Theory of Mass Culture," *Diogenes,* 3 (Summer 1953), 5. See also Dwight MacDonald, *Against the American Grain* (New York, 1962), pp. 3–75; D. W. Brogan, "The Problem of High Culture and Mass Culture," *Diogenes,* 5 (Winter 1954), 1–13; Edward Shils, "Daydreams and Nightmares: Reflections on the Criticisms of Mass Culture," *Sewanee Review,* 75 (1957), 587–608.

16. Bernard Iddings Bell, *Crowd Culture* (New York, 1952), pp. 13–47; Alan Valentine, *The Age of Conformity* (Chicago, 1954), p. 104. See also Daniel Bell, "Theory of Mass Society," *Commentary,* 22 (July 1956), 75–83; Joseph Wood Krutch, ed., *Is the Common Man too Common?* (Norman, Okla., 1954); Thomas Griffith, *The Waist-High Culture* (New York, 1959), p. 244.

17. Paul Goodman, *Utopian Essays* (New York, 1962), pp. 202–21; Norman Mailer, "Our Country and Our Culture," *Partisan Review,* XIX (May–June 1952), 299. See also Bruce Cook, *The Beat Generation* (New York, 1971), pp. 10–11, 48; Louis Kronenberger, *Company Manners* (Indianapolis, 1954), pp. 31–56.

18. Bell, *Crowd Culture,* pp. 140–41; Seymour Martin Lipset, *The First New Nation* (New York, 1963), p. 271; Parsons in Bell, ed., *Radical Right,* p. 192; Herberg, "Government by Rabble-Rousing," p. 16. See also Ferdinand Lundberg review in *The Yale Review,* XLIV (March 1955), 439–43; Bernard Rosenberg, "The 'New American Right,'" *Dissent,* 3 (Winter 1956), 45–50.

19. Bell, ed., *Radical Right,* pp. xi–xii; W. W. Rostow's essay is in Morison, ed., *American Style,* p. 301; Jessie Bernard, "Where Is the Modern Sociology of Conflict?", *American Journal of Sociology,* 56 (July 1950), 11–16; Ralf Dahren-

dorf, "Toward a Theory of Social Conflict," *Journal of Conflict Resolution*, 2 (June 1958), 170–83.

20. Louis Hartz, *The Liberal Tradition in America* (New York, 1955); Boorstin, *Genius*.

21. For a sampling of this sort of historiography see Richard Hofstadter, *The American Political Tradition* (New York, 1948); Robert E. Brown, *Middle-Class Democracy and the Revolution in Massachusetts* (Ithaca, 1955); Louis M. Hacker, *Alexander Hamilton in the American Tradition* (New York, 1957); Marvin Meyers, *The Jacksonian Persuasion* (New York, 1960); Daniel J. Boorstin, *The Americans: The Colonial Experience* (New York, 1958); Clement Eaton, *Henry Clay and the Art of American Politics* (Boston, 1957); Stanley M. Elkins, *Slavery: A Problem in American Institutional and Intellectual Life* (Chicago, 1959); David Donald, *Lincoln Reconsidered* (New York, 1956); Carl N. Degler, *Out of Our Past* (New York, 1959).

22. Diana Trilling is quoted in Harvey Swados, *A Radical's America* (Boston, 1962), pp. 265–73; McCarthy, *On the Contrary*, pp. 40–41; Parsons in Bell, ed., *Radical Right*, pp. 184–86; Harold Rosenberg, "Couch Liberalism and the Guilty Past," *Dissent*, II (Autumn 1955), 317–28.

23. Fiedler, *End to Innocence*, pp. vii–68.

24. Arthur M. Schlesinger, Jr., *The Vital Center* (Boston, 1962 ed.), pp. xxii–xxiii, 165–70; Eugene Victor Walter, "The Masses and the Elite," *Dissent*, 3 (Winter 1956), 77; Irving Howe, "This Age of Conformity," *Partisan Review*, 21 (Jan.–Feb. 1954), 23; Reinhold Niebuhr, *The Irony of American History* (New York, 1952), pp. 18–19, 83–84.

25. Schlesinger, *Vital Center*, p. 1; Robert Lindner, *Must You Conform?* (New York, 1956), pp. 22–23, 149–51; Archibald MacLeish, "The Alternative," *The Yale Review*, XLIV (June 1955), 481–82; Max Lerner, "The Flowering of Latter-Day Man," *American Scholar*, 25 (Winter 1955–56), 24; Kronenberger, *Company Manners*, p. 47.

26. Stevenson, *Major Campaign Speeches, 1952*, pp. 20–21, 117.

27. Kronenberger, *Company Manners*, pp. 16–20; Lewis Mumford, *In the Name of Sanity* (New York, 1954), pp. 4, 156, 161. See also Robert L. Heilbroner, *The Future of American History*, pp. 52–62; Niebuhr, *Irony*, p. 146; Griffith, *Waist-High Culture*, p. 263.

28. Delmore Schwartz, "Our Country and Our Culture," *Partisan Review*, XIX (Sept.–Oct. 1952), 594. See also Irving Howe, "Our Country and Our Culture," Ibid., pp. 579–80; Boorstin, *Genius*, pp. 157–60.

29. Griffith, *Waist-High*, p. 218.

30. James Rorty and Moshe Dexter, *McCarthy and the Communists* (Boston, 1954); Stevenson, *Major Campaign Speeches, 1952*, pp. xxv, 196; despite Stevenson's anticommunist campaign, Richard Nixon called him "Adlai the appeaser . . . who got a Ph.D. from Dean Acheson's College of Cowardly Communist Containment"; McCarthy shouted he wished he had a club to teach patriotism to "little Ad-lie." James Thurber, Section 2, New York *Times*, July 27, 1952; Viereck, *Shame and Glory*, pp. 292–93; Valentine, *Age of Conformity*, preface page.

31. Newtin Arvin, "Our Country and Our Culture," *Partisan Review*, XIX

(May–June 1952), 287; Sidney Hook, "Our Country and Our Culture," *Partisan Review*, XIX (Sept.–Oct. 1952), 569–74. See also Granville Hicks, "Liberalism in the Fifties," pp. 290–96. The editors of *Harper's* (February 1956), pp. 10–18, 68–72, went so far as to call for intellectuals to get together to produce a resounding "American manifesto."

32. Podhoretz is quoted in Wechsler, *Reflections*, pp. 21–22.

33. Norman Mailer, "David Riesman Reconsidered," *Dissent*, I (Autumn 1954), 358–59; Rahv, "Our Country," p. 304; Lionel Trilling, *The Liberal Imagination* (Garden City, 1953 ed.), p. vii.

34. Galbraith, *Economics*, p. 99; Hicks' review of Mills is quoted in Viereck, *Shame and Glory*, p. 215; Howe, "Age of Conformity," p. 12; McCarthy, *On the Contrary*, p. 39.

35. Quotation is from the first editorial in *Liberation* and is reprinted in Paul Goodman, ed., *Seeds of Liberation* (New York, 1964), p. 3.

36. *Dissent*, I (Winter 1954), 3; Lewis Coser, "What Shall We Do?" *Dissent*, 3 (Spring 1956), 156–65; a good sampling of *Liberation* articles from its founding to the early sixties is in Goodman, ed., *Seeds of Liberation*. Other important, but small-circulation publications of the left included *I. F. Stone's Weekly*, *Monthly Review*, and *The National Guardian*.

37. Buckley and *The National Review* that he edited opposed such things as social security, graduated income tax, the ban on religious teaching in public schools, and most government activities, except McCarthy-type witch hunting and the military build-up. Even conservative Viereck, *Shame and Glory*, pp. 60–63, dismissed Buckley's vision as a "moth-eaten mouse of petty economic privilege." See Buckley's *God and Man at Yale* (Chicago, 1951) and *Up From Liberalism* (New York, 1959).

38. Eric Hoffer, *The True Believer* (New York, 1958 ed.), first page of preface; Phillip C. Chapman, "The New Conservatism," *Political Science Quarterly*, LXXV (March 1960), 17–34; Bertram D. Sarason, "The Legend of Edmund Burke," *Dissent*, II (Summer 1955), 257–63; Eugene Victor Walter, "The Chimera of Conservatism," *Dissent*, II (Summer 1955), 250–56.

39. Viereck, *Shame and Glory*, pp. 8–9, 12, 111–14, 190–221; like the liberals, Viereck attacked utopian idealism and mass movements; he also characterized America's historical development in a manner similar to the consensus historians.

40. Arthur M. Schlesinger, Jr., review of Viereck's *Conservatism Revisited* is in New York *Times*, October 23, 1949, p. 49; Schlesinger's praise of Rossiter and Kirk's praise of Schlesinger are cited in Walter, "Chimera of Conservatism," pp. 250–56; Schlesinger's praise of Hoffer is quoted in the front page of the latter's *True Believer;* Hofstadter, *Age of Reform*, pp. 13–14.

41. Lionel Trilling, "Our Country and Our Culture," *Partisan Review*, XIX (May–June 1952), 319–21; Crawford H. Greenwalt, "The Culture of the Businessman," *Saturday Review*, January 19, 1957, pp. 11–13; Riesman and Glazer in Bell, ed., *Radical Right*, p. 100; Dan Wakefield, "Branding the Eggheads," *Nation*, November 24, 1956, pp. 456–57. See also Russell Lynes, *A Surfeit of Honey* (New York, 1957), p. 18.

42. Riesman's essay is in Eric Larrabee and Rolf Meyerson, eds., *Mass Leisure* (Glencoe, Ill., 1958), pp. 366–67. See also C. Wright Mills, "On Knowledge and Power," *Dissent*, II (Summer 1955), 203–4; Irving Howe, "America, the Country and the Myth," *Dissent*, II (Summer 1955), 242–44.

43. Riesman's essay is in Morison, ed., *American Style*, p. 365; Griffith, *Waist-High*, p. 271; Harvey Breit, "A Second Novel," *Partisan Review*, 27 (Summer 1960), 561.

44. *Prospect for America*, p. xv; TRB editorial is reprinted in Robert B. Luce, ed., *The Faces of Five Decades: Selections from Fifty Years of the New Republic* (New York, 1964), p. 405.

45. Goodman, *Utopian Essays*, p. xii. See also Swados, *Radical's America*, pp. 10–11, 128.

9

Showdown at the Little Red Schoolhouse

"*How Red Is the Little Red Schoolhouse?*" asked a 1950 booklet. To the National Council for American Education, the publishers of this pamphlet, the answer was obvious—the American public school system was being subverted by communists and their sympathizers. The pamphlet's cover pictured a Soviet soldier injecting a hypodermic labeled "Organized Communist Propaganda" into the little red schoolhouse. Within the booklet were headings (some in red ink): "The Treason Ring is out to make Reds of your Children" and "Textbooks can be Red propaganda."

This pamphlet was part of a concerted right-wing campaign against progressive education. The existence of such a crusade became evident in the wake of the 1950 firing of Pasadena's superintendent of schools, Dr. Willard E. Goslin. A nationally known progressive educator and president of the American Association of School Administrators, Goslin in the two years he directed the Pasadena schools had created a model system admired by progressive educators throughout the country. Yet in June 1950, his request for an increase in the school tax was voted down by more than a two-to-one margin. Attacks on Goslin mounted. In November citizen groups successfully pressured the board of education into demanding his resignation.

This might not have created a national stir except that an investigative reporter, David Hulburd, looked into the Goslin affair and in the spring of 1951 published *This Happened in Pasadena.* On Sunday, April 29, 1951, Hulburd's book received front-page reviews by James B. Conant in the New York *Times Book Review* and by John Hersey in the New York *Herald Tribune Book Review.* On the same Sunday the Washington *Post* also featured a long review by Agnes E. Meyer. The reviews, like Hulburd's book, favored Goslin and were alarmist. Dr. Conant, the former president of Harvard and one of the nation's most respected writers on education, warned "what happened in California in 1950 could happen to almost any community in the United States. . . . The importance . . . of what happened in Pasadena is the light the events shed not only on the exposed position of public educational systems but on the nature of certain reactionary forces at work in our democracy in these days of uncertainty and fear. . . . Indeed, this book is highly revealing of the reactionary temper of our times."[1]

What scared Conant and other educators was the nature of the attacks against Goslin and his school system and the belief that the Pasadena controversy was not an isolated incident. Hulburd's book showed Goslin to have been the victim of a well-planned right-wing campaign aimed at smearing progressive education. The Pasadena unit of Pro America charged the superintendent with belonging to the "Columbia cult of progressive educators" who aimed "to sell our children on the collapse of our way of life." Goslin was called a "traitor" to the American tradition and accused of introducing "socialism" and "communism" into the schools while not teaching students sufficient "Americanism." The National Council for American Education circulated their pamphlets *How Red Is the Little Red Schoolhouse?* and *Progressive Education Increases Delinquency.* These booklets linked progressivism with crime, irreligion, and Marxism. No wonder then that Conant concluded his review with the warning that "we must face the realities of the Nineteen Fifties: the tide of reaction is flowing strong; there are sincere opponents of all forms of non-denominational schools and colleges; there are others far from sincere who, as in every age, like to exert power by causing trouble, by urging the posse to lynch the victim, the mob to burn the dissenter's house, or the school board to fire the 'progressive' administrator. All this is made clear in the story of what happened in Pasadena."[2]

Even before the Pasadena affair, national media had been proclaiming a crisis in American education. *Life,* October 16, 1950, devoted an entire issue to the topic: "U.S. SCHOOLS: THEY FACE A CRISIS." But in reading the *Life* issue, it is clear that the Luce empire was not exactly sure what the crisis was. The issue did contain a scathing denunciation of progressive education by Bernard Iddings Bell. But the main editorial, written by historian Henry Steele Commager, was full of praise for American public schools.

After Pasadena the sense of crisis deepened and sides were taken. Articles in the *Saturday Evening Post* and *The Catholic World* blamed the problems at Pasadena on the excesses of the progressive educators. "A child educated strictly in the progressive method," claimed the *Catholic World* writer, "will tend to reject revelation." *Saturday Review,* on the other hand, ran a series of articles cautioning the public to be wary of extreme attacks against the schools. Similarly, *McCall's Magazine* featured as its September 1951 cover story an article by Arthur D. Morse, called, "Who's Trying to Ruin Our Schools?" This article opened: "Public education is under the heaviest attack in its history. The attack is not aimed at the improvement of free education. It is aimed at its destruction."[3]

Professional educators were particularly concerned about what they saw as the conspiratorial nature of the attacks on public education. The bookjacket for *This Happened in Pasadena* called the events there part of "a calculated, far-reaching plot." Goslin himself warned in his farewell speech "our freedom is in jeopardy. . . . I know of no better way to wreck everything we think is good in America than to begin to destroy ourselves, one by one, institution by institution, community by community, throughout the land." In July 1950, several months before Goslin's dismissal, Harold Benjamin, chairman of the National Commission for the Defense of Democracy Through Education, told assembled members that "a general attack on public education in the United States is now being organized. The enemy is trying out our line with a number of local, probing raids, attempting to find out where we are weak or strong, testing his methods of attack, recruiting and training his forces, building up his stock piles, filling his war chest, and organizing his propaganda units."[4]

Benjamin's speech no doubt struck some of his audience as unduly apprehensive. But in the post-Pasadena period, such charges by educators became commonplace. In February 1951 the American Association of School Administrators devoted its annual meeting entirely to discussing the varied assaults on public education. Shortly after this meeting Hulburd's book and a second carefully documented attack on the attackers, *American Education Under Fire* by Ernest Melby, were published. *Progressive Education*, the leading journal of progressive educators, employed two successive issues, October 1951 and January 1952, in "meeting the attacks on education."

From these and other studies there emerged a frightening picture of a carefully coordinated right-wing plot aimed at destroying progressive education. The attackers constituted a minority, according to Archibald W. Anderson, editor of *Progressive Education*, "but a minority that is skilled in tactics which distort the evidence, and which obscure the real issues and prevent their being considered in a calm, objective . . . way. This is the technique of 'confuse and control.' It constitutes a serious threat to American education." Anderson, while admitting there were some "honest and sincere" though "not so well informed" critics, lumped most educational dissidents under such mean labels as "congenital reactionaries," "witch hunters," "confirmed subversives," "tax conservatives," "disgruntled teachers," "unreasonable parents," "racketeers," "superpatriots," "race haters," "academic conservatives."[5]

In part Anderson was right. A variety of rightist groups were active in the early fifties. Education was one of their chief targets. Organizations such as Allen Zoll's National Council for American Education and Milo McDonald's American Education Association established local units in various parts of the country and launched campaigns accusing school systems of subversion, waste, and soft pedagogy. The Sons of the American Revolution and the American Legion joined the fray. The June 1952 issue of the *American Legion Magazine* featured an article entitled "Your Child Is Their Target," which charged progressive education with failing to teach the 3 R's, using communist-influenced textbooks, and employing subversive teachers.[6]

Schools were a very vulnerable target. They were community centered, dependent on local taxes, controlled by elected boards, and highly sensitive to organized pressures. More importantly, schools could serve as scapegoats. People, tense over world communism, Korean fighting, spy trials, nuclear weapons, could relieve their frustrations through attacks on the schools. After all, one could do little about the Soviet Union. It was thousands of miles away and hardly likely to be swayed by locally centered American pressure groups. But America's own public school system was another matter. Schools were everywhere and certainly were susceptible to such pressures. If, as people were repeatedly told in the fifties, the real battle between freedom and despotism was in the mind, then what better way to assure democracy's triumph than in purging the schools of any left-leaning teachers and tainted texts? For Americans agitated by the reforms of the New Deal, perturbed by World War II's lack of finality, alarmed by the Red menace, the school issue came to seem a tangible way of actively setting the world right. Progressive education was to be unveiled and destroyed. Then children would be taught not only the horrors of communism but of welfarism too. America would be saved, or so many believed.

The most serious and consistent conservative criticism was that progressive education and communism were one—or nearly so. Both, it was claimed, rested on a base of materialism and antireligion. "Progressive education," decried the author of the 1958 novel *The Pentagon Case*, "is education for socialism, and socialism is only a euphemism for communism." In a more academic but analogous statement, Dr. Lewis Haney, a New York University economics professor and Hearst newspaper columnist, identified progressive education as a "collectivist philosophy" that "comes down through Karl Marx, to John Dewey, [W. H.] Kilpatrick and the others, which is essentially the idea of taking the whole child out of the influence of the family and the church and subjecting him to a conditioning process, subordinating him to the group."[7]

Such attacks had a telling effect. In Los Angeles a right-wing pressure group with the backing of the Hearst press got materials about UNESCO dropped from the school system. In Indiana the story of Robin Hood was removed from school libraries and texts because it taught "communist doctrine." That state also passed a law requiring all teachers "to so arrange and present his or her instruction as to give special emphasis to common honesty, morality, courtesy, obedience to law, respect for the national flag, the Constitution of the United States and the Constitution of the State of Indiana, respect for the parents and the home, the dignity and necessity of honest labor, and other lessons of a steadying influence which tend to promote and develop an upright and desirable citizenry." The Board of Regents of the state of New York, overseer of all public education in the state except the universities, declared that public schools should "teach loyalty to our country as a primary duty." The Board established a special commission to investigate textbooks for patriotism. And so it went in state after state, community after community.[8]

Where legal action failed to silence progressive texts and teachers, extralegal methods often succeeded. Benjamin Fine, the New York *Times* education editor, reported in May 1952, that "a concerted campaign is under way over the country to censor school and college textbooks." He further advised that "voluntary groups are being formed in nearly every state to screen books for 'subversive' or un-American statements. These organizations, not accountable to any legal body, are sometimes doing great harm in their communities." Fine's was an understatement.

The major victims of these McCarthy-type campaigns were teachers and, of course, their students. Vigilante actions by local superpatriots frequently led to the dismissal of teachers whose loyalty was questioned, though the instructors' offenses were seldom more than holding a liberal opinion. In Houston, two teachers were suspended for reading a selection from D. H. Lawrence's *Studies in Classic American Literature* to their 15-year-old pupils. Elsewhere teachers were fired for supporting the National Education Association, the closest thing to a national teachers' union. The anticommunist witch hunts also took their toll. With few exceptions, teachers taking the Fifth Amendment before any kind of subversive investigating committee, however constituted, lost their jobs. Those fired were seldom accused of anything as concrete as past or present membership in the Communist party. New York, Pennsylvania, and California had laws encouraging the ouster of educators who failed to answer questions about their political opinions or membership in political organizations.[9]

The result of such pressure was the development of a stifling atmosphere of fear in which teachers were wary of publicly expressing potentially controversial opinions, joining organizations, crusading against injustice, or experimenting with new teaching techniques. The young and their mentors learned silence. The fear was tangible. Bernard Iddings Bell, though a critic of progressive education, found in extensive correspondence with public school teachers in the early fifties that "over three-fourths of my teacher correspondents are unwilling to be identified for fear of somebody or other."[10]

It was little wonder then that professional educators took fright. They decried having "to carry on their burdens in an atmosphere of widespread bitter public criticism and anti-democratic attacks which seek to change the fundamental character of our government as well as the character and spirit of our education."[11]

Yet what educators tended to overlook in the furor was that not all their critics fit conveniently into such categories as congenital reactionaries, witch hunters, superpatriots. Certainly there were scared old ladies who read communism into any textbook praise of the New Deal or disgruntled veterans who saw higher school taxes as some kind of Red threat. But among them were also serious and respectable intellectual critics of the educational system.

Dissatisfaction with schools for a variety of reasons had been building since the late 1940s. By the fifties it exploded into what both criticizers and criticized believed to be the deepest educational crisis in the nation's history. Paul Woodring, a professor of education, warned other teachers in 1952: "By this late date it must be obvious to everyone engaged in teaching that a strong ground swell is running against us. Entire issues of popular magazines and of journals of opinion have been devoted to critical examinations of public education, each year more books are published which attack current educational practices, and in meetings of boards of education more and more voices are being raised demanding changes in the schools."[12]

Woodring was not referring to the shrill voices of extremists. A thoughtful major assault on the schools had been launched in 1949 with the publications of Bernard Iddings Bell's *Crisis in Education* and Mortimer Smith's *And Madly Teach.* Both Bell and Smith were intellectually conservative. They were not, however, witch-hunting reactionaries. Their books were quite similar (Bell wrote the introduction to Smith's). Both studies leveled charges that would be reiterated time and again in the 1950s. Bell blamed the educational system for the sad state of mass culture. Education pampered students and, he felt, was too utilitarian at all levels. He advocated a return to basic subject matter, greater discipline, hard work, competition, less democracy, and above all the instilling of moral-religious values. He also criticized the schools for usurping domestic functions best left in the home. Smith echoed most of Bell's assertions, adding to them a biting tirade against John Dewey's educational philosophy and what he saw as the insidious power that Columbia Teachers College had in perpetuating Dewey's ideas. Both Smith and Bell agreed, as the latter stated, that schools following Dewey suffered "from complacent orthodoxy, from deadening devotion to a theory of man and a theory of knowledge that can only lead to disaster tomorrow."[13]

Other intellectuals, many of them liberals, came to concur with Smith and Bell. David Riesman's *The Lonely Crowd* (1950) was not ostensibly about schools. But this widely read and highly influential book pointed to the dominant educational philosophy as a major cause of the deterioration of American individualism.[14] In 1953 four major criticisms of the schools appeared: Albert Lynd, *Quackery in the Public Schools;* Robert Hutchins, *The Conflict in Education;* Paul Woodring, *Let's Talk Sense about Our Schools;* and Arthur Bestor, *Educational Wastelands.*

These authors and other critics dealt with a variety of problems: overcrowding of schools, the growing need for scientists and technicians, the shortage of adequately trained teachers, and the possibility (on most minds in the early fifties) that there might indeed be communist subversion in the schools. But the single major concern of all these authors was that the dominant educational philosophy—progressive education—had proved itself at least inadequate and perhaps a total disaster, depending on whom one read.

Progressive education had developed in the early decades of the twentieth century as part of the broad reform movement of the time. It aimed at democratizing the schools and making them more responsive to the needs of a complex urban-industrial society. Up to that time school curricula at all levels had been dictated by that of the colleges. This type of education had assumed that there existed a certain quantum of truth that all educated persons should know. It was a rigid aristocratic system with a heavy stress on classical liberal-arts subjects taught largely through drill and memorization.

Progressive educational theorists Dewey, Herbert Croly, Randolph Bourne, and others advocated altering the curriculum to better suit the practical needs of society and above all the interests, capacity, and happiness of the child. In line with the relativistic values implicit in Darwinian biology, Einsteinian physics, Freudian psychology, and pragmatic philosophy, these reformers saw the memorization of supposed universal truths and values as detrimental to real learning. Truth, they believed, was an ongoing process that could be approached in a variety of ways. These progressives urged that the schools be broadened to include a wider range of subjects and greater choice for the individual student. They also emphasized the need for schools to concern themselves with such nonscholastic matters as health, vocation, and the quality of family life. Education, they argued, should be tailored to different classes of children. Teaching methods were to be improved by adopting new principles from psychology and the social sciences. Ideally, teachers were to stimulate students to want to learn rather than imposing knowledge on them. Progressive education at its conception was a radical philosophy designed to remove elitism from education and make schools instruments for both individual development and social change.[15]

As progressive education became the new orthodoxy in the second quarter of the century, however, it was seldom practiced as originally preached. Much of the intellectual vitality of the movement seemed sapped. School curricula had been vastly expanded but often at the expense of learning basic skills thoroughly. In some schools students could choose from such subjects as how to date, dance, dress properly, drive a car, decorate a living room, flycast, shop, cook, curl hair, budget money. These were functional skills to be sure, but not when they nearly replaced reading, writing, and mathematics. As the progressive school mistress in Nabokov's classic fifties satire *Lolita* told the lecherous Humbert Humbert who had just put pubescent Lolita into her charge: "We are not so much concerned . . . with having our students become bookworms or to be able to reel off all the capitals of Europe which nobody knows anyway, or learn by heart the dates of forgotten battles. What we are concerned with is the adjustment to group life. This is why we stress the four D's: Dramatics, Dance, Debating and Dating. We are confronted by certain facts. Your delightful Dolly will presently enter an age group where dates, dating, date dress, date book, date etiquette, mean as much to her as say, business, business connections, business success mean to you, or as much as the happiness of my girls mean to me."[16] With slight allowance for satiric exaggeration, Nabokov's description fitted well all too many fifties schools. Under such a system it became possible for even a poor student to succeed with little effort, while superior students needed no exertion at all.

The first generation of progressive educators envisioned their reforms as a challenge to the status quo. What came out of their movement was anything but. Instead of encouraging students to develop ideas that might question society's values, teachers in the forties and fifties generally promoted adjustment to the group. The status quo became the norm to which students were expected to conform. This emphasis reached an extreme state in the late forties and early fifties with the emergence of the Life Adjustment movement. Originating in the Vocational Education Division of the United States Office of Education at a conference in 1946, the movement stressed that "functional experiences in the areas of practical arts, home and family life, health and physical fitness and civic competence" were basic to any educational program. The emphasis was on adjustment to existing conditions. In other words, the emphasis was on conformity.[17]

The fifties critics vehemently attacked this life adjustment approach. Its practice seemed glaringly damaging. "What I find," declared John Keats, "is that our schools pamper the jackasses, stuff the geniuses under the rug, and meanwhile envelop everyone in that fatuous diaperism they call life adjustment." "Modern young Americans," bemoaned Alan Valentine, "are probably the first victims of an educational system whose objective is not to make them wise but to make them adaptable."[18] *"You must adjust,"* sadly noted psychologist Robert Lindner. "This is the legend imprinted in every schoolbook, the invisible message on every blackboard. Our schools have become vast factories for the manufacture of robots."[19]

There were other absurdities that also lent themselves to harsh criticism. One professional educator, for example, addressing the National Association of Secondary-School Principals in the early fifties, rejected the notion that all students should master reading, writing, and arithmetic. "We shall some day accept the thought that it is just as illogical to assume that every boy must be able to read as it is that each one must be able to perform on the violin, that it is no more reasonable to require that each girl shall spell well than it is that each one shall bake a good cherry pie."[20]

But instead of attacking such concepts for what they were—absurd perversions of progressive philosophy—fifties critics blamed the entire progressive movement and advocated a virtual return to the rigid pedagogy of the 1890s. This was well illustrated in the writings of the most influential educational critic of the era, Arthur Bestor.

Bestor is an American historian whose closest contact with those in the teacher education business came when he taught briefly at Columbia Teachers College. In the 1950s he became obsessed with the supposed evils of the public school system. Beginning with a 1952 article "Liberal Education and a Liberal Nation" appearing in *American Scholar*, he followed with a series of articles in various popular and scholarly publications. Many of these were revised and incorporated into his 1953 book, *Educational Wastelands*. That work in turn was revised and expanded into *The Restoration of Learning*, published in 1955 and considered the most authoritative educational study of the decade. In 1956 the Council for Basic Education was founded with Bestor as one of its directors. On November 30, 1956, June 7, 1957, and January 24, 1958, *U.S. News & World Report* published lengthy interviews with Bestor under the titles "We Are Less Educated Than Fifty Years Ago" and "What Went Wrong with U.S. Schools?"

Bestor simplistically supposed that the issue in American education was "drawn between those who believe that good teaching should be directed to sound intellectual ends, and those who are content to dethrone intellectual values and cultivate the techniques of teaching for their own sake, in an intellectual and cultural vacuum." Like many of the educators whom he criticized, Bestor saw the educational crisis in conspiratorial terms. But where educators discerned a rightist plot, he beheld an "interlocking directorate" of professors of education, school administrators, and members of state departments of education conniving to prevent the Dicks and Janes of America from learning reading, writing, and arithmetic. To restore real learning, the power of the interlocking directorate would have to be drastically curbed, while strengthening the educational role of persons like himself—liberal arts professors in traditional disciplines.[21]

To Bestor the sole purpose of education was intellectual and moral training. This could come only through traditional academic disciplines—history, English, science, mathematics, and foreign languages. As the Council for Basic Education put it: "schools exist to provide the essential skills of language, numbers, and orderly thought, and to transmit in a reasoned pattern the intellectual, moral, and aesthetic heritage of civilized man." Like other critics of progressive education, Bestor admired the elitist educational systems of Western Europe and the rigid discipline of Soviet schools. Education for a democratic nation should differ from the traditional aristocratic systems only in the numbers whom it taught. This meant that electives should be cut to a minimum and all students, regardless of interest or ability, should be forced to master the traditional liberal arts subjects. What of those without the mentality to master such studies? According to Bestor that did not matter. They needed "the same kind of intellectual fare, only less of it."[22] In other words Bestor and others came close to advocating a return to the conservative, classical system of training, memorization, and intellectual discipline which had prevailed through the late-nineteenth century until it collapsed because of progressive criticisms and its own dire inadequacies.

By the mid-fifties critics like Bestor were markedly gaining in influence. In 1955 an Austrian-born lawyer teaching at New York University, Rudolf Flesch, published a slim volume, *Why Johnny Can't Read and What You Can Do About It.* "We too could have perfect readers," he assured his readers, "if we taught our children by the system used in Germany." His book was not specifically an attack on progressive education. It simply urged that reading be taught through phonetics. But as the book sat on the best-seller list week after week, giving rise to dozens of articles in national magazines, it strongly reinforced the notion that the progressive educators were the culprits.[23]

Then on October 4, 1957, the Soviets orbited Sputnik I, the first man-made earth satellite. Sputnik was less than 200 pounds. It was dismissed as a "hunk of iron almost anybody could launch" by Rear Admiral Rawson Bennett, the man in charge of the American satellite program.[24] But this satellite was followed a month later by the massive Sputnik II, weighing over 1,000 pounds and carrying a live dog. After these two Sputniks, the already swelling outcry against the educational system became a deafening roar. Everyone joined in—the President, the Vice-President, admirals, generals, morticians, grocers, bootblacks, bootleggers, realtors, racketeers—all lamenting the fact that *we* didn't have a hunk of metal orbiting the earth and blaming this tragedy on the sinister Deweyites who had plotted to keep little Johnny from learning to read. Special commissions were set up. Congressional hearings were held. TV and radio stations interrupted the flow of commercials and soap operas to air educational grievances. There is a "CRISIS IN EDUCATION" screamed, cover-to-cover, four successive self-proclaimed "Urgent" issues of *Life*. "The schools are in terrible shape," proclaimed the *Life* editors. "What has long been an ignored national problem, Sputnik has made a recognized crisis."[25]

A perceived educational crisis had, of course, existed throughout the fifties. But Sputnik catalyzed this crisis into a major consideration. In this respect Sputnik was to the educational crisis as McCarthy was to anticommunism. Neither Sputnik nor McCarthy caused these hysterias, but both focused them. Here in Sputnik was a tangible Soviet superiority for which the schools could be blamed. Earlier rightist complaints that America's educational system subverted national purpose seemed proved. Educational critics had a popular, concrete rallying point.

The cold war, which had hovered around the edges of the educational controversies throughout the fifties, now became the central issue. Senators, admirals, generals, university presidents, and even a few teachers poured out articles, books, and speeches comparing U.S. and Soviet education. Invariably the thesis ran: the Soviets yearly turn out more scientists and engineers; therefore, the Soviet system is better and we should alter our own system accordingly. Much of the first *Life* "CRISIS" issue was taken up comparing a supposedly typical Soviet 16-year-old, Alexei, with his American counterpart, Stephen. Alexei was pictured as a very serious student aiming at a future in nuclear physics. He studied three or four hours daily and was well read not only in Russian literature but in English, having read Shakespeare and Shaw. Even his leisure time had purpose. He kept in good physical shape with volleyball and mentally alert with chess, concerts, and piano practice. He did not smile much and was shy with women. But he was dedicated to his education, career, and country. Though finishing only his tenth year of school, Alexei was destined to enter the university the following year.

Poor Stephen, on the other hand, though in his eleventh year of school, would not go to college until the year after next. He had just managed to read Robert Louis Stevenson's *Kidnapped.* Stephen fooled around a lot and did not take the classroom too seriously. His classmates also appeared to trifle away their time. One *Life* photograph showed a girl in the back of Stephen's class reading *Modern Romances.* On the opposite page *Life* ran a contrasting picture of a disciplined technical class in Moscow. Stephen was failing geometry and mostly took easy courses like typing. He went steady and spent his spare time swimming on the team, doing the Rockin' Cha with his steady, rehearsing for the YMCA centennial, and leading prayers as student council chaplain. In case the message was not clear enough, the *Life* editors spelled it out: "a spartan Soviet system is producing many students better equipped to cope with the technicalities of the Space Age."[26]

Many persons saw the crisis as a conflict of the tender-minded progressives versus the tough-minded advocates of intellectual and moral discipline. Vice-President Nixon, in an address about a month after the second Sputnik, charged that "the most fundamental weakness" in American education "is that students are not allowed to face the challenge of failure." He attacked what he saw as too great an emphasis on democracy in schools and stressed instead the need for "competition," "backbone, standards, and guidance." We needed a tightening up of our educational system, sermonized William W. Brickman in *School and Society.* What we must have, he claimed, was "freedom with discipline." An Illinois minister quoted in *Life* asserted that "the study of science in both secondary and elementary schools should be made compulsory instead of elective. The schools should cut out the three H's—hoopin', hollerin', and hullabalooin'—and drill the three R's." Discipline was essential, everyone cried, for, in the words of a Louisiana housewife, "a child just naturally don't want to study."[27]

Not surprisingly in the post-Sputnik hysteria, a military man emerged as the most quoted educational expert. Admiral H. G. Rickover, the heralded father of the nation's nuclear navy, published *Education and Freedom* in 1959. Cold war concerns were foremost. Chapter titles read: "Education Is Our First Line of Defense—Make It Strong," "Lead Time and Military Strength" and so on. "Let us never forget that there can be no second place in a contest with Russia and that there will be no second chance if we lose." To win, he argued, intelligence was needed as never before. Intelligence that could be produced by "nothing short of a complete reorganization of American education, preceded by a revolutionary reversal of educational aims." That "complete reorganization" turned out to be much the same one Bestor and other critics had espoused earlier—a demand that the school's functions be contracted and that fundamentals be rigorously drilled into students. Rickover pressed this as a kind of national machismo—"our technological supremacy has been called into question." Education would be utterly absorbed into the cold war, become its tool, with students as regimented and drilled as the lowliest private.[28]

The Roman discipline demands also thrust forward massive, near hysterical, attacks on progressivism. *Life* editors told their readers that the real crisis in American education was "how to straighten out the debris left by 40 years of progressive educationists. . . ." "Dewey's world," they maintained was "demonstrably in tatters." Rickover agreed. He did concede that progressive educators had "a kindly spirit" and "the desire to make every child happy." Yet he was alarmed that they had "so complete a misunderstanding of the needs of young people in today's world." These needs, of course, were to have the young become the technicians in the cold war. Sloan Wilson of *Gray Flannel Suit* fame summed up a decade of accusations against progressive education. Under the progressive reign, he claimed, students had been "smothered with anxious concern, softened with lack of exercise, seduced with luxuries, then flung into the morass of excessive sex interest. . . . They are overfed and underworked. They have too much leisure and too little discipline." Liberals and conservatives united in outrage and the jeremiads went on and on, but the gist of each was the same—kids must be disciplined, trained, forced, if necessary, into becoming the technical and intellectual experts needed to keep America at the top of the hit parade of nations.[29]

In November 1957, shortly after the second Sputnik, the U. S. Government published *Education in the U.S.S.R.*, telling of the rigorous scientific and mathematical study of the Soviets. Two months later a prestigious group financed by the Rockefeller Brothers Fund issued a report calling for a full-scale federal scholarship program to encourage superior students. Such students, they argued, should be discovered by national examinations and given every encouragement, including special classes in the public schools, advanced placement in college, and scholarships. At about the same time as the Rockefeller report was issued, congressional hearings on education heard addresses by Rickover, Dr. James Killian, the President's science adviser, and Dr. Merle Tuve, director of Carnegie Institute. *Life* summed up their main points:

> We must raise the low standards of our secondary schools and eliminate their trivial courses.
>
> We must shore up the sagging quality of our science teaching, cut down on the teacher's extra jobs, give him time to become a professional scholar again.
>
> We must provide both opportunity and incentive for our gifted children. There must be an unremitting search for talent and intellectual giftedness.
>
> We must not slam the door in the faces of qualified people who want to teach, merely because they have not taken superfluous courses in teacher education.
>
> We must fight the pose that it is smart to be anti-intellectual and cultivate in our education a taste for what is excellent in intellect and spirit.[30]

And so America embarked on what might appear as a good Jeffersonian goal, the search for an aristocracy of talent. Unfortunately the talent hunt was largely limited to uncovering potential scientists and engineers who could serve the un-Jeffersonian ends of manning the military-industrial complex. Underscoring the cold war concern for a trained technological elite, Congress enacted the National Defense Education Act in September 1958. This law allocated nearly $900 million over a four-year period for scholarships and loans to encourage the study of science, mathematics, and modern foreign languages, especially Russian. All across the country scientifically minded youngsters became the objects of fond and anxious attention.

Such a scientific emphasis had its mental price. While Americans wanted to suddenly produce lots of scientists, some were ambivalent. Scientists after all were old men with long white hair and whiskers. They could be spies. As a pragmatic factory watchman from Kentucky said: "I believe that people who want to work in science should be thoroughly screened to make sure of their loyalty in the first place, before they are permitted to become scientists."

But for most Americans science became nearly as sacred as motherhood, anticommunism, and baseball.[31]

Such pressures brought about marked changes in public education. Even before the Sputnik lunacy, progressive education as a national movement had virtually ceased to be. On June 21, 1955, the New York *Times* announced that the Progressive Education Association would disband. The main reason for this, noted Benjamin Fine, was "the disrepute, even contempt in which the term 'progressive' has been held in recent years." The Association's journal, *Progressive Education,* folded two years later. As the historian of progressive education, Lawrence Cremin, wrote: "a movement that had for half a century enlisted the enthusiasm, the loyalty, the imagination, and the energy of large segments of the American public and the teaching profession became, in the decade following World War II, anathema." Cremin saw the movement as the victim of the "general swing toward conservatism in postwar political and social thought."[32]

The collapse of the Progressive Association did not, of course, mean the end of all progressive education. Truly progressive education, however, had always been extremely rare, requiring as it does teachers of incredible ingenuity with vast knowledge, great pedagogical skill, and psychological insight. Much of what went by the name progressive in the fifties was nearly as repressive as the system advocated by the Bestors and Rickovers. Progressive champion Paul Mort of Columbia Teachers College said shortly before his retirement in the spring of 1959: "I've probably seen more schools than anyone else alive, and I've seen exactly two progressive teachers—one an American, the other a Czechoslovak refugee in Bavaria."[33]

But there is no question that under such heavy attack in the fifties, progressivism even as an ideal languished. Those who considered themselves progressives tended to drop the "progressive" label in favor of "modern education." As Harold G. Shane, professor of education at Northwestern, wrote defensively in 1957: "Modern education, often given the vague label 'progressive' education, has long been accused of debasing our schools academically. Actually, modern educational practices have been maligned by writers who have given any shoddy educational practice the name 'progressive.' "[34]

In point of fact, by the mid-fifties the differences between the so-called progressives and their critics were not great, certainly not as vast as the furor would have led one to believe. In most places, ridiculous life-adjustment programs and simple "how to" courses had been quietly dropped. George B. Leonard, Jr., reported in 1957: "For a year and a half, this reporter has been visiting schools with no particular ax to grind. . . . Approaching the current controversy from this position, he found a surprisingly large amount of middle ground. Educators and critics are not so far apart as they think. . . . For every high school that offers a course in dating, 100 would have no part of it." In the post-Sputnik period, curricular and pedagogical changes were accelerated. But their conservative direction was already well laid out. Electives were reduced, academic standards were raised, science, math, and language programs were bolstered.[35] Much of this was to the good. By the late fifties superior students often were being challenged and a display of intellect, though only in certain subjects, was winning respect.

Yet these improvements were not accomplished without great loss. The near death of the progressive ideal left the schools dominated by conservative, cold war thinking and values. More than at any time since the nineteenth century, education enshrined the status quo, perpetuating elitism, sexism, racism, and militarism. Even the higher standards often failed of their purpose due to the rigid teaching manners. Ironically it was a conference of scientists and science teachers meeting at Woods Hole in 1959 that recommended progressive methods "unblocking intuition, giving youth confidence in himself, learning by doing, working with the life interests of each age group." The group's report urged dealing with large ideas, not memorizing the minutiae of accumulated facts. It saw almost any child as being capable, not just the elite few.[36] This advice went unheeded.

No wonder then that the decade witnessed so sharp a rise in student dropouts, juvenile delinquency, beatnikism, and other signs of disgust with the system. By the late fifties the anarchistic, satiric *Mad Magazine* was second in popularity only to *Life* among high school students. Many *Mad* readers were even more alienated by the authoritarian pedagogy of the post-Sputnik educators than they had been earlier in the decade by the pseudoprogressive fluff.[37]

Quite clearly the basic problem of establishing an educational system capable of meeting the needs of a complex industrial society, while at the same time maintaining democratic values and stimulating student creativity, had not been solved by decade's end. Fortunately, however, the years since 1960 have witnessed continued educational debate and, at least among some educators, the fight to recover and improve upon the original, radical, progressive ideal.

NOTES

1. James B. Conant, "The Superintendent Was the Target," New York *Times Book Review*, April 29, 1951, pp. 1, 27.

2. The best treatment of the Pasadena crisis remains Hulburd's *This Happened in Pasadena* (New York, 1951); see also Lawrence A. Cremin, *The Transformation of the School* (New York, 1961), p. 341; Joseph A. Brandt, "This, Too, Happened in Pasadena," *Harper's Magazine*, November 1952, pp. 76–79; Frank Chodorov, "Educators Should Be Warned by the Pasadena Revolt," *Saturday Evening Post*, July 14, 1951, p. 10; Conant, "Superintendent," pp. 1, 27.

3. Chodorov, "Educators Should Be Warned," p. 10; John B. Sheerin, "What Was the Question at Pasadena?", *The Catholic World*, October 1951, pp. 1–5; *Saturday Review*, September 8, 1951; Arthur D. Morse, "Who's Trying to Ruin Our Schools?", *McCall's Magazine*, September 1951, pp. 73–77. See also William W. Brickman, "Attack and Counterattack in American Education," *School and Society*, October 27, 1951, pp. 262–69.

4. Cremin, *Transformation*, p. 341; Goslin's speech and Benjamin's are both reprinted in Ernest O. Melby and Morton Puner, eds., *Freedom and Public Education* (New York, 1953), pp. 137–43.

5. Archibald W. Anderson, "The Cloak of Respectability: The Attackers and Their Methods," *Progressive Education*, 29 (January 1952), 66–82; Ernest Melby, *American Education Under Fire* (New York, 1951).

6. Cremin, *Transformation*, pp. 341–43; Anderson, "Cloak," pp. 70–74; Melby and Puner, eds., *Freedom*, pp. 155, 213.

7. Colonel Victor J. Fox (pseud.), *The Pentagon Case* (New York, 1958), p. 101; Haney's statement is in Melby and Puner, eds., *Freedom*, p. 193.

8. Robert Hutchins, *Some Observations on American Education* (Cambridge, Eng., 1956), pp. 74–77; Alan Valentine, *The Age of Conformity* (Chicago, 1954), pp. 157–58.

9. *Newsweek*, March 29, 1954, p. 58; Hutchins, *Some Observations*, pp. 70–74.

10. Bernard Iddings Bell, *Crowd Culture* (New York, 1952), p. 75.

11. Melby and Puner, eds., *Freedom*, pp. 10–13; *Progressive Education*, 29 (October 1951), 15.

12. Paul Woodring, "An Open Letter to Teachers," *Harper's Magazine*, July 1952, p. 28.

13. In addition to the books by Bell and Smith, one should consult Bell's

widely read articles: "Know How vs. Know Why," *Life*, October 16, 1950, pp. 89–98, and "The Fault Is Not the Teacher's," New York *Times Magazine*, November 18, 1951, pp. 18–24, 67–70.

14. David Riesman et al, *The Lonely Crowd* (Garden City, 1955 ed.), p. 80. Riesman complained after the fact that his criticism of progressive education was used by "virulent reactionaries"; Riesman, *Individualism Reconsidered* (Glencoe, Ill., 1954), p. 10.

15. The best history of the rise and fall of progressive education from its origins through the 1950s is Cremin, *Transformation.*

16. Vladimir Nabokov, *Lolita* (New York, 1963 ed.), pp. 161–62; also one should read Randall Jarrell's brilliant fifties academic novel, *Pictures from an Institution* (New York, 1964 ed.), p. 181, in which he has a German character recall reading a speech by Kaiser Wilhelm II, back in the 1890s, imploring parents and teachers "not to make their children study so hard, for many of the children had had their eyes ruined by their studies, and were no more good for soldiers. Your own American education is, I believe, of all the educations that have yet been devised the best for the eyes of the children."

17. United States Office of Education, *Life Adjustment Education for Every Youth* (Washington, D.C., n.d.), p. 17; Cremin, *Transformation*, pp. 333–38.

18. John Keats, "Are the Public Schools Doing Their Job? No," *Saturday Evening Post*, September 21, 1957, pp. 117–18; Valentine, *Age of Conformity*, pp. 155–56.

19. Robert Lindner, *Must You Conform?* (New York, 1956), p. 168.

20. Quoted in Arthur Bestor, "Aimlessness in Education," *Scientific Monthly*, LXXV (August 1952), 112.

21. Bestor, *The Restoration of Learning* (New York, 1955), pp. 17, 25, 102–11; Bestor, "Aimlessness," pp. 113–15.

22. Bestor, *Restoration*, pp. 25, 120; very revealing also is Bestor's review of Admiral H. G. Rickover, *Education and Freedom* in the New York *Times Book Review*, February 1, 1959, reprinted in C. Winfield Scott et al, eds., *The Great Debate: Our Schools in Crisis* (Englewood Cliffs, N.J., 1959), p. 147.

23. Rudolf Flesch, *Why Johnny Can't Read* (New York, 1955), p. 2; Scott et al, eds., *Great Debate*, p. 44.

24. Bennett quoted in William E. Leuchtenburg, *The Great Age of Change* (New York, 1964), pp. 130–31.

25. *Life*, March 24, 1958, p. 25.

26. *Life*, March 24, 1958; see also *Life*, March 3, 1958, p. 96; April 21, 1958, p. 34.

27. Nixon is quoted in *School and Society*, 86 (March 1, 1958), 104; Brickman is quoted in Ibid., 86 (January 18, 1958), 31; the Illinois minister and the Louisiana housewife are quoted in *Life*, March 3, 1958, p. 98; see also Sloan Wilson, "It's Time to Close Our Carnival: To Revitalize America's Educational Dream We Must Stop Kowtowing to the Mediocre," *Life*, March 24, 1958, pp. 36–37.

28. H. G. Rickover, *Education and Freedom* (New York, 1959), pp. 15–19, 23–24, 52, 186–90.

29. *Life,* March 31, 1958, p. 32; Rickover, *Education,* pp. 23–24; Wilson, "It's Time to Close Our Carnival," pp. 36–37.

30. *Prospect for America: The Rockefeller Panel Reports* (Garden City, 1961), pp. 337–92; *Life,* April 7, 1958, pp. 2, 89–96; see also *Christian Century,* November 27, 1957, p. 1404.

31. *Life,* March 3, 1958, p. 100, April 14, 1958, pp. 117–19; Henry M. Wriston, "Education and the National Interest," *Foreign Affairs,* 35 (July 1957), 564–80; William Benton, "Now the 'Cold War' of the Classrooms," New York *Times Magazine,* April 1, 1956, reprinted in Scott et al, eds., *Great Debate,* pp. 59–64.

32. Cremin, *Transformation,* pp. vii, 348; Hutchins, *Some Observations,* p. 40.

33. Mort is quoted in Martin Mayer, *The Schools* (New York, 1961), p. 64.

34. Shane is quoted in Scott et al, eds., *Great Debate,* pp. 133–34; see also Michael Walzer, "Education for a Democratic Culture," *Dissent,* 6 (Spring 1959), 107–18.

35. Leonard article is reprinted in Scott et al, eds., *Great Debate,* p. 42; *Life,* March 3, 1958, pp. 96, 98, April 21, 1958, p. 34. A Gallup poll taken in the spring of 1958 and quoted by *Life* revealed that fully 79 per cent of high school principals interviewed felt that their schools demanded too little work from students.

36. Paul Goodman, *Utopian Essays and Practical Proposals* (New York, 1962), pp. 257–58.

37. Ibid., p. 278; Goodman noted that the differentiation between *Life* and *Mad* readers was "deepening into polar groups of students, hostile to one another, the conformist and the totally disgusted."

10

Growing Up

"The teen-agers of today," remarked a mid-fifties commentator, "are stronger, smarter, more self-sufficient and more constructive than any other generation of teen-agers in history." To many observers, adolescents in the fifties seemed superior to any earlier generation. They were calmer, more confident, and utterly self-assured. Even the few rebellious exceptions did not mar the goodness of the rest. Leland Baldwin declared of them, "We are seeing the dawn of maturity. . . . Our long experience in democratic self-government has borne fruit."[1]

Today we do not think of fifties adolescence in such laudatory tones. Nor are maturity, self-confidence, or strength the usual words we would use to describe teens of that era. If anything, we tend instead to remember fifties youth in more superficial ways. We think of the musical tastes, the dress habits, the conformity and status anxiety, sexual repressions, and political apathy of the young. These provide much of the stuff of fifties nostalgia. We recall (and often smile at) these complicated artifacts. But we recall them with an odd mix of feelings: with the affection anyone feels for those lost days of youth, with fondness for that simpler time, perhaps even with amusement tinged by unexamined pain. We try (and usually succeed) at forgetting the difficulties of being young in those years. In the fifties, America, like many another culture, sought to mold the young after its adult dreams. But the terrible conflicts that characterized fifties culture themselves distorted the mold. America's divided messages were crucial in determining the ways kids accepted their world, how they came to assert themselves in it and, eventually, even the ways they chose to rebel.

Youth occupied a unique place in fifties America. Teens were perceived as different from other human beings and so were more set apart by a generation gap. The value of being young kept rising. At the same time, Americans were returning (after the disciplinarian interlude of the twenties and thirties) to their traditional permissive child-rearing practices. Many other factors also converged to create the fifties teen-ager. Unprecedented affluence was coupled to the growth of the luxury businesses. These businesses saw the need to identify (that is, create) a separate youth market. This proved mutually beneficial: Teens bought youth products for the status and the sense of identity they received, and businesses provided these luxury needs to make money.[2]

Other trends contributed to the growing segregation of the young. Progressive education, for instance, treated children as unique beings rather than imperfect adults. Freudian psychology also stressed the importance and uniqueness of childhood. The rise of the city, accompanied by the breakdown of community and the spread of the nuclear family, removed a major social control over the young. Added to these currents were the linked scientific and industrial revolutions. One of the most significant ideas resulting was the new worth placed on youth and novelty. To be old was to be obsolete. To be young was to be special.

Out of such concepts came Dr. Benjamin Spock's *Common Sense Book of Baby and Child Care*. First published in 1946, Spock's book attained almost instant popularity. This was not because it presented any new ideas, but rather because it was a successful pastiche of ideas rising into the public awareness. Spock miniaturized the culture's child-rearing ideas in his books, and so gave them a larger vogue. Spock, of course, never advocated the licentious permissiveness for which he has since been blamed. If he can be faulted for anything, it is the subtle totalitarianism of his ideas. As Philip Slater has pointed out, many "Spockian parents feel that it is their responsibility to make their child into the most all-around perfect adult possible. . . . The child has his entire being involved with parental aspirations. What the child is *not* permitted to do is to take his own personality for granted." This "mission to create a near-perfect being" was also one more instance of American product orientation.[3]

Still, it was only when Madison Avenue and the luxury industries got hold of the larger concept of unique youth that it changed. Fifties mass culture was, after all, dominated by business. And businesses generally expected people to indulge themselves with conspicuous consumption. Teens were no exception. Ads saturated the nation, and one of their major targets was young America. In these ads, youth became not the time when one's special character was molded but, instead, the time when one could expect to be totally indulged.[4]

Relations within the nuclear family are generally intense and demanding. But this social imperative for pampering created a new set of demands and repressions. Teen-agers, for instance, were forbidden by law and custom from exercising most adult prerogatives. This made them relatively unproductive members of society (except as consumers). Since the culture was biased in some ways in favor of the young, it was relatively easy for teens to express their resentments of this situation. Their opinions were courted, if only for monetary purposes. For instance, record firms and film companies took advantage of teen discontents through songs like "Yakety Yak" and films like *Blackboard Jungle* and *Rebel Without a Cause.* These only went so far as to articulate teen anxieties.

Adults in turn felt anger at the unproductive, demanding young. Yet they felt the need to swallow that anger. They often tried to explain their resentments by totally blaming them on the young. These were the years when America first came to be regarded as a "filiarchy," a society ruled by its children. In his *America as a Civilization* (1957), Max Lerner described the family as "child-centered anarchy." An article in a 1959 *Life,* "The U.S. Teen-Age Consumer," reported teens spent $10 billion annually. Mostly the money went to purchase consumer goods from the "Tower of

Baubles" *Life* depicted in glowing color. The tower included such items as cars, dogs, pimple cream, TV sets, lipsticks (alone worth $20 million in 1958), records, and phonographs. Adolescent spending power, *Life* stressed, was a crucial force. "If parents have any idea of organized revolt," the magazine concluded, "it is already too late. Teen-age spending is so important that such action would send quivers through the entire national economy."[5]

Life's attitude was not unusual. Its remarks did not reveal any actual powers adolescents might have. Rather, it pointed to some of teens' more evanescent strengths. In this society money was the primary index of one's power. Yet the young had no true economic clout. Industrial society had defined adolescence as a time of extended childhood rather than one of beginning maturity; and so the only fiscal power teens had was on sufferance from adults. Their only large-scale economic importance came as an easily exploitable youth market. They were conspicuous consumers of the soon obsolete. Even in this adolescents were usually dependent on parental indulgence. Thus, the child became a type of luxury, virtually an extension of the parents' spending habits.[6]

In that context, *Life*'s remarks about parental revolt, and the general trend to fix blame on the children, seemed rather shallow. However, the idea of filiarchy has never quite faded. One reason for this, in the fifties, was the period's other directedness. Adults typically explained their behavior by externalizing it. For instance, parents felt they could not confess "I'm moving to suburbia for myself, to improve my status." Instead, they perceived themselves as making great sacrifices for their children. Now, it cannot be doubted that sacrifices were made for kids in the fifties. Millions of women completely gave their lives over to child rearing. Millions of men took unpleasant jobs to maintain wife and children. But the fantastic thing was that the children (and wives) were ultimately faulted for these sacrifices. The phrase "for the sake of the children" came to be perceived as "the children made me do it."

Certainly this was far easier than considering the corrupting influences put on the young by the schools or the economic system. School and the pusher of the economy, advertising, might seem to be contradictory institutions. Ostensibly, one shaped children's minds to the intellectual and the necessary; the other sought instead to stimulate frivolous extravagance. But, by 1950, these were no longer incompatible areas—if, indeed, they had ever been except on the highest levels. The culture had accommodated itself (although not without guilt) to luxurious affluence and to the corporation. Public school had also achieved this accommodation. It became less and less the place to train the mind, and ever more the place where the culture's managers and consumers were prepared. This, of course, is not a particularly astounding fact: in any society, school's major purpose is not to pass on academic lessons but, rather, to inculcate cultural values.

While a tremendous amount of material about fifties school values exists, the most accessible of it concerns higher learning. To a very large extent, what happened in the colleges also happened in the public schools. However, among the significant differences was this: commentators who would never have criticized the public systems often felt free to scrutinize higher institutions. Partly this was because college still was a far more elitist institution than even today. Thus, it was safe to criticize college kids because they did not necessarily have to be regarded as typical citizens. Nevertheless, much of what was said in the fifties about higher institutions of learning was also quite true of the public schools.

Colleges and universities in the fifties emphatically embraced the complex values of their corporate culture. One sign of this was the growth of business as an area of study. By 1954, 19.4 per cent of all graduates were business or commerce students. Commercial fields of specialization grew more refined. One could study hotel and restaurant management, mobile homes, packaging. The personal attitudes of the students, too, were ever more geared toward business life. The fifties saw the rise of the organization student. *Parade* magazine interviewed one of the biggest men on the Iowa State University campus. He told the reporter, "you have to be very careful not to associate with the wrong clan of people, an introvert that isn't socially acceptable, guys who dress in the fashion of ten years ago, blue serge suits and loud ties. These people are just not accepted—and, if you associate with them, you're not accepted either."[7]

Students also had absorbed all the other values of their times. When Philip Jacob completed his study of *Changing Values in College* (1957), he remarked that they "fully accept the convention of the contemporary business society. They expect to conform to the economic status quo and to receive ample rewards." When Jacob asked freshmen at Michigan State University to respond to the statement, "a lot of teachers, these days, have radical ideas which need to be carefully watched," 59 per cent agreed. Jacob sampled student ideas across the country. Of his respondents, about 40 per cent felt the Communist party should be outlawed, that radicals of any sort should not teach, and that all conscientious objectors should be expelled from the country. Jacob finally concluded that, in the fifties, the major function of college was to persuade the individual "to reconsider aberrant values. It strengthens respect for the prevailing social order."[8]

Administrators themselves encouraged this process. Family life was not the only American institution to be reshaped by the corporation. College administrations began to evolve more and more toward the businesslike. Administrators spoke of their physical plants, their input and output, and the need to produce a good final product. The job placement center became fact at many institutions. At some schools, executives went so far as to admit students for their postgraduate business appeal. One dean of students told William H. Whyte, "we find that the best man is the one who's had an 80 or 85 average in school and plenty of extracurricular activities. We see little use for the 'brilliant' introvert who might spend the rest of his life turning out essays on obscure portions of D. H. Lawrence's letters."[9]

This eagerness to accommodate business naturally was not shared by every university scholar. But the array of values that forwarded the business attitude prevailed. In 1959, a University of Southern California professor named William S. Snyder wrote a letter to the *Nation*, charging "the commercialism and conformity in idea and action of the men who fill our faculties and the administrative posts in our colleges would nauseate the naive." Snyder went on to describe "the bowing and scraping . . . the uniformity of dress, speech, attitudes and behavior; the almost complete suppression of honesty and frankness" on the part of faculty people. What Snyder described so late in the decade characterized faculty behavior for most of the fifties. Not only conformity but the false populism of fear motivated academics. If students in college were cautious, commercial, status-seeking, conformist, politically naive, and apathetic, then only part of the reason was that they had brought these values to college with them. Higher learning is crucial to the young; in these years they are most open to change and challenge. In the fifties college kids largely learned to concentrate their social obedience—because most of their educators at every level simply increased the pressures of the conventional. Reward went to the privileged and the acquiescent.[10]

The values that would turn most of these youths into highly manageable consumers, of course, did not come purely from school. Rather, the educational system was one of several mainlines for this ethos. Other contributing institutions included the family and the mass media (particularly the new marketing-obsessed medium, TV). Church, too, grew in its shallow materialism in this period. The rise of Norman Vincent Peale was only one symptom of this. All these institutions were the membranes passing cultural messages to the young. The main currents of witch hunting, of nuclear terrorism, corporate bureaucracy, sexual doublethink, surrender to authority, and loss of individualism all vibrated through these means.

Since they seemed to have no choice, most kids came to believe in the mainstream message. It was "the reassuring truth," two *Collier's* reporters observed in 1951, "that the average young American is probably more conservative than you or your neighbor." But what the "average young American" really believed was not so much conservatism as caution. Many observers dubbed the youth of the fifties the "Silent Generation." This, though, was a misleading label. Young people in the fifties did not hesitate to say what they believed and wanted. But these ideas were so devoid of intellectual content, and so very trivial, that few adult observers could regard them as real. The unworded assumption seemed to be that these kids were holding something back.[11]

Such was not the case. Youth expressed itself quite clearly. On the surface, none of the young's conformist ideas should have been particularly startling to any sensible observer of American life. If anything, these attitudes indicated not so much youth's silence as its skillful understanding of adult pressures. They not only said what they thought adults wanted to hear; they actually decided to believe it. "Perhaps more than any of its predecessors," *Time* observed in 1951, "this generation wants a good, secure job." Security itself was the watchword, for youth as well as for adults. For girls, security meant marrying the right man and mothering a family. For boys, it meant having that family too, plus a nice corporate job. Even teens too young to marry pursued these domestic imperatives. They played courtship games like going steady.[12]

Certain material imperatives accompanied the dream. Boys and girls alike defined their future success in terms of suburban ranch homes, hi-fi sets, cars, TVs, and barbecues. Sure, some moral ideas existed alongside this consumerism. Just like their elders, most youths described themselves as liberals. But this liberalism had little political or moral reality. It merely implied a standard of interpersonal conduct. A liberal was gregarious, polite, cautious, apolitical (strong political faith being both rude and extremist), hazily religious, and even more hazily humanitarian. In practice, youths who bothered to express political opinions followed the prevailing winds. Often they did so rather cynically, very dimly aware of their alienation from political processes but unwilling to assert themselves for change. In the early fifties, for instance, most college men remained totally naive about the Korean conflict. They expressed a patriotic commitment to the anticommunist cause. But this was chiefly just verbal. Rarely did these young men go so far as to enlist —although they would obediently cooperate if drafted.[13]

There is much that is disturbing in such attitudes. These were ideas that were slick, careful, mediocre, and devoid of any daring. By purging oneself of all political taints (that is, of all idealism), and by hiding in the centrism of conventionality, the young had learned to avoid becoming targets in an age that searched for targets. Again, the apathy and materialism of fifties youth indicates the high degree to which the material imperative had penetrated their lives. They defined their futures only according to what they would be owning and consuming. The response of such good teens in the fifties was a mirror of American adult behavior at the time. But it was more. The American fifties teen was responding to the threats of the times much as all of twentieth-century Western society had responded: with a polite acceptance of the inroads against its humanity.

Youth's small expectations and nice manners marked the extreme limits they allowed the age to set on their awareness of culture, society, politics. They responded, finally, to such threats as McCarthyism and the bomb by pretending such issues did not exist. In a 1951 *Time*, a student commented: "This generation suffers from lack of worlds to conquer. . . . Sure, there are slums left—but another Federal housing project can clean up the worst. Most of the fights in labor have simmered down to arguments around the bargaining table. Would-be heroes are padded from harm—and hope—like lunatics in a cell." Such comments—and the educated young made similar remarks frequently through much of the fifties—reveal not only naivete but cynicism. The young, as much as their elders, were willing to overlook awkward, painful realities. In October 1956, when Hungarian students desperately rioted against the Soviet Army for their freedom, American students were rioting too—for the removal of losing football coaches. In 1954, officials of Oklahoma A & M surveyed students to discover their greatest fears and problems. The students' reply: their greatest worry in the world was finding a parking space.[14]

Now, these things are not just instances of mass idiocy. Both examples show that the young's cynicism was no more than a veneer. Peeled back, it revealed mock innocence, corruption, and appalling ignorance. But, in a negative sense, it also showed the way the young had come to accept the culture of the mass market. Its banal apolitics imbued their lives: self-expression and attitude were marked solely by one's purchases. When that shaped one's way of expressing the self, then inevitably there were few ways to truly express emotional imperatives (besides the emotion of greed). One had no language to talk about dissent, to communicate about the things that hurt, or shocked, frightened, or perplexed. One reason so many young people went along with the mainstream at this time was that they had no way to disagree, and no vocabulary to disagree in. The Oklahoma incident, in that light, demonstrated that the inability to express discontent was itself crippling and reshaping attitudes toward the world. If one had no way to say, for instance, "I worry about death," one tended to say other things. If these were feeble approximations of actual thoughts, one soothed things with a purchase.

The model of the ideal teen was thoroughly shaped by middle-class fantasies. The right kind of teen was liberal, clean-cut, concerned about reputation, rarely kissed on a first date, never went too far sexually, avoided delinquency, studied and planned for the future, and hung around the malt shop. This concept was at once superficial and demanding. It assumed, for instance, enough family money that the kid did not have to work and so could afford the time to study, date, lounge around. It assumed the kid was white and relatively privileged. It also assumed a home in an area where adolescent social life did not depend on the street corner or poolroom. The sexual idea was similarly limited, a combination of repression (if you feel it, don't do it) and ignorance (*sure* they don't do it). A youth from a social class unable to maintain such appearances was regarded as almost totally disadvantaged. The factors of poverty that might not be detrimental—for instance, the chance to learn independence or maturity earlier out of necessity—were ignored. In this age when poverty was perceived as a vanishing trivia, the poor were not so much people as deviants.

Deviance—the catchall label applied to anything outside mainstream awareness—also indicated the successful dissemination of psychology through culture. This field of thought contributed to the special status of youth in the fifties by defining childhood as unique. And psychology also had other, more indirect effects on the idea of youth. For instance, it popularized the notions of deviance and mental illness. Simultaneously, its rise disseminated the idea that anything mysterious or unfamiliar should be closely scrutinized. This was related to the era's other directedness: people expected to examine self and others for the telltale marks of nonconformity. Now, the generation gap already made the young seem strangers in the familiar American midst. All these ideas about monitoring the different, then either casting them out or curing them, led to such things as the spate of fifties articles seeking to explain youth. They were being closely watched.

Sometimes, of course, this scrutiny reached an absurd point. *Newsweek* reported in 1954 about the family of electronics tinkerer Jack Fletcher of West Covina, California. The Fletcher home, reported the magazine, was a "do-it-yourself nirvana." One of its most outstanding features was a "system of TV cameras and microphones installed throughout the house. . . . The Fletchers' three children, as a result, can be kept under their parents' eyes, while playing in their own bedrooms or romping in the yard outside." Such electronic surveillance of one's own children does make for an atypical anecdote. But its extremism was reduced to mere eccentricity in the *Newsweek* report: the publication's tone was one of proud approval, rather than shock, amusement, or skepticism. The Fletchers, in that sense, became one of the unsung forecasters of their times. They were precursors of the electronic invasions of the seventies.[15]

Similar extremes were reached on larger social scales. "In one Ohio town," *Newsweek* again reported, "parents worked out their own answer to the tearful plea: 'But all the other kids are doing

25. Marilyn Monroe engrossed in conversation with her playwright husband, Arthur Miller. The attention of newsmen was elsewhere as Marilyn put her best foot forward.

26. The bathrobe-clad Eisenhowers wave to a fond America in 1954.

27. In 1959, Beat poet Ray Bremser reads in the Gaslight, a Greenwich Village coffeehouse.

28. Allan Ginsberg, Gregor Corso, and William S. Burroughs sit in Washingt Square Park.

29. The audience at the premier of *Bwana Devil*, the first 3-D film, November 1952.

30. The hula hoop became a massive fad in the latter fifties.

31. Milton Berle was fondly dubbed "Uncle Miltie" and "Mr. Television." His comedy-variety series appeared in the early fifties.

32. Friday (Jack Webb), the stoic detective on the late-fifties *Dragnet,* unblinkingly brings down his man.

it!'" The way the town's parents solved this acute problem was to meet secretly and draft a code of behavior for their teen-age kids. The code determined such specifics as a curfew hour, a teen's permissible number of nights out a week, and the age a girl could begin attending dances. All the parents, *Newsweek* announced, would enforce the code. This rather desperate attempt to create a secure and universal social convention was praised by the magazine. "Thus," it concluded, "one of the most devastating arguments that an American teen-ager can raise was erased—because all the parents knew just exactly what all the other youngsters were doing."[16]

The Ohio example, like the Fletcher one, was an exaggerated instance. But it appears exaggerated only because the adults involved very slightly overstepped conventional boundaries. Their extremism was tiny enough to seem sensible to a mainstream publication like *Newsweek*. And this apparent sensibility could have been perceived as such only because the invasion of children's privacy was a cultural norm (and a corollary to the general invasion of privacy in the fifties). After all, only by such invasion could one make sure the kids turned out right.

Many kids, though, did not turn out right. Given the closely defined and superficial propriety of the era, this was not too surprising: any norm that excludes much of the range of humanity guarantees alienation and rebellion. Sometimes, of course, the rebellions were on no more than a fantasy scale. Reuel Denney noted in a 1953 *Bulletin of the Atomic Scientists* that "self-vanishing is what ten-year-old children wanted most according to a recent survey." Denney added that Americans "feel themselves pressured into social conformity, so that it satisfies them to involve themselves in fantasies of beating the world by vanishing from it." Young adults had their own version of self-vanishing. In a 1953 article entitled "Is This the Beat Generation?", novelist Robert Lowry described the young people who wanted to rebel but instead were completely caught up in consensus society. He showed how these people, who had good jobs, standard marriages, kids, homes in suburbia, imagined they were bohemians. They conformed at work all day and pretended to rebel at home: this convinced them their views and lives were really different and dangerous. They rebelled by disappearing into the mass.[17]

These mock rebels were, in their trivial defiance, far more understandable to the mainstream than the most glaring fifties rebellion of all: juvenile delinquency. Juvenile delinquency loomed disproportionately large in the decade's mind. Primarily, this was because all other national problems were being repressed. Poverty, militarism, racism, and sexism were seldom perceived as problems. Rather, these were only a problem to their victims: the classic example is that racism was seen as a Negro problem, not a white one or a human one. Through such thinking, young criminals became, as the *Saturday Evening Post* said, "The Shame of America." One sociologist went so far as to proclaim "no social problem has wrought deeper concern in the United States."[18]

In 1954, Benjamin Fine, then New York *Times* education reporter, published a book called *1,000,000 Delinquents.* His book was based on the estimate that, by 1954, that number of youths would get in trouble with the police each year. Fine's prediction turned out to be true. By 1956, it had been surpassed as well over one million kids "came to the attention of the police annually." That was an observation made by Richard Clendenen, executive director of the Senate Subcommittee on Juvenile Delinquency. Rates of delinquency, he noted, continued to rise dramatically, in both urban and rural areas. Many ever-younger criminals committed crimes against property. Car theft was the top juvenile crime. But startlingly often, the young also committed acts of inexplicable and pointless violence—rape, beatings, murders. True, statistically few of America's young were involved in such violent behavior. But the entire nation responded to the words of a Boston judge: "we have the spectacle of an entire city terrorized by one-half of one per cent of its residents. And the terrorists are children."[19]

How had this happened? How was it that one of society's greatest missions—protecting itself internally by teaching the young not to destroy within society—seemed to be failing? It came about, some observers felt, because of serious flaws in the individual delinquent. J. Edgar Hoover, for instance, pointed to irreligion and lack of family discipline as contributors to juvenile delinquency. "In practically all homes where juvenile delinquency is bred there is an absence of adequate religious training for children," Hoover said. "Most of them have never seen the inside of a church." Bishop Fulton J. Sheen pointed to the "3 D's," three types of parents he said created delinquent children: "doting, drinking, and discordant." The doter, giving the kids everything, raised "jaded children always seeking new thrills," and "that new thrill may be alcohol, marijuana, even murder." Drinkers, he felt, brought up children who were outwardly meek but who possessed "a terrific urge to violence." And fighting parents, Sheen went on, gave their children "a contempt for *all* law."[20]

Crucially, criticisms such as these depended on the perception of delinquents as deviants from a large, blessed, and closely defined norm. These kids were deviants only because they were undisciplined and/or overindulged. There was a solution. As one writer put it, "the clue is found in one word—DISCIPLINE." The problem boiled down to the failure within certain families to raise their children in the American way—and, even more, it boiled down to the lazy refusal of certain teens to cooperate with good society.[21] Effectively, by individualizing delinquency, such authorities as Hoover and Sheen sought to make society blameless for the young delinquent.

More liberal observers, in contrast, sought an answer in the larger environments of the delinquent. Here the first faltering steps toward recognizing some of America's cultural problems were made. Many of the worst delinquents, these observers said, were gang kids from lower-class urban slums. They could not help being what they were. They had been molded by their brutal environment. It was quite easy to blame the life of ghetto deprivation as a cause of child violence. Indeed, a whole genre of slum/sensationalism novels sprang up in the fifties. Samples of these include Irving Shulman's *Amboy Dukes* and Hal Ellson's *Jailbait Street*. These dwelled on the utter relentless animality of lower-class city life. The gist of such fictive theorizing was obvious: these kids are inevitably brutes. They are no longer sensitive human beings at all. Finally, this became not a humanitarian approach to the problem of urban delinquency, but one more way of dismissing the problem, and the people being destroyed by it. If one could portray only ghetto kids as delinquents, and then show them to be no more than animals, one need waste no time considering them (or any delinquents) as worthwhile humans.[22] The liberals' attitude, that is, was often as ineffective and insensitive as the conservatives'. Both ultimately dismissed the perceived delinquent, both labeled him or her an outcast or deviant. Again the mainstream emerged as pure and blameless.

To achieve this purity, many facts had to be ignored. For example, numerous middle-class kids, teens from families not at all fitting into Hoover's atheist accords or Sheen's 3 D's, were delinquents. Most young car thieves were not lower-class but middle-class. Again, many of the crimes of these young delinquents could not be precisely regarded as rebellion: they were distillation rather than defiance of adult values. As Paul Goodman wrote, "the group in society that most believes in the rat race as a source of value is the other underprivileged: the ignorant and resentful boys who form the delinquent gangs." These boys, he added, "esteem the rat race though they do not get its rewards." Dr. Robert Lindner, in his best-selling *Must You Conform?*, also noted this. "Our teen-age mutineers are above all conformists," he said. "In their behavior, they present us with a travesty of ourselves, having elevated conformity to the reigning passion of their lives."[23]

Conformity, of course, could not wholly explain nor justify the violence of juvenile delinquency. The frustration of living in an impulse-release society while being too young, too poor, too powerless, also had its overwhelming effect. Wrote Louis Yablonsky in *Commentary*, "the irony is that this world with its nightmare inversion of the official values of our society is nevertheless constructed out of elements that are implicitly or unconsciously approved . . . and that its purpose is to help the gang boy achieve the major value of respectable society: success."[24]

Much the same comments could be applied to many middle-class non-gang delinquents. They looked for "a quick, almost magical way of achieving power and prestige." In so many ways they seemed to be the logical, helpless outcome of Madison Avenue's demands. Much of the writing about these desperate children, however, went too far. Sometimes it sought to explain delinquency as solely a failure in communication. It is important to stress that, while many liberal critics recognized the damaging nature of fifties status materialism, very few felt this implied any criticism of the wasteful economic system itself. As Max Lerner wrote, "the violence with which intense slum youngsters imitate the values of culture, even while distorting them, may be seen as their own form of flattery. What they do is legally and morally wrong, but instead of being a sign of the decay of American life it may be taken almost as a sign of its vitality."[25]

Neither the liberal nor the conservative approach could be said to be wholly true, although both contained sensible elements. There was a kernel of truth in the disciplinarian idea that one could shape one's life—although, by the fifties, this had been perverted to imply not individualism but conformity. Similarly there was a kernel of truth in the liberal's idea of being molded by cultural conditions. Crucially, however, a synthesis between these notions (and the new cultural examinations such a synthesis implied) was avoided. This was largely because both sides had already posited the basic social ground to be wholesome, healthy, and viable. Criticism of it, therefore, slid off. Any rebellion, in such a definition, was causeless and meaningless. It was regarded not as the act of will it was, but rather as a failure of the will.

The many contradictions of the mainstream attitude toward juvenile delinquency therefore only worsened through the fifties. In 1956, Dr. Lindner's *Must You Conform?* seemed to offer some new ideas about the revolt of American youth. Psychiatrist Lindner used sophisticated language to discuss the general "mutiny" of America's young. But his conclusions about these rebels never transcended the smallness of mainstream attitudes. "The mutiny of the young," he wrote, "is not an ordinary social ailment, but a virulent epidemic affecting the race of men." Elsewhere, Lindner again wielded the language of psychiatry and mental illness to expel young criminals from the mainstream. "The youth of today is suffering from a severe, collective mental illness," he charged. Many of these sufferers, he went on, were no more than psychopaths, and many of the attempts to cure them only compounded "the conditions that generate the psychopathic virus."[26]

Lindner himself forwarded a common fifties habit of the educated. One facet of fifties culture was the lack of ways to express one's deepest suffering: the strictures of "cool" and of conformity each forbade this. Still, there was a semantic out, a way of indicating that one was feeling pain or misery. But it was a limited language: that of mental illness. Using this language to discuss problems did effectively indicate the existence of suffering. Simultaneously, though, it stigmatized. It harmed the person using it by labeling him or her as *sick*. Its other function was to stigmatize others, to term them deviants, perverts, strangers to the mass. Lindner, in saying the young had an "epidemic," "psychopathic virus," was doing this.[27] His well-educated version of the consensus attitude toward non-conformists was very damaging. To the question he posed with his book title *Must You Conform?*, Lindner finally answered: you don't have to conform, but if you don't you are sick.

Clearly, many commentators in the fifties did, however accidentally, manage to cite some of the factors contributing to the big picture of juvenile delinquency. As we have seen, many people recognized that the conspicuous consumption ethic might have a lot to do with delinquency. Yet another commonplace in American culture was its violence. America is a traditionally violent country. But usually we only notice violence when it is committed by out-groups; we have been trained from birth to ignore the far more massive violence committed in support of the status quo. In the fifties, the violence of juvenile delinquents was regarded as shocking, evil, and almost inexplicable. But violence committed against young criminals was quite acceptable.

One book, *Youth and the FBI*, offers several examples of this. The work was intended as a cautionary study of delinquency for the teen reader. Its authors sought to discourage teens from a life of crime with a number of object lessons. Many of their anecdotes end on a violent note. They conclude with such punch lines as "within a matter of months LaMarca was electrocuted," or "when we shoot we want the bullet to go to the right place. That's why we *shoot to kill*."[28]

One could cite dozens of similar examples from advice books to teens as well as from the mass media. But these would be only partial proofs of the fifties version of "might equals right." The fact underlying the entire direction of fifties America—whether its foreign policy, its military notions, its race relations, or even its affluence—was the American dependence on violence. W. E. B. DuBois wrote in a 1956 *Nation*, "our crime, especially juvenile crime, is increasing. Its increase is perfectly logical; for a generation we have been teaching our youth to kill, destroy, steal, and rape in war; what can we expect in peace?" In this decade of peacetime warmaking, of Rosenberg executions, bomb testing, racial conflict, global military expansion, people learned very quickly their lives and feelings were just not worth much. The violence wrought against the left in the early fifties, indeed, contributed on its own to the delinquent style. The events that culminated in the execution of the Rosenbergs provided innumerable object lessons in what happened to political rebels within the United States. Such violence shaped rebellion for many years, by assuring that it would become apolitical, disorganized, and sometimes so very personal—as in stealing a car—as to be the act of one individual alone. The lesson of mainstream violence, finally, could be summed up by another anecdote from *Youth and the FBI*. Its authors quoted an FBI agent. What he said was true not only for the hardened youths he referred to, but also for too many Americans in all walks of life. "To many youthful criminals," the agent said, "human life is cheap."[29]

The rigidity of personal standards itself also stimulated juvenile delinquency. Delinquency was often merely contextual: an act labeled delinquent in one place might be perfectly fine elsewhere. Sometimes, as in the case of teen girls' sexual delinquency, the actual delinquency might be blamed on only one partner, and the crime itself be essentially victimless. Perceptions of female delinquency themselves reveal much about mainstream attitudes toward rebellion. In the fifties, delinquent boys' crimes were almost wholly those of property or violence. The 20 per cent of delinquents who were female, in contrast, got in trouble usually for crimes pertaining to sex or autonomy. Nearly always, a girl was considered delinquent for running away from home or for participating in a mutually acquiescent sex act. The vague indictment of "promiscuity" was used even against girls who had not participated in sex acts, but who were merely perceived as sexually threatening. No comparable grounds existed for imprisoning boys. Rarely were male teens punished for running away, or for victimless sex acts.[30]

Both the loose definitions and the stricter punishments for female delinquency indicate certain things. Not the least of these is the need the society felt to enforce its sexual rules. The vagueness and hypocrisy of these rules, of course, was reflected in the discriminating and disproportionate punishments. Many such girls were sent to state institutions (reform schools). They received longer sentences and inferior services. Usually, though, it was lower-class girls who were so punished.

Middle-class families with problem daughters favored psychiatric therapy. A rebellious daughter might even be committed to a mental institution. Dr. F. J. Braceland testified at a court hearing how he would gladly commit an adolescent girl for victimless sex acts, solely on parental request: "If a man brings me his daughter from California [Braceland worked at a Washington, D.C., hospital] because she is in manifest danger of falling into vice . . . he doesn't expect me to let her loose in my hometown for the same thing to happen." As is obvious, whether or not the girl was mentally troubled, or even had already "fallen into vice," was irrelevant. Mental illness was so loosely defined as to include a girl's refusal to conform to her parents' concept of virtue. In such a light, the psychiatrist became little more than a fancy jailer for a social class ashamed of both autonomy and the genuine jail.[31]

The patriotism of waste; the transparency of sexual morals; the enforcement of conformity; the artificial democracy: all these cultural messages led Paul Goodman to say of the supposedly causeless rebels of the fifties, "perhaps there has *not* been a failure of communication. Perhaps the social message has been communicated clearly . . . and is unacceptable." We remember the fifties as a time of innocence and naivete. But that itself is a naive memory. In the fifties, many adolescents did perceive the confusion of their culture, its cruelty and absurdity. One of the major unspoken lessons of their culture was the need to look away from the contradictions and the threatening things. In learning this lesson, teens were cynically forced to acknowledge it. The delinquent, in that sense, was not simply a victim of poverty and greed, nor just a hungry believer in the American way. When a boy threw away his life for a service station robbery, when a girl threw away her virginity like it was a worn blouse, these people were not merely searching for attention, not merely engaging in the power barterings of culture. In their seemingly dumb, dull acts, they were making a serious value judgment. They were weighing their futures, and many of them were concluding that, as Paul Goodman would bitterly remark: "*the question is what it means to grow up into such a fact as 'During my productive years I will spend eight hours a day doing what is no good!*'"[32]

As the decade wore on, the American dream began to be almost a nightmare. Gradually, rebellion entered a renaissance in American culture. Many of its movements were rooted in the tremendous disaffection of the young. As Kenneth Rexroth warned in an early issue of *Evergreen Review,* "Listen you—do you *really* think your kids are like bobby soxers in those wholesome Coca-Cola ads? Don't you know that across the table from you at dinner sits somebody who looks on you as an enemy who is planning to kill him in the immediate future . . . ? Don't you know that if you were to say to your English class, 'It is raining,' they would take it for granted you were a liar? Don't you know they never tell you nothing? that they can't? that . . . they simply can't get through, can't, and won't even try anymore to communicate. Don't you know this, really? If you don't, you're heading for a terrible awakening."[33]

Such disaffection, in the latter fifties, introduced large-scale dissent into American culture. The birth of the New Left, the increasing popularity of pacifism and of the Beats, of rock and roll, civil rights activism, and even the increase of juvenile delinquency, all in their way represented a swing away from the monolithic pressures of the American mainstream. These movements, plus a number of cultural leaders, were highly important. Both a mass movement and a Martin Luther King, Jr., Allen Ginsberg, A. J. Muste, and James Dean were necessary to challenge people's perception of the world. In the late fifties, the rebellion began to grow.

Much of this early behavior was itself confused, shallow, unfocused, and naive. At no point, then or even at the counterculture's height, would it involve easy decisions and painless positions. But the mainstream had generated the need for a new American synthesis, and the youth of the late fifties began the movement toward that change. Perhaps the most predictive words about this evolution came from Nat Hentoff. These appeared in his remarkable essay on Lenny Bruce, "The Humorist as Grand Inquisitor." "Bruce is a distillation of the unfocussed rebelliousness among more and more of the young," Hentoff said. "They protest segregation and [bomb] testing and the hollowness of their parents, but they cannot yet say what they are for, what new society they desire. They are only *against*, but that at least is a beginning."[34]

NOTES

1. The mid-fifties commentator was Herman G. Stack, director of the State of California Youth Authority, quoted by Pat Boone in *'Twixt Twelve and Twenty* (Englewood Cliffs, 1958), pp. 38–39; Leland Baldwin, *The Meaning of America* (Pittsburgh, 1955), p. 286.

2. Paul Goodman, *Growing Up Absurd* (New York, 1960), pp. 218–27; Philip Slater, *The Pursuit of Loneliness* (Boston, 1970), p. 56.

3. Benjamin Spock, *Pocket Book of Baby and Child Care* (New York, 1955), a mid-fifties paperback edition of the *Common Sense* volume first published in 1946; Slater, *Pursuit,* pp. 57, 69. By 1957 Spock's book had gone

through 59 printings. The book sold about a million copies a year, becoming the biggest seller next to the Bible in American history.

4. Jules Henry, *Culture Against Man* (New York, 1963), particularly Chapter Two, "Advertising as a Philosophical System," pp. 45–99. Many of the remarks in this chapter were strongly influenced by Henry's book and Slater's *Pursuit.*

5. Max Lerner, *America as a Civilization* (New York, 1957), p. 564; Paul Benzaquin, "The U.S. Teen-Age Consumer," *Life,* August 31, 1959, pp. 78–87.

6. An interesting sidelight to this appears in the October 13, 1959, *Life,* in an article by a 19-year-old clerical worker recalling his $10,000 credit card binge. The youth, who earned $73 a week, had applied for the card as a joke. He was surprised to actually receive it. "That card was burning a hole in my pocket," he wrote. Within a couple of weeks the clerk had traveled to Montreal, Havana, Miami, and Las Vegas from his New York home. He bought hand-tailored silk shirts and silk pajamas, furs and a dog for girls he picked up, and stayed in the best hotel suites drinking champagne. Unfortunately, he also used the card as a reference to cash phony checks. This was his downfall. But, even after promising in the pages of *Life* to pay it all back, he felt no regrets: "that card gets you power and authority and respect," he wrote.—Joseph R. Miraglia, "My $10,000 Credit Card Binge."

7. Vance Packard, *The Status Seekers* (New York, 1959), p. 174; Jules Henry also discusses such ideas in *Culture Against Man,* particularly Chapter Seven, "Rome High School and its Students," and Chapter Eight, "Golden Rule Days," pp. 182–321.

8. Philip E. Jacob, *Changing Values in College* (New Haven, 1956), pp. 5–6, 38–39, 54.

9. William H. Whyte, Jr., *The Organization Man* (Garden City, 1956), pp. 88, 93, 94, 116; Robb Burlage, editor of the student paper *Daily Texan* at the University of Texas, quoted a New York *Times Magazine* comment: "Today the faculties at large universities work for the administration rather than the reverse, as was the case in earlier days. . . . A large and powerful bureaucracy, then, places a premium upon service to its ends, and these are not always coincident to the primary function of the teacher." (Burlage in *Nation,* May 16, 1959, pp. 444–45. Burlage's article is an early document of the New Left.)

10. "Academic Corruption," letter from William S. Snyder, *Nation,* July 5, 1958, inside cover; also see Edward D. Eddy, Jr., "Paradox in Parentheses," *Nation,* May 16, 1959, pp. 440–42; A. S. Link, *American Epoch* (New York, 1963), p. 657, on the way anticommunism and the loyalty oaths contributed to the destruction of academic freedom on the fifties campus "by identifying dissent and progressivism with Communism"; in the March 9, 1957, *Nation,* Charles Shapiro wrote that, at Wayne State University, "the campus socialist group was eliminated last year, just before Academic Freedom Week was celebrated on campus." Such authoritarian arrogance characterized the fifties campus, and continues to shape the seventies campus; the major difference the sixties introduced (evident as early as the late fifties) was the willingness of some few to defy it.

11. Judson T. Landis and Mary G. Landis, "Our Teen-Agers: How Good Are Their Morals?", *Collier's,* March 15, 1952, pp. 15–16; see, for instance, Caroline Bird, "The Unlost Generation," which originally appeared in a 1957 *Harper's Bazaar* and is quoted in Elting Morison, ed., *The American Style* (New York, 1958), p. 182.

12. "The Younger Generation," *Time,* November 5, 1951, pp. 46–47; *Newsweek,* November 2, 1953, pp. 52–54; Jacob, *Changing Values,* pp. 18–19; John Brooks, *The Great Leap* (New York, 1966), p. 240; David Riesman, "The Found Generation," *American Scholar,* 25 (Autumn 1956), 427–36; Whyte, *Organization Man,* pp. 78–82.

13. George Rawick, "The American Student: A Profile," *Dissent,* I (Autumn 1954), 395–96, was one of the first to acknowledge the cynicism behind student conformity and materialism; Jacob, *Changing Values,* p. 30, on the apolitical patriotism of college men; George D. Spindler, "Education in a Transforming American Culture," in Morison, ed., *American Style,* p. 167.

14. "Younger Generation," *Time,* pp. 46–47; *Nation,* May 16, 1959, p. 449, on American riots; Joseph Laffan Morse, ed., *Unicorn Book of 1954,* p. 429. As Slater has pointed out, American collegiates have always rioted in innocuous defiance of authority. But only when riots were politically motivated (as in the sixties and seventies) did people find this a cause for much concern.

15. *Newsweek,* December 13, 1954, p. 94, on the Fletchers.

16. Ibid., November 8, 1953, p. 30, on the Ohio town.

17. Reuel Denney, "Reactors of the Imagination," *Bulletin of the Atomic Scientists,* July 1953, p. 206; Robert Lowry, "Is This the Beat Generation?", *American Mercury,* January 1953, pp. 16–20—Lowry was a Beat novelist; also of interest are Russell Lynes' remarks about the so-called "Upper Bohemians" (upper middle-class couples whose rebellion consists of "slightly odd" tastes) in *Surfeit of Honey* (New York, 1957), pp. 31–46.

18. Richard Clendenen and Herbert W. Beaser, "The Shame of America," a five-part series in the *Saturday Evening Post* beginning January 8, 1955; Negley Teeters in foreword to Clyde Vedder, ed., *The Juvenile Offender* (Garden City, 1954), p. v.

19. Benjamin Fine, *1,000,000 Delinquents* (New York, 1957); "Why Teen-Agers Go Wrong," interview with Clendenen (executive director of the Senate Subcommittee on Juvenile Delinquency), in *U.S. News & World Report,* September 17, 1954—in this interview, Clendenen also gives a remarkably circular definition of the delinquent as "a child whose behavior is such that he could be adjudged delinquent under the laws of the state in which he lives"; Eric Goldman, *The Crucial Decade* (New York, 1955), p. 190; *Newsweek,* November 9, 1953, p. 29, quoting Judge John J. Connelly.

20. Hoover quoted in Vedder, *Juvenile,* p. 106; Fulton J. Sheen in *Reader's Digest,* June 1955, pp. 25–27.

21. John J. Floherty and Mike McGrady, *Youth and the FBI* (Philadelphia, 1960), p. 136.

22. Hal Ellson, *Jailbait Street* (Derby, Connecticut, 1959); Irving Shulman, *The Amboy Dukes* (New York, 1951).

23. Robert Lindner, *Must You Conform?* (New York, 1956), p. 34.

24. Louis Yablonsky, "The Violent Gang," *Commentary*, August 1960, pp. 125–30.

25. Max Lerner, *America as a Civilization*, p. 665—on page 575, Lerner compares the effect of the gang to "the playing fields of Eton." Leonard Bernstein and Stephen Sondheim, "Gee, Officer Krupke!" from *West Side Story*.

26. Lindner, *Conform*, pp. 5–11, 24–25, 27; see also "Rebels or Psychopaths?", *Time*, December 6, 1954, pp. 64–65.

27. Thomas Szasz, *The Myth of Mental Illness* (New York, 1961), pp. 296–302, discusses the imagery of mental "illness" and the flaw in using a "language" of such illness.

28. Floherty and McGrady, *Youth and the FBI*, pp. 22, 29, 38, 67. " 'I'd sure like to see some of those guns in action,' Buck said a trifle wistfully. 'No sooner said than done,' the agent replied . . ." and what he saw led Buck to conclude that "a kid would have to be crazy to buck the FBI."

29. W. E. B. DuBois, in *Nation*, October 20, 1956, p. 324. Shortly after this article appeared, the embittered DuBois emigrated to Ghana. Also Floherty and McGrady, *Youth and the FBI*, p. 86.

30. Noted Vedder in *Juvenile Offender*, "official charges of sexual intransigence do not appear with high frequency in the public records, except in the case of female offenders" (p. 124) and elsewhere, he comments, "most delinquencies committed by girls are sexual in nature whereas those delinquencies committed by boys and young men are mostly nonsexual." Since he made no mention of rampant female homosexuality, one must assume a discriminatory double standard. Also Floherty and McGrady, *Youth and the FBI*, pp. 109–10; *Newsweek*, November 9, 1953, p. 28; *Ms.*, April 1973, p. 116.

31. Braceland quoted by Thomas Szasz, *Manufacture of Mental Illness* (New York, 1970), pp. 46–47. Also see Leontine R. Young, "Delinquency from the Child's Viewpoint," in Vedder, *Juvenile Offender*, p. 62, on the institutionalization of an apparently sexy girl whose most concrete crime was to scream at her mother "that she would do just as she pleased."

32. Goodman, *Absurd*, pp. 29, 56, 102–3, 162–65.

33. Kenneth Rexroth, "San Francisco Letter," *Evergreen Review* (Spring 1957), p. 11.

34. Nat Hentoff, "The Humorist as Grand Inquisitor," anthologized in Paul Goodman, ed., *Seeds of Liberation* (New York, 1964), p. 250.

11

More than a Music

In April 1955, *Life* magazine ran a massive pictorial article about a mysterious new "frenzied teenage music craze" that was creating "a big fuss." *Life* seemed rather confused by the new phenomenon, not sure whether to use its usual tone of buoyant approval, or that of more rarely summoned anger. The article, consequently, is an odd mixture of these two moods: at once indulgent (aren't these kids cute?) and disturbed (these kids are in trouble!). Arthur Murray, for instance, was quoted as saying rock and roll dancing was healthy for kids. But then there was the fact that the New Haven, Connecticut, police chief had banned all rock and roll parties, and "other towns are following suit." *Life* went on, "some American parents, without quite knowing what it is their kids are up to, are worried that it's something they shouldn't be."[1]

By mid-decade, rock and roll was fast becoming teen-agers' music. This big change in musical habit rose out of several historical trends. One of the major factors was the altered state of teen-agers themselves. The widespread affluence of the fifties shifted adolescent status. Middle-class white kids were simply expected to go to school and have lots of wholesome spare time. This new standard created a sense of separation among teen-agers. They were obviously too mature to be considered children. But then teens were too young to wield the power of adults. In the limbo of transition and luxury, adolescents came to recognize themselves as unique, set apart, different. That perception marked the first throes of the developing postwar youth culture.

Before the popularizing of rock and roll, only a few emotional and consumer concerns provided a link between teens. There was lots of time to linger over such things. Teens came to devote that time to acting out the social roles they saw their parents practicing. Thus, courtship games gained overweening importance. Material conformity did too. A consumer youth market grew in economic consequence. Providing largely teen luxury items, it thrived on the sale of clothes, cosmetics, fast foods, cars, and other indulgences. But these things, the social practices and the consumer riches, were not enough. A more profound shock of recognition was needed to catalyze the separation into something new.

That the music came to do so involves a number of seemingly divergent factors. By 1950, the incredible rise of television was forcing radio into more music programming. At the same time, the mass migration of blacks out of the rural South and into urban centers was increasing. Radio reflected this population movement with a surge of "race" programming, and so rhythm and blues came to the urban airwaves. Before the mid-forties, rhythm and blues music had been relatively inaccessible to whites. Race records were sold in ghetto stores, far removed from the experience of most white kids. By 1950, however, rhythm and blues was within easy reach of anyone. All a kid had to do was roll a dial.

The music scene as a whole, too, made it nearly inevitable that teens would take to some unique part of it. The musical market in the early fifties was based on careful demarcations. Each market appealed to the tastes of a certain group. Thus, one's tastes could easily indicate one's social class. There was "longhair"—that is, classical—music for highbrows (the educated); country and western for whites who were probably lower class, probably of rural background; jazz, the music of blacks and white aesthetes; the pop, "Hit

Parade" ballads of the white middle class; and for city blacks there was rhythm and blues, the urban evolution of the blues. R & B, pop, and country music, as popular fields, all had their own separate charts rating a record's success. Rarely did a record "cross over." For instance, the pop white audience did not purchase R & B records such as the Orioles' "It's Too Soon to Know" (1948) or Louis Jordan's "Early in the Morning" (1947).[2]

Pop music, as the music of the white middle class, was sold to both teen-agers and their parents. No taste or social differences were acknowledged between young and old in the music's production. It was made to be mass-marketed. A new release would be decided on the basis of past hits. The decisions came from industry executives who were themselves middle-aged and so removed from any interest in young concerns. Such music reflected the attitudes of its adult producers and audience. Many of these attitudes can also be considered peculiar to fifties popular thought. Some of the main currents of emotion in the early fifties were the insistence on familiar security and on the facade of bland perfection. And what feelings could better describe the top tunes at this time? The music was, for the most part, very carefully made: mild, artificial, emotionless, cute. Any real feelings seemed to have been rendered out in a long and deliberate process. Pop records had the final passionate impact of marshmallow whip. Look, for example, at the way one could express one's deepest emotions to a loved one: "If I Knew You Were Coming I'd've Baked a Cake" (a 1951 hit for Eileen Barton), or "Come On-a My House" ("I'm gonna give you candy . . ."), a hit for Rosemary Clooney in 1951. The songs spoke of yearning, longing, caring—of emotions reduced to cliché as substitutes for actual feelings. Similarly, they spoke in such euphemisms for sexual passion as the embrace or the one kiss that quenches desire. These phrases were certainly code words for sexual intercourse. But the code was so repressed, so deeply buried in the cultural subconscious, that most people could pretend it was not a code at all. Thus, the euphemisms were widely regarded as the reality. Any basic moving experience or raw feeling beneath the one ultimate kiss was treated as nonexistent. To mention the things that this age of artifice repressed was perceived as a dangerous and explosive act. It was also regarded as commercially impractical, a block against a record's reaching the top ten and TV's "Your Hit Parade."[3]

The triteness and artificiality of early fifties pop was not the sole clue to its failure. Another indication of the way such songs were not satisfying the public was in the many unconventional records people purchased. The most obvious of these were the innumerable novelty hits of the early fifties. These were odd, unusual recordings. No matter how much fun or excitement they provided, novelties were by definition unrepeatable both as a success and as a musically significant event. The only musical trend created was an amorphous taste for generally amusing novelty records. But rather frequently such songs became best sellers. Sometimes these expressed the vague religiosity of the times. Frankie Laine's 1950 hit "I Believe" is the best example. Some few folk songs, also considered novelties, occasionally made the charts. The most famous folk group was the Weavers, who made such hits as the 1954 "On Top of Old Smoky." Many novelties were oriented toward sanitized ethnic fantasies. These ranged from emotional Jewish (Eddie Fisher, "Oh! My Pa-Pa," 1954) to mass-market Latino ("Vaya Con Dios," Les Paul and Mary Ford, 1953). There were orchestrated novelties like "The Typewriter" and "The Syncopated Clock," both issued in 1952. Conventional songs turned increasingly to novelty sound effects—for instance, the roulette wheel in the background of Kay Starr's 1952 "Wheel of Fortune," the squawking seagulls in the 1953 "Ebb Tide," the hammer-on-anvil of "Blacksmith Blues," sung by Ella Mae Morse in 1952. Even romantic tunes finally turned to a novelty approach. Patti Page's 1953 hit indicates a great deal about fifties music. Seeking a replacement for a lover, she musically wondered "How Much Is that Doggie in the Window?"[4]

There were other hints that pop music failed to satisfy the public. Many adults began to purchase records that were rather unique. The early fifties saw the rise of albums consisting purely of such sounds as racing car engines, jet-plane takeoffs, cattle stampedes, or trains-in-tunnels. Millions of these records were sold in the decade. The taste for sheer noise, that is, was not the later creation of rock and roll.[5] Perhaps the appeal of the sound-effects records rested in their strident attack on the enforced emotional stillness of those years.

Such trends sought specific people around whom to coalesce. The dissatisfaction with novelty and the growing taste for clamor found its first human outlet in 1952. That year, a skinny, half-deaf kid named Johnny Ray broke into the pop charts with a double-sided hit: "The Little White Cloud That Cried" backed with just plain "Cry." These titles more or less summed up Ray's musical approach. Ray's music was no different from the usual "Your Hit Parade" stream. But his performance was. Nicknamed the "Nabob of Sob" and the "Million Dollar Teardrop," he flaunted his neuroses and would ritually end every stage show collapsed and sobbing.[6] He would tremble, twist, choke in agony, squirm and buckle and most of all weep, aggressively and exhibitionistically. This won him lots of passionate fans, most of them teen-agers. Ray can be regarded as a portent of the future. But he can also be seen as a cultural transition point. He sang the familiar innocuous music of the pops. There was no challenge in that. But he introduced young white audiences to the idea that music could involve the raw emotions. To acknowledge that rawness was to admit to the pain, difficulty, and pleasure of the human experience, things often denied in the fifties. Particularly it was to appeal to the very adolescents who could spend so much time considering those stirrings.

Ray's fame was brief. Long before his momentary stardom, another American music had been developing that would eclipse Ray and his contemporaries. By the early fifties it was widening in importance. Sometime in 1951, a disc jockey named Alan Freed was visiting a record store in downtown Cleveland. He was surprised to see white teen-agers buying rhythm and blues records, and even dancing to the music in the store. "I wondered," he recalled later, "I wondered for about a week. Then I went to the station manager and talked him into permitting me to follow my classical program with a rock 'n' roll party." These represented two of Freed's greatest contributions to the fluctuating music scene. First, he had made a name change, but an all-important one. Freed shrewdly recognized that the name "rhythm and blues" stigmatized that music. The fact of American racism condemned black tastes in general and so "race records" in particular. Freed redubbed it "rock and roll"—a ghetto euphemism for both dancing and sex. In titling his show "Moondog's Rock and Roll Party," Freed also legitimized the music in another way for white kids. Before, some whites already listened to all-black R & B radio shows. But it was not a taste cultivated by the mass of whites. Freed, as a white DJ, put the music in a more familiar and acceptable format, reassuring the majority of repressed and nervous white kids.[7] His framework encouraged them to make the effort of overcoming their bland, stereotyped musical background. The R & B of Freed's early radio "party" was the strongest ancestor of the rock and roll that evolved a few years later.

Freed did more than begin playing black music for white audiences on the radio. Working on a medium that traditionally discriminated against black artists, Freed never forgot the R & B roots of rock, and always favored black performers on his shows. He entirely refused to play white cover versions of black songs. In 1957, Freed even banned all the recordings of Pat Boone from his program. Freed also disseminated the music through other media. For instance, he presented black artists to largely white audiences with stage shows. In 1953, one such program at the Cleveland Arena was canceled because 30,000 people turned up to fight for the 10,000 seats. Two thirds of the crowd was white. The show was produced later that year, and included R & B stars Red Prysock, Joe Turner, Fats Domino, the Drifters, Ella Johnson, and the Moonglows. Freed's success in bringing black music to white audiences was frequently noted in *Billboard*.[8]

Between 1952 and 1954, the broadening taste that Freed had recognized began to affect the national music market. In 1952 the Clovers' "One Mint Julep" broke from the race category to sell on some white charts. Bill Haley and the Comets, a white ex-country group, pioneered a crude new style with "Crazy Man Crazy" in 1953. That same year the Orioles' "Crying in the Chapel," a race ballad, hit the white charts, as did "Money Honey" by the Drifters, Faye Adams' "Shake a Hand," and the Clovers' "Good Lovin'."

In 1954, the Crows' "Gee," and "Sh-Boom," by the Chords, were the most outstanding of the crossovers sung by blacks. A cover version of the latter recorded by the Crew Cuts reached number five on the year's top ten. Haley hit the charts again with a cover of "Shake, Rattle and Roll."[9] To adults, these songs were all mysterious and somehow unpleasant. They were crude compared to the conventionalities of ballads. Only rarely did adults buy these records. It was growing clearer that, whatever else it might be, this music was for adolescents.

One of the most important things about these hits was that while the originals were performed by blacks, the best-sellers were recorded by whites. That was a characteristic of the musical industry up to 1956, and one that reveals the deep-set racism of the business. Only in part did this stem from the segregation of music charting.

Much more, it came about because of the perception of the black performance. That performance was generally banned from white-oriented airwaves. The justification for such censorship was frequently the objectionable or sexually explicit lyrics of black songs. The style of performance itself was often regarded as offensive—powerful rhythms and slurred pronunciations seemed unfamiliar, even ugly and corrupting to white ears. This was a pattern that would be repeated in the sixties when white kids began using drugs. The objectionable factor was considered fine for blacks, who were by implication already corrupt, but was perceived as poisonous to whites. In the case of fifties pop music, the mere fact that some of it was being performed in an R & B style by black artists was enough to condemn it.[10]

The ban was nearly universal among white pop disc jockeys. Yet starting in 1952 and 1953, R & B records grew in popularity with white buyers, particularly the young. This created a perceived need for white-performed cover versions of the songs. As long as the pop record industry existed, artists had recorded one another's songs. But what happened in the fifties was often a departure from this tradition. When Eddie Fisher cut "Dungaree Doll" in 1955, he performed it in his own distinctive belting style. He imposed his own talents and character on the record, and so his version was not an example of the white covers. But when Georgia Gibbs cut her cover of LaVern Baker's "Tweedle Dee," the Gibbs version was a complete copy of Baker's, down to the smallest nuances of drum and bass. Its only departures were slight, those of polish and smoothness, factors appealing to the bland musical background of the white majority. Gibbs did much the same thing in copying many other songs, such as "Roll With Me Henry." The changes imposed on her version of that record make the purpose of covers even clearer. In that song, any sexual euphemisms were obliterated. Even the title was changed to "Dance With Me Henry." These two Gibbs records sold in the millions. They were played on stations that would never play LaVern Baker, Joe Turner, or the Midnighters. That these records sold so well indicates the growing taste for R & B. But it just as much reveals the economic discrimination of the music business. Only 700 R & B disc jockeys existed in America, as opposed to 10,000 white pop jockeys, who would not play R & B. As one commentator more recently observed, "exposure was the name of the game."[11] By banning black singers, the taste of the white audience could still be manipulated, and sales of the weak imitation could be encouraged.

A number of white artists founded their success on recording packaged cover versions. Gibbs and Pat Boone were the most famous of these. Others included the Crew Cuts, the Fontane Sisters, and Tab Hunter. The only original recording the Crew Cuts ever made was a 1956 Budweiser commercial. The list of Boone's copies includes many of the greats of fifties rock: "Ain't That a Shame," by Fats Domino, Little Richard's "Tutti Frutti," the Flamingos' "I'll Be Home." "Not only do we like him," teens told *Billboard* about Boone at mid-decade, "but our parents do too." This showed a persistent teen concern with the power and authority of adults. Yet it also illustrated the transitory nature of this music at mid-decade. Many kids, having been educated on syrupy pops, were not completely ready for the earthiness and honesty of R & B. They bought records that educated them to a new taste, with more of the rhythms than pop possessed, although less of the impact than true rhythm and blues. Rock and roll, that is, was largely still in a becoming process around 1955. But parental music attitudes remained only a temporary concern. One of the most musically significant events of mid-decade was that, in 1956, Little Richard's "Long Tall Sally" outsold its sugary imitation by Pat Boone. It was the first black original to surpass its cover on the market.[12]

At the same time white singers were cleaning up on black tunes, another musical evolutionary step was being taken by Bill Haley and the Comets. Haley himself did some cleaned-up covers too. His version of "Shake, Rattle and Roll" significantly censored the lyrics of the Charles Calhoun tune originally sung by Joe Turner. Where Calhoun wrote "You wear low dresses,/The sun comes shinin' through," Haley revised the words to sing "You wear those dresses,/Your hair done up so nice." Haley also acquiesced to white sensibilities on stage, performing near-vaudeville tricks like playing the saxophone acrobatically. But the changes he imposed on such songs as "Shake, Rattle and Roll" represent an important aesthetic innovation. Haley's versions, unlike those of Boone or Gibbs, did not translate R & B into niceness. Nor were they straight imitations of the blues. What Haley did was to deliberately create a simple new formula for music, mixing up R & B with country. He took the basic African-originated beat and stripped away many musical effects—the loosely pronounced words, the complex and harmonious backing, the slurred note that is the blue note. He added some guitar work and other effects from "hillbilly" music. The results of his formula were not very good. Listening to any old Haley hit today is difficult. It's crude, insistent, oversimplified stuff, as primitive as its worst critics said it was. But it was important in that it was first. In spite of the dishonesty of his censored lyrics, Haley recordings contained an emotional excitement that acts in opposition to most white cover versions. While those intended to reassure, to tone down the unfamiliar and scary elements of sex, beat, and feeling, Haley's thumping and shouting delivery was a powerful and liberating force for a white teen-age audience previously restricted to the pops.[13]

Haley, of course, was only a musical transition point, too clumsy to last once his point became obvious. The synthesis of musical styles that he achieved increased into 1956. By that year, black artists were enjoying unprecedented successes selling to white audiences. In 1956, Little Richard's "Long Tall Sally" enjoyed its triumph. Adolescents came to purchase fully half the records pressed in America. And they bought black artists: Ray Charles, Little Richard, the Clovers, Chuck Berry ("Roll Over Beethoven"), Shirley and Lee ("Let the Good Times Roll"), the Five Satins ("In the Still of the Night"). All these performers had been impressed by the evolving musical scene. They all sang more lucidly, for instance, shunning the slurred pronunciation of blues tradition, to sell to whites as well as blacks.[14] They also recognized the implications of crossing over. Chuck Berry originally intended "Maybellene" to be "Ida Mae," for the country market, and indeed it has both a blues-based beat and country-style guitar work.

By 1956 the movie industry had produced several crucial films intended to debate the rise of juvenile delinquency. But these films wound up reshaping mass attitudes simply by disseminating a compelling vision. The first such film was Lazlo Benedek's *The Wild One* (1954). Marlon Brando starred as the motorcycle leader Johnny, whose gang rampages beyond his control, and who is then unjustly attacked by adult mobs. Johnny used primal antagonism as his tough male disguise hiding a sensitive nature. Teens, already recognizing adults' faint distrust of their behavior, could empathize with his brutal facade and actual heroism.

Two other movies helped focus this feeling even more. In *Rebel Without a Cause* (1955), James Dean and Natalie Wood were kids in trouble. But they were middle-class kids with quite believable family problems, rather than lower-class hoods like Johnny. Through this film, popular culture recognized the link between affluent teen-agers and rebellion.

Finally, the new musical aesthetic was joined to the whole in *Blackboard Jungle,* also a 1955 movie. *Jungle* is corny and sensationalistic. But it permanently joined juvenile delinquency and rock and roll in the mass mind. Bill Haley and the Comets performed the music in the picture. "Shake, Rattle and Roll," originally released in 1954, shot to fame because of this film. There was only a prurient and insensitive presentation of young problems in *Jungle.* Yet wherever one's sympathies rested, it was obvious that rock and roll was integral to the way these punks thought and acted.

The next major step was the one that gelled the entire musical scene. Its cultural implications—the big obvious ones and the lesser nuances—were great. Rarely when writing about any time can one cite an event as being inevitable. But the major rock event of 1956 was just such a thing.

Had Sam Phillips not discovered Elvis Presley in Memphis, it would have been necessary to invent him. By mid-decade all the cultural groundwork had been laid for just such a star, doing just what he did to the music and the people. That is one reason for Elvis' incredibly rapid rise. By mid-decade, R & B was making the white charts. The record business, though, was showing persistent hostility toward black artists. It remained impossible for most white kids to conceive of a black singer as beloved idol. Music was also hovering on some transitory brink. Bill Haley had demonstrated that the mixing of various musical styles had prodigious impact. Elvis, then, took the music scene one step farther. He was not just mixing up country and ballads and blues. Nor did Elvis clean up the then outrageous parts of his act to sell. His manager, Colonel Tom Parker, created an Elvis image in shrewd conjunction with the times. Parker recognized the importance of facade. Elvis looked tough, brutal, confidently sensual. But he was, deep down, a good religious country boy, who loved his mother and his capitalist success and eventually went into the army with a patriotic smile. Elvis looked delinquent, but he was safe. And he was white, and so even safer. Presley's tremendous talent and charisma completed his success. Singing, Elvis was the convergence of all the pop traditions. He drew on the elaborate sentimentality of country. He had the pure floating voice of a balladeer; and he loved the rawness and the beat of the blues. All these elements appeared in his best fifties songs: the tough and derisive "Hound Dog," the desperate "Heartbreak Hotel," or the light yet urgent "Don't Be Cruel."[15] But there was something more in his music. This was plainly a new musical form. It was not just a hack's tin pan alley synthesis but an evolutionary break.

One begins to get a feel for the sheer exciting newness of it all—of Elvis, of rock and roll—in looking at some statistics. Elvis was signed by RCA late in 1955. He recorded "Heartbreak Hotel." Within weeks it took the top position in both the pop and country charts, and was in the top five on the R & B chart. That this rapid rise and this crossing occurred was not completely unique. But Elvis continued to repeat that crosscultural success with a lengthy series of singles and albums. After six months, he had sold eight million records. In 1956, four of his singles in addition to "Heartbreak Hotel" sold amazingly. In the next two years, Elvis had a best-selling record during 55 of the 104 weeks.[16] The record business had literally never known any single performer to achieve such consistent gigantic success. Nor had the business ever seen such numbers of ardent fans. Elvis quickly came to represent an utterly different sensibility to the music business and, indeed, to America at large.

Elvis was not the only rocker to make the charts, but he was the most outstanding of a vital and expanding field. He illustrates important things about changing musical tastes. The record producers had long assumed that R & B was somehow distasteful to white kids. This assumption entailed certain American bugaboos: fear and dislike of blacks, fear of explicit sex, fear of sensual experience and of autonomous expression. The crooners before Elvis had been like Perry Como, relaxed, muted, low-key in performance, or else limited belters like Eddie Fisher. Elvis was anything but muted or limited. On stage he celebrated all sorts of then-outrageous notions. He would ride on in a gold Cadillac, wearing a gold lamé suit. He would move any way he wanted. He would intersperse hit songs with gospel songs, tunes by country singers like Carl Perkins with R & B standards from Big Boy Crudup. Where a crooner such as Como or Al Martino might sing of tragic love in tones more suggesting apathy or drowsiness, Elvis delivered the real feeling. His immense emotional range, of course, received less publicity than his stage presence. As one rock critic has since written, "there was no more pretense about moonlight and hand-holding; it was hard physical fact."[17]

It was also previously unheard of in the American mass market. Sexually explicit movements by a singer had been done before black audiences, or in sleazy bars or strip joints, but not before mainstream white America. The reaction against Elvis successfully obscured one of the great functions of such explicitness, a function drawn from the blues heritage. Originally, the blues was a means of expressing the hard facts of black existence. It was a safety valve. Moving expressively or singing about tragedy and cruelty made it possible to both acknowledge those parts of life and live with them. (This is in contradistinction to protest music that cites a social evil as exhortation, to provoke action.) The music made by Elvis in 1956 and 1957, and that by singers like Chuck Berry, Little Richard, Jerry Lee Lewis, Fats Domino, and others, performed this function too for its teen-age audience. Chuck Berry, indeed, perfectly realized this aspect of rock as pacifier/outlet in "School Days" (1957):

> Drop the coin right into the slot,
> You've got to hear something that's really hot,
> With the one you love you're making romance,
> All day long you've been wanting to dance.[18]

Adults, as the 1955 attitude of *Life* magazine indicated, had been unsure about just how to take to this new music. But by 1956, most adults knew: hostility was the rule. Elvis, as the king of rock, inevitably received much of the criticism. *Look* magazine's words seem to be a good metaphor for adult feelings toward the rock phenomenon as a whole. In an article entitled "He Can't Be—But He Is," the magazine moaned, "Presley is mostly nightmare." Consider the insular naivete and suspicion those quotes imply. Elvis, and by extension all his young fans, "can't be": there was no room for them in the mid-century conformity daydream. And so he could only be "nightmare." Presley was a bad dream personified because this "vulgar" man, as *Look* wrote, this gyrating, leering, sensual star was popular.[19] Popular with teen-agers. And not just the easily forgotten children of poor whites, of ghetto blacks, but with everyone's kids. No longer were the young mere extensions of their parents' musical tastes. Parents felt they were slipping out of control—if music was unfamiliar, what would be next?

Another *Look* article, talking about the Presley line of clothing and cosmetics, gratuitously injected an offhand comment that "the heavy divisions of the Presley force are half-grown females with half-baked ideas." That remark seems particularly strange considering the bulk of the article was puff for items like charm bracelets, sneakers, plaster of paris busts, and lipsticks (Hound Dog Orange, for instance). A Chicago radio station smashed Presley records on the air. Buffalo DJ Dick Biondi was fired for spinning Elvis records. A Cincinnati used-car dealer guaranteed to break fifty Presley records in the presence of every purchaser, and sold five cars in one day. Most animosity was directed toward the sensual implications of Elvis' act (and by extension, the implications of all rock and roll). But it was not just eroticism but self-expression in general that became the target of these angry adults. As *Look* magazine noted with disapproval, "When asked about the sex element in his act, he answers without blinking his big brown eyes, 'Ah don't see anything wrong with it. Ah just act the way Ah feel.'" Or, as New York *Times* reviewer Jack Gould commented after Elvis' famous Ed Sullivan appearance, "When Presley executes his bumps and grinds, it must be remembered by the Columbia Broadcasting System that even the 12-year-old's curiosity may be overstimulated."[20]

Overstimulated? Half-baked? Nightmare? The adult reaction to Elvis, and even more to rock music in general, provides a brilliant counterpoint illuminating American ideas of freedom in the fifties. As such, it also shows how patterns of rebellion, of counterculture if you will, are provoked. Rock did coalesce teen-agers, did give them a feeling of being a unique social group with particular characteristics. And it did specify certain material urgencies—like the faddism of "Blue Suede Shoes" or, more usually, romantic emotions. But there was no reason that any of this should have seemed politically revolutionary. Rebelliousness was the exception rather than the rule in the lyrics. The Coasters' generational conflict songs such as "Yakety Yak" and "Charlie Brown" were brilliant but atypical. Usually, very conventional mores were expressed—fidelity, male dominance, love, marriage. The material status quo was completely respected. Were it not for adult intervention in the music scene, rock and roll would have remained simply entertainment, at once identifying teen concerns and discharging social tensions. In *Brave*

New World Revisited, Aldous Huxley wrote how drugs had a tremendous potential for social control. They could very easily be not a rebel's defiant act, but a governmentally imposed tool for the enforcement of mass submission. Rock and roll could quite easily have gone that route: as just one more opiate, one more circus, one more distraction from the daily tedium. (This is not to say that rock has wholly avoided that function since the fifties.) It was how adults reacted to rock in the latter fifties that made it more than a music. Because without consciously doing so, the opponents of this music were articulating a cultural stance of inherent contradiction, a cultural stance not so much against the music as against the things it represented. Entertainment was on the way to becoming polemic.

Some of these elements have been illustrated in the reaction to Elvis. But just as crucial was the reaction to other performers, other songs—most of all to the ostensible effect of the music. In all this reaction one finds a single, central fear. The glowing core of that blurry fifties terror was a very real fear of autonomy and free expression. A quote from a book entitled *U.S.A. Confidential* is a good catchall of accusations against rock and roll. "Like a heathen religion, it is all tied up with tom-toms and hot jive and ritualistic orgies of erotic dancing, weed-smoking and mass mania, with African jungle background. Many music shops purvey dope; assignations are made in them. White girls are recruited for colored lovers. Another cog in the giant delinquency machine is the radio disc jockey. . . . We know that many platter-spinners are hopheads. Many others are Reds, left-wingers, or hecklers of social convention. . . . Through disc jocks, kids get to know colored and other hit musicians; they frequent places the radio oracles plug, which is done with design . . . to hook juves and guarantee a new generation subservient to the Mafia."[21] Nearly every phobia of American respectability at mid-century cropped up in exaggerated form in this paragraph. This, its authors insisted, was what rock and roll did to good white kids: it introduced them to their sexuality, to dope, to interracial contacts, to bizarre dance rituals involving the former; it taught them to distrust convention and finally it put them under Mafia rule. There are varying truths in all this. The Mafia accusation is dubious at best. Drugs were rarely part of the youth culture scene in the fifties—except for alcohol, a more acceptable vice. Probably rock's biggest contribution to racial equality was to economically enrich a few black artists—although white producers, southern white artists, and the cover singers really made the most money. Besides this, and the sort of interracial contacts made by sitting next to someone at a rock show, it is doubtful the music scene itself actually encouraged white girls to enlist with black lovers.

But it was in the dance-as-ritual and in the body discovered that rock made some of its greatest contributions. That it was easy to dance to was part of its aesthetic: that is why a record would be rated on the basis of "I can dance to it" on Dick Clark's *American Bandstand* television panels. And dancing to it, one could easily know that one occupied one's own body, rather than having to ignore it or fight its desires. People could become musical instruments, feeling and existing in the familiar repetition of a performance. As Elvis said, "Ah just act the way Ah feel." And that precisely cited the terror: in fifties America, to act happily and freely outside of conventional notions was not done. It was the greatest wrong.

In the final analysis this was the most basic paradox of fifties society. Inevitably, when this was at last precisely realized and questioned, the entire social outlook would begin to break down. Certainly adults tried to stave off that questioning. The censorship of rock and roll music was one instrument to that end. So-called objectionable content of rock triggered fierce parental and religious campaigns against songs, stations, record firms, and artists. A series of songs by the Midnighters was often cited as particularly evil, with its barely disguised ghetto euphemisms interpreted in newspapers everywhere: "Work With Me Annie," "Sexy Ways," and finally the ultimate divine retribution of "Annie Had a Baby" ("can't work no more"). That the ballad/pops contained euphemisms was generally ignored in this argument. When Rosemary Clooney sang "I'm gonna give you candy," did parents really think she was singing about fudge?

By 1957 and 1958 the opposition to R & B, black performers, and Elvis Presley grew in intensity as their popularity increased. But at the same time many adults reached a truce with rock and roll. They split from its attackers. One big reason for this split attitude was the mutations within the rock field. In certain respects, the image of rock was becoming more divergent as the music scene expanded in many directions. For instance, the last three or four years of the decade saw the rise of the clean white boy performers, the amateurs whose musical roots were not completely in the blues tradition. Their concerns were far more white, middle-class, and adolescent ones. They sang about naive first love, about dating, about nice, nearly sexless girls, about cars, going steady, and holding hands. These were very different and much more immature worries than those reflected in rhythm and blues, or even in country music. Such performers as the Everly Brothers, Neil Sedaka, Fabian, Buddy Holly, Paul Anka, and Bobby Darin varied tremendously in talent, but all shared the same relatively innocent teen outlook. They made adults perceive at least some aspects of rock and roll to be acceptable for the young.[22]

An equally important factor was the 1957 introduction to national audiences of a local Philadelphia TV show. ABC's *American Bandstand* was an unusual television program. It was not precisely an entertainment directed out at an audience. Rather it was a happening in which the viewer could participate, much as one participates in a party. The show brought brotherly, clean-cut Dick Clark, its master of ceremonies, into fame and fortune. More importantly, it furthered the domesticating of much of rock. The show emphasized wholesomeness. All the kids who appeared on *Bandstand* had to obey a strict dress code and behave properly. All the kids on the show (except occasional performing artists) were white. *Bandstand* music was oriented toward white teen-age tastes (as well as toward the record company interests of Dick Clark and others involved in producing the show).[23] But the harmless appearance of the show rubbed off on the music too. Everyone seemed to be having such a nice innocent middle-class time that no evil could be suspected. And this innocence was advertised every weekday afternoon on TV.

The suspicion of musical evil, of course, was merely redirected. Much of it was aimed at rockers like Elvis and the tough white singers who rose in the Elvis excitement, such as Jerry Lee Lewis and Carl Perkins. But by 1957–58, the many black performers who also had evolved beyond basic R & B had grown in popularity with white audiences: Chuck Berry, Ray Charles, Little Richard, the Drifters, and so many more musical giants. These black stars were distrusted by many white adults. Their effect on the young was regarded as dangerous.

Thus adults began directing various degrees of violence to the prevention of rock and roll. The mildest level was the banning of rock music on the radio. The next level of aggression came in the breaking or burning of rock records. Because of the memory of Nazi Germany, most Americans were highly opposed to the burning or censorship of books, but failed to generalise that morality to apply to other media, particularly records and comics. Innumerable critics in these years advised parents and teens to take an aggressive position against rock and roll. "Smash the records you possess which present a pagan culture and a pagan concept of life," urged *Contacts,* the newspaper of the Catholic Youth Center. "Some songwriters need a good swift kick. So do some singers. So do some disc jockeys." Such incitements to violence had their effects. Several disc jockeys were fired for airing rock tunes, or particular songs. A station in Portland, Oregon, KEX, fired a jockey for playing Presley's "White Christmas." Law-enforcement officials took the next step of seeking to censor or suppress rock and roll stage shows. When Elvis performed at the Pan Pacific auditorium in Los Angeles, police ordered he "clean up the show or else," and the vice squad monitored the entire performance to make sure he eliminated "all sexy overtones." Presley, of course, was not the only target. In Washington, D.C., authorities refused a permit for the "Biggest Stars of '58" show. Earlier that year, a show being presented in Boston by Alan Freed was interrupted by police, who upset the young crowd by turning on the house lights. Afterward some members of the audience spread through the city, fighting. One boy was killed and several beaten. Freed was charged with inciting to riot and with anarchy. It took him several years and a great deal of money to see these harassing charges finally thrown out of court.[24]

The attacks on the famous personalities of the rock world were scarcely the only result of such aggression. The hatred and racism inherent in attacks on rock created one notorious incident. This involved a singer not even remotely associated with rock and roll. Nat King Cole was performing before a large white audience at the Municipal Auditorium in Birmingham, Alabama, April 23, 1956. He had just finished singing "Autumn Leaves" when five men ran down the aisle, leaped on the stage, and began to beat him up. Police, who had been forewarned some sort of demonstration would occur, fended them off. The attack turned out to be linked to a White Citizens' Council campaign against "bop and Negro music."[25]

The attack on Cole illustrated the irrational nature of attacks on rock and roll. It was unusual only in its individual brutality. More often, less physical tactics were used; the violence was expressed in a more subtle manner. The late-decade payola scandals are the best example. These scandals grew out of congressional investigations into the TV quiz show corruptions. Payola is the giving of bribes to disc jockeys in order to secure airtime for certain records. It was a standard practice throughout the record industry. Significantly, the investigations and indictments made in the investigation against payola failed to examine the entire bribe-ridden music industry. Only rock and roll music—its producers and the jockeys who aired it—was the target. Congressional investigators literally assumed that rock was evil, "ugly," "unintelligible," "bad," that teen-agers were passive victims who never would have listened to it unless it had been forced on them by illegal activity. Among those disc jockeys indicted was Alan Freed.[26]

The scandal would ruin Freed. He eventually pleaded guilty to part of the charges and, in 1962, received a fine of only $300 and a suspended six-month sentence. But his career was wrecked. He lost his excellent job at WABC and WNEW. As Freed moved from station to station, other agencies pursued him with new indictments. He drank more and more. By 1965, at 43, Freed was dead of uremia.[27]

There is no doubt Freed was destroyed by the violence of the fifties mainstream, of people made hostile by changing times. One must also ask why Freed was the target. Another and bigger hero figure existed—Dick Clark. Clark was far more familiar to all American teen-agers. And, as congressional investigators were amazed to learn, he was far more implicated for profiting from his programming. Clark owned vast percentages of many records he aired, and of the companies that owned the records. The difference between Clark and Freed was largely one of perception. Clark had a better image. His public relations budget was much larger; he acted the ideal junior executive; his show featured wholesome white kids. Freed had a small PR budget and featured black musicians. Worse, he was abrasively vocal in denouncing the white imitators and opponents of rock and roll. Clark was cool, suave, a sharp businessman. Freed was emotional and outspoken, a much less attractive figure in the cool conforming fifties. And so Freed, identified with emotionalism and blacks, was destroyed, where the careful manners of Clark helped him thrive.[28]

Many commentators have since looked at the payola scandal as a sign of the decline of rock and roll. The late fifties and early sixties are presented as years of boredom, even dormancy, for the music. This is only partly true. Some things did get worse about rock. The late fifties, for instance, saw the decline of the personality disc jockey and the rise of Top Forty formula programming. This shrank talk, speeded the pace, and increased commercials. Records were to be played on the basis of singles sales alone.[29]

While this countered payola, it also tended to reflect only the less sophisticated tastes of the very young singles buyer. Album purchasers, who were older with more developed tastes, found their likings ignored in such radio programming. The rock that got played was less representative of the whole.

Other signs of the failing of rock could be discerned. Many of the great stars left the music scene by that time. Elvis went into the army and emerged a pop singer. Little Richard took the orbiting of Sputnik I as a sign from heaven and quit the music business. Jerry Lee Lewis married his 14-year-old cousin and was ostracized by the entire industry. Chuck Berry was, in the late fifties, charged with a violation of the Mann Act, for which he would go to jail in 1962. His time was also absorbed by business—in 1959, he sold his St. Louis nightclub and opened a vast amusement park. Some of the greats were dead—the Big Bopper, Buddy Holly, and Ritchie Valens all died in the same 1959 plane crash. Many young people, too, were turning away from rock. The liberalizing young (educated upper middle class) were looking to the virtues of folk music.[30]

But it is false to regard the entire rock music scene in those years as flaccid. The boy singers are indication of one direction of the music of the time. Critics interested in proving the collapse of rock at decade's end cite the worst performances of these boys as proof. And it is true that some of the all-decade lows in popular music were attained by a few of these kids. Fabian's "Turn Me Loose" shows almost as great an absence of socially redeeming qualities as does Bobby Rydell's "Kissin' Time." The main reason these two boys became stars was that they were packaged and promoted heavily by their record companies. But other adolescent boy singers did produce many exciting records, rock classics by themselves regardless of their teen attitude. The Everly Brothers created a consistent series of classics. There still is a tremendous excitement on such singles as Del Shannon's "Runaway" and Neil Sedaka's "Breaking Up Is Hard to Do." Even the utterly mediocre boy singers (like Frankie Avalon, Freddy Cannon, and Paul Anka) could very rarely produce thrilling songs (respectively, "Venus," "Palisades Park," and "Put Your Head on My Shoulder"). The teen sensibility of these performers did not necessarily interfere with the creation of danceable, compelling songs.

The late fifties and early sixties saw rock explode in many more directions. In the last years of the fifties, the black girl groups enjoyed their first fame. The roots of these groups were not wholly in the blues tradition, nor in white adolescent rock or even mid-decade rock and roll. They represent a unique sensibility, always female but never the passive feminine cliché the rest of rock preferred. The girl groups were all rough-edged, full-voiced, feeling, and rather aggressive. Their songs burst from the radio in an emotional fury, sometimes demanding, sometimes exulting, but never shy and retiring. Among the greatest of the girl groups were the Crystals, the Chiffons ("One Fine Day"), the Shirelles ("Will You Still Love Me Tomorrow?") and the Ronettes ("Be My Baby"). These groups, and the girl groups with one-record successes like the Teddy Bears ("To Know Him Is to Love Him") and Rosie and the Originals ("Angel Baby") were the ancestors of the later sixties white Shangri-Las, and of two important black girl groups, Martha and the Vandellas ("Dancing in the Street") and the supergroup, the Supremes.

Black male performers continued to enjoy successes in the late fifties and early sixties. In 1959, Ray Charles produced his most important fifties song, "What'd I Say." Lloyd Price sang "Stagger Lee" and "Personality." Jackie Wilson recorded "Lonely Teardrops." Brook Benton and Dinah Washington released two duets, "Baby (You've Got What It Takes)," and "A Rockin' Good Way (To Mess Around and Fall in Love)." Benton also released "It's Just a Matter of Time." Two black women released fine hits—LaVern Baker, with no cover competition, at last, had success with "I Cried a Tear," and Nina Simone had her first best-selling record with "I Loves You Porgy." Black male groups did very well in these years too: the Drifters, the Dominoes, the Coasters, many more. The list of excellent black performers, and of performances by whites trying hard to sound black, is long.

In no way, then, can the rock music scene of the late fifties be considered a dormant one. In its very complexity, it contained things to appeal to every taste and prejudice. Rock and roll of the period circa 1960, as well as of the mid-fifties, would have a profound effect on the next evolution of the musical scene—as much of an effect as did the pre-fifties pure blues. The Beatles, around whom the next rock revolution catalyzed, had been powerfully influenced both by whites like Elvis and Carl Perkins and by mid-fifties black rockers like Chuck Berry and Little Richard. Many of their early records are weak remakes such as "Long Tall Sally" and "Maybellene." One also finds strains of late-fifties adolescent fun music cropping up in such Beatles teen-oriented tunes as "I Wanna Hold Your Hand" and "She Loves You." Lloyd Price had enjoyed a hit in 1952 with "Lawdy Miss Clawdy." His song became one of the most influential of records. In the sixties it affected Johnny Rivers, the Hollies, the Dave Clark Five, and other British rockers. The Rolling Stones, even more than the Beatles, draw their music from American sources—especially from such performers as Berry and Richard, and the great blues musicians, particularly Robert Johnson. David Bowie also cites the fifties rockers, from Berry to Presley, as the most important influences on his life. Much mid-seventies music owes more to the teen-age rock sensibility of the period around 1960 than to earlier more R & B inspired music. The teen songs of that time, for instance, are ancestors to bubblegum music. The soul music of the sixties partly grew out of the works of Ray Charles and of Nina Simone, who both combined blues with gospel strains. Charles was also the biggest influence on Stevie Wonder, who began in 1963 with the bluesy "Fingertips" and has progressed incredibly since then.

One also finds amazing degrees of continuity within the industry. There are the obvious persistent stars, like Charles, Simone, Elvis. There are the stars who have returned to fame such as Chuck Berry and Little Richard. And then there are surprises. In the very early fifties, a chubby teen-age black girl named Little Esther had a lot of R & B hits, some of which crossed over onto pop charts. She emerged in the seventies as the distinctive Esther Phillips, won a 1974 Grammy for the album "From a Whisper to a Scream," and then released the sophisticated "What a Diff'rence a Day Makes."

Rock never really died. It is over two decades old and continues to explode all over the place. The affection for "oldies," itself interpreted as a sign of the weakness of the rock scene, is just a way of fondly remembering the history of rock on the part of those kids who themselves have so little history. For the young, by 1960, rock music was not dormant but managed to fulfill a number of functions. Some of these were contradictory. Even at its most furious the music had been unable to counter the life-programming most kids recognized as their future. Rock only provided a diversion from its colder constraints. But it was in the way rock and roll united teens as a self-acknowledged different group that the music performed its most challenging act: a challenge calling not for revolution but, more precisely, for reassessment. Once a teen-ager broke off from the music of adults, and especially once the parents began making bitter judgments about a simple matter of entertainment, a re-evaluation of more than the music was nearly inevitable. It was a re-evaluation refused, for the most part, until later years. But rock and roll did help contribute to a new attitude emerging in the late fifties. In that decade, America was a culture daydreaming of a false world, with Mr. Clean, Doris Day, General Ike, and universal luxury, without stress, Negroes, or genitalia. We were daydreaming, and rock was one of the forces that woke us up.

NOTES

1. *Life*, April 15, 1955, pp. 166–68.
2. Carl Belz, *The Story of Rock* (New York, 1969), pp. 16–25, describes the three major popular markets. "Early in the Morning" has all the elements of the great rock classics of the latter fifties. Louis Jordan's style would have been perfect for teen tastes a decade later. He was, in the late forties and early fifties, a major star of the so-called sepia market, but was unheard of in any other musical context.
3. Editors of *Time-Life* Books, *1950–1960* (New York, 1973), pp. 136–41, 152; Charlie Gillett, *The Sound of the City* (New York, 1970), p. 7; Arnold Shaw, *The Rockin' '50s* (New York, 1974), pp. 14–18.
4. *Time-Life, 1950–1960*, pp. 140–41, 152; Shaw, *Rockin'*, pp. 38–39.
5. Shaw, *Rockin'*, p. 159.
6. Gillett, *Sound*, p. 7; Nik Cohn, *Rock from the Beginning* (New York, 1969), pp. 11–12.
7. Gillett, *Sound*, pp. 15–17; Jeff Greenfield, *No Peace, No Place* (Garden City, 1973), pp. 46–48.
8. Shaw, *Rockin'*, pp. 104–8, 127, 222; Belz, *Story*, p. 51.
9. Gillett, *Sound*, p. 17; Greenfield, *No Peace*, p. 49; Cohn, *Rock*, pp. 18, 25–26.

10. Greenfield, *No Peace*, pp. 49–52.

11. Gillett, *Sound*, pp. 52, 53, 42; Shaw, *Rockin'*, pp. 125–26.

12. Russel B. Nye, *The Unembarrassed Muse* (New York, 1970), p. 350; Shaw, *Rockin'*, pp. 125–29. The Crew Cuts commercial appears on Increase Records' radio reproduction *Cruisin' 1956*, INCM 2001.

13. Gillett, *Sound*, pp. 25–26; Cohn, *Rock*, pp. 17–21.

14. Gillett, *Sound*, pp. 40, 46; Shaw, *Rockin'*, pp. 161–64, 167–68. James Brown also released his first record in 1956—"Please Please Please" with the Famous Flames.

15. Cohn, *Rock*, Chapter Three, "Elvis Presley," pp. 22–28; Nye, *Muse*, p. 350; Stanley Booth, "A Hound Dog to the Manor Born," anthologized in Jonathan Eisen, ed., *The Age of Rock* (New York, 1969), p. 51. See especially the greatest of the books on rock and roll, Greil Marcus, *Mystery Train* (New York, 1975), pp. 137–205.

16. Gillett, *Sound*, pp. 64–68; Cohn, *Rock*, p. 24.

17. Cohn, *Rock*, p. 25.

18. Gillett, *Sound*, p. 97.

19. "He Can't Be—But He Is," *Look*, August 7, 1956, pp. 82–84. See also *Time*, April 19, 1956, p. 14, for a letter censuring that magazine for its anti-Elvis remarks, signed by 43 fans.

20. "The Great Elvis Presley Industry," *Look*, November 13, 1956, pp. 98–104; Shaw, *Rockin'*, pp. 154, 211, 215; Gould quoted in *Time-Life, 1950–1960*, p. 145.

21. Jack Lait and Lee Mortimer, *U.S.A. Confidential* (New York, 1952), pp. 37–38. Innumerable remarks similar to this one, and not even diminished in exaggeration, appeared in these years. A Hartford, Connecticut, psychiatrist characterized rock and roll as "a communicable disease with music appealing to adolescent insecurity and driving teen-agers to do outlandish things." The psychiatrist's comments formed part of the pressure that encouraged Hartford authorities to revoke the license of the State Theater there following a three-day appearance of Freed's rock and roll review.

22. Shaw, *Rockin'*, pp. 182–84.

23. Ibid., pp. 175–81.

24. Belz, *Story*, p. 116; Shaw, *Rockin'*, pp. 154–55, 211, 215, 228, 235, 251.

25. Shaw, *Rockin'*, p. 160.

26. Gillett, *Sound*, pp. 24–25; Belz, *Story*, pp. 52, 109–16, offers the most cogent and intelligent analysis of the payola scandal available.

27. Shaw, *Rockin'*, pp. 225, 268–80.

28. Ibid., pp. 280–81.

29. Ibid., pp. 263–65.

30. *Time-Life, 1950–1960*, pp. 148–51; Shaw, *Rockin'*, pp. 147, 192, 209–10, 246. Eddie Cochran died in a car crash in 1960. The deaths of these four stars created almost instant cults around their brief lives. These were similar, although not as massive, as the deification of the dead James Dean by teen-agers.

12

Hollywood in Transition

"Hollywood's like Egypt," lamented producer David Selznick in 1951. "Full of crumbling pyramids. It'll never come back. It'll just keep on crumbling until finally the wind blows the last studio prop across the sands." By the early fifties Hollywood's problems were very evident, particularly at the box office. From a record weekly attendance of 82 million in 1946, film audiences alarmingly plummeted to about 36 million by 1950.[1] Labor troubles, higher production costs, adverse court rulings, highly publicized anticommunist hearings all hurt the movie industry. Added to this was the challenge of television. Hollywood, of course, survived all this. Movies are still an integral part of American popular culture. Yet in another sense the fifties did witness the demise of the old film-making system—the Hollywood of big studios, glamorous stars, formalized plots, packaged dreams, predictable profits.

Symbolic of the crises affecting Hollywood at mid-century was a perceptive Billy Wilder movie, *Sunset Boulevard* (1950). The film seemed to chronicle the rotten death of the Hollywood America had so admired up until that time. Gloria Swanson, whose original stardom had come in the twenties, bravely portrayed the faded silent star Norma Desmond. Norma lived wholly on past glories and present delusions. Her existence, and by implication the wonders of Hollywood, reeked of decay and corruption: a crumbling baroque mansion, a pet monkey's funeral, a menacing ex-husband chauffeur (Erich von Stroheim), a gigolo she murdered (William Holden). In the movie's last scene, Norma was about to be arrested for the crime. Convinced she was on a film set, grotesquely costumed as Salome, she descended the ornate stairs, posturing before police and reporters in whom she imagined adulation: "I'm ready for my close-up, Mr. DeMille."[2]

Film people saw Wilder's self-conscious, cynical portrait of a decadent Hollywood as an exaggeration. Nevertheless, by 1950 nearly everyone connected with the industry feared for its future. In a town where money was everything, declining profits forced Hollywood tycoons to seek other methods of reaching the public. Americans were losing their movie habits. By the early fifties more money was being spent on fishing tackle or on bowling than at the cinema. Corporate profits after taxes in the movie business fell from $181 million in 1946 to the industry-wide losses of $16 million in 1956.[3] Clearly something was wrong, and much of fifties film history can be seen as Hollywood's attempt to find new ways of luring back the crowds. A major transformation of the industry was to occur in the fifties. Hollywood remained, but it would never be the same.

Prior to the major challenge of television in the early fifties, the two most important factors undermining the traditional Hollywood system were anticommunist investigations of the industry and antitrust rulings against major production companies.

In 1951, a *Life* reporter, observing Hollywood reactions to news of an impending hearing on communist influences, wired her editor that the movie people put her in mind of "a group of marooned sailors on a flat desert island watching the approach of a tidal wave."[4] Investigations of communist influence in the motion picture industry were begun in 1947 by the House Un-American Activities Committee. Such probes continued intermittently through 1958, roughly paralleling the general anticommunist phobia discussed in chapter 1. It was not surprising that the superpatriots would subject Hollywood to close scrutiny, since movies were and are a significant purveyor of the national self-image and of the image that Americans have of other nations. Unfortunately, the film industry was particularly susceptible to such an inspection. Dependent on the financial support of conservative banking and industrial interests, needing a favorable press and public approval, and realizing that there were indeed some thirties radicals and even known former communists connected with the industry, studio heads quickly succumbed to McCarthyite bullying.[5]

The effect of the anticommunist mania on Hollywood was devastating. It seemed irrelevant that through all the endless investigations not a single American-made movie could be shown to be communist propaganda. The film industry bent over backward to prove its unreserved loyalty. As early as November 1947, Eric Johnson, president of the Motion Picture Association and former president of the American Chamber of Commerce, pledged that anyone refusing to cooperate with HUAC investigators would be barred from movie work. Initially, ten Hollywood figures were blacklisted and subsequently jailed, including screenwriters Ring Lardner, Jr., Albert Maltz, and Dalton Trumbo. By the early fifties, several hundred actors, writers, directors, and producers were so proscribed. (Though the exact number of blacklistees may never be known, five hundred would be a conservative estimate.) It mattered little that few of the victims were proven communists. Accusation was tantamount to guilt—even obviously mistaken accusation. Actor Everett Sloane, for instance, found himself blacklisted simply because his surname coincided with that of writer Allan Sloane who in turn was refused work for nothing more serious than criticizing the American Legion and bomb testing. Hollywood scenarist Louis Pollock for several years had his scripts rejected because he was confused with Louis Pollack, a clothing-store owner who had pleaded the Fifth Amendment before a subcommittee of HUAC. Actor Will Geer was blacklisted after poking fun at HUAC. When asked if he would be willing to fight for the United States in the event of war with the Soviets, the 49-year-old Geer had quipped that he would grow vegetables and entertain in hospitals as he had in World War II. For more than a decade, Geer was banned from movie and television roles. Yet he was one of the lucky ones. For many blacklisted Hollywood people, as well as Broadway, television, and radio personnel, unemployment in their chosen profession was permanent.[6]

As in the nation generally, governmental witch hunting was only the most visible manifestation of the anticommunist mania. In the case of Hollywood, the secular blacklisters proved even more formidable. In June 1950, three former FBI agents, the publishers of a small anticommunist newsletter, *Counterattack,* issued a 213-page paperback titled *Red Channels.* Most of this book consisted of an alphabetical listing of 151 actors, writers, musicians, and directors who were supposedly communist or supporting organizations "espousing Communist causes." The appearance of *Red Channels* coincided with the outbreak of the Korean War and the time when Joseph McCarthy's wild charges and the Hiss and Rosenberg cases were front-page news. In such an environment this right-wing book quickly became the most effective blacklist in the history of show business.[7]

Not only did anticommunist pressure cause the movie industry to silence or exile its left-wing dissenting voices. It also caused the industry to change the content of its product to conform to the national anti-radical, anticommunist mood. On one level this took the form of turning out unofficial cold war propaganda. Between 1948 and 1954, Hollywood produced more than 40 anticommunist films. The list includes movies such as *The Whip Hand* and *I Was a Communist for the FBI* (both 1951), and films on escape from behind the Iron Curtain—*The Steel Fist* (1952), *Never Let Me Go* and *Man on a Tightrope* (both 1953).

In 1952 Paramount Pictures produced *My Son John.* Better made than most propaganda efforts, which the industry saw as public relations films and not profit makers, *My Son John* starred Helen Hayes (lured out of a 17-year movie-making retirement) as the mother. Others in the cast included Robert Walker, Dean Jagger, and Van Heflin, as son John, the father, and the friendly FBI agent respectively. The film tells the tragic story of the Jefferson family, devout Irish-Catholics from small-town Anywhere, U.S.A. Two of the Jefferson boys, big blond football players, are about to go off to the war in Korea. But the third son, dark, sensitive, intellectual John, works for the State Department and has a deferment. The Legionnaire father suspects John of working for the communists (or "scummies" as he calls them). John went to college, associated with highbrow professors, used "two-dollar" words, did not play football, and worst of all, made fun of the parish priest. There are also hints that John may be gay and a narcotics user. Even John's adoring mother becomes suspicious. To relieve her fears, John swears on the family Bible that he "is not now nor has he ever been a member of the Communist party." The audience, however, is quickly reminded that nothing is sacred to "Commies." Finally, when the mother discovers that John has a key to the apartment of a suspected spy, she turns him in to the FBI. Even John's last-minute change of heart and ideology is to no avail; his former comrades assassinate him, gangland style, on the steps of the Lincoln Memorial.[8]

The film relied on and encouraged national, no-think stereotypes—a caricature of the American communist (an unnatural, evil alien without control of his destiny, the well-educated pinko dupe) and the good American (virile, small-town, puritan, American Legionnaire). It was the McCarthyite contrast between the red-blooded football player with faith and the effeminate godless egghead. *My Son John* even implied that the sacred unity of the family, so important in fifties popular culture, must give way to the need for national security. The repentance of the communist, like that of sinning women in Hollywood mythology of the time, brings no absolution. Most communist characters paid for their sins in death, either murdered like John, or as suicides (*The Red Menace*, 1949). Fortunately, such dangerous films were so lacking in humor, character development, drama, or subtlety that their audiences remained small.[9]

But the effect of anticommunism on Hollywood was not limited to studio blacklisting and the production of cold war propaganda films. The movie industry, again like the nation, became during these years exceedingly cautious, nervously conservative. As early as 1948, a film executive in charge of script approval reported confidentially: "I now read scripts through the eyes of the DAR. . . . I'm scared to death, and nobody can tell me it isn't because I'm afraid of being investigated." Movie companies hired private investigators to pry into the backgrounds of writers and actors. Some studios required signed loyalty oaths of all employees. The Motion Picture Alliance published an influential pamphlet by Ayn Rand, *Screen Guide for Americans*, with headings "Don't Smear the Free Enterprise System," "Don't Deify the Common Man," "Don't Smear Success," "Don't Glorify Failure." Rand proclaimed it the "moral duty of every decent man in the motion picture industry to throw into the ashcan, where it belongs, every story that smears industrialists."[10] In other words, films such as *Citizen Kane, The Grapes of Wrath,* or *Meet John Doe* were not to be produced.

The effect of such pressure was to enforce mediocrity. Films dealing with social, political, or psychological problems were reduced to a minimum. A statistical examination of feature-film content found that while the social problem film accounted for 28 per cent of all movies produced in 1947 (the first year of the HUAC investigations), by 1949 this percentage had dropped to 18. By 1953–54 only about nine per cent of movies dealt with social issues.[11] Like the other mass media and the academics, by the early fifties Hollywood films tended to portray America as one big, bland, middle-class paradise with problems no more serious than picking the right mate (*How to Marry a Millionnaire,* 1953) or paying for the wedding (*Father of the Bride,* 1950). Most films celebrated the myths of romantic happiness and material achievement, or they simply provided escape and entertainment (Westerns, gangster movies, musicals) in ways that had little to do with how people actually lived.

It is interesting to note how few Hollywood films were set in contemporary America. While this can be explained in part by the desire of film-makers to reach foreign as well as domestic audiences, the primary factor was to avoid controversy and the possible onus of radicalism. Why offend anyone with current drama (that could be perceived as social) when mass audiences could be gained through the pomp, costuming, adventure, and titillation of antique or biblical epics? Even good films dealing with real contemporary problems such as Elia Kazan's *On the Waterfront* (perhaps the best fifties film) or Stanley Kramer's *The Wild One* (both pictures starred Marlon Brando and were released in 1954) included apologetic prologues carefully explaining to audiences that, while what they were about to see might seem unsavory, the story represented an aberration from the real America of law-abiding patriots. Not until 1956 did Hollywood venture to produce a film mildly critical of McCarthy-type tactics, *Storm Center.* By then criticism of book-burning, *Storm Center*'s subject, was hardly daring.[12]

The second pretelevision challenge to Hollywood—the antitrust cases—though less dramatic than the communist controversy was equally important in changing the nature of the movie industry.

Traditionally the major studios had controlled every aspect of movie-making from production to distribution and exhibition. Either through outright ownership or contractual control of theaters, they had an assured market for a specific number of movies per year, regardless of film quality. This system produced fairly stable profits, at least during the thirties and forties when movie attendance was high. Naturally movie moguls enjoyed these traditional arrangements. They viewed them as necessary for stability. The United States Justice Department, on the other hand, saw such practices as monopolistic and restrictive of trade. The Justice Department won. As a result of several cases beginning in 1945 and culminating in 1950 when the Supreme Court rejected the industry's last appeals, the major studios were forced to divest themselves of theaters and to refrain from negotiating binding contracts with movie houses. In short, after 1950, production was divorced from exhibition. For the studios this meant that the films they made no longer were guaranteed a theater for their showing.

Had such a ruling occurred earlier, its effects might not have been so drastic. But coming when it did, it was crippling. Already public faith in Hollywood had been badly shaken by the anticommunist investigations. Now as the fifties opened, the movies faced their most severe challenge in the growing popularity of television. Attendance was dropping. Without guaranteed theaters to show productions the studios began to cut back heavily on production. While as late as 1951 Hollywood made nearly 400 feature films, by 1960 only 154 were produced. "B" films, shorts, and newsreels all but disappeared during the fifties. The cutbacks in production also meant personnel layoffs. The contract system in which producers, directors, actors, writers, and crew would be salaried by one studio for an extended period of time broke down. Job security vanished.

Under these new conditions, actual film production passed increasingly from the major studios to independents. The large companies assumed a new role as financier and distributor of films, leaving movie-making to independents on a movie by movie basis. This made it unnecessary for the studios to maintain their large lots. The success of early fifties independent productions such as *The African Queen* and *High Noon*, both released through United Artists, set a pattern. By the end of the decade less than a quarter of American films were turned out by the studios themselves. But to fully comprehend the extent of these changes, one must see them in the context of the television challenge.[13]

"Don't be a 'Living Room Captive,'" asserted a 1952 industry ad. "Step out and see a great movie!" A minor fad in the forties, television by the early fifties was an established part of American culture. By 1960, when Americans possessed some 50 million TV sets, a fifth of the nation's theaters had closed for lack of business. By then film footage shown on TV was at least five times greater than that released via Hollywood. Clearly a revolution in the public's entertainment habits had occurred.[14]

Initial Hollywood reactions to television took two tactical forms: ignoring it or fighting it. Those who took the ostrich approach saw TV as a passing fad. Surely, they reasoned, sensible Americans long accustomed to regular movie attendance would tire of squinting at the living-room tube, watching bad shows constantly interrupted by even worse commercials. More aggressively, studio managers forbade contract actors to appear on TV. They refused to sell old movies to the new medium, or to advertise new ones on it. Of course neither method worked. Americans rapidly were developing a TV habit even more serious than their earlier movie addiction. One's own living room was familiar and comfortable. Above all, once one had a set the viewing was virtually free.

The next Hollywood response (a typically American one) was to look to technology to save the day. Such devices as sharper, more riotous color, wider and larger screens, and new projection techniques were expected to lure the public back to theaters. Television may have been free, but it was a gray dwarf next to such colossal brilliancy.

The search for a technological panacea began in earnest on September 20, 1952, when an independent company opened *This Is Cinerama* in New York. This extra-wide-screen system utilized three synchronized projectors to put the picture on the screen in three sections. Although there was frequent distortion where the images joined, the overall effect was more lifelike than any previous technique. The expense of revamping theaters and acquiring the necessary equipment limited its spread. But playing fewer than 30 houses, the first Cinerama show grossed more than $25 million in five years. Hollywood took note.[15]

Movie people also paid close attention when an independent production released early in 1953 by United Artists began playing to packed houses throughout the country. The movie, *Bwana Devil,* was awful—a poorly made, badly acted story about big-game hunters and man-eating lions in Africa. Under usual circumstances it would have been a second-feature "B" film of limited appeal. But it had a gimmick. *Bwana Devil* was Hollywood's first 3-D movie—a two projector process which through the use of special polaroid glasses gave the illusion of depth.[16]

Three-D became an immediate fad. The major studios hastily cranked out cheap adventure films. All shared the illusion of things flying out at the audience—pies, arrows, spears, even spit in *The Charge at Feather River* (1953). Not until 1954 when Alfred Hitchcock made *Dial M for Murder* was a first-rate 3-D film produced. By then the fad was over, and *Dial M* was released flat in a non-3-D version.[17] Three-D had tremendous artistic potential. But it was wasted with stupid plots and shoddy production. Also, audiences found wearing 3-D glasses irritating, and many projection problems were not overcome. But the real deathblow for 3-D came late in 1953 with the introduction of Hollywood's first successful wide-screen process, CinemaScope.

Darryl Zanuck and Spyros Skouras of Twentieth Century-Fox were alarmed at declining audiences and intrigued by the success of Cinerama and 3-D. They decided to gamble with another new projection method. Their costliest picture of the year, the dreary religious epic *The Robe,* was filmed in CinemaScope and released in the fall of 1953. "Thanks to this modern miracle you can see without the use of glasses," touted the first CinemaScope ads. *The Robe* was a box-office smash. Fox studio quickly followed this with a second popular CinemaScope feature, the Marilyn Monroe comedy *How to Marry a Millionaire.* CinemaScope relies on an anamorphic lens, a compound lens that produces greater magnification in one direction than in another and is able to compress a large picture area on to a standard 35-millimeter frame. When the film is projected, another anamorphic lens spreads the picture over a large area which on a wide, slightly curved screen gives some illusion of depth. The financial returns from Fox's first CinemaScope productions assured continued use of the process. Other studios either leased it from Fox or produced similar wide-screen processes themselves (WarnerScope, SuperScope, Vista-Vision, Panavision, Todd-AO).[18]

While wide-screen spectaculars may have helped the movie industry at the box office, the adoption of the CinemaScope-type process in the fifties had negative effects on the artistic development of cinematic techniques. Size substituted for quality, though even before the advent of CinemaScope, quasi-religious spectacles such as *David and Bathsheba* (1951) and *Quo Vadis* (1951) had laid the groundwork for Hollywood's bigger-and-better mystique. In the case of *Quo Vadis,* its cost ($7 million) and statistics (32,000 costumes, 30,000 actors, 450 horses, 85 doves, 63 lions, 12 years of research, seven fighting bulls from Portugal, five teams of oxen, two cheetahs) were advertised by MGM as if they had something to do with the movie's merit. The big-screen techniques only accelerated this unfortunate trend. Like fifties autos, films became obsessed with bigness. The career of Cecil B. De Mille, whom serious film critics considered passé as early as the thirties, revived. His $13.5 million remake of *The Ten Commandments* (1956), a romantic biography of Moses, enjoyed great success. As one mid-fifties critic lamented, "the wide screen and the rediscovery of Christianity have restored films to their second childhood." This trend culminated in 1959 with the MGM production of *Ben-Hur,* another religious remake that could (and did) boast of a $15-million budget, 25,000 extras, five years in the making, and a larger-than-CinemaScope "Camera 65" wide-screen process. Such Bijou Christianity nicely reflected the decade's religiosity and offered spectacles difficult to duplicate on television. It was not, however, good cinema.[19]

The artistic deficiencies of big-screen filming were multiple. The switch from the standard screen which was nearly square to the rectangular wide screen brought peripheral vision into use. But it made close-ups difficult since they were either out of proportion or failed to fill the frame and hold audience interest. Commenting on this point, director George Stevens remarked, "CinemaScope is fine, if you want a system that shows a boa constrictor to better advantage than a man."[20] Effective wide-screen close-ups could, of course, still be made by an artful director. In Hitchcock's *To Catch a Thief* (1955), who could forget the vast Vista-Vision close-up of a woman's hand extinguishing a cigarette in the yolk of a giant fried egg? But the point is that the new process did not lend itself to subtle character development. Directors felt it necessary to stage their shots to make special use of the larger spatial areas. This meant that action—the chariot race or cavalry charge—became much more important than the nuances of plot or of character. Picturesque locations also assumed new significance, often to the point of dominating a picture. In general, CinemaScope directors had much less chance for variety, intimacy, or subtle emotions.

Reliance on big-screen blockbusters intensified the already conservative nature of Hollywood. Since the studios were cutting back sharply on the number of pictures produced each year, while spending much more per picture, each film became a major financial risk. A studio's fate often rested on the success or failure of a single film. Had *Ben-Hur* flopped, for example, MGM might well have gone bankrupt. The more expensive the picture, the bigger the audience it had to draw to make a profit. Consequently, producers and directors took as few risks as possible. The new, the daring, the controversial had no place in this scheme of things. Why risk a bundle on a contemporary social problem drama, when remaking a biblical epic or filming a smash Broadway musical seemed a sure thing?

Such tactics, together with the proliferation of drive-ins (a type of theater that did offer some competition to the comfortable TV living room),[21] helped Hollywood survive the dark days of the television boom. But survival came at a price. In the long run the film industry found it impossible to either ignore or to fight television. By the late fifties a symbiotic relationship had developed between the two competing media. A good example of this can be seen in the Academy Awards. The practice of granting annual prizes for the best film, actor, actress, director, and so on had been started by the American Academy of Motion Picture Arts and Sciences in 1927. But up until the early fifties, these awards, though prestigious, had not been basic to a film's financial success or failure. Television changed all this. The first televised Academy Oscarcast took place in 1952, and was watched by the largest single audience in television history to that date. With fewer people attending films regularly and fewer pictures being produced, movies recognized as Best Picture or gaining an acting award (or even a nomination) were assured big money. From 1952 on, Oscar winners consistently set box-office records. Five Best Pictures—*The Greatest Show on Earth* (1952), *From Here to Eternity* (1953), *Around the World in 80 Days* (1956), *The Bridge on the River Kwai* (1957), and *Ben-Hur*—each grossed well over $10 million. In this way television provided massive advertising for the movies while receiving in return a highly popular program.[22]

In other ways the film industry came to see the futility of fighting television. More money could be made through cooperation. As early as 1951, Columbia Pictures set up a subsidiary, Screen Gems, to make TV films. By mid-decade, Metro-Goldwyn-Mayer, owners of Hollywood's largest movie lot, was leasing space for filming TV productions and even commercials. RKO sold its lot outright to television comics Lucille Ball and Desi Arnaz who established Desilu Studios to produce both TV shows and movies. One of the most successful film-makers to utilize both media was Walt Disney. His "Disneyland" TV series, launched in 1954, served as a giant advertisement for Disney films and the new Disneyland amusement park at Anaheim. In the mid-fifties film companies sold or leased to television the broadcast rights to thousands of pre-1948 movies. And by the end of the decade movie studios were producing the majority of TV's prime-time action-adventure series. By then nearly three-fourths of the more than 40,000 persons employed in film-making in the Hollywood area worked for television. Film City had become, to a large extent, Television City.[23]

One potentially healthy change stimulated by the TV-movie competition was the breakdown of the film Production Code. Movie self-censorship went back to the twenties and had been formalized in 1930. Then, the Motion Picture Association of America, representing the major studios, had agreed to adhere to a Production Code—an extensive listing of all that should not be shown or even suggested on the screen. Designed "to recreate and rebuild human beings exhausted with the realities of living," the code created a mythic and naive world. Good had always to be rewarded and bad punished. Such sensitive subjects as miscegenation, suicide, drug addiction, rape, and incest were shunned. And even passionate kissing was limited to married couples (who always slept in separate beds). Walt Disney, on one occasion, was requested to remove the teats from a cartoon cow. As television began eroding movie audiences in the early fifties, Hollywood producers began bending and then breaking the code to lure back paying customers. One thing they well knew was that sex sold, and other forbidden topics might too.[24]

In 1953 Otto Preminger independently produced and directed an innocuous sex comedy, *The Moon Is Blue,* based on an already successful Broadway play. In retrospect, the film is mild. It jested about adultery and used such forbidden words as "seduction" and "virgin." Preminger, denied code approval, went ahead and distributed the film anyway. That was possible by 1953 since movie houses were no longer under studio control. The controversy surrounding *Moon* turned a minor comedy into a major money-maker. Preminger followed this with another prohibited subject, drug addiction, in the Frank Sinatra vehicle *The Man With the Golden Arm* (1955). The code was on its way out.

Television contributed to this change. By the mid-fifties TV programming was becoming less and less daring, more and more subservient to sponsors and pressure groups. In a sense the old code simply passed from one medium to the other. Television would restrict its subject matter, movies would become more permissive. This allowed film-makers greater freedom to treat new material and to use previously prohibited books and Broadway shows as the basis for scripts. Landmarks in the liberation of American cinema from code restrictions included *From Here to Eternity* (1953) with its famous beach necking scene; *Peyton Place* (1957) which though greatly watered down from the notorious best seller still came out as a small-town sex exposé; *Island in the Sun* (1957) which touched on miscegenation; *Compulsion* (1959) the first film to deal at all seriously with homosexuality; and *Blue Denim* (1959) the first film to treat abortion. Even in family-entertainment biblicals, revealing costumes and sensuous bathing scenes were becoming mandatory by mid-decade.

One of the chief promoters of the new sexual frankness on the screen was playwright Tennessee Williams. As early as 1951 the fine Elia Kazan direction of Williams' *A Streetcar Named Desire* had shocked audiences with its portrayal of the sexually frustrated older woman, Blanche DuBois (Vivian Leigh), and the young, animal-like Stanley Kowalski (Marlon Brando). Though in retrospect Williams' poetic portraits of neurotic people and frustrated sexual relations seem only escapist romanticism, such films as *The Rose Tattoo* (1955), *Cat on a Hot Tin Roof* (1958), *Suddenly Last Summer* (1959), and *The Fugitive Kind* (1959) were viewed as frank and sensational in the fifties. Williams' *Baby Doll* (1956), also directed by Kazan, caused the greatest furor. This story about the adulterous seduction of a child-wife (Carroll Baker) was the first film of a major Hollywood studio (Warner Brothers) to be condemned by the Legion of Decency. Despite this, or more likely be-

33. *Newsweek*, December 8, 1958, captioned this: "Smog-time in Los Angeles: For Want of Fresh air, hair turned green." By the late fifties, smog was a major threat in auto-infested Los Angeles.

34. Science-fiction films spoke to mass fears about radiation and red subversion. In this 1957 film, a bizarre atomic mist causes *The Incredible Shrinking Man* (Grant Williams) to dwindle away, landing him in all sorts of predicaments.

35. This "Classroom Scene, U.S.A.," part of *Life*'s post-Sputnik *Crisis in Education* series, stressed the apathy of American high school students.

36. Contrasting photo showed Soviet teens' academic rigor and eagerness.

37. This 1953 map demonstrates a magazine's conception of the radii of destruction resulting "If an H-bomb Hit Chicago."

38. Althea Gibson became the first black ever to play in the United States Lawn Tennis Championships. Here, she returns a shot in the 1956 French Championship, which she won.

39. Buying on credit became a staple of the fifties consumer economy. In 1955, Birmingham car dealer O. Z. Hall waves his arms over a sea of lures to credit buyers.

40. Giants star Willie Mays in 1954.

41. John Fitzgerald Kennedy campaigns in Elgin, Illinois, 1960.

cause of it, *Baby Doll* was a box-office hit and another force in loosening the restrictive code.[25]

A final factor undermining traditional Hollywood movie mores was the growing popularity of foreign films. Small art theaters showing the neorealistic French and Italian dramas or sophisticated English comedies grew in popularity during the fifties. People were attracted by the unsentimental realism and greater frankness of foreign offerings. In 1957 a French film, Roger Vadim's *And God Created Woman*, introduced Brigitte Bardot to art theater audiences. Her blatant sexuality combined with a childlike innocence thrilled and shocked U.S. viewers familiar with starlets more completely clothed. *Woman* grossed over $4 million in its initial American run. In retrospect one can see in the film an indication of the new Hollywood that would emerge in the sixties.[26]

Another French import, *The Lovers* (1959) played a similar role in breaking code and censorship barriers. Though not quite as popular as *Woman, The Lovers* gave American audiences the first nude love scenes shown in legitimate movie houses. Even more appalling to those offended by the nudity was the perceived immorality of the film. It tells the story of a wealthy woman (Jeanne Moreau) who with neither guilt nor anxiety abandons husband and child to go off with her lover of one night. When *The Lovers* played in Cleveland Heights, Ohio, the theater manager was prosecuted for obscenity. However, a precedent-setting U.S. Supreme Court decision ruled that the film did not come under the legal definition of obscenity.[27]

By the late fifties, then, Hollywood film-makers had greater freedoms than at any time since the early days of cinema. The code had virtually collapsed. The stranglehold of the major studios on production and distribution had been broken. Independent producers had become a major factor. New filming and projecting techniques were available.

How Hollywood used these new opportunities and techniques, however, is another matter. With few exceptions, fifties films, rather than leading cinematic art in exciting new directions, continued to crank out the same old kitsch—bigger and splashier than before, but seldom better. For every *Shane, African Queen*, or *North by Northwest*, Hollywood produced hundreds of *Lawless Streets, Muscle Beaches*, or *Hot Rod Girls*. While foreign directors were breaking new ground with such fifties films as *Rashomon* (Kurosawa,

1950), *Umberto D* (De Sica, 1952), *Pather Panchali* (Ray, 1954), *La Strada* (Fellini, 1954), *The Seventh Seal* (Bergman, 1956), *The 400 Blows* (Truffaut, 1958), Hollywood directors tended to rehash tired formulas. Even the so-called American movie breakthroughs, frequently applauded by cinema historians, seem rather trivial: the cowboy hero no longer enamored of killing (Gary Cooper in *High Noon,* Gregory Peck in *The Gun Fighter*), the love story about common city people (*Marty*), or the musical with a touch of ballet (*An American in Paris*). Although movies are a major source of popular culture, in the fifties, at least, Hollywood appears to have been largely a mirror of prevailing attitudes. The anticommunism, religiosity, and greater sexuality of films are examples of this. Such a trend can also be seen in examining film attitudes toward some of the topics already considered in this book such as women, minority groups, youth, and atomic power and science.

Independent women with dignity, wit, and style, though rare, had not been absent in thirties and forties films. Actresses such as Joan Crawford, Katharine Hepburn, Bette Davis, and Rosalind Russell frequently portrayed strong-willed, career-minded, autonomous heroines. Such female roles all but disappeared in the fifties. It is difficult to find a mid-century American film in which a female star dominated and carried a picture. In the few films where independent, unmarried women are portrayed—like Bette Davis in *All About Eve* (1950) or Gloria Swanson in *Sunset Boulevard*—they appear as neurotic, lonely persons whose lives lack real meaning. The ultimate 1950s characterizations of aging, lonely, slightly insane females are found in Tennessee Williams' films—Blanche in *Streetcar,* Anna Magnani's roles in *The Rose Tattoo* and *Fugitive Kind,* and Katharine Hepburn's portrayal of Mrs. Venable in *Suddenly Last Summer.* Williams' obsessed, romantic, self-destructive women offered meaty roles for actresses, but hardly served as useful models for encouraging female independence.[28]

A variant on the neurotic spinster theme was the unhappy middle-aged woman who finds redemption and fulfillment through a man. Hepburn starred in a number of such films—*The African Queen* (1951), *Summertime* (1955), *The Rainmaker* (1956). In *African Queen,* for instance, she played an inhibited British missionary's sister, a most formidable spinster, miraculously transformed into a beautiful responsive woman by the love of an unkempt riverboat captain (Humphrey Bogart). A related film subject was the tomboy made feminine (and so normal) through love. Two of the best examples of this pants-to-skirts transformation were the musicals *Annie Get Your Gun* (1950) with Betty Hutton as Annie Oakley and Doris Day's *Calamity Jane* (1953). Whether the transformation was of old maid or he-girl, the message was the same—a woman is only half a person until she has caught her man.

In Hollywood as in life, marriage-as-goal is what fifties womanhood was all about. Musicals and romantic comedies offered endless variations on the boy-meets-girl, love-marriage-happiness plot. In *Gigi*, the Academy Award winning 1958 musical, Leslie Caron plays an elfish French girl whose grandmother and great-aunt groom her to follow in the family tradition as an expensive mistress. Gigi, of course, rejects their training and ends up marrying Louis Jourdan. Even bad marriages were portrayed as worth saving. In George Cukor's *The Marrying Kind* (1951), for example, Judy Holliday and Aldo Ray tell a sympathetic judge what problems led them to divorce court after seven years of marriage and two children. In the end they are reconciled, even though their flashbacks and fantasies reveal the marriage to be rather tragic.[29] Most movie divorce in the fifties was depicted as the result of misunderstanding or comic quarrels. By the last reel, things were usually patched up and remarriage resulted.

Marty (1954), the greatly overpraised melodrama about a plain 34-year-old butcher (Ernest Borgnine) who courts an equally plain 29-year-old schoolteacher (Betsy Blair), conveyed the message that marriage was the only true source of happiness for men as well as women. With love and marriage, even the ugly, aging "little people" can be happy. As Marty tells his girl: "So you see, dogs like us, we ain't such dogs as we think we are."[30]

Doris Day and June Allyson frequently played the perfect fifties wife—a sacrificingly self-limited creature, totally dedicated to her man. Day's role in the musical biography of lyric writer Gus Kahn, *I'll See You in My Dreams* (1951), exemplifies the "good wife" ideal. Kahn (Danny Thomas), a poor boy who drives a wagon, is anxious to sell his lyrics. He meets Doris Day, who can write music. They team up and create a popular song. She then gives up her career so that Gus will be able to work with the very best songwriters. He is so impressed with her sacrifice that he marries her. From then on, Gus is a great success, with Doris drifting in and out of the plot only to have a baby or two. A dumb movie with a clear message for women: by giving up her career and helping her man, Doris got all a woman could want—marriage, children, and a successful husband.[31]

Even sex-goddess Marilyn Monroe almost invariably ended up married, about to be married, or unhappy because she was not married. In short, though there existed a range of female types in fifties films—frustrated career woman (the Joan Crawford type), virtuous fawnlike ingenue (Audrey Hepburn), perfect wife (Doris Day), blonde sex-bomb (Marilyn Monroe), teasing teen-age virgin (Sandra Dee)—women's interests invariably were depicted as centering on men, marriage, and family, or the resultant frustrations when these requirements for happiness were absent. In this respect, Hollywood both reflected and reinforced the dominant sexism of the age.

In the same way, Hollywood's treatment of minority groups mirrored mainstream American attitudes. Like the nation, moviemakers moved far from their earlier racial stereotypes while imagining they had moved much farther. In the early fifties blacks still occasionally could be seen playing maids or servants with grotesque comic accents and mannerisms. Blacks also still appeared as cowardly natives in African pictures. Films such as *King Solomon's Mines* (1950) or *Mogambo* (1953) employed blacks as foils for the heroics of the great white hunters. The first 3-D sensation, *Bwana Devil,* was filled with terrorized natives cringing before the vicious lions.

Yet the late forties and early fifties saw a conscious Hollywood effort to be liberal about race relations. Civil rights had become a major national issue; and, of course, Americans were aware that overt racism made for adverse cold war propaganda. Four controversial films of 1949–50 dealt specifically with racial prejudice. *Home of the Brave,* based on Arthur Laurent's play, treated a black soldier bullied and threatened by other members of his platoon until his heroism won him acceptance. Elia Kazan's *Pinky* dealt with a very light-skinned mulatto woman who, although passing for white as a nurse in the North, rejects her Yankee doctor suitor and returns South. She then inherits a large estate left her by a wealthy white woman (Ethel Barrymore). The film of William Faulkner's *Intruder in the Dust* included a lengthy, insightfully filmed section on the gathering of a white lynch mob. The black hero, unjustly jailed for murdering a white, is finally saved from the mob by good whites: a child, a lawyer, and an old lady who discover the real (white) killer.[32]

The last of these racially liberal films, Joseph Mankiewicz's *No Way Out*, was the most outspoken and prophetic. As a *Time* reviewer said: "The story comes directly to grips with racial prejudice in what is presumably an enlightened area of the U.S.: a big city north of the Mason-Dixon line." Sidney Poitier, in his first starring role, plays a prison-ward intern unable to save the life of a wounded white hold-up man. The patient's brother (Richard Widmark), described as a "thief and pathological Negro-hater," refuses to allow an autopsy that would clear Poitier of having caused the patient's death. Widmark proceeds to mercilessly bait the intern and later dupes the dead man's wife into inciting a race riot. Poitier has the unpleasant job of treating white riot victims who spit on him and call him "nigger." In the end, however, he is allowed to make the vindicating autopsy.[33]

None of these four films did very well financially, which may explain why no serious racial movies were attempted again until the late fifties. Instead, pictures such as *The Jackie Robinson Story* (1950) and *The Joe Louis Story* (1953) told Horatio Alger-type success stories with no hint of the real depth and nature of America's racial prejudice.

When serious black-white films were again produced, especially the Poitier and John Cassavetes *Edge of the City* (1957) and Poitier and Tony Curtis' *The Defiant Ones* (1958), the analyses of the causes of racism remained the same as in earlier efforts. The message was mainstream respectable liberalism: prejudice is bad, but it is an individual problem that education will solve. Like the Widmark character in *No Way Out*, racists were portrayed as blatantly sick, or they were misinformed and therefore easily corrected. In turn the blacks, who happen to be discriminated against, were shown as just like the middle-class boy (or girl) next door, only better. To get this message across, handsome Sidney Poitier and even handsomer Harry Belafonte were given most leads in fifties Negro-problem films. The part of the mulatto Pinky in the film of that title was played by the attractive white actress, Jeanne Crain. Poitier saw the type of role he played as "one-dimensional." White filmmakers, he said, put the Negro "on the screen in a saintly, unreal manner, because the Negro must represent a certain kind of character in order to help the white man absolve himself of certain guilt feelings and attitudes. . . . So they say, 'Well now, I'm going to make a wonderful humane statement with the presence of this Negro person who has lived under great handicaps and great denial all his life.' So they make a statement. And the statement finally is, 'You should be nice to your coloured friends. They too are human beings.' Well, this is messy, you know. That's why the black characters usually come out on the screen as saints, as the other-cheek-turners, as people who are not really people: who are so nice and good. It's messy. As a matter of fact, I'm just dying to play villains."[34] The kind of liberal wishful thinking Poitier described was perhaps a necessary step in helping white America toward less racist attitudes. But it can hardly be said that Hollywood took a leading role in the mounting struggle for equality and civil rights. Reality in such films was distorted with well-meaning smiles and lies.

Indians, too, fared slightly better in the minority-conscious Hollywood of the fifties. Twentieth Century-Fox was considered very advanced in 1950 in reversing the Indian-as-villain theme with (white) Jeff Chandler's sympathetic portrayal of the Apache leader, Cochise, in *Broken Arrow*. In this film the frontiersman hero (James Stewart) meets the Apaches soon after coming upon the mutilated bodies of two whites tortured by brutal savages. But this opening cliché is then dropped. The hero befriends good Cochise and comes to respect Indian ways, which is not surprising since the movie makes Indian civilization remarkably like that of whites. The opening tortures are never explained. Writer-director Delmer Daves became even less courageous in handling *Broken Arrow*'s love scene between Stewart and the beautiful Indian princess (played by white Debra Paget). Their idyllic marriage was not allowed to flourish. Paget is conveniently killed off in a skirmish, justified by a weak dialogue suggesting somehow that her death was not in vain because it brought Indians and whites closer together. Just how this was accomplished is never explained. But through the rest of the decade, Indian brides of white men always seemed to die off before the final reel, one more variant of "the only good Indian is a dead Indian."[35]

Broken Arrow set the pattern followed throughout the fifties. Indians became innocent victims, not savage aggressors. In *Sitting Bull* (1954), for instance, General Custer (Douglas Kennedy) was played as a bullheaded, stupid, double-dealing martinet. The Indians were blameless for his death. But, though they were more human than in previous film representations, the cinematic Indians of the fifties failed to achieve historic or anthropologic reality. They were still caricatures. More importantly, the problems confronting Indians were never presented as part of the whole system of white imperialism; as with blacks, Indians suffered at the hands of specific, atypical, usually neurotic, bad whites—the greedy trader, the vainglorious cavalry officer and so on. John Ford's *Rio Grande* (1950) is a good example. The villainous trader (Grant Withers), knowing that peace with the Indians will end his illicit gun and rum sales, deliberately causes white-Indian hostilities. Films such as *Two Flags West, Tomahawk,* and *The Last Frontier* are crowded with cheating traders and psychotic Indian-hating soldiers.[36] People could view such offerings, feel sympathy for the Indians, yet not become concerned about the very real exploitation of native Americans that was accelerating throughout the 1950s. The final irony is that just as Hollywood was revising its racial stereotypes to fit new liberal images, the release of many pre-1948 films to television brought all those bloody savages, cowering Africans, and clowning Rochesters right into America's comfortable living rooms.

Fifties society, alarmed by juvenile delinquency and the Beat phenomenon, made various attempts to find out what was going wrong with its young people. This issue increasingly made its way onto the screen as Hollywood began to find profit in such productions. The teen film emerged as a separate genre. Early examples of youth movies—*Hot Rod* (1950) and *Disc Jockey* (1951)—were shallow films that relied on sensationalism. The three classic youth-problem films of the fifties were released in 1954–55: *The Wild One* with Brando's moving portrayal of the tough but sensitive motorcycle gang leader; *Rebel Without a Cause,* the James Dean vehicle that took delinquency films out of the slums and into the suburbs, and *Blackboard Jungle,* which unequivocally associated delinquency with rock music. Although these films vaguely hint at larger social ills, they fail to explore them, and imply (as the title *Rebel Without a Cause* states) that serious rebelliousness has no real cause but can be attributed to individuals. Kids really want to do what's right, Hollywood seemed to say, if only parents and other authorities would provide proper guidance.[37]

Unfortunately even the superficial efforts at probing delinquency were dropped after the mid-fifties. Hollywood followed the box-office success of *Wild One, Rebel,* and *Blackboard* with literally hundreds of shoddy, sensational youth films. A few late fifties titles indicate the trend: *Crime in the Streets, Girls in Prison, The Flaming Teen Age, Rumble on the Docks, The Delinquents, Dragstrip Girl, Hot Rod Rumble, Reform School Girl, Eighteen and Anxious, High School Confidential,* and *Juvenile Jungle.* During these same years the teen-violence fad was joined by a monster fad in such forgettable films as *I Was a Teen-Age Werewolf, I Was a Teenage Frankenstein, Teen-Age Monster, Teen-age Cave Man, Monster on the Campus.*

Even though such films were made with an eye for the quick buck, and though they seldom went deeper into juvenile problems than common clichés, these youth films played an important causal role, and one that Hollywood never intended. For thousands of adolescent Americans, the film rebels (particularly Brando and Dean) personified their own feelings of alienation. They were seen as figures of moral purity rebelling against an inhuman environment, as individuals incapable of conforming in a society dominated by conformity and moral compromise. As such, these films and especially Brando and Dean were powerful forces shaping a separate culture of youth. *Wild One* and *Rebel,* like rock and the Beats, became integral parts of the late fifties and sixties emergence of the counterculture.[38] Even the teen monster films indicated a changing attitude. Instead of seeing themselves as the outwardly bad, secretly good Wild One, kids could fantasize along with the seemingly gentle, secretly threatening teen-age werewolf: I may look like a good clean kid, but I really am a weird, dangerous freak. This represented a major turnabout in self-image.

The cinematic treatment of atomic power and science largely reflected the popular mentality. Americans were ambivalent about the bomb and the science that created it. Hollywood was too. At the most inane and optimistic level were films such as the Dean Martin-Jerry Lewis comedy *Living It Up* (1954). The story concerns a gas-station attendant (Lewis) stranded in Desert Hole, New Mexico. From a local dump he procures a car that has been used at Los Alamos to test the effects of radiation. Although the car is no longer contaminated, Lewis spots a "Radioactive" label and collapses. Along comes Dr. Dean Martin who mistakenly diagnoses radiation poisoning. Before the doctor realizes his error, a news-hungry New York reporter (Janet Leigh) arranges for her paper to grant Jerry's last wish, to see New York City before he dies. The city and its mayor throw a big welcome. Lewis, as the title suggests, lives it up. But everyone becomes impatient when he does not die. Finally he submits to a staged state funeral in exchange for a street-cleaning job.[39] A superficial film like this corresponded with a good deal of official propaganda about the bomb and radiation, making both appear fairly safe and harmless.

More typical of Hollywood's treatment of atomic power was the proliferation of science-fiction films. Such movies had been made before the fifties, but they were isolated and did not represent a continuing trend. However, beginning in 1950, with *Destination Moon,* a pseudodocumentary about a trip to the moon, science fiction became a standard Hollywood genre. Many such films reflected varying degrees of anxiety about the future of atomic energy. An early example was *Rocketship X-M,* released in 1950 to compete with *Destination Moon.* An expedition sets out to the moon but is thrown off course and lands on Mars. There it is learned that atomic warfare has destroyed Martian civilization. The surviving Martians look fine (some of the women in fact are quite beautiful), but radiation has bestialized them. The American hero and heroine escape the contaminated planet. They lack fuel to return to earth, however, and are finally stranded, martyrs in space. A few films dealt directly with the specific dangers of atomic war. *On the Beach* (1959), a nuclear doomsday movie, is the best known of these. An earlier example, *Five* (1951), treated the earth's last survivors who, interestingly, were more concerned with the fact that one of their number was black than with the atomic holocaust.[40]

Most of the science-fiction disaster films, however, dealt with alien monsters who threatened American civilization. Many such monsters were brought forth by atomic explosions: either mutants created by radiation, or prehistoric brutes resuscitated by nuclear blasts. *The Beast, The Blob, The Creature from the Black Lagoon,* the giant ants that emerge from the Los Angeles sewers in *Them, Godzilla* (a Japanese atomic mutant popular in America), *The Deadly Mantis, The Spider, The Crab Monsters* were just a few of the deadly atomic offspring stalking or slithering through post-Hiroshiman cinema.

Other films dealt with menacing monsters of extraterrestrial origin. A 1951 film of this sort, *The Thing from Another World,* combined nearly all major American paranoias. Fear of an alien force, flying saucers, world destruction, extraterrestrial invasion, and atomic radiation are all exploited. The Thing crashes in a flying saucer and is quick-frozen into arctic ice. The creature is discovered by an American military expedition which includes several scientists and a reporter. When the Thing thaws it proves to be alive and dangerous. Though having the shape of a large human (James Arness played the part), this Thing turns out to be a radioactive vegetable that feeds on blood. After several disasters the military succeeds in destroying the monster. Yet the film ends with a direct exploitation of national anxieties: The reporter, Scotty (Douglas Spencer), faces the audience and warns: "watch the skies . . . watch everywhere . . . keep looking . . . *watch the skies!*"[41]

The Thing was a bad movie and gave rise to a host of even worse ones. But several of its themes were central to science-fiction films of the fifties, and to national anxieties. First, the threat to America is, like the communist fantasy, an insidious, alien Thing, different from us and very sinister. Second, it is the U.S. military that saves the day, through the use of force. In the case of the Thing they manage to electrocute it; in later sci-fi monster films atomic weapons often were used. Third, the film is anti-intellectual and particularly anti-science. Throughout the movie scientists are portrayed as deluded idealists, ineffectual men of mere ideas. This is presented in sharp contrast to the heroic men of action, the soldiers. The main scientist, Dr. Carrington (Robert Cornthwaite), a bearded, turtleneck-sweatered intellectual, wishes to communicate with and understand the alien. The film ridicules this notion—only destructive force can deal with the Thing. Fourth, atomic power is dangerous. This is symbolized in *The Thing* with the loud ticking of the Geiger counter reacting to the presence of the flying saucer and its occupant. Finally, while the military is able to annihilate this Thing, the danger remains. The subversive invader may try again, at any moment: "Watch the skies!" *The Thing* and its innumerable successors exploited popular neuroses while doing little to relieve or transform them.

Most fifties science-fiction films after *The Thing* contained similar themes. There were, however, a few exceptions. Another 1951 film, *The Day the Earth Stood Still,* is the outstanding example. Like *The Thing,* it deals with an alien being brought to earth by a flying saucer; there the comparison ends. The stranger, Klaatu (Michael Rennie), is a friendly alien, a representative of advanced civilizations come to bring to the destructive people of earth a solemn warning: "Don't play with the atomic bomb. You are irresponsible children whose powers exceed your wisdom. Grow up and stop playing with fire." When the President's secretary tells the alien, "You know there are on earth the forces of good and the forces of evil. We are the forces of good," Klaatu replies: "I'm not interested in such foolishness." To draw attention to his message, the stranger neutralized the earth's electrical and mechanical power for half an hour. The attempt is unavailing. Americans panic and the army is sent to destroy Klaatu. He is killed but revived by his robot, Gort, and together they leave earth.[42]

Unlike *The Thing, The Day the Earth Stood Still* offered no simple triumph of good over evil. Director Robert Wise did with this film what the best science fiction (indeed all great art) has always done—he forced people to question some of their most fundamental assumptions. It is an excellent picture and still worth seeing. That it was made in 1951 is remarkable. If it, rather than *The Thing,* had become the model for future science-fiction films, Hollywood might have played a valuable role in reshaping simplistic cold war attitudes. This was not the case.

In general, then, fifties films reflected majority attitudes. Movies were shaped by the dictates of commerce, fashion, and cold war politics. The overall images projected corresponded with official, established versions of reality: America was a comfortable, conservative, prosperous, classless, consensual paradise. The most vital issues were either not dealt with or were treated superficially. Even naming a problem, like drug addiction in *The Man with the Golden Arm,* was considered controversial. Seldom did movies intelligently probe beyond the surface of basic issues. Serious, intentional cinematic efforts to do so were invariably compromised by the industry's fear of hostile public reaction, low box-office returns, governmental interference, or censure.[43]

Despite this pandering to popular tastes, the movie industry continued to decline in public favor. In 1958, David Selznick sadly remarked: "People who say the movies are going to come back to the position they had ten years ago are just ostriches. Television has killed the habit of motion picture attendance." A year later another producer, Samuel Goldwyn, stated bluntly: "Conditions in the industry today are worse than I have ever known them in the 47 years I have been connected with pictures."[44] Hollywood panicked, stumbled, and groped its way through the fifties. In 1959 an unprecedented 11 Academy Awards went to *Ben-Hur,* the decade's costliest costume extravaganza—the epic that should have ended all epics. Old Hollywood was having a last fling in its quest for the elusive cinematic gold mine.

Yet there were some bright spots, and, of course, those who annually pronounced the industry on its deathbed were premature. For all the confusion, all the gloom and prophecies of doom, all the big-screen, lowbrow bonanzas, all the banal Abbott and Costellos and Francis the talking mules, American film-makers still managed to produce some good movies. There was Kazan's *On the Waterfront,* the taut, dramatic story of Terry Malloy's transformation from punk ex-boxer to singlehanded fighter against the gangsters dominating the longshoremen's union. Filmed in black and white on location along the grim streets and docks of Hoboken, the realistic acting of Brando, Eva Marie Saint, Karl Malden, Rod Steiger, and Lee J. Cobb helped create one of the century's great movies. The success of this film at the box office and the Academy Awards (Best Picture, Brando for Best Actor, Saint for Best Actress) also elevated realistic acting as taught at the Actors' Studio in New York to a place of importance in Hollywood. In addition to all the principals in *Waterfront,* other Actors' Studio alumni prominent in fifties films included Paul Newman, Ben Gazzara, Carroll Baker, Anthony Franciosa, Eli Wallach, Kim Stanley, Arthur Kennedy, Julie Harris, Pat Hingle, and James Dean. This was a bracing influence on an industry where a pretty face traditionally was more important than talent.

There were other memorable films too. One is Hitchcock's superb, irreverent, perverse comedy *The Trouble With Harry* (1956) —the story of an inconvenient body (Harry) with Shirley MacLaine in her debut role, and all filmed in the splendid colors of Vermont fall. Another outstanding fifties comedy is Billy Wilder's *Some Like It Hot* (1959). This Marilyn Monroe movie with Tony Curtis and Jack Lemmon doing female impersonations is exceptionally funny and anticipates comic trends of the sixties and seventies. Orson Welles' major fifties contribution, *Touch of Evil* (1958), was his best movie since *Citizen Kane* (1941). It is a complex thriller showing great diversity of character. Welles himself dominates the screen as the gross, corrupt detective. Though somewhat uneven, *Evil* is a powerful moral drama that explores a world of fear and violence.

There were a few good social-problem films of which Rod Serling's portrayal of primitive business ethics, *Patterns* (1956), and Sidney Lumet's exploration of prejudice and the jury system, *Twelve Angry Men* (1957), are outstanding. Both Serling and Lumet came to films from television, bringing new ideas to an industry dominated by directors and producers active since the thirties. Stanley Kubrick and Arthur Penn also made auspicious debuts as film directors in the fifties. Kubrick's *Paths of Glory* (1957) was undoubtedly the best antiwar film made until surpassed in 1964 by his *Dr. Strangelove*. Penn's first feature film, *The Left Handed Gun* (1958) is a Billy the Kid Western with psychological depth.

In these and a few other films, movie-makers went beyond the stereotyped recipes of traditional Hollywood. Professor of film Richard Dyer MacCann asked in 1962, "whether the 1950s will be remembered as the decade of strong new freedoms or simply as the decade of Hollywood's gradual, uncontrollable disintegration?"[45] It would not be too far wrong to answer both.

NOTES

1. Selznick is quoted in Ben Hecht, "Enter, the Movies," in David Talbot, ed., *Film* (New York, 1959), p. 583; Russel B. Nye, *The Unembarrassed Muse* (New York, 1970), p. 385; John Brooks, *The Great Leap* (New York, 1966), p. 168; Richard Schickel, *Movies* (New York, 1964), p. 164; John Cogley, *Report on Blacklisting*, vol. 1: *Movies* (n.p., 1956), 92.

2. Gordon Gow, *Hollywood in the Fifties* (New York, 1971), pp. 88, 147–48; Charles Higham, *The Art of the American Film* (Garden City, 1973), pp. 240–42, 250–52; Laurence Kardish, *Reel Plastic Magic* (Boston, 1972), pp. 210–11; Martin Quigley, Jr., and Richard Gertner, *Films in America* (New York, 1970), p. 193; Leslie Halliwell, *The Filmgoer's Companion* (London, 1965), p. 410.

3. Pauline Kael, "Movies the Desperate Art," in Talbot, ed., *Film*, p. 203; Arthur Link, *American Epoch* (New York, 1963), pp. 647–48.

4. Cogley, *Report*, 1:92.

5. Too frequently film historians attribute the anticommunist investigations of Hollywood to Senator Joseph McCarthy. For instance Leslie Halliwell, in the respected reference book *The Filmgoer's Companion*, lists Dalton Trumbo as "one of the 'Hollywood Ten' who were blacklisted by McCarthy" (p. 429). This is erroneous. As in the nation generally, the anticommunist mania hit Hollywood before McCarthy became the most noted witch hunter and continued after his 1954 censure. To view Hollywood's anticommunist troubles as caused by McCarthy is in fact doubly misleading. First, McCarthy took no

direct role in investigating show business. Second, and more important, to write about these events in terms of McCarthy is to see them as an aberration, something to be blamed on a single fanatic.

6. This sad episode of Hollywood history, though seldom mentioned in movie circles or in general film histories, has been the subject of several studies. One of the first and still an excellent one, Cogley, *Report on Blacklisting*, vol. 1: *Movies*, was itself the subject of an HUAC investigation. Other useful accounts include Stefan Kanfer, *A Journal of the Plague Years* (New York, 1973); Robert Vaughn, *Only Victims* (New York, 1972); Howard Suber, "The Anti-Communist Blacklist in the Hollywood Motion Picture Industry" (unpublished Ph.D. dissertation, University of California at Los Angeles, 1968); Alvah Bessie, *Inquisition in Eden* (New York, 1965); Murray Schumach, *The Face on the Cutting Room Floor* (New York, 1964), pp. 117–40; Les K. Adler, "The Politics of Culture: Hollywood and the Cold War," in Robert Griffith and Athan Theoharis, eds., *The Specter* (New York, 1974), pp. 240–60. The Sloane, Pollock, and Geer cases are treated in Kanfer, *Journal*, pp. 137, 214, 236–37, 286.

7. *Red Channels* (New York, 1950), the quote is from p. 9. See also Kanfer, *Journal*, pp. 98–122; John Howard Lawson, *Film* (New York, 1964), pp. 154–64.

8. While seeing this film is sufficient, a good discussion of it appears in Adler, "Politics of Culture," pp. 255–59. Contemporary reviews were critical of the film's script, not its message. See, for example, "Movies," *Newsweek*, April 14, 1952, p. 96.

9. For a discussion of the impact of anticommunism on film content see Dorothy B. Jones, "Communism and the Movies," in Cogley, *Report*, 1:196–233; Adler, "Politics of Culture," pp. 240–60.

10. Kanfer, *Journal*, pp. 81–97.

11. Cogley, *Report*, 1: 282, 219–20.

12. For a contemporary analysis of *Storm Center*, which starred Bette Davis as a small-town librarian defending the right for her library to possess (though not loan out) a book on communism, see Robert Hatch, "Films," *Nation*, October 27, 1956, p. 354.

13. These major fifties changes are discussed in Richard Dyer MacCann, *Hollywood in Transition* (Boston, 1962). See also Roger Manvell et al, *The International Encyclopedia of Film* (New York, 1972), pp. 484–85.

14. Quoted in MacCann, *Hollywood*, pp. x, 10; Kardish, *Reel Plastic*, p. 182.

15. Halliwell, *Filmgoer's*, p. 86; MacCann, *Hollywood*, pp. 20–21; Gow, *Hollywood*, pp. 12–14.

16. "A lion in your lap," claimed ads for *Bwana Devil*. Gow, *Hollywood*, pp. 14–15; MacCann, *Hollywood*, pp. 21–23; Quigley and Gertner, *Films*, p. 218; Philip Hartung, "The Screen," *Commonweal*, March 13, 1953, p. 575.

17. "A nine-day wonder," said Hitchcock of 3-D, "and I came in on the ninth day." Gow, *Hollywood*, pp. 15–17; Halliwell, *Filmgoer's*, p. 420; Kardish, *Reel Plastic*, pp. 186–87.

18. Quigley and Gertner, *Films*, p. 218; MacCann, *Hollywood*, pp. 23–26;

Gow, *Hollywood*, pp. 17–37; Schickel, *Movies*, pp. 166–68; Kardish, *Reel Plastic*, pp. 187–89; Nye, *Muse*, p. 385; Higham, *The Art of American Film*, p. 288.

19. The *Quo Vadis* statistics are cited in John McCarten, "The Current Cinema," *The New Yorker*, November 17, 1951, p. 119; the "second childhood" quote is from Kael, "Movies," pp. 190–94; Robert Hatch, "Theatre and Films," *Nation*, December 8, 1956, pp. 506–7; Tom F. Driver, "Hollywood in the Wilderness," *Christian Century*, LXXII (November 28, 1956), 1390–91; Moira Walsh, "Films," *America*, December 11, 1959, pp. 333–34.

20. Stevens is quoted in MacCann, *Hollywood*, pp. 25–26. An irritated reviewer of the big-screen Todd-AO *Oklahoma* (1955) described a "colossal close-up in which the heroine's left nostril alone is large enough to park a jeep in." "Cinema," *Time*, October 24, 1955, p. 106.

21. Drive-ins multiplied very rapidly in the late forties and early fifties. In 1948, there were 820 active drive-ins; by 1952 there were over 3,000. Drive-ins attempted to attract families with such features as playgrounds and laundromats. One even advertised a trout pond where you could fish. But, as might be expected, drive-ins' main appeal was to dating teen-agers and young adults. Al Hind, "The Drive-Ins," *Holiday*, July 1952, pp. 6–9; *Time*, September 18, 1950, p. 124.

22. George C. Likeness, *The Oscar People* (Mendota, Ill., 1965), pp. 59–61.

23. MacCann, *Hollywood*, pp. 12–19; William Kuhns, *Movies in America* (Dayton, 1972), pp. 189–90; Kardish, *Reel Plastic*, pp. 189–91.

24. Kardish, *Reel Plastic*, pp. 96–101.

25. Public reaction to *Baby Doll* is treated in *Time*, January 14, 1957, p. 100. See also MacCann, *Hollywood*, pp. 27–49; Gow, *Hollywood*, pp. 50–56; Quigley and Gertner, *Films*, p. 243.

26. Marjorie Rosen, *Popcorn Venus* (New York, 1973), pp. 280–81; Quigley and Gertner, *Films*, pp. 249–50.

27. Quigley and Gertner, *Films*, p. 262; Stanley Kauffmann, *A World on Film* (New York, 1967), pp. 222–23; John McCarten, "Love at a Glance," *The New Yorker*, November 7, 1959, p. 204; Robert Hatch, "Films," *Nation*, November 28, 1959, p. 407. Hatch's reaction to *The Lovers* was fairly typical. He condemned the film for not portraying guilt on the part of the woman: "When a woman walks out on a husband and child because a new acquaintance has roused and sated her, she pays some price for the change of alliance. If she pays no price, she is a moral idiot and unrewarding as a character of fiction."

28. Rosen, *Popcorn*, pp. 251–58.

29. "Cinema," *Time*, May 19, 1958, pp. 98–101; "Cinema," *Time*, March 17, 1952, p. 102; Wallace Markfield, "Sunnyside Down," *American Mercury*, August 1952, pp. 95–96; Gow, *Hollywood*, pp. 173–75.

30. Jerry Talmer, "Marty," in Daniel Wolf and Edwin Fancher, eds., *The Village Voice Reader* (Garden City, 1962), pp. 107–8; Robert Bingham, "Passion in the Bronx," *Reporter*, May 5, 1955, p. 36.

31. John McCarten, "The Current Cinema," *The New Yorker*, December 8, 1951, pp. 69–70; Rosen, *Popcorn*, p. 250; Bob Newhart, "June Allyson Never

Kicked Anybody in the Shins," in Arthur F. McClure, ed., *The Movies* (Rutherford, N.J., 1971), pp. 422–24.

32. V. J. Jerome, *The Negro in Hollywood Films* (New York, 1950); Kardish, *Reel Plastic*, pp. 174–75; Quigley and Gertner, *Films*, pp. 178–79, 182–83.

33. "Cinema," *Time*, April 21, 1950, p. 82; Andrew Dowdy, *Movies Are Better Than Ever* (New York, 1973), p. 69.

34. Poitier is quoted at length in Gow, *Hollywood*, pp. 97–98. A similar type of super-white, super-middle-class character also was used in portraying Jewish victims of discrimination in fifties films. In *It's a Big Country*, for instance, the Jewish soldier was the usual Jack Armstrong type; the woman's prejudice toward him was the product of sheer ignorance. See also Thomas R. Cripps, "The Death of Rastus: Negroes in American Films Since 1945," in McClure, *Movies*, pp. 266–75; Henry Popkin, "Hollywood Tackles the Race Issue," *Commentary*, October 1957, pp. 354–57.

35. George N. Fenin and William K. Everson, *The Western* (New York, 1973), pp. 17–19, 281. While white men had Indian film wives, they almost never had black wives.

36. Ibid., pp. 38–39, 282.

37. These seminal films are also discussed in chapter 11, pp. 299–300.

38. The auto death of Dean at age 24 in 1955 elevated the star into a permanent symbol of the moral outsider too sensitive to survive bureaucratized adult society. Two recent Dean biographies explore this phenomenon: David Dalton, *James Dean* (San Francisco, 1974) and Venable Herdon, *James Dean* (New York, 1974). See also Hollis Alpert, "It's Dean, Dean, Dean," *Saturday Review*, October 13, 1956, pp. 28–29; Ezra Goodman, "Delirium Over Dead Star," *Life*, September 24, 1956, pp. 75–88; Herbert Mitgang, "The Strange James Dean Death Cult," *Coronet*, November 1956, pp. 110–15.

39. "Cinema," *Time*, July 19, 1954, p. 76.

40. Richard Hodgens, "A Brief, Tragical History of the Science Fiction Film," *Film Quarterly*, 13 (Winter 1959), 30–39; Brian Murphy, "They Came from Beneath the Fifties," *Journal of Popular Film*, I (Winter 1972), 31–38; Kardish, *Reel Plastic*, p. 206.

41. Chris Steinbrunner and Burt Goldblatt, *Cinema of the Fantastic* (New York, 1972), pp. 221–34.

42. Pierre Kast, "Don't Play with Fire," in William Johnson, ed., *Focus on The Science Fiction Film* (Englewood Cliffs, 1972), pp. 68–70; "Movies," *Newsweek*, October 1, 1951, p. 90.

43. Government censorship took several forms. In addition to the pressure of official anticommunist hearings, the government encouraged films placing the United States and especially the military in a good light. Pentagon cooperation on a war film, according to Dore Schary of MGM, was worth between $1 and $2 million. Another government censorship tactic was for the U. S. Information Agency essentially to subsidize the distribution of certain American films in countries such as Turkey, Yugoslavia, Poland, and Viet Nam. The USIA had an approved list of titles that only included those films deemed to show the United States favorably. While this meant the exclusion of such bad films as *The*

Fly, or Elvis Presley's *Love Me Tender*, it also excluded such significant problem films as *Paths of Glory* and *The Defiant Ones*. Schary is quoted in Lawson, *Film*, pp. 158–61; USIA censorship is treated in MacCann, *Hollywood*, pp. 94–95.

44. Selznick and Goldwyn are quoted in MacCann, *Hollywood*, pp. 151, 159. The sense that Hollywood was in decline was pervasive at decade's end. See Hollis Alpert, "Are Foreign Films Better?" in McClure, ed., *The Movies*, pp. 249–54; Ezra Goodman, *The Fifty Year Decline and Fall of Hollywood* (New York, 1961).

45. MacCann, *Hollywood*, p. 118.

13

TV's the Thing

"One nice thing about television," a lady remarked to her husband as they sat before their set, "you don't have to pick out where to look."

This conversation took place in a 1951 Gardner Rea cartoon in *The New Yorker*. But it might as well have occurred in any of thousands of American living rooms that year. Before 1945, TV simply did not exist as a national phenomenon. It was a clumsy and expensive toy. The wartime invention of the Image Orthicon tube, however, made inexpensive good-quality television sets a reality. In 1946, 7,000 sets existed in the United States. In 1948, there were 148,000. By 1950, 4.4 million families had a TV, and people bought them at an acceleratingly feverish rate—20,000 *a day* by 1956. By 1960, 50 million televisions were owned in this country alone. In the short space of 15 years, watching TV had gone from freakish oddity to the perfectly usual.[1]

Americans found this sudden change only mildly surprising. TV, after all, answered the almost desperate need of the fearful early fifties for a simple mass diversion. Too, it seemed one more sign of the new American affluence. In those years, owning a television meant both status and entertainment. These apparently innocuous factors disguised the astounding changes TV introduced. Any successful invention, however small, induces change in its world. The economic pattern, the social system, the ways people look, act, and think are all affected. Consider, then, television, which in any analysis provided the most sudden and huge communication change in history.

In the late fifties and early sixties, many critics regarded TV as a "vast wasteland," an "idiot box," the empty brainless desert dotted by occasional intellectual oases. That, though, was a misleading attitude. To so completely reject TV was to avoid the medium's real force. For television was not (and is not) a wasteland. It was a lush jungle of messages, lessons, cues, and instructions on living in the material world. To an extent, TV mirrored American attitudes. But even more, it deepened and exaggerated certain outlooks and created new ones. Television has come to transform the cultural mind in many ways. What TV said, what it avoided saying, what good and what harm it did were all facets of that now permanent metamorphosis.

The young days of television as a mass medium, going into the early fifties, have since been called the "Golden Age of TV." That assessment, even allowing for the rosy hindsight of nostalgia, is moderately true. Those first years were fairly unique. This was primarily because TV had a semblance of balance in programming. The medium broadcast shows for widely disparate tastes, and this wide spectrum of shows appeared during prime time. One could choose opera (like the made-for-TV "Amahl and the Night Visitors"), the fights, live original dramas, quality documentaries like the "See It Now" series, Sid Caesar's satire or Milton Berle's hamming, in addition to situation comedies, musical variety shows, news, and adventure shows.

Added to this broad programming approach was the fact that much of TV in those years was broadcast live. Sometimes this made the medium seem clumsy. So many live shows have their tales of dangling microphones or intruding stagehands. But those little accidents only added to the excitement of TV. These stressed part of the medium's unique aesthetic: its immediacy. One could witness actual events unfolding in one's home. Nowhere was this more stressed than in two televised congressional hearings early in the decade—the 1950 Kefauver hearings on organized crime, and the 1954 proceedings in the Army–McCarthy case. Both events became surprise thrillers, complete with the unmasking of real-life bullies right in the nation's living rooms.

Television was a domestic presence far more intrusive than radio ever had been. It presented both sight and sound right in one's home. Moreover, after the initial set payments, TV was virtually free. Many changes in American entertainment patterns became almost immediately evident. People went out less and less in the evening. They devoted their spare time to the tube. This most drastically affected the movie and other entertainment industries. Watching TV was cheaper than going out, and involved less effort. No longer did one need literacy, great conversational wit, sporting talent, or even cash. Nor did one have to "pick out where to look." TV was easy to watch, easy to understand.

And this uncovered another aspect of the medium's aesthetic: TV functioned best when presenting simple messages in neat units, quickly replaced by more simple units. (That's why the essential TV program is the 30-second commercial.) This simplicity, of course, tended to contradict the complexity of real life. It favored instead a series of fast-moving images that produced an almost fictional version of reality. Television always tried to reduce life to the easy-to-understand. Thus it became a most seductive medium. The whole family could be entertained by this casual commodity, with only the minor exertion of turning on the set.

This intimate invasion seemed to imply that TV was that most egalitarian of media, the true universal communicator. Early in the fifties many commentators praised television for providing a broader vision of the world, and doing so in such a democratic manner. It was not just that TV was so accessible to the masses, but that it could potentially focus on anything, anywhere. Edward R. Murrow and Fred W. Friendly emphasized this in their series "See It Now," which always opened with two simultaneous shots: the Statue of Liberty and the Golden Gate Bridge, symbols of two ocean boundaries and so of the continent instantly spanned.

Similarly, the increasing ownership and viewing of TV sets appeared proof that America had truly become a middle-class yet classless and consensual society. TV was perceived as one of the solvents melting away the differences between Americans. It rendered them into one universal pool. It assured them that the American self-image of a nation of wholesome middle-class consumers was a positive fact of life. It promised to pass information between the millions of every-men and -women at a swift, effective pace.

But to regard TV as a democratic or even universal communicator was to forget certain things. For TV's was a flawed universality. It only functioned one way. TV could give incredible amounts of simple information to awesome numbers of people. But there was scarcely a return process. TV could influence the masses but the masses had little to do with influencing TV. The shape TV assumed in the fifties was authoritarian, commercial, and monolithic. It finally furthered the abdication of personal power that was already a fifties trend. Those who controlled the medium's messages gained unprecedented power. Many observers, most recently David Halberstam, have noted the way the public airwaves became dominated by private firms and individuals. These changes in the private sector naturally transformed the visible aspect of TV. By mid-decade, the wide-spectrum approach to programming was disappearing, as did any televised eccentricities of style or personality. These were replaced by a bland, non-live, fairly homogenized product.

The Red scares of the early fifties were among the things that encouraged this process. In 1950, three ex-FBI agents published a book called *Red Channels.* This book, and others like it, affected the young TV industry as it did radio, theater, and the movies. It provided both the justification and structure for systematic blacklisting. The logic supporting the lists was one of censorship. Certain people's mere presence was assumed to corrupt the audience.[2] That idea, resounding as it did of authoritarianism, of privileged information, of scorn for the public intellect, and of devious control of lives, was typical of early fifties culture. Countless actors, writers, directors, and others lost their livelihood to the blacklists. The censorship and purges became regular practice within the TV industry.

Another, more publicly obvious happening also contributed to the reshaping of TV. In a way, the "Hopalong Cassidy" series provided the major impetus. Hoppy, considered a movie has-been, got a cowboy series and became a children's idol. Department stores found the toys marketed to coincide with the Hoppy show so popular they could not be kept in stock. The fad grossed $100 million in business in 1950 before petering out.[3] But it left behind a firm lesson: TV reached into so many homes that it provided unprecedented advertising capacity.

Thanks in part to the junior cowboy fad, advertisers realized they must appeal to the greatest numbers of people. Thanks to the anticommunist purges, they learned oversensitive and simplistic notions of an audience's corruptibility or delicacy. Add to this the ad agencies' realization that sponsors' money paid for TV. Combined, these factors had an unpleasant result. TV became regarded as no more than a commercial medium. The public came to be seen as a childlike herd, easily swayed or spooked, capricious, and by turns greedy and anxious. The American people, indeed, were no longer regarded exactly as people. In the eyes of advertisers and network executives, they became not the public, but that pliant, eager, and ultimately dehumanized unit—the audience.

The effects of this attitude were clear. Revenue became the main obsession of the network corporations. While ad spending in general increased 258 per cent in the fifties, TV ad expenditures rose 1,000 per cent. Commercials brought the networks incredible profits. In 1953, CBS earned a profit of $8.9 million. The next year that network became the single largest advertising medium in the world. Its profits reached $11.4 million. By 1957, CBS profits totaled $22.2 million.[4]

The TV viewer provided a ceaselessly exploited market. Three giant networks effectively formed an oligopoly over national broadcasting. Each of the three would screen show material to lure a certain audience. These people were then surveyed in terms of age, sex, income, and sheer volume. Then this audience was sold to a corporate sponsor. The public, that is, was bought.[5]

A new system had to be devised to determine the cost of buying the public. The ratings system filled that need. During the fifties, CBS became the giant among networks by using the ratings system. When a program was rated high, it supposedly reached a larger audience than those low on the scale. Therefore it deserved higher advertising revenues. A popular show like "I Love Lucy" commanded several times the ad income of rival shows in the same time slot.[6] The sole purpose of the ratings, then, was mercantile. The job of a network executive became watching out for programming, but only as it affected profits. Other concerns were irrelevant.

Many retrospective studies of TV charge that, by 1956, sponsors had seized almost total control of programming. The networks are seen as helpless; the sponsors are faulted for the medium's commercialism and its programming decline. This is only partially true. It is more accurate to say that, by 1956, the networks looked first of all to pleasing the source of their profits. If they had not grown so eager for these immense profits, and so willing to dull the medium's message, sponsors would never have attained so great a sway. Moreover, the commercial captivity of television would be more forgivable were it not for the product it created. That televised result was almost uniform. With some few distinctive exceptions, TV's quality declined during the fifties on every channel. The concept of the lowest common denominator prevailed. Appealing to the largest possible audience was not in itself a bad idea. It was the abuses of its application that were bad. As a consequence of this extreme, imitative formula programming rose and balance vanished. By decade's end, the variety of TV's earlier years was nonexistent. Only the Hollywood distraction shows filled prime time: situation comedies, quiz shows, action programs. Most examples of these genres were nearly interchangeable. There was little difference in plot or emotion between "Route 66" and "77 Sunset Strip," or "The Untouchables" and "The Lawless Years," or "Wichita" and "The Deputy." A few limited ideas were endlessly replicated in almost all American homes. The unique and the stimulating scarcely existed.

The decline of TV did not take place in a vacuum. Innumerable critics protested the medium's flagging quality throughout the decade. But these protests were countered by members of the TV industry. These counterattacks asserted the critic was a highbrow, too intellectual to truly understand TV's pleasures. The industry performed an almost musical refrain: "we are only giving the public what it wants."[7]

But that was only the public relations attitude. To learn more, one must turn to the trade publications. These are the revealing documents. It is when members of an interest group think they are talking only among themselves that their words disclose the most. Such is the case here. As *Advertising Age* commented, "in very few instances do people know what they want, even when they think they do." There is a great contrast between these public and private expressions. Today, with the hindsight of a more skeptical time, such concealed acts come as little surprise. But in the fifties, people trusted leaders of business as well as of government. That is one reason they were willing to go along with the tastemaking process of TV. People believed that if certain material was aired so often, then it must be the stuff they liked. At least it was what they had to live with. One is reminded of the words of George Bernard Shaw, "Get what you want or you will be forced to like what you get."[8]

Corollary to the industry's "public wants" outlook was (and is) a resistance to seeing the larger effects of TV. That is, if TV gave the people what they wanted, then the medium did little or nothing to change their tastes. That concept is both culturally and historically inaccurate. Its most obvious flaw rests in advertising: if TV is not a major influence, why continue to run ads on the tube? What happened in television programming, in the last analysis, was very much a forceful act, very much the result of a paternalistic culture. From the imposed flood of information, people learned to like what they were told to like—which, in those pre-public TV days, was also the only choice they had.

The effect of TV's flood can also be looked at in terms of family entertainment patterns. For much of the fifties, both critics and lovers of TV felt the medium had only a salubrious effect on the family. As one writer noted, the automobile gave Americans rootless mobility. Fifty years later TV brought them back home, to happily share the entertainment. That is a naive view. In 1957, a study by Eleanor Maccoby indicated "that the increased family contact brought about by television is not social except in the most limited sense: that of being in the same room with other people."[9] Television, in the course of a very few years, completely changed our most personal family encounters. Before the electronics revolution, people could participate in entertaining each other as a matter of course. The mail-order catalogues from the turn of the century were filled with aids for social diversion. There were song sheets, parlor games, books of poetry, religious tales, and orations. Storytelling and conversation remained respected social arts. All these entertainments required human cooperation and contact. One can debate the actual amount of pleasure, community, or other intangibles such diversions afforded, but the essential active participation remained.

Radio began to erode that. With this first electronic entertainment, people no longer had to speak or assert themselves to have fun. But they still could share the entertainment, simply by looking at one another. That was the first sign of change: conversation and reading habits fading away, people seated around a receiver that imposed its efforts on them.

TV completed the process. A family might stay home together to watch it. But in doing so, they made no genuine contact with one another. They just sat, eyes riveted on an inanimate object, a flickering box. The viewer was alone in every respect except, perhaps, the physical. As the screen grew in social importance, conversation and interaction waned. One no longer had to assert oneself at all for diversion, just sit down and be programmed in. This could only encourage an inertia extending beyond the hours of TV-watching. Distant, powerful others even provided one's fun, and so one could surrender the will utterly. TV did not simply change the family's fun. It discouraged independence and activity. The medium depended on people's *not* thinking or acting for themselves. It instructed the audience to that end.

Sensory satisfaction changed too. TV only stimulates two senses—sight (in a flat, undetailed way) and sound (also distorted). The over 30 other sense experiences are frustrated. Even eating was affected. The TV dinner (introduced in 1954) was the first sign of mass media convenience food, of the diet subsumed by the all-encompassing screen. Mental starvation tended to be the rule too. By mid-decade, the typical show was aimed at what was considered the median audience intelligence level—that of 12-year-olds, and dull unadventurous 12-year-olds at that.[10] Intellectual boredom, or atrophy, was inevitable for the regular viewer.

Television might well have been a terrific force for communicating *to* huge amounts of people. But between them, it only served to eradicate communication, to foster a hypnotic passivity. It is not at all farfetched to accuse the industry of doing this consciously. By the latter fifties, advertisers had come to realize a quality TV program was undesirable. "Programs on television," one critic remarked at that time, "are simply a device to keep the advertisements and commercials from bumping loudly together. The message of the media is the commercial." If a program was interesting, people ignored the bracketing ads, since they were talking about the show. But more money was being spent on the ads (comprising 20 per cent of airtime) than on the remaining 80 per cent. Imperatively, commercials had to become more compelling than the programs. Thus programs became dumber and more imitative. The real focal point of TV became not entertainment but the commercial pitch. The solipsistic, the hypnotic, and even stupefying effect of television was designed deliberately.

As the decade wore on, certain circumscribed ideas, behaviors, actions, and emotions echoed across the land. In their repetition they became integral to the cultural landscape. These ideas, for the most part, were simplifications or exaggerations of already extant cultural fantasies. But the exaggeration, the simplification, and, especially, the dissemination of these dreams had a potent effect. Most obviously, this was a reshaping of the American dream world, of our mass myths and fantasies. Yet it cannot be thought that only our fantasies were affected by TV. Dreams do shape our waking. The medium reformed people's concepts of themselves by changing their dreams. In so doing, it reformed their waking, their acting, their behavior in the world.

TV's focus on commercials had a profound effect. Advertising depended (and depends) on one central emotion: a vague personal discontent. One bought stuff to alleviate feelings of inferiority. Most of the things sold in fifties America were luxury items—things not at all necessary to sustain life, fashionable things quickly rendered obsolete by shoddy construction or newer styles. The advertising of luxuries obviously was not unique to fifties TV. But only in that decade, and only through the television medium did advertising reach such barraging proportions. Never before had so many people heard so often that happiness and security rested in ceaseless acquisition. And this wasteful lifestyle was very much the American ideal in the fifties. Economist Robert Lekachman decried the climate that TV commercialism engendered: "We can only guess at the tensions and anxieties generated by this relentless pursuit of the emblems of success in our society, and shudder at what it might give rise to during an economic setback."[11]

But that TV's barrage of merchandise might be responsible for such anxiety was often dodged. Many also avoided regarding television's entire array of dubious effects. There are many cultural reasons for this. A general truth of fifties life was that people preferred to abdicate responsibility. TV's impact was overlooked as a matter of course. Americans also were skeptical of any ideas lacking scientific proof. Ideas were only allegations until confirmed by numbers, experiments, statistics, charts. Charges against TV were consequently denigrated as lacking scientific support.

Television was also shielded by other processes. For instance, critics could be attacked for supporting censorship. This was a most skillful technique. It obscured the way TV itself was a censored medium, but one censored in favor of conspicuous consumption, violence, and political apathy. Television was also protected in its status quo by popular attitudes toward free will. America then possessed an elegant rhetoric favoring democracy and autonomy. But largely this was just a verbal facade. One was free to conform to a conservative and commercial style, but not free to truly rebel. Thus, people who did not like what appeared on their sets were told they could always "vote" about the content by changing the channel.[12] That was a spurious and deceptive argument. Even ignoring the dependency TV fostered, the vote notion pretended a genuine selection of very different shows existed.

The question of choice was also part of the long argument about violence on television. As long as TV has been a truly mass medium, people have worried about the violence it presented. Robert Lewis Shayon's 1950 book *Television and Our Children* referred frequently to the late-forties protests against gratuitous violence on TV. In the fifties, the TV violence argument took on fairly simple proportions. One side held that television fantasy violence provided an excellent cathartic since evil was inevitably punished on the action shows. The opposing argument insisted children learned aggressive or violent behavior from watching it on television.[13]

"I like the idea of sadism," Quinn Martin, producer of "The Untouchables," told his scriptwriters in the fifties, "but I hope we can come up with another approach to it." Much of the justification for the accelerated violence on fifties TV was commercial. Sexual references were taboo. Rough language was also forbidden. Only "sadism" remained to hold an audience otherwise bored with inane repetition. Martin, like the people behind the other action shows, consequently had to contrive novel incidents of sadism for the home viewer: the machine-gunning of a crowd of Mexican prostitutes to open a program, the machine-gunning of a slip-clad woman just before a commercial pitch made to mothers, the machine-gunning of innumerable transitory gangland thugs. (One critic referred to the show as an "educational series on machine-gun usage.") All these examples have been selected from one series.[14] But much the same thing could be illustrated from almost any action show: "Whispering Smith," "Hawaiian Eye," "M Squad," "Gunslinger," "Hotel de Paree." The bad guys on such shows were always defeated, but that no longer was the point. Their defeat was inadequate to prove brutality or aggression a wrong, because the attractive good guys were equally responsible for the violent acts. They were always ready (that is, looking) for a fight. Sadism was the entire justification for their existence. That was one of TV's major lessons: violence and aggression are the stuff of life, the really worthwhile acts, the surest solution.

In creating a universe of easy battle triumph, TV provided the culture with a high-strung and violent vocabulary. One can say again and again that TV did not bring violence into the national character. That is quite true. The real stars of American history have always been the dollar and the gun. Americans have always turned too quickly to the latter (particularly to get the former). But TV took these complex myths and remade them, investing them with new power and impact. It not only simplified the worship of violence; it repeated its terms in every household.

This new vocabulary at once reinforced and justified other concepts. The cold war, for instance, depended on an aggressive and insensitive posture. Machismo was also forwarded by the gender emphasis of the action program. Too, the new language of TV stifled nonviolence. The adventure show heroes expressed only a bland confidence. Hurt might be done but was not communicated. Rarely, too, would opponents solve their problems with the pain of talk rather than the pain of bullets. Such a suggestion probably seems amusing or ludicrous. That this is so is one indication of our extreme conditioning. We expect (that is, have come to demand) our fiction and fantasies to include only the violent solution. Within such a culture it requires no feat of the imagination to conceive of oneself as a victim . . . or an aggressor.[15]

All these statements might be regarded as mere allegations. But the vivid repetition of television brutality is the first clue to the proof so often demanded in this debate. As early as the late forties, it was realized TV is a powerful educational medium of a special sort. Its teaching forte is rote. This is the basis of more recent shows like "Sesame Street." The rote effect on children was also obvious every time a tot repetitiously sang an advertising jingle. The implication is clear: violence was repeated on fifties TV, too. It appeared often and ritualistically, providing an intensely powerful lesson in its very redundancy. But, given nuclear culture blocks against recognizing brutality, given the mass surrender of personal power, given the virility and beauty fantasies people turned to in their stead, Americans mostly preferred to ignore the possible implications.

Only by the mid-seventies did psychologists and law-enforcement officials systematically confirm both long- and short-range evidence of the damaging effect of TV brutality. Working with two groups of kids (only one group regular TV watchers) scientists in the seventies found great "desensitization" to human suffering in the TV kids. The medium's aggressive fascination had already innured these very young ones to others' pain. The scientists involved in this study also linked extensive television watching to the commission of some of the most violent domestic crimes of recent years. The mid-seventies saw a string of grotesque crimes in direct imitation of TV: the gasoline burning of a Boston feminist, a robbery in which the bystander-hostages were forced to drink lye, a mail extortion plot directed against Sears Roebuck by children. One of the psychologists involved in the above study observed "the amount of television violence watched by children at age nine influences the amount and degree of aggressiveness at age 19. There is clear, documented evidence that watching violence for a few hours or even a few minutes can instigate violent behavior that had never happened before."[16]

One can speculate about the way this has shaped American history since 1950. How many of the roots of Vietnam lie in the televised repetition of the aggressive/violent answer? How much of the counterculture's decline into cheap easy confrontation was inspired by that model? How many assassins longed for the televised proclamation of their notoriety? The only area in which there need be no speculation is in the mad increase of violent crimes in recent years. TV, in that regard, is one of the two major triggers. The other is the availability of guns. These exist in direct relationship: television provides the emotional support for the brutal solution, and guns give the easy means.

Just as the run-and-shoot shows created certain expectations and expressions about violence, the prize shows aggravated mass attitudes about money. Variations on the idea of the prize show had been aired since TV's early days. "You Bet Your Life," emceed by Groucho Marx, was easily the best of these early prize shows. Introduced in 1950, the show offered relatively minor monetary compensation—$100 to the person who happened to guess the day's secret word and make the duck drop from the ceiling. The prize was rather irrelevant. "You Bet Your Life" had more to do with Groucho's behavior, which ranged from clever talk to crude insults.[17]

In contrast, the sob-story prize programs introduced to TV the idea of doing anything at all for the big reward. The early ones were transferred from radio. On "Strike It Rich," unfortunate women would singly relate their tales of misery and suffering. The audience would grant them "awards," and contestants also could win help via the show's "Heart Line," a telephone for outside contributors.[18]

Not so gentle a program was "Queen for a Day." On "Queen," three women would appear at once, each taking turns relating their tragic story. But this was not an everybody-wins show. Those three women were competing. The audience would pick the most pathetic of the three, and only she would get the prize plus the fake-ermine robe and the fake gold crown and the applause. Both "Queen" and "Strike It Rich" fostered a false picture of American poverty. They operated on the assumption that there were hardly any poor people left in America, and those few were all being gradually taken care of . . . on TV. Yes, emcees Warren Hull and Jack Baily seemed to say, we are helping these outcasts, lifting them up and up toward the mainstream's easy living. The losers, well, maybe they deserved to lose.

The idea of humiliation jumped from the sob shows to game shows with remarkable alacrity. The next logical step after "Queen for a Day" in the invasion of personal dignity was taken by shows like "Truth or Consequences." Humiliation, such prize programs insisted, can be fun. Even better, it can be materially rewarding. "Dollar a Second" and "Beat the Clock" were two examples of a crowded genre. (A modern descendant of these shows would be "Let's Make a Deal.") On these programs a contestant was required to do something contrived and foolish. This was the opposite of acting the prankster because it was an imposed act, one designed to pierce one's dignity or defenses rather than liberate them or respect them.[19] Contestants were further belittled because they had, after all, volunteered. At least the contestants on such shows would win cash or prizes. "Candid Camera" took the ridiculing aspect of these shows to its extreme: this show found uproarious humor in simple invasion of privacy with no quizzing or material rewards whatsoever. The cultural process of hilarious electronic invasion was so complete that even the invaded approved.

But the reward programs receiving the most attention in the fifties, while involving some of the elements of these shows, chose instead to offer the lure of gigantic amounts of money. "The $64,000 Question" debuted June 7, 1955. It set a pattern soon imitated by other programs like "The $100,000 Big Surprise," "$64,000 Challenge," and "Twenty-One": the attractive contestant answering obscure questions for lots of cash. The audience effect was astounding. "Question" quickly achieved vast popularity and also stimulated sales of the program's sponsor, Revlon.[20] It was denounced in little liberal magazines, imitated by other sponsors, parodied by *Mad*, and viewed by millions.

The appeal of all these prize shows is not too surprising. Mid-fifties America, trying hard to be cool and conform, could not permit itself many outlets for tension or excitement. The culture, too, still invested in the idea of the self-made success. As Horatio Alger had shaped that notion, triumph always depended on "luck and pluck," on a combination of capability and fortune. "Into the vacated myth of quick success," Dan Wakefield wrote in 1957, "the jackpot quiz shows came with an answer. They came to an audience hungry for glory, excitement, surprises and reassurance that the man in the anonymous street might still suddenly rise to a place in the golden sun."[21] Never before had so many people been able to participate in such a fantastic story of competition and success.

In 1958, a combination of congressional investigation and personal confessions revealed that the super-quiz shows had been rigged. Such contestants as Charles Van Doren (who had wanted to make intellectuals popular), an impoverished student named Herbert Stempel, actress Patty Duke, and a few others had accepted answers beforehand. "Entertainment value"—that is, enhanced ratings—was the ostensible excuse. As *Nation* said in 1959, "it is perhaps symbolic that even this simulation of fulfillment for the common man turned out to be a swindle." What, then, did the quiz show scandals do to the public that had been so fascinated with them? Dashed hopes were inevitable in such a corrupt situation. One must remember, too, that the late fifties was a time of economic re-evaluation. John Kenneth Galbraith published *The Affluent Society*, a critique of American wastefulness, revising his earlier, rosier pluralistic theories. New Leftism was starting up at some few schools. Innumerable other voices were beginning to question the tenets of a guns-and-butter economy. Those bare beginnings of a new American synthesis, though, were not successfully applied to a popular attack on the roots of the quiz shows. Ironically, the blame for the corruption only stigmatized a few individuals. These persons were certainly guilty but had been manipulated into that guilt. The corporations involved, such as Revlon and the networks, avoided penalty and reform. For a brief time, the moral and economic order was questioned—but only for a brief time. The passing of such shows as "Twenty-One" meant the end of the fixed TV giveaway program. But it did not mean the end of the TV giveaway program itself.[22] Tragically, the get-rich-quick-for-foolish-effort mystique still is perpetrated.

Another way the televised medium transformed American thinking was through its approach to public affairs. TV quickly proved to be the most remarkable medium for the dissemination of news. Radio had invaded the newspaper's province with instant reporting of events. This caused papers to shift to a more elaborate, soft-news function. They provided more non-news features, more story background and less hard reporting. The general family and news magazines flourished at this time, supplementing radio's audial aspect.

Television affected reporting and the print media even more. Since TV also showed the event, the pictorial aspect of printed news became less effective. People read less in general. They certainly read less news (usually fewer newspapers) in favor of watching TV news. When people did read, they turned to more specialized matter. Consequently, the general-entertainment magazines entered a decline. So did news photo publications and newspapers. This was the beginning of the end for magazines like *Collier's*, and eventually for *Life* and *Look*. Special-interest publications, however, gradually rose in popularity.

As advertisers shifted some of their revenues to television, the number of newspapers dwindled. More and more papers took an ever-softer approach to the news. This often meant a timid approach. It was also very directly shaped by televised news. Because television news stations tended to report government news releases as if these were actual events, papers began to echo this. They hastily would accept managed, packaged news without questioning its veracity. The late A. J. Liebling dubbed this newspaper practice "not-reporting."[23]

By the seventies, newspapers had shifted so much in function because of electronics reporting that a real hard news scoop might be disbelieved. This particularly occurred if the scoop contradicted the managed version of the news. When Bernstein and Woodward were using traditional police-beat techniques to uncover the Watergate story, when Hersh was working on My Lai, they found a profound reluctance on the part of most newspapers to even pick up the stories. Certainly this partly happened because of publishers' conservatism. Still, it was almost as though, because the facts had not shown up on TV, they did not exist.

The technique of TV newscasting also affected the news. Often, TV has been attacked for its slanted reportage. Regrettably, such deliberate bias did (and does) exist. This was particularly true in the formative years of TV newscasting. In his 1950 book, *The Great Audience*, Gilbert Seldes noted the first known instance of the televised faking of an event. The incident occurred during the 1948 broadcast of the Democratic presidential convention. A group of southern delegates stalked off the convention floor, dramatically stripping off their badges and hurling them on a table. The camera focused on the mounting pile of badges. When filming stopped, the delegates picked up their badges and returned to the floor. The entire gesture had been suggested by an NBC director.[24]

Such blatant manufacturing of news was far more infrequent than other possible distortions. Bias could be achieved subtly and with utter simplicity. For instance, the newscaster could insert just one volatile word in the brief moment accorded any event. More usually, an event could simply be ignored or misinterpreted. That was a practice so common that it came to shape the entire direction of early New Left politics. In the late fifties, the ban-the-bomb and pacifist demonstrators realized the best and, perhaps, only way to achieve a forum was by creating a quick, sensational event with big TV news appeal.[25]

Even the typical news show format tended to create a distorted picture. Partially this was because the world was approached in a spirit of haste. One often had the impression the announcer was cramming as many stories as possible into the non-commercial moments. The mannerly, measured, even compassionate approach had its failures too. Largely this occurred because of TV's sheer pictorial volume. Images tumbled before the viewer continually. When the camera focused on the victims of an earthquake or a war, then on the impeccable and kindly reporter, then on a jolly laxative ad, the network was not conspiring to distract people from active sympathy. Anything aired after those few shots of misery would be distracting. The particular quick-change format of the news itself discourages reflection. In this way the format counteracted the entire informative reason for broadcasting news.

The early fifties did enjoy a number of news programs that urged the viewer to reflect. The greatest of these was Edward R. Murrow's "See It Now" series on CBS. Murrow was one of the very few giants of TV journalism. His programs were important in themselves. But they also gave a small idea of the immense potential in the mature and moral documentary approach. Murrow's popular appeal, however, was taken as a personal threat by CBS chairman William S. Paley. Paley slowly eroded Murrow's strength, gradually removing him from prime time then from a weekly slot, and eventually from regular programming altogether. Murrow finally quit in disgust. He had been so popular at his height that if he had left CBS it would have badly hurt the network. Never again, Paley made sure, would such a threat exist from a journalist. And seldom afterward would documentaries be presented in a manner to provoke thought.[26]

With very few exceptions, Paley's squeeze against Murrow has shaped nonfiction commercial TV. Documentary journalism since the mid-fifties has taken pains not to move people, not to be provocative or controversial. The excuse has been balance: one must present both sides, and rouse no one. That is why TV documentaries were (and are) unpopular. They were boring. In avoiding making anyone mad, they also avoided making anyone interested. One watched only for a medicinal dose. Imagine the consequences if TV took equal pains to remove all affect from its sitcoms, crime thrillers, and soap operas.

Politicians initially regarded TV as a foolish nuisance. But in 1950, the congressional hearings on organized crime catapulted a little-known senator, Estes Kefauver, to national fame in a matter of weeks. Added to that political rise was another man's great fall. Four crucial TV broadcasts have been linked to McCarthy's decline: three "See It Now" shows on the excesses of anticommunism, and the 1954 televised Army-McCarthy hearings.[27] Somewhere between the elevation of Kefauver and the erosion of McCarthy lay a political possibility.

The mid-fifties, then, saw the birth of the show-biz politician. TV might have made the clumsy fraud obsolete. But the sincere fraud was given a new lease on life. In 1952, vice-presidential candidate Richard Nixon saved his political career by appearing on TV. Nixon gave his famous "Checkers Speech," in which he asserted his honesty in the face of charges he was a crook. In 1955, Nixon would comment "sincerity is the quality that comes through on television." Eventually, Nixon and every other politician in America would also learn that TV had conditioned people to expect not just a sincere but a photogenic image: the politician as pretty performer. The 1960 Kennedy-Nixon debates (JFK in well-defined dark suit, looking immaculate and youthful; Nixon in unfortunate light suit, thuggish five-o'clock shadow revealed under the studio lights) provided ample object lesson.[28]

The political mood of the country was also reflected on TV. During the early fifties witch hunts, for example, it was easiest to see the world in terms of both moral absolutes and respect for the vigilante/authority figure. Thus, clear-cut good/evil tales were the rule: "Wild Bill Hickok," "Hopalong Cassidy," even the singing cowboys such as Gene Autry and Roy Rogers. As the cold war eased around mid-decade, however, some few subtler shows were introduced. "Gunsmoke," "Maverick," and "Have Gun Will Travel" were the best in this mood, presenting worlds of moral complexity where the principle character might not even be a hero. James Garner's unathletic, unreliable, funny gambler Brett Maverick represented one peak of this style.[29] The simplistic tough guy shows still dominated action broadcasts by 1960. But more mature figures like Maverick, or like the epicurean Paladin (Richard Boone) of "Have Gun," had achieved a place. These were still Western adventures, still male- and violence-dominated shows. But presumably the programs were more mature because the heroes hesitated before pulling the trigger.

The TV industry avoided even a pretense of maturity regarding racial matters. Racism was both disseminated and encouraged by the medium. Partly this came about because of the timidity of sponsors and broadcasters. In 1958, for instance, Nat King Cole was to host his own musical variety program. Many top stars agreed to appear free of charge on the show. But the network was unable to find anyone willing to sponsor it. Cole's show was canceled.[30] A ballad singer, Cole could only have been a moderating presence on television: his style was so very far removed from emotional or cultural extremes. Eliminating his program was certainly a case of moral cowardice, but it also indicated the greed and anxiety of business in America, an anxiety that interpreted the presence of black skin as ample proof of extremism and controversy.

There had been a very few blacks on TV before Cole's cancellation. Bob Howard had a series called "Sing It Again" in the late forties. Enjoying little success, it was canceled. Most other appearances of blacks were either in the role of comic prop/servant (Rochester on the Jack Benny show) or, very rarely, in specials. Sidney Poitier performed in Robert Alan Aurthur's "A Man Is Ten Feet Tall" (the TV forerunner of the film *Edge of the City*). Ossie Davis acted as *The Emperor Jones*. "See It Now" once presented Marian Anderson; "Hallmark Hall of Fame" twice showed *Green Pastures*.[31] But overwhelmingly, television kept blacks out. They did not belong in the image TV wished to present of America. Indians only appeared in "horse operas," the fantasy Westerns. Other non-white groups similarly appeared in purely racist roles: wily, subtle Charlie Chan, wiggling Polynesian dancing girls, sleepy Mexicans with sombreros and serapes. Largely, the absence of non-whites, that falsehood, that void, was filled when the major networks purchased pre-1948 films. These, with their full complement of dead Indians and servile blacks, served to complete the racial fantasy.

It was easy for TV producers to imagine a world without blacks, but it was not easy for them to imagine one without laughter. The professional theater often employs a person with a big, silly laugh to warm up the audience. He sits in the house and starts laughing, right away, at all the punch lines, and pretty quickly the audience figures the show must be hilarious and then they laugh at all the punch lines too. That was the intention of canned laughter—to warm up the audience, and also to reassure them that what was going on was funny. One was not only being asked, then, to participate in the usual suspension of credibility that comes in watching a performed piece. The effect went further. People were accepting (and becoming addicted to) taped-in enjoyment not as mechanical interloper, but as a live audience's genuine pleasure. The laughs on tape performed a function similar to the commentary of the classical Greek chorus. But this time the process was incredibly vulgarized.

It was deceptive, not enlightening. Too often, canned laughter was a lie. It replaced the need to really laugh or even smile. TV could become more hypnotic than ever: simply tune in, and the medium did all the rest for you.

The genre most requiring canned laughs was, of course, the situation comedy. Nothing illustrates better the way TV constantly exhausts material, and so both creates a demand for novelty and a type of sophistication in the audience. It consumes ideas, jokes, shows, like no other medium ever did before. Unfortunately, given the many self-censoring strictures of TV in the fifties, fresh humorous material did not mean original or piercing stuff. Rather, comedy came to mean warmth and cuteness. The sitcoms depended on a gimmick: "Hey, Jeannie!" about a Scottish émigrée to America, "My Friend Irma" about a dumb blonde, Irma, and her roommate, Jane, in Mrs. O'Reilley's boarding house; "Father Knows Best," with superhuman suburban dad; "Guestward Ho!" about a Western resort. Early in the decade, a number of good-quality sitcoms did appear. "The Goldbergs" (beginning 1949) was easily the best of these, but far more than comedy it depended on perceptive analysis of relationships within the family. Occasionally a sitcom might be genuinely funny. "You'll Never Get Rich" (later "The Phil Silvers Show") sometimes hit the mark in portraying Ernie Bilko's money-making schemes. "Mr. Peepers" was an excellent, gentle, and low-key series of mid-decade starring Wally Cox. "The Burns and Allen Show," which debuted in 1950, was both funny and enduring.[32] More usually, however, the situation comedies skillfully avoided both perceptive analysis and laughter.

This became more true as the fifties went on. By decade's end, most of these shows were merely artificial: the extra-wholesome 1958-premiering "Donna Reed Show" (in one of its most vivid episodes, she offered to prepare an Armenian meal for an acquaintance, starting with pears and cottage cheese); "Happy" (1960), the baby who thought out loud; "Too Young to Go Steady" (1959), and countless other programs whose names have been mercifully forgotten. With such shows, canned laughter became essential, and not merely because no audience was present during the filming. Taped fun, in that context, was reassurance: this may be boring, it may be saccharine, and it may be just like the same boring saccharine stuff on all the other channels, but it is comedy. Hear the laughter?

Late-fifties sitcoms were the extreme opposite of the excellent humor TV had screened early in the decade. A major tragedy of the commerical takeover of TV was the cancellation of such programs as "Your Show of Shows," one of the most significant TV series ever. Starring Sid Caesar, this series also was a training ground for such great American comedians as Woody Allen and Mel Brooks. Caesar also created a taste in the American people for that sophisticated attitude, satire. His skits and sketches were fascinating: Caesar imitating a white sidewall tire, or doing a skit as the man of simple tastes whose entire dinner consists of boiled bread, or with Howard Morris, Imogene Coca, and Carl Reiner in the now-famous parody "From Here to Obscurity."

"The Ernie Kovacs Show" presented even more anarchistic comedy. It was unusual among high-quality shows in premiering as late as 1955. However, it did get canceled the next year. Until his death, Kovacs spent the remainder of his career as a guest performer on others' shows. That he, and an even greater influence on American comedy, Jonathan Winters, spent so much time in guest shots was significant. As the areas acceptable to TV broadcasts dwindled, so too did the scope of comedy. This was why situation comedy series focused on such unfunny affects as warmth or cuteness. As for individual comedians, only the cornball humorist could operate in the restricted atmosphere of latter-fifties shows. Stale jokes drove out creative ones. As Steve Allen said in 1958, "the humorist is a social critic." The genuinely critical comic could scarcely find a job in the industry. "There is this continuous business of 'They won't get it, you can't do this,'" another comedian noted. Steve Allen was able to persist on TV because he had many talents besides that of droll humorist, and presented them in a variety format. But many others were censored by a narrowing perception of not just acceptability but of the public mind.

Television humor came to lie, too, about the world and people in it. Because these programs obeyed all the taboos of TV, the sitcom generally depended on cultural stereotyping. Just as much, the genre avoided any of the troubles and tragedies of life. To be sure, one or two of these problem situations might crop up. But that would happen only as a temporary device to be solved by program's end. Trouble and anguish were, in this fantasy world, transitory.

One found much the same artificial approach in most fiction programming. In the fifties, a period when culture came up with innumerable ways to make people strangers among themselves, TV brilliantly helped unfit them for present and future. It taught that adversity was not the tempering stuff of life but something unreal, something brief and passing. The future shock of later stressful decades became inevitable.

One amazingly popular program able to perpetrate all sorts of untruths was also the first show ever to reach an audience of ten million people. "I Love Lucy" premiered in 1951. By fall 1952, the show had 34 million regular viewers. "Basically," felt one commentator, "it allowed husbands and wives to laugh at irritations in their own marriages."[33] But that was not the only function "Lucy" performed. Given the program's popularity, what it said about relations between the sexes was very important. American women in the fifties were not simply trapped in a paternalistic superstructure. Parts of that structure were in collapse. For instance, more females than ever were joining the commercial work force. But they were largely at the lowest economic levels. All the economic and social preconditions for a feminist movement were in the making. The discontent and rage that precipitate such a change had to be stifled, had to remain unacknowledged. Thus, a new mystique had to be created at some meeting place between the old roles and the new reality. "Lucy," in that context, was a force for its time.

Some elements of "I Love Lucy" seemingly catered to the changing reality of American women. Lucy, true, was not a working wife. But she could scarcely be described in any of the botanical terms so often applied to females: shrinking violet, clinging vine. Rather, Lucy Ricardo was played by Lucille Ball as an aggressive oddball, by turns tough and gentle in her behavior. Similarly, Ricky Ricardo (Desi Arnaz) as her Cuban bandleader husband was not the pure tough guy, nor even the stereotypical bland god of the suburban father school. He was a husband as explosively emotional as any female on TV. (This, however, can be attributed more to the Latino stereotype than to any desire to wear down sexual role-playing.)

But that was as far as the series' daring ever went. It was not simply that "Lucy" approached marriage problems as aberrations. The label of "aberrant" was transferred entirely to Lucy herself. Lucy habitually became involved in all sorts of silly and confusing mixups, which always had to be concealed from Ricky. She would call on her best friend, Ethel Mertz (Vivian Vance), to help her, making it necessary to conceal the mess from Fred Mertz (William Hawley) too. Guilt for the dumb errors in the plot usually fell along sexual lines. Week after week, Ricky discovered Lucy's error but let her go ahead with her crazy coverup anyhow; the husbands and wives acted in deceptive, graceless, greedy ways; one saw that the basis for this American marriage was dishonesty. That, certainly, was the source of most of the program's humor. Recalling the way TV stars tend to be regarded uncritically, as friends and ideals, that basic deceptive theme can only be mourned. Lucy portrayed the tough and intelligent woman as fool, as clown, as a being so mixed up she couldn't even cheat successfully. In Ricky, one saw the husband able to forgive out of his superior strength. At the same time one saw his almost shrugging acceptance: What can you do? he seemed to say. Women are all like this. And Ethel Mertz, Lucy's sidekick in mugging, provided the echo of proof. It was true that, at best, "Lucy" and its imitators (such as "My Little Margie") provided an outlet for marital stress. More usually, such shows simply disarmed the potential of the strong woman.

The soap operas were the only other TV shows featuring women in major roles. Their plots usually revolved about one central woman. She would be married, nearly sexless, and nearly middle-aged. Any men were weak-willed and error-prone. Any other women were treated as corrupt, because of youthful sexuality or careers. Women tended to watch such shows, as Molly Haskell has pointed out, because these provided their only available role-models. Unfortunately, the soaps provided a flawed model for females. True, the central heroine was a strong and determined woman. But hers was a costly strength. She gained it at great expense to herself, scorning education and intellect, shedding her own sexual pleasure and feeling contempt for anyone not just like her. Her dominance was also at the expense of others, who were the subjects of her scorn for trying to become anything outside the tiny expectations of the soap heroine's world. The best that can be said of these shows was that they eased the burden of certain housewives and provided them some consolation. But that, too, is an overly kind assessment. In later decades, the soaps would grow and mature. But in the fifties, they only sabotaged the self-respect of their fans.

So, too, did the action-adventure shows. While men in such programs were the authority figures, women were the incompetent window-dressing. Typically, "Hawaiian Eye" (1959) included Connie Stevens as the detectives' buddy, a singer named Cricket. She helped out the men by cluttering up the action, getting in the way, and cowering. Much the same was true of the women in all these programs, from "Martin Kane, Private Eye" (1949) through "Wire Service" (1956) to "Surfside 6" (1960) and well into the seventies. The female inevitably appeared in a part that labeled her as an auxiliary to a man: femme fatale, wife, sweetheart. But always she was no more than an excuse for the hero to swing into action. Women, that is, were simply impersonal props on this sort of show.

Not everything about TV was damaging. The medium still has a tremendous potential to create McLuhan's "global village," rather than simply make more walls between people. Too, it remains the most efficient entertainer around. But, particularly in the fifties, TV's message was a mixed one, a massage of good feelings and detrimental ones. Some few TV shows depicted a coherent and admirable world. Many of these bore the stigma highbrow and were one-time productions. But some important series shows did exist.

These shows made the best use of the TV aesthetic. One thinks of programs like Studs Terkel's "Studs' Corner," broadcast from a Chicago bar, and of "Garroway at Large." The latter, indeed, was the only whole TV series to be cited in the Museum of Modern Art's 1962 retrospective on television. Mid-decade saw Alistair Cooke's middlebrow series "Omnibus," which proved again that intelligent programming could be popular programming too. It was canceled anyway. Garroway was canceled too, replaced by televised boxing. Soon, it became virtually impossible to enjoy a plausible, gentle, and humane moment on TV. That was partial explanation for the popularity of the unassuming children's program, "Kukla, Fran and Ollie." That show presented a world in which diverse folk solved their problems peacefully. Affection and regard mattered. On "Kukla," two characters as different as a little clown and a toothy dragon could be loving friends.[34] It was a show that charmed both children and adults. It also worked against the crudeness of so many other shows kids watched.

The child, in the fifties, had a unique position as luxury member of society, with no useful work to perform. Lacking a well-defined work role, it was much harder for kids to learn about the adult world. TV, then, became distorted in importance to the child as the chief source of knowledge about grown-up behavior. Just as in any society, tremendous pressure was put on children to learn in a socially correct fashion. As Jeff Greenfield has pointed out, the children's programs could provide kids with subtle instructions in rebellion. Greenfield was fascinated with Clarabelle, the clown on the "Howdy Doody Show" (1947–60).[35] Clarabelle was the outlet for all that stress. He was mischievous, anarchistic, a prankster. Clarabelle constantly played jokes on the "Howdy Doody" adults. He usually got away with it, too. Clarabelle was also somewhat free of sexual role-playing, and indeed was rather androgynous: a male actor, reference to Clarabelle as "he," but the double-feminine name and the sexually unspecific and baggy costume. Clarabelle was the perfect escape from punishment, from learning the mystifying rules of the sexual game, from conformity and obedience. He was a rare fantasy alternative of impunity in a conforming world.

Such positive influences, however, were few and far between. Television, by the late fifties, had created a public taste for banality and violence. It also insulated people from reality. TV stifled the willingness to face the problems of surviving in the world. As Gilbert Seldes wrote in 1957, "the power of our new communications systems" is "the power to prevent people from understanding what is being communicated." One integral reason for this, Seldes and many others noted, was the way the electronics media tended to replace the print media. The Videotown study, in its tenth year (1958), revealed one proof of that. People who owned a TV read far less than before they had the set. These people read less than half the magazines they had beforehand.[36] Most obviously, this meant people were heavily dependent on the information they received from the tube. In light of the medium's distortions that was a most grave danger.

But at least equally significant was a likelihood Seldes himself predicted as early as 1957. "The half-observed phenomenon," he wrote, "is the arrival of a new form of communication on which a new culture can be based to combine with or supersede the culture based on the textbook, the novel . . . the work of scholarship, the editorial and—to be inclusive—the pulp magazine, the thriller, the tabloid."[37] Many observers feared TV would completely eradicate the print culture. Ray Bradbury's 1953 novel *Fahrenheit 451* was such a reaction. It depicted a future society where the printed word was totally illegal and the electronics media were the major tools of dictatorship. Seldes recognized a more likely process, however. He predicted a gradual combining of the two rather than the death of print.

That, so far, has been pretty much the case. As Marshall McLuhan felt, the presence of TV in all our lives has changed the attention span. One is no longer willing to spend hours listening to a single storyteller, he said. While this is a rather dubious suggestion, one can recall ways TV has influenced other arts. The early sixties Jerry Lewis movie *The Bellboy* was a series of little vignettes about bellhop Lewis in a hotel. It only could have been popular because it was preceded by years of televised commercials, brief messages with fast and vague plots. In that sense, TV ads, and then *The Bellboy,* were forerunners of such later productions as "Laugh-In," in which brevity was as important as comedy.

TV has also changed the look and even the sort of things people read and write, and thus the way they express themselves. By the mid-seventies, it was possible to observe some of this happening. By that time, an entire generation had grown up saturated by TV. These were not the rebels of the late sixties, who more likely were born in the years before TV's universality. The young adults of the seventies had, by virtue of their later birth, been exposed to TV much earlier and far more than any people before. People are inevitably shaped and controlled by the things making up their world. When TV is the major entertainment, a major babysitter, the major source of information for kids about the grown-up world, the passive moods and violent notions it insists on will be reflected in its young charges.

The person coming of age in the seventies, then, has likely spent tens of thousands of hours before a TV and has been strongly influenced by the medium. A number of traits can be observed among these young in relation to the print and electronic culture. The reading capacity of the average college student in the mid-seventies, for instance, was significantly lower than that of earlier groups of students. At Michigan State University in 1975, it was seriously debated by administrators that the average textbook level be reduced to that of the ninth grader. MSU is a useful example here. Unlike other schools complaining of reading incompetency, it has been admitting a broad spectrum of students for many years.[38]

The writing ability of the typical student is significantly lower, too. One finds a capably written linear essay less and less often. That, certainly, is a subjective judgment. Some critics blame the schools for failing to teach such essentials. But the kids writing many of these essays were TV-conditioned before they began school. They had already learned a way of thinking molded by its aesthetic: immediacy, intimacy, a barrage of simple and not necessarily related messages. Its effect on our previous concept of literacy is significant. In one MSU course taught over a period of nearly a decade, students were required to compose an intellectual autobiography. By the mid-seventies, the general writing style tended more and more to be remarkably like that of a television drama script. Bits of a lifetime would be told in short rhapsodic bursts that faded out to the next action scene. One paper went so far as to be pure adventure (attempted murder-by-auto, secret agents, FBI intervention, lurkings by night, and political suspicions). No intellectual development was betrayed at all. The star of the piece, instead of being a TV pretty-boy, was its young author. That young person never indicated enough awareness of the television to have been satirizing its dominant role in his life. But it was stamped on every sentence he molded.

In the early fifties, television had hinted at a terrific potential. Perhaps that potential was best reflected in the great performers of the TV screen: Edward R. Murrow, Sid Caesar, Lucille Ball, and "Mr. Television," Milton Berle. By the later fifties, TV's scope had shrunk. Only Ball, of these giants, remained (and she persisted by playing a little woman). The small talents prevailed as the most efficient purveyors of the commercial message. If one had to name a Mr. Television of 1960, it would more likely be a Bill Paley or a David Sarnoff, one of the behind-the-scenes media moguls who made their millions peddling banality and cruelty.

"Fantasy images are poor images," Ernest Becker wrote, "they never surprise us." TV's immense effect on American culture should come as no surprise. In many ways, it has merely perpetrated going aspects of fifties mainstream culture. But in too many other ways TV has given us back a different, new America: media simplifying life and life imitating media. The movies may have made our dreams and acts seem larger than life. But in the television age, everything, from food and fun through assassination and war, seems smaller than life, shrunk to the little screen's scale. The patterning process has often been insidious. It certainly has been ignored. But TV has put its hands on all our behaviors. Perhaps it is most appropriate to end this section with an anecdote told in the fifties by

Leonard Lyons, a story that unintentionally hints at the way TV has touched all our acts. Lyons told about a father who, returning home from work, found his young son seated before the TV. The child was wholly absorbed in a program but also clutching a suitcase. Puzzled, the father asked the mother for an explanation. "Well, he's running away from home," she said, "as soon as the program's over."[39]

NOTES

1. The Gardner Rea cartoon appears in *The New Yorker*, September 1, 1951, p. 25, and is also reproduced in this book; Russel B. Nye, *The Unembarrassed Muse* (New York, 1970), p. 406; William F. Leuchtenberg and the editors of *Life, The Great Age of Change* (New York, 1964), pp. 123, 147; Gilbert Seldes, *The Public Arts* (New York, 1956), p. 262. The number of TV broadcasting stations phenomenally grew in those years. In 1948, only 20 stations existed. By 1950 over 100 stations operated, and the number kept increasing during the decade—see John Brooks, *The Great Leap* (New York, 1961), p. 161.

2. American Business Consultants, *Red Channels: The Report of Communist Influence in Radio and Television* (New York, 1950); see also John Cogley, *Report on Blacklisting*, Vol. II, *Radio-Television* (n.p., 1956), published by the Fund for the Republic.

CBS even got TV mileage out of its own purges 20 years after the fact, in its special "Fear on Trial," shown in October 1975. "Fear" told the story of John Henry Faulk, a radio personality whose career was destroyed by his blacklisting. Faulk sued CBS and Aware Inc., the firm providing blacklist information. The TV show placed all the guilt on two individuals, especially Vincent Hartnett of Aware. The script conveniently forgot CBS' role in the trial, including its battery of lawyers and testifying officials who attacked Faulk. Only Hartnett's lawyer was shown, and both the lawyer and Hartnett were portrayed as prissy, aberrant people. CBS, it would seem, was innocent of the paranoid mood.

3. Dan Fowler, "Public Hero No. 1 . . . Hopalong Cassidy," *Look*, August 29, 1950, pp. 80–81.

4. Harold Mehling, *The Great Time-Killer* (Cleveland, 1962), pp. 38–45; David Halberstam, "CBS: The Power and the Profits," *Atlantic*, January 1976, p. 44. Halberstam adds that for CBS' first 25 years, ending in 1952, its profits leveled out annually around $4 or $5 million. In 1950, TV was just beginning on national hookup and CBS earned $4.1 million. By 1965, the network earned around $50 million, and this had more than doubled by 1975.

5. Lawrence S. Wittner, *Cold War America* (New York, 1974), p. 120. Wittner also quotes a young German writer: "Now people no longer have opinions; they have refrigerators. Instead of illusions, we have television; instead of tradition, the Volkswagen. The only way to catch the spirit of the times is

to write a handbook on home appliances." Jules Henry also approached the problem of commercialism in his *Culture Against Man* (New York, 1963).

6. Halberstam, "CBS," pp. 37–38, 44.

7. Robert Lewis Shayon, *Television and Our Children* (New York, 1951), pp. 51–59.

8. Vance Packard, *The Hidden Persuaders* (New York, 1957), p. 8; Shaw quoted in Shayon, *Television*, p. 71. As Henry Ford once said, "no one ever lost money underestimating the taste of the American people."

9. Eleanor Maccoby quoted by Rolf Meyerson, "Social Research in Television," Bernard Rosenberg and David Manning White, eds., *Mass Culture* (Glencoe, Ill., 1957), p. 350; Louis Kronenberger, *Company Manners* (Indianapolis, 1954), p. 79.

10. Wilson Bryan Key, *Subliminal Seduction* (New York, 1973), pp. 66–71; Eric Goldman, *The Crucial Decade and After* (New York, 1960), p. 266.

11. Wittner, *Cold War*, p. 120.

12. Seldes, *The Public Arts*, p. 208; Packard, *Hidden*, pp. 14–16, 114; Wittner, *Cold War*, pp. 120–22.

13. Shayon, *Television*, pp. 76–77, noted that as early as 1949 there existed citizen viewer groups already toting up statistics about TV violence.

14. Mehling, *Time-Killer*, pp. 144–55.

15. See Ernest Becker, *The Revolution in Psychiatry* (Glencoe, Ill., 1964), p. 57.

16. "In His Own Words," *People*, June 16, 1975, pp. 58–61, interview with Dr. Victor Cline, professor of psychology at the University of Utah; Key, *Subliminal*, p. 67, also contains important remarks on the educational nature of TV violence, as does Cline's anthology *Where Do You Draw the Line?* (Provo, Utah, 1973). Key speaks about the many studies of media violence and, too, on social techniques which "have been designed to maintain the system, not change it. If more money could be made by advertisers through the elimination of violence from TV as has been made by including it, a direct causal relationship would have been established years ago. It is entirely possible that both educational and governmental institutions . . . are victims of their own perceptual defenses."

17. "You Bet Your Life" is still rerun in some locations, often under the title "The Best of Groucho." While there are many brilliant moments on the show, it does much to dispel the view of Groucho as the eternally witty and sharp culture hero.

18. Arthur Shulman and Roger Youman, *How Sweet It Was* (New York, 1966), pp. 339–44; Jeff Greenfield, *No Peace No Place* (Garden City, 1973), pp. 127–28. Greenfield pointed out that, during the height of the sob-story shows, the Traveler's Aid Society found five cases daily of destitute families coming to New York, hoping only to appear on "Strike It Rich" to finance some desperately needed operation or massive illness.

19. Shulman and Youman, *Sweet*, pp. 341, 344, 346.

20. Mehling, *Time-Killer*, pp. 38–45.

21. Wakefield in *Nation*, March 30, 1957.

22. *Nation*, October 17, 1959, p. 223. Properly speaking, many TV quiz shows are still fixed. The difference is that, nowadays, a disclaimer (announcing

contestants were earlier informed of the answers) is briefly flashed in the final credits.

23. A. J. Liebling commented extensively on not-reporting in his *New Yorker* columns, anthologized in *The Press* (New York, 1961).

24. Seldes, *The Great Audience* (New York, 1950), p. 207.

25. Most usually, of course, the New Left was victim rather than beneficiary of such bias. Harlan Ellison, in *The Glass Teat,* told about TV camera operators at the 1968 Democratic Convention in Chicago. They avoided filming any demonstrators who looked like mainstream Americans, dressed in, say, suits or dresses and high-heeled shoes. Instead, the cameras focused on the most outrageously dressed young.

Juxtaposition was also an excellent discrediting technique. One simply reported on some very bizarre or absurd event, then promptly followed up by reporting on a serious political speech or protest. The context of ridicule in itself would effectively condemn the latter event. One very excellent example occurred on the June 23, 1975, "Today Show" (NBC). Reports on Sara Jane Moore, Lynette Fromme, and Patty Hearst were given in rapid succession. The effect was marvelous, calling up specters of Manson, witchcraft, too-aggressive women, assassins, FBI error, kidnaping, insanity, and finally and fully deriding the left.

26. Halberstam, "CBS," pp. 48, 52, 67–69.

27. Edward R. Murrow and Fred W. Friendly, *See It Now* (New York, 1955), pp. 31–42, 55–67.

28. Wittner, *Cold War,* p. 121. In 1960, Nixon had refused the advice of his TV consultant. When he appeared for the first debate he was recuperating from a wearing illness and looked it. Arriving at the studio, he also smashed a previously injured knee, making him look even more ill.

29. Shulman and Youman, *Sweet,* p. 309.

30. Ibid., p. 104.

31. Ibid., pp. 94, 104, 202, 119, 165, 190, 212.

32. "The Burns and Allen Show" is being rerun in some areas. It has survived surprisingly well, exhibiting far more charm than its contemporaries. All the comedies referred to in these and other paragraphs are briefly described by Shulman and Youman in *Sweet.*

33. Joseph N. Morse, ed., *The Unicorn Book of 1952* (New York, 1952), p. 376. Also see Seldes, *Public,* p. 225. Ball had once registered as a communist, to please her eccentric grandfather. When this was uncovered, long after her show's tremendous success began, it started a scandal. But the network staunchly refused to fire her. Seldes commented that their refusal "shows that, no matter how obscure a person may be, no matter how few millions are invested in him or her, America gives fair play to all. And, as Anatole France pointed out, the law in its sublime majesty forbids the rich as well as the poor to sleep under bridges."

"I Love Lucy" has never really gone off the air. In 1966, both CBS and NBC were broadcasting the Senate Foreign Relations Committee Vietnam hearings. CBS dropped the hearings when George Kennan, the first dove witness, testified. In its stead the network aired a fifth rerun of "I Love Lucy." Fred Friendly resigned in protest, and went on to write *Due to Circumstances Beyond*

Our Control (New York, 1967). In Spring 1976, "Lucy" cropped up again, being nostalgically parodied on NBC's "Saturday Night Live."

34. Museum of Modern Art Film Library, *Television U.S.A.: 13 Seasons* (Garden City, 1962), is the booklet about that 1962 exhibition, a retrospective of the best of TV since 1948. For the most part it cited individual high-quality productions of documentaries and drama. A very few individual episodes of series were cited, among them the May 24, 1952, "Your Show of Shows," the January 19, 1957, "Ernie Kovacs Show," the August 27, 1959, "Kukla, Fran and Ollie." The retrospective illuminated the major problems of approaching TV as art, a problem similar to that of critically approaching pornography or science fiction: the quality of the whole is so much lower than in most art forms, so that "quality" is rarer or itself inferior.

35. Greenfield, *No Peace,* pp. 133–34; Shulman and Youman, *Sweet,* pp. 356, 359.

36. Seldes, *Public,* pp. 231–32.

37. Ibid., pp. 261–62.

38. *Michigan State News,* Welcome Week edition, week of September 22, 1975; also that paper on October 6, 1975, reported national drops in SAT and ACT verbal and math scores. That article, however, attributed these drops to school and teaching failures, a somewhat naive assessment. Also see Keys, *Subliminal,* p. 71.

39. Becker, *Revolution,* pp. 57, 150; Lyons quoted by Kronenberger, *Company,* p. 79.

14

Beyond Alienation: Fiction in the Fifties

In 1951, *Time* magazine dismissed a new novel as unworthy of the reader's attention. The book, *Time* sneered, was just "one more recruit for the dread-despair-and-decay camp of American letters."[1]

Time was reviewing William Styron's novel, *Lie Down in Darkness,* which culminated with the suicide of Peyton Loftis. The theme of "dread-despair-decay" was not limited solely to this remarkable, angry book. In various forms, it occurred in most of the major novels of the fifties. More usually, however, it was called by a simpler name. It was alienation.

"When Edmund Wilson says that after reading *Life* magazine he feels that he does not belong to the country depicted there, that he does not live in that country, I think I understand what he means," Philip Roth said in a 1961 *Commentary* essay on American writing.[2] The sense of estrangement from one's world that Wilson and Roth felt was not, of course, limited only to writers in the fifties. If anything, it was gradually becoming a commonplace of the age. However, the spread of alienation through American culture was widely ignored. Perhaps the chief factor discouraging its recognition was the consensus fantasy of American culture. It was not a healthy, American act to talk about chaotic concepts like alienation. It was an admission that things were not the simple, pretty picture the fifties imagined. And this dodge points to the other major fifties syndrome: abdication. If alienation was a common fact of life, the main reason it was not acknowledged as such was due to the mass refusal to see. People chose not to think about the frightening, the threatening, the things they did which were inconsistent with their fantasy view of the world. Thus they chose not to act. They abdicated their responsibilities.

This produced a unique difficulty for novelists. "The American writer in the middle of the twentieth century," Roth said in *Commentary,* "has his hands full in trying to understand, and then describe, and then make *credible* much of the American reality. It stupefies, it sickens, it infuriates, and finally it is even a kind of embarrassment to one's own meager imagination."[3] Roth's comment may explain some of the depths of despair plumbed by fifties novelists. Suicide, betrayal, insanity, murder, rape were typical story devices. The grim ending (rather than the happy one of romance fiction or even the upbeat ending of thirties social-protest literature) came to be expected. It was as typical of the fifties form as was the extreme individualism each work possessed. Still, one of the most striking things about fifties fiction was that it discussed alienation at all. That this was the major theme of the decade's writing was proof of the main culture's failure to reach totalitarian proportions. Not everyone was hypnotized.

The fifties novels of alienation share a number of common traits. The tragic ending, or at least the ending that is disquieting and falsely happy, is one of the most significant of these. Two of Saul Bellow's novels provide a case. *Seize the Day* (1956) ends with the total collapse of loser Tommy Wilhelm. *Henderson the Rain King* (1959) has an ostensibly happy ending. Henderson appears to have found himself, and returns to America. But Bellow's conclusion contradicts this optimism. When Henderson tries to telephone his wife, the connection is too poor for her to understand him. On the plane, he meets a little boy who speaks only Persian. Waiting for the plane to refuel at Gander, he slides on the airfield ice, holding the child, in silent celebration. He rejoices in his frozen solitude. That is, any triumph Henderson might have found was meaningless. He was isolated from the world.[4]

Irving Howe has said of the fifties novels of alienation that they were highly asocial, almost totally subjective. There was little or no sense of an objective society providing any context. "The object perceived," Howe said, "seems always on the verge of being swallowed up by the perceiving agent, and the act of perception in danger of being exalted to the substance of reality." This repeatedly occurs in the great novels of the fifties. *Henderson* again provides the example. Gene Henderson feels himself confusingly estranged from his world. His brain obsessively repeats a mysterious message to him: "I want," it says. "I want, I want." Seeking to assuage his hunger and estrangement, to find meaning in his life, Henderson takes an African safari. But this Africa is so reduced to a journey through the white, male, Western psyche that it becomes no more than a dreamland. It is peopled by characters and events from a racist, machismo past: dusky loyal manservants, sexy sorceresses, philosopher-kings, tests of manhood involving lions, white men being acclaimed god, savior, rain king. Reality is swallowed.[5]

In the novels of this type, Howe continued, the world was depicted as "an apocalyptic cul-de-sac." Secular and technological progress was questioned. Human beliefs and purposes vanished. "Only the self" mattered and was worth saving. The protagonist, and only the protagonist, was the conscience of the typical fifties novel. Styron's *Lie Down in Darkness* allows its central character, Peyton Loftis, to mold much of the book's perception. But Styron put other people's perceptions in *Darkness* too. And he used Peyton, her brilliancy, beauty, and eventual insanity, to judge what he saw as American society's great failure. "They lost us," Peyton said of her parents and her parents' generation. In their shallow affluence the older generation of *Darkness* created a hollow, sterile, meaningless world. Even its most precious relics were absurd—for instance, the golf balls enshrined in the country club museum. In bemoaning the shallow materialism, the estrangement, even the violence of his culture (Peyton kills herself on Nagasaki day), Styron went beyond the usual strictures of the alienated novel. Of course, he fell into certain cultural traps. Peyton, for instance, is basically a stereotype of mid-century attitudes toward intelligent women. She is the brilliant female doomed by her intelligence, driven crazy simply because she is smart. But even so, her character is not the sole boundary of *Darkness*. Through Peyton, Styron created an apocalyptic vision of American society. It predicted only death, horror, and foreboding.[6]

Later fifties novels would exaggerate that sense of prophetic doom while rendering out any social themes. Saul Bellow's 1956 work *Seize the Day* is perhaps the quintessential fifties novel in this respect. The entire world of *Seize the Day* is simply that of Tommy Wilhelm, the perpetual failure. Tommy is alone, drifting, never able to seize the day and succeed, as he so desperately wishes to do. Everything goes wrong in his world: his rich, lucky father despises him; he has lost his job; he has left a rocky marriage for a mistress who no longer wants him; he is the victim of a stock market con that takes his last cash reserves. Nor is there any hope for salvation. In Tommy's world, people are virtual proof of Brownian movement. They are random atoms rendered human by greed. Sympathy, kindness, even love or definable personal philosophies do not exist. Repeatedly Bellow makes it clear that all the agonies of the book are being felt by one man alone. The plot, in a way, is a record of his coming to accept his solitary destruction. In the end, we see Tommy blundering into the funeral of a total stranger. He begins to weep, then surrenders to mourning—not for the stranger but for himself. And thus Tommy reaches the consummation of "his heart's ultimate need."[7]

The novel of alienation took such an utterly solipsistic, extreme form in the fifties for several reasons. Novels of alienation have been integral to American fiction since the late 1800s. But the mid-twentieth century pressure against criticizing society (while pronouncing America a land of, among other things, free speech) created a special tension. True, several important critical works on the American character emerged in the fifties. William Whyte's *Organization Man* and the writings of David Riesman are examples. But most of these studies, even while very cogently examining trends in culture, would ultimately surrender to them. In *Organization Man,* for instance, Whyte deplored the spread of corporate bureaucracy. But his answer to this gigantic problem was pathetically tiny. Deceive the system in little ways, he suggested, and he showed how to cheat on personnel exams. Whyte was responding in much the same way the solipsistic novelist responded to one great cultural pressure of the fifties: that against dissent. To criticize society *and* offer possible alternatives to it was to express dangerous ideology, hence to be immature, old-fashioned, and counterproductive. Naturally, critical dissent did exist in the fifties. But it was simply far more difficult to phrase (than, say, in the thirties or sixties); it was suppressed and attacked when it appeared; and most of all even its formation was tempered by a foreknowledge of such attacks. Instead, the apolitical, asocial, apathetic was encouraged.

Yet the novel has always been a didactic medium. Its form demands the drawing of broad social observations and moral conclusions. This was a very different imperative from the asocial pretense of the times. The two demands met, clashed, and eventually gave birth to the subjective novel. Considering the era's quasipolitical imperatives, much of fifties fiction had no choice. It had to become so subjective as to approach claustrophobia. This was many authors' only means of reconciling their need to write with the culture's need to deflect attack. Whyte, in *Organization Man,* had done no more than show the individual how to manage just for himself. In the subjective novel, only "a salvation by, of and for the self," as Howe wrote, came to matter. The fifties novel of subjectivity, by telling the inturned tale of one person, forestalled any possibility that the protagonist's sufferings and triumphs bore wider social meaning. No broad social demands were to be inferred. If any general moral wrong or cultural ill had been represented, it was just by accident.

This was a rather ironic result. After all, as the opening quote from *Time* demonstrated, to write at all about human alienation in America was to rouse mainstream ire. But the writer, in his arguments about alienation, tended to suppress the other central problem of the age: abdication. In a sense, the extremes of the fifties alienated novel forbade abdication from being treated. This was in itself an abdication. When Bellow or Salinger wrote about drifting individuals going to meet their doom, they sealed up the American sense of helplessness. They did not really prick consciences, or indicate the possibility of a way out of the mess.

There were exceptions to this abdication. Norman Mailer produced socially aware works throughout the fifties. His first novel of the decade, *Barbary Shore* (1951), bore a message of socialist hope and struggle. Unfortunately it was an elephantine, clumsy work. Then there was the furious *The Deer Park,* a Hollywood novel full of corrupted males and corrupting females. The only remotely decent men in *Deer Park* are the narrator, Sergius O'Shaughnessy, and the writer Charles Eitel. The writer has been summoned by a congressional anticommunist committee, and must decide whether to betray those around him. Finally Eitel talks, proving his own corruption; the narrator decides to save himself by leaving town. But even the angriest moments in *The Deer Park*, even its greatest criticisms of this rotten world, are lessened. Mailer himself described the book as simply a tale of a small, closed society rather than the larger surrounding one. His final book of the decade, *Advertisements for Myself* (1959), including the romantic, lying "White Negro", seems to embrace solipsism even in its title.[8]

Another novel which also dealt with the problem of abdication was Ralph Ellison's *Invisible Man* (1952). Oddly enough, at the time of its publication this book was regarded as just one more novel of alienation. Actually, Ellison's was one of the few social novels of the fifties, and the best of these few. One can see, though, how the novel was so misunderstood at first: the general ignorance about American racism, coupled with the novel's bizarre conclusion, could produce this effect. As we wrote in "Three-Fifths of a Person," the final meaning of the narrator's hermit existence was not really an expression of abdication. Ellison's protagonist might be alienated from white America, but he was not running away from it forever; he meant to struggle eventually.[9]

Retrospectively, some of the most interesting fiction of the fifties was written by J. D. Salinger. By 1960, this author was actually considered the major young American writer. He has published relatively few works, most of these in the latter fifties and early sixties; his only novel, *Catcher in the Rye*, appeared in 1956. Salinger's small, highly refined stories were extremely popular. He particularly enjoyed a following among educated youth. Salinger was one of the two fifties novelists to speak directly to the young's disaffection. (The other was Kerouac.) What, then, was his particular message? Why did he so impress the young?

Salinger's protagonists were all young people themselves. They were adolescents at the youngest; in their twenties at the latest. And inevitably they were sensitive, often spiritual souls trapped in a vulgar world. Holden Caulfield, in *Catcher*, is literally nauseated by the physicality of his universe. Sounds, smells, appearances assault and sicken him. Franny Glass, like Holden, is so shocked by the shallowness and phoniness of her world that, in *Franny and Zooey*, she finally suffers a complete nervous collapse in a restaurant. And her brother Seymour feels even more invaded by life. In "A Perfect Day for Bananafish," he commits suicide before his insensitive sleeping bride.[10]

But these are not just stories about the barbarisms of American culture. They are, in their own introspective ways, stories that pander to certain snobbish feelings in the reader. First, the characters exist in a banal America controlled by the insensitive and the crude. The drunks, boors, and phonies of Holden Caulfield's world are all simplistic but typical characters. Salinger made it very easy for the reader to concur in sneering at this vulgar, repulsive society. Simultaneously he flatters his audience; he pretends both reader and protagonist share an intelligence, sensitivity, and savvy far superior to that of the common folk. This appears only covertly. When Salinger comes close to facing such arrogant feelings, he quickly denies them, as when Seymour tells Franny she really loves that disgusting common personage the Fat Lady. If anything, one is left with a sense of noblesse oblige: these regular people are repulsive, stupid, and greedy, but we must love them to feel more pure.

In the character of Holden Caulfield, Salinger captured the suffering of every awkward adolescent in a hypocritical, repressive society. Yet Salinger, rather like the writers of soap operas, could not resist using this suffering simply as manipulation. The housewife was exploited by the soap opera without ever having her insularity challenged. Much the same was true of Salinger's manipulations of his readers through his characters' sufferings. Salinger did not seek to disarm or discharge misery, but rather to heighten it. Such suffering, in Holden and in the Glass children, was proof of their illness but also of their superior discernment. Nor did Salinger want them to wrest themselves out of their declines. Anything hopeful he granted them, even religion, worked out to be hollow and useless. True, religious aspects permeate many of his works. But actually, these are not so much examples of religion as of religiosity. In spite of Franny's Jesus chanting and Seymour's Zen quotations, the Glass kids have no thorough commitment to faith. They are echoes of Norman Vincent Peale and Dwight D. Eisenhower—simply fans of faith. While Holden Caulfield is not so much a Zen dilettante as are the Glass kids, he also inclines toward the vague pseudo-solution. He longs to be the catcher in the rye, the man who saves little children in the rye field before they plummet over the perilous fantasy cliff. If anything, the final message of a Salinger novel was the hopelessness of being happy and peaceful in this vulgar world. There is an obvious echo in Salinger of the ideas of American intellectuals in the fifties. Then, intellectuals expressed two contradictory notions. They at once praised American democracy and despised its popular culture. This type of thinking is resolved, in Salinger, by creating lovely, refined characters who are alienated from material crassness, and so are all doomed. Crucially, like the intellectuals of the fifties, Salinger denied his characters any chance of alternative fates. That is, he mourned alienation but depended on it. We are doomed by popular culture, but at least on the way down we can be charming, eclectic, witty, rich, and superior.

Perhaps it would not have been so hard for these writers to go beyond simple alienation (that is, to lead people to a new attitude toward their alienation) were it not for the outlook of the intellectual establishment. During the fifties, the academic and intellectual communities of America did make obeisance to a powerful literary establishment. Naturally its power was not total. It dominated the universities and the three major literary journals of the day—the *Hudson*, *Kenyon*, and *Partisan* reviews. The leaders of this establishment possessed tremendous clout in their limited sphere. Theirs was a coterie that had not truly existed before the fifties and would dissolve in the early sixties. But while it lived, its members dominated literary criticism—to the point where, as several commentators have observed, the writing of criticism and the critics' reaction surpassed the importance of the writing of fiction. Mailer, after publishing *The Deer Park* in 1957, agonized in the pages of *Esquire* about the way critics treated him. His reaction differed from other writers' only in its public visibility. Usually, literary historians have concentrated on the effect the literary coterie had on poetry. They overlook the less precise effect on the novel and on literature in general. Perhaps Mailer's reaction and the decline of the social novel should give the strongest clues. That is, not only did mass culture as a whole tend to support the novel of alienation, but the literary establishment expected a novel to express this idea. The social novel, critics insisted, had passed away. When a genuinely social novel appeared, it was ignored or misinterpreted.[11]

It was scarcely surprising that the critical establishment should misunderstand the emergence of a literary movement that was alienated but refused to abdicate social criticism. The Beats were the first socially aware artistic movement to emerge in the fifties.

Other novelists had attempted social themes, but they acted alone, like Ellison, or failed to unify their thematic approach, like Styron or Mailer. Yet the rise of the Beats, who comprised just one part of the avant-garde movement in Western society, did not intrigue members of the establishment as much as it infuriated them.

Initially, this was because these critics had been celebrating the death of the avant garde throughout the fifties. "The jobless, wandering artist is almost extinct," William Phillips wrote in a 1952 *Partisan Review* article about "the death of bohemianism." "The most serious artists are now concerned with sales, markets, publicity, and public response." Kenneth Rexroth, one of the Beat "elder statesmen," also described this outlook late in the decade: "This is a world in which over every door is written the slogan: 'The generation of experiment and revolt is over. Bohemia died in the twenties. There are no more little magazines.'" Actually, as Rexroth noted, more little magazines existed than ever before. Experiment and revolt were just beginning.[12]

Only partly did this revolt take the form of literature. Not all the Beats were writers, and most of the writers were poets or essayists. Those who did write, too, had great difficulties finding conventional publishers. Poet Lawrence Ferlinghetti, who also ran the City Lights Bookstore in San Francisco, eventually organized the City Lights publishing company to release experimental works. The first book he published was Allen Ginsberg's *Howl* (1956). In 1957, the little magazine that would prove the most enduring of the avant-garde periodicals, *Evergreen Review,* first appeared. The early issues of the review, read today, are virtually a compendium of the major avant-garde talents of recent times: Samuel Beckett, Henry Miller, Michael McClure, Gary Snyder, Jack Kerouac, William Burroughs, all appear in its pages.[13]

But such things would have had little national significance were it not for the San Francisco police. In 1956 they descended on Ferlinghetti's City Lights Bookstore and confiscated three publications as obscene. One of these was *Howl.* America has always been fascinated by its obscenity trials, focusing on them a blend of prurient titillation and genuine thoughtfulness. The *Howl* trial was no exception. The American Civil Liberties Union defended Ferlinghetti's publications. Lawyer for the defense was Jake "Never Plead Guilty" Ehrlich. In a landmark legal decision, *Howl* was ultimately vindicated. The most direct results of the trial were two: Jack

Kerouac, who was praised in *Howl's* dedication, finally found a publisher for the long-completed *On the Road;* and America discovered that it did, after all, harbor a genuine bunch of literary bohemians.[14]

The Beat writers are difficult to characterize as a literary group. They produced few major works, and only one truly enduring piece. Too, they were but one part of the avant-garde literary renaissance then beginning in Western society. The cultural effects of the Beat revolt, more than (but because of) its literary impact, eventually did affect American civilization. One of the main currents of the counterculture derived from the Beats. Yet this statement does not exclude two important factors. It does not deny the impact of the Beats on literature, nor does it contradict the fact that Beat ideas were very much drawn from the American mainstream, and that the revolt would have been nothing if not for those currents.

The Beats, and such literary fellow travelers as the Black Mountain poets, shared a unity of purpose. They all wished to restore literature and the arts to the people, to bring literature back from its dull sleep of obscure academic poems and alienated, apathy-inducing novels. Many of the most important Beat works themselves reflect a deep alienation from American society: *Howl's* denunciations of materialism and sexual repression, and the scorn for the middle class in *On the Road*, are only two instances. The romantic fascination with criminality that permeated much of Beat life also was a sign of its estrangement. But these were not simply statements of alienation. The Beats went beyond alienation to emphasize the need for a new American community. They tried to burst through (rather than simply reflect) a world of deadening politics, sexual hypocrisy, TV-induced numbness. As Allen Ginsberg would later put it, the Beat movement meant "the return to nature and the revolt against the machine. . . . It's either that or take that mass-produced self they keep trying to shove down your throat."[15]

Just as the public became very rapidly aware of the Beats in the latter fifties, the literary establishment very quickly developed a deep animosity toward this movement. This establishment already tended to favor the more solipsistic writers of alienation. Thus, covertly, they encouraged political and social apathy that favored right-wing politics. To those in literary power, an actual bohemian movement was enough of an affront. It contradicted the many announcements that the avant garde was extinct. But there was much more, beyond simply literary topics, that mattered here. The growth of a movement of writers who hinted at the possibility of challenging the American status quo, and who won terrific popularity when they said so, threatened the monolithic status and power of the literary establishment. The way this establishment approached the Beats finally became almost as important to later historical events as did the simple rise of the Beats alone. Examining the academics' attitude toward them becomes vital to any perspective of the fifties and of more recent years.

Both the tactics and attitudes of those intellectuals who organized against the Beats reflect basic fifties concepts. Very rarely did these critics examine Beat writings in their attacks. Nor did they deeply analyze the ideas expressed therein. Primarily, the method used to discredit the Beats was McCarthyist. In this sense, the reaction of the intellectuals against the Beats was just an analog to their early-fifties selling out to the anti-liberal reaction. Gene Baro, reviewing Lawrence Lipton's *The Holy Barbarians* (a 1959 explication of the Beat way of life), wrote that the book supported "promiscuous individual freedom at the expense of social regularity." James Wechsler labeled Jack Kerouac's writings "vulgar ramblings on a latrine wall." Norman Podhoretz reacted in perhaps the most extreme manner of all. "We are witnessing a revolt of all the forces hostile to civilization itself," he charged in an *Esquire* article. The Beats, he said, comprised "a movement of brute stupidity and know-nothingism that is trying to take over the country."[16]

One of the most interesting of the innumerable intellectuals' articles on the Beat menace is Diana Trilling's 1958 essay "The Other Night at Columbia." Ostensibly, this was a review of a Beat poetry reading. "For me," Trilling wrote, "it was of some note that the audience smelled fresh. I took one look at the crowd and was certain that it would smell bad. But I was mistaken. These people may think they're dirty inside and dress up to it." She also mentioned that Kerouac had been "clean" during an earlier event at Hunter College: "I've enquired about that." This may seem to be a lot of space expended discussing body odors, particularly in a poetry review. But that description demands revision. "The Other Night" is not a poetry review. It is, rather, very much what Trilling subtitled it: "A Report from the Academy." That is, hers was intended as the official intellectuals' overview of both this event and of the Beat phenomenon in an historical period when there was a literary establishment with official overviews. Because of this, Trilling did not have to waste her time actually considering the literature involved. Following the *Partisan Review* example, she merely issued pronouncements. Thus, much of "The Other Night" consists of superficial comments organized into a paternalistic and arrogant context. The audience is "children." The poets are too emotional. The girls are not pretty. The boys are pretty, and gay, and Trilling does not like the way anyone dresses. What she and her fellow thinkers wrote of the Beats was perhaps best summed up in a separate article by Norman Podhoretz. Podhoretz, who was the same age as many of the major Beats, felt that "what juvenile delinquency is to life, the San Francisco writers are to literature." He added that the Beat generation was a "conspiracy" to replace civilization with "the world of the adolescent street gangs."[17]

It was not surprising, given such a totally hostile intellectual response, that the mass media came to parrot these scornful words. The reasons for the mass media's attack on the Beats paralleled those of the literary establishment. Diana Trilling, in "The Other Night," had denied the Beats posed any "genuine, dangerous protest." But the nature of her article, and, even more crucially, the emotional violence expressed by such critics as Podhoretz and Gene Baro, contradicted that assessment. The Beats made the establishment afraid because they were a genuine bunch of dissenters; they were humanitarian, attractively hedonistic, very vaguely left wing, and, most of all, popular. That gave them a dangerous power. That is why virtually every established commentator overreacted so strongly against the Beats. The mass media, since it served the mainstream, had slightly different attitudes toward the Beat revolt than did the literary establishment. But their motivation was the same: a perceived need to smash this appealing movement by belittling it.

The innumerable articles such publications as *Time*, *Life*, and *Look* printed on the Beat Generation inevitably referred to the public's fascination with these figures. That fascination was also reflected in the many ways kids imitated Beats—in the proliferation of coffeehouses, poetry readings, jazz listening, and hip slang late in the decade. These were seemingly superficial things. But they were the most visible part of the disaffection young Americans were channeling in new directions. This disaffection, of course, had been reflected already by most of the modern novelists of alienation. But in the late fifties some few people understood it was time to do more than be cynical and disaffected. The Beats were among these people, and they were the first in the postwar years to use literature as one of their tools. They attracted so many young people because, through the mass media, they flamboyantly spoke of the possibilities of choice and change. Such ideas repelled the conservative forces in America, which needed abdication, acquiescence, or at least apathy to survive. Attacking the Beats was first of all a recognition that this statistically tiny group disproportionately countered such acquiescence.

A 1959 *Life* article entitled "The Only Rebellion Around" typifies such media attacks. Many of the comments made by its author, Paul O'Neil, are no more than the words of Trilling, or Podhoretz, simplified and fluffed up for the masses. "The wide public belief that Beats are simply dirty people in sandals is only a small but repellent part of the truth," O'Neil wrote. Their philosophy, he continued, was created solely to "offend the whole population." The reporter then described the three classes of people who became Beats: first, the "sick little bums"; second, the amateur or weekend Beats; and finally the "hostile little females." Many Beats were black or befriended blacks. Some were political radicals. All were sexually promiscuous. Sixty per cent were barely emotionally stable.

All O'Neil's sociological and psychological terms may seem familiar. They should be. These were the same accusations marshaled against any underclass that suddenly became a potent threat. Throughout this book we have seen how similar terms were applied against every group failing to conform to the mainstream. How easy, in those years, to raise the specters of penis envy or mental disease, to drag racist or political red herrings across the trail. That way, the genuine questions did not have to be asked, much less answered. The issues were well fogged. This short cut was so tempting that *Life* totally departed from the factual in its major photo accompanying O'Neil's article. The photo illustrated the essentials of "uncomfortable living" Beat-style. It included the black-clad Beat "chick," the Charlie Parker record, the coal stove, Chianti bottle, bare mattress, orange crates, bongos, and the beer cans for the obligatory pitiful baby to play with. And this entire "'pad' or household" was 100 per cent false. Or, as *Life* put it, "recreated in studio using paid models."[18]

There was a degree of truth in the anti-Beat attacks. Many Beats were immature, superficial, silly people whose idea of rebellion might involve no more than weird dress and irresponsibility. But the movement also included patient, disciplined writers like Rexroth, scholars like Gary Snyder, and innumerable other admirable figures. That the mass media chose to focus on the most idiotic behaviors of the Beats has a double-edged significance: first, it is a sign of the beginning rebellion against the mainstream concept of manners; but also it reveals the way the media attempted to manipulate the American situation. At the same time *Life* was touting the Beat generation as "The Only Rebellion Around," a number of other rebel movements were rising throughout the culture. The New Left was forming at schools like Berkeley and the University of Wisconsin. The civil rights, pacifist, and ban-the-bomb movements too were increasing in size, strength, and articulation. But these groups posed a graver threat to the media in that they could not be so easily belittled. Their members were highly articulate. They had no oddities of mannerism. The answer was to ignore these groups and concentrate instead on the Beats. One can only wonder to what degree this publicizing of a seemingly crazy target shaped the counterculture.

The joined efforts of the intellectuals and the mass media gave cultural permission to other groups to act against this avant garde. For instance, in March 1959, *Big Table,* a Chicago little magazine printing lots of Beat literature, was impounded for obscenity by the postal service. The tactics used against *Big Table* were similar to those used against other controversial publications. Its editor, Paul Carroll, was not informed of the impounding for a month. An official ruling on the charge was delayed much longer. This constituted a deliberate economic blow. Without an official ruling, the ACLU (which agreed to help Carroll) could not appeal the censorship. Nor could *Big Table* be mailed to its subscribers. Even though a legal triumph for the magazine was inevitable, the long deliberate delays proved fatal. As a writer commented in the *Nation* later that year, "the magazine will have escaped conviction, but not the sentence."[19]

If those in authority learned anything in the fifties, it was the great extent to which they could invade and manipulate people's lives. The *Big Table* anecdote, in this context, was but one minor instance of the broad pattern of extralegal repression practiced in America. Many intellectuals did little or nothing to oppose this destructiveness. Often, their words invited, nearly begged for, such suppression. Once the Beats were identified as the criminals of literature, it was no big step to treating them like criminals. Most other rebels were treated as such in the fifties anyhow.

The attack of the literary establishment on these upstarts had only negative results in the long run. Certainly, it must have been comforting at the time to so luxuriously lash out at such unfamiliar weirdos. Assaults and sneers involved less mental and emotional effort than attempting to tolerate or understand. It might have seemed funny: academic thinkers across the country twitching aside from this quivering Beat contagion. It might have seemed funny, that is, but much more it was dangerous. In belittling the vitality of such writers as Kerouac, Corso, Burroughs, Ginsberg, and in scorning their popularity among the young, the intellectuals helped create the gross chasm of later years between culture and counterculture. Such intellectual leaders chose not to understand what was going on in their own country. They chose not to mediate between mainstream and underground, but instead chose to lead the way in vilifying this new group of thinkers—this uprushing movement of a different sort of intellectual. In their unfortunate repetition of the McCarthy era's behavior, these people helped declare the terms of the sixties war of opposites. That is one of the great failures, the great tragedies of the fifties intellectuals. Having bowed to McCarthy early in the decade, they compounded their cowardice late in it. Many of the people we have been discussing were and remain among the most influential thinkers in America, despite the disintegration of the fifties literary establishment. These people helped set back the humanistic struggle in this country at least a decade, if not more, by their stubborn refusal. Beats, then hippies, New Leftists, and all that became the counterculture and the humanitarian movements of later years did not have to be perceived as vicious threats, nor as the enemy. That they were can be at least partially attributed to the failure of established thinkers to take an active critical role in society. Their error licensed every sort of mainstream intolerance.

Despite such intolerance, the anxieties of the fifties could only continue to grow into the righteous affirmation of the sixties. Literature before the Beats proved inadequate in that most basic artistic task: confronting, explaining, even transforming its world. The Beat avant-garde influence in the latter fifties was one of several forces necessary to reshape the popular consciousness. Unquestionably it aided in the renewal of spirit, temper, and intellect that would mark the next decade. This renewal in the profoundest way grew from the mainstream's social failures. As Gregory Corso wrote, "You may think unwell of us, but we are your natural children."[20]

By 1960, the Beat phenomenon seemed to be dying down. Its literary phase had foreshadowed giant changes in the direction of modern literature that have since occurred: the renaissance in poetry and the changing focus of prose. That literary change, in America, might be best characterized by the novels of John Barth. In the late fifties, he published two small novels of alienation, *The Floating Opera* and *End of the Road.* Then Barth departed completely from this type of novel with the great mythic *Sot-Weed Factor,* followed by *Giles Goat Boy* and other fabulist works. In the early sixties, when *Sot-Weed Factor* first appeared, the mass media announced the Beat movement was dead and concentrated instead on the renaissance Kennedy would come to symbolize. Actually, though, many of the Beats had not become ineffective but were quietly working for future change. And even that had been predicted as early as 1952. That year, John Clellon Holmes published *Go,* the first of the Beat novels to appear in print. Holmes' protagonist, like many other fifties characters, mused at length about the emotional, spiritual home he lacked and so desperately needed. But in Holmes' book the search was not one of failure and death. Rather he anticipated a possible change. *Go* ends on a note of muted, predictive hope: "'Where is our home?' he thought, for he could not see it yet."[21]

NOTES

1. *Time,* September 19, 1951, p. 83.
2. Philip Roth, "Writing American Fiction," *Commentary,* March 1961, p. 224.
3. Ibid., pp. 223–33.
4. Saul Bellow, *Henderson the Rain King* (New York, 1959).
5. Howe is quoted by John Leonard, "Confessions of a Cultural Commissar," *Esquire,* November 1975, p. 82.
6. William Styron, *Lie Down in Darkness* (New York, 1951); David L. Stevenson, "William Styron and the Fiction of the Fifties," anthologized in Joseph Waldmeir, ed., *Recent American Fiction* (Boston, 1963), pp. 265–71;

see also Paul Goodman, *Growing Up Absurd* (New York, 1960), for one way the general sense of alienation was absorbed into a new social philosophy.

7. Saul Bellow, *Seize the Day* (New York, 1956).

8. Norman Mailer, *Barbary Shore* (New York, 1951); *The Deer Park* (New York, 1955); and *Advertisements for Myself* (New York, 1959). The latter includes the essay "The White Negro," one of the most famous essays of the fifties. The piece concerned the hipster, that phenomenon of male city life compared by Mailer to the heroic pioneers, tough cowboys, and sensual blacks. Unfortunately the core of "The White Negro" is a falsehood. Mailer left out the central characteristic of the hipsters he idealized: they lived their tough daring night lives not in romantic spirit but in drug addiction.

9. Ralph Ellison, *Invisible Man* (New York, 1952). See also our chapter "Three-Fifths of a Person."

10. Salinger, *Catcher in the Rye* (New York, 1956).

11. Roth, "Writing," p. 233; Bruce Cook, *The Beat Generation* (New York, 1971), although often rather vague, is one of the major sources for those interested in the Beats and the fifties poetry scene. Other interesting sources are Allen Young's interview with Allen Ginsberg, published as the *Gay Sunshine Interview* (Bolinas, 1974), and Thomas F. Parkinson, ed., *Casebook on the Beat* (New York, 1961).

12. Rexroth is quoted in Gene Feldman and Max Gartenberg, eds., *The Beat Generation and the Angry Young Men* (New York, 1958), p. 334; William Phillips in "Our Country and Our Culture," *Partisan Review* XIX (Sept.–Oct. 1952), 586; see also Robert Graves, "The American Poet as Businessman," *Esquire,* October 1958, pp. 47–51.

13. Cook, *Beat,* pp. 151–52.

14. Parkinson, *Casebook.*

15. Cook, *Beat,* p. 104.

16. Gene Baro is quoted in the *Nation,* September 5, 1959, p. 115; James Wechsler, *Reflections of an Angry Middle-Aged Editor* (New York, 1960), pp. 1–18; Norman Podhoretz, "The Know-Nothing Bohemians," *Partisan Review,* Spring 1958, pp. 305–18.

17. Diana Trilling's essay is anthologized in her collection *Claremont Essays* (New York, 1964), pp. 154–63; Podhoretz, "Where is the Beat Generation Going?", *Esquire,* December 1958, pp. 147–50.

18. Paul O'Neil, "The Only Rebellion Around," *Life,* November 30, 1959, pp. 114–30; see also "Squaresville U.S.A. vs. Beatsville," in the September 21, 1959, *Life*—which includes several articles about Beats and regular folk. The genesis for these articles was the invitation some Hutchinson, Kansas, schoolgirls extended to Lawrence Lipton to visit their town. When he accepted, they hurriedly uninvited him. But the town reacted in terror, wondering if its youngsters might be incipient Beatniks. *Life* quoted a policeman: "A beatnik doesn't like work, any man that doesn't like work is a vagrant, and a vagrant goes to jail around here." The magazine also showed the Kansas kids trying out the garments of rebellion with no way to understand its substance. Clearly these kids felt a desperate need to escape their lives, a need *Life* refused to recognize. The only part of the article to penetrate the bland journalese was a comment by

an unnamed student: "I'd like to be one for a week. I'd like to do what I want to do and say what I want to say and have no worries, and know it wouldn't affect me in the future." The girls who invited Lipton were "whisked into seclusion by parents."

19. *Evergreen Review,* Spring 1959, p. 238, is an ad for *Big Table,* charging that the University of Chicago (its owner) had suppressed the Winter 1958 issue after the Autumn 1958 issue was attacked by a Chicago columnist as obscene. The University had ordered that the winter issue (to quote an administrator) "must contain nothing which would offend a sixteen-year-old girl."

20. Gregory Corso, "After Reading 'In the Clearing,'" in *Long Live Man* (Norfolk, Conn., 1962), p. 89.

21. John Clellon Holmes, *Go* (New York, 1952). Other works of interest include Jack Kerouac's novels, particularly *On the Road* (New York, 1957) and *The Dharma Bums* (New York, 1958); Ann Charter's excellent biography *Kerouac* (San Francisco, 1973).

Epilogue: Into the Sixties

America had been born of a dream: equality, liberty, the pursuit of happiness. Mid-twentieth-century Americans still paid homage to that dream. It was to be "the American Century." We would lead the free world and redeem the unfree.[1] Indeed, America emerged from the Second World War as *the* global power. To be sure, we saw the Soviet Union as an evil and nearly coequal power. But in reality, never since the days of the Roman Empire had world power been concentrated so completely. We had more powerful weaponry, more money, than anyone else. We had the chance 170 years of history had pointed to. What went wrong?

In each chapter we have ended up asking that question. It seems in retrospect not so much that the dream was betrayed. It was trivialized. Fear and prosperity combined to make us a mediocre people. We led by might, not idealism. We took pride in possessions, not achievements. We confused order with freedom, conformity with maturity, happiness with status, religion with "seven simple steps" to peace of mind and Dial-a-Prayer. The America of Lexington and Concord, Walden and Brook Farm had become the America of Detroit and Pittsburgh, Hollywood and Madison Avenue.

In 1950 the premier of Pakistan, Liaquat Ali Khan, said of our nation: "As I let myself ponder over this, I suddenly see the United States of America as an island—a fabulously prosperous island. And all around this island I see the unhealthy sea of misery, poverty, and squalor in which millions of human beings are trying to keep their heads above water. At such moments I fear for this great nation as one fears for a dear friend."[2] Few Americans saw so clearly.

Symbolic of the 1950s was a play, *The Flowering Peach,* written by Clifford Odets and produced on Broadway in 1954. Odets, whose best-known work *Waiting For Lefty* had epitomized the thirties theater of social protest, had, like most intellectuals, come to accept the established order. *The Flowering Peach* told the story of the aged Noah who at the conclusion of the play was forced to choose between living either with his radical or his rich son. He chose the latter. With him, he reflected, he would be "more comfortable."[3] In fifties America most of us were like Noah. We chose a seeming comfort. We ignored social ills.

Today's nostalgists paint the fifties picture in the soft pastels of that decade's tail-finned cars. Such a pink and baby blue portrait is both wrongheaded and dangerous. The sixties and seventies were not some sort of remarkable about-face, some magical transformation of the genial but "apathetic fifties." No, all the problems of recent years were present back then. Only the way we riveted our eyes on consensus made us not recognize them. Avoiding crucial issues, we aggravated them. Our own self-betrayals made the upheavals of later years inevitable.

Predicting the direction of change is always difficult, and few persons in the United States at fifties end foresaw either the excitements or crises that the near future had in store. It is true that the predictable mid-fifties (when the pin-striped Yankees inevitably won the World Series just as Ike was inevitably the Man of the Year) had given way to a less self-satisfied late fifties. Sputnik and Little Rock, Beatniks and delinquents had disturbed Americans. But to most people these seemed mere aberrations, bizarre flukes rather than portents of change. A speed-up of the growth rate of the GNP, a more flexible military establishment, and all would be well again. Or so it was believed.

Who could see the future: that the tiny civil rights and peace movements would grow so massively, that women would picket Miss America, that our creation of a puppet regime in South Vietnam would spark more than a decade of brutal Asian war, that college students would riot, that DDT was dangerous, that Presidents would be unmasked as crooks, that energy would be found to have limits, that a few disaffected Beats would give rise to hippies, yippies, freaks, and flower children, that rock and roll was here to stay?

Clark Kerr was representative of many establishment figures evaluating America at the end of the decade. In 1959, shortly after he had been installed as president of the University of California (one of the world's largest university systems), he said of students: "the employers are going to love this generation. . . . They are going to be easy to handle. There aren't going to be any riots."[4]

Even as Kerr spoke, his predictions were proving false. The times were (as Bob Dylan would soon tell us) a changin'. As early as 1958, some 10,000 black and white students had come to Washington to participate in a "Youth March for Integrated Schools"; a year later twice as many turned out to march for this cause. Racial inequality, nuclear testing, militarism, compulsory ROTC, and civil defense all stirred students to active protest in the last years of the fifties. In 1958 the student auxiliary of the National Committee for a Sane Nuclear Policy (Student SANE) was founded at Cornell University. The Student Peace Union began at the University of Chicago in 1959. That same year Wisconsin students started publishing the New Left journal *Studies on the Left.* The Cuban revolution, triumphing in 1959, also radicalized many young Americans, especially as the U. S. Government became increasingly hostile to the Castro regime.[5]

Nineteen sixty was a year of even greater change. A harbinger of what was to come occurred in January of that year when the Student League for Industrial Democracy, an offshoot of the old left League for Industrial Democracy, adopted a new name, Students for a Democratic Society. The creation of SDS was indicative of a growing moral outrage among the young, a resurgence of student activism. Such youthful commitment (though at first unconnected with SDS) gave rise to a massive sit-in movement. It all began on

February 1, when four black collegians sat down and ordered coffee at a white-only Woolworth lunch counter in Greensboro, North Carolina. Similar sit-ins followed and quickly captured national attention. Soon the tactics of non-violent direct action were being used to attack every form of public segregation, and these efforts were being coordinated by the newly formed Student Nonviolent Coordinating Committee (SNCC), which, along with SDS, would become a major focus for the emergent New Left student radicalism.[6]

In the spring of 1960, two additional protest issues attracted widespread publicity. Both capital punishment and the House Un-American Activities Committee came under student attack. On May 2, Caryl Chessman was executed in California. Originally sentenced to die in 1948, after being convicted of committing a number of non-murderous crimes, Chessman had for 12 years won a series of legal reprieves. During this prison period he had immersed himself in study, written a moving autobiography and numerous articles, letters, and appeals. Sympathy for him grew as his final death date neared. On the eve of his execution thousands of students from the San Francisco Bay region converged on San Quentin. For many people this highly publicized execution was a radicalizing experience.[7]

Less than two weeks after Chessman's death, on May 13, many of the same San Francisco and Berkeley students demonstrated against the House Un-American Activities Committee. At the time, HUAC was holding hearings on alleged communist activities in the Bay area. That day as student protestors gathered on the steps of San Francisco's City Hall where the hearings were being held, panicky police hosed and clubbed the passive students, claiming they were communist-inspired. But as Jessica Mitford noted in a report on the demonstrators in the *Nation*, these students had "gone far to shake the label of apathy and conformity that had stuck through the Fifties." In coming years, she predicted, such students would shape the world's future.[8]

That same May of the Chessman execution and the HUAC demonstrations, a less headlined event also heralded the changing future. On May 9, the U. S. Food and Drug Administration quietly announced approval of an oral contraceptive for women. The Pill would soon revolutionize relations between the sexes, freeing many women from the age-old fear of pregnancy.[9]

During this period, though not widely known at the time, Ralph Nader was investigating auto safety. Michael Harrington was uncovering poverty. Rachel Carson was amassing evidence on the deadly effects of pesticides. Betty Friedan was unveiling *The Feminine Mystique*.[10]

Finally, the election of John F. Kennedy, in November 1960, seemed to augment the already strong sense of change. Though Kennedy neither said nor did anything indicative of bold innovations, to many people, and especially the young, he exemplified a new public virtue and vigor. In this sense, even though he mouthed old political platitudes, he came to symbolize the end of complacency, the end of the fifties.[11]

With all this going on, some intellectuals did sense an ending, a break in the flow of history as the sixties began. Daniel Bell, for example, found "at the end of the fifties, a disconcerting caesura. In the West, among the intellectuals, the old passions are spent." But while Bell talked of the need for the youthful generation to seek "new purposes," he could not envision major change. "Social reform," he claimed, "does not have any unifying appeal, nor does it give a younger generation the outlet for 'self-expression' and 'self-definition.'" Utopianism was for him a deception. We had reached *The End of Ideology*. "The problem," he concluded, "is that the old politico-economic radicalism . . . has lost its meaning, while the stultifying aspects of contemporary culture (e.g., television) cannot be redressed in political terms."[12] Fifties complacency and consensus, in other words, would continue.

People like Daniel Bell spoke for a generation of American intellectuals who long since had moved from rebellion to "responsibility," from dissent to affirmation, from populism to pluralism, from radicalism to elitism, from social commitment to the ritual glorification of America. Pressured by past history, personal guilt, and world events, satisfied with domestic prosperity, the seeming success of the mixed economy and welfare state, these thinkers were ill prepared to deal with the nation's numerous and aggrandizing problems.[13]

Fortunately, however, there were intellectuals who took heart in the end of decade signs of youthful rebellion. In reviewing Bell's book, H. Stuart Hughes noted approvingly that "for the more imaginative and sensitive men and women under thirty, ideology and utopia are far from dead. They have suddenly and rather surprisingly come to life after ten blank years of slumber." C. Wright Mills in a prescient essay, "The New Left" (September 1960), also saw an emerging cultural radicalism, especially among students. "Let the old men ask sourly, 'Out of Apathy—into what?' The Age of Complacency is ending. Let the old women complain wisely about the 'end of ideology.' We are beginning to move again." Similarly, Paul Goodman concluded his immensely important *Growing Up Absurd* (1960) with the statement "that we of the previous generation who have been sickened and enraged to see earnest and honest effort and humane culture swamped by . . . muck, are heartened by the crazy young allies." He ventured to predict "that perhaps the future may make more sense than we dared hope."[14]

While not too many people in 1960 agreed with Hughes, Mills, and Goodman, these three proved to be a prophetic minority. Such thinkers and various youthful allies had begun a new search for the American dream. Rejecting the materialistic millennium of the fifties, they sought new alternatives to those the nation actually followed. They conceived of new goals besides those which were immediately visible. Their task would not be an easy one. But they realized that little positive would ever be accomplished if all possible objections had first to be overcome.

NOTES

1. Henry Luce in a 1941 *Life* editorial proclaimed this to be "The American Century." He extolled the United States as "the powerhouse of the ideals of Freedom and Justice." See Gilman M. Ostrander, *American Civilization in the First Machine Age* (New York, 1972), p. 361.

2. Premier Khan is quoted in Walter Johnson, *1600 Pennsylvania Avenue* (Boston, 1963), p. 266.

3. Harold Clurman, "The Frightened Fifties and Onward," in David Evanier and Stanley Silverzweig, eds., *The Nonconformers* (New York, 1961), pp. 119–24.

4. Kerr is quoted in William Manchester, *The Glory and the Dream* (Boston, 1974), p. 847.

5. Edward J. Bacciocco, Jr., *The New Left in America* (Stanford, 1974), pp. 1–24. C. Wright Mills, *Listen Yankee: The Revolution in Cuba* (New York, 1960) helped popularize the New Left view of the Cuban revolution.

6. Bacciocco, *New Left*, pp. 21–40; Kirkpatrick Sale, *SDS* (New York, 1973), pp. 15–34; Paul Jacobs and Saul Landau, *The New Radicals* (New York, 1966), pp. 3–41; Kenneth Rexroth, "Students Take Over," *New Left Review* (Sept.–Oct. 1960), pp. 38–41.

7. Bacciocco, *New Left*, pp. 24–26.

8. Mitford is quoted in Manchester, *Glory*, p. 849.

9. The Pill was Enovid. The story of FDA approval was carried on page 75 of the May 10, 1960, New York *Times*.

10. Nader, *Unsafe At Any Speed* (New York, 1965); Harrington, *The Other America* (New York, 1962); Carson, *The Silent Spring* (New York, 1962); Friedan, *The Feminine Mystique* (New York, 1963). All these influential books were begun in the late fifties.

11. I vividly remember attending a Kennedy campaign speech. In the fall of 1960, JFK came to Michigan State University where I was doing graduate work. To me and many of my friends this charismatic man played an important role in the growth of our political concern and awareness. Many of us would soon criticize Kennedy for not doing more to achieve equality and justice at home and for his aggressive policies in Cuba and Vietnam. Yet his influence on us was great and, I believe, positive.—DTM

12. Daniel Bell, *The End of Ideology: On the Exhaustion of Political Ideas in the Fifties* (New York, 1961 ed.), pp. 393–402.

13. C. Wright Mills wrote: "It is no exaggeration to say that since the end of World War II in . . . the United States smug conservatives, tired liberals and disillusioned radicals have carried on a weary discourse in which issues are blurred and potential debate muted; the sickness of complacency has prevailed, the bi-partisan banality flourished." Mills, "Letter to the New Left," *New Left Review* (Sept.–Oct. 1960), p. 18.

14. H. Stuart Hughes review of Daniel Bell, *The End of Ideology* in *Partisan Review*, 27 (Summer 1960), 564–68; Mills, "Letter to the New Left," p. 23; Paul Goodman, *Growing Up Absurd* (New York, 1960), p. 241.

CHRONOLOGY

1950

January 21: Alger Hiss is convicted of perjury in his second trial. The implications are that he spied for the Soviets during the thirties.

January 26: India becomes independent of Great Britain.

February 3: Klaus Fuchs is arrested in Britain as a Soviet spy. This leads to the arrest of Julius and Ethel Rosenberg, Morton Sobell, and Harry Gold in the United States.

February 9: McCarthy makes his "205 Communists" speech at Wheeling, West Virginia.

February 10: McCarthy, speaking in Utah, claims to have a list of "57 Communists" working in the government. The Red Scare, already in full swing by 1950, is given a single superstar around whom to rally.

March: Fuchs is convicted of espionage in Britain. McCarthy names Owen Lattimore as the top Soviet agent in America. Lattimore, though completely innocent, is never able to overcome suspicion against himself. Eventually he emigrates to Britain.

May: Senate hearings on organized crime begin and are televised nationally. These catapult Tennessee Senator Estes Kefauver to national fame. The hearings last into 1951.

June: Red Channels, the influential blacklist of entertainment people, is published.

June 5: The Supreme Court bans segregation in colleges and on railroad cars.

June 25: North Korea invades South Korea. Within days United Nations forces, dominated by American troops, join South Korea in the war.

July 3: William J. Levitt, the suburban developer, is pictured on the cover of *Time*. The suburban building boom is going full swing with 1.4 million new houses started in 1950 alone.

July 17: A Senate committee, headed by Maryland Democrat Millard Tydings, labels McCarthy "a fraud and a hoax." When Tydings comes up for re-election in November, he is defeated by a McCarthy candidate in a smear campaign.

August 27: Ezzard Charles defeats Joe Louis, thwarting the latter's comeback attempt to regain the heavyweight title.

September 18: Connie Mack, manager of the Philadelphia Athletics for 50 years, retires at age 87.

September 23: The McCarran Internal Security Act, a drastic anticommunist measure, passes.

November: Progressive educator Dr. Willard E. Goslin is fired as director of Pasadena schools.

November 1: Puerto Rican nationalist attempts to assassinate President Truman.

Truman gives the go-ahead for work on the hydrogen bomb.

Bomb-shelter plans become widely available for the first time. An official government pamphlet, *You Can Survive,* promises rather easy survival of atomic attack.

320 million pounds of potato chips and 750 million pounds of hot dogs are consumed in America. 4.4 million TVs are owned. More than 8 million automobiles are manufactured.

The CIA begins secretly funding the National Student Association.

David Riesman publishes *The Lonely Crowd* and Ray Bradbury publishes *The Martian Chronicles.* Best-selling books are Henry Morton Robinson, *The Cardinal* and *Betty Crocker's Picture Cook Book.* Lynn White, Jr., *Educating Our Daughters* is published, advocating separate, domestic training for college women. A right-wing pamphlet attacking progressive education, *How Red Is the Little Red Schoolhouse?*, also appears.

The Yankees win the World Series over the Phillies in four straight games.

United States Lawn Tennis Association singles champions: Arthur Larsen and Mrs. Margaret Osbourne.

The National Football Conference championship is won by the Cleveland Browns over the Los Angeles Rams 30 to 28.

The Academy Award for best picture goes to *All About Eve*. Other notable films include *Born Yesterday, Sunset Boulevard, Broken Arrow, Rio Grande,* and *Destination Moon.*

Top pop records are The Weavers, "Goodnight, Irene," Sammy Kaye, "It Isn't Fair," and Anton Karas, "Third Man Theme."

Dearborn, Michigan, crowns a "Miss Loyalty" at a beauty pageant.

The Diners Club is founded, the first of the special credit cards that proliferate in the fifties.

Census: U.S. population 150,697,361. 23.6 million Americans are homeowners.

1951

April 11: Truman dismisses MacArthur as commander of Korean forces. Korea is much in the news this year: many Americans cannot understand why an American-led victory has not occurred.

May 25: Willie Mays, age 20, bats for the first time as a New York Giant. He strikes out. By the end of the season, however, he earns Rookie of the Year award.

"Where you find an intellectual, you will probably find a Red."—*Washington Confidential*, a best seller. The years 1951–52 are the height of the loyalty-security mania.

New peak of women in the work force: 19,308,000.

An Indiana National Guard captain who suggests recruiting blacks into the guard is removed as company commander.

ATT becomes the first corporation with over one million stockholders.

Bobby Thompson's home run off Brooklyn Dodger pitcher Ralph Branca puts the New York Giants into the World Series. But the Yankees win the series four games to two.

Maureen Connolly becomes USLTA women's singles champ; Frank Sedgman takes the men's title.

Los Angeles Rams 24, Cleveland Browns 17 in National Football Conference championship.

Academy Award best film: *An American in Paris.* Other important movies include *Streetcar Named Desire, African Queen, Rashomon, The Day the Earth Stood Still,* and *The Thing from Another World.*

Edward R. Murrow's television news show *See It Now* premiers. CBS makes the first color telecast, although very few color TVs are in use.

A Pentagon bootblack who once gave $10 to the Scottsboro boys' defense fund is questioned 70 times this year by the FBI.

The 22nd Amendment to the Constitution passes, limiting the presidency to two terms.

"Amazingly real" plastic plants are manufactured on a large scale.

Best-selling books: James Jones, *From Here to Eternity* and Gaylord Hauser, *Look Younger, Live Longer*. Herman Wouk publishes *The Caine Mutiny*. Mickey Spillane's anticommunist thriller, *One Lonely Night*, sells 3 million copies. Other notable books include William F. Buckley, Jr., *God and Man at Yale*, Editors of *Fortune*, *U.S.A.: The Permanent Revolution*, Eric Hoffer, *True Believer*, David Hulburd, *This Happened in Pasadena*, Norman Mailer, *Barbary Shore*, and William Styron, *Lie Down in Darkness*.

Cleveland DJ Alan Freed, calling rhythm and blues records "rock and roll," begins to popularize black music among whites.

Top pop records are Patti Page, "Tennessee Waltz," Les Paul and Mary Ford, "How High the Moon," and Nat King Cole, "Too Young."

1952

Fall: Korea, Communism, and Corruption (K_1C_2) is the GOP anti-Democratic party slogan in the election campaign.

September 23: Richard Nixon makes his Checkers speech on TV and radio, denying he is a crook and saving his place as the Republican vice-presidential nominee. The same night, Rocky Marciano KOs Joe Walcott in the 13th round to win the heavyweight boxing title.

November 4: Eisenhower is elected President, defeating the Democratic candidate Adlai Stevenson. The Republicans also gain control of both houses of Congress.

November 26: Bwana Devil, the first 3-D movie, opens in Los Angeles.

November: First successful test of a hydrogen "device" by the United States destroys an entire Pacific island.

The B-52 bomber is developed.

A. J. Muste's pamphlet *Of Holy Disobedience* urges resistance to conscription and war.

TV Guide magazine begins.

Liberace makes his TV debut. "I Love Lucy" also begins and quickly becomes television's most popular show. "Dragnet" premiers.

Partisan Review publishes symposium, "Our Country and Our Culture," in which leading intellectuals celebrate America.

Best-selling books: Thomas B. Costain, *The Silver Chalice* and the Revised Standard Version of *The Holy Bible*. Ralph Ellison's *Invisible Man* is published. Other notable books are Frederick Lewis Allen, *The Big Change;* John Kenneth Galbraith, *American Capitalism;* Jack Lait and Lee Mortimer, *U.S.A. Confidential;* Bernard Malamud, *The Natural;* Reinhold Niebuhr, *The Irony of American History;* and I. F. Stone, *Hidden History of the Korean War.*

Pogo, chief character in Walt Kelly's comic strip of that name, runs for president with the slogan "I Go Pogo."

Academy Award for best film goes to *The Greatest Show on Earth.* Other notable films are *High Noon, Singin' in the Rain, This Is Cinerama, Mr. Hulot's Holiday, Umberto D,* and *My Son John.*

Nasser becomes President of the United Arab Republic.

Paint-by-number kits are introduced by a Detroit firm. The chlorophyll fad begins, with that chemical peddled in gum, deodorant, soap, and dog food.

Yankees win the World Series over the Dodgers, four games to two.

Sedgman and Connolly maintain their 1951 USLTA titles.

Detroit Lions 17, Cleveland Browns 7 in the National Football Conference championship.

Johnny Ray sobs to fame with "Cry" and "Little White Cloud That Cried." Other top pop records are Leroy Anderson, "Blue Tango," and Eddie Fisher, "Any Time."

1953

January: Eisenhower is inaugurated. He appoints John Foster Dulles as Secretary of State; Dulles will shape much of the decade's aggressive foreign policy.

March 5: Stalin dies.

April: Eisenhower issues Executive Order 10450 authorizing the most sweeping loyalty investigation of federal employees in American history.

June 2: Elizabeth II is crowned.

June 19: Julius and Ethel Rosenberg are executed at Sing Sing while demonstrators throughout the world plead for executive clemency.

July 27: An armistice ending the Korean War is signed at Panmunjom. U.S. casualties in the war totaled 165,485 with 54,246 of these killed.

August: The Soviet Union announces the successful development of their own H-bomb.

August 19: The CIA instigates a coup that overthrows the popularly elected Prime Minister of Iran, Mohammed Mossadegh, whose government had nationalized Iran's oil.

September: Earl Warren is appointed Chief Justice of the Supreme Court.

Atomic artillery shells are tested by the United States.

Charlie Chaplin, harassed by the FBI and the Internal Revenue Service because of his political opinions, surrenders his re-entry permit, refusing to return to America. Said Chaplin: "America is so terribly grim in spite of all that material prosperity. They no longer know how to weep. Compassion and the old neighborliness have gone, people stand by and do nothing when friends and neighbors are attacked, libeled and ruined."

Black income declines in relation to white.

Casey Stengel's Yankees win their fifth straight world championship, beating the Dodgers four games to two.

Rocky Marciano KOs Roland LaStanza to keep his heavyweight boxing title.

Maureen Connolly maintains the USLTA women's title; Tony Trabert wins the men's singles title.

The Detroit Lions again win the National Football Conference crown defeating the Cleveland Browns 17 to 16.

Two new conservative books are published and well received: Peter Viereck, *Shame and Glory of the Intellectuals* and Russell Kirk, *The Conservative Mind.* Arthur Clarke publishes *Childhood's End;* Kinsey issues *Sexual Behavior in the Human Female.* Best sellers are Lloyd C. Douglas, *The Robe*, and *The Holy Bible.*

1953–54 is the high point of comic book popularity with 650 titles in print having a combined circulation of 100 million monthly.

The Department of Health, Education and Welfare is created.

"The Today Show" debuts on TV.

Academy Award for best film goes to *From Here to Eternity.* Other important films include *Stalag 17, Shane, How to Marry a Millionaire, The Robe*, and *The Moon Is Blue.*

Top pop records are Percy Faith, "Song from the Moulin Rouge," Teresa Brewer, "Till I Waltz Again with You," and Lee Baxter, "April in Portugal." Notable rock songs are Bill Haley and His Comets, "Crazy Man Crazy," Ruth Brown, "Mama," and Clyde McPhatter's "Money Honey."

1954

January 12: Dulles announces policy of "massive retaliation." This leads to the rise of the Strategic Air Command, nuclear stockpiling, and many other cold war effects.

March 1: Three Puerto Rican nationalists wound five congressmen, firing from the House visitors' gallery.

April 22: The Army–McCarthy hearings begin. Broadcast on national TV, and running until June 17, they help discredit the Wisconsin senator.

May 7: The Viet Minh take Dien Bien Phu after a 55-day siege. This forces the French out of Vietnam. The United States paid France nearly $1 billion this year alone to fight the war. Vice-President Nixon at this time urges American intervention.

May 17: The Supreme Court rules in *Brown* v. *Board of Education of Topeka* that "the doctrine of 'separate but equal' has no place" in public education. "Separate education facilities are inherently unequal."

June: "Under God" is added to the pledge of allegiance. Later in the year, the Reverend Norman Vincent Peale is named one of the "Twelve Best U.S. Salesmen."

June 18: A CIA-financed and -planned right-wing coup overthrows the popularly elected government of Jacobo Arbenz in Guatemala after Arbenz had nationalized property of the United Fruit Company.

June 29: The Atomic Energy Commission refuses to renew the security clearance of J. Robert Oppenheimer. He is guilty not of disloyalty but of a "lack of enthusiasm."

September: SEATO is formed to contain communism in Asia.

November 1: The Algerian revolt against French rule begins.

November 2: The Democrats gain control of both houses of Congress.

December 2: McCarthy is condemned by the Senate.

December 15: The first Davy Crockett show debuts on "Disneyland."

Henry David Thoreau's *Walden* is banned from U.S. Information Service libraries on the grounds that it is "downright socialistic." Seventy-eight per cent of Americans polled in a national survey think it a good idea to report to the FBI any relatives or acquaintances they suspect of being communists.

Dissent magazine is founded.

The White Citizens Council begins organizing in the South to oppose the implementation of the *Brown* decision.

The first Newport Jazz Festival is held.

Top pop tunes are Kitty Kallen's "Little Things Mean a Lot," Rosemary Clooney, "Hey There," and Perry Como, "Wanted." The Crew Cuts' white cover version of The Chords' rock song "Sh-Boom" makes #5. Other memorable rock records are The Midnighters, "Work with Me Annie," and their follow-up, "Annie Had a Baby," The Drifters's "Honey Love," and Joe Turner's "Shake, Rattle and Roll."

Ernest Hemingway wins the Nobel Prize for literature.

Randall Jarrell publishes *Pictures from an Institution.* Clifford Odets' play *The Flowering Peach* is produced on Broadway. Best-selling books are Morton Thompson's *Not as a Stranger* and, again, *The Holy Bible*. Fredric Wertham publishes *The Seduction of the Innocent,* attacking violence in comic books. *Seduction* leads directly to the comic book industry's self-imposed censorship code and so its decline. Lawrence and Mary Frank publish *How to Be a Woman.*

TV dinner is invented and marketed: turkey, sweet potatoes, and peas.

Sports Illustrated begins.

Rocky Marciano keeps the heavyweight boxing title.

Cleveland Browns 56, Detroit Lions 10 in the NFL championships.

Vic Seixas wins men's singles in USLTA. Doris Hart takes the women's title.

Academy Award for best film is *On the Waterfront;* Marlon Brando also receives the best actor award for his role in *Waterfront*. Other important movies are *La Strada, Creature from the Black Lagoon, Rebel Without a Cause,* and *The Wild One.*

1955

January 1: American aid to South Vietnam, amounting to $216 million in 1955, begins. Diem, selected and groomed by Michigan State University professor Wesley Fischel, will come to power in South Vietnam this year.

February 3: Harvey Matusow, a frequent witness against leftists before the House Un-American Activities Committee and the FBI, admits that he did it for money and that he had consistently lied.

April 12: Scientists conclude that Salk vaccine is effective in preventing polio.

May 15: Allies and U.S.S.R. end ten-year occupation of Austria.

June: The Geneva summit conference is held between the major powers. This marks a "thaw" in the cold war.

August 28: Emmett Till, a 14-year-old black, is kidnaped from his Mississippi home after he had allegedly "whistled at a white woman." Four days later his body is recovered from the Tallahatchie River. The all-white jury acquits the two white men accused of the murder.

September 24: Ike has a heart attack in Denver.

September 30: James Dean dies in a car crash.

December 1: Rosa Parks refuses to give up her bus seat to a white man in Montgomery, Alabama. She is arrested. The black community rallies, starting a 54-week bus boycott that brings Martin Luther King, Jr., to national prominence and eventually wins moderate demands.

December 5: AFL-CIO forms by merger.

The Brooklyn Dodgers finally defeat the New York Yankees in the World Series four games to three.

Doris Hart keeps her USLTA women's singles title; Tony Trabert takes the men's title.

The Cleveland Browns take the NFL championship with a 38 to 14 win over the Los Angeles Rams.

Bill Haley's "Rock Around the Clock," made famous by the movie *Blackboard Jungle,* is the year's top record and helps to popularize rock. Bill Hayes' "Ballad of Davy Crockett" is the second best-selling single. Important rock releases are Chuck Berry's "Maybellene," The Clovers' "Devil or Angel," and Little Richard's "Tutti Frutti."

The first televised presidential press conference is held.

Three adult Westerns premier on TV: "Wyatt Earp," "Gunsmoke," and "The Rifleman." Also premiering is "The Lawrence Welk Show."

Charles Schulz's comic strip "Peanuts" begins.

Best-selling books are Herman Wouk, *Marjorie Morningstar* and Anne Morrow Lindbergh, *Gift from the Sea.* Other notable books include Daniel Bell, ed., *The Radical Right;* Arthur Bestor, *The Restoration of Learning;* Leslie Fiedler, *End to Innocence;* Rudolf Flesch, *Why Johnny Can't Read;* Will Herberg, *Protestant–Catholic–Jew;* Herbert Marcuse, *Eros and Civilization;* and Sloan Wilson, *The Man in the Gray Flannel Suit.*

Marian Anderson debuts at the Met singing Ulrica in *Un Ballo in Maschera,* breaking the color line.

Marty wins the Academy Award for best film. Also important are *The Rose Tattoo* and *Man with the Golden Arm.*

1956

February: Khrushchev denounces Stalin.

July: Egypt nationalizes the Suez Canal.

October 29: Middle East erupts into war: Israel, Britain, and France invade Egypt to destroy guerrilla bases and retake Suez. Pressured by the United States, they quickly withdraw.

November 4: The Hungarian revolt is crushed by the Soviet army. This ends a year of unrest and dissent in the Soviet satellites, including bread riots in Poland.

November 6: Ike is re-elected over Stevenson, though Congress goes to the Democrats.

Montgomery bus boycott continues into December.

Dulles announces "brinkmanship" policy–that the United States will go to the brink of war to keep world peace.

The phrase "People's Capitalism" is coined by the Advertising Council and comes into common usage in extolling America's economy.

Liberation Magazine begins.

The National Defense Highway Act passes, authorizing the construction of the multibillion dollar interstate highway system. Mass transportation is allowed to lag.

Elvis Presley records "Heartbreak Hotel," "Hound Dog," "Love Me Tender," and the year's top tune, "Don't Be Cruel." Ed Sullivan announces he will never permit Presley's smutty performance on his show. A few months later he recants, pays $50,000 for three Presley appearances which are photographed only from the waist up. *Look* magazine writes at this time: "Presley is mostly nightmare." The Platters' "Great Pretender" and "My Prayer" are the second and third top-selling records. Other notable records are Carl Perkins' "Blue Suede Shoes," Bill Doggett's "Honkey Tonk," Little Willie John's "Fever," and Shirley and Lee's "Let the Good Times Roll."

Cecil B. DeMille's *The Ten Commandments* is released. The Academy

Award for best film goes to *Around the World in 80 Days.* Other important films are *Giant, Bus Stop, The Seventh Seal, Baby Doll, The Trouble with Harry,* and *Patterns.*

Allen Ginsberg's book of poetry, *Howl,* is published. The best-selling books are William Brinkley, *Don't Go Near the Water* and Dan Dale Alexander, *Arthritis and Common Sense.* Other notable books include Saul Bellow, *Seize the Day;* Robert Lindner, *Must You Conform?;* Grace Metalious, *Peyton Place;* C. Wright Mills, *The Power Elite;* Linus Pauling, *No More War!;* and William H. Whyte, Jr., *The Organization Man.*

Joan Collins publishes *James Dean Returns,* a book of dictation from the dead star. She quotes him: "I am not dead. Those who believe I am not dead are right." The book sells 500,000 copies. Bits of Dean's death car start at $20. People are allowed to see the car for 25¢ and to sit behind the wheel for an additional 25¢.

Jackson Pollock dies in a car crash.

Diem cancels free elections in South Viet Nam with U.S. support. Elections had been scheduled for 1956 in the 1954 Geneva Accords, but an estimated 80 per cent of the people would have voted for Ho Chi Minh.

University of Alabama officials expel Autherine Lucy, their first black student, because her presence "threatened public order."

People buy TVs at the rate of over 20,000 every day. Over 500 TV stations are in operation. By this year Americans are spending more time watching TV than they spend working for pay.

Floyd Patterson wins the heavyweight title vacated by the undefeated Rocky Marciano, by knocking out Archie Moore in the fifth round.

The Yankees win the World Series over the Dodgers four games to three. They are helped by Bob Larsen pitching the first perfect no-hit game in series history.

Ken Rosewall takes the USLTA men's singles; Shirley Fry wins in women's singles.

The New York Giants win the NFL crown over the Chicago Bears by a score of 47 to 7.

1957

January 4: The final issue of *Collier's* magazine.

March 6: The Republic of Ghana is formed.

May 2: Senator Joseph McCarthy dies of "acute hepatitic failure."

August 29: Congress passes the first civil rights act in 82 years, establishing a weak civil rights commission.

September 25: Eisenhower sends one thousand army paratroopers to Central High School, Little Rock, Arkansas, to permit nine black students to attend the previously all-white school.

October 4: The Soviets orbit Sputnik I. Americans fear loss of world prestige.

November 3: The Soviets orbit Sputnik II, far heavier than the first satellite and carrying the dog Laika. The two Sputniks cause the United States to revamp its educational system to stress science.

November 26: Ike has a mild stroke.

December 6: A Vanguard rocket attempting to launch the first U.S. space satellite explodes on the pad at Cape Canaveral before a national TV audience; this is taken as a national disaster.

Recession begins, lasting well into 1958.

Martin Luther King, Jr., and others found the Southern Christian Leadership Conference.

Linus Pauling releases a petition signed by 11,000 scientists calling for an international nuclear test ban. Ban-the-bomb activism gains strength during the year with civil disobedience, organizing, and appeals.

Volkswagen sells nearly 200,000 beetles in the United States, the first sign of consumer rejection of huge Detroit cars.

Dick Clark's TV show *American Bandstand* begins bringing respectable rock to national audiences. Top pop tunes for the year are Debbie Reynolds, "Tammy," Pat Boone, "Love Letters in the Sand," and Johnny Mathis, "It's Not for Me to Say." Records such as Danny and the Juniors' "At the Hop," the Everly Brothers' "Wake Up, Little Susie," and Buddy Holly's "Peggy Sue" mark the growing popularity of white teen-age rock.

Marilyn Monroe weds Arthur Miller.

Academy Award for best film goes to *Bridge on the River Kwai.* Other important films are *Three Faces of Eve, And God Created Woman, The Incredible Shrinking Man, Edge of the City, Paths of Glory,* and *Twelve Angry Men.*

On the Road, Jack Kerouac's novel written early in the decade, is finally published. Also published are Nevil Shute, *On the Beach,* and Vance Packard, *The Hidden Persuaders.* John F. Kennedy's book *Profiles in Courage* is awarded a Pulitzer Prize. Best sellers are James Gould Cozzens, *By Love Possessed,* and Art Linkletter, *Kids Say the Darndest Things.*

Floyd Patterson KOs Pete Rademacher in the sixth round and retains the heavyweight title.

The Milwaukee Braves win the World Series over the Yankees four games to three.

Althea Gibson takes the USLTA women's singles title. Mal Anderson wins the men's title.

The Detroit Lions win the NFL crown defeating the Cleveland Browns by the score of 59 to 14.

1958

January 31: Army orbits Explorer I, the first successful U.S. space satellite, from Cape Canaveral.

April: Vice-President Nixon, on a good-will tour of Latin America, is showered with anti-U.S. pamphlets in Uruguay, stoned at the University of San Marcos in Peru, mobbed, spat on, and stoned in Venezuela.

The recession is major by spring. By summer, unemployment is at 7.5 per cent, the decade's peak.

May 1: Four pacifists are arrested by the Coast Guard as they attempt to sail their ship the *Golden Rule* into the U.S. atomic testing area in the Pacific. Protest of bomb testing is increasing.

June 1: Algerian unrest returns De Gaulle to power in France.

June 17: Imre Nagy, Hungarian ex-premier and leader of the anti-Soviet resistance, is executed.

July 10: Robert Earl Hughes, the world's heaviest human, dies at Bremen, Indiana, at age 32. He had weighed 1,067 lbs.

Summer: The National Committee for a Sane Nuclear Policy (SANE), founded in November 1957, possesses 130 chapters and 25,000 members.

August 23–October 6: Mainland China bombards Quemoy Island.

September: In response to Sputnik fears, Congress passes the National Defense Education Act.

September 22: Ike's closest advisor, Sherman Adams, resigns because he had accepted bribes.

Khrushchev becomes the Soviet premier. Thus the powers of that post and his other as party chief are concentrated in one man.

Ten thousand black and white students converge on Washington in a

"Youth March for Integrated Schools," one of the first signs of a new student activism.

Teen-agers buy fully 70 per cent of all records pressed, as the average age of pop music fans continues to drop. Top pop tunes are Domenico Modugno, "Volaré," Tommy Edwards, "It's All in the Game," and Perez Prado, "Patricia." The Coasters record "Yakety Yak." Other memorable records are Bobby Day's "Rockin' Robin," Chuck Berry's "Johnny B. Goode," and Bobby Freeman's "Do You Want to Dance?" The Kingston Trio's "Tom Dooley" sells 2 million copies and marks the beginning of folk music craze.

John Kenneth Galbraith publishes *The Affluent Society.*

Best sellers are Boris Pasternak, *Doctor Zhivago,* and Linkletter's *Kids Say the Darndest Things.* Some 350 million paperback books are sold. Other notable books include John Barth, *The End of the Road;* Martin Luther King, Jr., *Stride Toward Freedom;* and Vladimir Nabokov, *Lolita.*

The hula hoop fad reaches its peak.

The John Birch Society is founded.

The United States pays all the costs of the South Vietnamese armed forces and 80 per cent of all other government costs there.

Pacific Gas and Electric plans a nuclear power plant at Bodega Head, California. The proposed plant would have been a thousand feet from the San Andreas Fault. Construction is stopped only after years of court battles by environmental groups.

The Liz Taylor, Eddie Fisher, Debbie Reynolds affair highlights Hollywood gossip. Academy Award for best film goes to *Gigi.* Other important films include *Cat on a Hot Tin Roof, Touch of Evil, Black Orpheus, The 400 Blows,* and *The Defiant Ones.*

Floyd Patterson retains the heavyweight title by a TKO of Brian London.

The Yankees reverse their 1957 defeat and win the World Series from the Braves, four games to three.

Althea Gibson again wins the women's singles championship of the USLTA. Ashley Cooper takes the men's title.

The Baltimore Colts defeat the New York Giants 23 to 17 for the NFL title.

1959

January 1: Fidel Castro's guerrilla forces capture Havana and overthrow the Batista regime in Cuba. Initially the successful revolution is greeted with joy in the United States. But within six months Americans will become hostile to Cuba.

January 3: Alaska becomes the 49th state.

March 17: Dalai Lama flees to India when the Chinese crush a Tibetan revolt.

April 9: The first seven U.S. astronauts are selected.

June 8: The Supreme Court upholds the right of Congress and the states to investigate communism.

June 11: The Postmaster General bans D. H. Lawrence's *Lady Chatterley's Lover* from the mails.

June 26: The St. Lawrence seaway opens.

August 3: Nixon and Khrushchev exchange angry words in the so-called "kitchen debate" in Moscow.

August 21: Hawaii becomes the 50th state.

September 15: Khrushchev visits the United States but is refused permission to visit Disneyland.

November 2: Charles Van Doren confesses his deep involvement in rigged TV quiz shows, resigns his post at Columbia University. The TV scandal will also trigger the rock and roll radio payola scandal involving Alan Freed and based on the assumption that kids would never listen to rock unless corrupted to it.

Dulles, ill with terminal cancer, resigns as Secretary of State.

Synthetic penicillin is developed.

Studies on the Left is founded, the first New Left journal.

Rock stars Big Bopper, Buddy Holly, and Ritchie Valens die in a plane crash.

The top pop records are Bobby Darin, "Mack the Knife," Johnny Horton, "Battle of New Orleans," and Frankie Avalon, "Venus." Also of note are The Clovers, "Love Potion Number Nine," The Crests, "16 Candles," and Ray Charles, "What'd I Say." The teen rock craze continues with songs such as Dion and the Belmonts' "Teenager in Love," and Mark Dinning's "Teen Angel."

Ben-Hur wins the Academy Award for best picture. Also notable are *Some Like It Hot, On the Beach, The World of Apu, The Lovers, Room at the Top,* and *Hiroshima, Mon Amour.*

Best-selling books are Pat Boone, *'Twixt Twelve and Twenty,* and Leon Uris, *Exodus.* Other memorable books are Saul Bellow, *Henderson the Rain King;* Eleanor Flexner, *Century of Struggle;* Lawrence Lipton, *The Holy Barbarians;* Norman Mailer, *Advertisements for Myself;* Vance Packard, *The Status Seekers;* Admiral H. G. Rickover, *Education and Freedom;* and Leopold Stein, *Loathsome Women.*

Ingemar Johansson TKOs Floyd Patterson in the third round to win the heavyweight crown.

The Dodgers win the World Series over the Chicago White Sox four games to two.

Neale Fraser takes the USLTA. Maria Bueno wins the women's crown.

The Baltimore Colts defeat the New York Giants 31 to 16 to take the NFL title.

1960

February 1: Four black students sit-in at the segregated Woolworth's lunch counter in Greensboro, North Carolina. The sit-in movement is born. Within the year, 50,000 people will participate in similar demonstrations in over 100 cities and will succeed in desegregating many hotels, stores, theaters, parks, and lunch counters.

February 13: France explodes an atomic bomb.

February: Cuba, cut off from U.S. aid and trade, signs a trade agreement with the Soviet Union.

February 17: Eisenhower authorizes training by CIA of a force of Cuban exiles to invade Cuba.

Spring: Life and the New York *Times* run lengthy articles on the quest for a national purpose, reflecting American sense of loss and confusion.

May 2: Caryl Chessman is executed at San Quentin prison, California, despite worldwide protests.

May 5: Eleven days before a summit meeting, Khrushchev announces an American U-2 spy plane piloted by Francis Gary Powers has been shot down over the Soviet Union. The United States claims the plane to be a strayed weather observer. But on May 7 Khrushchev reveals that Powers is alive and has confessed to spying. The proposed summit collapses.

May 9: Enovid, an oral contraceptive pill for women, is approved for public sale by the Federal Drug Administration.

May 12: Students protesting House Un-American Activities Committee hearings in San Francisco are attacked by police.

June 30: Seventeen African nations gain independence on this day. One of them, the Congo, soon breaks out in civil war.

September 26–October 17: Four Kennedy-Nixon TV debates are held. These are viewed by an estimated 8 million people and help Kennedy defeat Nixon in the November presidential election.

Polio this year is reduced to 2,200 cases due to the Salk vaccine.

Average American incomes reach a record $2,218. Consumer indebtedness soars to $196 billion, while an annual $12 billion is spent on advertising.

A Jackson Pollock painting sells for $100,000.

TV is in 90 per cent of American homes.

A new civil rights act passes, appointing federal referees to help safeguard voting rights.

Americans consume 1,050 million pounds of hot dogs, along with 532 million pounds of potato chips.

Notable books include Daniel Bell, *The End of Ideology;* Paul Goodman, *Growing Up Absurd;* Herman Kahn, *On Thermonuclear War;* C. Wright Mills, *The Causes of World War Three;* and William Styron, *Set This House on Fire.*

The Student League for Industrial Democracy becomes Students for a Democratic Society (SDS). The Student Non-Violent Coordinating Committee (SNCC) is also formed.

Chubby Checker's "The Twist" starts a new dance craze. This is also the year of such recordings as "Angel Baby" by Rosie and the Originals, Roy Orbison's "Only the Lonely," and "Stay" by Maurice Williams and the Zodiacs.

Patterson KOs Johansson in the fifth round to become the first heavyweight to regain his title.

The Pittsburgh Pirates defeat the Yankees in the World Series four games to three, and Casey Stengel, age 70, is released as Yankee manager after 12 highly successful years.

Neale Fraser retains the USLTA men's singles title, while Darlene Hard wins the women's title.

The Philadelphia Eagles 17, the Green Bay Packers 13 for the NFL championship.

Census: 179,323,175 inhabitants; 32.8 million homeowners.

SELECTED BIBLIOGRAPHY

Since *The Fifties* is the first in-depth study of America's social and cultural history during that decade, our research was of necessity wide-ranging. What follows is an alphabetical listing of the more important published books consulted. For a more comprehensive bibliography, see the chapter notes.

Abrams, Charles. *Forbidden Neighbors*. New York, 1955.

Agar, Herbert. *The Price of Power: America Since 1945*. Chicago, 1957.

Allen, Frederick Lewis. *The Big Change: America Transforms Itself 1900–1950*. New York, 1952.

Alvarez, A. *The Savage God*. London, 1971.

American Business Consultants. *Red Channels*. New York, 1950.

Asimov, Isaac. *Foundation*. Garden City, 1951.

——. *Foundation and Empire*. Garden City, 1952.

——. *Second Foundation*. Garden City, 1953.

Balderston, John L., Jr., and Hewes, Gordon W. *Atomic Attack: A Manual for Survival*. Los Angeles, 1950.

Baldwin, Leland DeWitt. *The Meaning of America*. Pittsburgh, 1955.

Barth, John. *The End of the Road*. New York, 1958.
——. *The Sot-Weed Factor*. Garden City, 1960.
Barzun, Jacques. *God's Country and Mine*. Boston, 1954.
Bell, Bernard Iddings. *Crowd Culture*. New York, 1952.
Bell, Daniel. *The End of Ideology: On the Exhaustion of Political Ideas in the Fifties*. New York, 1961 ed.
——. ed. *The Radical Right*. Garden City, 1963.
Bellow, Saul. *Henderson the Rain King*. New York, 1959.
——. *Seize the Day*. New York, 1956.
Belz, Carl. *The Story of Rock*. New York, 1969.
Bentley, Eric, ed. *Thirty Years of Treason: Excerpts from Hearings before the House Committee on Un-American Activities 1938–1968*. New York, 1971.
Berle, Adolf A. *The 20th Century Capitalist Revolution*. New York, 1954.
Bessie, Alvah. *Inquisition in Eden*. New York, 1965.
Bestor, Arthur. *The Restoration of Learning*. New York, 1955.
Bettelheim, Bruno. *The Informed Heart*. New York, 1960.
Blanshard, Paul. *God and Man in Washington*. Boston, 1960.
Boone, Pat. *'Twixt Twelve and Twenty*. Englewood Cliffs, 1958.
Boorstin, Daniel J. *The Genius of American Politics*. Chicago, 1953.
Brooks, John. *The Great Leap*. New York, 1966.
Brooks, William Allan [pseud.]. *Girl Gangs*. New York, 1952.
Buckley, William F., Jr. *God and Man at Yale*. Chicago, 1951.
——. *Up from Liberalism*. New York, 1959.
Carson, Rachel. *Silent Spring*. Boston, 1962.
Chafe, William H. *The American Woman, 1920–1970*. New York, 1972.
Chambers, Whittaker. *Witness*. New York, 1952.
Childs, Marquis W. *Eisenhower, Captive Hero*. New York, 1958.
Christman, Henry A., ed. *A View of the Nation*. New York, 1960.
Civil Defense Education Project Staff, *Education for National Survival*. Washington, 1956.
Clayton, James L., ed. *Economic Impact of the Cold War*. New York, 1970.
Cochran, Bert. *The War System*. New York, 1965.
Cogley, John. *Report on Blacklisting*. Vol. I: *Movies*. Vol. II: *Radio-Television*. n.p., 1956.
Conant, James Bryant. *The Citadel of Learning*. New Haven, 1956.
Cook, Bruce. *The Beat Generation*. New York, 1971.
Cook, Fred J. *The Nightmare Decade*. New York, 1971.
——. *The Warfare State*. New York, 1962.
Cooke, Alistair. *A Generation on Trial: U.S.A. v. Alger Hiss*. New York, 1951.

Corso, Gregory. *Long Live Man.* Norfolk, Conn., 1962.
Cremin, Lawrence A. *The Transformation of the School.* New York, 1961.
Dalton, David. *James Dean.* San Francisco, 1974.
Daniels, Les. *The Comix.* New York, 1970.
Davis, Elmer. *But We Were Born Free.* Indianapolis, 1954.
Degler, Carl N. *Affluence and Anxiety, 1945–Present.* Glenview, Ill., 1968.
Denney, Reuel. *The Astonished Muse.* Chicago, 1957.
Drucker, Peter F. *The New Society.* New York, 1950.
DuBois, W. E. B. *In Battle for Peace.* New York, 1952.
——. *I Take My Stand for Peace.* New York, 1951.
Dykeman, Wilma, and Stokely, James. *Neither Black Nor White.* New York, 1959.
Editors of *Fortune. America in the Sixties.* New York, 1960.
——. *The Exploding Metropolis.* Garden City, 1958.
——. *The Fabulous Future: America in 1980.* New York, 1956.
——. *U.S.A.: The Permanent Revolution.* New York, 1951.
Editors of *Partisan Review. America and the Intellectuals, a Symposium.* New York, 1953.
Editors of *Time-Life. 1950–1960.* Vol. VI of *This Fabulous Century.* New York, 1970.
Eisenhower, Dwight D. *The White House Years: Mandate for Change, 1953–1956.* Garden City, 1963.
——. *The White House Years: Waging Peace, 1956–1961.* Garden City, 1965.
Ellison, Ralph. *Invisible Man.* New York, 1952.
Elson, Rev. Edward L. R. *America's Spiritual Recovery.* New York, 1954.
Ernst, Morris L. *Utopia 1976.* New York, 1955.
Evanier, David, and Silverzweig, Stanley, eds. *The Nonconformers.* New York, 1961.
Farnham, Marynia, M.D., and Lundberg, Ferdinand. *Modern Woman: The Lost Sex.* New York, 1947.
Feiffer, Jules. *Passionella.* New York, 1959.
Feldman, Gene, and Gartenberg, Max, eds. *The Beat Generation and the Angry Young Men.* New York, 1958.
Fenin, George N., and Everson, William K. *The Western.* New York, 1973.
Feuerlicht, Roberta Strauss. *Joe McCarthy and McCarthyism.* New York, 1972.
Fiedler, Leslie A. *An End to Innocence.* Boston, 1955.
Fine, Benjamin. *1,000,000 Delinquents.* New York, 1957 ed.
Flesch, Rudolf. *Why Johnny Can't Read and What You Can Do About It.* New York, 1955.
Flexner, Eleanor. *Century of Struggle.* Cambridge, Mass., 1959.

Floherty, John J., and McGrady, Mike. *Youth and the FBI*. Philadelphia, 1960.

Fox, Col. Victor J. [pseud.]. *The Pentagon Case*. New York, 1958.

Frank, Lawrence K., and Frank, Mary. *How to Be a Woman*. New York, 1954.

Freeland, Richard M. *The Truman Doctrine and the Origins of McCarthyism*. New York, 1972.

Friedan, Betty. *The Feminine Mystique*. New York, 1963.

Friendly, Fred W. *Due to Circumstances Beyond Our Control*. New York, 1967.

Fromm, Erich. *The Sane Society*. New York, 1955.

Galbraith, John Kenneth. *The Affluent Society*. Boston, 1958.

——. *American Capitalism: The Concept of Countervailing Power*. Boston, 1956 ed.

——. *Economics and the Art of Controversy*. New York, 1959 ed.

——. *The Liberal Hour*. Boston, 1960.

Gavin, James M. *War and Peace in the Space Age*. New York, 1958.

Gillett, Charlie. *The Sound of the City*. New York, 1970.

Ginsberg, Allen. *Howl and Other Poems*. San Francisco, 1956.

Glueck, Sheldon. *The Problem of Delinquency*. Boston, 1959.

Goldman, Albert. *Ladies and Gentlemen: Lenny Bruce*. New York, 1974.

Goldman, Eric F. *The Crucial Decade and After: America, 1945–1960*. New York, 1960.

Goldston, Robert. *The American Nightmare: Senator Joseph R. McCarthy and the Politics of Hate*. Indianapolis, 1973.

Goodman, Paul. *The Empire City*. Indianapolis, 1959.

——. *Growing Up Absurd*. New York, 1960.

——. ed. *Seeds of Liberation*. New York, 1964.

——. *Utopian Essays and Practical Proposals*. New York, 1962.

Goodman, Walter. *The Committee: The Extraordinary Career of the House Committee on Un-American Activities*. New York, 1968.

Gordon, Arthur. *Norman Vincent Peale*. New York, 1958.

Gow, Gordon. *Hollywood in the Fifties*. New York, 1971.

Greenfield, Jeff. *No Peace, No Place*. Garden City, 1973.

Griffin, John Howard. *Black Like Me*. New York, 1969 ed.

Griffith, Robert. *The Politics of Fear: Joseph R. McCarthy and the Senate*. Lexington, 1970.

——, and Theoharis, Athan, eds. *The Specter: Original Essays on the Cold War and the Origins of McCarthyism*. New York, 1974.

Griffith, Thomas. *The Waist-High Culture*. New York, 1959.

Gruenberg, Sidonie M., and Krech, Hilda Sidney. *The Many Lives of Modern Woman: A Guide to Happiness in Her Complex Role*. Garden City, 1952.

Haber, Heinz. *The Walt Disney Story of Our Friend the Atom.* New York, 1956.
Haight, Anne Lyon. *Banned Books.* New York, 1955.
Halliwell, Leslie. *The Filmgoer's Companion.* London, 1965.
Hargis, Billy James. *Communist America, Must It Be?* Tulsa, 1960.
Harrington, Michael. *The Accidental Century.* New York, 1966.
——. *The Other America.* New York, 1963.
Haskell, Molly. *From Reverence to Rape.* New York, 1974.
Haupt, Enid A. *The Seventeen Book of Young Living.* New York, 1957.
Heilbroner, Robert L. *The Future as History.* New York, 1960.
Henry, Jules. *Culture Against Man.* New York, 1963.
Herberg, Will. *Protestant–Catholic–Jew: An Essay in American Religious Sociology.* Garden City, 1960 ed.
Herdon, Venable. *James Dean.* New York, 1974.
Herlihy, James Leo, and Noble, William. *Blue Denim.* New York, 1959.
Higham, Charles. *The Art of the American Film, 1900–1971.* Garden City, 1973.
Hiss, Alger. *In the Court of Public Opinion.* New York, 1957.
Hoffer, Eric. *The True Believer: Thoughts on the Nature of Mass Movements.* New York, 1951.
Hofstadter, Richard. *The Age of Reform.* New York, 1955.
——. *The Paranoid Style in American Politics.* New York, 1965.
Hoover, J. Edgar. *Masters of Deceit.* New York, 1958.
Hughes, Emmet John. *The Ordeal of Power: A Political Memoir of the Eisenhower Years.* New York, 1963.
Hulburd, David. *This Happened in Pasadena.* New York, 1951.
Hutchins, Robert M. *Some Observations on American Education.* Cambridge, Eng., 1956.
Jacob, Philip E. *Changing Values in College.* New Haven, 1956.
Jacobs, Jane. *The Death and Life of Great American Cities.* New York, 1961.
Jacobs, Norman, ed. *Culture for the Millions?* Princeton, 1959.
Jarrell, Randall. *Pictures from an Institution.* New York, 1954.
Jerome, V. J. *The Negro in Hollywood Films.* New York, 1950.
Johnson, F. Ernest, ed. *Patterns of Faith in America Today.* New York, 1957.
Johnson, Walter. *1600 Pennsylvania Avenue.* Boston, 1960.
Johnson, William, ed. *Focus on the Science Fiction Film.* Englewood Cliffs, 1972.
Jowitt, Earl. *The Strange Case of Alger Hiss.* Garden City, 1953.
Kahn, Albert E. *High Treason: The Plot Against the People.* New York, 1950.
Kanfer, Stefan. *A Journal of the Plague Years.* New York, 1973.

Kardish, Laurence. *Reel Plastic Magic: A History of Films and Filmmaking in America.* Boston, 1972.
Karp, David. *Escape to Nowhere.* New York, 1955.
Karson, Albert, and Gianakos, Perry E., eds. *American Civilization Since World War II.* Belmont, Cal., 1968.
Kauffmann, Stanley. *A World on Film.* New York, 1967.
Keats, John. *The Crack in the Picture Window.* Boston, 1957.
——. *The Insolent Chariots.* Philadelphia, 1958.
Kelly, Walt. *Ten Ever-Lovin' Blue-Eyed Years with Pogo, 1949–1959.* New York, 1972 ed.
Kempton, Murray. *America Comes of Middle Age.* Boston, 1963.
Kerouac, Jack. *The Dharma Bums.* New York, 1958.
——. *On the Road.* New York, 1957.
King, Martin Luther, Jr. *Stride Toward Freedom.* New York, 1958.
Kirk, Russell. *Academic Freedom.* Chicago, 1955.
Knoerr, Alvin W., and Lutjen, George P. *Prospecting for Atomic Minerals.* New York, 1955.
Kolko, Gabriel. *Wealth and Power in America.* New York, 1962.
Kronenberger, Louis. *Company Manners: A Cultural Inquiry into American Life.* Indianapolis, 1954.
Krutch, Joseph Wood, ed. *Is the Common Man Too Common?* Norman, Okla., 1954.
Lait, Jack, and Mortimer, Lee. *U.S.A. Confidential.* New York, 1952.
Landis, Paul H. *Making the Most of Your Marriage.* New York, 1955.
——. *Your Marriage and Family Living.* St. Louis, 1954.
Lapp, Ralph E. *Atoms and People.* New York, 1956.
——. *The Voyage of the Lucky Dragon.* New York, 1958.
Larrabee, Eric. *The Self-Conscious Society.* Garden City, 1960.
——, and Meyersohn, Rolf, eds. *Mass Leisure.* Glencoe, Ill., 1958.
Latham, Earl. *The Communist Controversy in Washington: From the New Deal to McCarthy.* Cambridge, Mass., 1966.
Lee, Gordon C. *An Introduction to Education in Modern America.* New York, 1957.
Lerner, Max. *America As a Civilization.* New York, 1957.
Leuchtenberg, William E., and the Editors of *Life. The Great Age of Change.* Vol. 12: *From 1945.* New York, 1964.
Lewis, Richard S. *The Nuclear Power Rebellion.* New York, 1972.
Liebling, A. J. *The Press.* New York, 1961.
Lilienthal, David E. *Big Business: A New Era.* New York, 1953.
Lincoln, C. Eric. *The Black Muslims in America.* Boston, 1961.
Lindner, Robert. *Must You Conform?* New York, 1956.
Lindstrom, Carl E. *The Fading American Newspaper.* Gloucester, Mass., 1964 ed.

Lipton, Lawrence. *The Holy Barbarians*. New York, 1959.
Lomax, Louis. *The Negro Revolt*. New York, 1962.
Luce, Robert B., ed. *The Faces of Five Decades: Selections from The New Republic, 1914–1964*. New York, 1964.
Ludden, Allen. *Plain Talk for Men Under 21!* New York, 1957.
——. *Plain Talk for Women Under 21!* New York, 1957.
Lynd, Albert. *Quackery in the Public Schools*. Boston, 1953.
Lynes, Russell. *A Surfeit of Honey*. New York, 1957.
MacCann, Richard Dyer. *Hollywood in Transition*. Boston, 1962.
McCarthy, Mary. *On the Contrary*. New York, 1961.
McClellan, Grant S., ed. *Juvenile Delinquency*. New York, 1956.
McClure, Arthur F. *The Movies: An American Idiom*. Rutherford, 1971.
McCullough, C. Rogers, ed. *Safety Aspects of Nuclear Reactors*. Princeton, 1957.
MacDonald, Dwight. *Against the American Grain*. New York, 1962.
MacLeish, Archibald. *J. B.* Cambridge, Mass., 1958.
McLuhan, Marshall H. *The Gutenberg Galaxy*. Toronto, 1962.
——. *The Mechanical Bride*. New York, 1951.
Mailer, Norman. *Advertisements for Myself*. New York, 1959.
——. *Barbary Shore*. New York, 1951.
——. *Deer Park*. New York, 1955.
Malamud, Bernard. *The Natural*. New York, 1952.
Manchester, William. *The Glory and the Dream: A Narrative History of America 1932–1972*. Boston, 1974.
Mapp, Edward. *Blacks in American Films*. Metuchen, N.J., 1972.
Marcuse, Herbert. *Eros and Civilization*. Boston, 1955.
Maritain, Jacques. *Reflections on America*. New York, 1958.
Marty, Martin E. *The New Shape of American Religion*. New York, 1959.
May, Ernest R., ed. *Anxiety and Affluence: 1945–1965*. New York, 1966.
Mayer, Frederick. *Philosophy of Education for Our Time*. New York, 1958.
Mayer, Martin. *The Schools*. New York, 1961.
Meeropol, Robert and Michael. *We Are Your Sons*. Boston, 1975.
Mehling, Harold. *The Great Time-Killer*. Cleveland, 1962.
Melby, Ernest O., and Puner, Morton, eds. *Freedom and Public Education*. New York, 1953.
Merriam, Eve. *After Nora Slammed the Door*. Cleveland, 1964.
Meyer, Donald. *The Positive Thinkers*. Garden City, 1966.
Miller, William Lee. *Piety Along the Potomac: Notes on Politics and Morals in the Fifties*. Boston, 1964.
Millett, Kate. *Sexual Politics*. Garden City, 1970.
Mills, C. Wright. *The Causes of World War Three*. New York, 1960.
——. *Listen Yankee: The Revolution in Cuba*. New York, 1960.

———. *The Power Elite*. New York, 1956.
———. *White Collar: The American Middle Classes*. New York, 1951.
Moore, Barrington. *Political Power and Social Theory*. Cambridge, Mass., 1958.
Morison, Elting E., ed. *The American Style: Essays in Value and Performance*. New York, 1958.
Moss, Norman. *Men Who Play God*. New York, 1958.
Mumford, Lewis. *The City in History*. New York, 1961.
———. *In the Name of Sanity*. New York, 1954.
Nabokov, Vladimir. *Lolita*. New York, 1963 ed.
Nader, Ralph. *Unsafe at Any Speed*. New York, 1965.
Nadler, M. *People's Capitalism*. New York, 1956.
Nelkin, Dorothy. *Nuclear Power and Its Critics*. Ithaca, 1971.
Niebuhr, Reinhold. *The Irony of American History*. New York, 1952.
Nixon, Richard M. *Six Crises*. Garden City, 1967.
Novick, Sheldon. *The Careless Atom*. Boston, 1969.
Nuttall, Jeff. *Bomb Culture*. New York, 1968.
Office of Civil and Defense Mobilization. *The Family Fallout Shelter*. Washington, D.C., 1959.
———. *Individual and Family Survival Requirements*. Washington, D.C., 1959.
O'Neill, William L., ed. *American Society Since 1945*. Chicago, 1969.
Packard, Vance. *The Hidden Persuaders*. New York, 1957.
———. *The Status Seekers*. New York, 1959.
Parenti, Michael. *The Anti-Communist Impulse*. New York, 1969.
Paterson, Thomas G., ed. *Cold War Critics*. Chicago, 1971.
Pauling, Linus. *No More War!* New York, 1958.
Peale, Norman Vincent. *The Power of Positive Thinking*. New York, 1952.
Peck, Jim. *We Who Would Not Kill*. New York, 1958.
Peters, William. *The Southern Temper*. Garden City, 1959.
Potter, David M. *People of Plenty: Economic Abundance and American Character*. Chicago, 1954.
Prospect for America: The Rockefeller Panel Reports. Garden City, 1961.
Quigley, Martin, Jr., and Gertner, Richard. *Films in America, 1929–1969*. New York, 1970.
Reich, Wilhelm. *The Function of the Orgasm*. New York, 1961 ed.
Reynolds, Earle. *The Forbidden Voyage*. New York, 1961.
Rickover, H. G. *Education and Freedom*. New York, 1959.
Riesman, David. *Individualism Reconsidered*. Glencoe, Ill., 1954.
———. et al. *The Lonely Crowd: A Study of the Changing American Character*. Garden City, 1955 ed.
Rogin, Michael Paul. *The Intellectuals and McCarthy: The Radical Specter*. Cambridge, Mass., 1967.

Rosen, Marjorie. *Popcorn Venus: Women, Movies and the American Dream.* New York, 1973.

Rosenberg, Bernard, and White, David Manning, eds. *Mass Culture.* Glencoe, Ill., 1957.

Rovere, Richard H. *The American Establishment and Other Reports, Opinions, and Speculations.* New York, 1962.

——. *Senator Joe McCarthy.* New York, 1959.

Rustin, Bayard. *Down the Line.* Chicago, 1971.

Salinger, J. D. *The Catcher in the Rye.* New York, 1961 ed.

——. *Franny and Zooey.* Boston, 1961.

——. *Nine Stories.* New York, 1959.

Sarratt, Reed. *The Ordeal of Desegregation: The First Decade.* New York, 1966.

Schickel, Richard. *Movies: The History of an Art and an Institution.* New York, 1964.

Schindler, John A., M.D. *Woman's Guide to Better Living.* Garden City, 1958.

Schlesinger, Arthur M., Jr. *The Vital Center: The Politics of Freedom.* Boston, 1962 ed.

Schneider, Louis, and Dornbusch, Sanford M. *Popular Religion: Inspirational Books in America.* Chicago, 1958.

Schumach, Murray. *The Face on the Cutting Room Floor.* New York, 1964.

Scott, C. Winfield, and Hill, Clyde M., eds. *The Great Debate: Our Schools in Crisis.* Englewood Cliffs, 1959.

——, eds. *Public Education Under Criticism.* New York, 1954.

Seldes, Gilbert. *The Great Audience.* New York, 1950.

——. *The Public Arts.* New York, 1956.

Shannon, David A. *The Decline of American Communism: A History of the Communist Party in the United States Since 1945.* New York, 1959.

Shayon, Robert Lewis. *Television and Our Children.* New York, 1951.

Sheen, Fulton J. *Life Is Worth Living.* New York, 1953.

Shils, Edward A. *The Intellectuals and the Powers.* Chicago, 1972.

Shulman, Arthur, and Youman, Roger. *How Sweet It Was.* New York, 1966.

Shute, Nevil. *On the Beach.* New York, 1957.

Silberman, Charles E. *Crisis In Black and White.* New York, 1964.

Sitney, P. Adams, ed. *Film Culture Reader.* New York, 1970.

Spectorsky, A. C. *The Exurbanites.* New York, 1955.

Spillane, Mickey. *One Lonely Night.* New York, 1951.

——. *Vengeance Is Mine.* New York, 1950.

Spiller, Robert E., and Larrabee, Eric, eds. *American Perspectives: The*

National Self-Image in the Twentieth Century. Cambridge, Mass., 1961.

Spock, Dr. Benjamin. *Pocket Book of Baby and Child Care*. New York, 1955 ed.

Stein, Leopold. *Loathsome Women*. New York, 1959.

Steinbrunner, Chris, and Goldblatt, Burt. *Cinema of the Fantastic*. New York, 1972.

Sternglass, Dr. Ernest. *Low-Level Radiation*. New York, 1972.

Stevenson, Adlai E. *Major Campaign Speeches of Adlai E. Stevenson, 1952*. New York, 1953.

Stone, I. F., *The Haunted Fifties*. New York, 1963.

——. *Hidden History of the Korean War*. New York, 1952.

Stouffer, Samuel A. *Communism, Conformity, and Civil Liberties*. Garden City, 1955.

Styron, William. *Lie Down in Darkness*. New York, 1951.

——. *Set This House on Fire*. New York, 1960.

Sutton, Francis X., et al. *The American Business Creed*. Cambridge, Mass., 1956.

Swados, Harvey. *On the Line*. New York, 1960 ed.

——. *A Radical's America*. Boston, 1962.

Szasz, Thomas. *Law, Liberty and Psychiatry*. New York, 1963.

——. *The Manufacture of Mental Illness*. New York, 1970.

——. *The Myth of Mental Illness*. New York, 1961.

Talbot, Daniel, ed. *Film: An Anthology*. New York, 1959.

Taylor, Maxwell D. *The Uncertain Trumpet*. New York, 1960.

Theoharis, Athan. *Seeds of Repression: Harry S Truman and the Origins of McCarthyism*. Chicago, 1971.

Thruelsen, Richard, and Kobler, John, eds. *Adventures of the Mind From the Saturday Evening Post*. New York, 1960.

Trilling, Diana. *Claremont Essays*. New York, 1964.

Trilling, Lionel. *A Gathering of Fugitives*. Boston, 1956.

——. *The Liberal Imagination*. New York, 1950.

Truman, Harry S. *Memoirs*. 2 vols., Garden City, 1955–56.

U. S. National Security Resources Board, *You Can Survive*. Washington, D.C., 1950.

Valentine, Alan. *The Age of Conformity*. Chicago, 1954.

Vatter, Harold G. *The U. S. Economy in the 1950's: An Economic History*. New York, 1963.

Vaughn, Robert. *Only Victims: A Study of Show Business Blacklisting*. New York, 1972.

Vedder, Clyde B. *The Juvenile Offender*. Garden City, 1954.

Viereck, Peter. *Shame and Glory of the Intellectuals: Babbitt Jr. vs. the Rediscovery of Values*. Boston, 1953.

Wattenberg, Ben J. *This U.S.A.: An Unexpected Family Portrait of 194,067,296 Americans Drawn from the Census.* Garden City, 1965.

Wechsler, James A. *Reflections of an Angry Middle-Aged Editor.* New York, 1960.

Wertham, Fredric, M.D. *Seduction of the Innocent.* New York, 1954.

White, Lynn, Jr. *Educating Our Daughters.* New York, 1950.

Whitehead, Don. *The FBI Story.* New York, 1956.

Whyte, William H., Jr. *The Organization Man.* Garden City, 1956.

Williams, J. Paul. *What Americans Believe and How They Worship.* New York, 1952.

Wilson, Sloan. *The Man in the Gray Flannel Suit.* New York, 1956 ed.

Wittner, Lawrence S. *Cold War America: From Hiroshima to Watergate.* New York, 1974.

Woodring, Paul. *Let's Talk Sense About Our Schools.* New York, 1953.

Woodward, C. Vann. *The Strange Career of Jim Crow.* New York, 1955.

Wright, Richard. *White Man, Listen!* Garden City, 1957.

Zeligs, Meyer. *Friendship and Fratricide.* New York, 1967.

Zinn, Howard. *Postwar America, 1945–1971.* Indianapolis, 1973.

Zornow, William Frank. *America at Mid-Century.* Cleveland, 1959.

INDEX

PHOTO CREDITS

1–4. Courtesy of Michigan State Archives
7, 8, 22, 27, 34, 42. United Press International, Inc.
9, 10, 12, 13, 15, 16, 26, 32. Wide World Photos
28, 29. Burt Glinn, © 1966 Magnum Photos
5. Eric Schaal for Time-Life Picture Agency, © Time, Inc.
6. Drawing by Gardner Rea, © 1951 The New Yorker Magazine, Inc.
11. Grey Villet for Time-Life Picture Agency, © Time, Inc.
14. Andreas Feininger for Time-Life Picture Agency, © Time, Inc.
17. Art Shay for Time-Life Picture Agency, © Time, Inc.
18. Francis Miller for Time-Life Picture Agency, © Time, Inc.
19. Charles L. Trainor for The Miami *News*
20. Allan Grant for Time-Life Picture Agency, © Time, Inc.
21. Movie Star News
23. Don Cravens
24. Hank Walker for Time-Life Picture Agency, © Time, Inc.
25. Loomis Dean for Time-Life Picture Agency, © Time, Inc.
30. J. R. Eyerman for Time-Life Picture Agency, © Time, Inc.
31. Ralph Morse for Time-Life Picture Agency, © Time, Inc.
33. From *How Sweet It Was,* published by Shorecrest, Inc.
35. Movie Star News
36. Stan Wayman for Time-Life Picture Agency, © Time, Inc.
37. Howard Sochurek for Time-Life Picture Agency, © Time, Inc.
38. Reprinted from *U.S. News & World Report,* © 1953 U.S. News & World Report
39. Thomas D. McAvoy for Time-Life Picture Agency, © Time, Inc.
40. Robert W. Kelley for Time-Life Picture Agency, © Time, Inc.
41. Loomis Dean for Time-Life Picture Agency, © Time, Inc.